THE LIFE AND TIMES OF
SIDNEY AND BEATRICE WEBB

The Life and Times of Sidney and Beatrice Webb

1858–1905: The Formative Years

Royden J. Harrison
Emeritus Professor of Social History
University of Warwick

First published in Great Britain 2000 by
MACMILLAN PRESS LTD
Houndmills, Basingstoke, Hampshire RG21 6XS and London
Companies and representatives throughout the world

A catalogue record for this book is available from the British Library.

ISBN 0–333–77343–8

First published in the United States of America 2000 by
ST. MARTIN'S PRESS, INC.,
Scholarly and Reference Division,
175 Fifth Avenue, New York, N.Y. 10010

ISBN 0–312–22641–1

Library of Congress Cataloging-in-Publication Data
Harrison, Royden.
The life and times of Sidney and Beatrice Webb : 1858–1905, the
formative years / Royden J. Harrison.
   p.   cm.
Includes bibliographical references and index.
ISBN 0–312–22641–1
1. Webb, Sidney, 1859–1947.   2. Webb, Beatrice Potter, 1858–1943.
3. Socialists—Great Britain—Biography.   4. Socialism—Great
Britain—History.   I. Title.
HX244.7.W42H37   1999
335'.14'092241—dc21
[B]   99–15616
                                                                            CIP

This book is printed on paper suitable for recycling and made from fully managed and
sustained forest sources.

10   9   8   7   6   5   4   3   2
09   08   07   06   05   04   03   02   01   00

Printed and bound in Great Britain by
Antony Rowe Ltd, Chippenham, Wiltshire

Contents

List of Plates

List of Abbreviations

BP	Beatrice Potter
BW	Beatrice Webb
CWN	Charles Webb Notes
D	The Diary of Beatrice Webb 1873–1932
GBS	George Bernard Shaw
GW	Graham Wallas
ID	*Industrial Democracy*
L	The Letters of Sidney and Beatrice Webb
MA	*My Apprenticeship*
OP	*Our Partnership*
PAS	Passfield Papers, British Library of Political and Economic Science
RCL	Royal Commission on Labour
SW	Sidney Webb
TU	*The History of Trade Unionism*

Introduction

At the end of their lives the Webbs established a body to be known as the Passfield Trustees. Its task was to benefit the institutions which they had a hand in creating: the Fabian Society, the London School of Economics, the Labour Party, the *New Statesman*, the *Political Quarterly*, *Tribune* and so forth. In distributing the proceeds of the Webbs' estate the trustees rightly felt that it was the LSE with which Sidney and Beatrice had the longest and most continuous identification. The chairman of the trust was Sir Alexander Carr-Saunders, the noted demographic sociologist, who was also the director of the school. William Robson, Professor of Public Administration in the LSE, was also an active trustee. It was to the school and those who worked in it that most of the resources went. The school presence was not equally apparent in all the trustees. For example, Margaret Cole was there as being along with her husband, G.D.H. Cole, a life-long adversary and friend of the Webbs. John Parker MP evidently stood primarily, but not exclusively, for the Labour Party connection. These trustees were required by the last instruction to appoint a biographer.

Beatrice in her journal – a better title for her diary – states that she spent much time in contemplating the character of the 'unemployed intellectual' who would be given that task. When in the mid-sixties I was invited to come and meet the trustees in the House of Commons I had some doubts about whether the noun applied to me. I was certain the adjective did not.

Bertrand Russell declared that nobody had ever dared to call him an 'intellectual'. He understood by that term someone who pretended to have more intellect than he really had. 'Unemployed' I was not. I had just returned from a very busy semester in Madison, Wisconsin, where I had been teaching modern British and European history and was trying to readjust to my duties as a teacher of Industrial Studies in Sheffield. I was now academic adviser for the day-release programmes for coal miners and steelworkers. The Director of the Extramural Department was among those pressing me to put myself forward for a new 'chair' in politics in the university. I was greatly relieved when this appointment went to Bernard Crick. I was greatly flattered when Crick asked me to join his department. No sooner had I accepted than I was confronted with a challenge from my old friend and comrade Edward Thompson to come and partner him in the direction of the Centre for the Study of Social History at the University of Warwick. I declined, but a few weeks later the university was convulsed by a crisis: Edward resigned as director of the centre; the vice-chancellor invited me to come to Warwick to consider the succession. I agreed to do so provided I was to be made a professor or accorded equivalent powers within the Warwick University constitution. I also insisted that before I met the Warwick appointments board I should discuss with the librarian the creation of an archive of primary sources in British labour and social history. This was the beginning of what is now the Modern Records Centre, which houses the records of the Trades Union Congress, the Confederation of British Industry and numerous trade unions and companies. However, my first task at Warwick was to supervise the existing student population, which was largely employed in writing theses on crime and criminals in the eighteenth century, a subject area which was certainly not mine. Thompson told me that he considered my appointment would be good for Warwick, but probably not for me. I doubt whether he was right on either count.

All these developments put back progress on the Webbs, as did my inability to resist temptations to visit Japan and Australasia. Every night the shades of Sidney and Beatrice visited me with curious and reproachful stares and interrogated me as to why I was taking so long. 'Can you write a biography?' enquired Margaret Cole. I did not know the answer. I was trying to find out, encouraged by the evident assurance of the other Passfield Trustees. They were not only helpful collectively but, like Margaret Cole, Sir Alexander, Professor Robson and especially John Parker MP gave me their recollections of the Webbs. They also encouraged me to interview others who had known them: Lord Attlee, Lady Simon of Wythenshawe, Leonard Woolf, Kingsley Martin and the most helpful of all, Bertrand Russell. (It was on my own initiative that I went to Moscow to talk to Ivan Maisky, the sometime Soviet Ambassador to the United Kingdom.) In particular I am indebted to Margaret Cole for reminding me that while it may be desirable to wait until one has read all the existing literature concerning the relationship between the Webbs and the person to be interviewed, such persons will not be around for ever. So it was when I was just beginning that I set off for Wales to see Russell and to Moscow to see Maisky.

I was made hesitant in my response to Margaret Cole's key question because I already sensed the social historian's problem: how can you see the tree for the wood? I was determined to manage a life and times: one that had, almost as much, to be a times as a life. The trustees were inclined to press me down to one volume and a couple of years. To the best of my recollection we fully agreed that the Webbs were not to be separated. We left undisturbed other potentially controversial matters.

I had not been at work for more than a few weeks before they rose to the surface. I was at work in the library of the LSE when I discovered that I was not alone in writing a Webb biography. Mrs Kitty Muggeridge was already benefiting from the infinite helpfulness and learning of the librarian and his staff. Neither then nor upon subsequent occasions did I want to deny access to the Webb material. Yet I had worries about the Muggeridge connection. What, I wondered, was one to make of Malcolm Muggeridge's letters to his 'Aunt Bo', in which he tried to discuss with her the incidence of masturbation in Welwyn Garden City or his contention that the Soviet Union was a terrible place? Perhaps there was a reasonable contention here, but what of the remark that it was only fit for 'hunchbacks, perverts and Jews'? Mr Muggeridge was the only eminent person who declined to grant me an interview. He explained, what by chance I already knew, that his wife was writing a life. I found this 'a bit rich' and said so to the trustees. Why had they not told me about the Muggeridge activities? Professor Robson replied that I had never asked about them. Did I think they could deny access to a niece? (I had hoped that I would be spared the connection of a second cousin once removed.)

Robson went on to ask me to record any references to himself which I came across in the papers. This was a request that could not be met. Was I to tell him that Sidney regarded him as the most boring person on earth? He did not bore Beatrice, since she enjoyed asking herself why he was such a bore!

Then I discovered that I had very nearly had a most distinguished predecessor. In 1947 the Passfield Trustees had asked R.H. Tawney to write a biography of Sidney. By 1949 the work was under way and Tawney had found a research assistant in the shape of Henry Pelling. It was only then that he discovered that one of the Trustees, Margaret Cole, had embarked upon her own biographical endeavour without troubling to inform him about it. Incredibly she had chosen for her title one which Tawney had used himself in his memorial lecture of 1945: *The Webbs and Their Work*. Tawney felt that this episode made his work impossible. I found it made my own difficult.

Next I found what I took to be a still more damaging challenge. Professor Norman MacKenzie asked to stay in my house in Sheffield to discuss his editorial work on the diary of Beatrice Webb and the letters between Sidney and Beatrice. His wife Jeanne was assisting him. She went beyond the editorial role when she wrote *A Victorian Courtship: The Story of Beatrice Potter and Sidney Webb*, 1979. This offering was unhelpful. When the second invader on the field of the 'authorised biographer' appeared, Professor Robson was no longer with us. My previous question could not be put again!

Amidst these numerous challenges I felt the Webbs to be less pressing than others might have done. I think Sidney would have had some sympathy with my attitude. I doubt whether Beatrice would have been quite so emancipated.

Yet despite all the difficulties I still feel a deep sense of gratitude to the Passfield Trustees for commissioning me. Since Margaret Cole was the only one I knew, albeit slightly, I suspected that she was my main supporter. (As an 'advanced student' at Oxford I had worked under the supervision of her late husband, G.D.H. Cole.) I felt – and still feel – deeply indebted to the Universities of Sheffield and Warwick, which both granted me leave of absence with generous financial support. In addition I owe a debt to the Social Science Research Council and to the Leverhulme Foundation for enabling me to employ two research assistants. Jean McCrindle helped me – under very difficult circumstances – with the start of the project. Dr David Martin provided me with invaluable material for Webb at the Colonial Office and has been helpful in other ways. Most of my other debts must be acknowledged at a later date and elsewhere. However my old friend and colleague John Halstead must be recognised for mobilising a secretarial pool consisting of Maria Baldam, Audrey Elcock, Julie Goode, Aileen Jones, Justine Perkins and Barbara Zeun. He also provided a demanding editorial eye by which I was occasionally corrected and sometimes encouraged. I am grateful to him too for dealing with matters during my period of hospitalisation.

ROYDEN J. HARRISON

Part I
The Man with
No Inside:
Sidney Webb 1859–90

And still they gazed, and still the wonder grew,
That one small head could carry all he knew.

Oliver Goldsmith

Let me say at once that I have no intention of writing an autobiography.
I am, I believe, 'not that sort'. Indeed, I have very little knowledge of what
has happened to me internally. I am, I suppose, what is nowadays called
an extrovert. Things impinge on me and I react to the impact, occasionally,
with ideas and suggestions that prove interesting ... I can supply nothing
but a series of disconnected accounts of impacts and reactions.

'Reminiscences', *St Martin's Review*, October 1926

Sidney Webb is a door that will never be unlocked.

A.J.P. Taylor

1

The Shaping of a Professional Man 1859–85

1859—Webb's birth and family, early education and schools in Switzerland and Germany—Enters the civil service—Further education and examination successes—First-division clerk at the Colonial Office—Meets Sydney Olivier—Cambridge and the Whewell Scholarship—Antipathy to the classical, literary, aristocratic tradition—Life in the Zetetical Society—Sidney's first paper (1881) and pessimism—Disposition towards positivism—Webb's personality and attraction—Sidney and George Bernard Shaw—Influence of Olivier and Wallas—Activity in the 'Lambeth Parliament'—The engagement with Henry George and Karl Marx—Webb, Marshall and the 'rent of ability' leading to the doctrine of Renunciation.

Sidney was born in the heart of London on 13 July 1859. 1859 was a momentous year. In publishing it saw the first appearances of Darwin's *The Origin of the Species* and of Marx's *A Contribution to the Critique of Political Economy*. (Marx wrote in German and published in Germany, but he lived in London, within easy walking distance of the Webb household. It was at the Highgate Cemetery that Engels announced that Marx had done for human history what Darwin had done for nature.) Webb and Engels were to establish a respectful hostility at the Democratic Club. More important and interesting for the life of Sidney was the appearance in 1859 of J.S. Mill's *Essay on Liberty*, probably the most influential of all Mill's books and yet the one least congenial to the Webb spirit. Certainly it compared unfavourably with the contempt for mere money-making contained in the latter editions of the *Political Economy*, never mind the posthumously published essays on *Socialism* (1879). Sidney's father is supposed to have been actively identified with Mill's candidature when he stood for Parliament, but no hard evidence for this has been found. Of more immediate and obvious importance was the fact that 1859 saw the coincidence of Mill's *On Liberty* and Samuel Smiles' *Self-Help*. Both books

3

have been seen as unqualified celebrations of individual liberty, meaning the absence of restraint or doing what one desired. This is possible, but only upon a careless reading. 1859 saw significant advances in collective self-help: the theory and practice of positive freedom among workmen. A fresh ambition and fresh self-confidence among the 'pompous trades and proud mechanics'. It was during the prolonged strike and lockout in the London building trades that began in 1859 that the London Trades Council was established and the principles of the 'New Model' unionism that first conquered in engineering, extended to carpenters and joiners, bricklayers, and less successfully, among painters and plasterers.

These proletarian developments roughly coincided with the rise of professionalism among the middle classes. Even lawyers and doctors, parsons and army officers, the archetypal professional gentlemen, began to come under challenge from professional associations that devised standards and enforced them. In the crucial instance of the civil service, the Northcote–Trevelyan Report of 1853 took many years to implement the system of employment by open competitive examination as against the privilege of nomination. It was in 1859 that it was enacted, with limited exceptions, that no one should for the purposes of superannuation be deemed to have served in the civil service unless he had a certificate from the Civil Service Commissioners who were first established in 1855.

As to party politics, 1859 belonged in the small minority of years that the Tories were in office between 1844 and 1874. When Reform was a question out of doors it was too alarming to be a matter for the House. When it was a parliamentary preoccupation it was too minimal or trivial or boring to engage the attention of 'the masses'. It was not until Sidney was about eight or nine years old that an extension of the franchise concerned men both outside and inside parliament so that democracy became what Bentham would have termed agenda. As for the government of London, it remained in many respects in the Dark Ages. In 1859 it was a long way behind other great urban centres in the matter of democratic reform.

Sidney Webb's mother was born, Elizabeth Mary Stacey, in East Anglia in 1825. Her father was a sea captain from Wivenhoe, near Colchester, employed in the coastal trade. The other members of her family were farmers or small property-owners living in Essex and Suffolk. Her father Benjamin and her mother died while she was still a child, and one or other of her aunts brought her up. In 1848 a brother-in-law lent her a few hundred pounds, and by 1851 she had established herself as a hairdresser and a keeper of a shop selling ladies' toilet requisites at 45 Cranbourn(e) Street, Leicester Square.[1]

Across the way at number 46 Cranbourn Street there lived the family of a finisher named William Webb.[2] One may conjecture that it was through these neighbours that Elizabeth came to meet Charles Webb of Catherine

Street, Pimlico, whom she married at St George's Parish Church, Hanover Square, on 14 May 1854.[3] He was four years younger than she was, but he came from much the same milieu. It was the world of small property-owners in sleepy towns and villages of southern England, affected by the industrial revolution through its impact upon the market, rather than by its presence as a way of life. Charles Webb's father, James, kept the Duke's Head public house in Peckham, and accumulated a fortune of several thousand pounds. However, his family was large, and most of the other members of it were in decidedly modest circumstances. His brother Thomas was a general servant or agricultural labourer. His eldest son William became a master tailor in the village. There were many relatives and dependants.[4] When Charles Webb married Elizabeth he described himself as a 'hairdresser' and he was so described on Sidney Webb's birth certificate. On Sidney's own copy of the certificate, the word 'hairdresser' was erased, and replaced by 'accountant'. One assumes that this reflected a concern with accuracy rather than gentility. Charles Webb was no doubt an accountant, but he appears to have pursued that occupation intermittently and on a freelance basis. The hairdresser's shop provided the largest and steadiest part of the family income, and as head of the household Charles assumed the formal control of it, at least for a time. However, his real interests were in public service rather than business. He was a sergeant in the Queen's Westminster Rifle Volunteers, and a crack shot. He was also a vestryman – which explains why he was sometimes described as a rate-collector – and a Poor Law Guardian.[5] He was reported to be a keen Radical and to have been a member of John Stuart Mill's committee when the 'Saint of Rationalism' contested the Westminster election of 1865.[6] However, his name did not appear on the published list.[7]

Such evidence as there is concerning Elizabeth and Charles Webb suggests that she was a resourceful and industrious woman, and that he was an intelligent and public-spirited man. On the face of it, their marriage was a success. In 1946 Bernard Shaw remarked to Sidney: 'You had wonderful parents: I have never met a more gentle, conscientious, thoroughly likeable pair in my life. It was largely due to them that I can also say that I never met a man who combined your extraordinary ability with your unique simplicity and integrity of character.'[8]

Sidney, who was born at Cranbourn Street on 13 July 1859, confirmed that his was a 'happy family'.[9] His eldest brother Charles and his younger sister Ada came to live, in their own very different ways, lives as contented and fulfilled as his own. Yet happy though they were, Sidney came to feel that one great influence was missing. He envied Ruskin who could recall as the chief blessing of his boyhood that it had taught him peace. Peace was not to be had in Cranbourn Street. The Webbs were always 'in the thick of the fight'.[10] They were not poor. In 1861 they appear to have employed three shop assistants as well as one resident servant in the house.[11] The rateable value of the shop and the house together came to £188.[12] Allowing for Charles Webb's contribution to the household, the family income must have been fully £500 a year. Yet they were not beyond the reach of poverty. An illness or a commercial depression might make serious inroads on their slender resources. Elizabeth and Charles both came from families of the 'middling sort', in which 'rising' and 'falling' in the social scale was a familiar experience. Their neighbours in Cranbourn Street – small merchants, dressmakers, drapers, window-blind makers, and importers of French stays – lived precariously in the unsettled regions of the lower middle class. And close by, in the teeming streets, in the maze of courts and alleyways, dwelt a small part of that great and as yet unmeasured mass, the London poor. As a young man in his twenties, Sidney declared that there was something worse than poverty, and that was the fear of it.[13]

Like most of us, Sidney received his earliest education at his mother's knee, and like most of us, he could remember nothing at all about it. He fancied that he taught himself to read 'very largely from the books and notices in the shop windows'.[14] His mother took him to a succession of churches and chapels 'in search of an eloquent preacher free from sacer-dotalism', but he never went to Sunday school.[15] She also took him, as a very little boy, to see the Lord Mayor's Show from the steps of St Martin's Church, telling him that if he was a good boy he might himself be Lord Mayor of London. His father, as a strong Radical, doubtless had a more exact knowledge of the qualifications required for that particular office. Besides, Sidney was not always a good boy. If he managed to wander endlessly through miles of streets without ever being robbed or molested, he sometimes fell foul of authority. Once when he and his brother, elegantly and respectably attired in kilts, were playing round the Duke of York's Column, they were chased by a policeman. To the end of his days Charles Webb recalled how Sidney 'tore off his Scotch cap and flew down to steps to the Park'. Charles might enjoy recalling such escapades, but for Sidney they were no less disagreeable in recollection than they had been at the time. At the age of twenty-two he found:

> I can recall most easily instances of trivial blunders or sins committed, which caused me intense mental discomfort at the time, such as shame, remorse, etc., though occurring at least fourteen years ago: and this with a vividness and consequent repetition of the pain, which makes it a very unpleasant psychological experiment.[16]

London seemed to Sidney to have been his first and greatest school. In the streets he became 'precociously familiar' with many aspects of life.

He recalled that

> It used to take me a full hour to get the whole length of Fleet Street, so absorbing were the pages of periodicals there exposed to view. I found more instruction in the reputedly arid pages of Kelly's London Directory, then already a ponderous tome, than in any other single volume to which my childhood had access.[17]

This great, free and informal process of self-education was supplemented by attendance at a reputable private school just round the corner from Sidney's home, in St Martin's Lane.[18] The headmaster bore the ominous name of Mr Pincher, but although Sidney came to consider that fear of punishment had been one great factor in his moral development,[19] it is doubtful whether he was often the subject of Mr Pincher's severities. He was far too intelligent, industrious and sensitive a child to have allowed it. Sidney detested punishment considered as retribution and doubted whether it had ever had much use in improving the character of those upon whom it was inflicted, but he did hold that 'a good whipping of the first culprit has deterred many a whole school from following his example.'[20]

When Sidney went to school he went to learn. In 1871 his parents, acting on the advice of a friendly customer, sent their sons to a school at Herveville on the Lake of Rienne, near Neuchâtel in Switzerland. This was a delightful place, with its own vineyard sweeping down to the lakeside. At vintage time the boys picked the grapes and were allowed to eat all that they wished. Sidney fared as well as the rest, but he also worked so diligently that within three months he could hold his own in French dictation against the French-speaking Swiss boys. About 1873 the boys left Switzerland to complete their education in Germany, where they were placed in the care of a Lutheran pastor in Mecklenburg-Schwerin. The story that Sidney was shipwrecked on the voyage from England to Germany has no foundation in fact. If he got wet, it was through playing about in the boats in Wismar harbour.[21]

It is possible that in the early seventies certain differences arose between Sidney's parents, and this partly explained their decision to send the boys abroad. In his old age Sidney received a letter from Canada by someone who claimed to be his sister. He responded that he could not remember her. He does not appear to have told Beatrice about this. No invitation was sent to this person to come to the great family party, which was arranged about this time. The sister – or half-sister – was barely literate, but she employed a lawyer to follow up her claim. Sidney did inform his brother, who congratulated him upon his management of the matter despite the fact that he was, as he wrote, not in the habit of 'handing out bouquets'. This suggests a strong possibility that Charles Webb senior

fathered a child – possibly by the living-in servant. This unwelcome birth
would have been more likely to occasion the foreign schooling of Sidney
and his brother than the advice of a friendly customer. However that may
be, their hope that a mastery of French and German would help them to
find secure employment proved to be fully justified. If as a twelve-year-
old Sidney objected to being dispatched to the Continent and held
that London was the only place on earth to live,[22] he and his brother
immediately on their return found useful and progressive employment.
While Charles went into Marshall & Snelgrove, the department store, the
sixteen-year-old Sidney, ten days after his arrival back in England in 1875,
was a clerk in a colonial broker's. He did so well there that his fortune
seemed assured. The broker was so impressed with his recruit that he
offered him a partnership when he was twenty-one if only he would stay
with him.[23] With her sons safely established in business, Elizabeth Webb
sold her shop and moved to 27 Keppel Street, where she and her husband
spent the rest of their lives in modest comfort together with their daughter
Ada (who was as brilliant an examinee as Sidney himself)[24] and their dog
Prince. Charles Webb junior married in 1883, and neither he nor Sidney
were 'home birds', but Sidney introduced his parents to Bernard Shaw,
Graham Wallas and the other friends he made during the next ten years.

   Despite the tempting offers of his new employer, Sidney Webb had –
unlike his brother – no ambition for a successful business career. If he had
his mother's industry, resourcefulness and unusually powerful memory,
he seems to have resembled his father in culture and outlook. He even followed him so far as to become, for a time, a volunteer. More to the point,
he subscribed to paternal influence so far as the merits of John Stuart Mill
were concerned. Mill was not only the great teacher to be respected, but
also the model to be followed. As he had chosen a career in the East India
Company, as a means to security and leisure for continued learning, so
Webb elected to enter the Civil Service, eventually reaching the Colonial
Office.[25] The end of his formal schooling marked the beginning of a ten-
year period of intensive further education, associated with entry into the
public service and continuous promotion within it. Sidney was a voracious reader, whose reading was distinguished by its phenomenal range
and speed. He became a member of the London Library and a reader at
the British Museum and devoured books at a rate that left his friends –
and his examiners – humbled and aghast. The introduction of an examination system, rigorous and systematic, was one of the most characteristic
features of English life in the third quarter of the nineteenth century. It
was essential to that rise of the professional man, as distinct from the professional gentleman, which was one of the important characteristics of
English social development at this time.[26] The older professions, such as
medicine, developed in the 1850s associations with an established 'ethic',

and acquired, with the help of legislation, control over entry. But the newer ones, such as engineering, architecture, dentistry and schoolteaching, sought to create and perfect examination systems, providing objective criteria of a man's fitness to practise. High connections, or experience of the public schools, or of Oxford and Cambridge still counted for much but – to the alarm of the old landed oligarchy – they were ceasing to be necessary or sufficient conditions of entry into the new and growing categories of professional employment. To succeed, one needed to be a good examinee, and in the history of mankind there can have been few examinees that could compare in point of excellence with Sidney Webb. The challenge of an examination brought him to exactly the right pitch of competitive excitement. His memory furnished him with everything he needed. His sure sense of relevance and his lucid style allowed him to express himself with clarity and economy. He swept all before him.

At the end of 1876 Sidney took a first-class certificate in German from the City of London College. This institution was one of several established around 1848, with the object of providing some useful employment for the intelligent artisan and as a counter-attraction to Chartist meetings on the Kennington Common. In point of fact few working men went to such establishments, and those that did sometimes caused the clerical directorate so much trouble that the police had to be called in to evict them. Most of the students were men of much the same social level as Sidney himself.[27] They were clerks who wore collars and ties and had smooth hands. Once he had left the colonial broker's Sidney could settle down to real work. Between November 1878 and December 1880 he received twenty educational awards from the City of London College. He took first-class certificates in arithmetic, book-keeping, English grammar, French and geology. In 1878 he won the Cotton Prize for modern language, as well as the Phenean Essay Prize. Next year he took the Thompson Prize in arithmetic and the Cobden Club Prize in political economy. He also made off with the Medhurst Prize for proficiency, punctuality and regularity. In 1880 he contented himself with the Cutler Law Prize, prizes in commerce and in geology, and the Lubbock Testimonial Scholarship for the highest aggregate number of marks in three of the subjects of examination. Lest this should be taken to mark a falling-off in ambition, it should be explained that he simultaneously enrolled at four institutions of continuing education in London. These were the Society for the Extension of Further Education, the Society for the Extension of University Teaching (where he took a first in geology) and the Society for the Encouragement of the Arts, Manufacturers and Commerce (where he took three certificates and several prizes). Also the Birkbeck Literary and Scientific Institution, where he secured eleven certificates between the end of 1879 and the close of the following year. If he did chance to be placed in the second division, he generally took the subject again and was placed in the first. 1879 at Birkbeck was particularly good. He was awarded the English Essay Prize and the Mednyansky Essay Prize, the Henken Prize in correspondence and the Ravenscroft Prize for English grammar. In addition to the Birkbeck Prize for mental science, he took prizes for logic and geology, along with the Chester Prize in political economy.[28]

While at Birkbeck, Sidney led his first public movement for institutional reform. He served as secretary to a committee formed to secure the better representation of the students in the institution. He led 'a large minority' of his fellow students in 'earnest protest' against an alteration of the constitution that made a two-thirds majority necessary before there could be any change of rule. Holding that 'unanimity of opinion can only be outlined by the sacrifice of either invaluable individuality, or of that healthy general interest in the affairs of the institution, which is the best guarantee for its stability', the protesters denounced the new rule. It would stereotype the institution and diminish its capacity for change. Under the pretence of protecting the minority, it established the dominion of a minority. The rule, approved by a simple majority, required a two-thirds majority to rescind it. Anticipating the discoveries of Michels, the protesters argued that

> No measure opposed by the Committee will have a chance of being passed: the Committee alone will practically be able to reject any alteration brought forward by the body of members. A committee – through its official position – its organisation – the numerous acquaintances of its members and their esprit de corps – necessarily commands great power in a meeting. This power is now rendered irresistible. The issue had been treated as a question of confidence, and this had prejudiced the decision in a most unwarrantable manner. The change had its origin in a determination to prevent lady subscribers from acquiring the full privilege of members. We contend that such a serious matter as an alteration of rules likely to last for generations should not be brought forward in order to defeat any particular resolution; still less, a resolution supported by so large a minority of student-members, and against which arguments may not be adduced.

The governing committee at Birkbeck was much displeased with Sidney Webb and firmly resolved that his protest should not be entered in their minutes.[29]

While Webb was troubling and triumphing at Birkbeck, he was simultaneously advancing up the civil service by examination. He had entered the War Office in 1878 as a lower-division clerk. In the following year he went into the Inland Revenue as a Surveyor of Taxes. Finally, in 1881, after an examination in which he offered neither of the favoured subjects of classics and mathematics and yet secured 'an almost incredible number of marks',[30] he went into the Colonial Office as a first division clerk. Such a clerkship in the Colonial Office was worth a starting salary of £250 a year. The duties were not onerous. The doors did not open for public business before 11 o'clock even if one had to stay on until 7.30 in the evening. The blight of the Office, which came to weary Sidney more and more as the years passed, was procrastination and 'bottling'. The old staff, who formed the first-class upper division clerks, were a product of the patronage system. Some were sleepy and easy-going, others were men with shattered nerves who suffered from a suppressed phobia which made them paper-shy. All suffered from a 'potterers' rot'. The second class of the upper division was made up of university men recruited by competition – like Sydney Olivier – along with a 'younger, more intelligent class of men' – like Sidney Webb. (The near namesakes, who were both for a time in the West Indian department as well as being resident clerks together, soon became firm friends.) Beneath were the subordinate clerks of the lower division: men who entered the service at about seventeen, having had a lower-middle-class education. Finally there were the writers, who spent their time copying out the dispatches.

'In the afternoons, exercise was provided in the large First-class Clerks' room of the Eastern Department in the form of cricket, played with a paper ball tightly lashed with string, and a long tin map case for bat.'[31] One could well understand how Sidney, who probably neglected the cricket, found ample time to prepare himself for the Bar. This process normally cost about £130, but Webb made it more than pay for itself by winning £450 in academic prizes.[32] After being placed in the first division of classes in the intermediate examinations for the Bachelor of Laws, he 'came a mucker', as he put it, and finished in the third class. The reasons for this comparative failure will be made apparent in the next chapter, but there was an earlier disappointment which must be noticed first, for it must have made Sidney ponder the strange association between social divisions and administrative hierarchy in the Colonial Office.

In 1883 Sidney competed for the Whewell Scholarships in international law awarded by Trinity College, Cambridge. He secured the second scholarship, but was unable to take it up because his Colonial Office duties would not allow him to meet the condition that he must reside in the college. Sidney sought to demonstrate – and he did it very persuasively – that the Master and the Fellows of Trinity had a discretionary power under the Statutes, which would allow them to waive this condition if they chose to do so. The Permanent Under-Secretary, Sir Robert Hundert, commended him on the skill with which he made out his case. The Earl of Derby wrote to the Master of Trinity on Webb's behalf. Sidney drafted a letter to Sedgwick in the hope of mustering Millite understanding in his interests. It was of no avail. Trinity could not be induced to make a concession. Sidney certainly felt that he had been cheated, and that the episode was of larger than personal significance. He filed all the correspondence together under the jocular heading, 'Memories pour servir à l'histoire de notre siècle.'[33] When he gave his first series of public lectures at the Working Men's College, he proudly and defiantly described himself as 'Second Whewell Scholar in International Law'. When Mark Pattison's *Memoirs* were published in 1885, Sidney became engrossed in them. He found in Pattison a kindred spirit.[34] Here was a remarkably hard-working and conscientious man, having (so he said) no history but a mental history, who directed all his energy to self-improvement and the forming of his own mind free 'from the bondage of unreason'. At Oxford, Pattison felt ill at ease among contemporaries whose social background and graces he did not share. In his *Memoirs* he recorded how his new ideas on teaching and university administration had brought him up against the archaic college establishment that had sought to deprive him of his fellowship.[35] 'It would be interesting', said Sidney,

> to know how much has been lost to England by the unfortunate chance which placed both its ancient Universities in malarial marshes, instead of on high ground, swept by bracing sea-breezes and watered by rapidly flowing streams, which at any rate, know their own minds.[36]

A 'full, true and particular account of the great Whewell Scholarship case' has its place in any explanation of Sidney's complex, but basically antipathetic, attitude towards the classical, literary and aristocratic cultural tradition of Oxford and Cambridge. It was an interesting episode that brought into relief social and cultural divisions which were to be fully confirmed by later experiences. The new race of professional men who struggled to make their way as gentlemen (since everybody thought it was their duty to try to become gentlemen) could only make their way forward through evening institutes and other establishments which had been created for 'practical' purposes. And they were largely imbued with the traditions of scientific, provincial, bourgeois culture. Those who rose through this process were likely to sense that they were at once more professional than their counterparts from the ancient universities, while being less assured in their manners and their tastes.

The belief that the great benefit of an education at Oxford or Cambridge lies in the opportunities it affords for young men to thrash out informally the ultimate problems of meaning and purpose, human and divine is one of those exemplary half-truths. 'The Apostles' or the 'Society of Mumbo-Jumbo' have always been affairs of minorities. If those reared in the tradition of provincial bourgeois culture had to spend longer in the lecture room and on 'cram', they also managed to create their own societies, in which some at least of the same issues were debated. Sidney delivered his first lecture when he was exactly seventeen years old. His audience probably consisted of fellow students at Birkbeck, and his subject was 'The Existence of Evil'.[37] It was evidently well received, for it was followed by another on 'The Service of God'.[38] In these lectures Sidney swiftly dispatched the Almighty – although in a very tolerant, reasonable and sympathetic manner that was wholly becoming to an admirer of the late John Stuart Mill. He noticed that

> the infliction of punishment is now regarded as a defect even by our poor human educators. Their business is to govern by developing the sympathies, by moral persuasion, by the influence of high example, and in proportion as they fail in this, and have to resort to harsher proceedings, they give the measure of their incapacity. How much more then must severity be discreditable in an all-powerful Deity? Besides, not one of God's punishments is educational; all have the character of wanton ferocity. Adam, having sinned once, is punished forever.

He concluded that

> the pain and sin here below is not God's punishment on our sins, not yet a trial of our virtue. If we believe in God, I think it follows that his attributes are infinite power and love. Predestination and original sin are *not* consistent with justice, and therefore *not* with love. These cannot be the causes of sin and evil.

As for the service of God: the problem was that if He was infinitely rational, powerful and loving, 'What good can the so-called service be to such a One?' If service meant prayer and prayer mean petition then 'God is not a weak-minded fool to be changed by every petition addressed to Him.' Yet Sidney, at seventeen, was of the opinion that religious belief, if sincere, was the most valuable for the conduct of life. He affirmed that 'any religion is better than no religion'. Prayer might have beneficial effects even if it was of no practical use, and even if a large proportion of those worth respecting had been claimed by secularism. 'Is there', he asked, 'a religion of the heart, even if not of the head?' If so it must be something more than a merely allegorical statement of Utilitarian principles, with the service of God made all one with the services of man.

Sidney's unbelief began with a growing sense of the logical and moral inadequacy of Christianity. He stopped accompanying his mother to church and when on some rare occasion he did so, it made him cross. As 'best man' at his brother's wedding, he found the service

> a most lugubrious and disgraceful remnant of superstition. The mild officiating curate gave us the entire animal, concluding with 'two short rules for happiness in the new state', evidently attributed by some Church organ. These were gracious heavens, the whole duty of married man – first to join together in morning prayer, second to attend church. And this is the institution which is in touch with the national life![39]

He had already been vexed by considerations of this sort before he began to encounter the problems of reconciling theology with the teachings of the geologists and biologists, or came to regard the clergy as hirelings of peace and order battening on the 'surplus value' produced by the proletariat.[40] Yet like most of the emancipated members of his generation he felt the cravings of religious need, and was haunted by the difficulty of finding new sanctions for morality bereft of its traditional theological support.

From a student debating club Sidney moved on in 1879 to the Zetetical Society: the oddly named meeting place of religious-minded agnostics, faddists, and the more intellectual and progressive sort of lower-middle-class enthusiast. The term 'zetetic' was apparently coined in the seventeenth century. In the 1820s there had been zetetical societies which had organised working-class infidels.[41] But this one, established at 9 Conduit Street, Regent Street, was emphatically neither infidel nor working-class. It was concerned with social, political and philosophical subjects, and it had a special philosophical section which met monthly to hear the more technical papers on political economy, as well as metaphysics, logic, ethics and psychology. The Zetetical Society declared that

> its primary object is to search for truth in all matters affecting the interests of the human race; hence no topic, theological or otherwise, discussed with decorum, is excluded from its programme: and that the Society may not become identified with any particular opinion or school of thought, no vote is taken except on its business affairs, and its doors are thereby thrown open to all who, whatever their opinion may be, desire to arrive at truth.

The subscription was five shillings per session. The society's committee consisted of young men and women, who tended to get married to each other, had not been to university and who wrote books about managerial problems such as the keeping of factory accounts – or so it would seem from the sparse information that is available. At least 5 of the 13 members of the committee subsequently became Fabians: among these were George

Bernard Shaw and Sidney Webb, who met each other for the first time at a Zetetical meeting in 1879.[42]

Despite its avowal of an impartial and Socratic spirit, the Zetetical had a radically progressive and avant-garde character. Between 1880 and 1882 it was addressed by a number of distinguished and worthy, if now mostly forgotten, radicals. Dr C. R. Drysdale spoke on the Malthusian state remedy for poverty and dear food. He was the president of the Malthusian League, which had been established in 1878. The Bradlaugh–Besant trial, and the outrageous sentence of four months' imprisonment on the devoted and courageous publisher Edward Truelove in 1878–9, 'went far to make legal the general, free discussion of contraceptive knowledge' by provoking a violent popular reaction.[43] Dr Charles Drysdale, unlike his brother George, was more concerned with the economic and social implications of contraception than with its medical technique. It may be assumed that he had no difficulty in abiding by the rule respecting 'decorum'. For many years the young Webb was a very decided Malthusian, and he took a particularly deep interest in the mortality of rich and poor, a subject on which Charles Drysdale had just spoken to the Medical Society of London.

Sidney probably already knew James Beal, who spoke on the great reforms and reformers. Beal, auctioneer and land agent, had his offices at 20 Regent Street, close to the rooms of the Zetetical Society. Along with Sidney's father he had allegedly been a member of John Stuart Mill's election committee in 1865. Beal had a splendid reformist record. He had been associated with Place and Hetherington in the campaign against the taxes on knowledge. He had addressed a series of trenchant letters to the Bishop of London on 'certain Popish practices' observed in the churches of St Paul, Wilton Place, and of St Barnabas, Pimlico. With some success he had challenged the legality of ritualism before the Privy Council. Of still greater interest, he was a pioneer in the struggle to reform London. In 1857 he began a long struggle against the London gas companies which culminated in the passing of the Metropolitan Gas Act in 1860. This measure improved the quality of the gas supply, limited its prices, curtailed dividends and effected a net saving to the consumers of £625 000 per annum. He was also an energetic and effective advocate of an improved water supply for the metropolis. In 1876 he broke new and important ground:

> Fearing lest an increased education rate should render the cause of scholastic enlightenment unpopular, he set himself to investigate other possible sources of revenue, and an altogether remarkable series of papers on 'The Corporation Guilds and Charities of the City of London', contributed to the *Dispatch* and signed 'Nemesis', was the result.

He exposed endless anomalies and gigantic abuses, and demonstrated that what was wanted was a single municipality for the whole of London. Here was a career perfectly suited to inspire and instruct Sidney. But there was more to it than that

> for Beal, with all his fiery zeal, has a wonderful knack of converting foes into friends, if only an opportunity of exerting his personal influence is afforded him. His own mind is so thoroughly made up, that he will speedily make up yours if you are not on your guard.

Here was a character from whom much could be learned.[44]

The association with Mill was maintained in the person of Helen Taylor, who talked to the society on the Irish Land League. Richard Congreve, who had inaugurated organised positivism in England in the year of Sidney's birth, came before the Zetetical in his role as backroom Pope of the new religion of humanity. Congreve had resigned his fellowship at Wadham College, Oxford, in the hope of teaching larger and maturer audiences to find salvation through following the more up-to-date curriculum devised by Comte out of the inheritance of Saint-Simon and the tradition of *L'École polytechnique*. When he talked to the Zetetical Society in October 1881, Congreve had already broken up his own following, partly through insistence on the quaint, sacerdotal side of positivism. But there was much else in Comte that appealed to him immensely, and that continued to influence him with varying degrees of intensity until the end of his life. He followed Comte in rejecting metaphysics, and making philosophy only a science of the sciences, and depository for the most general and important scientific truths. If he shared Mill's contempt for the details of Comte's new religion, he had a broad sympathy with his attempt to bring religious feeling into harmony with the conclusions of scientific enquiry. In particular, he applauded the attempt to establish a positivist polity founded upon the final science – the new historical discipline of sociology. The reconciliation of order and progress; the alliance of the philosopher and the proletariat; the moralisation of the capitalist; the ordered planning of the economy through the concentration of capital, and the direction of the banks – these were among the items in the Comtian repertoire which for a time captivated Webb and left some permanent impression upon him.[45]

The Zetetical Society was by no means solely an affair of distinguished speakers. Many of the members themselves prepared and discussed papers. They ranged far and wide: from the origin of civilisation to Cobbett and vaccination; from vegetarianism to the political emancipation of women; from spelling reform to the future of the working classes; not to mention Shelley, Ireland, utopia, Athens, India, parliamentary oaths and national insurance as a remedy for pauperism. Sidney read his first paper to the society in 1881 when he was twenty-two years of age. He gave it the impressive but obscure title of the 'Ethics of Existence'.[46] It was prompted by Mallock's *Is Life Worth Living?*, a work which the young lecturer found to be a 'dull, incomplete and shallow criticism on Utilitarianism and Materialism'. It was also – although Webb hardly confessed it – prompted by J.S. Mill's *Autobiography*.

It may be recalled that when Mill was twenty he was

in a dull state of nerves, such as everybody is occasionally liable to; unsusceptible to enjoyment or pleasurable excitement; one of those moods when what is pleasure at other times becomes insipid or indifferent; the state, I should think, in which converts to Methodism usually are when smitten by their first 'conviction of sin'. In this frame of mind it occurred to me to put the question directly to myself: 'Suppose that all your objects in life were realised: that all the changes in institutions and opinions which you are looking forward to could be completely effected at this very instant: would this be a great joy and happiness to you?' And an irrepressible self-consciousness distinctly answered: 'No!' At this my heart sank within me: the whole foundation on which my life was constructed fell down. All my happiness was to have been found in the continual pursuit of this end. The end had ceased to charm, and how could there ever again be any interest in the means? I seemed to have nothing left to live for.

Mill claimed that Coleridge had exactly described his case:

A grief without a pang, void, dark and drear,
A drowsy, stifled, unimpassioned grief,
Which finds no natural outlet or relief
In word, or sigh, or tear.[47]

This was Webb's mood in 1881; it was, he allowed, as Mill himself did, a state of mind passed through by most reflective men, even if they are not usually confirmed for ever in melancholy. But while Mill could find none but Coleridge to express his feelings, Webb marshalled his supporters from the entire history of world literature, in proof of

How weary, stale, flat and unprofitable
Seem all the uses of this world.

He began with Johnson:

Ye who listen with credulity to the whispers of fancy, and pursue with eagerness the phantoms of hope, who expect that age will perform the promises of youth, and that the deficiency of the present will be supplied by the morrow – attend to the history of Rasselas, Prince of Abyssinia.

He continued with Tennyson:

> I stretch the lame hands of faith, and grope,
> And gather dust and chaff, and call
> To what I feel is Lord of all,
> And faintly trust the larger hope.

> Most of my hearers [said Sidney] will, I think, know something of this state, so prevalent at the present day. Its leading feature is a deep sense of unsatisfactoryness, of unrest, of discord. This is no new thing. We trace the influence of fits of pessimism in the Psalms and especially in Ecclesiastes, in ancient Greek and Roman literature, and in the middle ages. But as we come down to our day the names become thicker, until there is hardly a poet of the present century whose views are not more or less tinged with melancholy. Take as instances Shelley, Byron, Heine, Lamartine, Leopardi, Tennyson and Browning.

Sidney had no wish to follow Schopenhauer and attempt to build up to a logical conclusion of pessimism by arguing from the facts of the universe and of the nature of man. 'These German metaphysicians seem like so many cobwebs to the average Englishman.' He wanted to describe this state of mind and to account for it in commonsense terms. This he did by making reference to the prevalence of indigestion, 'a potent cause of melancholia: mental overwork; and there is I think one other special physical cause that cannot be dwelt upon.'

It may occur to the reader that this explanation, although admirable in its way, would hardly suffice to explain a growing tendency to pessimism. However, Sidney had anticipated this objection: indigestion arose from want of exercise, light and air. In short, 'from the necessary conditions of the life of great cities'. It was the paradox of progress that, while its march made cities grow, so the oxidation per head decreased. He maintained that there was little that could be done to alter the material conditions of life:

> If increasing knowledge makes accidents less frequent, increasing the use of machinery will keep the average equal. If increasing justice shares the earth's return to labour more justly among the labourers, Malthusians know it is quite visionary to suppose a time when severe labour will cease to be necessary for the maintenance of the race.

There was however, one other source of pessimism – acuteness of sensibility, for which some treatment might be prescribed. As sensibility increased, excruciating pains came far to exceed in intensity corresponding pleasures. Since inducing a state of placid sluggishness or dull stupidity was unlikely to be a course which would commend itself to a Zetetical Society, and least of all to Sidney Webb himself, he recommended precisely the plan followed by John Stuart Mill: avoid introspection; discover 'the efficacy of an absorbing interest in removing grief'. Without mentioning Mill at all, he too subscribed to the view that

> happiness is the test of all rules of conduct, and the end of life. But … those only are happy … who have their minds fixed on some object other than their own happiness: on the happiness of others, on the improvement of mankind, even on some art or pursuit followed not as a means, but itself as an ideal end. Aiming thus at something else, they find happiness by the way. The enjoyments of life (such was now my theory) are sufficient to make it a pleasant thing when they are taken en passant without being a principal object. Once make them so, and they are immediately felt to be insufficient. They will not bear a scrutinising examination. Ask yourself whether you are happy, and you cease to be so.[48]

The pessimism of 1881 was no mere youthful affectation. Webb was a settled pessimist for at least ten years. Nor was his paper out of keeping with the rest of the Zetetical Society's programme: a programme that was strikingly representative of the preoccupation of the time, and so evidently formative of the minds of its most distinguished members. Pessimism, positivism and socialism were a progression common to many of the ablest young professional men of the 1880s Great Depression.[49] Schopenauer appeared in an English translation early in the decade, and this no doubt encouraged the belief that pessimism was the mode of thought and the essential feeling of all great writers. He also insisted, as Sidney has been shown to do, on a great line of distinction between the man of feeling and thought, and the ordinary unthinking and unfeeling man. But pessimism bore no necessary relation to misanthropy. On the contrary, considered as a thesis to be defended, it may have helped to direct attention to the extent of poverty and social evil. If it was a warning against a utopian dream that took no account of reality, it could, through its recommendation to negate the individual will, prepare men to dedicate themselves to causes and submerge themselves in active association. Positivism, with its maxim *vivre pour autres* and its repudiation of the 'metaphysical' language of individual rights in favour of a positive science of morals emphasising social duties, offered the individual submission to

the interests of humanity. It announced itself to be the last and final outcome of modern science, yet it issued in a religion in which the head was
to be subordinated to the heart, and knowledge was to be directed by sympathy and compassion. Although positivism was optimistic about the ultimate destiny of mankind, it held out no hope of immediate or painless
deliverance; it insisted upon the need to elaborate and develop social science; it offered no run-and-read solutions. Finally, socialism came to suggest that where the positivist was content to educate and to convert, one
might properly seek the enforcement of morals and wisely regulate what a
purified public opinion proved powerless to control.

The influence of his father and the whole quality of his education disposed Sidney Webb towards positivism – considered, in the first place, not
as a specifically Comtist doctrine, but as a whole stream of tendency in
modern European thought. He contended that, outside mathematics, we
owed little to the ancients. Knowledge had grown more in the last four
hundred years than in all preceding periods put together. The end of the
eighteenth century had seen the inauguration of what he termed 'the second Renaissance'. James Mill and Bentham had given us most of the fundamental ideas of psychology, ethics and jurisprudence. Adam Smith and
Malthus had literally created political economy, while in philology the
same honour belonged to von Humboldt, Grimm and Schlegel. These
were the opening men of an epoch of which John Stuart Mill was the last
considerable representative. Sidney declared: 'I yield to no one in my
admiration for the two Mills.' Yet he considered that J.S. Mill had
belonged to what was now recognisably a pre-scientific age. He had
known little of the natural sciences and less of biology:

> In fact his education in this respect belonged to the old-fashioned type.
> His work in logic and political economy is unshaken because there biol-
> ogy has but little influence, but I contend that his Psychology, his Ethics
> and above all else his Metaphysics, his theory of things, want correcting
> by later ideas.

Mill was a destructive. 'The great generalisations which I contend must
change the whole drift of our Philosophy, are especially the conservation
of Energy and Evolution.' It was not John Stuart Mill, but Herbert
Spencer, who must be acclaimed the Bacon of the Second Renaissance.[50]

On 22 March 1882 Sidney gave a paper to the Zetetical Society in which
he attempted to make good these contentions concerning the new learning of the nineteenth century. He called his talk 'Heredity as a Factor
in Psychology and Ethics'.[51] He began with an assertion that would have
had more warrant had it been made in 1892 than in 1882: namely, that
the theory of heredity had made great advances in the course of the

nineteenth century. In conformity with a general rule illustrated by Newton in physics and Darwin in biology, 'the advance is not so much in the facts which science inductively demonstrates, as in the theories in which the facts are summed up, and in the new light thrown upon other facts by the deductive application of the theories.' Darwin himself had asserted: 'we may look at the following law ... as fairly well established. ... A tendency in *every* character new and old, to be transmitted by ... generation, though often counteracted by various known and unknown causes.'[52] According to Sidney, this applied to structure: 'from the species dog, nothing can be produced but dogs', and this with reference to individual peculiarities a well as the general typical form. Racial and national characteristics were inherited. It was 'inevitable' that peculiarities of function were equally transmissible. And here Sidney paused to elaborate the point in a manner that was to become the hallmark of Webb for the next fifty years:

> it must suffice to remind you that peculiarities of taste and smell, of hearing, sight and touch are all frequently recognised as inherited, including near-sight, long sight, dull sight, squinting, cataract, amaurosis, day-blindness, daltonism, deafness, dumbness and left-handedness. In fact diseases generally – which are nothing but morbid peculiarities of structure – have nearly all been proved to be derivable from ancestors. Instances are especially well known in the cases of such various disorders as Gout, Insanity, Consumption, Leprosy, Catalepsy, Epilepsy, Apoplexy, Asthma, Elephantiasis, Stone, Cancer, Sebaceous Tumours, Plica Polonica, Ichthyosis, Psoriasis, Dipsomania, Sonambulism, General Nervousness and Suicidal Mania.

The point was that nothing was too trifling or too momentous to be transmitted, including – according to the still conventional wisdom of Lamarck – 'scars and wounds'. But the key contention was the inheritance of psychical as well as physical characteristics. Sidney held that 'we imply this clearly [*sic*] when we talk of the courage of the Plantagenets; the obstinacy of the Bourbons; or the pertinacity of the Hohenzollerns.' It was neglect of this circumstance that put John Stuart Mill behind the level of the age. To grasp this great 'fact' was to place oneself in a position that allowed certain long-standing problems to be solved, or more adequately approached. For example, this applied to the celebrated debate between Mill and the empiricists, on the one hand, and intuitionists like Hamilton on the other, concerning innate ideas. The empiricists were, according to Sidney, incomparably superior to their opponents, and entirely right in contending that all our ideas are derived from experience. What they missed – thanks to their ignorance of biology – was that 'our experience must be understood to relate not merely to individual experience but also to that of our ancestors. Consequently they were unable to rebut convincingly the contention of the intuitionists that such propositions as $2+2=4$ could never have acquired such fixity and certainty merely through upbringing and being particularly well-attested inductive generalisations. We do feel an unusual degree of assurance about these propositions. But this feeling, declared Sidney, was to be explained not by the different logical or epistemological status of these propositions, but because the experience of the race 'had fixed and embodied them in the brain cells we inherit'. Similarly, there were long-standing problems arising from Berkeley's theory of vision, which could be resolved thanks to the scientific observation of new-born chicks by Sir Joseph Banks.

What interested Sidney most was the light that he imagined new notions of heredity shed upon the problems that J.S. Mill discussed in his essay *On Liberty*:

> Following the lead of Humboldt and John Mill, advanced liberals have generally gone to such an extreme of liberty as has unfortunately caused them to be separated by a great gulf from the practical politicians who have to work the government machine, and upon whom they might have had an important influence for good … The philosophical radical had found a theory, that self-regarding actions should not be interfered with by the government, and he thereupon called upon the government to hold its hand in such cases as vaccination, education, sanitation and what not, because he chose to assert that these were self-regarding actions. The stupidity of officialdom and sagacity of statesmanship, not understanding why he was wrong, but simply perceiving by that inherited intuition of common-sense, that he was wrong, have held on their course and the philosophical radical has blindly persisted in his vituperation of moderate interference, with the effect of throwing away that beneficial influence upon radical politicians which seems to have been exercised by Bentham and James Mill, the Fathers of the Tribe.
>
> For, if we believe in the universal potency of heredity, it must at once become evident that, in this particular world at least, there is no such thing as purely self-regarding action, and the fundamental axiom and world-moving level of the philosophic radicals becomes a mere scholastic fulmination of no immediate practical application.

However, the conclusion of Webb's argument pointed to Positivism rather than to Socialism: 'Should Government then interfere with each and every act? God forbid that any such conclusion should be drawn.' Bentham – so much wiser than his declared disciples – 'said that the proper sphere of government was to be determined by a laborious and far-reaching examination of each particular case.' What heredity brought home was the proof of the Positivist notion of inter-generational independence and indebtedness:

> We can, alas, no longer hold the comfortable doctrine that God made this world and the sin and the shame and the misery which is in it. Our ancestors made this world and its imperfections, and if we are impressed by the pain of our fellow creatures: if we feel the shame of the plundered toiling lives of the millions of England; if we hear of the unspeakable atrocities which all over the world the strong man is committing on the weak; if we know that the dark places of the earth are *full* of cruelty; let us at all times remember that if our ancestors have made these horrors, it is we who have in our hands the making of the future world … Our petty lives are a trust for which we are fully responsible, not to God, but at the bar of our conscience: a trust for the exercise of which we have the clearest instructions written in the groans and blood of murdered humanity where, for instance, the skeletons of those who fell on the battlefield of South Africa, and of those who died of starvation in England last year, alike cry out a solemn warning against aggression by the strong on the weak, by the rich on the poor.

Such was Sidney Webb in the days of the Zetetical Society: a youth of astonishing learning: ingenious and bold – if still somewhat jejune – in speculation; by temperament a sensitive, introspective pessimist; by education, a Positivist inclining increasingly to Comtism, and passionately eager to serve suffering mankind. Although it was already evident that he had the makings of an outstanding teacher, he had no great presence and he still needed to write out his speeches in full rather than deliver them from his notes. He was small – no more than 5 feet 4 inches tall – and ill-proportioned, the head being exceedingly large in relation to the body.[53] He was short-sighted, and his blue eyes were very bright and prominent below a high and well-shaped forehead.[54] His hair was dark and thick. He grew an imperial and preferred to be photographed in profile. He spoke rapidly and forcibly and with what – to aristocratic ears – was taken to be a cockney accent.[55] However, a young woman who studied him closely, and who was to be the first of many writers to report him in fiction, found the evidences of culture in 'voice, manner and diction.' If he was small, he had no 'superfluous flesh'. If his head was large in relation to his body, it was 'a fine and rugged head'. If his background should have sunk him into 'a complete rut of commonplace', he was highly attractive and immensely impressive. And it was as a teacher that he was at his best. Not only had he

> an unusual mastery over words, a clearness and simplicity of thought and a fearlessness of expression that drove the sentence out in well-directed

blows, but in the matter of his lecture he himself had an indomitable faith. Deft and ingenious in the logical application of argument he might be, but the main quality was burning conviction and absolute sincerity. To a girl accustomed to the superior didactic manner, the scholarly hesitation, and the careful non-self-committal of a Cambridge lecturer, this fire of sincerity was something astounding. Moreover there was humour and racy originality in the turn of some the lecturer's phrases, pointing to a very deep streak of the quality which should be common to all men, but which has been almost lost to the race in the process of civilisation – and that is of humanness.[56]

Sidney could be attractive to women. Throughout his life they noticed his small, finely shaped hands.[57]

To a tall, young, red-haired Irishman, Webb was not small: he was 'rather below middle height'; he was not merely unusually well read and able: he was already the most knowledgeable and most able man in England. He was not merely an admirer of John Stuart Mill, trying to work his way through problems in the positivist tradition; but a 'disciple … [who] had grasped the economic certainty that private property in the sources of production plus freedom of contract must produce a plutocracy face to face with a proletariat, and substitute class-war for genuine democracy.'[58] Probably something of this idealised picture entered into Bernard Shaw's impression of Sidney Webb when he first saw him; but, for the rest, Shaw's attractive account telescopes the developments of a decade or so in the most misleading manner. Sidney came as no *deus ex machina* either to Shaw or to the Fabian Society. In the days of the Zetetical, Sidney showed neither the clearness nor the coolness that Shaw retrospectively attributed to him.

Yet that they met there is incontrovertible, as that their friendship was of high importance for them both and for socialism in England. GBS recalled that: 'Quite the wisest thing I ever did was to force my friendship on him and to keep it; for from that time I was not merely a futile Shaw, but a committee of Webb and Shaw.'[59] He told Sidney:

Fortunately … I had a musical mother, and was stuffed with first-class music, National Gallery pictures, and uncensored literature: in short, very highly educated on one side before I was ten. When we met, you knew everything that I didn't know and I knew everything that you didn't know. We had everything to learn from one another and brains enough to do it.[60]

On another occasion he remarked: 'The balancing instinct in Nature is remarkable. Alarmed at her work in 1856, she produced you three years later as my complement. It was one of her few successes.'[61]

Sidney was as persuaded as Shaw that they were complementary. It was a union of outrageous paradox with invincible common sense; of egotistical exuberance with selfless dedication: of wit and eloquence with industry and learning; of the platform with the committee. Beginning with the comic, sophisticated innocence of the newly wise, their partnership proved to be effective and durable. The one whose whole life was in display and self-advertisement could enter into an equal relationship with the other: he who came to renounce personal power in favour of a pervasive, self-effacing influence. That they could use each other is clear. That they came to a deeply affectionate mutual regard courses against the probabilities and enlarges hope.

Yet Shaw was mistaken in implying that there was a fair exchange of education between them. It was he, rather than Sidney, who benefited on this account. Webb saw to it that Shaw was 'documented'; Shaw failed, if he ever seriously tried, to widen and deepen Sidney's artistic sensibilities. The young Webb never appears to have attended a concert or discussed music. He never referred to painting beyond remarking that the Sansisto Madonna was the only ancient picture that really touched him. He went to the theatre; he was enthusiastically with William Morris in being Anti-Scrape; but he trusted his own judgement of the arts only in relation to literature. He was fond of poetry and he frequently read novels, being as well acquainted with Zola and Freytag as with Dickens and Thackeray. However, his favourite novelist was George Eliot, and it was intense disappointment with the inadequacies of George Eliot that persuaded Shaw that he was capable of becoming a successful writer.[62] What Sidney valued in *Silas Marner*, *Romola* and *Midddlemarch* was the plausible description of bourgeois life, and persuasive insistence on positivist morals. As Sidney reflected: 'The aristocracy is after all a small class, and the world consists chiefly [*sic*] of that vast and undefined middle class to which nearly all George Eliot's characters belong.' The standard complaint that she was too gloomy and pessimistic, and too prone to indulge in explicit scientific analysis of character, was rejected by Webb. For him, the world was really like that, and it was natural to one of her culture and education to take the reader into the dissecting room. Her books were unrivalled as culture for the feelings and as carriers 'of the great lessons of Work, Renunciation and Submission'.[63]

It was not from Shaw, another cultural outsider and autodidact, but from Sydney Olivier and Graham Wallas that Webb felt that he had most to contend against and most to learn. From about 1882 Olivier and Webb were living together in the Colonial Office as resident clerks, the fate of the British Empire being regularly left in their hands overnight. One evening Wallas called to see Olivier with whom he had struck up a friendship at Oxford. Olivier was out, and he passed the time until his return by playing chess with Sidney Webb and arguing about the world in general.[64] Sidney's friendship with these two men was, throughout the 1880s, singularly warm and deep. For a time Olivier had served as a tutor to the children of Henry Crompton, the leading Positivist, and Webb and he were both attracted to Comte. Wallas was a schoolteacher ready to be impressed by the limitations as well as the strengths of the classical and literary tradition of Oxford. He shared Webb's large ambitions for improvement and his generous social sympathies, but discovered that Sidney's education had given him clarity of purpose and efficiency in method and resource that he lacked.[65] Sidney recalled that

> Wallas had enjoyed what was then declared in England, to be the best education that the world could give. I had almost the diametrical opposite … constantly to be meeting him in intimate converse was, to me, a liberal education beyond price …[66]

Although Shaw was quickly brought in to complete the quartet, it was Wallas and Olivier who widened his historical understanding, particularly of classical antiquity, and they helped him to instruct himself and his sister Ada in studying Virgil and Horace, Cicero and Lucian.[67] Olivier and Wallas helped to enlarge Webb's knowledge rather than to modify his values or redirect his attitude. If Sidney was to acquire the elements of a classical education at second hand, his mind – as Wallas complained – was to the end that of an Aristoteleian rather than a Platonist. His attitude to the literary and architectural remains of classical antiquity was obstinately 'philistine'. Thus, upon reading Lucian, he concluded that little of it would be accepted by a publisher nowadays.[68] A visit to Hadrian's Wall only served to lower his already low opinion of the Romans: as a feat of engineering it did not begin to compare with the London Underground. As Sidney remarked to Wallas:

> However important the Greeks, like the Celts, have been to our development, we are not bound to find either their drama or their stone axes as good as ours:
>
> > John P
> > Robinson he
> > Said they didn't know everything down in
> > Judee.
>
> There![69]

In expressing his debt to Wallas for a liberal education, Webb was not confusing it with a classical one. It was one thing to point up the difference between an educated man and one who had merely been trained for his *métier*, and another to make the correct and elegant translation from Latin and Greek the unique and distinctive attribute of cultural excellence. If Olivier and Wallas helped Sidney to see the inadequacy and shallowness of arguing for an education in useful knowledge, while leaving the training of the mind to look after itself, he saw with Sidgwick that the correct teaching of useful knowledge might afford as valuable a training in method as any other kind of teaching.[70] Greek might be indispensable to clergymen and lawyers might be better for being able to read Latin, but the dead languages offered little to medical men or to those who were entering the newer professions. It was impossible for a man of Sidney's learning and education to be intimidated into a sense of inferiority by the claims made for classical education as training of the mind. It was certain that such a man would detect behind this pretension attempts to retain an exclusive character in higher education, just as political, scientific and administrative progress was rendering it more and more futile. It was equally certain that a man with his capacity for learning would not be indifferent to the cultural tradition in which his friends and colleagues had been reared. But as we shall see towards the end of this chapter he discovered within that tradition conclusions which they had never suspected.

Yet in 1882–3 Sidney appears to have been far closer to the established Liberalism or Radicalism than his friends. He was as prepared as they were to seek a wider audience than that afforded by the Zetetical Society, but he had scruples against any organisation that might be thought to have designs on private property. In 1883 and 1884 he was active in the 'Lambeth Parliament'. He served as 'Foreign Secretary' and then as 'Colonial Secretary' in successive Liberal 'administrations'. The government was an advanced Radical one, which abolished oaths, disestablished the Church and amended the Education Act of 1870 so as to provide for 'national, free, secular, compulsory education'. But when a Conservative administration took over and introduced an Artisans' and Labourers' Dwelling Bill, Sidney opposed it:

> the leading principle of the Bill was the power it gave to the local authorities to acquire sites and erect artisans' dwellings. If they attempted to hand this over to the imperial department, or worse still to the miserable vestries, the jobbery, incompetence, mismanagement and gross extravagance would be something beyond comparison.[71]

Towards Henry George, whose agitation provided one of the most important gates for entry into the infant Socialist movement, Webb defined his attitude in a lecture, which he delivered in a Congregational church at the beginning of 1884. He found *Progress and Poverty* to be a 'wonderful book', although it was the awareness of poverty, not poverty itself, which was growing. As for rent, George could not abolish that; 'Difference in land did exist, and rent existed; and that was the difference.'

It was not rent which caused poverty, but the rise in population that increased rent by widening the gap between poor and good soils. The socialists were more consistent than George, but even if you added the nationalisation of capital to that of land, it would not remove poverty. 'It might do much if the increase of population went on exacting ever more toil to equal grinding poverty. This was an iron law – it was vain to kick against it. Without "prudential limits" to population, all other expedients were as but draining water into a sieve.' He could 'see no better system than the un-Christian, competitive, devil-take-the-hindmost system of private property'; but of this he was certain: 'because we seized the produce of the poor, they died.' The rich must cease to live in luxury. They should invest their wealth, which would reach the poor and make them better – it would be 'twice blessed'.[72] When Shaw invited him to join the Land Reform Union, one of several organisations that flourished under the impact of Henry George's propaganda for land nationalisation, Sidney declined except under certain conditions:

> I am, I think, an enthusiastic land law reformer, and I brought in a mild Bill last session to the Lambeth parliament … and an integral part of that scheme was a revision of the land tax, though this could not appear in the Bill. But although I am entirely in favour of the restitution of the land to the people – if it could be done – I am at present not a land nationaliser. Even if I were, I should not see in this any wonderful panacea. It would enable us to abolish all indirect taxation, which might be a good thing, but I am not enthusiastic at the prospect of cheap gin. It is certainly not worth a revolution, and even a revolution would not abolish rent, that presumed destroyer of wages. I enclose 2s 6d and should like to be a member of your society, if nationalisation is not an article of faith … but if the committee should not care about such a cold-blooded member, please return the 2s 6d …[73]

Shaw was already falling under the spell of Marx. He encouraged his friends to take part in a 'Karl Marx Club' or seminar, which was held in Hampstead under the auspices of Mrs Charlotte Wilson, a lady who wished to entertain very advanced opinions. Sidney's intended conversion was indefinitely postponed as a result of the absence of Shaw and the presence of the well-known economist, Edgeworth. Sidney described the scene for the benefit of GBS:

> We were eleven, and you were the faithless apostle. Mrs Wilson – who appeared to my astonished gaze as a 'Rosetti' young woman with dense

hair – read a most elaborate analysis of Chapter I of Marx, in English, over which she must have spent weeks. F.Y. Edgeworth, who was in the chair, then opened the proceedings by expressing his intense contempt for Karl and all his works, and snorted generally on the subject, as Ricardo might have done to an errant economist of the period. The company, most of whom were apparently under the impression that we were assembled for the purpose of reverently drinking in the wisdom of the great seer, were speechless with amazement; and Edgeworth's voice was followed by a silence which was thick enough to have been cut with a knife. In despair he appealed to me. I rushed in, and the rest of the evening was a kind of Scotch reel *a deux*, Edgeworth and I gaily dancing on the unfortunate K.M. trampling him remorselessly under- foot, amid occasional feeble protests and enquiries from Mrs Wilson (who had thrown away her young love upon him …)

Now this sort of thing is demoralising – I mean to me. Of course you will have already noticed how demoralising it must have been to the others. But unless some utterly unscrupulous socialistic dialectician like yourself turns up there, we shall have discarded *Le Capital* within a month, and be found studying the gospel of Ricardo! Please therefore appear there next meeting, Wednesday 12th. in great force to defend Chapters 2 and 3 on money. I am going to bring Olivier to assist you, if possible; but he alone would not be sufficiently 'brazen' in argument on the subject.[74]

Whether Shaw appeared at the next meeting or not, discarding *Le Capital* took more than a month. Almost a year later Sidney bought Volume II in German. 'I fear a very bad investment. Still it is something to be relieved of the sense of privation. (Without having read the book) I am prepared to assert that it is worth little. Everything is still put off – this time until the third volume.'[75] While Shaw still hoped to convert Sidney to Marx, Sidney hoped to convert Marx into a means of teaching Shaw some German. They read two pages in two hours, Sidney accompanying each word with a philosophical dissertation.[76]

Notwithstanding these appearances to the contrary, Sidney generally adopted a respectful attitude towards the founder of scientific socialism. For four years between 1883 and 1886 he led a prolonged discussion with his three friends and others on Marx methodology, his theory of value and his concept of socialism. It was not until 1886 when he wrote a paper on 'Rent, Interest & Wages: Being a Criticism of Karl Marx and a Statement of Economic Theory' that he arrived at any settled opinion.[77] Throughout, Webb recognised that Marx was a man of great learning and acute intelli- gence. He had set the cat among the pigeons by pointing up the failure of the orthodox economists to give an adequate account of profits or of the natural laws that regulated the distribution of income among the several classes. Early in 1884 he found that

> the chief value of the book of Karl Marx is the very plain account of the exploitation of labour. There is, however, nothing new in the explanation except the point of view, although this, perhaps, makes all the difference … he utterly and repeatedly smashes, pulverises and destroys the absurd idea that money breeds money, or that capital or machinery produce anything: an idea however that is still widely current … Marx pursues this subject with great ability, and has some instructive chapters on the rate and progress of exploitation.[78]

In 1886 Sidney was still commending Marx's summary of exploitation as 'a marvel of forcible exposition', while denying that, as a piece of applied economics, it had originality. Marx was inventive only with respect to terminology. Webb maintained that such a term as 'the degree of exploitation' was only a new expression for the rate of wages. At the most Marx's service had been to expose the problems which the orthodox economists had hushed up, but which were capable of being solved by orthodox methods.

It was with respect to Marx's methodology that Sidney's opinions went through their sharpest vicissitudes before he finally shrugged it off. In 1885 he had either forgotten about the 'instructive chapters on the rate and progress of exploitation', or else he had come to regard them as excursions into economic and social history, and standing in no logical relationship to the core of the analysis. In a paper on 'Economic Method',[79] Marx is described as the father of the 'abstract–intuitive' school, which differed from J.S. Mill and the advocates of the 'concrete–deductive' method in

> ignoring all the present facts of society, starting from premises of assumed primordial and necessary elements in human nature only … Karl Marx, as I understand him, would oust from the data of Political Economy all references to the political and social conditions of men, and would admit only human nature in the abstract, as it nowhere actually exists or has existed … The followers of Marx appeal confidently in their justification to the example of pure mathematics … To them man is man, and not capitalist employer, serf, slave or peasant proprietor … As economists they have produced nothing, corrected nothing, discovered nothing, and the only useful method in Political Economy remains the much abused, but still triumphant, Concrete Deductive Method of Ricardo, Mill and Cairns.

By the following year Sidney had discarded this remarkable opinion and come to the conclusion that Marx was also a follower of the concrete–deductive method, although he concealed this from himself and from others.

The first necessity for a due appreciation of Marx's work is a proper understanding of his point of view and method. To acquire such an understanding it is perhaps not too much to say that we should ignore all his professions and explanations on the subject, and pass resolutely over all his definitions. The mental twist – dare we call it affectation? – which constantly led him to enshrine his acute remarks in esoteric and philosophic terminology, or obscure metaphysical arrangement, only darkens counsel, and we quickly discover that he has no special means of discovering truth, but only a Teutonic capacity for over-subtle analysis.[80]

Marx, just like Mill, had to proceed by abstracting certain relationships from the influence of all modifying and counteracting factors, and to assume universal selfishness and perfect competition.

In classifying economic methods Sidney did not always relate the methodology to the distinctive aims and preoccupations of the various schools of economists. So far as he considered aims at all, he thought of them in their normative rather than in their analytic aspect. The 'theological school' in which he placed Ruskin and Henry George deduced certain principles from assumed ontological data, and Marx's labour theory of value was similarly a prop for his ethical conclusions. He did not consider the labour theory in relation to the avowed aim of discovering the laws of capitalist development. He considered it in its relation to the determination of prices in the market. In 1884 he evidently was teaching that 'free competition by removal of legal restraints, causes commodities freely produced … to exchange for each other in proportion to the labour expended on them'.[81] But he was already recommending his students and friends to read Marshall's *Economics of Industry*,[82] and by 1886 he had thoroughly convinced himself of the correctness of the Jevons type of marginal analysis. 'The peculiarity of the Marx theory is the determined exclusion of every fragment of scarcity value from the normal case, whereas it may plausibly be argued that the factor of possible scarcity does enter into every conceivable exchange.'[83] This left the problem of furnishing some alternative to the Marxist account of the distribution of income and of cyclical crises. By extending the Ricardian theory of rent, and through a special application of the Jevonian marginalist analysis, Sidney began to try and offer a new socialist account of exploitation. This task was by no means completed in 1886. As for the problem of explaining crises of overproduction, Sidney and his friends did not seriously attempt this in the eighties, and it was destined to remain as their most fundamental and long-standing omission.

It might plausibly be maintained that in relation to the theory of value, Webb and the Marxists were at cross-purposes, and that the general muddle resulted from a failure on both sides to see the actual role and function performed by the labour theory of value in Karl Marx's thought. However the young Webb objected not only that it was a mere prop to an ethical conclusion, but also that it was disposed to qualify that conclusion and to reject what were commonly taken to be its political and administrative implications.

The trouble with Marx was that he did not recognise the economic function of the middle classes in general and of the professional middle class in particular. Thus, in 1884, while conceding that the middle class was on trial, and it was open to the reproach that it had neither the skill to produce the wealth it controlled, nor the taste with which to enjoy it, Sidney held that it nevertheless performed indispensable functions. One stratum of it worked by hand and brain in distribution. Another performed the managerial functions of engineering modern business: superintending inferiors and promoting enterprise, invention and efficiency. Another performed the function of saving, so as to increase future capital. Last but not least there were the professional men who supplied us with law and letters, engineering and education, the arts of war and administration. All these strata combined to supply by their example elevating standards of life and comfort. They maintained and developed the sense of beauty and general culture, and helped to diffuse them through society. In 1884 Sidney found that Marx and the socialists totally excluded these indispensable people from the designation of 'workers', and lumped them together with landlords and mere rentiers. Two years later he was still making the same complaint. Marx classes rent, interest and profits in one mass as the fruit of 'exploitation'. Consequently, 'no light is thrown by Marx on the amount of the remuneration of superintendents, managers, foremen and indeed, skilled labourers of any sort.' Marx habitually ignored 'the great difficulty of managing this great force (capital) which is at present performed by a part of the class he would abolish.'[84] Moreover, since Lassalle, so much has been made of the 'reward of abstinence', that economic socialists are afraid to use this serious, expressive phrase. But it may be suggested that the turning of income into capital, by abstinence and saving, is a necessary social function. That it is one costing to the saver considerable effort and often self-denial and pain; and that its due fulfilment is absolutely essential to the increased production of the future. Even in Marxian economics this painful social duty, the fulfilment of which increases the product, would seem to merit a share of such increased production. Thanks to the law of diminishing marginal utility, Webb could now (1886) assert that there was a 'surplus value of utility strictly analogous to the Marxian surplus value of commodities'. This surplus value merely placed at the disposal of society 'at a price determined, not by cost of production but by relative scarcity, the use of social product indispensable to the world, but under individual control'.[85]

The crucial concept in Webb's economic thought was the notion of the rent of special ability, as the reward of a distinct, scarce and monopolised factor of production. As recipients of one of the three rents, the manager or professional man appeared to be in an analogous position to the landlords with their rents, and the capitalists with their interest. (In consequence the notion of profit acquired an unsettled or equivocal status.) The unravelling of the relations between this class of rent receivers and the other two was a complicated problem to which Sidney gave prolonged attention. Plainly it presented, morally and administratively, special difficulties for the socialist bent on expropriating surplus value. In 1884 he deprecated the proletarian contempt for 'useless' study, which was made possible only by easy circumstances. 'State endowment of research might effect the same end, but one shudders to think of the fate of Comte and Herbert Spencer, Blake and Rosetti, Browning and Matthew Arnold, at the hands of never so enlightened a Home Secretary.'[86]

Webb had shown that the middle class performed indispensable functions. However, along with the other two classes of rent receivers, they secured the lion's share of the national income. They supplied their services at exorbitant cost that bore no proportion to their real value, and could have no warrant by the elementary principles of distributive justice. The middle class enveloped itself in idleness. Political economy was 'the child of the bourgeoisie':

> The current political economy of the bourgeoisie is still compounded of shreds of empirical maxims bound up with perverted pieces of M'Culloch and Bastiat: in possession of this powerful *horum organum* he [the bourgeois] still appeals loudly to the Science of Political Economy and he has, alas, been able to use this pasteboard armour with only too successful results.[87]

Apart from restoring and extending the science of political economy, what was to be done? In 1884–5 Webb declared:

> I am, I am sorry to say, no believer in State Socialism, the impossibility of which I need not here attempt to demonstrate. I am a strictly orthodox believer in Political Economy as expounded, say, by Marshall. I am not even a believer in land nationalisation in the ordinary sense.[88]

At this time Sidney explicitly rejected the view that socialism could be equated with the further extension of state regulation of industry, and increasing state control of health and housing. If socialism meant anything it meant not the regulation of the monopolist, but his suppression by the state. The practical extension of *laissez-faire* had gone far. Instead of shedding bitter tears, as the philosophic radicals foretold, we 'clanged our chains in exulting triumph'. But socialism, even land nationalisation, could be accomplished only by revolution.[89] Besides he considered that it meant immoral confiscation. 'This, however is perhaps due to my bourgeois training, and results doubtless from a warping prejudice in favour of bourgeois dishonesty.'[90]

In the mid-eighties and even perhaps in 1886 only two remedies appeared to offer any hope. The first was that labour should organise itself into a monopoly capable of bargaining effectively with other monopolies. A labour monopoly would lead to an 'armed quadrilateral' of countervailing power;[91] no idyllic vision, but something to be preferred to the present subjection of the labourer. The difficulty was that anyone who knew his Malthus, or who was aware of the unpromising and stationary character of the trade union movement, could entertain little hope of much progress being made in this direction. The second was the moralisation of the capitalist:

> This may seem a perfectly visionary ideal, and certainly when we think of the absolute unconsciousness of the British bourgeoisie of the real nature of interest, and still more of the ability wages; when we remember his insatiable appetite for middle class luxuries which he calls 'comfort', we may well despair. Yet much has already been done … looking at the power of English capital, and the still greater power of English ability; looking again to the stolid stupidity and unreceptivity of the English bourgeois. I would warn them [the Marxists] seriously that they have undertaken a very difficult task: they will find it easier to moralise the monopolist than to expropriate him.[92]

This thesis which had been advanced before the London Dialectical Society in February 1884 was developed in a paper entitled 'The Way Out' which Sidney read almost exactly a year later.[93] He argued that the lot of more than half the people of England was deplorable, and 'it is simply absurd for the more fortunate classes to lay the flattering unction to their souls that the discomfort of the poor is due chiefly, or largely, to vice and improvidence.' The misery of the poor was due to their poverty: their poverty was due to the inequality with which the produce of labour was shared. His solution to this Condition of England question through taxation and collectivism was more Roman than Greek, as he demonstrated in 1888.[94] Just as the positivist, Professor Beesly, was able to make Roman history a vehicle for commentary on the contemporary human condition,[95] so Sidney found in Rome material for what he called a 'sociological sermon'. According to Sidney the classicists were apt to exaggerate the influence of Rome. 'We inherited from the World-Empire scarcely a single institution of social organisation or administration, and not one public office.' As for the torch of learning, about which so much as written, Rome failed to hand on even what it had received from Greece. In consequence,

> Teutonic literature was able to rise in its pure originality uncontami-
> nated by the corruption and feeble prettiness of the later Roman
> writers. We could probably not otherwise have had a Nibelungenlied
> or even the Canterbury Tales, these leading straight, as they do, to
> Shakespeare and Goethe.

Sidney's command of German allowed him to be familiar with the work of Mommsen and the German school. It was on this that he relied in presenting the Rome 'manufactured' in his own generation: the Rome which was, 'to a great extent merely the Broken Spectre of its own personality reflected on the mists of antiquity'. What the personality of Sidney found in the typical Roman was a subordination 'to the preservation of Rome, and this not the Rome composed of himself and his fellows, but a pure abstraction, the State apart from the citizens.' While 'the happiness of Romans was of course the ultimate unconscious aim ... the public spirit of the Roman led him ... over and over again [to declare] for the ultimate interests of the abstract entity'. In Rome, unlike Athens, where 'the supremacy of the individual became more and more recognised', the Romans were remarkable in recognising, as a universal conviction, that their duty 'lay in somehow promoting the permanent national welfare at any cost of individual sacrifice'. While the Athenians believed in themselves, 'the Romans rightly believed in their State'. The stern utilitarianism of the early Roman character, which was unfortunately suborned as 'the poison of the higher individualism' stole 'insidiously in' with an 'Attic philosophy and elegance', recovered itself for a time under an acceptance of the Stoic philosophy. This subject, said Sidney, leads us to the point: 'the necessity in life of fixed rules'. On the question of freedom, 'the perfectly free man is he whose impulses issue into action untrammelled by rules, even rules of thought.' While 'perfect individual development' is 'only rendered possible by the following up of all natural instincts' and the full play of all suggestions of thought, 'the perfectly Socialised' put constraint upon themselves in every direction. 'The Ego stands ever ready as a watchful guardian, remorselessly checking and strangling those monstrous births and strange abortions which all minds bear, but only foolish or bad minds bring to light.' Yet this 'autonomic internal rule of the perfect man' is insufficient for 'imperfect mortals'. The Romans recognised from the beginning the necessity of law by which rule would apply to those who had not yet 'let the ape and tiger die' within them. Roman law, Sidney adjudged to be 'the noblest native product of the Empire'. The 'scientific completeness' with which it covered the whole field of ancient life was in marked contrast to the scanty jurisprudence of the barbarians, and, indeed, of early Rome itself. While in Athens every case was argued on first principles and decided according to the momentary impulses and temporary ethical views of the popular judges for the time being, the Romans recognised that it is infinitely better to have any fixed rule. This even if its strict observance produced hard cases in exceptional instances. To the Roman, liberty meant the 'freedom to choose your laws and your law-givers' and this was not inconsistent with the most rigid subjection to them when once chosen. Liberty in the sense of freedom *from* law or restraint was to the Roman immoral licentiousness. The benefit that accrued from the Roman acceptance of this view and was embodied in Roman Collectivism as against Greek Individualism was enjoyment for the first time of the benefits of world commerce and the international division of labour. As a general rule, at least down to the Empire, Sidney argues on the authority of Mommsen that 'the income drawn from the provinces was not properly a taxation of the subjects for the benefit of the mother state.' It was, rather, revenue by which the latter defrayed the expenses of the administration. In contrast to the Egyptian and the Carthaginian cases, the Roman Treasury was but the joint military chest of the allied peoples. What Rome teaches in sociology is that 'if the progress of humanity be the ultimate end, and not merely our own personal happiness, we must have regard not only to the development of the individual, but also to that of the Social Organism.' The special lesson of Rome with respect to 'the type' of social organism is

> the necessity … of the universal reign of law in society. Man's perfect state is constant subjection. Freedom is the choice of, not absence, of rule, and at every turn the good citizen finds as the rule of life Goethe's emphatic motto.
> 'Thou shalt renounce, renounce, renounce'.
> It is the master of the house who is bound: the brutish slave is free. The momentary impulse to the permanent will, the present to the future, the individual to the mass, the generation to the race – all is subjection: in the perfect commonwealth man 'never is, but always to be blest'; and, oddly enough, finds his highest joy therein. Our wrongheaded refusal willingly to bow the neck to this yoke is the one unpardonable social sin; the obstinate 'will to live' an individual life which is the survival of the brute in man.

If it was the social question and Karl Marx, not Horace or Ovid, that he and Wallas, Olivier and Shaw were most concerned with when their friendship was formed in 1882–3, by 1888 Roman history, at least, had become a vehicle whereby Sidney could express some basis for a solution.

2

The Prevailing Fabian
1885–90

Sidney joins the Fabian Society—The personal preoccupations of 1885—Fabian Society activity and the critique of anarchism—The Fabian Parliamentary League—Webb and 'The Mistakes of the Socialists' —*Facts for Socialists* and the distancing from Positivism—The Basis—The Charing Cross Parliament—Distances Socialism from ethical speculation and Marxism—The *Fabian Essays*, the 'Historic Basis of Socialism' and the emergence of the distinctive features of Fabianism—Fabianism as heir to Positivism and Utilitarianism—Fabianism and economics—Webb's growing reputation as a lecturer and writer and recognition as a political organiser—His introspection towards the end of the decade.

Sidney first spoke to the Fabian Society in March 1885. He was elected a member along with Sydney Olivier in May. By the following year he was on the executive.[1] This does not imply that he exchanged Positivism for socialism between March and May 1885 or even that he must have been a socialist in 1886. The 'Basis', which laid down that 'The Fabian Society consists of socialists,' was not adopted until 1887. But 1885 was a propitious year for a new departure in British politics in general and in British socialism in particular. It witnessed the beginning of 'the most dramatic thirteen months in modern English party history'.[2] To appearance, the two-party system had broken down, and Parnell, challenging English rule in Ireland, had succeeded in establishing Irish rule in England. In reality, the Liberal Party under Gladstone had gone over permanently to Home Rule, and so ensured the continuity of the two-party system while itself ceasing to be capable of furnishing the normal government of the country which was, henceforth, Tory. Joseph Chamberlain and Randolph Churchill were the rising stars of political life, each assailing his respective 'old gang' with the help of radical programmes and extra-parliamentary party organisations. The Irish difficulty helped to popularise the theory, if not the practice, of a new social radicalism in England. It did this first by causing the Tories to bring in measures such as Lord Ashbourne's Act – the first state-assisted scheme of land purchase. It worked to the same effect by encouraging imperialists like Chamberlain and Churchill to hope that they could break out of the vice in which Ireland seemed to hold them fast by such radical projects as the 'unauthorised programme' which announced that socialism was no stigma, but a 'modern tendency pressing for recognition'.[3] Whether he was numbered in the Liberal or in the Tory ranks, Chamberlain's doctrine that the rich ought to pay – and must be induced to pay – 'a ransom' for their privileged access to land and capital, continued to receive a wide and increasingly sympathetic hearing. But while established Radicalism swore that it shared the intentions of Jack Cade, it was, under the disorganised conditions of parties, unable to 'deliver the goods'. Socialism was in a similar predicament. As a school of thought it was making – thanks to the support of men of the distinction of William Morris – considerable progress. But as an organised movement it was to discredit itself. H.M. Hyndman's Social Democratic Federation, which had been founded in 1881 as a broad radical alliance, had become possessed by the most narrow Marxist sectarianism, at once rigid and romantic. By accepting subsidies from the Tory Party in 1885 it had allowed itself to become the object of contempt and derision. William Morris and the Socialist League were being caught up in the coils of anarchism. Between 1884 and 1887 unemployment was running at an exceptionally high rate. In 1886 more than 10 per cent of all British trade unionists were out of work, a figure not to be reached again until after the First World War. But when, in the parks and the streets, the socialists led the unemployed into actions against the police they were, from a military point of view, soundly beaten.

Thus, the political and economic situation could hardly have been more favourable for a restatement of socialism in terms that would make it seem relevant and effective. Unfortunately the Fabian Society was in no condition to make the most of the opportunities. It had indeed succeeded in separating itself from the Society of the New Life, and stopped harking after community-building of the old-fashioned Utopian sort, but it had acquired no decided character of its own. It collected its members from among people of the most varied and unsettled opinions, and was divided evenly on the land question, positivism, Marxism and anarchism. Anarchism had indeed a considerable following among the Fabians of 1885. It was by no means the monopoly of Mrs Charlotte Wilson. The first number of *The Anarchist* included a contribution from Bernard Shaw, who had been a Fabian for a year or so, in which he asserted that

> The Collectivists would drive the money-chargers from Westminster only to replace them with a central administration of public safety, or what not. Instead of 'Victoria by the Grace of God', they would give us 'the superintendent of such and such an industry, by the authority of

the Democratic Federation,' or whatever body we are to make our master under the new dispensation.[4]

Another future Fabian Essayist, William Clarke, also declared that he accepted the anarchist platform, and started a paper called the *Wageworker*, in which he apparently differed from his fellow anarchists only in advocating permeation of political machinery in the interests of hastening its destruction.[5] E.R. Pease, the future secretary of the Fabian Society, donated £1 to the propaganda fund of *The Anarchist*.[6]

To many of these young Fabians it appeared, at least in retrospect, as if Sidney Webb had been sent by Providence to deliver them from these or similar delusions. He certainly never had any patience with anarchism, although he translated two Gedichte in Prison for *The Anarchist*.[7] He thought it had set itself against the immanent tendency in modern society to increasingly complex organisation. He doubted whether it would be either feasible or desirable to rely on such social pressures as ostracism, to do the work of government: any sane person would prefer to be tried in a court of law rather than by public opinion. He disputed whether a sense of freedom made for happiness, or whether law necessarily reduced freedom: 'Only those laws are restrictions which I feel as such.' He considered that anarchism was a case of atavism rather than any avant-courier of the future golden age.[8] This was perfectly consistent with his admiration for John Stuart Mill, for the Mill he admired was the author of the *Logic* and the *Political Economy*, not of the *Essay on Liberty*. There were three compelling reasons for rejecting the idea of the freely developing autonomous individual. First, there were no self-regarding actions. This was one of the first and one of the most settled opinions of Sidney Webb. Second, it was the monopolists of the factors of production who pre-empted liberty for themselves at the expense of the majority of mankind:

> Loss of liberty and independence, what of these? This is perhaps felt to be the weightiest objection to collectivism, but one that Mill himself thought to weigh but as dust in the balance of advantages offered by Socialism; and this present liberty and independence of the comfortable classes, on what are they based? The King's House at Dahomey is a great square building. The mighty corner piles stand solid in the African sand, and their solidity is secured – so the natives will tell you – by the blood of the slave girls crushed in the holes in which the piles are driven.[9]

Yes, socialism meant the loss of liberty of mill-owners and their like to squander wealth in luxury and to travel where they pleased. Third, it was not through liberty but through work, submission, renunciation in favour of the organisation of the commonweal that men would find, if not happiness, the highest fulfilment. Sidney's slowly but steadily maturing conception of the soul of man under socialism was as distant from Oscar

Wilde's with respect to the soul, as it was to the socialism. Miss Brooke knew her man when, in her novel *Transition*, she made Sidney say: 'We've got to fight the anarchists. If you want to point out to me the genuine enemy of practical socialism, show me an anarchist.' Miss Brooke's anarchists attempt to assassinate Webb, but otherwise his relations with them are faithfully depicted.

If Webb in 1885 was able to free minds from anarchism, he was by no means prepared to introduce them to a new and finished socialism. Far from having thought Mill to his logical conclusion, he had hardly arrived at Mill's own very tentative and qualified acceptance of socialism. Far from having glanced at the first volume of *Capital* and instantly found it wanting, he was in the midst of a prolonged struggle to arrive at some adequate appraisal of that work. Far from dismissing Comte, he was in some essential particulars a positivist. His social ideal was the moralisation of the capitalist, and he did not conceal the fact that he had discovered it in Comte. He was not, however, a young Beesly or a Semerie. Far from being a Positivist of the Left, he never discussed the role of a militant trade union movement in inducing the capitalist to treat his capital as a public trust, nor did he ever refer to the possibility, envisaged by Comte, of a provisional dictatorship of a proletarian governor. 'The labour metaphysic', the 'romantic' view of the proletariat, had no attraction for Webb. This may well have been one of the reasons why he never formally associated himself with organised Positivism in England, although the difference of generation between himself and Beesly, Harrison or Compton probably had something to do with it.

Sidney became the prevailing Fabian, but he was far from this in 1885. He did not appear to be a *deus ex machina* – or perhaps a *machina ex deo* – come to save the society from vague rhetoric and high-minded sentimentalities. No doubt it would be easy to demonstrate that it was historically inevitable that a new professional, practical, calm, cool and collected socialism should appear in 1885, and that such a man as Sidney Webb should arrive and be its prophet. History filled the sky with omens, but it had to wait a little longer – for Webb far from being cool or practical, was far too wretched to be fit for much political work.

When Sidney Webb joined the Fabian Society he was intensely preoccupied with his own misfortunes and inadequacies. Shortly after he had become a Fabian he apologised to Shaw for having taken up so much of his time with his woes:

> How like I am to everybody else – a reflection which has come home to me a good deal lately. My consolation is that I was furnishing you with heaps of material, and perhaps even preventing you from making confessions to me. But a better excuse is the very bitter and overwhelming

reality of the matter to me – the extent of which I shall fail to make you realise. I really am very sick – however absurd it may be.[10]

He impressed Graham Wallas with the 'bitter and overwhelming reality of the matter' during a long walk and talk. However, despite the exercise and the conversation and the beer and the bus and the bed, he had a sleepless night: 'But this lying in a dreamy state, with will and judgement suspended, consciousness languidly following out its aimless thread, has become not unpleasant to me.'[11] Wallas left his cane and Sidney felt 'debauched' by it, but carefully preserved it, and returned it along with a novel called *But Yet A Woman*. Sidney was very much attached to this book and wanted Graham to 'please enjoy and appreciate it'. There was, he insisted, so much of himself in it. This applied to the hero, but still more to the villain. (Both characters appear to a reader at the end of the twentieth century as almost equally preposterous. However, they are drawn in such emphatic lines that one can be left in no doubt as to what Sidney meant.)

The hero is a young doctor who is both made for society and hates it. He uses the pressure of his professional duties to protect himself from people:

> It is not so difficult to know oneself as to confess to the knowledge – and beneath his desire to lose himself in his profession, beneath the armour which he wore, he knew the man, like other men, with nerves ready to tremble, and pulses that obey smiles and frowns … He was what he was [a cynic] because he wished to be, not because he could not help it.

The villain was a journalist and a royalist conspirator against the Third French Republic. He was selfish, lustful, vain and prudent. 'Before the altars of great principles he did not bow – he stood upon them; they were the pedestals of a statue … All the force of his affection was retroactive. With him it seemed necessary to have lost, to love at all.' Although the reader is assured that there was good as well as evil in this character, he might well be excused for being flummoxed by the heroine's question: 'How did you expect one to love you, M. de Marzac, when one knows you?'[12]

Sidney was not alone in his troubles. Shaw was busily defending (unsuccessfully) his virginity from Jenny Patterson of Brompton Square,[13] and Wallas had lost his school-teaching appointment in Highgate over a question of religious conformity. Webb instantly offered to come to Wallas's rescue. He urged him not to be in too much of a hurry to find another post: 'I want to say, before I forget it, that what I said at

Hampstead about your not hurrying too much to get a place, if delay was any use – about the money in fact – was fully meant and you can rely on it.'[14] He continued:

> Character is always the safest investment – of good or of evil. There alone are we quite sure to find the bread after many days. And if Sophocles regarded too exclusively the non-human element in the production of events – we are a little apt to go to other extreme and think that we are entirely 'the master of things'. Providence – a blind and unconscious and therefore not a malignant Providence, still has the greatest share in running the concern: and I am (partly and occasionally at any rate) a disciple of Mr Micawber, with a faith in things unseen but about to turn up. At any rate much more comes to us than we have worked for, and of this not much more than half is evil.

He warned him:

> Don't be like me, wanting at each step to see my life in advance ... this has landed me in the 'Impasse dur du bureau des Colonies' instead of on the 'Avenue directe a Mon Désir' to use a directory-al metaphor. If you can only bring yourself to wait calmly, and utilise the time just as though your future were secure, there can be little doubt that it would pay you. So much easier is it to preach than to practice.[15]

Although in future years their friendship was to be clouded by differences of policy and temperament, Graham Wallas never forgot how 'extraordinarily kind and helpful' Sidney had been in the summer of 1885.[16]

Yet concern for his friend brought no release from his own anguish. Nor did a holiday in Brussels followed by long walks round Stonehenge and through the West Country. For a moment Salisbury charmed him, until he pulled himself up and acknowledged 'better fifty years of London than a cycle of decay.' Walking from Amesbury he felt 'almost happy' in his thoughts and built 'all sorts of Castles' until he remembered that he had been drinking beer 'which always gets into my head'.[17] From Brussels he warned Wallas:

> You are only in fashion in being in low spirits. It seems to me that my acquaintances all round are in trouble, (Only Olivier excepted – he is most unreasonably and inhumanely happy, I know). Some who have money are sick about other things. Some are sick about money. Those whose external circumstances are darkest are not the most unhappy. And I, whom nearly all envy; and whom they all persist in regarding as filled with joy, now pass my life in endeavouring to persuade them that

I am a hopeless fraud and entitled to a commiseration which their hard hearts deny – all this means (beyond dull rainy weather) that in my opinion individual happiness is (1) not attainable at all (2) a fixed quantum in each personality, irrespective of events and circumstances (3) nearly the same in each one (4) not worth consideration so far as, with the help of Dr Heidenhoff,[18] we can avoid so doing. (I am afraid a logical deduction would be (1) alcohol (2) opium (3) suicide, but I can't pursue the argument now ...

As to Else (?), she is very well but I am not in love with her and leaving out of account this inexplicable emotion which 'bloweth where it listeth' beyond all ken or reason, I don't think I should have married her. She was not reasonable enough. The Doctor (as Freytag meant) was quite right in objecting to that 'das Leben des geistes sie ist so weit entfernt wie die heilige Elisabeth.' Much of what followed arose simply from her not possessing enough of the calm reason of her husband. I am still convinced that this calm reason unbiased by any prejudice, instinct or emotion, is the highest and best in the world – that it leads only to unhappiness is only of a piece with the rest. I, at least, am not bound to prove everything to be good, just when I feel nearly everything for the bad.

Therefore, since we are both unhappy – or at least not happy – (and both without any real striking reason dazu) let us frankly admire and pity ourselves. Quant à moi, for a miserable man I am still capable of much enjoyment. (Olivier, however, says that my unhappiness is largely due to an ascetic avoidance of enjoyments: ce n'est pas vrai – it is only indolence.) The best enjoyment is in friendly intercourse. When I get back I mean to throw myself metaphorically at the feet of Mrs Olivier (as I have already done in 2 or 3 other households), confess my unhealthy state of mind, and request her to allow me to come occasionally, like Saul, to be comforted by David. Please aid me.

The colour of the wallpaper opposite which I write this, is not unpleasant. There are perhaps other circumstances which adequately account for my being today more than usually discontented with myself (i.e. with the world at large et le bon dieu). It is odd that after having been Pessimist by profession for at least seven years, I should not yet have exhausted all the shock of ever-new surprise and disappointment at finding the world an uncomfortable one. The momentum of existence – the flywheel which alone carries our lives over the 'dead-spot' in the revolution is certainly the most strongly optimistically possible. As indeed it should be, being only the instinct of self-preservation evolved in the race by many aeons' struggle. (Hence by the way the Buddhist Nirvana is wrong – evolutionary false. Query: also George Eliotism?) This is a strange letter. You may find it interesting, even amusing. Hence I send it. I think it is really from yours sincerely, Sidney Webb.[19]

He was still the same Webb at the end of the month. 'I want you to bear with me whatever I may do as I feel desolate indeed. Why did God put such a thing into life?'[20] In mid-August he had still 'no repose of mind but a dull self-devouring, which is very restless and impatient'. Wallas had found a post in Germany and had apparently proposed that Webb should take a further continental holiday:

> I see no reason [wrote Sidney] why it should not come off, but every-thing, great and small, has gone wrong with me this year down to my losing 5 shillings at cards the other night – quite unusual for me. It is my 'Pechjar', my star has gone out, and from being a child of fortune, I am reduced to an ordinary mortal.

He explained that although he did not believe in luck, he believed in the belief in it – a rather difficult accomplishment. 'However', he continued, 'it remains still that I was born on a Wednesday':

> Now as to my convalescence, I used to feel myself all over every day to see how much I was hurt, and as it were, take the temperature and pulse. My deepest depth lasted about 17–18 days, which seems very short. About the 18th day it occurred to me that after all yesterday was not so bad and had really gone off with comfort. I had been moved into a milder compartment with less flame. There I have been ever since. It is compatible with occasional enjoyment and general absence of acute pain. But periodically I go down into Hell again, no doubt when my 'light is low' and 'all the wheels of being slack'. But the more usual feel-ing is one of dullness and blackness of things, not acute but massive.
>
> I don't think that the experience is good for character. I noticed, (con-firmatory of *But Yet a Woman* and *Through One Administration*) that, a little while I was distinctly more moral than usual. I did one or two unselfish things which I should not have done usually. But that is evanescent. There is an additional cynicism and 'hardness'. I can't charge it with my Pessimism, but because that was real, sincere and thorough five years ago; but it is now realler, sincerer and thorougher. I have no *impulse* to suicide, tho' the thought has never been totally absent from my mind for years. That shows the benefit of settling such questions and also, I think, it is a consequence of more robust health.
>
> It is interesting to notice how much man is still nine-tenths an irra-tional animal – how little influence the intellect has, compared with that exercised by the emotions. It has been a lesson to me. One sees how

explanations may seem complete, and yet how very far they are from taking account of everything.

I think Dr Heidenhoff is so much needed that he must exist some where. What a sale Lethe-Water would have, done up like Appolinaris, and sent all over the world by a limited Liability Company. Can't you discover such a spring somewhere near Weimar?

One more reflection – as has been said often, it is faith-destroying. I am distinctly *more* atheistic than before and I am afraid also more unsettled as to the Ethical Standard and its application.

I have fallen back into my old life here, reading and loafing and play-ing cards.[21]

Sidney moved in fear and trembling of something uncomfortable turning up, and his holiday was spoilt by a whole succession of minor mishaps and bouts of severe melancholy. He returned to England in October and could report by the end of the following month:

I have settled down to a very dead level of life – 'no hope no fear' sort of existence, which is not incompatible with comfort, although it is with reading or writing much. I think my special disturbing influence has passed off – that is so far as its own form is concerned – and I am much as I was 18 months ago, plus experience and several memories, and a certain unrest, and minus some of my youth and hope.[22]

His brother's marriage on Christmas Eve can hardly have improved mat-ters for him. He did not conceal his envy of happily married friends, nor his fear that their marriages would draw them away from him. He ended the year playing chess and whist and lamenting Wallas's absence in Heidelberg: could he not come home and manage a private adventure school where he could experiment? He helped his sister Ada with Virgil and Horace, but went into his LL B exam in January 'just as I am, without any cram'. In consequence he had to tell Wallas:

I have gone rather a mucker (for me) in the Honours exam, as I am only in the Third Class. But only seven have passed at all (against some 12 last year) out of over twenty, and there is no first class and only one sec-ond. Still – it was the equity, which was in fact most iniquitous.[23]

Thus Sidney came out of 1885 'hardened' by disappointment and emo-tional disturbance, and finally freed from the duty of preparing for the next examination. He was already a Fabian, but this as yet signified little. If the society was socialist, it was so only in the vaguest sense. Webb could certainly not have joined the SDF or the Socialist League because these were, so far as the bulk of their memberships were concerned, predominantly proletarian bodies. Moreover they tended to obscure their own confusion about the nature of socialism and the transition to it behind a show of doctrinal assurance and certainty. The Fabian Society, on the other hand, was decidedly middle-class, and its characteristic members were teachers, journalists or civil servants like Podmore, Olivier or Webb himself. Sidney was much more at home than he would have been in the company of proletarians in whose political capacity he had little trust, and who were too inclined to measure their progress in terms of the latest demonstration in the parks or clash with the police in the streets, rather than by the quality of the discussion. The Fabian might bark about civil war preferable to 'such another century of suffering as the present one has been',[24] but this did not commit him to organising an insurrection. If he had bees in his bonnet he knew they were there, and would be grateful to you for removing them. Yet Sidney's identification with the society appears to have developed slowly, and it is highly doubtful whether he would have been able to accept the Fabian 'Basis', with its explicit and unequivocal commitment to socialism, much before the time of its introduction in 1887. In 1885 the society already associated itself with organised socialism. It did so, for example, shortly after Sidney became a member, when it sent a delegate to sit on the Vigilance Committee that arose out of the Dod Street conflict.[25] It assumed responsibility for the reputation of socialism in England, when on 4 December 1885 it formally condemned the SDF for disgracing the movement by accepting Tory gold during the general elections.[26] The Society was indeed split on this subject and it was through the resignation of its secretary, Frederic Keddell, that a vacancy arose on the executive that Webb came to fill.[27] But he appears to have been far too absorbed in his own personal affairs to pay much attention to these events. He looked on the election results from a conventional Liberal standpoint, remarking: 'We have gone a tremendous crash in the towns.' It was the fault, he thought, of Chamberlainism and the 'atheist taint' attaching to the 'Free Schools' slogan, although he acknowledged that it also pointed to the strength of the Church, the 'Free Trade' cry, the Primrose League, discontent with foreign policy, and the defection of the Irish. He expected politics in future to be dominated by the issue of disestablishment.[28]

Such activity that Sidney engaged in after he joined the Fabian was directed to the critique of anarchism. If this was true of the small part he played in 1885, it applied largely to what he did in the following year. He helped to produce a Tract, *What Socialism Is*, which was designed not so much to propagate a particular doctrine as to clarify the issue between anarchism and collectivism. The conflict between these two tendencies was making itself felt throughout the international labour movement.[29]

The importance of Sidney's contribution to the debate was that in demolishing anarchism he was bound to propel himself towards collectivism. The more effectively he conducted the polemic against the anarchists the more he undermined the basis of his own Positivist position. It was not easy to complain that the anarchists took an altogether utopian view of the possibility of moralising society at large, while clinging to the view that the captains of industry – of all people – might be made amenable to moral suasion. After all, the anarchists themselves dismissed that as a quite unrealistic expectation.

It must be remembered that Sidney and his friends were still wrestling with Marx, and had not yet arrived at an alternative socialist economic theory. That did not prevent them from summoning a great conference in June 1886 which was attended by delegates from 53 radical, secularist and other such clubs and societies. It was addressed by William Morris and Edward Aveling of the Socialist League; by the anarchist Wordsworth Donisthorpe; by Stewart Headlam for the Christian Socialists; by three Members of Parliament (Bradlaugh, Saunders and Dr G.B. Clark) and many others. Annie Besant, who had joined the Fabian Society shortly after Webb, spoke and so did Sidney himself, but it was a fiasco.[30] In fact, Webb's paper illustrated how little the Fabians had to offer at this time. He called it 'The Need for Capital'.[31] The emphasis was not on the maldistribution of the national income, but rather on the miserably inadequate size of the national product. Too many workers toiled with too few machines. The solution was increased saving along with the introduction of the eight-hour working day and the three-shift system, so as to ensure the fullest utilisation of the productive resources. This would produce more social profit than nationalisation of the land or of interest. The fault of capitalism was not that its property relations were increasingly restricting the development of production – Sidney expressly endorsed Say's law of the market – but that the capitalists, who were alone in a position to save and invest, neglected their duty:

> We socialists, following therein the orthodox economists such as Mill and Cairns, accordingly impeach the idle monopolists for a grave dereliction of moral duty, in thus consuming for their own selfish personal benefit so much of the toll wrung from the toil of their less fortunate brethren …

London was crying out to be rebuilt. 'In every house we want hydraulic lifts, the electric light, the telephone in every home …'

'We socialists' – socialism meant at this stage 'the enforcement of moral duty', or rather, that is what state socialism meant, for socialists were held to be divided between 'moralisers' and state socialists. The Webb of 1885 had been clearly in the first of these two categories. The Webb of 1886 was plainly becoming closer to the second. He had been forced forwards by the logic of his polemic with the anarchists; by the difficulty of coping with the objections to Positivism raised by Podmore and other Fabians; by the hardening effect of his own personal disillusionments; and by the impact of increasingly bitter social and political conflicts of 1885–6 at which the London unemployed stood near the centre. He now stated: 'I am not a Positivist, and I am by no means sure that the capitalist can be moralised, and I call myself a socialist because I am desirous to remove from the capitalist the temptation to use his capital for his own exclusive ends. Still the capitalist may do good by accumulation.' He was of the opinion that 'Positivists, so far as they have thought out their economic system, came clearly under the definition of socialism.'[32] Although he was losing his simple faith in the moralisation of capital, Sidney retained throughout his life a keen appreciation of the merits of Comte and of his English followers. In fact, his mind was so deeply impregnated with these ideas that they entered as a permanent element into his social thinking, causing him to trust to the conscience of the rich as an agency of change, and a condition allowing socialism to emerge as a result of a growing consensus in its favour.

However, the word 'socialism' was not usually employed in the nineteenth century to mean more than the regulation by public opinion or the state of the functions performed by the capitalist. A defining feature of socialism was its belief in the expropriation of the capitalist and performance of the function of accumulation, either by a democratic state or through other institutions of a collective, equalitarian and democratic character. The agitation involving the London unemployed, and culminating in the trial of Hyndman, Burns, Williams and Champion for sedition, directly occasioned Webb's first proposals aimed at enlarging the operations of government to the point at which it assumed the function of the employer. Concurrently with the organisation of the conference at which he spoke on the 'Need for Capital', he helped Frank Podmore to draw up a report on 'The Government Organisation of Unemployed Labour'. The state cultivation of tobacco was hardly a revolutionary – or very sensible – proposal for dealing with unemployment, but it was a beginning. If the report failed to win much support or attention within the Fabian Society or without, it did contain other, more convincing evidence of the inventiveness (and realism) of its authors. It recommends the revival of social life in the villages, so as to diminish the supposed migration from the countryside to the slums; the docks companies were advised to introduce a scheme for the decasualisation of the labour force; the unemployed must be trained for some new trade or calling; technical education and labour bureaux were advocated, along with the municipalisaton of the drink supply, the nationalisation of the railways and universal military train-ing.[33] It was odd and inadequate, but a recognisable start along a path which was to prove distinctive, even when it was not always rewarding.

Sidney was in much better heart by the summer of 1886. He went on a week's walking tour with Pease in Northumberland before joining a party of friends for a holiday in Scandinavia. In Northumberland they went down the Walker colliery 'and realised some of Germinal – but our partic-ular conductor was a most prosperous man, house full of furniture, and a Conservative! He was a "viewer", however, a sort of foreman.' But only a small part of the time was spent in social investigation. What Sidney noticed at York – apart from the fact that the whole population seemed to be in transit – was 'a most Romanish reredos in the shape of a triptych by Tinworth of the Crucifixion'. Hull was made memorable, not by the docks, 'but the worst statue I ever saw. There is one of William the Third on Horseback, William dressed like Julius Caesar, with bare head and palm leaves round it, horse and figure completely gilt.'[34] In Salisbury in the pre-vious year, he had found the town chiefly remarkable for alehouses, but

the Cathedralosity impressed me; not the thing itself, for that is swept and garnished like a modern workhouse, smells of the builder, all fine new, in the worst nineteenth century style. I don't deny there may be fragments of the old surviving, but the trail of the restoring serpent is over them all and the general impressions of newness. Why, they have actually polished the new pillars, until you can trace each shining Paludina (it is freshwater limestone 'Purbeck marble') across the church. On the roof there are hideous paintings. I fell into the hands of a specially fatuous verger, who recited his mechanical tale into my ear: 'On removing the yellow wash they discovered sufficient of the old paintings to enable the interior to be restored'. 'Why', I exclaimed, 'you don't mean to say it is thought that the ancients painted like that?' He looked at me for a moment, more in pitying sorrow at my stupidity, than in anger, and then began again: 'On removing the yellow wash, etc.' And then, most unkindest cut of all, I contributed 6d towards com-pleting the vandalism![35]

If Sidney shared the values of William Morris when it came to Anti-Scrape[36] (though Morris would certainly not have parted with the 6d) they were now to make a decisive break politically. On 17 September 1886, a socialist conference was convened by the Fabians at Anderton's Hotel. Webb does not appear to have been a participant, but he certainly supported the majority who favoured organising the socialists into a political party as against the minority, led by Morris, who held that no parliamentary party could exist without compromise and concessions that must hinder the advance to socialism. So as to save Mrs Wilson and the small band of anarchists whose main base was in the Fabian Society, it was decided to establish a Fabian Parliamentary League. The style and spirit of this League was from the first Webb's and duly became that of the entire Society.[37]

Yet in 1886 Sidney was one of the most detached, academic and perverse of Fabians. If he called himself a socialist he enjoyed the prospect of tormenting enthusiasts with the orthodox wisdom. He asked Wallas:

> What do you think of running a series of lectures in the Fabian this winter on 'The Mistakes of Socialists'? 'Just like the Fabians', they would say. But we must have some new thing. The only other wild suggestion I have is to run a series of lectures to different classes: Address to Aristocrats; Warning to Women; Reproof to Reprobates; Problems for Politicians; and so on. If we could only dare to have an address 'To Men Only' our future would be made. I am afraid one 'To Women Only', say by Mrs B., would not draw.[38]

'The Mistakes of Socialists' duly appeared as a series of articles entitled 'Some Errors of Socialists and Others'.[39] The first error was 'that industrial Progress diminishes the need for technical education'. The second, 'that a large fortune must necessarily have been obtained to the detriment of the wage workers.' Sidney argued that this was not so since large business incomes frequently arose from economic rent of land or rent of ability:

> No – the capitalist who makes a large income is not particularly the enemy of the wage-workers he employs; still less is he their enemy if he abstains from consuming this income, and allows it to accumulate. We want many more of such capable 'captains of industry' … it is not robbery of individual wage-workers against which we plead, but embezzlement for private uses of what should be devoted to general public purposes.

This aroused a satisfactory amount of indignation, after which Sidney's demonstrations that the freeholder was not the only landlord, that socialists should not be in favour of the reduction of tithes, and that the distributor was a productive worker came rather as an anti-climax.

These articles serve to conceal that 1887 was a decisive year for the Fabian Society: the year in which Sidney really took it in hand and in which almost all the most distinguished and enduring features of Fabianism emerged. It saw the publication of *Facts for Socialists*; the formation of the Parliamentary League; the adoption of the socialist 'Basis'; and – in the immediate wake of 'Bloody Sunday' – the first formulation of socialism (by socialists) as the deliberate extension of the current administrative practices of going institutional concerns.

Facts for Socialists was first published in January 1887. It went through fifty editions and became, perhaps, the most useful, famous and distinctive of all Fabian publications. Yet it was no more than a skilfully ordered and carefully documented version of the first half of the paper on 'The Way Out' which Sidney presented to the Society in March 1885. Its primary purpose was to demonstrate that two-thirds of the national product went to the recipients of the three rents, and that this inequality was the major agency responsible for poverty and distress. As in 1885 he had maintained: 'It is not wise unnecessarily to incur, as the socialists have done, the opposition of the statisticians and economists by decrying their results, when theory results really prove your own case;' so he supported every proposition by reference to recognised and orthodox authority. In part, it was a magnificent *argumentum ad hominem*: essentially, it was an example of a superb and perfectly legitimate literary opportunism.

He began with a quotation from Robert Giffen, who had become the *bête noir* of Hyndman and the SDF, thanks to a paper on 'The Progress of the Working Classes in the Last Half Century'.[40] Sidney, unlike Hyndman, had acquainted himself with Giffen's entire literary output. And on p. 393 of the second volume of *Essays on Finance*, he fell upon the following: 'No one can contemplate the present condition of the masses of the people without desiring something like a revolution for the better.' This was duly placed at the head of the Tract. If such diligent looking was rewarded even on stony ground like this, it reaped a rich harvest when applied to J.S. Mill or other Liberal authorities. Mill indeed was introduced so as to fill in Giffen's vague admission: 'It is the great error of reformers and philanthropists in our time, to nibble at the consequences of unjust power, instead of redressing the injustice itself.'

The Tract was brilliantly arranged and illustrated with simple and telling diagrams. The size of the nation's income; who produced it; who the producers were; how the idle rich lived; the shares of rent and of interest; of profits and salaries – all this led into the final sections which summed up the division of the product between the classes and the masses, and showed its consequence in 'The Two Nations'. Section X was entitled 'The Class War':

Between the two classes there is perpetual strife. Disguise it as we may by feudal benevolence, or the kindly attempts of philanthropists, the material interest of the small nation privileged to exact rent for its monopolies, and of the great nation thereby driven to receive only the remnant of the product, are permanently opposed. The more there is allotted to labour, the less will remain to be appropriated as rent

(Fawcett, *Manual of Political Economy*, p. 123) ... The force by which this conflict of interest is maintained without the conscious contrivance of either party, is competition, diverted, like other forces, from its legitimate social use. The legal disposers of the great natural monopolies are able, by means of legally licensed competition, to exact the full amount of their economic rents; and the political economists tell us that so long as these natural monopolies are left practically unrestrained in private hands, a thorough remedy is impossible.

In its penultimate section, the Tract pointed to 'Some of the Victims of the Struggle': the fifty annual deaths, exclusive of infants, from starvation in London; the streets which were proscribed by the insurance companies because the occupants were bad risks; the 15 312 deaths from industrial injury; the army of 3 000 000 paupers costing £10 250 000 per annum. Since the Tract was concerned with 'facts', the prolonged discussion of 'remedies', which had comprised the second part of 'The Way Out', was dropped in favour of the simple conclusion:

> Socialists affirm that the evil can never be remedied until the 'Two Nations' are united by the restitution to public purposes of rent and interest of every kind, and by the growth of social sympathy promoted by the accompanying cessation of class distinctions.

There was no clear indication that this was to be accomplished by statutory rather than by moral methods. It was not until the tenth edition appeared early in the twentieth century that a new section was added which described 'Some Steps Already Taken Towards Socialism'. Once these references to municipal enterprises and death duties made their appearance, the section on 'The Class War' was re-entitled 'The Competitive Struggle' and its first line, 'Between the two classes there is perpetual strife', was deleted.

Sidney was slowly but perceptibly distancing himself from Positivism. The Positivists, who were cited among the authorities in *Facts for Socialists*, were formally abstentionists when it came to holding elected office. A month after Tract 5 had appeared, showing that socialist conclusions could be made to issue out of orthodox economic sources, the formation of the Fabian Parliamentary League signalled commitment to the view that it could equally be made to issue out of existing institutions. Sidney, along with Shaw, Olivier, Bland and Russell, drew up the rules:[41]

> The Fabian Parliamentary League is composed of socialists who believe that socialism may be most quickly and most surely realised by utilising the political power already possessed by the people ...

The League will endeavour to organise socialist opinion, and to bring it to bear upon parliament, municipalities and other representative bodies; it will by lectures and publications seek to deal with the political questions of the day, analysing the ultimate tendencies of measures, as well as their immediate effects, and working for or against proposed measures of social reform according as they tend towards, or away from, the socialist ideal.

The League will take an active part in all general and local elections. Until a fitting opportunity arises for putting forward socialist candidates to form the nucleus of a socialist party in parliament, it will confine itself to supporting those candidates who will go furthest in the direction of socialism. It will not ally itself absolutely with any political party; it will jealously avoid being made use of for party purposes.

It was stressed that members of the League must make it a duty to take part in the public life of their district. They were to take part in elections, keep watch on public officials, bring pressure to bear on their MPs and make the best use of the local press. They were also expected to 'visit the workhouses of their neighbourhood: and should exercise a careful supervision of local funds'.

In June the Society adopted its celebrated 'Basis', the test of admission, which opened with the words: 'The Fabian Society consists of Socialists'. This did little more than ratify what had become apparent for at least six months. Sidney was now as ready as Shaw and the others to call himself a socialist, and thus go beyond the initial agreement of Fabians in opposing 'the Competitive system' and calling for society to be 'reconstituted in such a way as to secure the general welfare and happiness'. The Basis committed Fabians to work 'for the extinction of private property in land' and

for the transfer to the community of the administration of such industrial Capital as can conveniently be managed socially … If these measures be carried out, without compensation (though not without such relief to expropriated individuals as may seem fit to the community), Rent and Interest will be added to the reward of labour, the idle class now living on the labour of others will necessarily disappear, and practical equality of opportunity will be maintained by the spontaneous action of economic force, with much less interference with personal liberty than the present system entails.

The Basis concluded by stressing that it was to the development and spread of enlightened opinion that the Society looked for an agency to promote the progress of socialism.

Sidney, unlike Shaw and many other Fabians, was never tempted to consider the advance of socialism in England in any way other than through peaceful progress of law and opinion; through patient educational work and steady use of the existing constitutional machinery of local and central government. 'The doctrines of Socialism can only be extended by bringing about a slowly dawning conviction in the minds of men; it is certain that no more forcible revolution organised by a minority can ever avail, either in England or elsewhere.'[42] Bloody Sunday, 13 November 1887, appeared to Shaw and others to confirm the correctness of this view. The SDF had identified Socialism with the organisation of the unemployed, and from 1885 they had led them in repeated clashes with the police. There had been moments when they had alarmed respectable society into improving benefits for the jobless, and there had been times when the skill and courage of socialist advocacy appeared to be winning a new respect and prestige for the cause. On 8 November Sir Charles Warren, chief of Metropolitan Police, announced that he was prohibiting all further meetings in Trafalgar Square. On the following Sunday the Radicals, the Irish Nationalists and the socialists marched in defence of the right of public meeting. They were dispersed with great efficiency and brutality by soldiers and mounted police. Shaw recalled:

> We skedaddled, and never drew rein until we were safe on Hampstead or thereabouts. Tarleton found us paralysed with terror and brought me on to the Square, the police kindly letting me through in consideration of my genteel appearance. On the whole I think it was the most abjectly disgraceful defeat ever suffered by a band of heroes outnumbering their foes a 1,000 to 1.[43]

> Not one, not one, nor thousands must they slay,
> But one and all, if they would dusk the day.

So sang William Morris in his *Death Song for Alfred Linnell*, a victim of police violence. But Sidney was almost certainly not among the marchers, being neither physically nor temperamentally suited to street fighting. Increasingly he was living for the cause, but he was not disposed to think that there was much use in dying for it. Freedom of speech and public meeting was essential to his kind of socialism, as much as it was for the verities favoured by Morris or Hyndman, but he did not speak out of doors. He preferred the debating society, the lecture room, the conference hall and forum supplied by the local parliaments in Lambeth or elsewhere. And just at the time when the socialism of massive class struggles was discovering how far short it fell in mind and organisation for the task it had set itself, Sidney was beginning to detect the first signs of his own influence on public affairs. In August 1887 the Earl of Wemyss treated the House of Lords to a long address on recent socialist legislation.[44] He read a long list – what was soon to be thought of as a long Webb-like list – of Bills interfering with freedom of contract, all of which had found their way into law since 1870. 'The upas-tree of Socialism,' cried Wemyss, 'planted by Mr Gladstone in 1870 was now overshadowing our land and attracting every kind of bird of prey to roost in its branches ... nowadays Conservatism appeared to be nothing but the fifth wheel in the socialistic coach.' There were three sorts of socialism: of the streets; of the professors; of the statesmen. The last was far the worst. Politicians of all parties 'truckling to the Saxon with his vote and the Irish tenant with his gun', were in furious competition to reduce liberty and confiscate property. 'La democratie c'est l'envie,' and, it might be added, 'c'est le vol.' The Earl found it necessary to draw attention to

> the great number of debating Clubs in which socialist doctrines were advocated. In many of these clubs there was a close imitation of parliamentary forms ... There was one in particular which met near where their Lordships were assembled, and was called the Charing Cross Debating Society. The Prime Minister and First Lord of the Treasury was Mr Champion. Mrs Besant also held office, and the Chief Secretary was the Rev. Stewart Headlam, a member of the Society of Jesus [sic]. The noble earl then read extracts from the Queen's speech in which deep regret was expressed at the unequal distribution of property, at the luxury of the rich and idle classes which tended to the depression of the poor, and to the wasteful and unbusinesslike management of public departments.[45]

Sidney was delighted:

> He told Wallas, he seems to have read our Queen's Speech to the House. I have heard nothing about the Parliament except a letter form Headlam threatening to resign because our Budget contains no special taxation of ground rents. I am to bring it in on Friday.

The Charing Cross Parliament was founded in the summer of 1887 and in July H.H. Champion was able to inform the House that he had succeeded in forming a Socialist ministry. He was supported by Annie Besant as Home Secretary, GBS at the Local Government Board, Hubert Bland at the Foreign Office, Graham Wallas at the Board of Trade and Sydney Olivier as Colonial Secretary.[46] Sidney Webb as Chancellor of the Exchequer introduced his Budget resolutions on 19 July. He abolished all taxes on foodstuffs; all duties on hawkers and peddlers, hackney carriage licences;

and inhabited house duty. He put income tax at 2s in the pound, but with the abatement of one-third if the income was earned and an additional one-third if the income was under £1000 a year. He maintained present exemptions.[47] (In the real world, the standard rate was 8d. It did not reach 2s until the middle of the First World War.)[48]

But what mattered was not primarily that Wemyss should notice Sidney playing Colonial Secretary at Lambeth or Chancellor at Charing Cross, but that he suggested a measure for the advance of socialism which Sidney had earlier rejected but now found relevant and acceptable. Indeed, by adopting and elaborating Wemyss's criteria, he was able to offer a much more optimistic perspective and prospect for socialism than anyone else. Harcourt had still to discover that 'we are all Socialists now,' but Sidney saw the possibilities, from the standpoint of the socialist stage army, of exploiting the neurotic anxieties of the Liberty and Property Defence League. As Webb was ready to surprise the world with the conclusions that he could derive from Ricardo, Mill or Jevons, he was equally prepared to astonish it by discovering that Lord Wemyss was perfectly well balanced. The 'upas-tree' of socialism, far from belonging to the delirium of aristocratic coal-owners, was a reality not to be gainsaid. In 1885 Sidney had impatiently dismissed Chamberlain's assurances that 'the path of legislative progress in England has been for years, and must continue to be, distinctly socialistic'.[49] In 1887 he began to treat the regulation of the monopolist, not as something opposed to his suppression, but as the beginning of a process which must culminate in it.

A month or two after Wemyss's speech Sidney spoke to the Hampstead Society for the Study of Socialism on 'The Economic Basis of Socialism and its Political Programme'.[50] For the first time he carefully and publicly distinguished Fabian socialism from ethical and utopian speculations on the one hand and from Marxism on the other. Socialism was not to be reduced to applied Christianity or to a mere ethical theory:

> Socialism is a statement of the principles of social organisation and is, I think, compatible with any ethic which recognises the existence of the social organism, and acknowledges human welfare as at least one of human ends. But it is something more than Christianity or any other ethical system, in that it is the incorporation of positive knowledge of the laws of sociological development, and the deduction therefrom of concrete principles of social organisation.

Utopianism was repudiated. 'Auguste Comte, in fact, could foresee no better ideal community than a glorified wage-slavery, with human masters guided by philosophic priests.' As for the fancy sketches of Godwin,

Fourier or Cabet, they had become 'outworn and impossible to use', thanks to an understanding of evolution and of the historic method.

So far Webb went with 'scientific socialism' – but he went still further: 'The key to the confused history of European progress is this notion of a struggle for surplus value, and all revolutions can be shown to have had an economic basis, although our historians have usually ignored it.' The main instrument for the exaction of surplus value had been the organisation of labour. In the early stages, the organisation of labour beyond the family seems to have required slavery, which had once been the only means of social progress. But the power over the labourer has not necessarily always been merely physical. Theological influence has been used to 'divert a portion of the surplus value to "spiritual uses", nourishing (like the meats offered to idols) whole classes of non-producers'.

But with Marx, thus far and no further:

There will never become a moment when we can say '*now*, socialism is established.' The principles of social organisation must have already secured partial adoption as a condition of the continued existence of every social organism, and the progress of socialism is but their more complete recognition, and their conscious social acceptance as the line of advance upon which social improvement depends.

Thus, socialism may have as one of its aspects the continued struggle for surplus value. But more fundamentally it simply develops and perfects institutions and controls, forms of public authority which have long been present, and which the rise of democracy and the problems posed by the industrial revolution require to be raised to a new level.

It was this thesis which Sidney elaborated before the Sunday Lecture Society in the following year and in the Fabian essays in 1889. Hampstead was, appropriately enough, the scene of most of the discussions, formal and informal, out of which Fabianism emerged. The Argosy, which Sidney joined in November 1882, always met there.[51] Mrs Wilson's 'Economic Tea Club' and the Hampstead Public Library furnished the setting for the prolonged discussion of Marx. By the end of 1887, with Shaw's conversion to marginal analysis complete, the Fabians had settled their account with Marxism, and were indeed becoming weary and dissatisfied with walking up the hill to meetings of the Hampstead Society for the Study of Socialism, or to the Hampstead Historic. Early in 1888, Wallas remarked to Olivier, Shaw and Webb:

We shall not long be able to work together – I e.g. may at any moment have to leave London and become an usher in a country school – any of

us may knock up or die – especially we ought not to neglect the tim
between our last H.H.C meeting and Webb's departure for America.

(Sidney had secured, in view of his excellent services at the Coloni
Office, special permission to take three months' leave to visit Americ
with E.R. Pease).[52] 'The summer is really the best time for this kind c
work and we shall not have so much lecturing to do.' What Wallas had i
mind was a series of tracts on the law of rent or other economic problem
'We could write clearly but scientifically ... *Our Corner* would take then
or better *Reynolds* ... We might offer them to the Fabian to take or leave
He felt that the four of them should work alone, 'since we are the onl
four people in England who are agreed about anything.'[53]

Sidney concurred in Wallas's proposal. They should tell Miss Brook
(secretary to the Hampstead Historic) that they were going to vote again:
the continuation of the club. The four of them should 'enrich the worlc
with six tracts, each to be begun as an essay, discussed, and revised in th
light of discussion. However he was not persuaded that Wallas had quil
correctly indicated the area that should be covered. Olivier fully share
Wallas's opinion of 'our pre-eminence in our generation'. It was unnece:
sary to invite lots of socialists to hear the four of them discussing. H
thought that the papers should be reprinted 'at the expense of a join
stock company, for which reason selected millionaires should be invited t
the preliminary discussion'. Shaw dissented from Olivier's view tha
they should meet centrally and that the walk to Hampstead was a tire
some nuisance. On the contrary, the walk was the most useful feature c
the Hampstead Historic. He thought that they should write a socia
democratic history for working men.

Such was the genesis of *Fabian Essays*, arguably the most important sir
gle volume ever produced by English socialism. The credit for the origina
proposal belongs to Wallas. Shaw did the editorial work. It was ver
much a collective enterprise. Yet Sidney was plainly *primus inter pares*. Hi
contribution was outstanding and crucial to the entire argument of th
volume, and in so far as there was a general standpoint that pervaded th
book, it was he who had done most to forge it. Of the four friends wh
were responsible for the bulk of the work, he was the acknowledged intel
lectual leader, and it was he who shaped what was most distinctive an
consequential in its pages. This was fully apparent to a knowledgeabl
and attentive reader such as William Morris, who saw – and deplored
the Sidney Webb spirit with which the book was pervaded.[54]

Shaw, who opened the volume with an entertaining exposition of th
theory of rent, was unique as a writer, but as an economist spoke only a
one chastened by Wicksteed and captured by Webb. It was Sidney, not GBS
who first discovered how to derive socialist conclusions from the premise

of orthodox economic thought. Yet this chapter, together with the following one by Sidney himself, provided all the fundamental ideas of the book.

In the 'Historic Basis of Socialism', Sidney elaborated the ideas which he had first publicly advanced before the Hampstead Society in December 1887. He wasted no time before coming to his major idea:

> So little element of permanence was there in ... individualistic order that, with the progress of political emancipation, private ownership of the means of production has been, in one direction or another, successively regulated, limited and superseded, until it may now fairly be claimed that Socialist philosophy of today is but the conscious and explicit assertion of principles of social organisation which have been already in great part consciously adopted.

Utopia, even in the form signed by Auguste Comte, has to be rejected as incompatible with our understanding of evolution and our grasp of historical method:

> No philosopher now looks for anything but the gradual evolution of the new order from the old, without breach of continuity or abrupt change of the entire social tissue at any point during the process ... History shows us no example of the modern substitution of Utopian and revolutionary romance.

Fabianism conjoins even as it superseded the old radicalism and the old utopian socialism. As a socialism it accepts the Radical inheritance which teaches that changes must be acceptable to the majority, gradual and – 'in this country at any rate' – constitutional and peaceful. As itself a radicalism it accepts that a mere political levelling is 'insufficient to save a State from anarchy and despair'. Thus, Fabianism set out to achieve that convergence of radicalism and socialism which Hyndman had sought to effect in 1881, not by the submission of the pre-socialist 'Left', but through a theoretical and practical compromise: a compromise within which neither side is expected to experience any sense of loss.

Next, Sidney described the disintegration of the old pre-industrial synthesis: an affair of the 'vast impersonal forces'. Where Marx had referred to the bourgeois recruiting its own gravediggers in the shape of the proletariat, Sidney was content to make the steam engine the Frankenstein of capitalist production: the agent immediately responsible for urban democracy, political economy and socialism. Similarly, English political history was not so much a record of 'the battle of democracy' as 'the record of the reluctant enfranchisement of one class after another, by mere force of the tendencies of the age'. In a manner which has since become part of the conventional wisdom, the Second Reform Act is treated as neither the

product of a belief in democracy nor of fear of the ultimate revolutiona
politics of the masses, but of competition with the opposing faction. Th
leads to the conclusion that: 'The industrial revolution has left tl
labourer a landless stranger in his own country. The political evolution
rapidly making him its ruler. Samson is feeling for his grip on the pillars
However, the blind giant has no need to pull the temple of individua
ism down about his ears. The creed taught in this temple is that of tl
philosophic radicals. The Chartists, the Owenites, the Tories, the democra
the Christian Socialists and finally those like Comte, J.S. Mill, Darwin an
Spencer who have gained a conception of the organic quality of societ
started to drive out the money-changers and to expose utilitarianism as
creed of Murdstones and Gradgrinds'. Still more to the point – 'the pract
cal man has been irresistibly driven' beyond individualism. 'The liberty
the property-owner to oppress the property-less by the levy of econom
tribute of rent and interest began to be circumscribed, pared awa
obstructed and forbidden in various directions.' There follow instructi
lists of the industries and services once left to private enterprise and no
wholly or partially left to the community. Joint stock companies, succes
fully conducted by salaried managers, run about one-third of Englis
business. The functionless shareholders of these concerns could be expr
priated without dislocation:

> Besides its direct suppression of private enterprise, the State now regi
> ters, inspects and controls nearly all of the industrial functions which
> has not yet absorbed … the State registers all solicitors, barrister
> notaries, patent agents, brokers, newspaper proprietors, playing ca
> makers, brewers, bankers, seamen, captains, mates, doctors, cabme
> hawkers … Nor is the registration a mere form. Most of the foregoin
> are also inspected and criticised, as are all railways, tramways, ship
> mines, factories, canal-boats, public conveyances, fisheries, slaughte
> houses, dairies, milkshops, bakeries, baby-farms, gas-meters, schools
> anatomy, vivisection laboratories, explosive works, Scotch herrings an
> common lodging houses.

In short, the capitalist 'is being registered, inspected, controlled and ever
tually superseded by the community; and in the meantime he is con
pelled to cede for public purposes an ever-increasing share of rent an
interest'.

The municipalities, as Sidney argued, have done most to socialis
industrial life. The 'current radical programme' in London served to sta
current socialist demands for legislation: the shifting of the whole tax bu
den on to the recipients of rent and interest, and the gradual taxation t
extinction of these categories of income; extension of the Factory Act

with the recognition of minimum wages and maximum hours; all children to obtain 'the best education they are capable of'; without relaxing the tests against supporting able-bodied idleness; generous provision without stigma for the aged, sick and unemployed; the gradual extension of municipal activity; completion of the remaining planks in the classic radical or Chartist programme.

We were now, so Sidney concluded, on the eve of a 'new synthesis'. This was marked by a recognition of the organic nature of society as something more than an aggregate of its individual units, and the awareness that 'perfect and fitting development of each individual is not necessarily the utmost and highest cultivation of his own personality, but the filling, in the best possible way, of his humble function in the great social machine.'[55] The conditions for social health were a matter of scientific investigation. The 'greatest happiness' principle was quite acceptable. What could be plainly shown was that it was consistent neither with Benthamite economics nor with the law of rent.

Most of the other essays simply elaborate or apply these ideas. Olivier, assuming a 'positive ethical science', tried to demonstrate that socialist moral ideas already were coming to permeate society, and that 'socialist morality, like that of all preceding systems, is only that morality which the conditions of human existence have made necessary.' Annie Besant, with an exaggeration which Sidney may have found embarrassing, declared that Mr Ritchie had, through the creation of county councils, 'established the Commune'. Society was well on the way to socialism even though there would never be a moment, as Sidney had pointed out, when one could say 'now Socialism has arrived'. Wallas and Clarke and Shaw can all be shown to have borrowed authorities and instances from Webb's armoury. The excitement of the whole volume arises from its confident sense of a world seen afresh, and having thus been seen, becoming impossible to view again in old ways. The sense of socialism, not as imminent revolution, but as an imminent, going institutional concern was peculiarly, although not exclusively, the Webbian contribution to *Fabian Essays*.

The presence of discordant voices among the essayists, whether muttering their reservations *sotto voce*, or crying out in unmistakable protest, served only to point up the distinctive Webbian tone. Shaw's second essay ended with a valedictory address expressing nostalgia for revolutionary socialism even as he gave it up for the Webbian inevitability of a 'sordid, slow, reluctant, cowardly path to justice'. Clarke, while treating the Webbian dose as incontestably necessary, foresaw that some probably 'inefficient method of taxation and public control' over trusts was likely before men came to see the true solution. Annie Besant allowed the possibility of the temporary subordination of the public to the private sector and a consequent 'serfdom' for municipal employees. But only Hubert

Bland rose to an explicit critique of Webb's position. Sidney had acknowledged that the Zeitgeist was potent but did not pass Acts of Parliament without legislatures; Bland made altogether more of the need for proletarian class-consciousness and, in particular, for the rise of a distinct Labour Party. While he too went with Sidney in holding that 'the trend of things to Socialism is best shown by the changed attitude of men towards State interference and control,' he added, 'still it must not be forgotten that although Socialism involves State control, State control does not imply Socialism ...' Bland dismissed with contempt Webb's pointing to hawkers' licences as an instance of the progress of socialism and searched, although with modest success, for criteria by which the mere growth of state regulation might be distinguished from socialism properly so called. Allowing that the transition to socialism must be gradual, Bland yet maintained that there was no occasion for halting agnosticism when it came to whether any society was socialist:

> We shall be able to say that we have a socialist state on the day on which no man or group of men holds, over the means of production, property rights by which the labour of producers can be subjected to exploitation ...[56]

With the appearance of the *Essays* almost, but not quite all, the distinctive features if Fabianism had emerged. Indeed, by 1887 they would have all been apparent to an informed and discerning observer. Fabianism was a distinctively English socialism, recruiting its leaders and supporters from the new race of professional men, as distinct from professional gentlemen. Its nature was profoundly influenced by the absence in England, during its formative period, of a mass workers' party, and the presence of a tradition, established by the philosophic radicals and continued by the Positivists, of small intellectual ginger groups that reputedly worked to some effect upon law and opinion. In economic theory, Fabianism was distinguished among socialisms by its repudiation of the labour theory of value in favour of a development and adaptation of Ricardian and Jevonian thought. The principal effects of this substitution were to make socialism appear as a conclusion derived from the premises of orthodox political economy; to point up through the notion of 'rent of ability' the important and equivocal position of the professional man; to make socialism depend upon a consumer's economics, emphasising the demand side, rather than a producer's economics emphasising the supply side; and to direct attention away from crises and the long-run tendencies of capitalist production in favour of a kind of static microanalysis which was useful in relation to the critique of particular institutions and in preparation of proposals for administrative innovation. However, the Fabians' essential achievement did not consist of replacing one kind of socialist economic theory by another. They were more interested in institutional relationships than in economic ones. They saw socialism not as the outcome of a class struggle which could grow ever sharper as capitalism developed, but as the result of a growing consensus which was already emerging around going institutional concerns. Just as socialism was a conclusion immanent within orthodox economic thought, so it was even more seen as immanent within existing administrative practice; it was nothing but such practice fully clothed and in its right mind. 'I draw my conclusions', declared Sidney Webb, 'from other men's premises.' To which Bertrand Russell replied: 'Well, Webb, either the conclusions follow anyway, or else you are guilty of sophistry.'[57] To this neat bit of repartee there was but one possible response. What Sidney Webb meant was that he appropriated major premises, adding the minor ones so as to arrive at the desired conclusion. And this was a very essential part of Fabianism that had hardly made its appearance in 1889. The Fabians, much more than the philosophic radicals or the Positivists, came to make explicit the *minor* premise of their age. Their speciality lay in formulating axiomata media – the propositions that connect the fundamental principle to the particular project. These were the vital links, as the Fabians subsequently taught, without which large principles are of no practical moment, and particular projects 'mere empiricism'! Such middle axioms as

> To raise compulsorily the Standard of Life; to enforce a National Minimum in each important point; Collective regulation of all matters of common concern, and so on … are the instruments by which your fundamental principles can be applied – the lathes in which particular reforms are but the cutting tools to be changed from time to time as the task requires.[58]

The Radical programme which Sidney had cited in his essay came close to formulating some such axiomata media, but they had not yet received the prominence they were subsequently to be given. In all other major respects Fabianism had established its essential identity by the end of the eighties.

Before returning to the circumstances of Sidney's personal life it will be useful to explore this summary account of the Fabian presence rather more closely.

Whether considered socially, theoretically or practically the Fabians of the eighties and nineties were the heirs of a tradition stretching back to the philosophic radicals of the twenties and of the Positivists of the sixties and seventies. Although the philosophic radicals have been described as 'intellectuals', this claim could only be validated by reference to their attitudes and their political conduct – hardly with respect to their social situation.[59] The intellectuals, in England, were not seen to be specific social stratum in the first half of the nineteenth century. James Mill fully identified himself with the 'people', by which he frankly understood the 'middle rank' to be the exemplar and the prophet. The values of utilitarianism, which Sidney characterised as 'Protestantism of sociology',[60] were preeminently those of the triumphant bourgeois – economy, efficiency and uniformity. Yet as writers, a part of what the Duke of Wellington called 'the scribbling set', and as public servants, the philosophic radicals appeared as precursors of the new tribe of professional men. The positivists, thanks to Comte and to the influence of developments in France, were the first – apart, perhaps from John Stuart Mill – to have a clear sense of the alienation of the man of thought from the bourgeois and of the supposed common interest between the intellectual (seen as doctor, teacher and secular priest) and the proletariat.[61] With the positivists there were not only men who spent a large part of their time in unpaid public service on commissions, as Frederic Harrison did, but men who were public employees, like J.H. Bridges and Henry Crompton. In the case of the Fabians there is no mistaking their consciousness of themselves as a contingent almost exclusively recruited from a *nouvelle couche sociale*: the shabby genteel intellectual proletariat.[62] It is the rise of the newer professions that sets their social tone: administration, accountancy, teaching, journalism. To follow these occupations was to cut oneself off from the rest of bourgeois society, because entry into them was increasingly restricted by formal requirements, and the most successful pursuit of them involved the following of truth or beauty or efficiency for their own sakes. Indeed the pervasive influence of the acquisitive society was held a principal reason for the failure of successful professional practice, which always required the sacred spark of critical detachment, which mercenary interests threatened to extinguish.

If the Fabians had a sharper sense of their own distinct social location, that merely reflected the slow progress of the English intellectuals considered as a distinct social stratum. Like the philosophic radicals and the positivists they arose not merely out of the same social formation, but out of the prolonged personal friendship. As Graham Wallas observed:

> The history of any definite 'school' of philosophic or political opinion will generally show that its foundation was made possible by personal friendship. So few men can devote themselves to continuous thought, that if several think on the same lines for many years it is almost always because they have encouraged each other to proceed. And varieties of opinion and temperament are so infinite, that those who accept ... each other's utterances, are generally bound by personal loyalty as well as by intellectual agreement.[63]

The friendship of Bentham and James Mill, of the Positivists' mumbo-jumbo at Wadham in the mid-century, and of Webb, Shaw, Olivier and Wallas himself confirm the point. It is also significant that the friendship out of which these schools emerged were all London-based. Admittedly this had sometimes a negative impact on their fortunes, but generally it meant that they were all well placed for lobbying and wire-pulling.

The philosophic radicals expressed the values, not of a mere social stratum, still less of an esoteric school, but of a whole class, or at least of the most ambitious, hegemonic part of it. They expressed, most clearly, the opposition of the vigorous, scientific and practical, provincial bourgeois culture to the relatively effete, classical, literary and aristocratic culture of the ancient universities. The Positivists and the Fabians were ultimately at one with their utilitarian precursors in this respect. For both positivist and Fabian were, after all, utilitarian – believing actions are to be judged by their consequences, and impatient with theological or metaphysical arguments. All three groups were equally short with appeals to abstract rightness, and ready to dismiss them as 'nonsense on stilts'. Each of these small groups would have echoed De Tocqueville: 'We need a new science of politics for a new world.' Each believed that it was on the way to discovering that science, urged on, as Bentham said 'by the groans of all'. Sharing certain leading preoccupations – with trade unions, the poor law and education, for example – they were all wire-pullers exploiting a remarkable range of socio-political contacts. All were thought radical and shocking, and all of them wearied of the frivolities and irrelevancies of existing party conflict. Each in turn was to be torn between the hope of capturing one of the existing parties and the possibility of starting *de novo*. Despite this predicament, each succeeded in working to much effect and each endured repeated disappointment with a calm born of the belief that it came as the herald of an immanent consensus that would issue from reason or of history.

Certainly neither utilitarian, nor positivist nor Fabian would have been prepared to serve as crew on that Oakshottian boat which has no destination, no harbour, no floor for anchorage. To keep the ship of state afloat was a necessary but insufficient purpose in politics. What was wanted was a science that could accomplish the organic unity of analysis and ideal. Bentham did it by reducing morality to a kind of 'transcendental physiology': 'Nature has placed mankind under the governance two sovereign masters, pain and pleasure. It is for them alone to point out what we ought to do, as well as to determine what we shall do.' The positivists did it through the law of the three stages, which were at once an epistemology, a philosophy of history and a programme of social reconstruction. The Fabian did it, although with much more diffidence, by demonstrating that socialism was both the desirable and the inevitable outcome of the conjunction of democracy and modern industry, and to this discovery of a science of society and a scientific polity is necessarily connected a more or less pronounced tendency to secular religiosity and the cult of the expert. The doctrine of the old faith opens a gap between facts and values. Science, which has torn them asunder, must reconnect them and place ethical judgements upon a sound demonstrable basis. If men are to be delivered only by a new science of politics then – until education has improved the 'average sensual man' – much must devolve upon the scientifically trained expert. A certain distrust of the masses was present in the thinking of all these groups, although it was much less pronounced among the positivists, in the relatively quiet mid-Victorian years, than it was in the case of the philosophic radicals or the Fabians. All were disposed, on certain occasions, to play the same kind of equivocal role as the Benthamites played in 1831–2: at once seeking to raise the waves of popular disturbance and to calm them; to rouse a wholesome terror in the ruling class while keeping the actual danger within bounds. This tendency to blow hot and cold was rationalised, principally by James Mill, into a political strategy.[64]

The philosophic radicals, the Comtists and the Fabians comprise a single tradition by virtue of their positivist spirit and their *modus operandi*. But one must resist the temptation of taking them to constitute a progression to the 'left'. In terms of militancy and a disposition to play with fire, the Benthamites and the Positivists showed much more daring than the Fabians. Mrs Grote was not alone in scorning 'piddling, domestic detail and amelioration'. Bentham himself despised gradualism and longed for 'utter, organic, sweeping change':

> Ought it not, – this and every reform – ought it not to be temperate? Well then – to be temperate it must be gradual – to be *well* done it must be *gradually* done. Fellow Citizens! as often as you meet a man holding to you this language, say to him: 'Sir, we have our dictionary: what you are saying we perfectly understand: *done gradually* means left undone, left undone for ever if possible …'[65]

Marx acknowledged that the Positivist Beesly had an understanding of crises, and there was indeed an apocalyptic tone in many of his pronouncements.[66] With the Fabians, visions of catastrophe – if they appeared at all – were always remote and heavily veiled. It is perhaps necessary to make this point, since in their programmes the three schools undoubtedly exhibited a fairly steady progression from individualism to collectivism. The Benthamite enthusiasm for the free play of market forces and enlightened selfishness is replaced by the Positivist insistence on the need for organisation and the moralisation of the capitalist, and finally by the Fabian call for planning and the statutory enforcement of morals. These changes required a corresponding development in economic thought. The philosophic radicals, particularly through Ricardo, had made an immense contribution. Yet even in Ricardo, not to mention Bentham, they had imposed upon that science a 'bourgeois taint'. Frederic Harrison and the Positivists protested against 'plutonomy' – the turning of economy into a code of morals. Yet apart from J.K. Ingram they numbered no distinguished economist in their ranks. Their critique appeared to be directed merely at changing the terms of discussion, rather than advancing the analysis itself. There was about it too much generality, an air of amateurism. Webb and the Fabians placed themselves deliberately in the line of economic orthodoxy. The crucial paradox about Fabian economics was that it was simultaneously socialist and professional.[67] Marx was the last great amateur economist, as Darwin was the last great amateur in natural science.

The Fabians habitually talked as if their rejection of the labour theory of value in favour of their own development of Ricardo, and partial adoption of Jevons, constituted their decisive contribution to socialist thought. Wallas, for instance, supposed that it was this which allowed the Fabians to escape from the remorseless logic of a catastrophic class struggle and to offer a perspective of 'more or less'; of a gradual progress towards socialism.[68] In fact, in their judgement, it makes no difference whether the income of non-workmen is described as a rent secured by monopolists of scarce factors of production, or as a form of surplus value which arises from the difference between the value of labour power and the value it produces. A conflict of interests between the classes is pointed up by either interpretation, and the possibility of either gradually encroaching on the wealth and income of the idlers, or of expropriating them at one blow, would appear to be open on both views. The consequences that flowed from this substitution of Ricardo–Jevons for Marx were more limited, although still highly important. First, the Fabians were, through the concept of the rent of ability, to emphasise both the importance and the guilt of the professional stratum to which they themselves belonged. Webb and other Fabians frequently reproached Marx with obscuring the decisive role of trained and skilled management, and of professional administrators. The analytic demonstration that professional men were rent-receivers but not idlers, guilty but useful, supported the powerful sense which they had of their own equivocal position. Second, by introducing Jevons, the Fabians turned socialist economics away from the 'supply' side towards the demand side. They made it over into a consumer's economics. But in doing so they directed attention away from dynamic towards static relationships. They were left with a socialist economics that offered no account of cyclical movements of capitalist crises.

The Achilles' heel of Fabian economics was not any failure to explain the 'realities of exploitation', but its inability to account for the periodic convulsions of the capitalist system.

Yet the Fabians, it must be insisted, were mistaken in imagining that their most novel contribution lay in their economic theory. That was not, whether in *Fabian Essays* or in their other publications, where the main emphasis tended to be placed. What most distinguished them among contemporary socialists was their preoccupation with institutional relationships rather than with economic ones. What most distinguished man, what was most crucial to being human, was not the continuous self-transmutation of his nature through work but uniqueness as the maker and moulder of institutions.[69] Social institutions were at once the most influential and the most malleable part of his environment. Contrary to the generally received opinion, what separated the Fabians from the Marxists was less their economics, less their preference for describing property-derived incomes as 'rent' rather than 'surplus value', than their rejection of historical materialism and the class struggle, in favour of an institutional interpretation of history. In a subordinate aspect, socialism might indeed be seen as the continuation in modern form of the long struggle for surplus value. At a deeper level it had to be regarded as the final outcome of a permanent and ever-enlarging principle of social organisation:

> The principles of social organisation must already have secured partial adoption as a condition of the continued existence of every social organism ... the progress of socialism is but their more complete recognition and their conscious acceptance as the line of advance upon which social improvement depends.[70]

Marx, attending to the laws of motion of capitalist production, discovered that the working class, alone of revolutionary classes, could have nothing of its own which it aspired to extend or fortify.[71] It was the most revolutionary class in history because it alone could not emancipate itself without abolishing its own conditions of appropriation. Webb and the Fabians, focusing on the trend of institutional development in nineteenth-century England, discovered that socialism was already an active principle and going concern. The workers had everything to gain by enlarging the area of public ownership, service, administration and control. The force of things, political and industrial, was necessarily making in that direction: 'There will never come a moment when we and say: "*now* Socialism is established!"' Morris and the Marxist might complain that the Fabians reduced socialism to mere machinery; that they confused form with substance; but could they deny that the Ten Hours Act, or sanitary and other legislation, had checked, and indeed reversed, the trend to increasing immiseration? The demand for the legally enforceable eight-hour day became – at the end of the eighties and the beginning of the nineties – the rallying point for English labour, and indeed for international labour. It served to mask the gap that separated Marxism from both Fabianism and empiricism. Marx had encouraged demands for the legal limitation of working hours. He had helped to write them into the programme of the International. He had announced that victory on such a score would be a triumph for the political economy of labour ('social production controlled by social foresight') over the political economy of capital.[72] As Marx wrote, 'In enforcing such laws, the working class do not fortify governmental power. On the contrary, they transform that power now used against them, into their own agency.'[73] Sidney took a very active part in the campaign for the legal eight-hour day, although he employed himself in rebutting objections rather than rousing the demand for it.[74] There were enlightened employers who could be brought to accept the proposed measure. If it was legitimate and proper, why not demands for a minimum standard of life? Why not an endless programme of encroachment at the expense of capitalist wealth, income and power? Engels might complain that Sidney and his friends hushed up the class struggle, but he had to concede that as well-documented and effective propagandists they were unmatched.[75]

Such were the distinguishing characteristics of Fabianism as they had come to shape themselves by 1887 and as they became known to a wider public in 1888. In terms of each and of all these characteristics Sidney Webb clearly emerges as the prevailing Fabian. Admittedly Olivier and Podmore were also, as first-division clerks in the civil service, types of the new professional men. But they came from Oxford not Birkbeck. Wallas was fascinated by Bentham and philosophic radicalism and Annie Besant had been deeply impressed by Comte. But no other Fabian could claim, as Sidney could, to be so immersed in the relevant tradition – to have had Bentham for his first teacher, J.S. Mill for his model, and the moralisation of the capitalist as his earliest social idea. Shaw introduced Sidney to Marx, but it was Sidney, as the most professional of Fabian economists, who led the way in wrestling with the German and in supplanting him.

While Shaw was preparing *Fabian Essays* for the press, Sidney was taking three months' holiday in the United Sates in the company of Edward Pease. They toured an area bounded by Quebec in the north, Richmond in the south and Chicago in the west.[76] They spent much of their time in Boston where Sidney was deeply impressed by the Massachusetts Institute of Technology and where he enjoyed the company of General F.A. Walker, the president of the American Economic Association. Apart from Walt Whitman – who was ill – Walker appears to have been the most distinguished American with whom they were able to make an acquaintance.

He had coined the phrase 'rent of ability' in an article in the *Quarterly Journal of Economics* in 1887, and it was in the course of the discussion that arose out of this that Sidney had first publicly advanced what was to become known as the Fabian theory of rent.[77] Webb found Walker to be 'typical ex-militaire, square solid face, great self-reliance and strength; received us very kindly, remembered me, and asked us to dinner, putting us up also at his club'. This was the Tavern Club, a Bohemian institution of only 125 members, who were admitted for their talent. Walker's economics course at MIT was the best Sidney had ever heard of 'but mainly historical and statistical – laboratory methods'.[78]

The buildings in New York were 'high and gorgeous' but the city was generally mean, slovenly and untidy.[79] Boston was 'good value', but America as a whole was not worth much.

Sidney had taken 300 – 'or was it 100?'[80] – introductions to the United States. He was already on the way to becoming a public figure well known in London and beyond. From 1884 he had – without noticeably slackening his activity in local discussion groups, 'Parliaments' and debating clubs – taken to formal teaching. Once more following in Positivist footsteps, he had become a lecturer in Political Economy at the Working Men's College. But whereas Frederic Harrison never managed to establish a Church of Humanity among the 'semi-middle class youths ... aspiring to be correct',[81] Sidney soon had a flourishing Fabian 'Group' among the students.[82] From 1887 he began increasingly to lecture at the City of London College where he himself had once been a student. By 1888 he had so far 'arrived' that he could be invited to address the Sunday Lecture Society: a body which entertained only the most distinguished and famous authorities.[83] At the same time he spent Sunday after Sunday addressing local Liberal or Radical associations, branches of the SDF or the William Morris connection at Kelmscott House. While Shaw could choose to speak on some large perennial issue such as 'Wages or Social Democracy', Sidney's contributions were distinguished by their precision and their relevance to some immediate political or social issue.[84] He worked at teaching, continuously recasting and refreshing his material. Thus, when he returned from America he gave a course of lectures on economic principles in relation to American experience.[85] One of his most successful enterprises was a course entitled 'Political Economy from *The Times*'.[86] This was no lazy, chance affair of waiting for something to turn up. The lectures derived from the settled form of the paper rather than from particular news items. The births and deaths column opened a discussion of population, and the social differential in fertility and mortality rates; the appointments column became the occasion for discussion of the supply of labour and the rent of ability; while students were assured that 'nothing in all political economy is so fascinating as the esoteric side of the "shipping intelligence". *The Gazette* may be made more interesting than the last new novel.'[87] He knew how to make the dry bones live, and continuous support of his classes bore out the press opinion that he was 'a trenchant and convincing speaker, an admirable lecturer on political economy, [who] has the rare gift of combining close and accurate thinking with a really popular presentation of economic subjects'.[88]

His writings meant that his prestige grew beyond the circle of his students and the membership of London Radical Clubs and socialist branches. He was required to deal with the intellectual difficulties and the moral perplexities of strangers who wrote to him for counsel. Sir H.B. Bacon wanted to know what were the legislative proposals of the socialists. He was told that

> Socialists do not claim to have any panacea in the shape of practical legislation immediately to set things right. Socialism, indeed, emphatically negatives such hope, by asserting that the whole basis of social organisation must be (and is being) changed, before things will be well. Bills in Parliament it leaves merely to party politicians, the chief work at present being to change the *principles* on which these politicians, and the voters, act in social matters.

Having disclaimed any ambition to project legislative programmes, Sidney immediately proceeded to do so, following the exact lines of the Radical programme to which he was to refer in his Fabian essay. Such a programme, he declared, was supported by 'most thoughtful politicians, as well as supported by the political economists. But they are delayed by the opposition of those who would be (as a class) extinguished by them: i.e. those who now live on rent and interest.'[89]

Some of those who lived on rent and interest found it morally disturbing. Thus E.R. Pease, left £3000 by his father in 1884, resolved two years later to become a carpenter. He held down a job for an hour in America; a week in north London and three months in Red Lion Square making knick-knacks. Webb saw that he was a born secretary and secured his services for himself and the Fabian Society.[90] He could give no such directly practical aid to Jane Burdon Sanderson who wrote begging for his advice. He told her it would do no good simply to refuse to draw her rent and interest. This would be but to cede them to the persons paying them; by no means necessarily to the worker. Besides, rent and interest properly belonged to the entire community and not just to the individual workers. (Early in 1880 he had demolished Edward Carpenter's recommendation for passing on wealth, showing it to be useless and probably harmful.)[91] Her duty was to work according to her ability and to consume no more than she needed.

Unless each individual does work equal in utility to the utility of the commodities he consumes, he is a dead loss to the world. The lives of the workers would be happier if he did not exist. This is an appalling reflection and, when once realised, it may serve to correct the inevitable personal bias which leads us to give ourselves to the benefit of the doubt.

However, to work for not less than eight hours a day (it might be unpaid social or political work) and to consume no more than the equivalent of the services she rendered, was not her whole duty. 'It is part of the natural duty of work of rich persons to look after the disposition of their wealth.' For example, to harass the directors of companies in which she might own shares, in the interests of decent working conditions for those they employed:

> Even then the present system makes you almost helpless. Women and children will be oppressed and starved *with your capital* whatever you do. If you resent this and groan under the necessity, it seems to me that you should do what you can to alter the system i.e. throw your energy and ability into the cause of Socialism …. It is impossible that all persons can be equally moralised; therefore the laws and institutions must be altered so as to prevent the immoral people any longer preying unwittingly on the world.

There was a duty to 'spread the light' and to join 'some militant organisation'.[92]

By the late eighties Sidney was becoming known not only as a gifted and energetic lecturer and writer, but as a potentially formidable political organiser. The *Star* described him as 'that rare combination – adroit manager of men and the enthusiast'.[93] He appeared in both these capacities when as secretary of the Holborn Society Liberal & Radical Association he engaged Gladstone in a correspondence at the end of 1888. The Council of the Association told the Liberal leader that it regretted that the party programme was so little calculated to solve the pressing problem of urban poverty. It called upon the party to tax ground rents and values; to improve artisans' dwellings and sanitation; to provide more technical education and evening instruction and recreation for young people; to promote the further utilisation of city endowments; and to work to reducing the hours of labour and bettering the condition of the unemployed. Gladstone could only explain that he had done his best, but had been thwarted by the Tories and the dissentient Liberals.[94] Gladstone and his friends were to become increasingly aware of the Fabian presence. It was already making itself felt in London politics and in the London press, but these first exercises in permeation are best described in the following chapter.

In the labour movement too, Sidney cut a figure. He was respected and sought out even by those who were remote from him politically. Thus he was invited to become a member of the Committee of the Central Democratic Club, an institution which was intended to provide a meeting place for the leading personalities of the labour, Radical and socialist movements.[95] In 1889 he enjoyed a very good dinner, at one shilling a head, in the company of Mahon, the club manager, and many others. These included J. Harrison Davidson (brother of the wandering scholar who had founded the Fabian Society's precursor, the Fellowship of the New Life), Eduard Bernstein, Tom Mann, Friedrich Engels and Eleanor Marx. In his after-dinner speech Sidney stressed that friendship was compatible with differences of opinion and dwelt upon the international character of the club. Engels was equally conciliatory, affirming that each nation must determine its own method of propaganda for itself, and seeing beyond all differences, great progress, 'certain victory'. Tom Mann sang 'The Flowers that Bloom in the Spring', adding a 'democratic' verse of his own. Aveling recited Shelley's 'Men of England'. The entire company then roared out, to the tune of 'John Brown', William Morris's 'March of the Workers':

> Hark! the rolling of the thunder!
> Lo the sun! and lo thereunder
> Riseth wrath, and hope, and wonder,
> And the host comes marching on.

Sidney and Friedrich Engels went out into the Grays Inn Road and agreed that the wines would have been better for a little more warmth, but were otherwise seemingly well satisfied with the occasion.[96] It was regrettably not an evening to be repeated, and the club did not prosper. Despite such convivial occasions and despite his growing public reputation, Sidney Webb at the end of the eighties was still beset by his sense of personal inadequacy, still inclined to introspection and to pessimism, still disturbed by sharp recollections of the pain he had endured in 1885. When Pease became engaged to Emily Davidson, Sidney wrote her one of his longest and most self-revealing letters.[97]

27 Keppel Street
Russell Square
12th December 1888

Dear Miss Davidson

I take the very earliest of my opportunities since my return to London yesterday afternoon, to write to you. I am very sorry that you were

away from London so that we cannot talk face to face of the momento▸
secret which I am strictly enjoined not to impart to anyone – thoug
there are no doubt about 59 similar possessors similarly circumscribe
If you ever come up to London (e.g. to do some shopping) and esp
cially if you are going through London on your way North, please l
me have a chance of seeing you, here or elsewhere.

For I have a great desire for your friendship, with the very smalle
capacity for acquiring it. I have often envied the ease with which othe
'catch on' to congenial spirits (E.R.P. for instance, is one such lucky ◂
clever person),[98] where I simply remain outside.

I am very busy of course, somewhat serious, very analytic and intr
spective – but I hope passably honest, sincere, and not obviously hat
ful or repulsive. Yet I seem 'left out' in more than one case, and in mo▸
than one department of life. (This, however, is by the way) I am at ar
rate going to begin by a long intimate letter *to yourself*. One of the dif▸
culties incidental to your present position is my uncertainty as to yo▸
exact personality. I am writing to you, or to Pease and you, or to y▸
plus Pease? The copyright of a letter remains vested in the writer, anc
am compelled to avow a desire that I may be understood as writi▸
only to you, and not to you, plus Pease. I do not forbid you to pass ▸
this letter but should prefer you not to. My own theory of marria▸
does not involve the merging of identities. I am even against an intelle
tual communion. Let me assume for the nonce that it is to be a me▸
partnership. I write to one of the partners only.

I was very pleased when Pease told me his great news soon after v▸
met at Queenstown. Nothing could have pleased me more than th
you should marry Pease – unless it was that Pease should marry you
and here as both events happening together. Nevertheless you will pe
haps understand that it was with a 'contraction' of the heart that I hea▸
the news; and an old wound, which still embitters me was torn ope
and bled, as it bleeds now while I write to you these words and I thir
again of Heine's song, (Do you remember Ein Mädchen liebt e
Andern – I forget whether you read German), and the whole mournf
swing of Schubert's setting of some of them – 'Der arme Peter', f▸
instance comes back to me, and so on and so on. I mean I am very cro
with things in general, and I realise that I am 'left out'. I am afraid
have a great deal of 'Langsam' in me – I knew it when I read Ma▸
Pattison's Autobiography.

However my own little woes – now some five years old – are n
your fault and I am not irrational enough to grudge others better luc
But I must not disguise the fact that one grievance against you I have
which you must atone for. 'L'ami quise marie se perd'. I am near
thirty and during the last five years (just those five years too) I have lo

five intimate friends by marriage. With Pease I had become intellectually intimate, though living afar off, and America has made us real
friends. We are as Shaw would say 'even on quarrelling terms'. Now
you are to come in and carry him off from me just as our friendship
ripens. C'est dur. The loss is irreparable whatever you may intend to
say. It rests indeed with you to furnish compensation by becoming
yourself a friend. I warn you that it is hard to be 'friends' with me –
I am an exacting person, needing more to be loved, it may be, than
capable of loving – a kind of stone wall on which fruit *will* grow but
needing a good deal of sun. (NB you didn't know that I was so poetical
did you?)

Having frankly avowed my position towards you I proceed to
America. How did you enjoy *your* visit to America? For though to the
vulgar eye, and to that of the ticket collector, Pease and I were alone
you and I and Pease know that it was a case of 'one and one and a shadowy third'. Where we went, your wraith went also: what we saw we
saw with you, what we thought we discussed in your presence and
even for your sake, and I am not sure whether that exacting Goddess
whom we all three serve, I mean Humanity, was not sometimes
eclipsed by one human.

Now don't go and suppose that this increase of the party was
unpleasant to me. I trust that you will permit me to say that I too felt
that I had an interest in the matter, and many and many a time the
threeness of our party gave a new zest to the intellectual stimulus of
our mutual intercourse. I do not deny that your peculiar relation to us,
(as the perpetually present absentee) was occasionally an abnormal factor in our action. For instance, the Post Office became the only public
building in each city that we cared ever to visit: we were invariably
under the impression that it was the most pressing of our social obligations on each particular day, it seemed inevitably to lie on the nearest
road from any point to any other point (which can hardly be possible
outside of two-deminsional space) and the quality of the city, the value
of our local friends, and even the punctuality of the mails and of those
privileged intercommunicators Kennedy Todd & Co. Nor do I deny that
I felt a little 'out of it' on each of these occasions. That you must forgive
me, other people's old wounds smart when the East wind blows, but
mine smart in anybody else's sunshine. I *could* not write when I was in
Pease's company, the influence was too strong, of his presence and consequently of your own presence, but I hope you understood that, and
that my congratulations were not really delayed, even if not actually
translated into words and curves of ink.

Now as to the future. I am pleased that your are at Cheltenham, but
don't put off the marriage. Has Pease ever told you of Stepniak's saying

as to how fiercely Russian Nihilists love, because they know that any moment the end may come. We are all in that position here. Any moment the end may come – do not delay.

And remember the Comtist maxim – one of the many good ones of the Positivists – 'live openly'. Do not make a mystery or secret of your position now or hereafter. There is no such thing as a self-regarding act. The world is entitled to know exactly how you stand and not only discreditable mysteries, but all mysteries are bad and evil bringing. I began life badly and entangled myself in several private mysteries. These cling around me still, though I have tried to work out of them. This is partly why I have urged Pease to come back to England quickly. I want you to press him to do so. His services would be very valuable in London just now, we are on the crest of a wave, and all hands are needed to keep up the progress and press our advantage. There are astonishingly few workers: and none with just Pease's qualities, and America was not as fertile as we hoped. There is very little for him to learn there.

This leads me to another point. Do you remember in *Felix Holt* his bitter address to his inamorata as to the pernicious influence of women in dragging men away from lofty ideals and unselfish ends, down to the merely personal claims of family, (of course I do not fear any such evil influence from you – at least, not consciously) – you will not be a 'basil plant' but you are undertaking a great responsibility. For good or for evil you are stepping into a position of enormous influence over one mind and centre of action. What influence will that be? This is a very pretty problem in psychology (I hope you don't mind it being called by so learned a name) and I confess I am a little doubtful as to the result. I had almost wished that Pease had married a stronger 'Collectivist'. He possesses as Mrs Wilson acutely says the Anarchist mind. His mere existence – proper and decent existence, of course – is a main end to him. He is wedded to an incurable (and vain) personal optimism, which leads him to act in and for himself alone, according to his momentary impulses, extremely well trained impulses, but still *mere* impulses. This is necessarily fatal to social and combined action which I try to think is my own ideal. One person alone can follow his impulses safely, e.g. in crossing a crowded street, but two people together crossing the street must act deliberately in concert, or else separate, or else face the inevitable result, a smash. Now my theory of life is to feel at every moment that I am acting as a member of a committee, and for that committee – in some affairs a committee of my own family merely, in others again a committee as wide as the Aryan race. But I aspire *never* to act alone, or for myself. This theoretically combined action involves rules, deliberation, discussion, concert, the disregard of one's own impulses, and in fact is Collectivism or Communism. The contrary habit is logically Anarchism.

Of course Pease is not an Anarchist. He is too clever not to see clearly the obvious inequalities and iniquities of unlimited Individualism, that is – he understands the Law of Rent in its fullest extent, and as he is one of the most unselfish men I know, he acts, in all weighty matters, on Collectivist lines. But he reserves a large sphere of minor matters as practically self-regarding and in these he is an Anarchist. Did you ever hear of the prophecy that a lately married common friend would, although most kind and unselfish, one day eat all the butter on the table, unconscious that his wife had none? (and he *did* too). That will be true – in the spirit – of Pease, unless you send him off on slightly different rails. He has lived too long and too much his own life, to be quite qualified for a Communist Colony. You too, I am afraid, have somewhat of an Anarchist mind. You too have had to live your own life, and to be at any rate intellectually alone. Beware lest you intensify each others individualism in the small matters which make up four-fifths of life, and each of which is unconsciously moulding the character which will hereafter deal with the larger matters – admittedly to be done on Collectivist lines. This need not imply that I am in favour of 'Merger' or even of Communism in marriage. Let it be a mere partnership. But let the partners, in every detail, act in and for the partnership – except in such spheres as they may severally act in and for larger Committees. I should like you to read (may I say over again) my paper on 'Rome', printed in July and August numbers of *Our Corner*, especially the conclusion. This will throw some light on the criticism I am making. Of course just now this will seem unnecessary to you. One element of your common position is the mutual harmony of thought and action which it implies. (Shaw once said that when we 'superior intellects' fell in love, we always felt and said that we were not under any illusion like the common herd, we knew his or her faults and defects perfectly well, and our own position, free from the usual glamour. This, he said, was simply that we were under the spell of just one illusion the more.) Pease is certainly in that position. Are you? Not that I would have you imagine that I am referring particularly to the little trials of married life, or that I am counselling you 'How to be happy though married'. You will, I think, understand that I am referring to the whole of life's action, and its effect on the character, and thus on all future action – and the world for ever.

Pease never would discuss plans of travel, we quarrelled daily on this point – as I would not give way. He said that you alone made all his plans when he was with you, and he simply accepted them. This is bad, even ignoble – if it is to be your future habit. It is merely the old bad

theory of marriage inverted. My interest lies in its evil effect on chara-
ter, his and yours. I want you throughout life, to deliberate, discuss, an
concert your every act, in free communion with those with whom yc
are acting, whether one or many. I am of course aware that all this
very frank – even to impertinence, but it is what I have said to Pease a
forcibly as I could and what I would say to you were we togethe
Beware lest you do the Socialist cause *harm* by marrying one of its mo
useful members – see you improve his character, and not deteriorate 1
see that you increase his energy, and the width of his altruism, n-
diminish them. See that Pease plus Davidson – *more* than Davidson an
Pease separately, not, as is so usual much less. However I won't go c
preaching, especially as I have no title to be heard in the matter. I ho
that one day we may be friendly enough to talk over such things free

Pease told me that you thought me unfriendly to you. That mu
have been my unfortunate infirmity. From the beginning I had nothir
but kindest feelings towards you – yet without the capacity for allowir
them to be seen. We scarcely ever met except at Hampstead, thoug
you did once show me how short we all are at 27 Keppel Street. M
mother and sister are perhaps matter of fact and sharers in my ow
coldness, but I can assure you that they would be very glad if yc
would make them friends.

I have just had a letter from Pease at Philadelphia which I enclose.
will of course take him some time to get to work and be hard for hir
Don't let him stay too long.

Will you let me know about work? Perhaps I can help yo
Remember that I am rather great at vague knowledge of things in gei
eral, and that I have access to the most perfect storehouses. Send me
line when you want to know *anything* and I will find out.

The election of Mrs B Headlam, and another Socialist person, on tl
London School Board may be of use to you. Do not look for oi
moment for anything out of London. There is literally no other pla-
worth living in. I have seen a great many others and *I know*.

I can't write all I want to say. I never wrote so long a letter before 1
anyone, but I have not yet done. Yet I must stop, and so adieu.

Sidney Webb
13/12/88

Webb remarked in his old age that

I have very little knowledge of what has happened to me internall
I am, I suppose, what is nowadays called an extrovert. Things imping
on me and I react to the impact, occasionally with ideas and suggestioi

that prove interesting ... I can supply nothing but a series of disconnected accounts, impacts and reactions.

This was a truthful account of what he had trained himself to become,
rather than an accurate report of what he had always been. For Sidney at
thirty was an introvert whose pugnacious self-assurance in public life
hardly concealed his profound sense of personal inadequacy. For him, self-
denial meant not renunciation but release. One must recall how intensely
he suffered from the pangs of shame and remorse; how they were as vivid
and acute in recollection as they had been at the time of commission and
discovery; the settled pessimism; the sense of being small and ugly and
personally insignificant and unlovable. Where was Dr Heidenhoff with his
process of thought extirpation: the process which would select for oblivion
the memory of failure and humiliation? He might try to follow Mill's
counsel and find happiness as something incidental to work for humanity
but, so long as he conceived of humanity as Mill did, its emancipation
appeared not merely as unsatisfying, but as dreadful. The will to live an
individual life was the survival of the brute in man. One must combat this
wrong-headed refusal willingly to bow the neck to the yoke: reject the
highest cultivation of our own personality in favour of filling, in the best
possible way, our function in the great social machine. Man is a being who
forms committees; he must aspire never to act alone.

This is not to deny the reality of Sidney's social conscience, nor does it
in any way invalidate his critique of individualism as the mask of
exploitation and chaos. But part of the secret of his effectiveness lay in the
harmony between his sense of public duty, and his fear of personal freedom and individuality. It is commonly supposed that Webb, like Darwin,
sacrificed his own all-round development to politics and investigation.[99]
But was it too much time among the earthworms which led to social inadequacy and cultural one-sidedness, or was it not rather the inadequacy
and one-sidedness which sent him to the earthworms in the first place? In
this dialectic, what appears first as effect comes subsequently as cause.
Webb became, like Darwin, an anaesthetised man, which is not at all the
same as being unfeeling. It is the result of a too acute sensibility. The
anaesthetised man tries – sometimes with but indifferent success – to
localise the anaesthetic and to numb only part of himself. The young
Webb loved London, and cared deeply for Wallas and other friends. But
this love and friendship came through a purposive rapport. How could
such a rapport be achieved in every relationship in life? One could not
escape from oneself until the vacant place was filled in the last, the smallest and the important committee. Sidney had to bear the burden of autobiographical reflection, of introspection, of self-pity, until he could submit to
that happy yoke.

'Men are like planets,' remarked the hero of *But Yet a Woman*, 'as part of a system they behave themselves well enough, but any one of them, freed from the restraints of others, would rush to destruction.' Happily for Sidney, the stars were in their courses, and within six months he felt the first faint gravitational pull. He was reviewing Charles Booth's great book with its 'terrible numbering of the people'. There he found that 'Miss Beatrice Potter contributes lucid papers on "the Docks", "the tailoring trade" and "the Jewish Community". Though sometimes a little hard in tone, and too individualist in economics, these afford important information on disputed points.'[100]

It is to be hoped that A.J.P. Taylor's opinion that Sidney Webb is 'a door that can never be unlocked' may be revised. The reader should be able to do this for himself without more explicit help from the biographer. Far from being the incorrigible extrovert that he made himself out to be in later life, the young Webb was exceptionally sensitive and vulnerable, one who suffered from shame and embarrassment even more after the event than during it. He longed for 'Dr Heidenhoff's process' and cultivated self-deadness in the professional civil service. An admirer of John Stuart Mill, he must have been familiar with the celebrated message in the *Autobiography* where the author recalled the personal discovery that personal happiness was to be found, not in the search for it for oneself, but in the pursuit of it for others. This was the meaning of the innumerable joinings of societies, clubs, 'parliaments', reform associations and, indeed, the Fabian Society itself which he came to belong to and then to shape. He was entirely satisfied that Shaw should come to be the predominant performer on the *platform* while he prevailed within the *committee*. Shaw found it aggravating that Webb should diminish himself. Webb found it easy and necessary. When it came to the formation of the partnership he found it delightful.[101]

Part II
The Divided Self:
Beatrice Potter 1858–90

You are young, pretty, rich, clever, what more do you want? I expect you get on well in Society. Why cannot you be satisfied?

Maggie Harkness to her cousin Beatrice Potter, n.d. [1878?]

A woman, in all the relations of life, should be sought.

Beatrice Potter, Diary, 27 November 1887

Why should not the girls have freedom now and then?
And if a girl likes a man, why should she not propose?
Why should the little girls always be led by the nose?

A work girls' song recorded by Miss Beatrice Potter while she was employed in an East End sweat shop in 1888

Slowly the poison the whole blood stream fills.
It is not the failure nor the effort tires.
The waste remains, the waste remains and kills.

William Empson, Missing Dates

3

The Making of a Gilded Spinster 1858–85

The social distance between the Potters and the Webbs—The 'Glorified Spinsters' and the lower middle class—Contrasting trainings, but a common education—The importance of Herbert Spencer—Between Spencer and Chamberlain—Joseph Chamberlain as more than an episode and more than a non-event.

During the prolonged and difficult negotiations, which culminated in the formation of the partnership, Sidney advanced his cause as best he might. Indeed, in his desperation no argument appeared too bizarre to be denied a trial. In one bad moment he even assured Miss Beatrice Potter that whatever else might distance them, they were not separated by the barriers of class.[1] Miss Potter did not record her response to this assurance. But whatever it was may be made the subject of safe conjecture: Mr Webb was an incompetent social investigator or he was impertinent. The possibilities were not mutually exclusive.

Upon no known criteria could Sidney Webb and Beatrice Potter be placed in the same social class. While he was a public employee, the son of a self-employed hairdresser and of a doubtfully qualified professional man, she was the eighth child and eighth daughter of a great capitalist. Richard Potter was so great a capitalist that he could not possibly have known the names of all those who were in his direct employ, let alone of those who were indirectly dependent upon him for their livelihood. He had, to be sure, a first-hand acquaintance with Sidney's 'fear of poverty which is worse than poverty itself'. But this had belonged to a particular moment in his career: a moment long since past and one from which he protected his beloved daughters by the size and balance of his portfolio. During the sharp commercial and political crisis of 1847–8 he had lost the greater part of his inherited wealth which he held in French stocks.[2] He had had to turn his back upon a life as a rentier and a gentleman and become, as his forebears had been, an energetic businessman. He rapidly recouped all that he had lost thanks to a partnership in a timber-works

The Potter family tree

Richard Potter = Laurencina Heyworth
1817–1892   1821–1882

| Lawrencina, 1845–1906 m. Robt. Durning Holt d. 1908 | Catherine, 1847–1929 m. Rt. Hon. Leonard Courtney (Lt. Courtney of Penwith) d. 1918 | Mary, 1848–1923 m. Arthur Twisden Playne d. 1923 | Georgina, 1850–1914 m. Daniel Meinertzhagen d. 1908 | Blanche, 1851–1905 m. W. Harrison Cripps d. 1923 | Theresa, 1852–1893 m. C. Alfred Cripps (Lt. Parmoor of Frieth) d. 1941 | Margaret, 1854–1921 m. Rt. Hon. Henry Hobhouse d. 1937 | Beatrice, 1858–1943 m. Sidney Webb (Ld. Passfield) d. 1947 | Richard, 1862–1864 | Rosalind, 1865–1949 m. 1. A.D. Williams d. 1896 2. G.C. Dobbs d. 1946 |

Figure 3.1 *The marriages of the Potter sisters into distinguished families. Beatrice and Catherine's unions' were childless but the others produced 43 children.*

that made a fortune out of the Crimean War. By the time of Beatrice's birth in 1858 he had found his way onto the board of the Great Western Railway, subsequently becoming president of the Grand Trunk. Henceforth, the family's wealth was affected by economic fluctuations, but they did not disturb its style of life.

Richard Potter's recovery from the shock of 1848 was not entirely due to those traits of character that he might have inherited from his father or grandfather. If he shared their aptitude for business, he affected to have no taste for it. In 1837 he advised his father that he preferred the Bar to entering the family's warehouse in Manchester.[3] But only a short experience of practising law was needed to persuade him that this profession was equally disagreeable. After his marriage in 1844 he retired, intending to live gracefully in the South of England. It was the crisis that aroused his slumbering energies and showed that he had his father's calculating intelligence and will to success. To these he joined advantages unknown to his father and still less to his grandfather. He had been sent to Clifton and to University College, London – the infidel institution in Gower Street – the appropriate centre of learning for the son of 'radical Dick', Manchester capitalist and MP for Wigan. It was an old schoolfriend who offered Richard the partnership in the timber-works. His wife, Lawrencina Heyworth, was the daughter of a Liverpool merchant and Radical parliamentarian and had a family background much like his own. It was through her that he entered the world of railways and big capital. Thus, social connection and the increasingly influential cousinhood of the rich provided a safety net for those who fell. Such nets might not be held in place forever. However, Richard Potter, without qualifying for inclusion in the annals of *Self-Help*, answered sufficiently to its values. He was not afraid of work once it became necessary, nor was he one of those dissipated young fops who became 'sodden with pleasure' and unfit for the competitive struggle. He was a fortunate, able and cultivated man, ruthless and cynical in business, loving and indulgent in his relationships with his wife, his daughters and his friends. As his fortune became indestructible, he switched from the Liberals and exchanged Nonconformity for the Establishment; he turned to the Tories during the political crisis of 1866–7. Yet he was not to be passionately engaged by religion or politics.[4] His attitudes were easy and civilised. He neither disowned his forebears nor did he feel uneasy or disturbed when he was in the company of those who still affected to despise commerce.

The Potter daughters spent most of their early years in Standish, a mansion some eight miles from the timber merchant's firm in Gloucester. When they were not in Gloucestershire or in their London house they were to be found at Rusland Hall in Westmorland or at their mother's favourite residence, the Argoed, in Monmouthshire. Richard Potter frequently travelled abroad in the company of one or more of his daughters.

But if the family can properly be said to have had a home, it was Standish, overlooking the vale of the Severn. Beatrice was born there on 2 January 1858. The house was divided into two parts. The front, facing south-west, was linked by heavily carpeted corridors. In these one passed by the doors of endless bedrooms and sitting rooms, the best drawing room and mother's boudoir, the dining room; then on to the back of the house, to the library and study, the smoking and billiard room. Stone steps and bare, flagged passages connected the rooms at the rear. Here were the house-keeper's room, the rooms of governesses; then, one descended, down through the butlers' and the upper servants' quarters to the lower ser-vants' quarters. Here also were the day and night nurseries, the one bath-room, and the schoolroom where Miss Potter – easily wearying of her lessons – might look down at her friends the laundresses hurrying across the servants' yard or past them to the grooms working in the stables beyond.[5]

All Beatrice's sisters got married before she did. With the partial excep-tion of her one younger sister, Rosie, all of them married their social equals. Three of the elder girls found husbands with substantial property. Lawrencina ('Lallie'), the eldest, married R.D. Holt, who had important interests in Liverpool shipping companies and played a prominent part in the life of that city as a member of one of the ruling Unitarian and Liberal families. Mary, the third daughter, married Arthur Playne, the owner of a cloth mill in Gloucestershire, the only brother-in-law who might have passed for a squire or been described as 'aristocratic'. Beatrice went to the United States with her father and the Playnes two days after her fourth sis-ter, Georgina, married the banker, Daniel Meinertzhagen. Georgina tended to be impatient with young Beatrice for her intellectual pretensions.

The next group of marriages brought Beatrice brothers-in-law who were rather more to her taste. Her second sister, Kate, had been a member of the party that went to America in 1873. While they were making their way back from California, Beatrice was attacked by scarlet fever and had to be carried off the train at Chicago by her father and George Pullman. Scarlet fever was followed by rheumatic fever. Then came the measles. Kate played the nurse and proved herself 'a dear kind devoted sister'. In her diary young Beatrice confided: 'I really have not found out one seri-ous fault.' However, the Potter parents were displeased with Kate since she wished to withdraw from society and devote herself to philanthropic work under the direction of Miss Octavia Hill. Kate's tenacious claim to serve the poor and the suffering was rewarded in 1875 when she was allowed to become a rent-collector in the East End of London.[6] Despite this renunciation of the world of the gay and splendid she made, in 1883, a highly successful marriage to Leonard Courtney, then Financial Secretary to the Treasury in Gladstone's second administration. Despite his 'massive intelligence' and immense integrity Courtney never managed higher office. Although she had generous recollections of his contribution to the family's intellectual life,[7] Beatrice was somewhat disappointed with Leonard in the early eighties. As her father said, he tended to treat politics as if it was a trade secret.[8] Indeed, the fifth sister, Blanche, by her marriage to the distinguished surgeon William Harrison Cripps, appears to have contributed more to her young sister's education. Beatrice took to some laboratory work under his direction.

The sixth sister, Theresa, married Charles Alfred Cripps, brother to William and subsequent father of Stafford. When he married Theresa, Cripps was a successful young barrister. His complicated and powerful intelligence fascinated Beatrice. He was to enter Parliament as a Conservative in 1895. The seventh sister, Margaret, married a future Liberal Unionist MP, Henry Hobhouse, the elder cousin of the sociologist L.T. Hobhouse. While Beatrice respected Hobhouse, she felt that he was hardly worthy of her favourite sister, the closest to her in years, in interests and in temperament. He lacked liveliness. He took her from the friendly competitor for fatherly regard, who was also a rival in literary accomplishment and a companion in walking, smoking and arguing about political economy or the Religion of Humanity.[9] On holiday with the Hobhouses in 1881, she noted that Maggie was 'seedy and miserable; the natural result of the conditions of married existence.'[10] The following year she found that she liked Henry better, but that her sister had improved neither intellectually or spiritually. Her powerful faculties were under-employed and she was no longer at peace with herself. Beatrice considered her sister's attachment to individual freedom was deadening her sympathies. She was

> strongly averse to the breaking down of the barrier of respectability between the endowed classes and the outer mob of the uneducated and unclothed. And intimacy with the barbarians is dangerous except it be for the purpose of impressing upon them moral maxims which will lead them to a peaceful resignation as they watch those who Have enjoying and wasting while they are dying of hunger. 'Independent circumstances' is the test of superiority; independence is the luxury which will develop virtue, struggling, battling, helping, nothing good will come of it – the pride of respectability will be worn away without which man is the human animal, the lawless passion and fearful power.[11]

This suggests that Beatrice in 1882 had attained to an independent, critical and emancipated position with respect to class society. In fact no single passage from her early writings could convey the complexity of her attitudes. She had an absorbing interest in social differences. Her snobbery was nicely regulated, allowing her to despise it when it was paraded by others while enjoying a suitably reserved indulgence in it herself. Thus, while on holiday in the Alps in July 1882 she chanced to meet a Christian Lady who explained to her the perilous nature of foreign travel:

> Then *this* morning I sat down on a bench near quite a *ladylike* looking girl: where do you think she came from?
> No! Where?
> From *Birmingham*!

'Dear me', replied Beatrice sympathetically while silently remarking the strange compromise with the manner of worldliness in a self-professed follower of Jesus of Nazareth. The woman was, she concluded, 'steeped in class prejudice'.[12]

Yet Miss Potter herself had very decided feelings respecting the limitations of the provincial bourgeoisie. These were apparent when she went to Cornwall in the company of her sister Kate to attend the 'Courtney Demonstration'. Here she noticed with interest and satisfaction that Bolitho (the tough country gentleman and great property-owner for whom Leonard had once worked as a bank-clerk) attended the proceedings. Moving on to Plymouth, she then met the local dignitaries and Beatrice studied her sister's class-consciousness. Kate would never have allowed herself to be kissed by the daughter of the leading journalist. Beatrice did permit it and felt warmed by it. But she did not exempt herself from the rule that when Potters felt really superior it was in the presence of smaller bourgeoisie. 'I felt, in the society of the Plymouth worthies, the presence of inferior animals with smaller intellects and colder hearts – but none of the subtle antagonism and contempt of the wholesale trader to his retail brother.'[13]

Only a month or two before her first meeting with Sidney, Beatrice returned to her reflections on the lower middle class. One of the closest friends of her girlhood had been Carry Darling, a school teacher. They spent six months together in Germany. It was Beatrice's first friendship outside her family. In Wiesbaden they would sit together far into the night, their feet cocked high on the China stove, smoking cigarettes and talking philosophy. Friends had helped Carry to spend two years at Newnham. The daughter of the illegitimate son of a squire, she had to seek her own livelihood. Beatrice found Carry's nature 'intensely loveable', but so did others. 'Twice or three times she was engaged or "kept company" for her lower middle class origin showed itself in her love affairs if nowhere else.'[14] She used to pity Beatrice the round of 'Society': riding in the Row, wasting Sundays receiving calls from eligible young men. During the 1880s she went to take up a headship in Australia and formed a passionate attachment to a married man. Beatrice conjectured that since he was the English master at the boys' grammar school he was 'probably the first really cultivated and attractive man she had come across – for her old loves were of the lower middle class type.'[15] Carry went off to meet her lover in Japan and 'in a sort of queer way' became engaged to the captain of the ship! 'God preserve me', Beatrice concluded, 'from a lover between 35 and 45: no woman can resist a man's importunity during the last years of an unrealised womanhood.'[16] Presumably resistance would be somewhat easier – as well as the more imperative – if the man in question happened to be 'lower middle class'!

But if Carry Darling belonged to a class which Beatrice despised she was also a member of an order with which Beatrice sympathised and with which she felt herself to be closely associated. One of the most distinctive features of English society in the 1880s was the rise of the Glorified Spinster.[17] The Glorified Spinster liked to think of herself in terms of freedom rather than necessity, of heightened ambition rather than reduced circumstances. Yet her connections were decidedly with the lower middle class. Typically she belonged to a child-rich family of one of the less successful members of the business or professional community, a family persuaded of its increasing poverty by anxiety about the butcher's bill and boys too big for their cricket suits. The daughters in such households were apt to fear that they were going to be numbered among the 'superfluous woman'. Privately they were prone to contemplate the advantages of polygamy or the Chinese way with female infants. They were also apt to be 'rebellious' daughters who liked to see themselves striking out for an independent life rather than being compelled to make their own way in the world as a result of altered circumstances. As the supply of employable girls increased so did the demand for their services as nurses, teachers, book-keepers, clerks, librarians, journalists or rent-collectors, or as heads of departments in laundries or other businesses where the habit of giving commands to working-class females was more important than mastery over the technical processes of production.[18] The average income in such employment might amount to between two and three pounds a week, an amount that often signified defeat and drudgery for a married man, but sufficiency for an emancipated girl. Having no one but herself to support and often receiving some occasional help from the more tolerant or affluent members of her family, she might visit the theatre, buy books and take the occasional holiday abroad. Out of the modest comfort of her bed-sitting-room, she proclaimed that if an Old Maid was something less than a woman, a Glorified Spinster was something more. She showed it by her display of perfect indifference towards the weather, her calmness in crowds, her readiness to run for the omnibus. When she met her friends they soothed each others' nerves with the help of cigarettes while discussing the redistribution of property, the possibilities of euthanasia and the moral lawfulness of suicide.

While the Glorified Spinster was a recognisable type, she often had only a precarious hold upon her own identity. While she might argue with acquaintances about rejecting marriage and breaking with a life of dependence upon her relatives, among her peers she was inclined to admit that it was 'no use blinking the fact that nothing can make up to us women for the loss of human ties.'[19] One could bury one's care under a load of work, but only for limited intervals. Such women had grown apart from their parents. They hoped to see them so rarely that old affection would do instead of sympathy in thought and feeling; but a vague sense of insecurity as well as a sense of obligation to their fathers prevented them from making any clean breaks. As to marriage, they thought it disgusting that men discussed matrimonial matters as they did. 'They talk a girl over; speak of her as if she was an animal; and always imagine she is in love with them unless she snubs them, and then they hate her.'[20] But few of them were prepared to renounce marriage altogether. They supposed that there were some men left who believed in women. If they became engaged to one they rejoiced. It would grieve them to give up their work, but 'glorified spinsterhood plus a future to look forward to – even at the cost of losing its halo – is a very jolly form of life.'[21] But if marriage was problematical, so was employment – despite the increased opportunities of securing it. The root of the problem was inadequate educational preparation: 'Girls brought up at home in a school room or shut up all day with a woman, who perhaps possesses no mind whatsoever, are not fit to live alone or work for themselves or their fellow-creatures.'[22] If women with strong individualities were not meant for marriage, what were they meant for? Beatrice's close friend and cousin Maggie Harkness was an excellent example of the Glorified Spinster, but she found great difficulty in discovering work that would satisfy her. She tried nursing and journalism. She thought that the happiest career would be that of an actress. She might have been a doctor, but her own concept of femininity was one of the obstacles in her path: 'If I were a man I should be a doctor – as a woman I can't. I do not believe in women having nerves for operating. I could not cut up a little child.'[23] So she became a political adventuress instead, playing the part of a mysterious, exciting and cynical go-between among socialists and politicians.[24]

In the early and mid-eighties the Glorified Spinster was identified more by her attempts at leading an 'independent life' rather than by any distinctive independence of thought. In religious matters she tended to attitudes nostalgic and mature. One of Beatrice's dearest friends after 1885, Ella Pycroft, found the old devotional books full of a faith that she no longer shared, but which she still found almost as soothing as the cigarettes to which Beatrice helped to introduce her.[25]

Ella worked among the poor and she did so in a way that points up the equivocal situation of the Glorified Spinster. She was in a great tradition, for it was allowed that caring for the poor was a decently feminine interest. But whereas this had been seen as an extension of the domestic obligations of respectable women, it was becoming a professional undertaking for those who had no domestic life of their own. The forms of self-indulgence that it masked were changing. As caring for the poor became professionalised it ceased to be an extension of the domestic round and become a possible release from its tedium and emptiness. In place of the satisfaction of playing the great lady were the subtler rewards that some women found in escaping from their own social diffidence or insecurity.[26] If upper- and middle-class ladies could always feel more sure of themselves when they were with the poor, the Glorified Spinsters were inclined to think that they could be themselves better when they were with them.

It was with this version of the Glorified Spinster that Beatrice felt herself to be particularly close. Going into the East End in the company of Ella Pycroft, working as rent collector, charity organiser or social investigator, she enjoyed herself. She rejoiced in the absences of restraints that she would have felt in another sphere of life. She discovered that she could visit working men in their rooms without arousing the sexual expectations that would have been present in the case of males from any other class of society.[27] A bed was only disturbing if the man was in the habit of flavouring haddock by keeping it behind the mattress.[28]

But while the Glorified Spinster had lower-middle-class associations, it was despite these that Beatrice valued her. These women, just because they were women striving to become professional people, were much superior to the petit bourgeois. This seemed to her to be manifestly true of the energetic, self-respecting, simple, warm, organised working people of the northern factory towns.[29] It was also partly true of the vital and humorous casual labourers of East London. This leisure class at the foot of society was envied rather than pitied.[30] From an economic point of view a clerk or shopkeeper might be fit for life, as this 'residuum' was not – but if one sometimes feared this self-indulgent sensual mass, one did not have the contempt for it occasioned by the pathetic pretensions and total want of distinction that – so Beatrice believed – characterised the lower middle class.

It must be understood that the Glorified Spinster generally managed to live down her class origins, and that unlike Carry she succeeded in staying on the right side of respectability. If Ella Pycroft or Maggie Harkness had relations with men that were not entirely orthodox they did not positively flout convention. The young Beatrice came to accept what she could not admire. When Ella Pycroft became engaged to Maurice Paul (who was ten years her junior), Beatrice seems to have felt much as she did when her friend Benjamin Jones, the co-operator, declared that he limited the size of his family by the use of contraceptives. It was distasteful, but it was difficult to formulate an objection to it in a rational form.[31] However she was quite decided that she was not going to be guilty of lapses that might cut her off from her family or turn her into a social outcast. Thus, after Maggie Harkness introduced her into the 'British Museum set' she bumped into Karl Marx's daughter, Tussy. Miss Potter at once recognised that Miss Marx was no mere Glorified Spinster. It was all very well to proclaim oneself a socialist and an atheist; it was allowable to argue that Christ lacked heroism. But a suspicion of over-indulgences in drugs and of enjoyment of 'natural' relations with the opposite sex was quite another matter. Accordingly, Miss Marx's invitation to Miss Potter to visit her was regretfully ignored. Tussy might be 'comely', her eyes might be 'fine' and 'full of life and sympathy', but 'the chances were against her staying long within the pale of respectable society'. Beatrice saw her own social position as one that conferred upon her great opportunities to play the participant observer, but that social position itself was not to be jeopardised. If she mixed with this fascinating woman she would become more or less connected with her. So Miss Potter parted with Miss Marx and went on to a meeting of the Charity Organisation Society instead.[32]

If Eleanor Marx in 1883 seemed likely to become notorious, Mrs Annie Beasant in 1887 had already achieved this distinction. In November of that year Beatrice went along to hear her speak at the Eleusis Club. While acknowledging that Mrs Besant was a real orator, Miss Potter felt that it was a revolting spectacle to witness a woman upon a public platform: 'to see her speak made me shudder. It is not womanly to thrust yourself before the world. A woman, in all the relations of life, should be sought.'[33] Beatrice was perfectly capable of sympathising with Mrs Besant, who had been 'robbed of her child', but she was not inclined to associate herself with her. She sensed the insecurity of Annie's relations with the socialists. There was nothing permanent about the lady. She was here today and gone tomorrow. The young Beatrice was not afraid to travel, but she took care never to go on a journey without making sure that she had a return ticket.

Sidney Webb and Graham Wallas were among those who failed to get into the crowded meeting held at the Eleusis in November 1887.[34] It was just as well. Had Mr Webb met Miss Potter on that occasion they could not have hit it off. To begin with, Sidney still fell far short of the celebrity that he was to attain subsequently. He would have been bound to defend Mrs Besant as the foremost Fabian of the day, but her opinions on the nationalisation of the railways were not sufficiently well founded to impress the eighth daughter of a great railway director. Indeed, Mrs Besant's ignorance of the whole subject made Beatrice depressed. How could her attitude towards Fabian socialism have been improved by a presumptuous little clerk, looking up at her out of a grubby collar and daring to lisp out his contradictions in a cockney accent?[35] Far from being the same social class as herself, this Mr Webb would be expected to make contact with a Potter only as a passenger (possibly steerage) on the Holt's Blue Funnel Line, as a singularly impecunious client at the bank of the Meinhertzhagens, or perhaps as a patient with a sufficiently interesting ailment to engage the attention of Willie Cripps. Most probably he would meet a Potter only in his role as a deferential civil servant, where he might expect to wait upon a Courtney, a Cripps or a Hobhouse when one or more of them attained to ministerial rank. Perhaps Miss Potter would have eventually recognised that men like Mr Webb were not without interest as the subject of sociological enquiry and were not devoid of merit and political importance. She might – despite his inadequate table manners – have invited him to a meal; but to share anything else with him would have been unthinkable.

*   *   *

Thus, the unfortunate Sidney, in asking Beatrice to allow that they were of the same social class, had chosen the line of argument least likely to succeed. He would have done far better to suggest that class differences were irrelevant or unlikely to last than to pretend that they did not exist. Beatrice was acutely conscious of their reality and their importance. She was imbued with class pride and it was only in relation to foreigners that her prejudices were still more pronounced.[36] His claim to a community of interest with her was far better founded when he pointed not to class, but to culture.

A culture may have its source in the experiences and the aspirations of a class, but it can never be narrowly confined to one. The forms of truth that it most prizes; the standards by which it distinguishes between the beautiful and the ugly; the content that it gives to the impartial rules governing right conduct, may all be recognised to have their origin in a particular social tradition and still be felt to have a universal validity. Thus Sidney Webb and Beatrice Potter shared not a common education but rather an overlapping range of concerns and a common intellectual inheritance.

The experience of formal education was dissimilar if only because Beatrice can hardly have been said to have had much. She did her best to avoid the formal instruction offered to her in the Standish schoolroom, and in this she appears to have had considerable success.[37] Mr Pincher had no equivalent in her childhood experience and she never sat an examination of any consequence in her life. Her frequent illnesses, real or imagined, and an indulgent father who could see little reason why his young daughter should suffer a rigorous discipline, spared her from ordeals in which Sidney delighted. Perhaps it left her without his capacity for unremitting toil or his sense of complete accomplishment. She applied herself to studies, which she enjoyed, but became impatient when she had difficulty, as with mathematics or political economy.[38] What began as impatience with herself tended to become impatience with the offending subject and led her to a switch of attention. Her mother's conviction that Beatrice was the least intellectually able of all her children was hardly helpful in correcting this fault.[39]

Yet the households in Cranbourn Street and in Standish were both libertarian and free-thinking. If the values of hard work were impressed upon the children – always more upon boys than upon girls – this was done by example rather than by attempts at compulsion. If both the mothers were concerned with religious truth, they were free from fanaticism and not alarmed by a spirit of free enquiry. By the standards of the ruling oligarchy, classical antiquity was allowed less than its due importance, but science and useful knowledge were highly valued. Concepts of evolution, the idea of progress and the assumption that methods of natural science might be used productively in relation to social disorders were commonplace. If they were not accepted without question, they were acknowledged to be excellent topics for debate.

If Beatrice took longer than Sidney to make her acquaintance with *Kelly's Directory*, this was not because there was any class of literature which was regarded as undesirably stimulating for young girls. From the Potter library she could take whatever books she chose. With her father or her sisters she enjoyed the greatest freedom of discussion. It was not as a result of overt family pressures that she tended to arrive during her adolescence at suitably maidenly and conventional conclusions. At seventeen she read *Jane Eyre* and found it to be an 'an impure book'.[40] Victor Hugo was pure. George Sand had an undercurrent of hidden sensuality and was 'impure'.[41] She was her own censor trying, evidently with indifferent success, to protect herself from writers who encouraged her in her own propensity to build fanciful castles in the air: love scenes and death-bed scenes, romance and melodrama. She sometimes felt that the very freedom of her upbringing was a burden to her. It made it hard for her not to waste her time on romantic fantasies. Worse still, when one was encouraged to make up one's mind it was hard to sustain any settled faith in God.[42] By the time she was in her early twenties Beatrice had discovered George Eliot. Like Sidney she had the greatest affection and admiration for her work. She was her favourite novelist and retained that status until

1881. In that year Beatrice first read Balzac and was fascinated and quite overwhelmed. Never before had she read 'such disgustingly true analysis of mean, base, thought and feeling'.[43] A year later she was trying her hand at translation:

> Financially speaking M. Goriot was a hybrid between the tiger and the boa constrictor. He knew how to lie in wait, to crouch watching and examining his prey, then opening the cavern of his purse gulp down a mass of gold and, like a gorged serpent resting, digest, methodical, cold and quiescent.[44]

The appalling thought that her father, outside the decencies of domestic life, might behave like that, or that that might not disturb her dear sister Maggie Hobhouse, may have flickered across her mind. In 1882 at the age of twenty-four, she first toyed with the idea of trying to write something publishable. It was to have been an article on Balzac.[45]

In literature, Beatrice firmly preferred prose to poetry. She seems hardly to have read poetry. Most of her recorded reading from late adolescence onwards was in philosophy or history. She read Plato wearily and Bacon with pleasure and benefit. Her studies were under no close direction, but their bias was quite apparent. At nineteen, Harriet Martineau gave her a higher idea of the religion of science, while Buckle's *History of Civilisation in England* left her deeply impressed.[46] In the next year or two Ruskin and Goethe were mentioned favourably, but it was Lecky, Lewes, J.S. Mill and Auguste Comte who were the authors for whom she had the highest regard and to whom she paid the closest attention. Her reading was not uncritical. Thus Lecky prompted her to question whether there was a correspondence between progress and happiness.[47] But while she was not as immersed in the English Utilitarian tradition as Sidney, she was carried along by the powerful currents of positivism. It was not surprising that Herbert Spencer, who was supposed to have given the positivist tradition its definitive form, was her closest friend and teacher. The synthetic philosopher, a great but merely literary influence so far as Sidney was concerned, was one of the most important characters in Beatrice's life.

Richard Potter and Herbert Spencer were old friends. They shared a common background in the rising, reforming, non-conforming middle class of the North – or the Midlands in Spencer's case. Their families – with a fearful and predictable monotony – were for the First Reform Act and the New Poor Law and against the Corn Laws and Chartism. Just as Richard Potter had been to University College and had accomplishments outside money making, so Herbert Spencer had practical experience in the running of railways and would have hotly protested against the notion that he was a mere pedagogue like Auguste Comte. As Potter had

about him something of the self-made man who had arrived, Spencer w
a self-taught man who had won for himself a position of great eminen
in English thought. In the mid-Victorian years, in the eighteen sixties a
seventies when Beatrice was a girl, Herbert Spencer was at the height
his powers. The prophet of Evolution and of Progress, he was revered
Darwin. The scourge of classicists, he satisfied the demand that knov
edge should be useful in content and systematic in form. He was t
dreaded adversary of clericalism, militarism and superstition; his am
tion to be a walking encyclopaedia was merely incidental to his purpc
of applying the methods of science to the study of society: the creation
sociology. Sociology was indispensable. Once moral rules had lost the
supernatural sanctions, right conduct could only be determined a
upheld by being shown to be another way of expressing the laws
human survival and development.[48]

Spencer's first book, *Social Statics* (1851), was the best approximatie
which English middle-class Radicalism could produce to the *Commun*
Manifesto. If Cobden's sense for the social foundation of politics and
passionate conviction that bourgeois interest ultimately coincided wi
those of humanity makes it proper to describe him as a middle-cla
Marxist, Spencer's sense for the logic of historical process seen as
agency working through, but beyond, human consciousness might ea
him the same description. Arguably this is more like the positiv
Marxism of Engels than of the dialectical Marxism of Marx. Man's selfi
and aggressive nature was the inheritance of his earliest struggles to su
vive. Granted that men had become selfish there was no avoiding t
corollary that all power that is not made accountable to others will be se
ishly exercised. Monarchy, feudalism: the record of the latter Europe
aristocracies provided proofs more than were wanted that all irrespons
ble rulers always had and always would sacrifice the public good to the
own benefit. The English landed oligarchy merely furnished the late
example in this squalid story. From the Black Act (9th of George I) whi
had provided for death without benefit of clergy for those suspected
circumstantial evidence of poaching; through the Enclosure Acts; throug
reduced taxation of land while other taxes enormously increased; throug
the perversion of the funds of the public schools – the sorry story ran in
the present day. England was still suffering from an electoral system th
gave undue weight to the landed interest and the consequences of th
were to be seen in the game laws, the law enabling a landlord to anti
pate other creditors, to obtain his rent by immediate seizure of his tenant
property and much else besides. 'If, therefore, class-legislation is the co
sequence of class-power, there is no escape from the conclusion that th
interest of the society can be secured, only by giving power into the hand
of the people.'

What gave interest to this democratic rhetoric was not that it was carried rather far and included a demand for the nationalisation of land, but that it was grounded in a form of philosophical determinism. 'The course of civilisation', according to Spencer, 'could not possibly have been other than it has been.'

Social Statics was not just democratic rhetoric carried to the point of a demand for land nationalisation. It might indeed be usefully considered as a critique of the hunt, that cherished institution of landed society, but it was a critique. It raised the usual sentimental protest against blood sports and the iniquity of the game laws to quite a different level.

Man in his aboriginal state could survive only by exterminating the lower forms of life that tenanted the earth. He could obtain his happiness only at the expense of other beings. His nature had to become adapted to his circumstances. He had to develop a desire to kill and the capacity to enjoy the sight of pain and anguish. The behaviour of men to the lower animals and their behaviour to each other bear a constant relationship:

> The blind desire to inflict suffering, distinguishes not between the creatures who exhibit that suffering, but obtains gratification indifferently from the agonies of beast and human being – delights equally in worrying a brute, and in putting a prisoner to the rack.[49]

This truth was illustrated, according to Spencer, by

> the spectators in the Roman amphitheatres [who] were as much delighted by the slaying of gladiators as by the death-struggles of wild beasts. The ages during which Europe was thinly peopled, and hunting a chief occupation, were also the ages of feudal violence, universal brigandage, dungeons, tortures. Here in England a whole province depopulated to make game preserves, and a law sentencing to death a serf who killed a stag, show how great activity of the predatory instinct and utter indifference to human happiness coexisted.[50]

However, lying dormant within man was a capacity to maximise his own happiness by rejoicing in the happiness of others. This propensity dictated the 'law of equal freedom', according to which all men might do as they chose so long as they did not infringe on the right of other men to do likewise. After accomplishing its appointed purpose man's earlier nature must evolve through further functional adaptation into its ultimate state. But this adaptation takes place slowly. The circumstances of human life do not undergo sudden and permanent changes:

> Note further that where the destructive propensities have almost fulfilled their purpose, and are on the eve of losing their gratification, they make to themselves an artificial sphere of exercise by game-preserving,

and are so kept in activity after they would otherwise have become dormant. But note chiefly that the old predatory disposition is in a certain sense self-maintained. For it generates between men and men a hostile relationship, similar to that which it generates between men and inferior animals; and by doing so provides for itself a lasting source of excitement. This happens inevitably.

(This was not a chance expression. As already noted, Spencer insisted that the 'course of civilisation could not possibly have been other than it has been.') The desires of the savage acting, as we have seen, indiscriminately, necessarily lead him to perpetual trespasses against his fellows and consequently to endless antagonisms – 'to quarrels of individuals, to fighting of tribes, to feuds of clan with clan, to wars of nations. And thus being by their constitutions made mutual foes, as well as foes to the lower races, men keep alive in each other the old propensities after the original need for them has in great measure ceased.'[51]

In modern industrial society men were so mutually dependent upon each other that functional adaptation had to take the form of developing the sympathetic rather than the predatory capacities. The ground for this had been prepared by an earlier clearing away of the inferior races of men: conquests generally have marked the victory of social over antisocial man. Similarly slavery, once a necessary condition for the acquisition of work discipline, had indirectly aided the development of the civilisation which it otherwise confronted as its opposite. The time for the supersession of war and bondage came when the moral sense of men, in adaptation to the changing social state, pronounced them wrong. But 'during man's apprenticeship to the social state there must predominate in him some impulse corresponding to the arrangements requisite ...' Savage selfishness required hero-worship and boundless state power. Changes in the savage character were required to bring about an incongruity with the existing institutions, then revolution more or less successfully (usually less) began to restore equilibrium. But

> the same causes which render a better social state possible, render the successive modifications of it easier. These occur under less pressure; with smaller disturbance; and more frequently: until, by a gradual diminution in the amounts and intervals of change, the process merges into one of uninterrupted growth.[52]

Morality, according to Spencer, was 'a species of transcendental physiology'. Evolutionary progress was, in all its forms, discovered to be the tendency to individuation. By the time Beatrice was five years old he was in possession of that conception of evolution as a cosmic principle which was universally present in organic and organic matter; in the animal kingdom and in human society. It was, accordingly to *First Principles*, 'a change from an indefinite, incoherent, homogeneity, to a definite coherent heterogeneity, through continuous differentiations and integration'.[53] In the words of a mischievous parody, it was 'a change from a no-howish, untalkaboutable, by continuous somethingelsifications and sticktogetherations.'[54] Right conduct consisted in acting in accordance with the cosmic principle against all despotisms whether of caste, custom, sex or whatever sought to limit individuality.

Already in *Social Statics* Spencer was well supplied with learned illustrations of his evolutionary law as exhibited in the progress from the creatures consisting of nothing but amorphous semi-fluid jelly in the phylum Porifera on to the beings in the Alcyonidae with their digestive sacs and accompanying mouths and tentacles, through to the Corallidae and the Tubiporidae and much, much more besides, but all subserving the same point that evolutionary progress is marked by increasing variety of senses, instincts powers and qualities; a rising distinction and complexity; a more marked individuality. But paradoxically, this tendency to increasing individuality had to be joined with the greatest mutual dependence – a difficulty to be removed only by the adaptation of men such that desires inconsistent with a perfect social organisation would die out. As Karl Marx imagined the communist society of the future as one in which the free development of each had become the condition of the free development of all, so Spencer insisted that within existing society one could witness the maturing of the ultimate man whose individual claims would coincide with public wants:

> He will be that manner of man who, in spontaneously fulfilling his own nature, incidentally performs the functions of a social unit; and yet is only enabled so to fulfil his own nature by all others doing the like.[55]

The celebration of bourgeois society was joined to stern lessons for the rich. Woe betide those who kept their eyes too close to the ledger and sold adulterated goods. The young Spencer did not, indeed, go as far as his French counterpart, Auguste Comte, and raise an impertinent cry for the 'moralisation' of capitalists: he was content to demonstrate that mere pocket prudence should induce them to further human welfare.

At the time of Beatrice's birth, Herbert Spencer was already established as sensibly *avant-garde*, respectably radical, utopian in a generally commendable and rather painless way. But he was a radical. Full of the new learning, he was savaging the classicists and calling into question all the assumptions of received educational policy. Like the great Bentham, he accepted nothing because it was customary. Every institution and practice had to justify itself before the bar of a scientific intelligence applying the test of utility. In his *Education: Intellectual, Moral and Physical* (1861) he complained that the comparative worth of different kinds of knowledge had remained unconsidered. The debate on the relative merit of classics and mathematics was a wholly inadequate substitute for the systematic reflection that was required. Education ought to be a preparation for life. Accordingly, it ought to start with a knowledge of the sciences of physiology, hygiene, physics and chemistry which bore most closely upon its preservation. Next come those sciences most closely related to the pursuit of the practical arts involved in the efficient production of food, clothing and shelter. Third in order of importance came everything bearing upon the rearing of offspring. Then came the social sciences capable of making boys and girls into intelligent citizens and good neighbours. Only finally did one reach knowledge of foreign languages and literature; things fit to occupy leisure, but which a leisured class made into nearly the whole curriculum. Since it failed to start with the immediate interests of the child and neglected to develop powers of observation, established educational method was distinguished by an insistence on drill and learning by rote. Instead of being an enjoyable experience of freedom, education became a harsh discipline enforced by unreasoning authority. Following Rousseau, Spencer held that moral training should take the form of allowing the child to suffer the natural consequences of his own action.

Thus, when the philosopher visited Standish he was welcomed as a liberator to the children and a scourge to the governesses. 'Submission not desirable!' he cried as he pointed to the deficiencies of 'stupid persons who taught irrelevant facts in an unintelligible way'.[56] Beatrice's mother was uneasy. The governess despite being an 'old-fashioned dame' opened her 'pursed-up lips' to good effect: 'You can go out this morning, my dears, with Mr. Spencer and mind you follow his teaching and do exactly what you have a mind to.'[57] This they did. Scientific expeditions in search of fossils, flowers and insects were likely to become frolics in which Spencer was pelted with dead leaves by the elder Miss Potters while the younger ones engaged in still more direct forms of assault. 'Your children are r-r-rude children,' he exclaimed to their mother before leading them off on another outing.[58] Beatrice loved him very much. When he died she recalled that: 'As a little child he was perhaps the only person who persistently cared for me – or rather who singled me out as one who was worthy of being trained and looked after.'[59] Nor was that judgement an extravagance occasioned by his passing. She affirmed many years later that: 'It was the philosopher on the hearth who, alone among my elders, was concerned about my chronic ill-health, and was constantly suggesting this or that remedy for my ailments; who encouraged me in my lonely studies ...'[60]

Beatrice's need for Spencer was surely associated with the birth and death of the only son of Richard and Lawrencina. Being the next child after Beatrice, he might well have been regarded as far too successful a competitor for her mother's affection and attention. Beatrice evidently felt the need to protest her love for her baby brother. Yet in her autobiography she hardly mentions his existence and makes no reference to the wonderfully Victorian scene at his death-bed where the little fellow on Christmas Day promised the adoring and anguished mother that he would never be a bad boy again.[61] Whatever dark and unacknowledged thankfulness Beatrice may have felt at his departure was ill-judged: the boy was soon to be replaced by another daughter; an inadequate substitute, no doubt, but a sufficient reason for continued neglect of the she who was sentenced to be the last but one. Spencer, on his side, had a great need of affection and modest success in securing it. A confirmed bachelor, he flattered himself that George Eliot had been in love with him and that it was only her ugliness that had prevented him proposing to her. He was – as Beatrice herself came to see – anxious to claim her as a substitute for a child and a lover.[62]

It was not until she was approaching twenty that Beatrice could be expected to tackle the successive volumes of the synthetic philosophy which had been coming from the printers from her infancy onwards and were only now nearing completion. *First Principles* in 1862 had been followed by the *Principles of Biology* two years later. The *Principles of Psychology* went in to a new and revised edition in the early seventies and the *Principles of Sociology* and the *Principles of Ethics* had appeared, at least in part, before the end of that decade. Beatrice went to Spencer in the hope of some release from the torments of religious doubt.

Since she had been fourteen they had periodically afflicted her. In the autumn of 1872 she had caught herself trying to surpass her sisters in the presence of gentlemen. She knew that she was '*very, very*, wicked' and that her faith was slipping from her. 'I feel [as] if Christ can never listen to me again.'[63] Three years later she found herself more devout and went off to take the Holy Sacrament, but she was still worried by mysteries such as the doctrine of the Atonement, which she found repugnant.[64] A year later she had shaken off the chains of the beautiful old faith in exchange for Herbert Spencer's doctrine of 'harmony and progress'. She declared herself impressed by his teaching that it was through consciousness of the 'unknowable' that science and religion were to be reconciled.[65] Apparently this conclusion was not inconsistent with some experiments in spiritualism. (The spirits made the interesting suggestion that she should try to involve her mother in these enquiries.)[66] Visiting St Peter's in 1880, she felt the temptation to commit intellectual suicide and convert to Catholicism:

> My intellectual or logical faculty drives me to the conclusion that outside the knowledge of the relative or phenomenal, I know nothing except

that there must be an Absolute, a something which is unknowable. But whether the very fact that it is unknowable does not prevent me from considering it, or thinking about it, or contemplating it, is a question which Mr Spencer's logic has not set at rest … But I possess another faculty, the emotional – which is the dominant one in all my better and nobler moments – This spirit unceasingly insists that there is something above and around us which is worthy of absolute devotion and devout worship.[67]

While Beatrice had these understandable difficulties with the 'unknowable' she made her way to a form of reverential agnosticism. This should be understood as having been a balanced regulation of competing moods rather than as a successful reconciliation of hostile intellectual tendencies. Her path forward was not an easy one.

When her mother died in 1882 it was Beatrice who was with her while the other sisters waited downstairs. She died of a bowel condition; her death was noisy, smelly and painful. It left Beatrice with even less faith in the possibility of another life:

As I looked at our Mother dying – I felt it was a final dissolution of body and soul – an end of the personality which we call the spirit. This was an intuitive conviction – on this great question we cannot reason. But though my disbelief in immortality was strengthened, a new and wondrous faith has arisen within me – a faith in goodness – in God – I must pray, I do pray and I feel better for it, and more able to put aside all compromise with worldliness and to devote myself with singleheartedness to my duty'.[68]

She did indeed try to resume the old clothes of religion, but she found that she dared not study Christianity. She knew that it would undermine her faith. 'It is', she recognised, 'unworthy to shrink from examination; unworthy alike of the spirit of the faith and the spirit of the enquiry. God help me!'[69] But neither God nor Mr Spencer could remove the difficulty. Neither her understanding of the All Mighty nor of the Unknowable could satisfy the conflicting claims of intelligence and sensibility, nor could one more than the other effect the organic unity of analysis and ideal which was so much wanted. She could only acknowledge the conflicting imperatives and allow that they answered to different sides of her nature. All her life she needed prayer without ever being able to give, or even wanting to give, a compelling account of the power to whom her prayers were addressed. Prayer might be best in the context of religious music or architecture, but its validity was quite independent of any theological dogma. It was the occasion of a release from personal ambition or vanity: a joining of awe and love in the interests of a recovery from littleness: a rejuvenation of moral sense. If it puzzled her, the important thing was that it worked. She felt happier and better for it. Of course, Spencer was undismayed by awe. It had a secure place within his system. 'Awe', he reassured her, 'is quite legitimate. It arises in our minds from a perception of power.'[70] However, she ought always to remember that the Princes of the Church were as bloodthirsty as their secular neighbours. But that was not in dispute.

Even if Beatrice had not met Joseph Chamberlain in 1883, it is doubtful whether she would have long remained the faithful disciple of Herbert Spencer. There is an irony that overtakes the best – precisely the best – of pedagogues: the capacity that they develop in their pupils makes them into rebels rather than into soldiers of the line. At the same time, this fate is well deserved if the Master pretends to be the creator of a definitive system of thought while insisting that Progress is the central idea of his system. Yet before she was twenty-six Beatrice hardly ventured on any serious or sustained criticism of her teacher. She allowed herself some gentle mockery of the pedantic philistinism with which he responded to Cologne Cathedral. Even he refrained from criticising the interior, but he objected to the curved outline of the spires. ' "In architecture what I require", he spoke, "is that the lines should be defined, that either they should be continuous or definitely broken. Moreover, the curve is especially objectionable in this case – in so far as Gothic architecture is perpendicular." '[71] She glimpsed that it might be a mistake to ransack the universe for illustrations of one's principles instead of finding ways of testing them: Spencer was obsessed with order rather than – as she came to put it – with making 'the order of thought' correspond to the 'order of things'. She began to understand why others might find him repulsive. In his craze for system-building he came to develop one faculty at the expense of all the rest: draining away his capacity for sympathy and a full enjoyment of life, he became more and more crotchety, vain and egotistical.[72] Indeed, after the appearance of his *The Man Versus the State,* which was full of conviction and intensity of feeling, it became clear that he must pay the price of his ambition to supply a definitive philosophy. It left him with no employment for his declining years but a defence of his principle and an elaboration of it which grew ever more tedious. Already Beatrice sensed what was happening to him. In taking his temperature before embarking on a journey, or looking with trepidation upon each new dish, his hypochondria far surpassed her own. He became increasingly irritated with a world that was out of sorts and stupid enough to question the necessity and desirability of increasing individuation. He came to welcome death even upon his own bleak view of that prospect. Long before the appointed hour arrived he was uttering fearful moans and asking: 'Why more tomorrows?' By that time not even his beloved disciple could suggest an answer.[73]

Yet in 1883 she was not tempted to dissent at any point from the conclusions of *The Man Versus the State*, the last great manifesto of the nineteenth century in favour of full-blooded *laissez-faire* written by a thinker of the first order.[74] She certainly did not detect the signs of self-contradiction and apostasy that socialists, overjoyed by such a notice, believed they had discovered. Spencer did, very much despite himself, make socialists. But if he made Beatrice into one, it was in the most roundabout, remote and indirect way.

It is tempting to conclude that Spencer contributed to the socialist revival only when his influence was topped up with that of Comte.[75] It could plausibly be argued that this was true both of Sidney and of Beatrice herself.[76] However, there was a host of ways in which his influence worked itself out while corresponding not at all with his mature intentions: the combative and challenging spirit of his early radicalism; the style of thought and conduct that sent him deliberately to set his face against the churchgoers on Sunday mornings and walk in the opposite direction; his contempt for the privileged status of landed society and his early advocacy of land nationalisation; his bold and uncompromising denunciation of swindling company directors and of shopkeepers who adulterated their goods; his championship of the law of equal freedom and sure sense for a society in which the condition of the free development of each would become the condition of the free development of all; all these things made his defence of unregulated capitalism appear to many of his former admirers to mark him down as a renegade. It was said that he had made more men socialists than the late Dr Marx himself.[77] Moreover, he had taught a whole generation to think in terms of evolution, progress and the possibility of a science of society based upon the 'organic analogy'. Beatrice recalled that her lasting debt to Spencer was that he taught her 'to look on all social institutions as if they were plants or animals.'[78] This may appear to be a thoroughly inadequate and pernicious habit of mind in our century, but it constituted an insight into the human condition rather than a denial of it in the last one. The concept of a functional adaptation of social structures, which proceeded willy-nilly and independently of the consciousness of those who furnished the personnel of such institutions, could be rewarding and even revolutionary. Beatrice was to deploy it to good effect in her first book.[79] For the time being she was oblivious to its more disturbing implications, real or imagined.

In 1883 she was just as oblivious to the contradictions in Spencer that took others forward towards socialism. As early as 1871, T.H. Huxley, a friend of the Potters as well as the champion of Darwin, had argued that 'administrative nihilism' accorded ill with the 'organic analogy'.[80] If the development of society was analogous to that of organisms, then, surely, one would expect its progress to be marked by ever increasing conscious direction as against dependence upon merely instinctive controls and mindless adaptations. Probably both Spencer and his opponents attached quite undue weight and importance to the organic analogy, but there is no doubt that socialists fancied that they had caught the philosopher out and that they rejoiced in the belief that, whatever Spencer thought he was doing, he was in fact furnishing a scientific foundation for socialism.[81] Beyond this, socialists might point out that *The Man Versus the State* described a process of alleged degeneration which was scarcely explicable on the author's own principles. In that work Spencer drew a picture of the slow but remorseless growth of state control and provision. His illustrative lists running from the Factory Acts through to state education and free admission to museums were indistinguishable from those drawn up by Sidney Webb except that Webb compiled his six years later, made them longer, and saw in the process something entirely wholesome.[82] There must have been many readers of *The Man Versus the State* who found it a self-defeating book: the *reductio ad absurdum* of classic individualism. Instead of drawing back aghast at all this evidence of legislative enactments that have restricted the freedom of the capitalist in the interests of producers and consumers, they were encouraged to project new measures which were bound to appear as so many despotic and salutary inroads upon the rights of property.

Among these reckless and misguided spirits whom Spencer encouraged rather than subdued were the rediscoverers of poverty: the socialists, and the new radicals of the Great Liberal Party who, under the leadership of Joseph Chamberlain, were busy 'fouling their own nest'. In strict accordance with Spencerian principles the progress of English Radicalism was distinguished by an increasing specialisation of differentiation of function. Whereas in the 1840s the leaders of middle-class radicalism had moved easily from the world of business to the world of politics and the world of letters, by the 1880s they tended to confront each other at the head of distinct establishments. The friendship of Richard Potter and Herbert Spencer depended upon common memories rather than upon any present coincidence of need or purpose. Beatrice's father regarded the philosopher with a benign contempt. He might be an agreeable companion, but he had ceased to be of any practical importance.[83] Chamberlain, like Potter, had risen above the hurly-burly of competition to a position of monopolistic or oligopolistic power, but he then chose to renounce entrepreneurial life for political life. Seemingly the politician answered to a different system of controls from the great manufacturer of bolts and screws. It had not always been so. The progress of a culture was experienced as disintegration.

1883 opened with Beatrice fully preoccupied with the syllabus according to Spencer. He might not have proved the positive existence of the Absolute, but his work was a landmark in the history of thought. In particular, he had fully persuaded her that 'comparative physiology – that is, knowledge of the development of animal life, is the only key to and the only basis for a science of sociology'. In mid-February she had to leave Rusland Hall to take possession of their London home at 47 Princes Gate. She mourned the departure of the student and the entry of the society woman, but the student had not been over-active nor was the life of the society woman to be unrelieved by study.[84] In Westmorland she had done little sustained work beyond reflecting on whether culture did not increase the power to act while diminishing the desire to do so and whether the application of scientific method was not simply the introduction of justice into our intellectual relationships. In London she was able to find time for a close reading of Willie Cripps's *Adenoid Diseases of the Rectum* – not the choicest topic in fashionable circles – and to engage in some laboratory work under Cripps's direction. She prepared specimens of tumour and peppered her diary with such instructive observations as 'the epidermis and all its appendages are extra vascular'.[85]

The move to London was not, of course, decided upon out of regard for improving Beatrice's skill in preparing specimens. In March Kate was to make her late but brilliant marriage to Leonard Courtney. This left Beatrice as the one unmarried Potter girl of eligible years. Mournfully she concluded: 'I was not made to be loved, there must be something repulsive in my character.'[86] Perhaps it was her attitude to 'Society', which she entered consciously as a participant observer. She asked herself whether she was not an 'unmitigated prig' to approach Society to learn rather than to amuse.[87] The trouble was that she could not pretend to be wholly detached from this atmosphere of 'ease, satiety and boredom, with prospect and retrospect of gratified and mortified vanity'.[88] She was tempted by the prizes and inclined to imagine that her relative lack of success in making off with them was due to her superior attitude. After a huge party at the Speakers, one or two of which would have sufficed for a lifetime, she fancied that the 'mental superiority of men [is] greatest in our class. Could it be otherwise with the daily life of ladies in Society ...', a life dominated by a desire to inch oneself further up the social scale and by dreary and unimaginative discourses on the 'servant problem'?[89] 'At present', wrote Beatrice in the early spring of 1883, 'I feel like a caged animal, bound up by the luxury, comfort and respectability of my position. I can't find a training that I want without neglecting my duty.'[90]

Her duties were diminished by packing her younger sister, Rosie, off to school. This welcome departure occasioned one of Beatrice's few generous references to the youngest Potter as a 'sweet, touching character'.[91]

Doubtless, Rosie was the least accomplished of the girls, but she also lacked the Potter characteristic of 'a hard self-assertiveness'.

This quality was surfacing again in the father. Recovering from the shock of his wife's death, he began to plan a great new railway amalgamation. Beatrice noticed his shrewdness and sharpness, his cynical depreciation of men and their ways as things foreign to his nature. In his personal relationships he was utterly unselfish and unselfconscious.[92] She had much conversation with him and asked him for his opinion on schemes for co-operative production. He dismissed them, holding that the efficient operation of industry required the fullest identification between ownership and control. The salaried manager was an inferior being. The best result to be expected from co-operative production would be nothing but the appearance of a new race of capitalists.[93] Beatrice was inclined to reason, after the manner of the wages fund theorists, that there was little hope for workmen unless they could restrict their numbers. But she had not studied political economy and felt more than ever a 'wretched little frog' without title to a serious opinion on the subject.[94]

Now that Kate had exchanged her philanthropic activities for marriage, Beatrice was allowed to take her place. In April 1883 she joined the Charity Organisation Society.[95] This body had been established in 1869 as the Society for Organising Charitable Relief and Repressing Mendicity.[96] Its leading idea was that indiscriminate and unregulated charity did more to promote poverty than it did to relieve it. In ever expanding towns and cities the traditional forms of social control and well-judged acts of charity gave place – so it was thought – to a dangerous remoteness between social classes and an environment favourable to the 'clever' pauper. He was allowed to defeat the salutary purposes of the New Poor Law. He escaped from the principle of relief within the workhouse, under the principle of 'less eligibility', by joining the anonymous, faceless, army of the poor and using his ragged wife and seemingly hungry children to make a 'touch'. Against those who degraded themselves and others by professing poverty and living on their hard luck, it was necessary to mobilise the spirit of business efficiency and of scientific verification. Deeply impressed by the possibility that poverty was becoming a trade, the COS was committed to turning philanthropy into a profession. This meant – along with much else besides – a scrupulous attention to 'case work'. It was not long before Beatrice was making the acquaintance of Mr Pavey, a dispenser who took opium and left his wife to support their three children on fifteen shillings a week. She subdued her feelings of righteous indignation.[97] It was immediately apparent to her that the COS was an improvement on the former state of things:

One thing is clear to my mind, it is distinctly *advantageous to us* to go amongst the poor. We can get from them an experience of life which is novel and interesting; the study of their lives and surroundings gives us the facts wherewith we can attempt to solve the social problems; contact with them develops on the whole our finer qualities; disgusting us with our false and worldly appreciation of men and things and educating us in a thoughtful benevolence. Perhaps the worst result for us is that our philanthropy is sometimes the cause of pharasaical self-congratulation.[98]

This was all very well, but what form was 'thoughtful benevolence' to take in the case of Mr Pavey and his family? Beatrice appears to have had recourse to highly effective measures. Ella Pycroft asked:

Do you remember telling me when I first knew you how you had helped to bring about the death of an opium eater in Soho? I couldn't understand then how you could have done such a thing, but now I have come to think that you were right, and right in a most large minded, far-seeing way. I am coming to see more and more that it is useless to help the helpless, that the truly kind thing is to let the weak go to the wall and get out of the strong people's way as fast as possible.[99]

There was more than one way of sharing Louise Michel's conviction: '*La philanthropie, c'est une mensonge!*' Leonard Courtney was fond of repeating that expression over lunch. He would draw his shaggy eyebrows together and parting his capacious lips declare that: 'every day I believe more in undiluted political economy.'[100] Depriving the undeserving poor of life was only a logical extension of depriving them of their liberties, and it was even more economical. One hopes that Mr Pavey's widow grasped these truths, even though her expression of gratitude to Beatrice may have given rise to 'pharisaical self-congratulation'.

However, Beatrice had chosen to join the COS just at the moment when rising unemployment was causing such confirmed advocates of sternness as the Revd S.A. Barnett of St Jude's, Whitechapel, to reconsider their position. During the bad winter of 1880–1 he had favoured giving distressed families relief only on condition that the father was deprived of his liberty of entering the workhouse.[101] He noticed that this policy was highly successful in reducing pauperism, but unfortunately did nothing to diminish poverty. Accordingly, in the very month in which Beatrice joined the COS, he published an article on 'Practicable Socialism'. Without making a clean break with the COS, he announced his conversion to the view that the state should provide for the poor. Only the state could release the labourer from a vision of the future dominated by the shadow of the workhouse and the grave. Describing himself as a socialist, Barnett announced that it was to the government which one must look for better housing, education, medical attention, schools of industry for those fit to work, and pensions for those incapable of working. The costs of these necessary provisions would have to be made by introducing a system of graduated taxation.[102] In the following year Barnett became the first Warden of Toynbee Hall. Beatrice became friendly with him and with his wife. Yet it was not this acquaintance that first disturbed her faith in doctrines that seemed to license her to take the lives of the poor and the worthless.

In June 1883 Miss Beatrice Potter first made the acquaintance of Miss Beatrice Chamberlain: 'essentially provincial: in the good and bad sense'. Also of Miss Chamberlain's father: 'I do and I don't like him.'[103]

She got to know him better in the following month. At a dinner, a Whig peer sat on one side of her while he sat on the other. The peer talked of his possessions; Mr Chamberlain talked of confiscating those possessions for the masses.

Herbert Spencer said that Mr Chamberlain was 'a man who may mean well, but who does, and will do, an incalculable amount of mischief'.

Joseph Chamberlain said that Mr Spencer was, fortunately, in his writings unintelligible: 'otherwise his life would have been spent doing harm.'[104]

Miss Potter was still distant from a position in which she could see that both of them were correct.

Joseph Chamberlain was twenty-two years senior to Beatrice. When she was thirteen or fourteen he was Mayor of Birmingham and master of the Liberal Caucus which had emerged after the passing of the Second Reform Act. In those days he had dared to associate himself with the short-lived republican movement and had earned the royal displeasure. If he had been an insolent nuisance in the early seventies, by the early eighties he had come to be regarded as the most dangerous man in England. As President of the Board of Trade in Gladstone's second administration he had determined to do for the whole country what he had already accomplished for his own city: 'Parked, paved, assized, marketed, gas-and-watered and improved.' He declined to be muzzled by office. 'Electrified' by the writings of Henry George and impressed, if not entirely convinced, by Alfred Russel Wallace's case for land nationalisation,[105] he was certain that such works were bound to capture the imagination of the masses and make them eager for political and social reform. Before the Second Reform Act, Richard Cobden had positively complained about the non-appearance of Spartacus; before the Third, Joseph Chamberlain appeared to respectable society to be grooming himself for the part – although the grooming in the strict sense of the term was decidedly incongruous: wearing his monocle and his orchid and sustained by a fortune made out of his monopoly in bolts and screws, he may have appeared an unusual prophet of republican simplicity. Yet he carried conviction among friend and foe alike. He began by prompting Engels's advice to those who might aspire to form a Labour Party: he took as his rallying point the unrealised points of the Charter. He was for manhood suffrage, equal electoral districts, one vote one value and payment of members. He also fully understood that a mere programme of political reform was no longer enough. The parody had to be extended to include 'the Charter and something more'.[106]

When Beatrice first made his acquaintance he was embarking on a great programme of public meetings and demonstrations. In March 1883 the Leader of the Opposition, Lord Salisbury, made a courageous sortie into the Birmingham fortress, but only played into Chamberlain's hands. The counter-attack was immediate:

> Lord Salisbury constitutes himself the spokesman of a class – of the class to which he himself belongs, who toil not neither do they spin (great cheering), whose fortunes, as in his case, have originated by grants made in times gone by for the services which courtiers made the Kings (renewed cheers), and have since grown and increased while they have slept by levying an increased share on all that other men have done by toil and labour to add to the general wealth and prosperity of the country ...[107]

This was widely interpreted as incitement to class hatred, but worse was to follow. In June, Chamberlain participated in a great demonstration in honour of John Bright, a fellow Member of Parliament for Birmingham and the finest representative of a phase of bourgeois radicalism that Chamberlain was bent on superseding. Remarking on the absence of public expenditure or military display on this occasion, he added: 'The brilliant uniforms, the crowds of high officials, the representatives of Royalty – they were absent (loud laughter and cheers) – and nobody missed them (renewed laughter and cheering).'[108] Such words were unforgivable from one who had kissed hands and who was still in office. Whigs and Tories were demented with rage. The Queen conveyed to the Prime Minister her most severe displeasure. The wretched Gladstone was obliged to require the President of the Board of Trade to apologise – which he did, but only in terms of which made matters worse. Radical workmen were delighted. Even revolutionary socialists like Tom Maguire began to look on Chamberlain as something more than an ambitious opportunist, important only as a straw in the wind.[109]

Beatrice did not know now what to make of him. They met frequently and had long conversations together in June and July. After these meetings she spent nights sleepless from excitement.[110] She was unable to work and found it impossible to think about anything but his striking personality, his political passion, his immense will power. In one sense the experience did accelerate her progress towards sociology. In September she reiterated her faith in comparative physiology as the basis, but expressed a distrust of over-much reliance upon arguments from analogy. She began to insist that the sociologist should experience the types of mental forces he must study. 'To be a great sociologist', she concluded, 'you must more or less resume in your own nature the complex ingredients mixed in varying proportions, in the units with which you have to deal.'[111] Accordingly, she was able to find a scholarly justification for spending a whole week with the Chamberlains in Birmingham at the end of that month:

> Much might be learnt by studying the life and thought of such a man; discovering how *representative* he was, how much his convictions were the result of individual characteristics and how much they were the effect of surrounding circumstances. They are *convictions passionately* held; his whole energy is thrown into the attempt to realise them. Is the basis of these convictions honest experience and thought or were they originally the tool of ambition, now become inextricably woven into the love of power, and to his own mind no longer distinguishable from it? What is his principle? Is the Government the interpretation [interpreter?] of the people's wants? Is it the business of the governing class to gratify the sensations of the great social organism or should the advice of the most intelligent portion of the community be taken as the remedies irrespective of the longings of the patient?[112]

Chamberlain's provincial bourgeois background was, on balance, reassuring: 'Coming from such honest surroundings he surely must be straight in intention.'[113] But it was not only his political intentions that interested her. Chamberlain's first wife had died in childbirth, as had his second, Florence. He had remained unmarried for eight years. It seems likely that Beatrice half expected, and certainly hoped, that he would propose to her. He excited her. Such a marriage would be an immense triumph. Chamberlain was a far bigger figure than Courtney or Hobhouse. He might well become Prime Minister, and his wife might exercise an immense influence over him and over events. But did he want her? If he wished to marry her would she be able to influence his intellectual and political development? And if he would allow this, how should that influence be exercised?[114]

For the moment the questions were unanswerable. She had lost her mother in whom she would have confided, the one to whom she felt she had become so much closer during the last months of her life. Here was a subject that would have allowed her to achieve the sort of intimacy and admiration that she had missed so much. In the event she turned to her old nurse, Martha Mills, and filled the autumn evenings at the Argoed with reminiscence. Martha had witnessed her mother's courtship. Martha and her mother came from the same stock in the northern manufacturing town of Bacup. Beatrice proposed that she should accompany 'Da', as Martha was called, upon her next visit to the place. ' "Well, you know I can always go; there's no occasion to wait for that," answered the dear old woman, "but my friends up there would be astonished to see a Miss Potter coming along with us; they are not accustomed to such grand folk. I think they would be what they call 'flayed' by you!" "Oh," cried I, jumping up with the delightful consciousness of an original idea, "I wouldn't be Miss Potter, I would be Miss Jones, farmer's daughter, near Monmouth." '[115] Thus, this famous visit was a sentimental journey before it was a scientific expedition, an attempt to escape an obsessive preoccupation with new attachments through a renewal of old ones. Upon her return, Beatrice decided not to write up her experiences, but save them, to bank them as security for her claims to 'an individual life'.

In Bacup, Beatrice found no hopeless poverty wasting itself away; no coarse humour and no low, sensual excitements. There were no opium eaters who needed to be put down, no bitter cry to answer or subdue. In Bacup the world exhibited an order pleasing to political economy, charity organisations, and Mr Herbert Spencer. If the meek and the gentle-hearted were sad, that could be attributed to the melancholia and the suicidal mania that Beatrice attributed to the Akeds, her mother's side of the family. If some of the weavers were out of work and trade was worse than could ever be remembered, there was comparatively little poverty. Nobody suggested that it was impossible to get on or improve without individual exertion and voluntary co-operation: 'na makin' of laws', they said, 'can alter that'. Here were working people whose company was charming and restful. They were pious, innocent and dignified. They provided for the needs of this world in their co-operative stores and for their needs in the next through chapels. Beatrice found a community that was not merely reassuring, but admirable in its creativity and simplicity. It persuaded her that: 'one of the best preventatives against the socialistic tendency of the coming democracy would lie in local government.'[116]

Her account of 'real' working-class life delighted Herbert Spencer. He was very disappointed that she found it – despite her ambition for literary fame – inexpedient to publish. This was just the kind of material that would correct the sensationalism of such tracts as *The Bitter Cry of Outcast London*.[117] The sentimental outpourings of clerical enthusiasts were calculated to stoke the engines of socialistic agitations and encourage the pernicious political tendencies associated with demagogues like Joseph Chamberlain. But 'while the old political philosopher [was] discussing with the Editor of the *Nineteenth Century* the desirability of encouraging a beloved disciple to come into the literary arena; the same beloved disciple [was] entertaining – with no untender feeling – the arch enemy; the very embodiment of the pernicious tendency.'[118]

Her tortured state could not endure 'The "to be or not to be"', she wrongly concluded, would soon be settled.[119] The first report in the journal of the momentous visit was dated 12 January 1884, a week after it had taken place:

> Another small episode of my life over. After six weeks of feverish indecision, the day comes. Lounge full of young people and the three last days past in dancing and games: I feel all the while as if I were dancing in a dream towards some precipice. Saturday 5th: remainder of the ball party chatting round the afternoon tea table, the great man's son and daughter amongst them. The door opens: 'Mr Chamberlain': general uprising. I advance from among them and, in my nervousness, almost press six pounds just received into his hand. General feeling of discomfort; no one quite understanding the reason of Mr Chamberlain's advent. There exists evidently no cordiality between him and his host; for Father in a few minutes retires to play patience with an absent and distressed look utterly disgusted at the *supposed* intentions of his visitor. At dinner, after some shyness, we plunged into essentials and he began to delicately hint his requirements. That evening and the next morning until lunch we are on 'susceptible terms'. A dispute over state education breaks the charm. 'It is a question of authority with women, if you believe in Herbert Spencer you won't believe in me'. This opens the battle. By a silent arrangement we found ourselves in the garden. 'It pains me to hear any of my views controverted' and with this preface he began with stern exactitude to lay down the articles of his political creed. I remain modestly silent; but noticing my silence he remarks that he requires 'intelligent sympathy' from women. 'Servility, Mr Chamberlain' think I, not sympathy, but intelligent servility; what many women give men, but the difficulty lies in changing one's master, in jumping from one *tone* of thought to the exact opposite – *with intelligence*.[120]

Unable, rather than unwilling, to accept his mastery and to meet his requirements, she advanced as boldly as she dared her 'feeble objections' to his general propositions. She owed it to herself and to him to be absolutely sincere:

> He refutes my assertions by re-asserting his convictions passionately, his expression becoming every minute more gloomy and determined.

He told me the history of his political career, how his creed grew up on a basis of experience and sympathy; how his desire to benefit the many had become gradually a passion absorbing within itself his whole nature. 'Hitherto the well-to-do have governed the country for their own interest; and I will do them this credit – they have achieved their object. Now I trust the time is approaching for those who work and have not. My aim in life is to make life pleasanter for the great majority; I do not care if it becomes in the process less pleasant for the well-to-do minority. Take America, for instance. Cultured persons complain that the society there is vulgar; less agreeable to the delicate tastes of delicately trained minds. But it is infinitely preferable to the ordinary worker.'

To this Beatrice attempted the rejoinder that the American workers owed any superior equalisation of conditions to the riches of their continent rather than to their political system. She went on to suggest that the American plutocracy seemed richer and more powerful 'owing to the generally corrupt nature of American institutions'. This was hardly calculated to endear her to the brilliant imitator of the American caucus: the British statesman who was 'electrified' by Henry George and whose political style most closely resembled the United States populists:

Not a suspicion of feeling did he show towards me. He was simply determined to assert his convictions. If I remained silent he watched my expression narrowly, I felt his curious scrutinising eyes noting each movement as if he were anxious to ascertain whether I yielded to his absolute supremacy. If I objected to or ventured to qualify his theories or his statements, he smashed objection and qualification by an absolute denial and continued his assertion. He remarked as we came in that he felt as if he had been making a speech. I felt utterly exhausted. We hardly spoke to each other the rest of the day. The next morning when the Playnes had left, he suggested some more 'exercise'. I *think* that both of us felt that all was over between us, so that we talked more *pleasantly*, but even then he insisted on bringing me back from trivialities to a discussion of the intellectual subordination of women. 'I have only one domestic trouble, my sister and daughter are bitten with the women's rights mania. I don't allow any action on the subject.'

'You don't allow any division of opinion in your household, Mr Chamberlain.'

'I can't help people thinking differently from me.'

'But you don't allow the expression of the difference?'

'No.'

And that little word ended our intercourse. Now that the pain and indecision are over, I can't help regretting that absorption in the peculiar nature of our relationship left me so little capable of taking the opportunities he gave me of knowing him.

The Political creed is the whole man – the outcome of his peculiar physical and mental temperament. He is neither a reasoner, nor an observer in the scientific sense. He does not deduce his opinions by the aid of certain well-thought-out principles, from certain carefully ascertained facts. He aims, rather, at being the organ to express the *desires* …

He was a great leader because he intuitively understood the wants of a class; was capable of articulating them; could reimpress them upon what would otherwise have been a dull, indifferent multitude. His influence would 'depend on the relative power of the class he is adopted to represent':

By temperament he is an enthusiast and a despot. A deep sympathy with the misery and incompleteness of most men's lives and an earnest desire to right this, transforms political action into a religious crusade; but running alongside this genuine enthusiasm is a passionate desire to *crush* opposition to *his will*, a longing to feel his foot on the necks of others, though he would persuade himself that he represents the right and his adversaries the wrong.

She shrewdly recognised that he must hate moderate men most: that he must prefer the adversary who regarded him as the incarnation of the 'evil one'. 'And now that it is all over I have a stunned feeling as I gradually wake up to the old surroundings, and look forward to new modifications of them … Undoubtedly the Bacup trip is the right direction …'.[121]

Yet throughout 1884 she found it was a direction which was hard to take. He, who could summon up the political spirit in 'the average sensual man', still held her enchanted. Denied this sorcerer, she was still unfit to be the apprentice. And matters were made worse, the denial seeming less than final. In March 1884 she received a pressing invitation from Miss Chamberlain to spend two days in Birmingham. She accepted, noting in her journal: 'I am afraid there is a dash of the adventuress about me and it struck me as rather comically interesting to investigate the topmost of the Caucus …' For a moment she maintained the superior person tone. In Highbury – the Chamberlain establishment – 'there is very much taste and all very bad … You long for a bare floor and a plain deal table.' When Mr Chamberlain condescended to appear from his exotic greenhouse he gave her a 'constrainedly polite welcome'. Whereupon Beatrice asked herself, as she sank into a perfectly constructed armchair, 'are we about to take part in a funeral procession?' John Bright came in and Chamberlain assumed that he knew her: '"not me", say I humbly, "but I think you knew my grandfather, Lawrence Heyworth." "Lawrence Heyworth", replies the old man with slow emphasis, "Yes – then you are the daughter of Lawrencina Heyworth – one of the two or three women a man remembers to the end of his life as beautiful in expression and form." '[122]

Her mother's triumph with the father of the older Radicalism can hardly have failed to contrast with her relations with his successor. With Chamberlain she stumbled uncertainly to success and to failure. When she suggested that the side of the Englishman's nature that had formerly been absorbed in religious enthusiasm was now informing political life, he declared that he agreed with her. 'I rejoice in it,' said he. 'I have always had a grudge against religion as absorbing the passion in man's nature.' But when he showed her his orchids she blurted out that that the only flowers she loved were wild ones. Under the circumstances it was hardly fair of her to observe that Joseph Chamberlain had great diplomatic talent, but not in *'la recherche d'une femme.'*

'Is it', she asked herself,

> cold-blooded to write truthfully of one's relationship to a man? If one tells anything one should tell all ... All the small *affaires de cœur* of past years I have left unmentioned simply because they have not interested me. But Joseph Chamberlain with his gloom and seriousness, with absence of any gallantry or faculty for saying pretty nothings; the simple way in which he assumes – almost asserts – that you stand on a level far beneath him and that all that concerns you is trivial; that you yourself are without importance in the world except in so far as you might be related to him: this sort of courtship (if it is to be called courtship) fascinates, at least, my imagination ... I don't know how it will all end: certainly not in *my happiness.* As it is, his personality absorbs all my thoughts ... And if the fates should unite us (against *my will*) all joy and light heartedness will go from me. I shall be absorbed into the life of a man whose aims are not my aims ... I hate every form of despotism.[123]

She went to the Town Hall in the company of Joseph's son, Austen. Opinion was to be aroused for the coming Reform Bill. She attended to Chamberlain, not to his arguments. She watched closely his brute exercise of powers of command: his extraordinary ability to attract the sympathies of his audience. She cursed her education in relation to Chamberlain much as D.H. Lawrence was to curse his in relation to the snake. How ironical that Spencer – the aged, pedantic, flibbertigibbet who had come to hate life, but who had offered her decisive help in overcoming the shock of rejection – should now be the occasion of a second and seemingly worse rejection. The training she had received from him appeared as a barrier in the way of her union with the man she loved; the education she had received from him appeared as an insuperable obstacle to it. She might unlearn *laissez-faire*, but she could not unlearn 'submission not desirable', even when it seemed as eminently desirable as it did in this case.

There was an unbearable element of uncertainty. In April she reflected that if her refusal to consent to subordination and absolute dependence had 'cured all desire on the other side', then she would be 'mortified' but relieved:

> Ambition and superstition began the feeling. A desire to play a part in the world and a belief that as the wife of a great man I should play a bigger part than as a spinster or an ordinary married woman

led her on –

> His temperament and his character are intensely attractive to me. I feel I could reduce the gloom, could understand the mixed motive and the difficulties of a nature in which genuine enthusiasm and personal ambition are so curiously interwoven ... Do I believe in the drift of his political views and do I believe that the means employed are *honest*? ... Once married, I should of course subordinate my views to my husband's: should, as regards his own profession, accept implicitly his view of right and wrong, but I cannot shrink the responsibility of my judgement before I acknowledge his authority. Social questions are the vital questions of today. They take the place of Religion ... Their solution seems largely a matter of temperament.[124]

She had no devotion to his goals and had to twist her reasoning in order to tolerate them. This was not so serious as her reservations about his means; her suspicion that Chamberlain would never scruple to act from ulterior motives; that he used his supporters for purposes of his own which were distinct from theirs. She despaired of her power to improve him and found some consolation in knowing that she could not do it. 'I should *not* influence him. He has shown me that distinctly ... It is only when I have simulated "la femme complaisante", turned the conversation from principles to personalities, that he has desired me.'[125] She was certainly correct. Chamberlain wanted a helpmate, a reliable admirer, not a partner; an intelligent woman capable of following his political career and not confining her interests to merely personal and domestic life, but one who was totally submissive to his will and purposes.[126] As May came without further word from Highbury, Beatrice acknowledged: 'The woman's nature has been stirred to its depths; I have loved and lost.'[127] Without ignoring her need for the theatrical and a certain romantic reward, which she found in the role of the disappointed lover, she was doubtless at a low point. 'Both ideals have fallen, life alone, life together, remaining only the seemingly commonplace round of private duties.'[128] For the rest of the year she repeatedly committed herself to one last word on the subject. In October she wrote: 'passion – with its burning heat, an emotion which had long smouldered unnoticed, burst out into flame and burnt down intellectual interests, personal ambition, and all other self-developing motive.'[129] Longing for love and a settled occupation, desiring the personal prestige that she might have acquired, she resolved that, being unable to live without the help of others, she must live for others. But it was easier said than done: by the end of the year she was asking what she would not give for a mother now. How was it that anyone cared for life?

Despite her misery, Beatrice began to develop new relationships. In November 1884 she noted that she was becoming more intimate with the Booths. In January 1885 Ella Pycroft spent three days with her. Ella was plain-looking, strong, with an attractive sincerity. She was a free-thing, anxious for work and otherwise indifferent to life. 'We shall', remarked Beatrice, 'get on.'[130] And so they did. They worked together in the Katherine Buildings near the docks. In February Beatrice studied the papers delivered at the Industrial Remuneration Conference and was particularly impressed by those presented by Benjamin Jones concerning the Co-operative Wholesale Society and one Sidney Taylor on profit sharing.[131] But she was still far away from a condition in which Chamberlain would cease to be her ruling obsession. It remained an open question with her as to whether her observation of East End life and her study of social questions were to be a preparation for life with the Great Man or for a profession in sociology in the style of the Philosopher.

In January 1885 she was expecting Chamberlain to make his intentions towards her clear. The old delusion returned in the spring when he dined with them. He told her that her brother-in-law, Leonard Courtney, was 'an ass'. Nevertheless the Courtneys arranged a picnic so that she could meet him again. 'That day will always remain engraved on my memory as the most painful one of my life. The scene under the Burnham beeches, forcing me to tell his fortune – afterwards behaving with a marked rudeness and indifference.'[132] Courtney tried to console her and asked her not to seek a life of 'barren brilliances'.[133] Kate also advised her that a marriage to Chamberlain would be a 'tragedy: a murder of your independent nature'.[134]

In 1885 Chamberlain had reached his most leftward point. He began the year with his 'Ransom' speech. Addressing the working men of Birmingham he warned them that the new Reform Act would not bring the triumph of democracy unless they organised: 'If the interest of the great majority is without discipline and without recognised leaders, it will be like a mob that disperses before the steady tread of a few policemen, or before the charge of a handful of cavalry.' But the masses, once organised, would insist that social subjects received far more attention in the legislature than had been the case in the past:

> If you will go back to the early history of our social system you will find that … every man was born into the world with natural rights, with a right to a share in the great inheritance of the community, with a right to a part of the land of his birth … Private ownership has taken the place of these communal rights, and this system has become so interwoven with our habits and usages, it has been so sanctioned by law and protected by custom, that it might be very difficult and perhaps impossible to reverse it. But then I ask what ransom will property pay for the security it enjoys?[135]

A few days later he exchanged the term 'ransom' for 'insurance': 'What insurance will wealth find it to its advantage to provide?' The answer was free education; local government reform; 'the provision of healthy decent dwellings in our large towns at fair rents; and in the country, facilities for the labourer to obtain a small plot of land.'[136] These and the other measures he was soon to weave into the Unauthorised Programme were to be paid for by graduated taxation, new death duties and expropriation of unearned increments. Far from being a socialist programme, it was an anti-socialist programme, but few saw it in this light. Gladstone told Lord Acton that he was 'entangled' by it and regarded it as a 'taking into the hands of the State the business of the individual man'.[137] *Punch* saw Chamberlain as a clown touching the backsides of respectable citizens with a hot poker labelled 'Socialism'.[138] Whatever he meant, Chamberlain had certainly succeeded in raising the political temperature and drawing the future of private property into the centre of political debate.

In August 1885 Beatrice tried to understand and to stumble along behind him, but she found it hard going. Spencer's past influence was 'over-powering' and she was drawn back to her old teacher's view of the duties of the state:

> the free and right administration of *justice* between individuals. But because there has been no justice or rather injustice administered to great classes of men, owing to their powerlessness, great wrongs have arisen. Can these wrongs be redressed? Certainly not by the simple administration of justice – that must be based on the *status quo*. Ought

we then to take from a whole class of individuals that which has been stolen (we will admit the theft) by past individuals of that class in past times from other classes – shall we not offend actively against the very principle we wish to establish? That is the crucial question.[139]

Without explicitly referring to Chamberlain she continued to protest against the language of 'rights'. It was not rights but renunciation which individuals and classes had to learn. 'That false metaphysical idea of rights', said she following Comte, 'as some unalterable result, determined in quantity and quality, due to all men alike, is working its wicked way in our political life.'[140] Yet she was beginning to see the terms in which a compromise might be effected between Spencer and Chamberlain. Socialists who aimed to levelling *inherited* conditions might be practical. More, this might actually accelerate evolutionary progress by promoting the survival of the fittest. Inherited qualities were, of course, quite a different matter.

Among the motives that led Beatrice to these reflections and that sent her into East End buildings was the sense that there was still a possibility of an alliance with Chamberlain: that her increasing knowledge of social conditions and her growing understanding of his principles would make her more useful and attractive to him. She could not bring herself to believe that all chance of marriage had gone. She declined to give up the hope even when Chamberlain's sister told her that the brother had never considered it – a proposition that Beatrice could not credit since the sister herself had examined Beatrice about her attitude towards him.[141] Accordingly, when in February 1886, she received a letter in the Great Man's handwriting she was 'ominously excited'.[142]

Chamberlain had just been disappointed in his hopes of getting the Colonial Office in Gladstone's third administration and had accepted the position of President of the Local Government Board. Conscious of his impending break with Gladstone and anxious to prepare a comprehensive Local Government Bill, he was obliged to turn his immediate attention to the dangerous situation associated with the unemployed workers' riots. His doctrine of 'ransom' appeared to be entering the arena of practical politics when, under the stimulus of shattered windows in Pall Mall, the Lord Mayor's relief fund leapt up to £79 000 in a few days. The socialist leaders were arrested, but the government was uncertain how to respond. Campbell-Bannerman, the Secretary of State for War, thought in terms of throwing up earthworks at the mouths of great commercial rivers as a pretext for supplying jobs. The press was full of comments on this and related projects as well as hair-raising accounts of the 'rioters in their lair'. It was at this moment that Chamberlain's eye fell upon a letter from Miss Beatrice Potter in the *Pall Mall Gazette*.

In it was her first publication opposed to public works for the unemployed. 'I am a rent collector', she wrote, 'on a large block of working class dwellings situated near the London docks, designed and adapted to house the lowest class of working poor.' 'Lack of employment in the East End,' so she argued, 'was not so much the result of a general depression of trade but of the characteristics of a specific, local labour market. During the last half century there had been a decline in the once flourishing trades of the metropolis. They had departed. Unfortunately the workers were not inclined to follow their masters down river or out to the suburbs. There were three main classes of East End workmen: a small number brought up in the traditional trades of the neighbourhood; foreigners attracted by reports of high English wages; and the largest group of all – countrymen pressed out of the ranks of trade in provincial towns and rural districts who thoughtlessly drifted to the great centre of odd jobs and indiscriminate charity.'[143] They became a 'leisured and parasitic class'. 'The loudly proclaimed "right to work"', said she, 'is only too often translated in their minds to the right to work when, how and as much as they like.' Given that metropolitan life already attracted large numbers of low-class labourers who were already depressing the conditions of life of the stratum immediately above, how foolish it would be to go in for a policy of public works. 'The condition of the London unemployed would be altered in no other way than by the additional discontent involved in the disappointment of false expectations and by the establishment in their minds of a falsely understood right.'[144]

Chamberlain asked if he could come and talk to her about this letter which he had read with 'great interest and agreement'. He confessed:

My Department knows all about Paupers and Pauperism, but has no official cognizance of distress above the Pauper line. Yet this is surely the serious part of the problem. I am trying to collect facts from different sources but it is difficult to make them complete. I am convinced, however, that the suffering of the industrious non-pauper class is very great and is increasing. What is to be done for them? I do not quite follow your suggestion. Surely the reason of the distress is that there is an actual insufficiency of employment and not merely that the workers do not know where to find work which actually exists somewhere for them … If the distress becomes greater something *must* be done to make work. The rich must pay to keep the poor alive … It will be necessary in each district to find some poorly remunerated employment which

    a) will not tempt him to remain in it longer than is absolutely necessary,

    b) will not be degrading in its character,

    c) will not enter into competition with workers at present in employment, and

d) is of such a kind that every workman whatever he has done hitherto can turn his hand to it.

Perhaps something like spade labour was wanted to test the sincerity of
those who were in want of temporary assistance. Would Miss Potter
please let him have her opinion with respect to these 'rather crude suggestions'.[145]

Beatrice replied to Chamberlain on 'York House paper' but from Bourne-
mouth in a letter of uncertain date.

You take me out of my depth! When I leave London and the peculiar
conditions surrounding the familiar working-class there, I am lost in a
sea of general principles and crotchets.

As I read your letter, a suspicion flashed across me that you wished
for some further proof of the incapacity of a woman's intellect to deal
with such large matters – now if it will in any way serve you, I willingly
offer up my thoughts and give that which is needful!

I agree that 'the rich *must* keep the poor alive': always supposing that
the continued existence of that section of the poor, with liberty to
increase, is *not* injurious to the community at large. And this depends
primarily on facts of which *I* have no knowledge ... You say, that
poverty is 'increased and increasing': is it permanent? If the depression
be due to a permanent relapse from the abnormal activity produced
by the extension of railways etc, depopulation is to some extent a necessity?

But if the lack of employment be temporary, then the question
resolves itself into the easier one: will the public works you propose
(1) attract the labourer out of unemployment? (2) will they keep the
labourer in good, or even in fair, working condition, so that he will be
available for true productive service after the bad time has passed?

My objection to Public works within the metropolis was not based on
the larger question, upon which I have no right to an opinion, but simply upon the conviction that the conditions to which the state labourer
would be subjected within the metropolis, would be hopelessly demoralising. I feel very strongly about this.

Then as to the nature of the work offered. I think there would be two
practical drawbacks – and I will illustrate one by a curious Whitechapel
fact. 135 men applied to the Relief Committee. They were offered street
sweeping at 2/- a day 3d extra for each child. Only 15 accepted, 11 of
them went to the work, and 5 stayed. We were much disgusted and
thought this was additional proof of the demoralisation of the East
End 'out o' works'. But in discussing the matter quietly with the men

attending the meeting room of Katherine Buildings, we found that there was a strong feeling among the better class that unless they were prepared to sink permanently into the ranks of less skilled labour, acceptance of this work would injure their chance (some said irretrievably) of gaining employment in their own trade.

I confess I do not attach much importance to this objection: still it was urged by men who were themselves in work.

To my mind the grand difficulty – would be enforcing good quality and sufficient quantity of work – It would seem to me to require almost a slave-driving body of overseers.

And my impression is, I admit it is not founded on experience, that if the work were sufficiently unskilled *not* to enter into competition with other employment, it *would* be degrading in its nature, likely to become a sham test, and by the subsistence it afforded would increase a parasitic class injurious to the community.

I fail to grasp the principle 'something must be done'.

It is terribly sad that 100 men should die of semi-starvation, should prefer that slow death to the almost penal servitude offered them by the workhouse – but quite apart from the communities' [sic] point of view – if by relieving these 100 men you practically create 500 more – surely the unsatisfactory nature of these men's lives outweighs in misery the death of the smaller number (this statement overlooks the possibility of emigration).

Death after all is a slight evil compared to life under many conditions?

We hear the death-groans of the 100, we do not hear the life-groans of the 500, until it is too late!

If I am wrong, it is not from shallow hard-heartedness, but because I have not sufficient intelligence to see how the measures you propose would work towards the good of the community or even towards the happiness of the class you would relieve …

I must have expressed myself badly in my last letter. I did not mean the thorough investigation of low-class society in London to affect immediately the present question of want of employment – but –

I think I won't explain myself – you will say it is a 'crotchet'!

I have no proposal to make except sternness of the state, and love and self-devotion from individuals, a very old and self-evident remedy!

But is it not rather unkind of you to ask me to tell you what I think? I have tried to be perfectly truthful. Still it *is* a ludicrous idea that an ordinary woman should be called upon to review the suggestions of Her Majesty's ablest Minister! especially when I know that he has a slight opinion of even a superior woman's intelligence in these matters (I agree with him) and a dislike to any independence of thought.

I have long ceased to believe in free-will in ideas. We may sacrifice our thought, as we may sacrifice our life, but so long as we live and so long as we think, we must live and think according to our own natures? – even though *we* may be the first to admit that our constitution is [discussed?] and our thought wrong. You will say, this is not relevant to 'Public Works for the Unemployed'. It is only a feeble excuse for daring to obey you – to obey you in the spirit as well as in the letter!

Believe me.

Yours very sincerely
Beatrice Potter

In a subsequent letter she added an impetuous note.

Now I see I was right not to deceive you. I could not lie to the man I loved. But why have worded it so cruelly, why give unnecessary pain; surely we suffer sufficiently – thank God! – that when our own happiness is destroyed there are others to live for. Do not think that I do not consider your decision as *final* and destroy this.[146]

When she talked about being unable to deceive him she was presumably referring to her opinions about poverty and public works. But this second letter was an extraordinary and even hysterical one. Her father had had a bad stroke at the end of 1885.[147] In January 1886 Beatrice had despaired of life and drawn up her own last will and testament.[148] Her balance of mind was disturbed.

After Beatrice's first letter, Chamberlain had replied that:

I thought we understood each other pretty well. I fear I was mistaken. In the hurry of this life it is not easy to get a clear conception of any other person's principles and opinions. But you are quite wrong in supposing that I undervalue the opinion of an intelligent woman. There are many questions on which I would follow it blindly, although I dislike the flippant self-sufficiency of some female politicians. Neither do I dislike independence of thought ...

I hardly know why I defend myself, for I admit that it does not much matter what I think or feel on these subjects. On the main question your letter is discouraging; but I fear it is true. I shall go on, however, as if it were not true, for it we once admit the impossibility of remedying the evils of society, we shall all sink below the level of the brutes. Such a creed is the justification of absolute, unadulterated, selfishness, and so we must go on rolling the stone up the hill even though it is almost certain that it will roll down again and perhaps crush us. I do not think that your practical objections to public work of the kind I suggest are conclusive.

And here he went on to reveal his cynical accomplishment as a statesman:

> It will remove one great danger; viz. that public sentiment should go wholly to the unemployed and render impossible that State sternness to which you and I equally attach importance. By offering reasonable work, even at the lowest wage, to the really industrious, we may secure the power of being very strict with the loafer and the confirmed pauper.[149]

Accordingly, Chamberlain disregarded Beatrice's counsel and issued a circular concerning municipal relief works. The President of the Local Government Board took as his major premise that it was

> not desirable that the working classes should be familiarised with Poor Law Relief … The spirit of independence which leads so many of the working-classes to make great personal sacrifices rather than incur the stigma of pauperism is one which deserves the greatest sympathy and respect, and which it is the duty and interest of the community to maintain by all the means at its disposal.[150]

The local authorities must supply relief work under two conditions. First, the men employed should be engaged on the commendation of the Guardians as persons it would be inappropriate to send to the workhouse because of their previous good character and respectable circumstances. Second, the wages paid would not constitute relief and would not be associated with disenfranchisement, but they should be something less than ordinary wages paid for similar work. Thus, the strongest incentive was to be given to those so employed to return to their previous occupations at the earliest opportunity. This circular was a major innovation, in so far as it accepted public responsibility for the provision of employment in times of exceptional distress.[151] For the rest, its policy was close to that of the COS in requiring Guardians to show a new discrimination through what amounted to the casework approach. The dangers which Beatrice anticipated were hardly likely to arise. The only justification for her attitude was her correct perception that the East End labour market was in a state of chronic over-supply. In this part of London misery was permanent and not dependent upon a particular phase in the trade cycle.

Within months or so of his last letter to her, Chamberlain had broken with Gladstone on the Irish question. She went to the House of Commons to hear the magnificent debate, but she expressed no opinion on the merits of the contending forces. Having accepted Chamberlain's views that democracy and poverty were the questions of the age, she was not disposed to depart from that agenda because he chose to reorder it. Ireland became the ruling idea in British politics and the occasion for a far-reaching reconstruction of political parties, but Beatrice maintained the most complete silence on that subject. She was content to notice how Chamberlain 'won for himself the cheers of the higher class portion of the House' – he who had so recently been denounced as the 'English Robespierre'.[152]

Chamberlain had made an important and exceedingly complicated contribution to Beatrice's development. She had 'been humbled as far down as a woman can be humbled'.[153] Yet it seemed that it was her own intellectual independence and pride which was, in fact, responsible for her disappointed hopes. She had no wish to reject society, in items of either 'the simple happiness of a woman's life'[154] or social success; *she* had been rejected. But if she had not defied society, she had not diminished herself to suit its requirements. Chamberlain had drawn her away from intellectual pursuits and yet made her return to them with a new sense of urgency. She had been profoundly impressed by the manner in which he seemed to have brought the twin questions of democracy and poverty to the forefront of the public debate. She wished to share his ideals, but she could not fathom his 'principle'. Under his influence she had begun to question the doctrines of Spencer; but she could not bring herself to disregard Spencer's method.[155] She needed an alternative philosophical framework within which political action could be given rational justification and scientific authority. These were not Chamberlain's concerns. His life lay in political action informed with passion and instinct. This left Beatrice with a sense of unseemliness of the struggle for power. She distrusted his practices. She doubted whether his goals were capable of realisation.

*   *   *

The President of the Local Government Board was not alone in writing to the author of 'A Lady's View of the Unemployed at the East'. It will be recalled that Beatrice, referring to her work in co-operation with Ella Pycroft in the Katherine Buildings, began her article by describing herself as a rent-collector in dwellings 'designed and adapted to house the lowest class of the London poor'. In the dark winter of 1885-6 Beatrice may well have imagined that she would never see the tenants again. She would have to nurse her father and manage his business affairs. She would have to act as guardian to her younger sister, who was showing herself to be increasingly selfish, stupid and unbalanced.[156] Possibly she assumed that the tenants would not see her article. If so, she was mistaken. It was drawn to their attention and it aroused their bitter indignation.

During 1885 her relations with many of them had been less than happy. She did not want to have to follow the policy of Peabody and Octavia Hill and recruit as tenants only those who were respectable and in secure employment. She sought to fill the rooms while being as proud as Ella of reducing arrears of rent. But in the summer of 1885 she mishandled at least one of the 'roughs' or 'aborigines', having recourse to summary measures where softness would have paid better than hardness.[157] It was easy to see that the right rule of conduct was firmness in enforcing obligations combined with a patient gentleness in the manner of doing so, but it was difficult to apply in practice. The theory was that the respectable tenants would raise the level of the rest. In fact, the respectable kept rigidly to themselves. Sadly Beatrice concluded that this self-imposed isolation was 'the acme of social morality: the only creed one dare preach'.[158] A sweater and his wife, a Prussian Catholic, confirmed her view of the poor tenants as mostly members of a dissolute leisured class. These devout, hard-working sweaters were forced to go into the pubs to round up their workers. They were rewarded with bad work, cadging and thieving. The terrible irony of the 'pub' was that it tended to destroy the fittest and to spare the meanest natures.[159] In the buildings the boys and girls congregated in the water closets on the landings, while for the adults there was no other social centre but the 'pub'. 'A woman, diseased with drink, came up screaming to me; in her hand the quart pot; her face directed to the "public". What could I say? Why dissuade her? She is halfway to death – let her go – if death ends all.'[160] Beatrice had toyed with the idea of trying to get the tenants to run the buildings themselves on co-operative lines. But it was unimaginable that the spirit of the Bacup could be introduced into the Katherine Buildings. 'How can one help these people if they are not worthy of life from an economic point of view?'[161]

However, in February 1886, against the background of the rioting, which had placed the West End in the hands of the 'mob', Beatrice began to receive reports from Ella Pycroft of a new spirit among the tenants:

It has been a very exciting week at the Buildings, there was a regular mutiny last Tuesday at a concert; they (the men) sang songs I very much disapproved of and Mr Aarons brought forward a friend to sing and dance although Mr Paul and I had distinctly said we would not have it. My black looks stopped the man and Aarons went off to the back of the room in a huff, leaving me to announce the next song. Then Elliott came forward to sing (to help me out of my difficulty I thought) but he made a speech most insolently finding fault with my conduct and I had to answer him and assert my authority; and then Aarons appealed to the people to know if he hadn't succeeded in amusing them and all the low set applauded him. It was horrid. I talked to the two men after the concert was over and said we were not going to quarrel, but such a thing must never happen again and that I should talk to them another time. And then I went away with my friend Miss Black, the only lady who was there, and got hissed by the rough set as we went out … they must never have a loose rein again. It has been all my fault for trusting them too much.[162]

Ella went on to report that every room but one in the Buildings was occupied, but the directors showed no gratitude for her reports. One of their respectable tenants, a 'preferable' on the docks, had offered others work, but Mr Gibbs was too lazy to get out of bed to go to it, which just showed how long it took to find the truth about people: 'if a man is constantly out of work it is generally his own fault'. As for the Tripconys and Mrs Sullivan, they would sooner or later have to be evicted just as Beatrice herself had evicted two women for leading a low life.[163] 'Mrs Sullivan was lent money to start old clothes work and it strikes me she has spent it mostly otherwise. She has been ill so it has been a great temptation, but I should have expected her to be more honest.' It was all so much easier for Miss Octavia Hill who had a more respectable type of tenant and ran only £1 arrears on a £12 rental and was able to make it a condition of allowing arrears during a first illness that the tenant should join a club or savings bank on recovery.

In her next letter Ella described the reception of the article in the *Pall Mall Gazette*. She herself thought its conclusions were correct, but 'if you were in the midst of the excitement about this dreadful relief fund, you would have written even more strongly against extra relief.'[164] Maurice Paul saw that one boy read it to the others and great discussion followed:

The excitement amongst our men à propos of socialism, relief works and funds and the eight-hour movement is intense. The talk is of nothing else in the Club room. When we abuse the relief fund and relief works in general and point out the evil that must ensue the men can't help seeing it and agreeing with us, but they come back always to saying 'something must be done'.

Nagle senior was the first to apply for relief at the Mansion House, and, much against my will, I had to say that his story was true. Now numbers are applying. Canon Bradby has to distribute some of the money. At first I said I'd tell him nothing about the people or help the fund in any way, but he simply told me I must … We are going to get the papers of the Social Democratic Federation to read up the question of the day … to take down to the club for the men's benefit. They are all fair traders. I don't think they'd read any book that gave them much trouble though they are so excited about such subjects … I feel as if a big pan, too heavy to lift, were on the point of boiling over and I was hunting in vain for something cold to put in it and stop it; perhaps the necessary something may be found yet, or the fire may go out. I wish you were here. How you would enjoy arguing with the men.[165]

The men were not prepared to wait for the pleasure of Miss Potter's company. A week later Ella wrote further:

Aarons was busily inditing a letter to you last night, so I hope you will receive it in time to send a reply by Monday. Mr Paul says he has told you all the commotion your letter has made, and that you doubted our wisdom in showing the paper to the tenants [but] after all, the results would have been much worse if we had not shown it and they had chanced to find it for themselves. It is satisfactory that they all agree with your opinion as to relief works; and also that there are at least three people who, having read the article dispassionately, understand it and agree with it all. The three are Elliott, Buckley and Lyons.

It would perhaps have been better if we had kept the paper back till we could read it to them and talk over it then and there. It would have prevented the spread of false reports which I have had to contradict all over the Buildings. But, on the other hand, the excitement produced by their misunderstanding your words has made them think over things and acknowledge a few wholesome truths. Aarons was specially angry at your saying the Buildings were 'designed and adapted' for the lowest class of workmen; partly because he will take 'low' to mean 'disreputable'; and partly because he shares our feelings about the construction of the Buildings. But I told him you did not mean to express approval of their construction, but on the contrary had written so strongly against it to Mr Bond that the plans for the new block had been altered.[166]

Aarons wrote:

Having read your article in the *PMG* and given it due attention and study, I would venture to point out some errors, likewise some passages that we do not concur with. Before I proceed with this subject we would pay all due deference to the views most ably expressed by you with regard to metropolitan relief works,[167] which I consider to be the main point in your article, but – in dealing with the characteristics of a people – we cannot observe too much caution in our remarks. In sharing the opinion of many others, permit me to add, that I believe you have the best and kindest of intentions in conjunction with the welfare of the poorer working classes. Tis' an unfortunate fact but the most illiterate mind is too apt to misconstrue *that* which it does not readily and easily perceive, the sequel is it jumps at too hasty conclusions. Such is the case with your article: for, since its publication, it has caused much discontent among us here. We have argued different points over and concluded that you have erred in different respects. There are some passages too which we think require a more definite explanation and which I will make it my duty to point out so that if you will kindly explain these points to our general satisfaction we shall only be too happy to re-establish the good feeling that has hitherto existed among us here towards you.

In the first place you observe, or rather I should say you use this observation, 'I am a rent collector in a large block of working class dwellings, situated near the London Docks, *designed* and *adapted* to house the lowest class of working poor.' That they are most disgracefully constructed I am prepared to show.

Let us first of all look to the sanitary arrangements here, and although the subject is of a somewhat delicate nature, yet the consequences arising from the bad construction and mismanagement thereof are too serious and evil to pass lightly over. It is true that people of both sexes come in too close contact: nothing more than a thin wooden partition separates the male from the female, so that it invariably follows that should two people of opposite sexes occupy their different sections at one time they must become cognisant of the fact. That horrible vulgarity and wretched depravity have ensued on this very account my own wife and child can testify. You are at liberty to question them on the point if you choose. I would therefore venture to observe that the mode of construction of these places, have [*sic*] not a tendency to improve the condition or impart a finer tone of morality to a people they were *designed and adapted* for, and the sooner some remedy is suggested and acted upon to remove this prevailing evil, the better for all those immediately concerned.

Now turn we to house accommodation. I do not wish to enter too minutely into details, but what I wish to imply is we are not accommodated with even the common and proper facilities for enabling us to keep our homes in common and proper order. Now what is most practically necessary here to those who have a desire to live in cleanliness is a cupboard: 'the thousand and one little sundries', if I may be allowed to use the term, which are indispensable in a home, must be stowed away under the bedstead or hidden in obscure corners. By those who have no regard for even this poor apology for tidiness, they may be found strewn and scattered upon the floor in all directions. Can people possibly be expected or prevailed upon to keep their homes in proper order while this state of things exists?

There are still a number of discomforts experienced here and felt just as keenly as those I have attempted to describe. For instance, smelly and defective chimneys; draught pouring in from doors and windows (from which understandable sickness has arisen) but above all the horrible stench that arises from the closets (and particularly experienced by the tenants who occupy the double rooms when the so-called system of flushing does not act. When the drainage pipes have been stopped the water has to be cut off or the closets would over-flow). No one passing by the building could fail to notice this nauseous smell all last Summer and how it escaped the attention of the sanitary inspectors I am at a loss to understand. Perhaps nothing but an outbreak of Cholera here next Summer will open the eyes of our directors to the serious consequences which would inevitably await them. In concluding this important subject allow me to observe that there are two important facts laid bare viz that in the construction of these buildings great mismanagement and inexperience has been displayed or an utter disregard and contempt for the virtue, morality, cleanliness, health and comfort of a large body of people, namely the poorer working classes. Having pointed out these facts, the stern duty of the directors is plain. Let them therefore come forward and show their willingness *to act* ere our health becomes endangered and even our children become demoralised and corrupted. Having given you my views upon the subject, let me beg you to accept and frankly acknowledge that the words *designed and adapted* are wholly out of place and too hastily written.[168]

Maurice Paul and Ella Pycroft approved the terms of Beatrice's reply and read it to the men:

I don't know that they quite understood it all [remarked Ella], very few of them would be likely to acknowledge that brain-workers were not, many of them, idlers. I suspect they put you down as one and Mr Paul has had to argue hard to convince the boys that he is not one. I don't know what their opinion of me is – perhaps carrying a bag and putting down figures in rent books may be looked upon as some slight work, but of course they would think it much easier to do than hauling about casks in the dockyard … I was a little sorry that you said your letter was to be destroyed. If it had been left in the room for a day after having been read to the men, I think its 'educational influence' would have been greater. But it was accepted as a peace offering and that was the great point.[169]

In fact, Beatrice did not return to the buildings for any length of time until the late summer of 1886. By then she was persuaded that they had been an 'utter failure'.[170] In arriving at this conclusion she was ignoring the financial aspect. Ella and her co-workers thought 'it would be dreadful if one failed to make the Buildings pay enough percentage.' Thanks to their heroic efforts, the directors had no cause for dissatisfaction on this score. The rents for the 281 separate rooms amounted to £934 at the half year ending in June 1886. Arrears at £31 were less than the weekly collection and bad debts amounted to £8.15s. 6d.[171] Ella thought these results quite good enough to justify putting in some shelves upon which the tenants might place their saucepans and kettles. But the directors were slow to appreciate the efforts of their rent-collectors and displayed a large ignorance of the realities of working-class life. If 10 or 20 tenants out of 200 came home drunk on Saturday night, they were apt to think that there was need for greater sternness and for more evictions.[172] They were ready enough to pay for a warden to arm himself with a bullseye and prowl about at night driving vagrants from the landings, but they had no suggestions to make about rooms in which the bugs were so numerous that they could not be cleared out by sulphur.

Discipline was a great difficulty and it sometimes required considerable courage to impose it:

> Saturdays are always trying days in the Buildings and today I was pursued and bullied by two people on whose goods I had made the broker levy a distraint, till I didn't know whether I weren't the brute they seemed to think me. I think in one case I was. I had carelessly forgotten to say that the bed wasn't to be seized.[173]

On another day:

> I had to give so many notices for quarrelling and to refuse to listen to so many appeals. The Fishers are gone at last and Mrs Fisher is [such] a good-hearted woman in spite of her rowdiness that I hated giving her notice. Her husband burnt the notice before my eyes and they shouted at me until I was really frightened, but we parted the best of friends, poor things.[174]

But far worse than the ordeal of having to 'county court' bad tenants for every penny they owed was the consciousness of the hopelessness of help. Injury or sickness was frequently the cause of the most pitiful destitution:

> I am trying to bolster up a woman in Katherine Buildings who has been half-starved and she will come back from a Convalescent Home (to which she is going) pretty strong and then it will begin all over again

and I know (or think I do) that if I had left her to die, it would have been shorter misery for her. And I half feel that I am doing wrong to help her and yet I couldn't help it. I wonder if in the next generation people will be strong enough to crush their compassionate feelings and act wisely?[175]

In the view of Pycroft, when men got compensation for accidents at work it did them no good. She reported the case of Mr Downs, a steady fellow, who got his ribs and collarbone broken at the docks. Being paid £60 compensation ruined him. For while he banked half of it and paid his debts, he left home on Monday morning in a temper leaving his wife with four shillings – her own earnings and her boy's. He had a pension of £4 a year, which he received for having served 21 years and 125 days in the army. Bradlaugh and Labouchere taught him that it was at the beginning of and end of all injustice that he should get so little when the cowardly officers who had failed in action during the Crimean War had honours heaped upon them. He declared he did not care how little he got so long as they got nothing. Miss Pycroft feared for his sanity.[176] But she also feared for others who received no compensation and no pensions. Thus, Mr Sherman was run over by a cart and his hand was so badly damaged that he could not work. Since he could not pay his rent, she had to tell him that he must go into the Infirmary:

> But the tears ran down his cheeks at the thought. The one thing he has is his liberty to sit in his room or hobble to the balcony. He said that he might as well drown himself and for the first time in my life I thought that suicide might be justifiable.[177]

Beatrice paid Mr Sherman's rent.[178] She was also the largest subscriber to the boys' club, which was run by Maurice Paul. Maurice Paul considered that 'hardness' was the chief of all the virtues, but when he thought no one was looking he helped Mr Elliott to pay his arrears.[179] Ella Pycroft believed socialists contradicted each other and themselves and was quite sodden with the truths of political economy. But she knew that a woman would rather starve on a pinch of tea in her own teapot – even if the spout were off – than endure quasi-military discipline in some heartless institution.[180]

*   *   *

Beatrice had never intended to devote her life to rent collection. At dinner with the Barnetts she dared to quarrel with the redoubtable Octavia Hill when that lady suggested it was work that mattered and there was no need to conduct a systematic enquiry into where tenants came from, how much they earned, or why they left or got evicted.[181] Barnett was much more sympathetic to Beatrice's position. He warmly approved and endorsed the spirit of her contribution to the *Pall Mall Gazette*:

> By bold advertisement [he told her], the rich proclaim £60,000 to be given away. The poor loafers who think themselves hardly treated coming up from the country. (The Common Lodging Houses have filled and the Casual Wards in London have emptied). The dissolute and the idle crowd into the offices opened for relief. At Whitechapel I never saw a sadder group; sad not only because the men and women were thin and ragged, but because they were dissolute, vacant, and full of bitterness. The Police said many were known … and their talk was low and brutal. Threats to break windows were considered and the lowest morality was boasted of. In Bethnal Green the rush has been so great that many police have been employed and fights are common.

He urged her to write more about the chief effects of the Mansion House Fund. At the same time, he advised her that it was necessary to go beyond COS orthodoxy. The poor might live on third-rate food, but they could not survive on third-rate medical attention.[182]

Beatrice resolved to use such time as could be spared from caring for her father for study. It was necessary to discover the facts and it was imperative to clear one's head with respect to theory. Accordingly, she joined the board of Charles Booth's statistical research unit. Booth was a cousin. She had been seeing more and more of Booth and his wife and – despite his rather smelly house – affection and respect was growing on both sides. Booth was imbued with the tradition of provincial statistical societies that had long been engaged in the collection and enumeration of social and economic facts. He had the moral earnestness of the professional men who built the recently defunct National Association for the Promotion of Social Science.[183] Under the stimulus of distress, unemployed riots and socialist agitation, he was bent on conducting an exhaustive enquiry into the extent and nature of poverty in London. Along with Beatrice he recruited Maurice Paul, Benjamin Jones, 'Secretary of the Working Men's Co-operative Society', and a trade union secretary named Radley. He subsequently secured the help of other friends, including Canon Barnett, 'a queer, ugly little man, with no attraction of body or manner – but with a *certain* power.'[184] Barnett was knowledgeable and dedicated, but like all the other members of the board he could offer her no satisfactory house of theory. Beatrice was contemptuous of his shallow theology. As for Booth himself, he had positivist sympathies, but for the rest saw the great primary intellectual duty to be the discovery of the facts, their exhaustive enumeration and the expression of conclusions which were to take the form of statistical series.

If Beatrice was apprenticed to anyone it was Booth. She thought of him as the boldest pioneer of the methodology of the social sciences in the nineteenth century.[185] Mayhew's *London Labour and the London Poor* was 'good material spoilt by bad dressing. It is a mine of information – both of personal observation and of statistical enquiry – but there is no opening to it nor any destination reached.'[186] Following a suggestion made by Joseph Chamberlain, Booth used school attendance officers to help him build up a picture of East End life house by house. These reports were then subjected to a process of cross-verification by testing them against census enumerators' returns and information supplied by the Charity Organisation Society and by other bodies. It was, indeed, a Herculean effort carried through without benefit of sampling techniques. Beatrice was the only founding member of Booth's team who was still associated with him when the first volume of findings appeared in 1889. She played little part in the accumulation of the statistics through the interviewing programme, but it impressed her as being one of the indispensable elements in the new social science. The other was personal observation, and in the next three years it was with this task that she was most concerned. But before she could undertake it she felt a need to settle theoretical accounts: a need which she felt much more strongly than Booth himself. They were agreed that the defenders of *laissez-faire* sheltered from facts behind their assumptions, while interventionists tended to get the facts out of proportion and fall victim (so they thought) to the fallacy of selective instances. Yet it was Beatrice who felt most keenly the gap between Grand Theory and mindless empiricism. She grasped more readily than he the force of Darwin's great maxim that one cannot be a good observer without being an active theoriser.[187]

In the summer of 1886 she decided that it was imperative for her to come to grips with 'economical science'. Her response to Chamberlain's proposal for public works revealed the extent to which her thought was imbued with the spirit and conclusions of vulgar political economy. She found the subject to be

> hateful – the most hateful drudgery. Still, it is evident to me I *must* master it and, what is more, I must master the *growth* of it – for each fresh development corresponded with some unconscious observation of the leading features of the contemporary industrial life.[188]

Fortunately, this back-breaking task did not take as long as might have been anticipated. Within a week or two she found that she had 'broken the back of economical science so far as I want it'.[189] In short, she had liberated herself from it rather than mastered it – which is not to diminish or disparage her accomplishment. If economics was not a subject to be deep-searched with such saucy looks, they might yet be sufficient to detect that it was an impostor when it presented itself as if it were a code of morals and good government. The influence of Comte and his English followers was evident. She followed the Master in making an exception of Adam Smith. Comte had put him in his Calendar of Great Men and correctly perceived that he was a moral philosopher who did moral philosophy openly and intelligently and not covertly and badly as so many of his successors had done. Smith did not rely upon a diminished and deformed conception of human nature described as economic man. He did not abstract economic activity from all the surrounding areas of life. He had the historical sense. Beatrice's self-imposed 'drudgery' led her to recover these conclusions and allowed her a sense of making them her own. 'The generalisations upon which he [Adam Smith] based his reasoning were wider and were drawn more from direct observation than from an *à priori* idea of man made up on unconscious generalisation of one type of man, the city man, only.'[190] Ricardo and Marx were, she thought, mistaken in assuming that the acquisitive instinct was equally present in all men. Reserving Marx for subsequent consideration, she presented herself with a good 'Marxist' question: if

> the political economy of Adam Smith was the scientific expression of the impassioned crusade of the eighteenth century against class tyranny and the oppression of the Many by the Few; by what silent revolution of events, by what unconscious transformation of thought, did it change itself into the Employers' Gospel of the nineteenth century?

She tried to express her conclusions in two papers which she hoped might find their way to publication: the first was on the Rise and Progress of English Economics; the second – which was not written until the winter – was on Karl Marx's *Capital*. With neither of them did she achieve much public success. Booth told her that the first ought to be put away in a drawer and allowed to mature whilst Spencer and Courtney protested against it very vigorously. Beatrice had objected to the economists' habit of dismissing unemployment or other blemishes on the market mechanisms as 'frictions'. Spencer told her that the economists ought not to be reproached. Characteristically he made his objection through an argument by analogy which depended upon a rigid departmentalisation of thought. Economics was compared to physiology. 'Physiology formulates the laws of the bodily functions in a state of health, and absolutely ignores pathology.' How ridiculous it would be if we tried to readjust physiology to adapt it to pathological states!

> Just so it is with the account of the normal relations of industrial actions constituting political economy properly so-called. No account can be

taken by it of disorder among these actions, or impediments to them ... And moreover, if these pathological states are due to the traversing of free competition and free contract which political economy assumes, the course of treatment is not the readjustment of the principles of political economy, but the establishment as far as possible of free competition and free contract. If, as I understand you, you would so modify politico-economical principles as to take practical cognisance of pathological states, [then] you would simply organise pathological states, and things would go from bad to worse.[191]

Beatrice now saw through this sophistry. Spencer's letter showed that he had 'no historical sense'. As a matter of historical fact physiology had grown out of the study of life in all its manifestations including disease and death. Second, she had no intention of prescribing a course of treatment. She was pointing to the limitations of a mode of thought that might explain some phenomena but could not explain others. Finally, she detected the question-begging way in which Spencer identified 'health' with the normal functioning of a capitalist economy. 'The object of science is to discover what is; not to tell us according to some social ideal what ought to be.'[192]

But while she was breaking free from the hold of vulgar political economy, Beatrice was not prepared to embrace Marx. She came to the conclusion that the labour theory of value was radically defective. Marx reduced all labour to manual labour. He utterly failed to recognise the importance of people like her father who exercised crucially important judgements: whose hunches and intuitions about what to produce when and where were as vital to the satisfaction of social needs as were the physical efforts of labourers. It was hopelessly one-sided to think of exchange value being determined solely by the amount of socially necessary labour time incorporated in a commodity. She made out of Marx's concept of commodity fetishism, not a critique of capitalism, but a critique of Marx. 'In the weird Marxist world' – not at all recognisably the world of Richard Potter –

> whilst men are automata, commodities have souls; money is incarnated life, and capital has a life process of its own! The idea of an 'automaton owner', thus making profit without even being conscious of the existence of any desire to be satisfied, is, to any one who has lived within financial or industrial undertakings, in its glaring discrepancy with facts, nothing less than grotesque.[193]

Thus, Marx's concepts of the objective laws of capitalist development were falsified for Beatrice when put to the test of subjective experience: the experience of a class, which was defined for her by its power of command.[194] And this was occurring just at the time when her objective experience of East End life was encouraging her to question the subjectivity of the 'old philosopher'. But what had she to put in the place of the discarded constructions of rival theoreticians? At first sight, little beyond the linguistic innovations which inexperienced, impatient and ambitious students have always been ready to pass off as original discoveries. Exchange value, so she suggested, was to be understood as the product of 'faculty' on the one side and 'desire' on the other. Even as a mere exchange for the term 'supply' and 'demand', this appeared to be of doubtful originality since Booth employed this language.[195] Yet Beatrice's proposal for amending the vocabulary of economics ought not to be dismissed too quickly as being nothing but an attempt at innovation, pretentious in its intention and awkward in result.

'Supply' and 'demand', it may be conjectured, suggested to her the presence of inhuman agencies tending to find equilibrium in a stationary state. The terms 'faculty' and 'desire' constantly reminded one that economics should be about human attributes and behaviour in the context of the confusion of human nature and not in isolation or detachment from it. 'Faculty' might have a history as 'supply' could not: 'desire' was a far richer concept than 'demand' and much more could be said about it than it was 'fickle' or 'fluctuating'. Thus, to talk in terms of 'faculty' and 'desire' was to open one's mind to the observation of the real changes which they underwent in the life of social institutions, while 'supply' and 'demand' invited one to engage in a priori reasoning. With 'faculty' and 'desire' one comes upon questions to be investigated; with 'supply' and 'demand' as one's analytic tools the conclusions reached in advance of the enquiry: they offer explanations of what must be the case whether it is the case or not. Thus, it follows from the law of supply and demand that labour goes where it is best paid. But Beatrice knew, as a matter of direct observations, that labour often stayed where it was worst paid. With the demoralised casual labourer who was physically and spiritually unfit for work it made more sense to refer to the economic faculty being 'intermittent' than to remark that their labour was over-supplied. Whereas 'supply' and 'demand' suggested the presence of a self-correcting mechanism; 'faculty' and 'desire' allowed for the possibility that the former might deteriorate into an 'intermittent state' while the latter, being satisfied without the obligation to work, ceased to generate activity and became wholly parasitic.

However muddled and incomplete her observations were about political economy, she had the sense of being released as a social observer free to investigate without coming upon foredoomed conclusions.

She was not about to be seriously discouraged by the suggestions of Booth, or Willie Cripps or Leonard Courtney or E.S. Beesly, that her conclusions about Karl Marx or about 'economical science' were jejune or mistaken.[196] She felt that she had released herself from submission to iron laws and that she might proceed upon her career as social investigator with a new freedom. In October she went to Bacup where her 'dear Lancashire folk' were not even as far along the road to emancipation from the conventional wisdom as she was. All the men she met took 'little or no interest in politics (they have no votes), their thoughts (are) set on getting on in this world and the next; their conversation consisted chiefly of personalities and religion.'[197] In contrast to the men and women of the East End of London, they seemed to live a life of well-earned, well-paid work in which a tendency to suffer excessive overtime seemed to be the only serious problem. In the East End, she asked,

> where is the wish for better things in the myriads of beings hurrying along the streets night and day? Even their careless sensual laugh, the coarse jokes and unloving words, depress one as one presses through the crowd and almost shudders to touch them. It is not so much the actual vice, it is the low level of monotonous and yet excited life – the regular recurrence of street sensations in quarrels and fights, the greedy street bargaining, and the petty theft and gambling.[198]

Benjamin Jones blamed the dock employers for paying them so badly; Beatrice blamed them for paying them at all.[199] But this apparent hardness and a continual tendency to return to the old, rigid attitudes of the COS were becoming mixed with a deeper and more rounded concept of East End life. Thus these 'hereditary casuals' who might not be fit to live (economically speaking) had their own splendid qualities even if they were not the same as the workmen of Bacup. So they lived on stimulants and tobacco varied with bread and tea and salt fish, hated regular employment and lived for gambling and other paltry excitements. Yet, if they were late risers, they were also

> sharp-witted talkers, and, above all, they have that agreeable tolerance for their own and each other's vices which seems characteristic of a purely leisure class, whether it lies at the top or the bottom of society. But if we compare them with their brothers and sisters in the London Club and West-End drawing-room we must admit that in one respect they are strikingly superior. The stern reality of ever-pressing starvation draws all together. Communism is a necessity of their life; they share all with one another, and as a class they are quixotically generous. It is this virtue and the courage with which they face privation that lend a charm to life among them.[200]

In the spring and summer of 1887 Beatrice was enjoying an increasingly wide range of acquaintances – from Huxley, a 'broken down old lion',[201] to Stephen Sim, the stevedores' secretary.[202] From Arthur Balfour, saying 'cynical and clever things that are meant to be cleverer than they turn out to be',[203] to Mr Hoffman, foreman in a shoe factory, student of the sweating system and a Methodist preacher ever ready to denounce the wicked indifference of the rich.[204] She felt that she was daily learning more and more and she had an encouraging sense of her own increasing powers. She felt an increasing security and happiness in her friendship with the Booths, the Barnetts, Ella Pycroft, Maggie Harkness, Bella Fisher and Carry Darling.[205] But she could not bring herself to break altogether with the Chamberlain connection and maintained friendly relations with his daughter and sister. In May 1887 he wrote to her remarking that he had breakfasted with Booth and wanted to know what had to be done about the East End. Charity was hardly imaginable on a sufficient scale:

> State employment would give rise to every form of jobbing and extravagance and would interfere with business and private enterprise. Emigration is quite unsuitable to the class most in need of relief. I do not see my way at all and yet I fear that the problem may at any moment be forced upon us in an acute form and while we are still quite unprepared to deal with it.[206]

Since their correspondence in 1886 he had tried every means to renew the acquaintance. Six or seven times in the year she had refused his overtures.[207] Now she gave way. Before going to see him in Birmingham she spent a week in Brighton with Herbert Spencer, but her thoughts were elsewhere. She arrived in Birmingham in time to hear him address a meeting of his old supporters. 'And after he sat down it was natural our eyes should meet in the old way.'[208] Despite the fact that they had been moving in different directions since February 1886 and he now appeared as the guardian of law and order: despite the fact that he behaved towards her like 'the triumphant lover' – as a man who is sure of his conquest – she invited him to visit her father and herself. He came but it only served to add a week's unhappiness to the long chain of misery. Again feeling overrode dignity: she told him that she 'cared for him passionately'.[209] Having told him that, she desired that they should not see each other again. He appealed to her generosity:

> Why are we never to see each other again? Why can we not be friends – 'camarades' – to use your own expression? I like you very much – I respect and esteem you I enjoy your conversation and society and I have often wished that fate had thrown us more together. If you share this feeling to any extent why should we surrender a friendship which ought to be good for both of us?

I have so much confidence in your generosity as well as in your good sense that I am encouraged to make this appeal to you in what I feel to be a very delicate matter.

The circumstances of my past life have made me solitary and reserved, but it is hard that I should lose one of the few friends whose just opinions I value and the sense of close regard and sympathy would be a strength and support to me. I cannot say more. You must decide, and if it is for your happiness that we should henceforth be strangers I will make no complaint.

I return your letter, as you wish it, but there is surely no reason why you should be ashamed of feelings which are purely womanly and for which I have nothing but gratitude and respect.

I am always

Yours very sincerely
Joseph Chamberlain[210]

Beatrice tore out the pages of her diary for June to August 1887 and put them in an envelope along with this letter of Chamberlain's. She did not look at them again until May 1890. She caught herself gloating over his political setbacks as a heaven-sent vengeance on her deep humiliation – a humiliation which she accused him of glorying in and wishing to prolong. She was ashamed of these feelings. She tried to understand how she must have appeared to him:

> First, … as a self-opinionated person, too full of her own ideas to sympathise with his. At other times as an uncontrolled emotional woman – now refusing to see him, then expressing in naked written language the depth of her feeling. Naturally enough he was puzzled – dreading to be refused – frightened of being caught – and amazed by my perfect self-possession in conversation and argument. In short – whatever may have been his faults towards me – there were ample in myself to account for all the suffering I passed through. Can I be brave and sensible and once for all vow that I will forgive and forget?[211]

After the summer of 1887 there were no more emotional encounters between them. In the following year his engagement was announced to the daughter of the American Secretary of State for War. She gasped as if she had been stabbed.[212] She went to pray in the still, silent spaces of St Paul's. The week of his marriage was spent in a state of utter nervous collapse. Yet she saw with increasing clarity that there was something wrong with the political tone which could allow him to become 'the darling of aristocracy'. She was able to tell herself with growing assurance that the development of an important part of her personality would have been stopped or stunted had she married him. But she also came to take satisfaction in recording how men had found her attractive only to be dismissed by her with contemptuous indifference. Thus, when she saw that the eccentric anarchist, Auberon Herbert, was considering a proposal of marriage, she asked herself: 'Did I laugh or did I shudder?'[213] When Professor Edgeworth – fresh from dancing on Karl Marx's grave in the company of Sidney Webb[214] – showed her 'the furtive glance of unsatisfied desire', she remarked: 'Tiresome man. He misunderstands my characteristic frankness and takes it for encouragement to friendship.'[215] She recovered from the last disastrous meeting with Chamberlain by visiting the Booths. She had developed a close and intimate relation with Charlie, 'but without passion or the dawning of passion'.[216] Yet early in 1889 she noticed that: 'It would be strange if the close personal relationship between me and (Charlie) had not ended. Mary (Booth) has been generous – thoroughly generous – but for the last year the warm affection between us has been cooling.'[217] Mary tried to make up for it by signing her letters: 'Yours ever, with love and love again in good measure, pressed down and shaken together and running over.'[218] As Beatrice remarked, 'God knows celibacy is as painful to a woman (even from the physical standpoint) as it is to a man. It could not be more painful than it is to a woman.'[219]

4

From Social Investigator to Socialist 1885–90

'A Lady's View of the Unemployed at the East'—Its reception by the tenants, by Canon Barnett and by the President of the Local Government Board—Emancipation from political economy and rejection of Karl Marx - The firm of Paul, Potter and the work of Charles Booth—Evidence to the Lords Committee on Sweating—The pleasures of slumming and the duty of sternness—Beatrice's progress towards collectivism in practice and in recollection—Bertrand Russell's paradox and the divided self.

In her old age, Beatrice offered a tidy and persuasive account of how she came through social investigation to socialism. In her recollection it appeared as a smooth, logical progression. It began in her experience of East End life. It was this that led her to the recognition that the landlord and the capitalist must be made subject to all-pervasive control. Subsequently she saw that control was not enough: it was powerless to eliminate cyclic crises of capitalist production or to establish a 'national minimum' of civilised existence. Nor could any amount of regulation touch the morally debasing character of profit-making. Finally, it was the co-operative movement, with its 'production for use', which led her to perceive an alternative to modern business enterprise. Beatrice affirmed that this line of theoretic progress had been completed by 1890, but she did not attempt to date each successive phase.[1] The problem about her recollections is how far this 'order of thought' corresponded with the 'order of things' and in terms of what sort of time-scale.

'A Lady's View of the Unemployed at the East' gave no hint that she had embarked on this progression, for it was in perfect accord with COS orthodoxy. She was opposed to public works. She saw the main difficulty in terms of hordes of rustics being attracted into London by the prospect of sensual excitements and indiscriminate charity. She had nothing to offer but loving kindliness from individuals and sternness from the state. Admittedly she did show an historical sense not usually found in charity organisers. She drew attention to the decline of London's traditional industries and she pointed to what is called the 'vertical disintegration of production' which characterised the tailoring and furniture trades.[2]

She did not publish again until October of the following year. Yet despite the fact that she had by now studied the political economists and found them wanting, and spent much time talking to dockers and port employers, her position was still largely consistent with COS attitudes. She deplored the failure to find substitutes for traditional forms of social control. 'Respectability and culture have fled, the natural leaders of the working class have deserted their post; the lowest element sets the tone of East End existence.'[3] Heavy blame was still attached to those who – acting out of a combination of fear and stricken conscience – supplied indiscriminate charity. Yet she began to see that indiscriminate employment – the habit of the dock companies of offering work without reference to character – might be a yet more important consideration. Casual employment on the docks was identified as encouraging parasitism. It was not merely the failure to distinguish the 'deserving' from the 'undeserving poor', but the failure to attend to the distinction between the regularly and the casually employed which was responsible for so much suffering and demoralisation. By carefully noticing the difference between the permanent employees on the docks (the 'Royals' and the 'ticket' men) on the one side, and the mass of casuals plus the two thousand members of the really 'criminal class' on the other, Beatrice helped to break up the conventional view of dock life in which the 'dockers' were seen as the undifferentiated refuse of the labour market. Once her distinctions were recognised, the way was opened up to protecting those who were economically 'fit' by restricting competition from the 'unfit': the parasites who were 'eating the life out of the working class, demoralising and discrediting it'.[4]

In short, by the end of 1887 she was coming to see that the organisation of the labour market might be more important than the organisation of charity so far as dock workers were concerned. She blamed 'individualism run wild' and complained that everything was ordered for that 'spoilt child of the nineteenth century – the consumer'. She went on to argue that

> The only radical remedy is a kind of municipal socialism, which many of us would hesitate to adopt, and which in the case of the docks and the waterside would take the form of amalgamation under a Public Trust. This would facilitate a better organisation of trade and admit the dovetailing of business.[5]

This won for Miss Potter the affectionate regard and respect of the more advanced section of dock workers who were striving to build up trade union organisation. In November she attended a dockers' meeting addressed by Ben Tillett. Although she declined to speak herself – being nervous of doing so and thinking it unwomanly – she was cheered to the echo. She found Tillett well intentioned, but given to sensationalism and intellectually inadequate.[6] She had herself made it plain that experiments in municipal socialism were fit subjects for consideration rather than for immediate adoption.

Her article on dock life had concluded with the words: 'In short, if society is to be reconstructed on a socialistic basis, the workhouse of today will only foreshadow in the severity of its regulations the workhouse of the future.'[7] She assumed that the better organisation of the labour market would simply make the case of the demoralised and destitute workless worse than ever. For them, society could have nothing to offer but the bare necessities of existence supplied within the conditions of restraint. Beatrice could understand the temptation of the 'socialist' docker who could not resist pilfering tobacco before it was burned as 'undeclared' by Customs House officials.[8] Like Charles Booth,[9] she could enjoy the East End and respect the quick wits and the generous practical communism that lent a charm to life among the people there. But her sympathetic insight never extended to an indulgence when it came to work discipline. She would have had no patience with the docker who remarked: 'If you are made permanent you are made a white slave of directly; you are transferable from here to there and everywhere.'[10] From her standpoint that freedom could be secured only by perpetuating a process of deterioration, parasitism and decay. Accordingly, she had not placed herself outside the pale so far as the COS was concerned. Indeed, at the beginning of 1888 she wrote an article in the *Charity Organisation Review* in which she reiterated that the root of the trouble in the East End was not to be found in a system of employment nor in a method of trading, but in 'the mental and physical shortcomings of the human material'.[11]

However, she tried to persuade the COS that even if the shortcomings of the 'human material' were basic, the structure of the labour market was important. If a public trust might help in the docks then the growth of large-scale trading, as against small-scale, might do much to alleviate suffering in the tailoring trade. She had become a friend of John Burnett, sometime secretary of the engineering union and subsequently Labour Correspondent to the Board of Trade. She was impressed by his account of how the rise of the sewing machine had, allegedly, transformed the journeyman tailor.[12] 'Instead of a complete tailor, we have cutters, basters, machinists, fellers, buttonhole workers, and general workers, all brought to bear on the construction of a coat.'[13] She was ready to accept Burnett's definition of 'sweating' as an evil resulting from the excess and abuse of the 'contract system' under which work was let out by middlemen.

Direct experience of working in the sweatshops contributed to a revision of her opinions. She began learning how to 'sweat'. In April she settled at 56 Great Prescott Street to begin life as a working woman. She went off to a co-operative workroom to be taught how to finish a pair of trousers. Without really having mastered the art of 'besting' she went off trudging around the East End in search of employment.[14] It was no easy task to find it:

The sun's rays beat fiercely on the crowded alleys of the Jewish settlement: the air is moist from the heavy rains. An unsavoury steam rises from the downtrodden slime of the East End streets and mixes with the stronger odours of the fried fish, the decomposing vegetables, and the second-hand [sic] meat, which assert their presence to the eyes and nostrils of the passers-by.

For a brief interval the 'whirr' of the sewing machines and the muffled sound of the presser's iron have ceased. Machinists and pressers, well-clothed and decorated with heavy watch-chains; Jewish girls with flashy hats, full figures and large bustles; furtive-eyed Polish immigrants with their pallid faces and crouching forms; and here and there are poverty-stricken Christian women – all alike hurry to and from the midday meal; while the labour-masters, with their wives and daughters, sit or lounge about the house-door, and exchange notes on the incompetency of 'season hands', the low price of work, the blackmail of shop foremen; or else discuss the more agreeable topic of the last 'deal' in Petticoat Lane and the last venture on race-horses.[15]

Miss Potter, aping the manner and accent of a work-girl, enquires 'do you want a plain 'and?' She is embarrassed by the awkwardness of her own performance and rouses the suspicion and curiosity of her respondents. Eventually she finds employment at a shop run by a one-eyed Jewess at 198 Mile End Road. Her co-op training has not equipped her for the work of an unskilled trouser hand. A neat and respectable married woman sacrifices her own time (she is paid by the piece) to teach her the task. But respectability is not the keynote. The pressers use much foul language propositioning the younger girls around the table while the older women exchange gossip. One girl is said to have had three babies by her father and another has had one by her brother. Beatrice thinks that most of the girls are decent enough but 'full of enjoyment of low life and promiscuous courting':[16]

'I say, Milly' shouts one to the other, 'you can tell that bl—y brother of yours that I waits 'alf an 'our for 'im houtside the Paragon last night. I'll be blessed before I serves as 'is Round the Corner ag'in.'

The pale girl who sits beside Beatrice is a quick worker, but she can earn no more than one shilling a day. At the tea break she offers her neighbour some bread and butter:

'No thank you', I answer.
'Sure?' and without more to do she lays a thick slice in my lap and turns away to avoid my thanks. A little bit of human kindness that goes to the heart and brings tears into the eyes of the investigator.

After twelve hours in a sweatshop Beatrice went home:

'I'll be married in a week' are the last words I hear passing from Jo to Harry, 'and then my wife shall keep me.'
'I'll go to the bl—y workhouse', jokes Harry, 'if I don't get a gal to keep me. I won't sweat here any longer for 5s. a day.'[17]

Beatrice subsequently worked for a few hours at two other shops, but found them of no interest. When she was invited to give evidence before the Select Committee of the House of Lords which was enquiring into the sweating system she did so on the understanding that she would not be asked to speak on the basis of her own direct experience.

She appeared before the Committee on 11 May 1888. Her evidence showed that she had made a considerable advance from the position that she had adopted, under the influence of Burnett, five or six months earlier:

'How would you define the sweating system?' enquired the Earl of Dunraven from the Chair.
'I should say that an enquiry into the sweating system was practically an inquiry into all labour employed in manufacture which has escaped the regulations of the Factory Act and trades unions.'[18]

She explicitly repudiated the view that 'sweating' could be regarded as a consequence of the subcontracting method of trading, drawing attention to worse cases of sweating where there was no subcontract. In particular, she pointed to women out-workers who generally got less than those employed in the workshops. She held that the irresponsibility and bad work done meant that employers 'have to take it out in one way or another. There is an enormous number of goods spoilt and not brought in on time, and that sort of thing, so that the honest have to pay for the dishonest ...'
Thus, in May 1888 Beatrice had a useful analytical definition of sweating. It hardly prepared their Lordships for the descriptive and prescriptive parts of her evidence.

'Should we leave it all alone or not?'
'I really have not any opinion about it.'
'But do you not think that there is a very strong case for legislation?'
'Not in the tailoring trade.'[19]

There were two considerations that accounted for Beatrice's caution and agnosticism. First, she was persuaded that sentimentality and sensationalism had to be avoided at all costs. As in the case of the docks, so in the case of the tailoring trade: it was necessary to distinguish between the different types of work being done and the contrasting situation of different types of worker. She was anxious to discredit the view of the sweater as an all-powerful exploiter draining away the life-blood of the wage-earners. 'In the busy season', she explained, 'they [machinists and pressers] swear at their employers; in the slack season employers swear at them.'[20] She apparently left some members of the Select Committee with the sense that she was heartlessly minimising the amount of suffering. Lord Sandhurst remarked:

'We have had some very strong evidence on this Committee as to the exceptional poverty of the tailors and tailoresses; from what you have seen of them do you consider that they are a population in extremely miserable circumstances?'
'Not the Jewish section and not the coat trade.'
'But the gentile population?'
'Trouser, vest and juvenile suit makers are exceptionally poor.'
'Did you hear of any cases of starvation?'
'Not of actual starvation.'[21]

Earlier she had been asked:

'Do you think the coat makers are able to take care of themselves?'
'Yes, except as regards sanitation. In the lowest class of domestic workshop the standard of sanitation and over-crowding is very low; no doubt about it; but that is their particular taste.'
'You think they do not feel it?'
'I do not think they feel it very much.'[22]

But it was not only this *sang froid* attitude which stopped Beatrice calling for legislation. Having conceded that sanitary standards were low, she was asked: 'Do you think there would be any danger if better sanitation were insisted upon that it might raise the cost of producing these goods?' She replied that

'it would tend to drive the trade into the lower channels of home work, and that you would have that fringe, as I call it, of the women making a coat for 7d, getting bigger and bigger. I think if you touch anything you must take the whole thing, and deal with the home work too.'

'Your principal remedies or suggestions would be that the landlord should be made responsible, and that sanitation should be better looked after?'

'Yes, if you do anything. Of course, I think there is a good deal to be said for doing nothing; but if you do anything, I think you must extend the remedy over the area of the evil. You must not just take the top part of it and deal with that alone, and drive the trade into lower channels.'[23]

In retrospect Beatrice was profoundly distressed by the character of the evidence she gave to the Lords committee and by what she imagined to be the way in which it had been received by the press. Her Superior Person dismissal of the committee – it was 'not made of stuff fit for investigation' – swiftly gave way to a fear that she had misled it and that she had been detected by the *Pall Mall Gazette*.[24] Chamberlain's engagement had been placarded all over London at the end of April. She was suffering intensely and the thought that she had been found out as a liar made 'the laudanum bottle loom large as the dominant figure.'[25] According to the printed report she concluded her testimony in the following manner:

'How long have you been at work in the tailoring trade?'
'Three weeks inclusive of the training I got.'
'The whole time in one shop?'
'No I worked altogether in five shops, but I could not keep my place in the coat shops, for the reason that coat work is so very much more skilled than other work.'
'You worked the usual twelve hours a day?'
'Yes.'
'Besides that, you have had a large personal experience of the way work is carried on in people's homes?'
'Yes as a rent-collector.'[26]

In fact, she had told the Committee that she had worked in sweatshops for a longer period than three weeks. When she received the proof of her evidence she corrected her 'hasty exaggeration' by pretending that the mistake had not been made by her, but by the short-hand writer or the compositor.[27] But even this 'corrected' statement was still most misleading. She had worked the twelve-hour day on only two days running and over a much longer period than three *consecutive* weeks. It was not merely her incompetence that prevented her from working for longer periods: it 'would simply imply more mental and physical endurance than I possess'.[28] Had she made that confession to the Committee it might seriously have diminished the weight that was attached to her testimony. The opponents of the sweating system, whose 'hysterical' and 'sensational' statements she was anxious to discredit, would have been quick to point out that her experience supported their view that a sweatshop was 'unendurable'. Thus, she had not even got to the point where Herbert Spencer's caution was relevant. He advised her:

> Bear in mind ... that the experiences which you thus gain [by participant observation] are misleading experiences; for what you think and feel under such conditions are unlike what is felt and thought by those whose experiences you would describe.[29]

Tortured by her own conscience and terrified that she would be detected as a liar, Beatrice imagined that the press had found her out. In fact the *Pall Mall Gazette* did not question her veracity, but her competence and sensibility. However, it did so in exactly the terms that she would find most wounding. It mocked her as a 'lady amateur' and scorned her for suggesting that the victims of the sweating system were 'rather well off'.[30] Her friends advised her against making any response or explanation. Lord Thring assured her that the *Pall Mall Gazette* was not admitted into his house and that the Archbishop of Canterbury and all the other members of the select committee 'thought that you gave most valuable evidence in a ladylike and unassuming manner.'[31] Booth was particularly firm in advising her against drawing any further attention to the episode.[32]

Beatrice wisely took Booth's advice. She followed up her evidence with an article on East London labour. While maintaining her stance as the discriminating realist opposed to the undiscriminating sentimentalist, she broke new ground. Earnings were not, she insisted, uniformly low. Excluding the general hand of the domestic slop-shop whose earnings never exceeded one shilling and sixpence and frequently fell below one shilling for twelve hours' work, East End coat-making allowed a rate of four pence and a halfpenny per hour for males. Females received two pence and a halfpenny, while nine pence an hour and six pence an hour were high watermarks. The middleman – supposedly occupying a crucial exploitative position between the wholesaler and the retailer – was largely a myth. The Jew competed with the provincial factory workers, not with skilled English tradesmen working on the old traditional lines of one man, one garment. Moreover, the well-to-do sweaters ran workshops where physical conditions often compared favourably with those prevailing in the ordinary, provincial clothing factories. But 80 per cent of sweaters were small men. Big employers in London were handicapped by high rents, high costs of fuel and the irregularity of demand. This was good observation and it furnished support for the anti-socialist (or a-socialist) conclusion that it was exactly the absence of the capitalist employer, independent of and distinct from, the wholesale trader, able, to some extent, to resist the constant pressure of competing firms in the direction of cheap, intermittent, and low-class production that was the curse of the East End.[33] The multiplication of small masters was due to the ease of entry into the trade and the Jewish love of *profit* as distinct from other forms of money-earning.

Yet while she maintained much of the 'tough-minded' tone of her testimony to the Lords Committee, Beatrice began to offer a rather fuller account of sweating. To the committee she had identified it analytically; now she did so descriptively. Sweating meant over-crowded and insanitary workshops or living rooms; long and irregular hours; constantly falling prices and a comparatively low rate of wages for the mass of the workers. Its condition was – as she had said – the absence of regulation whether by trades unions or by the state. The soul of the sweater was not merely to be found in the ignorant consumer buying 'balloon coats' held together with soap; nor in the grinding wholesale slop trader; nor in the rack-renting landlord; but in the 'evil spirit of the age, unrestrained competition'.[34] She now paid warm tributes to the efforts of the trade unions. The solution must lie either in the restriction of the supply of labour or else in enforcing a higher standard of life among female, foreign and unskilled English workers through the extension of the Factory Acts or the Public Health Acts.[35]

In her last article of the 1880s, Beatrice turned her attention to the problem of Jewish immigration. As had become her habit, she prepared to write the piece through an extensive programme of meetings and interviews. She wrote:

> I feel uncomfortable every time I see these dear, kind Jews – they have been overwhelmingly kind to me; but I fear they will look upon my paper as an unwarranted attack upon the Jews; they will take all I say good of them as mere truism and will resent the rest.[36]

In fact, the main weight of her article was directed against such anti-Semitic slanderers as Arnold White, who painted a picture of the Jews as 'destitute foreigners' living in conditions which resembled 'those of animals'.[37] Beatrice thought that experience of Christian brutality and the virtue of training in the Talmud had made the Jews much superior to their Gentile neighbours in the East End. 'In the Jewish inhabitants of East London we see ... a race of brainworkers competing with a class of manual labourers.'[38] She saw that the Jewish Board of Guardians ought not to be confused with an English parochial body and that it was a vulgar prejudice to suppose that it performed analogous functions. The records of organised Jewry illustrated

> the skill, the tenacity, and, above all, the admirable temper with which our Hebrew fellow-countrymen have insinuated themselves into the life of the nations, without forsaking the faith of their forefathers or sacrificing as a community the purity of their race.

But while Beatrice saw that 'Jewish charity does not tend towards the demoralisation of individual recipients', she did believe – and rightly – that the Jewish Board of Guardians fostered 'the artificial multiplication of small masters.'[39] This was achieved by loans to men who had qualified themselves to become sweaters by working at starvation wages and for an enormous number of hours. In an earlier piece she had maintained that 'the strongest impelling motive of the Jewish race was the love of *profit* as distinct from other forms of money-earning'.[40] She now maintained that 'though possessed of many first class virtues, the immigrant Jew is deficient in that highest and latest development of human sentiment – social morality'. She did not mean to imply that they were anything other than law-abiding. Quite the contrary, but

> the Jew is quick to perceive that 'law and order' and the 'sanctity of contract' are the *sine qua non* of a full and free competition in the open market ... in the case of foreign Jews it is a competition unrestrained by the personal dignity of a definite standard of life, and unchecked by the social feelings of class loyalty and trade integrity.[41]

This judgement of 1889 points more definitely to Beatrice's rising faith in the capacity of the labour movement than to any prejudice against Jews. She never suggested that Jewish immigration was a major factor making for sweating. She thought that there was something distinctively Jewish in the division of labour in the tailoring trade, but she saw that this was competitive with provincial factory production rather than with the skilled English tailor making high-quality goods. She thought that the Jewish community in East London was progressive in that it was constantly sending out successful immigrants even while new fugitives from the pogroms came in. This flow of Jewish immigrants needs to be contrasted with the stagnant pool of unskilled female labour in which one found the most exploited and dispirited labourers in the East End. And the terrible but progressive experience of the Jew was associated with the permanent helpless and hopeless state of his Gentile neighbours. Rather like Marx himself, she saw in the Jew – or rather the immigrant Jew – the embodiment of the idea of capitalism.[42] He seemed

> to justify by his existence those strange assumptions which figured for
> *man* in the political economy of Ricardo – an always Enlightened
> Selfishness, seeking employment or profit with an absolute mobility of
> body and mind, without pride, without preference, without interests
> outside the struggle for the existence and welfare of the individual and
> the family. We see these assumptions verified in the Jewish inhabitants
> of Whitechapel; and in the Jewish East End Trades we may watch the
> prophetic deduction of the Hebrew economist actually fulfilled – in a
> perpetually recurring bare subsistence wage for the great majority of
> manual workers.[43]

The study of the Jewish community first appeared in Charles Booth's *Life and Labour* (1889). The volume also contained reprints of two earlier articles by Beatrice. Booth stressed the general community of view between himself and his contributors and called for 'limited socialism – a socialism which shall leave untouched the forces of individualism and the sources of wealth.'[44] Perhaps it was out of deference to this commitment to 'limited socialism' that Beatrice struck out from her piece on the dock workers the conclusion relating to the increased severity of workhouse regulations in a socialistic society. Sentimentalists and libertarians might have thought that a serious objection to socialism, although it is doubtful whether Beatrice or Booth would have thought so.[45] In the year in which she expressed that opinion Beatrice remarked that the Cornish Christians thought of individual suffering to be relieved rather than of the common good. 'And I maintain that *I* am the true socialist through my willingness to sacrifice the individual to the community.'[46]

There is no other evidence that she ever described herself or thought of herself as being a socialist in the 1880s. Her evidence to the Select Committee and her studies of East End dockers, tailors and Jews show how slow she was to advance towards socialism. She had indeed cautiously advocated the setting up of a public trust or board to regulate employment in the docks, but what she wanted to restrict was competition; she never argued that public ownership was preferable to private ownership *per se*. Despite the recollection of her old age which placed her recognition of the need for 'an all pervading control, in the interest of the community, of the economic activity of the landlord and the capitalist' in the 1880s it was not until May 1890 that she passed from opposition to such control, or from a halting agnosticism concerning its feasibility, to open and vigorous advocacy of it.

*   *   *

What was it that transformed her attitude between the time when she gave evidence to the Lords Committee and the presentation of its report? First, perhaps, the report itself, along with the preceding volumes of evidence: 'the whole staff of working factory inspectors, and the whole body of trade unionists examined by the Committee, recommended the extension of factory jurisdiction to the sanitation of all workshops.'[47]

Sanitation was exactly the matter about which Beatrice in May 1888 had been most ready to allow the need for legislative action. However, in June 1890 she dismissed with scorn a restriction of reform to this one subject. The noble lords proposed 'that for sanitary purposes all workshops (domestic and otherwise) should be treated as factories'. 'But why should we stop here?' asked Beatrice. Showing quite a new mastery of the Workshop and Factory Act of 1878 and the Public Health Act of 1875, she went on to propose detailed amendments of those measures together with changes in the Local Government Act, to achieve 'the tuning of these three great legislative instruments to one common note of strength and harmony'. If public opinion was not ripe for the socialist answer to the labour problem, then the employer had to be made responsible for the performance of his duty by legislative enactments reinforced by the pressure of public opinion and by trade unionism. Only thus could the 'hideous social evils known as the Sweating System' be rooted out.

Between the last of Beatrice's descriptive studies of East End life and this programmatic piece written in the spring of 1890 lay months of increasing involvement in the affairs of the labour movement. The editor of the *Nineteenth Century* had asked her for an article on co-operation. The subject had already occurred to her and she resisted the advice of Alfred Marshall and others to turn her attention to women's employment and leave co-operation to others better qualified in economic science.[48] She began the work in February 1889, after long talks with her most intimate working-class friends Burns, Benjamin Jones and J.J. Dent. She also went back to Bacup and other northern towns. At Hebden Bridge she stayed with the widow of an ironfounder and rejoiced in her 'true Yorkshire straightforwardness and cordiality'.[49] She saw many co-operators and attended their meetings. She also met a number of young men from Oxford and noted that they and the co-operative working-class people formed a mutual admiration society: 'common condemnation of the capitalist class and money-making brainworkers: a condemnation the form of which bordered precariously on cant, and was clearly the outcome of ignorance'. Yet after having spent six months in close association with the co-operators and their leaders at every level, having scrupulously observed what she took to be their strengths and their weaknesses, she could observe:

how inexpressibly ugly are the manners and ways of a typical middle-class man, brought up in the atmosphere of small [sic] profit-making [securing profit by] 'driving other chaps' – a phrase which represents in Howard Collins' mind the great world of invention and enterprise; for the small manufacturing and retailing tradesman's business is a matter of driving and 'doing' workers and customers. And experience of this class makes me wonder whether 'profit' is not on the whole a demoralising force, whether a system of standard salaries and standard wages, such as is being gradually evolved by joint-stock and co-operative enterprise, is not a higher form of industrial organisation? Should not the use of a man's faculties after he has received his maintenance be dedicated to society? [She had become well acquainted with the head of the immense Co-operative Wholesale Society, J.T.W. Mitchell, who lived in small lodgings in Rochdale on £150 a year.] Is not profit-making the sharing of unlawful gain? And are … not … the forces of public opinion and the natural evolution of industry tending in that way?

Some such conclusion I am coming to in my study of the Co-operative Movement. It seems to me to have been essentially a movement *not* towards the sharing of profits by workers, but towards an unconscious realisation of the socialist ideal of officially managed business on the basis of voluntary association.[50]

But co-operators were muddled about much. They did not know how to regulate their relations with the trade unions. This – together with the great dock strike of the summer of 1889 – increased Beatrice's interest in the whole world of labour. She had no first-hand acquaintance with the gas-workers or the match-girls who had led the first struggles of the new unions of the unskilled, but she was an authority on the docks. In the great struggle organised around the demand for 'the tanner' – that is, a basic wage of sixpence an hour – she found a new and astonishing evidence of the vitality and creativity of the organised working class. By the end of August she was becoming more and more excited by the success of John Burns and her old friend of two years back, Ben Tillett:

> Certainly the 'solidarity of labour' at the East End is a new thought to me … an extraordinary manifestation of practical sympathy, of effectual help, has been evolved among all classes at East London – skilled artisans making common cause with casuals.[51]

She thought that it proved the possibility of an 'organised Labour Party in London' which would have a powerful lever for 'working its own will'. Yet she feared that success would be as transient as in the great battles waged by the dockers in the early seventies: battles of which she had learned in long conversations with management and men during her investigations in 1887. But her own work in that year seemed irrelevant: 'the great instinctive movements of the mass are perhaps, after all, more likely to [have an] effect than the carefully reasoned judgements of the scientific (or pseudo-scientific?) observer.'[52]

It was in the midst of the dockers' struggle that she went off to the Trades Union Congress at Dundee. She had already had some slight experience of these large trade union gatherings and had noticed that the established labour leaders regarded the lower grades of workmen as almost as objectionable as the capitalist employers. At Dundee she soon made the acquaintance of the leaders of the 'old unionism', the chairman and the secretary of the Parliamentary Committee of the TUC:

> This morning, while I was breakfasting Shipton ... joined me. His view of the dock strike is strongly adverse to the men and is visibly biased by his antipathy to, I might almost say hatred, of Burns ... 'The way the strike was begun', he remarked, 'was illegitimate. No responsible leader of a Trade Union which had funds of its own to lose would treat employers in that fashion. Ben Tillett drew up a letter demanding certain concessions and sent it with a letter asserting that if these demands were not conceded by 12 o'clock that morning, the men would come out. Just fancy expecting a manager to decide a question of enormous financial importance without consulting his directors! Then Burns came on the scene with his intense desire for notoriety and his foreign ideas of the solidarity of labour which he is trying to foist on trade unionists. But it won't work. Each trade has its own interests and technicalities ... Look how the Knights of Labour have failed! That sort of thing is bound to break up in the end. Capital has only to sit still with folded hands. If the Dock companies stand out – if they are able to resist the other capitalist interests which are causing the strike to get their own way – if they can resist this pressure the whole combination will break down and the workers will dribble back.'

So spoke Shipton. Clearly, whatever might be his sympathy for dock labour his dislike of a socialist victory was the stronger feeling:

> Shipton is not an attractive man. Small, with a weasel-like body and uncertain manner; an uneasy contorted expression; grey eyes with an absolute lack of candour or frankness – with that curious film over them which usually denotes an 'irregular' life (he is a widower of some fifty years old who neglected his wife) deep furrows under the eyes and stretching from the nostrils round his mouth. A black beard, neatly trimmed – a general attempt at middle class smartness – completes the outward man ... I should imagine that in his heart of hearts he has little

sympathy with the workmen: that he prizes his position as an official for the power it brings.[53]

After breakfast with the chairman of the Parliamentary Committee, Beatrice took luncheon two days later with its secretary, the formidable Henry Broadhurst MP, the first workman to secure office in a government and the *bête noir* of Keir Hardie and the socialists. She smoked a cigarette with him steady in the belief that the cigarette would be 'the wand' with which the woman of the future would wield influence over men.[54] What ever influence the cigarette may have had on Broadhurst's attitude towards her was as little compared with his relief on learning that she was an anti-suffrage woman, one of a number of distinguished ladies who had signed a piece in the *Nineteenth Century*. Broadhurst immediately thought that she must be sensible when he discovered she had signed a document declaring that the 'emancipating process has now reached the limits fixed by the physical constitution of women'. And that giving women the vote would only change them from sympathetic and disinterested creatures into hotter partisans than men.[55] Beatrice received his congratulations with a thankful-ness that was mingled with an unexpressed contempt. She saw that he was a 'middle-class philistine to the backbone; … his view of women is typical of all his other views: he lives in platitudes and commonplaces.'[56]

Yet these hard and accurate judgements of the leaders of the 'old' unions did not imply any uncritical or easy admiration of their rivals. The veterans like Shipton and Broadhurst were at least knowledgeable, which was more than could be said for many of the socialist leaders who indulged in dirty, personalised attacks which were full of envy and malice and showed a contempt and hatred for the facts. From her dear but unscrupulous friend, Maggie Harkness, Beatrice had formed the impres-sion that many of the socialists and new unionists were hirelings of the Tory caucus. For the rest, they were 'beardless enthusiasts and dream-ers of all ages and conditions'.[57] As for the socialist laird and MP, Cunninghame Graham, he was swiftly dismissed as a 'poseur', an 'enthu-siast' and an 'unmitigated fool'.[58] Indeed, at Dundee it was only John Burns who impressed her as a man of conscience and of will, but she sensed that he was destined to depart from the socialist camp. As she sailed down the river or sat at the head of the table at a reception, she con-cluded that most of the delegates were a 'fine-looking, able set of men', but with a great trust in the established leaders and a profound suspicion of the socialist parvenus.

In the following month the dockers carried off their 'brilliant victory' and in November she went to hear Tom Mann address a meeting of co-operators at Toynbee Hall. How much more impressive he was than the famous men of parliamentary Liberalism that she had come across in the last few months! Even when he was only groping after the facts, he compared favourably with John Morley – terrified of the socialist challenge in Newcastle, and talking about social questions without beginning to understand them.[59] Even when he was recklessly boasting that the workers could wring anything out of the dock directors, he seemed a man of purpose and of earnestness when put alongside Sir Edward Grey, who had confided to her how torn he was between his love of sport and his sense of public duty.[60] Beatrice was deeply impressed by Mann's assertion: 'Socialism means the co-operative organisation of industry when no one shall be outside. This was the ideal state towards which they were all striving. But so-called co-operation, like the trade unionism of the fossil unions, had denied this faith.' She noticed the contradiction that occurred as he went on to discuss the task before the dockers. She noticed it but she did not revel in it:

> We are determined [said he] to eliminate the riff-raff: the wretched wastrels that have disgraced the docks. The end of this week we close our books. We must be hard-hearted and clear-headed; it is no use gushing over the out o'works. We want men who grasp the problem, who see that if we are to raise the status of our members we must keep them with sufficient wages to provide food, to keep up their physical strength, with constant employment to prevent them from being loafers. The other men at the Dock Gates must 'clear off'; with us there is no room for them; no doubt there are other social movements to provide for them; but our movement is to eliminate them.[61]

Tom Mann impressed her, but only a month earlier she had projected collaboration with Auberon Herbert in writing an 'individualist' novel.[62]

For Beatrice, 1890 began with a further crisis in her father's health. She loved him, yet she found herself wishing for the release which would come with his death. While he lived he seemed to exile her from the triumphant upsurge of the new trade unionism which had made – whatever its limitations – the magnificent conquest of the docks. She retained her friendship with the representatives of the older trade unionism, but it was Tom Mann, Ben Tillett and John Burns who seemed to have evoked unsuspected forces beyond routines of store and chapel on the one hand, and the chaotic parasitism of a lost residuum on the other. Together with the philosophic spirit of Dent, the opportunism of Benjamin Jones, the marvellous business capacity of Mitchell, they seemed to be the harbingers of a new world of labour: makers of a labour movement full of dynamic possibilities. Then there were the able young men who had written *Fabian Essays*, who commanded respect and who might prove of first-rate importance once the surge forward of trade unionism had received its first check.[63] What with her brothers-in-law supplying her with an entrée into the life of established society, what with her privileged social position, she ought to have a unique opportunity to observe and, perhaps, to influence events. She heard now – more distinctly than before – the voices of the wrecks, the waifs and strays of civilisation echo off the walls of the luxurious homes of her relatives. Yet it was not these voices that made up the 'bitter cry' to which she had to harken. The cry she most attended to was that of brains, doomed to the treadmill of manual labour, asking for a career in which ability would lead; this – for her – was 'the bitter cry of the nineteenth century woman'.[64] It was the women and the workmen, as Comte had said it would be, but it summoned her beyond Positivism:

> And the whole seems a whirl of contending actions, aspirations and aims, out of which I dimly see the tendency towards a socialist community, in which there will be individual freedom and public property, instead of class slavery and private possession of the means of subsistence of the whole people. At last I am a socialist![65]

Miss Beatrice Potter first met Mr Sidney Webb in January 1890. It was not until after that meeting that she declared herself a socialist. It was not until after that meeting that she saw how the pervasive control of the landlord and the capitalist might be established in practice. Before then she had doubted whether it was either possible or desirable. Very sensibly, she had regarded 'half-measures' as likely to prove worse than useless. Yet this conviction that pervasive control was necessary was recalled as the starting-point of her journey towards socialism. Perhaps she had seen that 'whole measures' were desirable at a much earlier date, but, if so, she had not known how to devise them. As for the cyclic crises – which she remembered as the second item in her instruction – she had shown next to no appreciation of their reality since she was far too preoccupied with the problem of the chronic over-supply of labour in the London labour market to trouble about them. Her distaste for the acquisitive motive at the heart of capitalist production had been made more evident – but not much more. It was not getting rid of capitalists, but ending capitalist *competition*, which had been the distinguished preoccupation of her early writings. As for 'co-operative production for use' – as distinct from co-operative organisation for retail distribution – she may have shown more sympathy for it than her father had done; but she had no more confidence than he had in its ultimate success.

In short, her recollection of 'how I became a socialist' is better read as a persuasive statement of why her reader should become one than as a true record of her own progress. What stood between the pessimistic, *sang froid* testimony to the Lords Committee in May 1888 and the optimistic affirmations of February and June 1890 was the 'explosion' of the new unionism and the exceptional knowledge of administrative law and the extraordinary capacity for administrative innovation of Mr Sidney Webb.

*   *   *

Bertrand Russell once remarked that: 'If you set down a list of Beatrice's leading characteristics you would say – "What a dreadful woman!" But in fact she was very nice. I had a great liking and respect for her. I was always delighted by a chance of meeting her.'[66] Unfortunately he declined to enlarge upon this paradox or to attempt an explanation of it. When it was reported to others who had known and admired her, they felt confident that Russell was saying something shrewd but they were unable to explain what it was.[67]

Perhaps the 'Russell paradox' should be understood as a reference to the 'divided self': the nasty characteristics belonging to a 'false-self system' which concealed a second self which was nicer and 'more real' than the first.[68] Undoubtedly, Beatrice had a precarious sense of her own identity. She saw her early life in terms of a struggle 'to be herself'. For most of the time that struggle was regarded in quite a commonplace way: it was a matter of circumstances that were beyond her control. She was trapped between her duty to her father and her desire for an independent life. Her mother's death, her father's illness and her sisters' marriages left her with a duty that seemed to her undeniable and inescapable. But Beatrice was well aware that this was a superficial and inadequate way of thinking about her predicament. Beyond the rivalry between the dutiful daughter and the Glorified Spinster there were deeper and more permanent divisions. When she came to discuss them in public it was in terms of the continuous controversy between an ego that affirmed and an ego that denied. Yet that account of her divided self – moving and truthful as it was – stopped short of completeness. Of course she was torn between affirming and denying the possibility of a social science, just as she was restlessly preoccupied with the problem of how the conclusions of such a science might be related to the affirmations of her religious and moral experience,[69] but in *My Apprenticeship* this discussion of the divisions in her internal life was made to accommodate conflicting purposes. After all, the dilemma that she described could be counted an eloquent proposal of certain problems that existed in their own right and that could be shared with the reader. At the same time, it could be taken as an oblique reference to depths of personal experience, which could not be easily disclosed. The ego that affirmed and the ego that denied were made to appear respectable by being presented as contenders from different logical worlds, rather than the representatives of warring psychic states. The opposition between religion and science was not merely the opposition of heart to head, but of self to self. *My Apprenticeship* offered an 'acceptable' account of an aspect of her alienation in place of a full account of it.[70]

Beatrice saw her mother as a 'divided personality': a woman who was for ever repressing her humanity out of regard for her class responsibilities and her deference to the teachings of political economy. After her mother's death, Beatrice felt much closer to her than when she had been alive.[71] She persuaded herself that she too was a 'duplex personality'. She referred to 'the nether being in me; the despondent, vain, grasping person – the Heyworth – doomed to failure. Linked to this nethermost being was the phantom of mother – the gloomy, religious [person] affecting asceticism and dominated by superstition.' The second self was

> essentially a realist in intellectual questions, a rationalist in metaphysics and therefore a sceptic of religion. This is the happiest and perhaps the highest expression of my ego. But alas! This being has its life and origin in my sensual nature: it springs from vigorous senses and keen perceptions. If I were a man, this creature would be free, though not dissolute, in its morals; a lover of women. These feelings would be subordinate to the intellectual and practical interests, but still the strong physical nature upon which the intellectual is based, would be satisfied. And as I am a woman, these feelings unless fulfilled in marriage (which would mean destruction of the intellectual being) must remain controlled and unsatisfied, finding their only vent in one quality of the phantom companion of the nethermost personality – religious exhaltation.'[72]

Doubts about her own identity were not confined to a particular moment, nor were they always expressed in terms of the division between being a Heyworth and being a Potter. As hinted at earlier, when she contemplated Catholicism she rejected it as a 'suicide': an execution of one ego by another.[73] She asked herself to whom it was that she writing in her diary. The question perplexed her in terms of her own internal life and not in relation to the public or to posterity.[74] There were times – as in the matter of her evidence to the Lords Committee or at critical moments in her relations with Chamberlain – when she found in her conduct an 'irresponsibility' which resembled being occupied or possessed by someone else. Perhaps part of the attraction of playing at being other people – Miss Jones, the farmer's daughter from Monmouth, or a representative of Singer's sewing machines or a Jewish immigrant or a sweated worker – was that the participant observer's rational duality was a comforting release from the irrational duality of her ordinary experience.

The 'false-self system' is supposed to have its origins in the attempts of a child to respond to what he thinks is demanded of him by his family: a response which is made at the expense of his capacity for independent experience and a free relatedness to others. In Beatrice's case, her problem of identity was most closely connected to her femininity. As a child she felt unwanted and unloved by her mother. Her mother, reared by and with men, disliked women. Her father, having no sons, treated his daughters as if they had the intellectual capabilities of men and something more. The death of 'Dicky' made it all the more important to achieve 'masculine standards'. This meant defying the ruling idea of femininity as signifying sentimentality, softness and want of intellectual powers. Spencer's notion of the scientific attitude, his belief that people could be studied just like plants or animals, encouraged a frame of mind in which callousness could be confused with detachment. If she was to be noticed and valued, Beatrice imagined that she had to deny herself as a woman, not merely in immediately sexual terms, but also in terms which left other aspects of her nature unfulfilled. Her sex had a reputation, which had to be lived down by cultivating 'hardness' and 'inhumanity'. In no other way would her testimony as a social investigator be taken seriously, nor would she achieve the literary fame that had eluded her mother.

To insist that Beatrice felt she was divided against herself is to draw attention to one of her most pronounced characteristics, but it is not to assert that she was 'schizoid'. She managed far too well for that description to be applied to her. To explain her 'hardness' by reference to a false-self system is not to explain it away, nor is it to uncritically subscribe to a concept of human nature in which all negative characteristics are dismissed as 'unreal' or 'unnatural'. Some of her least lovable qualities can be quite sufficiently understood in terms of her class experience and not in terms of her particular position within her family. Her snobbery and arrogance were convincingly spontaneous and were produced without any special effort on her part. They survived her recognition that she had been born into a class that gave orders rather than obeyed them.[75] They rarely figured as the subject of her periodic exercises in self-criticism.

Yet while resisting an interpretation of Beatrice's personality which is cast within some ready-made and tidy scheme, it remains a fact that Russell must have been referring – in some sense – to her divided self. Otherwise, he was talking nonsense and just the sort of nonsense that he – beyond any other Englishman – was least likely to talk. Therefore, it must be presumed that he intended to point to a division in Beatrice's behaviour which was seen, perhaps, as a contrast between the more conspicuous and 'public' aspects of it and the less easily identified and enumerated 'private' aspects. Moreover, he may have detected that few of her faults and limitations enjoyed security of tenure. There was scarcely an assumption underlying her thought and conduct which might not come to be summoned up for review: interrogated and – if found wanting – dismissed. It was as if she had contrived to match each flaw in her nature with some complicating or countervailing tendency.

Thus, it was decidedly disagreeable that she described the weakness and the wickedness of her fellow humans with far more relish and with far more memorable exactitude than she displayed in the short notices that she accorded to their virtues. Moreover, she could be merciless and hard in practice as well as in theory. She was prompt to punish, prompt to hurt and even destroy those whom she regarded as 'worthless'. Her habit of severe self-criticism cannot entirely excuse her. Her protracted attempts to be honest with herself, to condemn herself for pride or for vanity, too often had a Rousseauesque touch about them. Her ready acknowledgement of her own faults was noticed, stood on its head and turned into grounds for further self-congratulation. Yet it was a mark of her integrity that she found herself out when she played this game.[76] Moreover, when others also found her out, the love that she had for her friends was strong enough to endure their cruelty towards her. Thus, Maggie Harkness was repeatedly 'bitchy' and treacherous in her relations with Beatrice and yet Beatrice remained loyal and loving towards her.[77]

Next to her 'hardness', Beatrice exhibited arrogance; a willingness to play the boss, whether in relation to her invalid father, her younger sister or the unfortunate tenants at the buildings. The fact that she had noticed the despotic disposition of Octavia Hill did not prevent her from displaying, from time to time, a similar trait herself. Yet she recognised the moral excellence of collective self-help. She respected and admired the culture of the co-operative societies. She wanted the tenants to manage the Buildings. Her opposition to co-operative production depended upon convictions about the efficient organisation of business and not upon hostility towards the ideal of self-management as such. Democratic collectives might replace capitalists; but she denied that they could dispense with the services of professional experts. How proletarian democracy was to come to terms with professional managers and administrators was one of the crucial areas in which the debate between the ego that affirmed and the ego that denied was carried on.

In addition to a convincing show of hardness, arrogance and snobbery, Beatrice also gave an impression of narrow-mindedness and philistinism. She displayed indifference amounting to disdain for the pleasures of eating and drinking. She occasionally went riding (first horses and later bicycles), but she had no interest in sport or games. She had virtually no appreciation of art other than literature and in literature her enjoyment was almost completely derived from modern prose works in English or French. She had little or no taste for poetry, nor in her early life for music. In intellectual matters she seemed to exhibit an obsessional singlemindedness. There was something in her inhumanity and isolation of mind that was reminiscent of Spencer. But whereas he led 'a spider-like existence; sitting alone in the centre of his theoretical web catching facts', she deliberately repudiated universality in favour of hunting down the facts relating to one or other of her 'specialities'. Yet if one watched her closely it became apparent that she was restricting her field of vision in the interests of efficiency rather than through an inability to do otherwise. Beyond Beatrice the active investigator was the contemplative Beatrice, a ruminative and critical person. She never put aside for more than brief intervals ultimate philosophical questions. Perhaps if she had been to a university she would have had all that nonsense about the relationship between facts and values knocked out of her before she was twenty-five. But one doubts it. Her spirit of restless and devoted questioning never left her, and this helps to explain the affection and respect Bertrand Russell felt for her.

A descriptive summary of Beatrice's character may be cast in the form of a balance sheet, but the character itself can only begin to be understood in terms of the dynamics of a divided self. The fact that the horrors of the sweating system so slowly and imperfectly aroused her compassion or her indignation is indeed explained by the standards that shaped her false self. It was not simply class selfishness that prevented her from believing that there was much that could be done. It was more to the point that she imagined she ought not to feel like a woman if she was to become a competent social investigator whose testimony would be taken seriously. She had therefore to deny the prompting of her own nature if she was to become the sort of person she thought she wanted to be.

Such a divided self necessarily had an aggravating, half-emancipated character. But those who are inclined to scorn Miss Potter for her failure to make a clean break from her family and with established orthodoxies and conventions need to remember that in late Victorian England there was no intelligentsia in the continental sense of the term. There was no sizeable and well-defined order of men and women in which all aspired to independent thought and rejected all authority in heaven or on earth. Even William Morris or Bertrand Russell lacked the kind of rootlessness that was required. In the 1880s a lot of talk about apocalyptic crisis and claims to millenarian vision needed to be treated with scepticism. Secularists, socialists, libertarians and vegetarians might all proclaim the existence of two camps and enquire which one you were going to join, but the suggestion that they promised a comprehensive change rarely carried conviction even among themselves. Beatrice had, accordingly, to make her way forward with painful, halting steps. Granted the traditional wisdom that holds that two is company but three a crowd, the discordant and divided self must find a companion who is 'selfless' in the strictest possible way. The divided self needs another who has no internal life, but who is fulfilled in living vicariously in the collectives to which he belongs. One who is ready to treat marriage as a partnership, as the ultimate committee within or over which he will preside as an intelligent, helpful and disinterested chairman. Such men are hard to find. They must be tested in fire and in flood before their credentials are recognised.

APPENDIX: BEATRICE POTTER VERSUS BEATRICE WEBB: TOWARDS AN AUTOCRITIQUE

Like Jean-Jacques Rousseau, Beatrice Potter had the gift of intimacy. She did not confront her readers; she enticed them. *My Apprenticeship* is one of the compulsory delights for the student of late-Victorian England. This masterpiece was first published in 1926. In that case, the reader may ask, why not reserve an account of it for a later volume?

The short answer is that such a conventional treatment would make unreasonable calls upon the reader's memory or send the reader back to the chapter which they have just read or else involve an unacceptable amount of repetition. The device represented by a note like this may disturb the conventional notion of a biography, but that is a small matter.

Readers will probably recall how Beatrice introduced *My Apprenticeship* by reference to a

> continuous debate between an Ego that affirms and an Ego that denies … Can there be a science of social organisation in the sense in which we have a science of mechanics or a science of chemistry, enabling us to forecast what will happen, and perhaps to alter the event by taking appropriate action or persuading others to take it. And secondly, assuming that there be, or will be, such a science of society, is man's capacity for scientific discovery the only faculty required of the reorganisation of society according to an ideal? Or do we need religion as well as science, emotional faith as well as intellectual curiosity?[78]

The reader should have been left in no doubt that this was a central preoccupation for the young Beatrice. As she indicated, it was also a crucial question for her sister Margaret as well as for some of her most influential teachers such as Frederic Harrison. Yet it is misleading in so far as it is *over-cognitive*. The divided self inhabited worlds below the cerebral one. The need to satisfy her strong sexual desires and to make a marriage as socially distinguished as that of her elder sisters was in conflict with her pursuit of intellectual independence and intellectual distinction. Which was it to be? Her suitors shared her doubts on the subject and drew back before the adverse possibility. The divided self has to be understood in terms of the trials and the struggles of women in mid- to late-Victorian England, particularly for Glorified Spinsters, which had more immediate terms of reference than the rivalry between science and religion.

BEATRICE POTTER'S MENSTRUAL CYCLE FOR 1886

Date	Jan	Feb	Mar	April	May	June	July	Aug	Sept	Oct	Nov	Dec
1	?D	D				P	P					D
2		P	P	P		P	D					
3		P	P	P		P						
4	P	P	PdD	PpD	P	P						P
5	PD	P	PdD	D	PD			D				P
6	P	P			PD							P
7	P	P			P					D		P
8	P	PD			PD						PdD	P
9	P				P	D					PdD	P
10	P	dD			P						P	P
11	P										P	PmdD
12				dmD			Dd				P	
13		D			D					P	P	
14		D	D							P		
15		D			D		D		PD	P		
16									P	PD		
17				D	D		D		P	PpD		
18				D	D				PD	P		
19						D	D	P	P	D		D
20								PD	P			
21								P				
22		D					P	P				
23							P	P				
24						Dd	P	P				D
25					D	P	P	P				D
26	D					P	P					Dd
27			D			P	P					
28	D				D	P						
29			PD	D	P	P			dmD			
30			P		P		D					
31	D		P		P		D	D		D		P

Key

P = supposed regular paramenstruation on the assumption that this lasted seven days and 20 August was the third of these.

D = Diary entry

d = depression, irritability or lethargy

dm = mixed with the above

Notes

During 1886 Beatrice Potter made 33 entries in her diary: of these 10 were made during her presumed paramenstruation, while 7 more were made within 3 days of either end of it. There is, therefore, a tendency to greater frequency of entry during the paramenstruation – around a third instead of nearly a quarter. Of the 33 entries, 7 exhibit total, or almost total depression, irritability and lethargy; of these 5 were made during the presumed paramenstruation and 1 of the remaining 2 could be accommodated on the assumption of a 3-day span of irregularity.

Note that the 'hysterical' letter of, or about, 6 March, from Beatrice to Joseph Chamberlain would have been written close to or during the cycle. Was one of the functions of the diary to allow the painless expression of depression, irritability and lethargy? Was there a going into purdah among middle-class women at such times? May we assume that Beatrice, as one of so many sisters, would be relatively well informed when she judged (20 August 1886) 'not that I suffer much'? Would she have noticed irregularity? She noticed only lethargy – to be unaware of the source of depression and irritability seems unusual: see K. Dalton, *The Menstrual Cycle*, 1969. Harriet Blodgett, in her admirable *Centuries of Female Days: English Women's Private Diaries*, 1988, p. 42, draws attention to the extreme rarity of references to 'the curse'. She misses the references in Beatrice's diary, even though Beatrice is treated as one of her leading cases.

Beatrice's opposition to feminism and to political equality between the sexes was not primarily a matter of the opposition of many feminists to special factory legislation for women. As a young woman she herself was strongly opposed to it. Her conviction that women should keep their distance from politics in general and the Irish question in particular related to her love for Joseph Chamberlain, a love which had a depth and importance not fully disclosed in *My Apprenticeship*. To go for politics in general and the Irish question in particular opened fresh possibilities of differences with the 'Great Man'. It was best to distance oneself from them and concentrate on matters of social welfare and reform. After all this was simply an enlargement of the woman's accepted traditional role of carer for the poor, the frail and unfortunate, raised to a new level by a 'masculine' cast of mind. The neglect of the Irish question is one of the great deficiencies of *My Apprenticeship* considered as a guide to contemporary politics.

That great book is more deficient still when it comes to the discussion of the alleged growth of social compunction among the middle class, which Beatrice in retrospect discovered to be one of the grand facts of the 1880s. How did this grand fact relate to the rising importance of the Charity Organisation Society and the stern policing of mendicity in the metropolis and further afield? It was hardly honest of Beatrice to pass over her own part in bringing about the death of a drug addict and her murderous attitude to those who were thought to be unfit for economic life. As has been shown, the young Beatrice was one of the many middle-class observers who treated political economy as a code of morals and concluded that the best place for many of the wretched of the earth was simply beneath it. Of course she became a socialist. However, her account of how this happened can be shown to be rather misleading if her autobiography is compared with her journals. Mrs Webb's account of her conversion is neat and tidy. Its function is to persuade you to become a socialist, not to explain how she became one.[79] According to *My Apprenticeship* it all began with her experience of East End life, which brought a conviction of the need for an all-pervading control, in the interests of the community, of the economic activities of 'the landlord and the capitalist'. (This conviction was not prominently displayed in Miss Potter's testimony to the Lords Committee on the Sweating System.) But she concluded that state regulation and trade union intervention could not correct cyclic crises: the alternate spells of over-work and unemployment, inflation and depression. (This was not the ascendant difficulty in the East End where there was a chronic *over-supply* of labour.) Yet Mrs Webb recalled that, 'This national minimum of civilised existence to be legally ensured for every citizen, was the second state in my progress towards socialism.'[80] The third stage came with pondering upon 'the psychological evils of a community permanently divided into a nation of the rich and a nation of the poor, into a minority always giving orders and a vast majority always obeying orders'. Matthew Arnold, unheeded by his own generation, had been right! 'Our inequality materialises our upper class, vulgarises our middle class, brutalises our lower.'

Finally, Mrs Webb recalled that it was her study of the co-operative movement and her subsequent work on trade unionism that impressed upon her the possibility of Britain without capitalists: 'a possible alternative to modern business enterprise'. Although *My Apprenticeship* acknowledged that it was the presence of Sidney Webb that immediately preceded the discovery, 'At last I am a Socialist',[81] his contribution is understated, as we shall see in the next chapter.

What was the diary for? Was it no more than an exercise yard for the development of her literary skills? Was it always her intention that it should be only for her own eyes? Did she imagine that it would be an aid to her development as a writer, but also a means of keeping a watch upon herself and becoming an instrument of her own moral improvement? It performed all these functions, their relative importance changing over time. However a few generalisations are possible.

The length of the entries varied inversely with the importance of what she was doing. A Victorian lady's diary was likely to be best tended when she had 'the curse'. She was likely to have gone into purdah once a month. Beatrice was able to compare her own experience with that of her nine sisters. She considered that she did not have too bad a time of it. One entry in the diary – better journal – allows a prediction and retroaction of her menstrual cycle.[82] This can then be related to the degree of depression and misery in the journal. The whole exercise is highly conjectural and subjective.

The 'discoveries' (concerning the menstrual cycle) must not be allowed to obscure the far more interesting division within Beatrice Potter-Webb's divided self. The paradox identified by Bertrand Russell between Beatrice's most conspicious and unpleasant characteristics and her delightful and engaging ones has already been noted and it is appropriate to conclude these observations by pointing up this enigma. How could the greatest modern British philosopher, the heroic defender of common sense, find a reality beyond appearances, an essence in Beatrice that was so at odds with her outward show? The provisional answer is that she never stopped asking questions.[83]

Part III
The Early Years of
the Partnership 1890–2

She is too rich, too beautiful, too clever. But there is no class divergence between us.

Sidney, in the 1890s

[He is a cross] somewhat between a London card and a German professor.

Beatrice

Together we could move the world. Marriage is a partnership. It is the ultimate committee.

Sidney

If you lose at Deptford, I will spend the whole day kissing you.

Beatrice

I was lifted shoulder-high ... I felt inclined to go round by Cannon Street, in order, like Jack Cade, to smite London stone with my umbrella and to shout into the night: 'Now is Mortimer Lord of London.' But I went to the Central Telegraph Office instead.

Sidney

5

The Formation of the Partnership 1890–2

Beatrice and Sidney compared—The engagement with co-operation and the compact between Sidney and Beatrice at Glasgow—Sidney's reaction to Beatrice's mistrust—The vicissitudes of the 'working' compact and the relationship—Sidney leaves the Colonial Office and takes to journalism—*The Eight-Hour Day*—Collaboration leading to intervals for 'human nature'—Proposed marriage and the Potter family—The rebellion in the Fabian Society against the 'Webb party'—*The London Programme* and the London County Council—Marriage.

Beatrice never expressed anything but admiration for Sidney's learning and industry. As for physical appearance or sexual attractiveness, he was no match for Joseph Chamberlain. It was not merely that Chamberlain's social and political position was far more impressive and prestigious. He was not simply in Parliament and the cabinet. He was making a bid for national and imperial supremacy. The monocle and the orchid were more commanding than the pince-nez and the goatee. The tall, commanding man from Birmingham had a presence received to the somewhat Cockney Londoner of Cranbourn Street. Yet Webb's physical appearance was not to be despised. Bernard Shaw pointed out that he resembled an improved version of Napoleon III. Emma Brooke, the novelist and Fabian, found Sidney an attractive and desirable figure. She cast him as the hero in one of her works. She had him, as an attractive as well as an exceedingly able man, assassinated by an anarchist!

Beatrice's feelings towards Sidney must remain the subject of speculation because he was trying out how to impress her; because her feelings were not constant; because she had strong sexual disappointments and sexual desires; because she occasioned strong feelings of social as well as sexual failure; because she enjoyed passing herself off as the disappointed lover; because she imagined it was Woman whom he was worshipping through her. She experienced a whole complex of feelings associated with prolonged virginity and deferred adolescence. Sidney suffered from colds and other commonplace ailments. Beatrice appears not to have cared to notice these minor maladies. She came to welcome what she termed 'intervals for human nature'. This precluded all forms of nursing or mothering.

They were drawn together by a common culture; a similar cast of mind; closely shared political and social ideals; and the close fit between their different attainments, skills, experiences and goals. They were both the products of the provincial bourgeois culture of which Herbert Spencer was the prophet: Spencer, who had been Beatrice's earliest friend and teacher, and whom Sidney had saluted from afar as 'the Bacon of the Second Renaissance'. They both retained Spencer's love of systematically arranged facts, as well as something of his complacency about problems of ultimate value. They both gradually came to recognise that Spencer's 'social organism was never organic',[1] and that there was a basic contradiction between his appeal to this principle and his insistence on individuality as the goal of life. They both turned towards Comte in search of some correction for Spencer's extreme doctrinaire individualism, which appeared year by year to become more untenable and preposterous. In the founder of sociology they found a critique of 'metaphysical' individualism, an acknowledgement of the claims of organisation, and of the proletariat. They found also an attempt to meet the demand of religious-minded agnosticism for liturgical forms and – more important – reconciliation between the world of fact and of value which the nineteenth century had torn asunder.

It was from Spencer and from Comte that they derived their taste for that 'delicious positivism' that discloses the gap between pretension and performance, and sets the world by its ears even as it puts it back on its feet. Sidney had uncovered the unconscious socialism that underpinned legislative programmes and administrative actions; Beatrice was in the process of disclosing that the co-operative movement was about a democracy of consumers rather than, as it obstinately supposed, about a democracy of producers. Each was disclosing realities that had been obscured by defunct ideologies, justifying and rationalising those realities and, in doing so, alerting streams of tendency into currents of thought. Some thinkers pretend to raise thought to action; Sidney and Beatrice were equally inclined to pretend that they did the reverse: that their thoughts were but statements of the principles of going institutional concerns. Progress implied a coincidence between impending change and moral imperative: between necessity and desire.

Marx could be made to reinforce these dispositions. Both of them had, in the same year, tried to settle their accounts with him. Sidney wrote with more learning and competence than Beatrice, but to much the same effect. The principal flaw in the labour theory of value and in the labour metaphysic was its failure to allow for the varieties of work and the crucial importance of managerial and professional functions. They did not wholly deny the political capacity of the working class. Sidney knew the London working men's clubs and made a high estimate of their political importance. Beatrice admired the democracy of consumers, which she found in the co-operative movement. But they were as impressed by the inadequacies and limitations of these institutions as they were by their successes. The complete emancipation of the proletariat could not be secured by its own unaided efforts. The 'Labour Party' needed the administrative and political experience of the younger radicals, just as it had to be informed with socialist ideas and understanding which had to be brought to it from without. Similarly Beatrice was convinced that the workers could not secure the control of industry through their own producers' associations which necessarily lacked the capital, the commercial skills and the line of command needed for the efficient operation of modern business.[2] When she asked him why there had been no revolution in England during the Napoleonic wars, he answered:

> There might have been a Jacquerie or a bread riot, but the descendants of Cromwell's Ironsides were too busy running cotton mills and fitting out ships; and without them, I think there could, at that time, have been no strength anywhere.[3]

In Sidney's opinion there never was a time when the working people could achieve a revolutionary reconstruction of society, relying on themselves alone.

Other middle-class socialists, like Hyndman or William Morris, were content to appear as mavericks who had broken with their class, but Sidney and Beatrice saw themselves as members of an advance party recruited from among a new social stratum which was in the course of coming over to socialism. They were, both of them, self-consciously 'professional people', impatient with amateurism whether in social service, research or administration. Each had had to work and sacrifice to become a professional person. And both of them felt, along with the joy and significance of disciplined intellectual effort, a high sense of responsibility (and an oppressive weight of guilt) about how they used their faculties and how they disposed of their 'rent of ability'.

Yet Sidney's self-denial went altogether deeper and was more literal than Beatrice's. His ambition, which she – unconsciously, no doubt – helped him to realise, was to cease to have any meaningful 'internal' life. To become unconscious of personal history and identity; to respond actively and usefully to external stimuli; to obliterate the distinction between public and private faces – hence Sidney's baffling simplicity. Once the minimum demands of that part of his nature that could not be compounded had been met, he could wholly renounce personality and personal power in favour of anonymous influence. In this he was like

Lenin: he combined a unique simplicity and integrity with a ruthless, calculating and complex political strategy. Kant's maxim, that a man should always be treated as an end and never as a means, can never impress those who treat themselves as means. He was the most disinterested of schemers. He was an intriguer who was 'spiritually unveiled'.[4] He left all but a handful of his political opponents at a loss. Even as he bribed them or coerced them, they knew that he reproached them. He was, not only intellectually, but also morally, an extremely formidable man.

For Beatrice, self-obliteration was also a programme, but one she could never realise. She told him that she had been warning herself

> against the personal note – the intolerable 'I' or 'our' – against the consciousness, quite as much as the expression of egotism. Undoubtedly it is inexpedient – because it arouses antagonism and creates a silent distinction which grows in the day of success and bursts into flame in the day of failure.[5]

But characteristically the concealment of self was, for Beatrice, not a condition of her moral being so much as a matter of good manners.

> Superficially well-bred persons learn to hide their consciousness of self – hence the charm of good society – really well-bred people have not got it – hence *Social leadership* – when breeding is combined with capacity.[6]

She was left, as he was not, with time on her hands, cut off from her work and from public concerns. Again and again she summoned herself to appear before that private tribunal in which she was the accused, the prosecutor and the judge. Here she was charged with vanity; cross-examined about self-pity; condemned for indulgence and sentenced to hard labour. Yet she was a habitual offender: a veritable old lag in relation to the stringent requirements of that exacting moral law that she would impose upon herself. Unlike Sidney, her consciousness of self was ineradicable. He needed her so that he might lose himself in the last collective; she needed him as an extension of herself.

Both of them had an overwhelming sense, ascetic and evangelical, of duty: of self-denial, renunciation and submission, which were hardly consistent with the direct exercise of personal power. Sidney, without ever aspiring to be the Man of Destiny, was eager to be his confidential clerk. Nor was he above an occasional chuckle at the great man stumbling over his lines. How, he wondered, could Mill ever have imagined that life could become uninteresting in a mass democracy?

> To play on these millions of minds, to watch them slowly respond to an unseen stimulus, to guide their aspirations often without their

knowledge – all this, whether in high capacities or in humble, is ... [an] endless game of chess, of even extravagant excitement.[7]

He wanted Beatrice to help him move the world. And she too felt the romance of the great machine of government, longed to use it to make the homes of the poor as 'dignified, restful and orderly as the official residence'. She deliberately planned to do it through developing a 'close intimacy' with the permanent officials of the departments of state and the leaders of popular organisations.[8] For such large and selfless ends they would intrigue and scheme; Sidney finding pleasure in it, Beatrice some sadness, in that 'Florence Nightingale, Octavia Hill and Tom Mann should distrust her as one who was prepared to exploit her influence over men for her own ends'.[9]

Sidney and Beatrice complemented each other. He had a deep emotional need for her: she needed to arm herself with his immense capacity for work. She thought of herself as an originator rather than as an executant. She was wearied and exhausted by prolonged application to the 'mechanics' of learning. Moreover, he brought experience of the workings of central government; a lively sense of the possibilities of municipal enterprise; and an acknowledged position in the leadership of metropolitan radicalism and socialism. She, in turn, had access to 'Society', which meant opening the doors, not merely of the 'gay and the splendid', but of the grave and the earnest. The Courtneys and the Hobhouses belonged to the heart of the prosperous and assured, humane and improving, established and respectable Liberalism, which Sidney had hitherto had to approach from without. Still more important, Beatrice had begun to acquire a feeling for the qualities of provincial working-class life, and had begun to acquire an understanding some of its institutions. The co-operative movement had far more vitality and importance in Lancashire or Durham than it had in the metropolis. As Beatrice identified the limitations, as well as the successes, of the voluntary social and industrial institutions of the working people, so Sidney was impressed by the inadequacy of a merely working-class socialism or labour politics. By putting their insights and conclusions together, separate and competing movements could be shown to complement each other. Sidney and Beatrice discovered their personal need for each other while they were in the process of redefining the labour movement. This was, indeed, what they were doing. The dynamic, institutional, tripartite conception of the world of labour was at once their discovery and their programme. Sidney brought more to this redefinition than Beatrice, for he had largely anticipated her critique of the co-operative movement. However, he lacked her sharp appreciation of its positive achievements, and before he met her he tended to treat the co-operators as competitors of the socialists in the

work of social reconstruction.[10] *Fabian Essays* displayed a complete ind
ference to co-operation and to trade unionism.

Sidney and Beatrice knew that they were complementary, but they c
not make this discovery at once nor did they make it simultaneously
powerful forces drew them together, there were others, seemingly no l
powerful, that worked to keep them apart. They were divided by cl
and style of life; by manner and by physical presence; as well as by app
ent differences of temperament and disposition. Sidney, who fell 'he
over heels' in love with her at their first meeting,[11] now doggedly deni
now furiously strove to overcome, all the impediments she discovered
the way of their union. He conceded that

> There is much to be said in presumption against marriage out of on
> *class* – if by class is meant that very real difference which is the prod
> of different educations, social traditions etc. But there is surely
> much to be said against marriage out of one's *position*, i.e. the positi
> of one's family.[12]

However, Beatrice's favourite sister, Margaret Hobhouse, was adama
'Better marry a man with heart disease than some little fellow with
position.'[13] In the end, Beatrice advised Margaret to mind her own bu
ness, but before that stage had been reached the 'ego that denied' h
enjoyed many a triumph over 'the ego that affirmed'. The forces that dr
them together worked powerfully to cement the relationship; but th
were not well adapted to initiating it. Only Sidney's astonishing pers
tence and determination protected the partnership and allowed it
emerge out of the terrible storms and buffetings to which it was perio
cally subjected throughout the course of its future.

During the development of the partnership both Sidney and Beatr
had recourse to the graphic arts to describe their hopes and fears w
respect to their relationship. Sidney presented his suit thus:

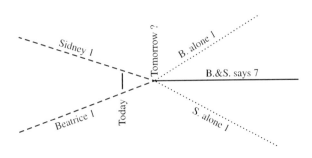

(4 December 18

Beatrice expressed her feelings by the means of the following strange device. She drew Sidney's particular attention to the need to focus his 'morbid effort' in 'Humility' while at the centre she placed a blob of sealing wax explaining that she was simply devoting herself to keeping these qualities constantly before her.

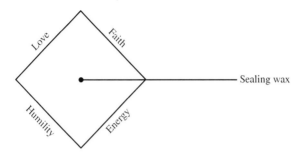

(January 1891?)

Under these circumstances it seems appropriate to supply the diligent reader with a chart of the history of their courtship, taking Sidney's emotional temperature as the most convenient guide and measure.

He was in love with her from that first meeting which had been arranged by Margaret Harkness early in January 1890. She took an instinctive liking to him but – as always with Beatrice – this was fully consistent with her most merciless criticism. She thought that he was

somewhat between a London card and a German professor. To keep to externals: his pronunciation is Cockney, his 'Hs' are shaky, his attitudes by no means eloquent – with his thumbs fixed pugnaciously in a far from immaculate waistcoat, with his bulky head thrown back and his little body forward, he struts even when he stands, delivering himself with extraordinary rapidity of thought and utterance and with an expression of inexhaustible self-complacency.[14]

By April Beatrice had carried her analysis beyond the 'externals':

'I have done everything I intended to do', said the little man. 'I have a belief in my own Star.' 'Take care, Mr Webb,' say I in a motherly tone, 'don't be complacent about small successes.' Poor Sidney Webb: I surprised him by my sympathy and 'unholy knowledge' (as he termed it, of men's feelings) into a whole history of his life, his thought, feeling and action. 'You reduced me to a pulp by your sympathy, and then

impressed your view on me; you have made me feel horribly small –
you have given me an altogether different sense of proportion – and yet
I don't believe that I look at things in a disproportionate way,' says the
little man defiantly. 'Come, Mr Webb, you can feel that you have humbled me by making me a socialist.'

I am not sure as to the future of that man. His tiny tadpole body, his
unhealthy skin, lack of manner, Cockney pronunciation, poverty, are all
against him. He has the conceit of [a] man who has raised himself out of
the most insignificant surroundings into a position of power – how
much power no one quite knows. This self-complacent egotism, this
disproportionate view of his own position is at once repulsive and ludicrous. On the other [hand], looked at by the light of his personal history,
it was inevitable. And he can learn; he is quick and sensitive and ready
to adapt himself. This sensitiveness, combined as it undoubtedly is with
great power, may carry him far. If the opportunity occurs, I think the
man will appear. In the meantime he is an interesting study. A London
retail tradesman with the aims of a Napoleon! A queer monstrosity to
be justified only by success. And above all a loop-hole into the Socialist
party: one of the small body of men with whom I may sooner or later
throw in my lot for good and all.[15]

Sidney thanked her for her frank friendliness, an attitude which was, he
thought, 'as valuable as it is rare'.[16] He declared that she had humbled
him – and much more seriously than she realised. He confessed to further
faults and weaknesses. He was, he confided, extremely liable to be influenced by those around him and, far from being a 'fatuously self-confident
person' was prone to a sinking of the heart and a feeling of despair as he
approached each new intellectual challenge.[17] He described himself as
'timid and cursed with looking before and after, fearing to hear the
"ground whirl of the perished leaves of hope". (Did you credit me with
knowing my Rosetti?)'[18]

Yet he yielded nothing to her intellectually. He told her, in tones of confident pugnacity, of

the long rolling fight all over the country into which the Fabian Society,
and I in particular, am being more and more drawn. You need not fear
our taking up any impractical or sectarian attitude: we are indeed constantly seeking chances of translating the crude abstractions of the doctrinaire socialist into the language of practical politics. But it is difficult
to know how to treat the Liberal leaders. They are generally such poor
creatures and so hopelessly 'out of it'. I wish their education could be
taken in hand in some way that would save the Fabian Society from
becoming more and more conceited. But really every day makes me
inclined to say 'I told you so' over some event or other.[19]

1 Beatrice Potter's birthplace, Standish House, near Gloucester (as it appeared on a postcard from *c.* 1914–18). This was one of the three country houses owned by the Potter family.

2 Sidney Webb's birthplace, 44–45 Cranbourn Street, near Leicester Square (as photographed for the London Transport Executive in 1904). These were the Webb family's only properties. The hairdressing sign would have been present in the year of Sidney's birth.

3 A Potter family group in 1865. Lawrencina and Richard Potter (*seated*) with daughters Georgina, Mary, Margaret, Beatrice, Theresa and Blanche (*left to right*).

4 Charles Webb, Sidney's father, in the uniform of The Queen's Westminster Volunteer Rifles.

5 Elizabeth Mary Stacey, Sidney's mother.

6 Joseph Chamberlain (as he appeared on a visiting card presented to the Potter household).

7 Sidney Webb.

8 Sidney Webb (as he appeared at about the time of his marriage to Beatrice).

9 Beatrice Webb (as she appeared at about the time of her marriage to Sidney).

10 Sydney Olivier.

11 Graham Wallas.

12 Bertrand Russell.

13 George Bernard Shaw.

Four of Sidney Webb's key Fabian friends

He disagreed with Beatrice regarding the poor law. He held that there was no point in tinkering with it. It needed to be entirely replaced by a great, organic, democratic and generous reform while it was still 'safe'. 'I cannot promise to obey,' he warned her. 'I will however learn.'[20]

It was with respect to the co-operative movement rather than the poor law that Sidney had the best opportunity of learning from her and he seized it eagerly. She suggested that he should accompany Ella Pycroft and herself to the co-operative conference which was to be held in Glasgow at the end of May 1890. On the first day of the meeting Sidney and Benjamin Jones publicly made a compact between the co-operators and the socialists:[21] a compact which Sidney and his fellow Fabians followed up with letters to the *Co-operative News*. The Fabian Society offered to supply free of charge lectures to any co-operative society in the United Kingdom. Many old co-operators thought that a 'good spirit-stirring speech was better than any lecture', and others – like E.O. Greening – objected that the Fabians were opposed to co-operation; neglected the need for gradualness; and wanted to subject the workers to the rule of petty politicians. Sidney skilfully avoided all polemic; won the guarded support of G.J. Holyoake; got numerous Fabian lecture courses established. He taught that 'the real import of the Co-operative movement … is not profit-sharing but the collective control of the consumer over industry: not the division of so-called "profits" among a large number, but their elimination as far as is safely possible'.

At the same time he struck a new and conciliatory note which he had learned from Beatrice. 'The "democratisation" of the retail trade and of some branches of industry can, it has been triumphantly proven, be effected by the Store and the Wholesale, where neither the national government nor the local authority could yet venture to step in.'[22]

The Fabian 'offensive' in the co-operative movement in 1890 was, in its way, as much of a positive contribution towards developing a new sense of the labour movement as was the effort of socialists, Mann and Tillett to the organisation of the unskilled.

But there was another compact or 'concordat' concluded at Glasgow. Unlike the one concluded between Sidney and Benjamin Jones, it was private as well as being far more ambiguous. On a bridge above the Clyde two socialists reached a working compact. She warned him that it was 100 to 1 against its leading to more than friendship. 'If it weakens you', said she, 'give it up. Do you promise?' He promised, adding,

'However it ends I will make it serve my life – my work shall be both more vigorous and higher in tone for it. I will *make* you help me, and I will insist on helping you – our relationship shall be judged solely by the helpfulness to each other's work. Forgive me if I say that I believe that if we were united we could do great things together – I will not bother you with that; but I will vow solemnly that even if after a time we part, I will do better things for our friendship than I could have done without it.'

'One more thing', said Beatrice, 'promise me not to let your mind dwell on the purely personal part of your feeling. I know how that feeling unfulfilled saps all the vigour out of a man's life. Promise me to deliberately turn your mind away from it – to think of me as a married woman, as the wife of your friend.'

'That I can hardly promise. But I will look at the whole question from the point of view of Health: as you say, I will not allow myself to dwell on it – I will suppress the purely personal feeling – I will direct my imagination to strengthening the working tie between us.'

One clasp of the hands and they were soon in a warm discussion of economics. '*Finis*', wrote Beatrice in her diary,[23] but Sidney spent the night in reading the book of Job in his hotel bedroom, and conjecturing whether the pious donors of bibles had ever imagined that it might serve a need such as his.

On returning to London Beatrice too spent a sleepless night, perplexed and miserable about the misunderstandings that she felt surrounded their concordat. She wrote to Sidney:

Do not let us misunderstand each other. It is the first time in my life that I have granted friendship to a man who has desired something more. But the motive which has led me to depart from what I conceive to be the safe and honourable course, has not been that I think there is any probability (I might almost say *possibility*) of a closer tie, but that I regard our work of greater importance than our happiness, and that I feel the enormous help we may be to each other. But I feel that this is a one-sided bargain, since your happiness is more involved than mine – it is you and not I who runs the risk of suffering. Now, I almost fear from your last words yesterday, that you look upon our working friendship as a *means* and not as an *end* – that you hope and expect that it will lead to something more; and that in your words and manner to me you will be constantly expressing that hope and that expectation.

I want you to think this over very seriously; I want you not only to consider your own health and happiness as of the utmost importance (since the value of your work depends on them) but I want you to realise that you will be betraying my confidence and trust, if you allow yourself to build up a hope or allow others to suspect, that we are more to each other than frank friends with a common faith and common ends.

Personal happiness to me is an utterly remote thing; and I am to that extent 'heartless' that I regard everything from the point of view of making my own or another's life serve the community more effectively.

But you are still young and have life before you; you can hope for happiness as well as work – if your imagination were free you might find one who could give you the love of a young life – of a life which has not been forced through the fire and forged into a simple instrument for work.

I have tried to put the question of the continuance of our friendship from *your* point of view. My own point of view is simply this: if I find that our friendship leads to constant perplexity and anxiety on my side, or if I find that it leads to surmises and expectations in the minds of others, I shall retire absolutely and entirely from it. I do not want mystery and perplexity to hinder the little bit of work I have to do, and I cannot afford to lose my reputation as an honourable and healthy-minded woman.[24]

Sidney was appalled by her mistrust: mistrust of him, of herself, of all warmheartedness. He told himself he could live on cold iron, but he feared even to consider it. He assured her that he could not and would not wreck his life. That he was in love, as Austria goes to war, with limited liability. 'It does not mean that I love you less, but that duty has so far become organic with me. *That* you at any rate will understand and believe.' And yet in the next breath he confessed: 'I am horribly afraid now it would be too much for me.' He begged for a detailed concordat:

No one could be less skilled than I am in 'making love'. I could not woo you by my manner even did I wish. I *did*, and realised how completely I failed, even to make you suspect. (How *glad* I am that I failed, for you would not otherwise have suggested to me to go to Glasgow.) You can torture me horribly. I had vaguely thought that I would give no woman this power over me – in my pride!

He was willing to wait seven years, if need be, even if his Rachel failed him in the end:

But you said some horrible things on Friday night; you inevitably made me fear that you might possibly *refuse* to recognise any possible chance of change. You almost posed as being willing to sacrifice everything to your intellectual work – to sacrifice not only any potential feeling of your own, but with it all another's life. Now I do not need to remind you, who see all these things so clearly, that you have scarcely any right to do that. You would be wanting in faith and honour and justice. You would be making an idol unto yourself. Your altruism would become an egoism. And your work would unconsciously suffer. You would lose your subtle sympathy. You would still believe that you could see, with an even clearer vision, and you would be all the while becoming blind – blind to all the finer shades and impalpable differences which make the difference between Truth and Untruth. You would have dried up 'warm-heartedness' in order to get Truth – and you would not even get Truth.

I am capable of sacrificing more than you dream of. I could be as great an adjunct to your intellectual life as you are to my moral being. Of course I stand to gain by far the most, because I gain your intellect too, and cannot give you moral help. But *together we could move the world*.[25]

Beatrice responded:

Let it be as you say. I will not withdraw my friendship unless you *force* me to do so, by treating me otherwise than as a friend, or by making it apparent to the world that there is ought but 'camaraderies' between us … Your letter has touched me deeply *but it must be the last word of personal feeling* – I shall try to grow worthy of that reverence you are giving 'Woman' – through me – a reverence which must ennoble the nature that receives.[26]

(He had remarked that he now knew what Comte was driving at by his apotheosised woman.) She spent the last afternoon in May praying in Westminster Abbey that she would be worthy of having a man's soul in her keeping.[27] At the beginning of June she was kneeling in the cathedral at Cologne meditating on the dark and bright sides of tenderness:

I prayed – I prayed – I implored help and guidance to be humble and pure – to be worthy of the position of influence I have gained. My life is passing by swiftly, like the strong current of the Rhine … And thus I thought of the worship a man is giving me – not me, but Woman through me – and I prayed again that I might make my life a temple of purity wherein to receive it. And I, so vain, so impure – God help me.[28]

She returned to London in July:

I go this morning to take the Sacrament in St. Paul's. Two months of enjoyment and rest – of friendship and beauty – must now be followed by nine months of strenuous work – enlightened by love and guarded by purity – body and soul [a] living sacrifice to humanity – to obtaining the noblest outcome for Humanity.

Temptations have passed from me since last I took the Holy Sacrament. The sin of egotistical despair and discouragements, the sharp pangs of bitter hardness, no longer attract and taunt me. But with success in work [she was about to begin writing her book on the co-operative movement] and love in relationship arise the subtler sins of self-congratulation and self-indulgence. Now that I rest in the consciousness of fulfilment, in the blessedness of Love, I ought to fight against these more hidden enemies.[29]

Sidney was never able to find in old or new liturgical forms any help in rededicating himself to humanity. On his thirty-first birthday he thought a lot about the value and purpose of life, but he did not consecrate himself to the service of man:

> That is not our English way, but I resolved that I would be resolute against my two great temptations (1) Undue devotion to my own fixed purposes and (2) that indolence which disguises itself beneath the feeling of 'inability to create today'.[30]

From the end of May until mid-August the partnership was maintained as the kind of working compact that Beatrice found acceptable. On political matters, Sidney was as uncompromising as ever. For example, he told her quite frankly that, despite their merits, her proposals for outlawing sweating 'fell below maximum political effectiveness'. But with respect to his personal manners and conduct he was suitably distant when he was not being patient and humble:

> Yes you are quite right in your criticism of my egotistical loquacity. I must and will learn reticence ... My loquacity has led me to be frankness itself in all my diplomacy and, like Bismarck, I have acquired thereby a reputation for deepness and even duplicity. I agree that this is an evil and I will learn reticence ... I treasure up what you say about not boasting of my small successes in manipulation. I *will* be more reticent – *mit deiner Hilfe*! Now tell me of other faults.[31]

She did so. In gratitude he cried out: 'Surely Comte was right in making women the inspirers and guardians of morality.'[32] But no one should suspect the identity of his Clothilde de Vaux. On that subject at least, he would be reticent. And yet while he was at her feet and while he was avowing that he had no lover's arts and that even if he had, the notion of 'winning' her favour was abhorrent to him, he was subtly suggesting that her lack of feeling for him might signal a defect in her moral nature. Goethe, he warned her, was 'an awful example of the result of pure intellect'. What was its culmination but selfish anarchism? Goethe talked of self-mastery, but surely this must be a special demon of temptation. What did Goethe ever renounce? He never learned to see himself as a soldier in the great army of humanity. He never saw that 'we have no right to live our own lives'. Aloof, denying his manhood, fancying that everything could be settled by pure intellect, he diminished his effectiveness as a teacher. He proposed to give up all for truth, and ended with his absurd refutation of Newton's option which made him the laughing stock of scientific Europe.[33]

This was sufficiently dignified and Aesopian to be received without protest. Before he left on his holiday, and immediately after she had returned from hers, they met. To his delight he found her *'ravissante'* and 'angel-good'. It was all he could do to avoid saying goodbye in a way which would have broken their concordat at once.[34] Thus dangerously encouraged, he went off with Shaw to Oberammergau and there, sitting on the hill of the Silver Crucifix, he wrote to her:

> Did you see in Frankfurt the Ariadne of Bannecker? It is a wonderful but meretricious nude, supposed to represent earthly love – but she is not in love at all – *il y a toujours un qui aime et une qui se laisse aimer* – (alas) – and this is merely *'une qui se laisse aimer'*. You see by this time I know the difference. It is not a moral but an immoral sculpture, it does not make one understand the highest, but only the lowest side of life.[35]

'Another time,' replied Beatrice, 'write such a letter if you like but do not post it.' It was an 'abominable' letter and had it not been the outcome of evident emotion, she would have been obliged to describe it as a 'gross impertinence':

> If you value the continuance of our friendship, exercise a little more self-control – and occasionally think of me, and of my comfort – do not be always brooding on my effect on your life and your own feelings. It is truly masculine! I do not quite know what the word 'Love' conveys to a man's mind; but that is not what a woman understands by Love – Love to us has in it some element of self-control and self-sacrifice. I can now say that I have honestly tried to be as frank as I know how – it remains for you to determine whether I am to feel free to be 'as kind as I can'; or whether I am to treat you … as one against whose assumptions I must be perpetually protecting myself. I have lent you friendship – on trust – it is for you to pay me back that – before you ask me to give you more … For Heaven's sake let us have no more of it – I am sick and weary of the question – don't provoke me again.[36]

'I will not offend again,' he replied, 'you shall not need to write me another such letter: a terrible letter.'[37] Yet what was he to do? It seemed to him that she had called him into full being only in order to torture and diminish him. Was the comic who was inwardly sober a more pathetic figure than he who was reputedly conceited while all the time he was torn by diffidence and self-distrust? He told her:

> I think you are partly responsible for this. You called me into consciousness of myself by believing in me, and since then I have been much oppressed by responsibility. You pointed out some of my faults and thus destroyed what self-satisfaction I ever had – and I don't think I ever had much of *that* form of self-deceit.[38]

She began to exert a profound influence on the direction of his activities. She made him gradually diminish the amount of time that he spent on ephemeral journalism and the day's propaganda and organisation, although this was what he thought he did best. Although she looked to him to help her to master Marshall she discouraged him from attempting his own *Principles*. On her advice he gave it up, but this left him with a sense of failure.[39] More positively, it was her influence that helped him to project the lecturing campaign, which the Fabians mounted within the co-operative movement at the end of 1890. Still, when Beatrice asked for criticism, she got it. He told her that she underestimated the power of 'party' in social reform:

> It hurts me to believe that you have never belonged to a Liberal Association! Is that so? Consider how hard it is for the labourers round you to pluck up courage even to run a Liberal Association, which is the elementary form out of which all revolts grow. And I think you will one day feel the need of more obviously and actively repenting about woman's suffrage. Are you quite 'honest' about that? All of which I feel very impertinent.[40]

He risked 'impertinence' again by dissenting from Beatrice's interpretation of the Passion Play which they had both separately seen that summer at Oberammergau. She thought it had the feeling of a social revolt. He dissented:

> Pontius Pilate somewhat restored my male self-complacency. My profession made me realise entirely his position. I should have acted just as he did. And I can't help feeling that Jesus did not give him a chance. The least bit of energetic defence would have enabled Pilate to save him … The fact is that I do not greatly worship the Jesus type: you will understand why I have a vague feeling that he ought to have 'taken it fighting' to some extent, at any rate to the extent of making a reasonable defence. No wonder the disciples 'scattered'. The beauty of sacrifice qua

sacrifice does not adequately appeal to me. There ought to be a reasonable calculation of means to ends, an attempt at adaptation to the environment – not necessarily precluding such actions as that of John Brown … It is sometimes one's duty to 'use oneself up' as a cannon ball.[41]

Beatrice, despite her occasional revulsion of feeling, liked Sidney. If she was occasionally imperious and exacting, she had a high regard for his intelligence and learning. She wanted to retain his friendship and the friendship of his friends. She specially liked Graham Wallas, Sidney's closest friend:

He is so perfectly sincere and naively enthusiastic. And he has [here she showed her acuteness] quite a teacher's faculty for imparting all he knows, and great generosity in giving it. But what charms me is the perfect sort of relations between your little knot of men – it is singularly trustful – you really care for each other …[42]

Wallas visited her while Sidney was away in Europe. She had less success with Shaw. He announced himself outraged at her suggestion that a poverty-stricken, busy man like him should be imperiously summoned down to talk to her. 'To think that I should have lived to be sampled – to be sent down on approval or return – to be inspected by daylight by a fastidious young lady in search of an eligible socialist society to join.' He commanded her to practise her speaking and to turn no more socialist heads with her wiles.[43]

The concordat restored, she went off to Yorkshire to attend the Economic Section of the British Association. She and Sidney stayed in the Midland Hotel, Leeds. They travelled back from Bradford together along with Llewellyn Smith. They were in a third-class compartment. At 11.30 p.m.

A variety artist jumps in – a pretty, smart, foreign Jewess, decidedly the worse for liquor – forthwith addresses herself to the gentlemen in the carriage; these leaving us at the next station, turns to my two companions. Tells us the details of her life, becoming more and more racy. L. Smith collapses in the corner, looking alternatively severe and unalterably amused. SW, by whom she sits, tries to keep her in order by enquiring, in the most fatherly manner, into her earnings and into the statistical side of her profession. Whereupon I get interested and show signs of listening. She immediately brightens up and leaning across SW tells me in a loud whisper about her latest tights and the sensation they created, remarking that she did not mind speaking of such a subject to a husband and wife. I bury myself in the corner; L. Smith shakes with laughing and SW begins hurriedly another statistical enquiry. And it ends by the young lady offering to introduce him as a performer on the variety stage, looking doubtfully the while at his big head and little body![44]

On the way back to London they travelled 'first' and were spared all intrusion. Sidney told her about his examination successes and read her to sleep with Morris's *A Dream of John Ball*.[45]

Thus in September 1890 the relationship appeared to be tightening. In the following month Sidney visited Charles Booth and tried to convince him that the municipalities and the co-operatives could be efficient without competition. Since Booth was one of Beatrice's closest and most respected friends, he was desperately anxious to stand well with him. But their meeting was not a success. 'I cannot,' wrote Sidney, 'be other than myself, and I can and will not meet people, even my superiors in years and experience, except on terms of intellectual equality and sincerity.'[46] Unfortunately Beatrice had confided in the Booths, and Charles warned her that Sidney was not man enough for her and that she would grow out of him.[47] This warning appears to have had its effect and throughout the autumn her heart was hardening against her friend.

At the end of November Haldane came to see her to discuss the possibility of an alliance between the progressive Liberals and the Fabian socialists. She felt well prepared for the encounter since Graham Wallas had only just left her and she fancied she was quite *au fait* with Fabian strategy. After seven hours of negotiations, Haldane began to explore the possibilities of an alliance of another sort. She tried to impress him with the advantages of celibacy for the Apostles of the new creed, but he continued to send out scouts in all directions. At last she said: 'Ah, Mr Haldane, I will let you into the secret of woman's unmarried life. In my days of deep depression I brood over matrimony – but it is an alternative to suicide.'[48] Haldane threw up his hands with an 'uncomfortable laugh' – as well he might, for Beatrice had more than half persuaded herself that she meant it. Family responsibility kept her from her work. Marriage, particularly marriage to an active politician, would present fresh impediments to her career. It would be 'an act of *felo de se* for a speculation in personal happiness'. And what a speculation! She became more than ever decided that personal passion had burned itself out and that what little might remain haunted her memories of Joseph Chamberlain.

Sidney sensed the change of attitude and fought desperately against it:

I am not deceived. I know that I deceive myself when I pretend to estimate you and criticise you, and count up your good qualities and your drawbacks. It is the 'indefinable you' that I want – bother your qualities and the defects of your qualities.[49]

If it was the painful memory of Chamberlain that came between them, let her remember Shaw's saying that 'grief of two-years' standing is nothing but a bad habit,' as he had been told in his own case in 1885 – 'Don't nurse your *Kummer*'. He sent her *Dr Heidenhoff's Process*, which he considered a very good guide to 'cerebral hygiene'.

> I believe that good cerebral hygiene consists largely in 'selecting' one's impressions so that the mind dwells upon those only that have a good effect on the mind … Remorse e.g. is very dangerous. We need just remorse enough i) to make us remember that it is *disagreeable* to sin, ii) to impress us with the need for *caution* when again approaching the chance for sin.[50]

But outside Heidenhoff's laboratory, the sponge of oblivion cannot be passed over an item of memory without reducing the capacity for feeling and experience. As the recollection of her 'humiliation' receded, Beatrice became more convinced that, although she was susceptible to the charm of being loved, she was not capable of loving. Sidney complained:

> You have an undercurrent of 'anti-male' feeling, which no doubt answers to some part of your rather wide experience, but which I simply don't understand … I think the 'subjection of women' is bringing a growing anti-male tension which seems to me (though not unmerited) very bad in its results. It would be an evil thing if women, in any sense, formed a huge Trades Union or protective confederacy against men.[51]

Since she was unmoved by the rather clammy sensuality of Rossetti, he decided that she must be afraid of the claims of romantic love. He told her of the German girl who had remarked that no woman would ever marry Sidney Webb because she could only be his '*Zweite Braut*'. 'I *hope* you will never be more than this – I have tried and I intend to try to make this so – with your help.'[52]

But at the end of the year – while he lay stricken with scarlet fever – she told him that she did not love him: that she found him personally unattractive: that she doubted whether she ever could bring herself to submit to a close relationship with him. She sometimes felt that even his friendship was distasteful to her and that friendship led to misunderstandings. He took her 'playful words' seriously and became presumptuous. Therefore it would be best if they saw nothing of each other and stopped being intimate friends.[53]

O love, my love! If I no more should see
Thyself, nor on the earth the shadow of thee,
Nor image of thine eyes in any spring.
How then should sound
Upon Life's darkening slope
The ground whirl of the perished leaves of hope
The wind of Death's imperishable wing!

Dante Gabriel Rossetti

He raged. He burnt some of her letters. He cursed and abused his best friend, Graham Wallas, for no reason, and he could not explain himself to Wallas or anyone else for she had forbidden him to mention her. He told Beatrice that she had been principally responsible for the misunderstandings that had wrecked his suit. He would never have dreamed of 'precipitating things', had it not been for an oversight of hers.[54]

Yet it was characteristic of Beatrice that, while she told herself that all was over, and while she acted out the drama of breaking the tie asunder, she left herself a loophole which would allow some relationship to be maintained. If he swore to stop writing her intimate letters; returned all the ones that he had received; swore that no more letters existed; and declared that if friendship should lead again to hope, he would not reproach her if she married another man – then he might still write to her provided he addressed her as 'Miss Potter'.[55] He accepted that, 'I am like Auguste Comte: as I cannot have what I want, I make a virtue of wanting only what I can have! But the friendship of Clothilde de Vaux was invaluable to Comte, in developing all the better side of his nature.'[56] (It can hardly be said to have improved the Frenchman's sense of humour. Sidney managed a wry joke – he would really have to get the Liberal Party to write 'the abolition of scarlet fever' into its programme. John Morley would accept this, since scarlet fever was a serious infringement of individual liberty and totally inconsistent with self-help.)[57]

While he was convalescing, Sidney meditated a new plan of life. Beatrice had told him that she would far rather marry a clerk in the Colonial Office than a parliamentarian,[58] but since she would not marry him he would ignore this. He had to conquer his 'bourgeois' preoccupation with security. Despite the fact that it would come as a grave shock to his parents, he decided to leave the Civil Service and to try and earn his living by journalism and scraps of practice at the bar.[59] He had already finished his *Socialism in England,* was working at a book on the eight-hour day with Harold Cox and was preparing another on *The London Programme*. In association with Massingham he already had half a career in daily and weekly journalism. Closer association with Haldane and Grey only persuaded him that the need for someone in Parliament, or at least on the London County Council, was very great.[60]

Beatrice, on his insistence, sent her subscription to the Fabian Society, but she was going through a crisis with respect to her new-found faith in socialism, and was questioning whether political commitment was consistent with scientific research and scholarly distinction.[61]

While allowing that he might sacrifice thought to action too much, he reminded her that there were advantages in 'joining one's party'.[62] For the rest, he used the distance which Beatrice had imposed upon him to become 'placidly aggravating'. Late in January 1891, Beatrice's friend, Mrs Green, widow of the political philosopher, used some remark of Sidney's as a pretext for asking about her attitude towards him. Beatrice, in turn, used the incident to revert to her imperious, exacting and threatening tone. She told him that

> Mrs Green's surprise and curiosity were very painful to me. Moreover it makes it increasingly difficult for me to remain on terms of friendship. I have no intention of losing her respect, or of hiding things from her, or even of going out of my way to explain my motives. But you have forced my hand, and laid me open to the reflection of being rather a vulgar coquette. I regret all the more this slip as hitherto you have acted with so much honourable discretion – so that you have made a delicate position possible for me.[63]

He dismissed this in a line or two, remarking that it was no fault of his that Mrs Green suspected their relationship – or rather what had been their relationship. He went on to discuss London politics and Buxton's Bill against sweating.[64] It began to dawn on Miss Potter that she had to reckon with a form of Gresham's law in this matter of reprimanding Sidney and consigning him to outer darkness. Besides, the man was so extraordinarily industrious and useful. In between engaging in a polemic against Courtney in the *Economic Journal* in February and finishing his book on *The London Programme* in April, he complained about Harold Cox not being able to keep up with him on their eight hours book.[65] At the same time he read the manuscript of Beatrice's work on co-operation:

> Shall I be quite candid? Do not take it amiss if I confess to a slight feeling that you have taken too long over it. The book will not be a *very* great work; and you could have written it more quickly if you could have had anything of the nature of what the racer calls a 'pace-maker'.[66]

As her thoughts turned to a big work on trade unionism, he encouraged her to consider collaboration with Llewellyn Smith. He told her:

> You do not write quickly or easily: what you ought to get for this work – perhaps this is what you seek in Llewellyn Smith – is a secretary who could seize your ideas, arrange your materials, and leave you only

to revise the MSS and rewrite just where you felt inclined. This is how most of the great statesmen do their work, and I think it is economical.[67]

Showing no jealousy of Llewellyn Smith, he suggested that she should invite Wallas – for whom he had never felt any jealousy – down to stay with her. In the middle of March he did allow himself one line of personal feeling: 'The great secret of life is not to expect too much from it. After all the world is neither black nor white, but grey – a kind of pepper and salt mixture – and only children cry for sugar instead. (I am a child) Yrs, Sidney Webb.'[68]

The following month Beatrice went for a six weeks' stay with Alice Green. They went together to the co-operative congress at Lincoln, and Sidney accompanied them. On the way back he placed his hand on hers and it was not withdrawn. Beatrice was being taken more and more into public life. She had given her first series of lectures before a distinguished audience that included Herbert Spencer, Frederic Harrison, Haldane and Massingham.[69] She was working to secure an appointment for herself as a sub-commissioner to the Royal Commission on Labour over which her brother-in-law, Leonard Courtney, presided. She was 'cheeky and impertinent' to him and he was contemptuous of her, so nothing came of it except a closer identification with Sidney, who had already crossed swords with Courtney.[70] Her thoughts were increasingly taken up with plans for a great book on trade unions. She knew that she needed Sidney. She was drawn to him by affection and gratitude, although marrying him would be 'an act of renunciation and not indulgence of self as it would have been in the other case'.[71] Considered as renunciation, she decided that there was much to be said for it. On 20 May 1891, in the Devonshire House Hotel, they became secretly engaged and embraced each other for the first time.

For Sidney their relationship had to be described in cosmographic imagery. They were to be thought of neither as sun and planet, nor as planet and satellite, but as each an entire solar system, and when solar systems came together, it was a big thing.[72] He knew that man was a planet who needed to be part of a system, if he was not to rush to destruction. He did not admire dated Ptolemaic systems but – if she willed it – there should be an improvement on Copernicus, and 'Bee' should be the sun in the new Webbian cosmology.[73] He loved the way she dilated her nostrils; he loved her 'chiffy blouse'; he loved her haughty and imperious manner; he loved her faults:

Your wilfulness, your natural ambition – indeed they are not in themselves faults at all … What the world wants is not men and women ideally perfect in character, but warm-hearted, thinking, throbbing, *erring* fellow creatures – truth through warmheartedness, character through action.[74]

With her it was different:

> On the face of it [she wrote] it seems an extraordinary end for the once brilliant Beatrice Potter (but it is just because it is not an end that she has gone into it) to marry an ugly little man with no social position and less means – whose only recommendation – so some may say – is a certain pushing ability. And I am not 'in love', not as I was.[75]

She did not let him forget that it was a case of beauty and the beast. He acknowledged that it was so and begged only that it might not turn out to be an affair of Titania and Bottom.[76] He kissed her photograph and, never having dreams (or at least having no recollection of having had them) – wished to dream. Did she ever, he wondered, kiss his photograph? 'No dear, I do not even look at your photograph. It is too hideous for anything. Do be done in a grey suit by Elliot & Fry and let me have your head only – it is the head only that I am marrying!'[77] She advised him: 'Get a new tie and string to your pince-nez and look after your pronunciation. You can't afford not to be careful about externals!'[78] He sent her a new portrait:

> I fear I can't put a better part of me, and perhaps by upright living I may get some kind of light in my face which will take off its ugliness. But if it has found favour with you, I can easily put up with caricatures and repulsion of others.[79]

Beatrice had brought Sidney almost to the point of accepting the Comtian doctrine respecting the moral superiority of women. But it was Sidney rather than Beatrice who practised Comte's maxim: 'Live Openly'. He was free, as she was not, from doubts and equivocations. He responded to life with a warmth, simplicity and directness which she found it difficult to attain. When it seemed likely that there would be a renewal of the struggle in the docks, he told her: 'I had a real "rush" of pity, and I felt I could give up life and even give up you, if I could prevent the suffering it will cause.'[80] She admired the genius of Tom Mann, but thought that 'even the best of the dockers bear the brand of London cunning and London restlessness.'[81]

She told herself that she regretted having to sacrifice her capacity for appreciating art and music and literature so that she could investigate labour movements:

> We will try to have a little culture … try with a humble and reverent attitude; we shall enjoy the atmosphere of culture even if we do not

acquire the substance; and by a judicious choice of friends, we may get glimpses into the land of promise, which we will do our level best to make possible for others.[82]

'Dearest,' he wrote, 'I confess to a low taste. I *like* the kitchen of life.' Yet he saw that 'we must save our whole selves alive if we are to do our best work'.[83] He therefore asked her to help him learn the language of the arts. This was surely an unintended irony, for in literature at any rate, his knowledge was far wider and his judgement surer than hers.

In the autumn of 1891 Beatrice helped C.T. Ritchie to organise a debating club in the Stroud Valley. At first all went well and Sidney was invited to come down and speak. Before he was due to arrive, Beatrice gave an address which caused great excitement and thoroughly annoyed Sir John Douglass, the great Tory landlord. Mary Playne was much distressed and begged her to get Sidney to cancel his visit. Beatrice decided to comply with her sister's wishes, despite the fact that she thought it good to rouse the valley out of its deadening torpor. Sidney, however, refused to write a letter to Ritchie pretending that he had another engagement.

> Surely [she wrote] you owe it to me to make my relations with my family as pleasant as possible – it is not too much to ask of you to throw over a wretched little Club! Of course I can't force you to do it, but if you care for my feelings at all, you will write by the evening's post to Mr Ritchie stating simply that you are unavoidably prevented by an important political engagement from coming down to Gloucestershire on 28th. Anyway, I can't have you here on the 28th.[84]

'Dearest Bee,' he answered, 'do not love me less because I *could* not do what you asked.'[85] She had taught him a franker, simpler truthfulness. She would not expect him to be subservient to her every word. They ought to add together, not to merge, their moral intuitions.[86] In the end he gave way, but only after he discovered that she had already said that he would not be coming.

At the end of 1891 Richard Potter's long illness was drawing to its close and Beatrice was understandably torn between sorrow and relief. She was perplexed as to how she ought to feel. He told her:

> If you feel on the whole glad, – feel glad and say so. If you feel solemn, be solemn. Do not feel or say or think what you imagine you ought to feel, say or think – that is the usual horrible mockery of an English funeral.
>
> There is death on earth, but no *Death* with a big D. This personification of Death – a kind of bogey man – is answerable for much of our

false sentimentality on the subject. Dearest – *moi qui vous parle* – I am feeling horribly faint at the thought that either you or I must be 'lost' one day, to the other. It is no use crying 'Peace, Peace' where there is no peace. I am not reconciled to death – we must bear it, but I will not pretend that I will acquiesce in it.

And since we *must* part one day and our bodies – Sweet, *qui nous appartient à toujours* – must be put away – and our minds cease – since it must be so, let it add a new sanctity to our love – not only that but to our view of human life. A few precious years is all we have for each other and for the world – let us never profane those years. The greatest Blasphemy seems to me to be doubt – of love, of life, of progress. Help me to keep us both from Doubt.[87]

It was the wholeheartedness of Sidney's love and his perfect integrity that gradually conquered Beatrice's doubts. She had doubted whether marriage would really aid her work. 'I love you,' she told him, 'but I love my work better.'[88] He showed her that this was a false antithesis. He was tempted by opportunities of entering the House of Commons, but if this seemed to threaten her career, he would be well content with a career of usefulness in the LCC. If his socialism meant that some of the 'old' unionists might be more reluctant to talk to Beatrice about trade unionism, lists of provincial Fabians furnished by Sidney could supply useful contacts. If the great task which she had set herself seemed overwhelming, he would find her a research assistant and come himself to help her sort and arrange the ever mounting mass of facts. As early as August 1891 she was recording: 'We allowed half an hour for confidential talk and "human nature" and then worked hard at the Ironfounders' Records. Then lunch, cigarettes, a little more "human nature", and then another two hours work.'[89]

Nor did she find these intervals for 'human nature' disagreeable. 'It is very sweet, this warm and close companionship in work.'[90] Her engagement in May had been a cool, deliberate step: by the end of the year she found in it a source of unconscious, growing happiness.[91] In October she had chanced to see Chamberlain and his wife, who travelled part of the way on the same train as she did. She had doubted whether she could ever again feel for any man as she had felt for him. Now she could tell Sidney:

Dearest – it caused me no pang; he was looking self-complacent and self-conscious (he has lost his old look of fervid intentness) and I thanked Providence that I was travelling third class in search of knowledge and not first class in his train. The little wife looked plain and insignificant, but good and sweet – somewhat doll-like. They seemed to

me an absolutely suited pair – both enveloped in a sense of social prestige and material comfort: he the dominant male and she – *la femme
complaisante*. I felt a grim satisfaction that he was so mated; and I grieve
to say that I felt a bit contemptuous (it was unchristian to say the least
of it). Perhaps if he had seen the elderly spinster occupant of a 3rd.
Class carriage, he would have felt like feelings.[92]

A few days after Richard Potter's death on 1 January 1892, Ella Pycroft
heard that Beatrice was going to marry Sidney:

> I'm just going to tell you the absolute truth, Bee – and that is that I
> should be quite genuinely glad if I thought you cared for him one half
> as much as he does for you – but you know when we were talking of
> marriage the other day I felt as if you hadn't the remotest idea of what
> love meant in my sense of the word – perhaps I'm wrong, and at any
> rate you may learn to know if you don't know, and then it would be all
> right. You're quite right, one wants intimacy of thought and comrade-
> ship, but marriage ought to be something much more than that.[93]

Ella's wise cautions would have been appropriate at the time of the
engagement; by now they were already out of date, and every passing day
made them less relevant. All the elements of hardness and cruelty went
out of Beatrice's writing. 'We love each other devotedly,' she wrote. 'We
are intensely interested in the same work. We have freedom and means to
devote our whole lives to the work we believe in. Never did I imagine
such happiness open to me. May I deserve it.'[94] Sidney asked: 'Can't you
be a little haughty or imperious or exacting for a change? I have a sense –
delightful – of getting deeper and deeper into your debt.'[95] By the spring
of 1892 she did gently reproach him for having more of the husband's
manner, but then she herself was writing like a wife. 'I have been meaning
to advise you not to bring the thick flannel night-shirt. I notice you always
have a cold when you return home and I am pretty sure that it comes
from changing from flannel to cotton night-shirts.'[96] He had written earlier in May: 'I don't feel today as I have done on former days when we
have parted. This time we have gone beyond the former stage: I feel as if I
was separated – not from my love – but from my wife.'[97] (From this point
until their marriage in July their letters are incomplete and many sheets
are missing. Deeply as they cared for historical accuracy and completeness
there were evidently some phases of their life which they thought better
closed against prying eyes, even those of the 'great-grand niece' or 'unemployed intellectual' who would come to write their biography.)

There were of course difficulties with families and friends. She dreaded
the cramped, ugly, lower-middle-class character of Sidney's home, until

gradually her dislike of these unfamiliar surroundings 'disappeared in the blessedness of love'.[98] The Booths did not want to know Sidney and she cried about it.[99] Spencer took away his literary executorship from her and she managed to laugh:

> 'I cannot congratulate you,' observed the philosopher, 'that would be insincere.' 'You see that he has succeeded in marrying me, Mr Spencer – that shows he has a will.' 'Undoubtedly,' groaned out the philosopher, 'that is exactly what I fear – you both have wills – and they *must* clash.'[100]

Sidney had the rather painful and laborious task of calling upon her sisters and her brothers-in-law:

> Dearest, my impression is that your sisters are not very able women in the intellectual way. Really, Mrs Holt is the cleverest of the lot; and your trained intellect stands out as quite alien to them all. I have been amused to watch how they all rush at me with futile little arguments, utterly lacking in logic or acumen, their husbands meanwhile looking on indulgently and, when appealed to, sweetly and quietly putting them straight – I don't wonder that you got on best with the said husbands … a set of remarkable men, each in his own way. (I except the Williamses whom I have not seen, and the Playnes whom I have not seen for two years.)
>
> But I don't want to 'run down' your sisters. They have all been exceedingly kind, and they are at least as clever as the ordinary women of society, and the ordinary mother of a family. Only, you see, one expected *your* sisters to be something more. Especially does one miss the logic and the intellectual atmosphere which you bring to everything. Mrs H[obhouse] talked most about Luxury – its evil, and yet how impossible it was to have things orderly and clean without accepting the whole conventions of one class. She said the servants would not allow any deviation.
>
> As you say, these people are not really conscious of the existence of Poverty. Indeed Mrs H. struck me as unconscious that there were any individuals of the same *species* as herself who had less than £5000 a year.
>
> Mrs Hobhouse had discussed the impending wedding. I said I hoped there would be no ceremony. She said: 'Where will it be? I suppose the Registry Office. I much prefer the Church.' I said I supposed it depended on one's opinions. She replied, 'O not at all. I myself am advanced!' And then I fled.[101]

In fact not all the sisters were 'extremely kind', and he had one of his colds which he felt made him 'more than necessarily mean and small and ugly'.[102]

Mrs Playne vexed me with her ostentation of cynicism; her admiration for Lottie Collins, the singer and dancer of 'Ta-ra-ra' and so on. She seemed to be bent, probably, quite unconsciously on sounding all the depths of me that she disliked. I am quite sure she thinks me horrid, and oddly enough, still on entirely wrong grounds.[103]

It was not pleasant to be quite so frankly despised. And if the Hobhouses or the Courtneys did not regard him as vulgar, he had the impression that they did see him as rather like Chamberlain at the corresponding stage of his career: cool; superficially able; somewhat unscrupulous politically; a pushing, rising young man. This too was 'a little horrid'. He did not think he was in danger of Chamberlain's fate but he begged his Bee to save him from it.[104]

Sidney was probably quite right about how the Hobhouses regarded him. But in their eyes it was decidedly to his advantage that he was noticed in *Times* leaders, and coming to be spoken of as an important man in radical and socialist politics. He was within their political world, even if he had entered it by another door and occupied a different position inside it. After all, he had just been returned eighth behind Lord Carrington to the Executive of the National Liberal Club.[105] He dined with Sir Edward and Lady Grey, acted as a private legislative draftsman for Sydney Buxton and was a close friend of R.B. Haldane's. These men were political opponents to Liberal Unionists like Courtney or Hobhouse, but they were not beyond the pale. Webb was lower-middle-class, a socialist wire-puller, but he might have been far worse. Had he been committed to independent working-class politics and appeared as the spokesman of the 'Labour Party', communication would have been infinitely more difficult, and the barriers of class would have been far higher. A little playful radicalism or socialism was one thing; the organisation of an independent class party of the proletariat were quite another. Here there was a departure between the conditions that were formative of the partnership and those that favoured a fully defined consciousness of what the labour movement was and must become. Beatrice and Sidney were drawn together by the discovery of how the great voluntary associations of co-operation and trade unionism, in which she was primarily interested, needed to be complemented by what he had already projected in terms of socialist policies for local and central government. Much of the charm of their association lay in the way in which the interests, knowledge and experience of one seemed to disclose the appropriate sphere of activity for the institutions with which the other was concerned. Thus, Beatrice had identified the barriers to the further extension of the co-operative movement.[106] For example, there were social barriers. The very rich (who did not matter) and the very poor (who did) were shut out. Sidney's response was to argue that: 'As we cannot make co-operation fit our residuum, we must make our residuum fit for co-operation.'[107] The co-operative store flourished in regions such as Lancashire, where the Factory Acts had done most for the compulsory elevation of the poor. Again, Beatrice found that large-scale enterprise presented administrative and financial barriers to the advance of co-operation, but Sidney could demonstrate that these barriers could not stand against the claims of municipal enterprise. But while they thought about trade unionism and co-operation in class terms, they did not think that socialism required a third working-class institution: a Labour Party. Had Sidney been any other kind of socialist than a Fabian one, had he trusted, as other socialists did, in the political capacity of the working class, it is doubtful whether Beatrice would ever have had the patience to develop their work and their friendship.[108] But had Beatrice not come from the world of prosperous, humane and established liberalism, Sidney might have been more strongly tempted than he was to pursue the tactic of pressure from without rather than permeation from within. He might have arrived earlier than he did at the full, modern, tripartite conception of the labour movement. In fact he always equivocated about the necessary class character of a socialist party – but then, that kind of equivocation surrounded the Labour Party itself.

It was when Sidney's hopes of marrying Beatrice had all but perished that he resolved to spurn the security of the Colonial Office and take full-time to journalism and politics. The founding of the *Star* in January 1888 under the editorship of T.P. O'Connor MP had opened doors for him. Not that O'Connor was sympathetic, but H.W. Massingham, the assistant editor, was a radical with Fabian leanings. The inevitable rows culminated in O'Connor selling out in July 1890. 'The paper', declared Webb, 'will remain under Stuart[109] and Massingham, that is (I say it to you only) me. I need hardly say that this will further exalt our power.'[110] And so, for a time, it did. Sidney and Shaw were able to get any inspired 'par' into it whenever they liked. The foundation of the *Speaker* under the editorship of T. Wemyss Reid in January 1890 also – despite Shaw's initial misgivings[111] – supplied them with another valuable medium. Massingham quarrelled with Stuart who drew £1000 a year for himself out of the *Star* and finally resigned from it in January 1891. A couple of months later he went on to the Fabian executive. When Sidney finally left the Colonial Office in September 1891, he and Massingham went into a kind of partnership, Sidney being paid £200 a year for writing a half-column of a London Letter which they prepared for *The Bradford Observer* and other provincial papers.[112] If he pushed himself, Sidney found he could manage as many as ten articles (including London Letters) in seven days.[113] In the first seven and a half months that followed his resignation from the civil service, he earned £200 from daily journalism, contributions to learned journals or heavier periodicals, and royalties on his books. On the top of this he had made investments which brought him in £80 during this period.[114] Massingham advised him to marry a woman with £1000 a year:

'You mean Beatrice Potter?' 'No, no. Potterism is to be taken with a large grain of salt. I don't know that you wouldn't find that you had *bitten off more than you could chew*. And I don't think that she has much money, she doesn't live like it. No, don't marry a clever woman, they're too much trouble.'[115]

But three months earlier, walking hand in hand across the moors of northern Norway, Sidney had been in earnest conversation with Miss Potter:

I don't want to influence you [she said] in the detail of what you do, for everyone must work out the detail of his own life; but I think it is time you deliberately planned what you intend to be – and that you made everything else fall in with that.

You forget [he answered] that has been impossible hitherto. I have decided that I want to take part in the government of the country according to socialist principles. I also want to think out the problems of socialist administration before they come up for settlement.

Quite so. That is exactly my view of what you want to be. But writing 'London Letters' … won't help you to *that*. You know that I think more highly of your abilities than you do yourself. So I don't mind saying that in order to become a first-rate administrator you want more education in the technique of administration, and in order to think over the various social problems, you want technical knowledge of those very questions! The LCC will give you the one – helping me will give you the other.

I agree with you about my deficiencies [said he] but I think there is a danger that in trying for big things we may diminish our usefulness – that in refusing the smaller influence one gains by casual journalism, one may be neglecting the only work one is capable of doing well. To help you will be one of my principal aims – but for other reasons. What I am undecided about is whether you are not (and I also) too ambitious for me – whether you are not expecting too much from me.

No, I don't expect anything in particular from you. I do not know whether you unite the qualities and whether the opportunity will offer itself for you to become a really big man. About that I do not much care. We are not responsible for your abilities or for the natural circumstances which might make those abilities 'the talent of the hour'. But it is clear that your abilities are sufficiently good to enable you to do first-rate work on the County Council for instance. In the County Council alone there is a magnificent field for administrative ability – and for that handling of men in committees in which you excel. And that work is infinitely more important at the present moment than any amount of smart journalism. And what is equally significant, there are apparently few (if any) men who are at once willing and able to do it – while journalists of every degree of smartness abound, and after all, though I do not think you are a first-rate political instrument – so far as we can see there are no men in political life who are at once good instruments for making Public Opinion and good instruments for executing it. You unite these qualities of thinking and acting; though we are uncertain to what degree; and you also have the means to do the work which is most useful to the community. We are both of us second-rate minds; but we are curiously combined – I am the investigator, and [you] the executor – and we have a wide and varied experience of men and things between us. We have also an unearned salary. This forms our unique circumstances. A considerable work should be the result; if we use and combine our talents with a deliberate and consistent purpose.[116]

As soon as he was out of the Colonial Office Sidney let it be known that he was in search of a winnable seat on the LCC. Offers to nominate him came in from many constituencies in London. He settled for Deptford. Beatrice sent him £100, which he imagined would cover his expenses. It was given and received in a simple manner without the slightest embarrassment on either side. 'Yes, you shall give me a cheque for the County Council expenses; it won't come to £100 at most – and I shall be the Member for Potter!'[117]

However, this comradely attitude towards Sidney's election campaign did not extend to the Fabian Society. For a year Shaw had been predicting trouble: 'The seismological signs indicate that we are all spoiling for a fight. What is more, the revolt is going to be against the Webbian opportunism.'[118] It duly began in December 1891 when Sidney, at the age of 32, found that he had 'lost the confidence of a certain section of the younger members by entering upon public life as a candidate'. The revolt was headed by John Burns and Hubert Bland, both of whom made 'bitter and malicious' speeches.[119]

Sidney liked to think of the Fabians as the 'Society of Jesus' of socialism – 'without, I hope, the mental subjection which Protestants accuse the Jesuits of, and also without the moral shiftiness'.[120] The rebellion made him feel 'very weak and incapable, and full of a sense of my own unworthiness and want of strength to cope with the difficulties of democracy'.[121] Although he tried to persuade Beatrice that the Society did not mean much in his life, this was manifestly untrue. It was the only place where he could hope to speak his whole mind and where he felt completely at ease socially. If he went to the National Liberal Club he knew that half the members thought of him as a vulgar and subversive figure, and that John Morley suspected him of intriguing against him.[122] If he went for a beer with a dozen socialist gas stokers and sang the Marseillaise in English, he knew that they were struck by the difference between his hands and theirs, and that they suspected him of being a trimmer.[123] He was himself perfectly clear about where he stood: 'Whatever John Morley may think, I am a Girondin not a Jacobin.'[124] He added: 'I don't *want* to be a Girondin but it is so necessary to protest against those who wish to be extreme at all costs, even with loss of practicability, that I always expect to rank as a Girondin.'[125] Having thus placed himself in the revolutionary tradition, he concluded: 'It seems evident that the Fabian Society is by no means exempt from the usual failings of revolutionary movements ... the revolution devours its children, I have always foreseen it.'[126]

Although his candidature was the immediate issue involved in the rebellion against him, there was a complex background of personal and political antagonisms. His relations with John Burns and the proper shape to be given to the demand for the eight-hour day; his quarrel with Hubert Bland and the problem of the bearing of socialism upon the rise of a 'Labour Party'; his own personality and the subtle interdependence of his notion of socialist strategy with his conception of socialism itself – all these were elements in the struggle.

John Burns was a handsome, witty, forceful labour leader who exiled himself to the vastness of his own unconquerable vanity. Sidney had helped him in private and 'boomed' him in public,[127] but Burns did not welcome the prospect of sharing the limelight with Webb on the LCC. Besides, there was a real issue of principle between them on the eight hours question. It will be recalled that this was the decisive rallying point for all the forward forces in the world of labour during the last two decades of the nineteenth century. This was the slogan that promoted the transition from radicalism to socialism, which linked socialism to the new unionism, which aided in the recovery of the tradition of the International and the spirit of internationalism. Burns's reputation, like those of Mann, Champion and Hardie, was bound up with advocacy of the eight-hour day. So was Sidney's. Along with Harold Cox, he had made the fullest, clearest, most detailed and lucid case for legislation.[128] Burns knew very well that Webb was the man with the telling facts who could show that 82 per cent of the drivers and firemen employed on the railways in March 1890 were working more than 12 hours at a time. That he could discover a tramcar conductor in Bradford who regularly worked 115 hours a week for three shillings a day. But Sidney distinguished himself from Burns and other socialists, not merely by gladly undertaking to meet and to beat the economists on their own ground, but by taking pains to minimise the 'true' conflict of interests between employers and employed, and by making only sternly practical and gradualist proposals. One had, Webb insisted, to make allowances for different types and classes of worker, and one had to take proper account of the implications of shift systems, overtime, waiting time and emergencies. He said that

> in industrial organisation any sudden change – however good – produced a serious dislocation; but almost any gradual change – however important – could be endured without social injury. Time was of the essence of the matter.[129]

He therefore presented the advance to the eight-hour day as a matter of stages. It should be inaugurated by being applied in all work for public authorities and made a condition for securing government contracts. This should be followed by the limitation of the hours of labour in industries and services in which such hours were excessive, and where there was no direct problem of foreign competition: for example in transport, gas and distribution. Finally, the government ought to adopt the principle of 'trade option' - a principle which the Fabians had advanced as a novelty in a draft bill they had prepared in 1889 and subsequently discovered to be already incorporated in a Factory Act introduced in Victoria, Australia, in 1885.

Burns rejected the principle of trade option – contracting in to the eight-hour day, in favour of 'trade exemption' – contracting out of the eight-hour day. In Sidney's view this showed him at his worst. The important thing was to carry any eight-hour resolution at the TUC and that – he thought – would be quite difficult enough.[130] In the event Burns was proved right, for he succeeded in carrying his 'hard' version of eight hours at the Congress of 1890. Sidney acknowledged that this was splendid, as well as surprising. Yet he clung to the old position of trade option because he thought it important to conciliate the powerful forces in Lancashire and in Northumberland and Durham which appeared to remain unalterably opposed, and because he wanted to 'build a bridge for the opponents' of the whole concept. 'But,' as he added, 'Burns no doubt is thinking more of the influence on the masses.'[131]

Bland, at the head of the younger and more impatient element within the Fabian Society, was now also thinking in terms of 'influence on the masses' and wanted to throw the whole movement 'into the Labour Party'. Sidney, in an unsuccessful speech, resisted this demand (and defended his candidature as a 'progressive' for the LCC). He contended that: 'Our business is to convert the whole community to socialism.' Every Fabian ought to do what best he could, whether in Liberal or Labour circles, to win men for socialism, for they must reach all sorts of people if socialism was to triumph. Certainly one might try to imitate the Irish Nationalists and create a small, determined, disciplined party in the

Commons that would sell its votes for 'Labour' measures. But this would be a degradation of politics, and it might be doubted whether concessions wrung from reluctant leaders and carried out by unbelieving ministers would ever be ultimately effective. What was wanted was not a mere Labour Party, but a collectivist party. 'Labour', with its energy and determination, was an indispensable element within such a new organisation, but it was quite insufficient, taken by itself. The new party required the support of the younger radicals who could bring to it experience of public life and of administration, and the ideals and the principles of the socialists, upon which its action must be based. The Fabian Society should play a great but unobtrusive part in the formation of this party. But if it was to do so, it must not delude itself that workmen were spontaneous socialists, and it must no more 'give itself away' to the Labour than to the Liberal Party.[132]

Bland and his young supporters were unconvinced that you could thus hunt with socialist hounds while running (in Deptford) with the Liberal hares. Had they known of the full extent of Sidney's involvement with Schnadhorst, Stuart and the other Liberal organisers, they would certainly have pointed to the contradictions – although not to any want of integrity – that characterised this policy. Thus, before he had gone to the United States in 1888, Sidney, in his capacity as a member of the Holborn, the Westminster and the London University Liberal and Radical Associations had printed a private and confidential memorandum addressed to the leaders of London Liberalism.[133] The object was to indicate how the mass of metropolitan wage earners was to be united to the Liberal Party. The Tories and the Unionists held 51 out of London's 62 seats. Sidney showed the 'chill indifference of the masses' to official Liberalism by graphically demonstrating the geographical distribution of electoral apathy. While London Liberalism had seen the flight of the 'money-bags' to the Unionist seceders, the rapidly growing workers' clubs, many of which were organised in the Metropolitan Radical Federation, scornfully repudiated the word 'Liberal', mingling derision with indifference when presented with the party's official programme. In Sidney's view:

> Further evidence of this alienation can be seen in the new 'Labour Party'. Scarcely a week passes without some attempt to form a local branch, or a local 'Labour Union' of some sort. The air is thick with their draft constitutions, draft programmes, draft titles and so on. Most of them come to nothing, and it may well be doubted whether the time is ripe for a separate National Labour Party, but every attempt at its formation indicates working-class disgust with official Liberalism.

Nor was there any occasion for surprise that workmen should talk of Liberalism as a sham, when the most brutal employers – like Bryant & May – went in for Gladstone worship. And the Party's Nottingham programme (1887) offered the dock labourers and sweated trouser-hands of 'outcast London' nothing but Home Rule, registration reform, abolition of entail, disestablishment of the Scottish Church and local government reform. Was it not shameful, conscious hypocrisy to pretend that 'one man, one vote' meant manhood suffrage when all that was intended was the abolition of plural voting, or to talk about 'free land' when all that was meant was the abolition of entail? Sidney concluded that if the Liberals were to survive in London they would have to adopt a 'Labour Programme' as frankly and as wholeheartedly as they had adopted Home Rule. But in the same document he clearly indicated the difficulty:

The continued support of the capitalist as such necessarily involves the continued alienation of his 'hands'. It is perhaps irrelevant to enquire which, for 'the Party of the Masses', is the honest course. The masses still however expect some honesty even in politicians.

He confronted the Liberal Party leaders with a stark statement of the realities of class:

The material interests of these two great parties [*classes*, RH] are diametrically opposed to each other. No last compromise between them is even possible. On the one hand is the great mass of the workers by hand or brain, who will naturally insist on social arrangements which shall enable them collectively to enjoy the whole produce of their toil. On the other hand stand the classes which such social arrangements would necessarily completely eliminate: the idle recipients (from their unseen economic slaves) of tribute, called by the euphonious names of rent and interest. Between these two economic classes stands the middle class, the great majority of its members receiving, under the name of profit, both wages and interest. By its education, its share of the economic tribute, and its social aspirations, this middle class is always being subtly drawn towards the other 'classes', which, as a class, it dislikes and envies. By its history, its traditions, its politico-religious feelings and its dislike of aristocratic rule, it is impelled to resist those classes.

Thus, Bland and his comrades could have pointed out that Sidney's strategy depended on the highly dubious assumption that such vague and uncertain considerations as 'history', 'tradition' and 'politico-religious feeling' could be effectively appealed to and made to override the sharp promptings of 'economic tribute', 'education' and 'social aspiration'. As for the wire-pullers and party managers to whom Sidney was more especially appealing, would they not defer the hour when they would be compelled to make the choice with which he said they were confronted? Webb himself had admitted that there would probably be many more attempts to divert attention from the central social issues by going in for a 'cry' against the House of Lords or enlarging on the splendours of jingoism.[134] How long must they wait before they cleared the political ground of such irrelevancies? Sidney declared that he wanted to save the Liberal Party from becoming a merely middle-class party, like the German National Liberal *Partei*. 'I believe that would be bad and I have played to save it from that fate, even if it should imply Morley's resignation.'[135] But why would it be bad? Why did he ignore the fact that the shrinking of German Liberalism down to a mere middle-class grouping was associated with the rise of the first mass socialist workers' party in Europe? No doubt because that was a Marxist, an impossibilist party, which did not recognise that socialism was a matter for 'the whole community'. And also because there were good people in the English Liberal Party: people who accepted the claims of Labour and were inclined towards socialistic measures. Who were these good people? Well, Sidney's host when he stayed at Hanover House, Leeds, was the second most influential man on the executive of the National Liberal Federation:

> He is a good honest fellow, evidently a pattern of all the bourgeois virtues, anxious to do as much for the Labour Party as he can, and believing in its *future* influence, but as he is also the most influential man ... what he can *do* is not very much.[136]

Bland and the young guard were in rebellion against the 'Webb party' and the policies that gave rise to such a paradox as this. They were impatient with the politics of influence, which they associated, quite rightly, with a whole host of compromises and equivocations. They wanted to escape from them by making a clean break in favour of a Labour Party. But they themselves were ill-placed to play much part in that game. They might triumph over Sidney for a moment, but they could not consolidate their victory, or make it a genuine point of departure in the history of the Fabian Society. Sidney's strength lay in the fact that no one in the Fabians could doubt his personal disinterestedness:

> No one has the least ground for saying [he wrote] that I have ever tried to form a 'Webb' party; or that I have been loath to lend an anonymous hand to any movement. I am, in fact, much too proud inwardly to care very much about getting the actual credit of any piece of work. I want things done – I do not want to do them myself.[137]

His candidature for the LCC might momentarily obscure this from the eyes of the younger Fabians, but it could not be in question among the older ones. It was this reputation for personal integrity, which shielded him when he got himself into equivocal situations. And, of course, the politics of permeation did lead to endless equivocations: to a constant tendency to exaggerate successes and to minimise costs. Given that projects for launching a labour party were in the air, it was rather invidious for a leading socialist to have repeated secret talks with Schnadhorst about lists of 'Labour' – i.e. Lib-Lab–candidates.[138] Again, since the Fabian Society was associated with other socialist organisations in a public agitation for the restoration of free speech in the metropolis, it was risky for Webb to have private interviews with government representatives aimed at a mutually acceptable accommodation.[139] It might also be thought odd that Webb, as the author of a singularly objective and impartial history of socialism in England, which encouraged Hyndman to hope that he might yet become a Marxist,[140] should anonymously contribute to the *Financial Reform Almanack*.[141] This was, after all, a handbook of middle-class radicalism that bore on its cover a portrait of Cobden, and declared itself for 'Economical Government, Just Taxation, Perfect Freedom of Trade'.[142] The fact that he had warm disagreements with Schnadhorst, got free speech restored without bloodshed as a result of his talks with Sir Charles Russell, and said nothing that he did not believe in the Cobdenite journal, was not to the point. In the eyes of militants and men of principle he was keeping company with the enemy. He did feel uneasy about these charges. And, whatever Shaw might say, it was the case that 'permeation' did mean compromising, and 'soft-pedalling' and 'back-scratching'. Not all the concessions could be expected to come from one side. Thus, when Sidney was looking for a seat on the LCC he promised to help non-socialist politicians to get the workers' vote.[143] Sidney knew that he was a Girondin and he confessed that he was prone to the typical Girondin failing:

> Time was I shrank
>   from what was right
> For fear of what was wrong.[144]

Behind the debate in the Fabian Society on permeation versus independence – and still more manifestly behind that controversy within the British labour movement as a whole – lay a more fundamental dispute about the nature of socialism itself. Bland had already taken Sidney to task about this matter in *Fabian Essays*, where he had disassociated himself from the view that socialism could be equated with the indefinite extension of state ownership, regulation and control. William Morris, in a criticism of Edward Bellamy, had disclosed the issue much more adequately and explicitly. According to Morris, Bellamy was

> perfectly satisfied with modern civilisation, if only the injustice, misery and waste of class society *could* be got rid of; which half-change seems

possible to him. The only ideal of life which such a man can see is that of the industrious *professional* middle-class men of today purified from their crime of complicity.

Bellamy's mind was 'fixed firmly on the mere machinery of life'.[145]

It has been shown that Webb had a high regard for Bellamy. The 'half-change' in the life of the individual, which Bellamy had imagined in *Dr Heidenhoff's Process,* had been treated by Webb as more than an acceptable fictional device. He thought it a guide to cerebral hygiene. Much as one might cut out a diseased appendix, individual life could be renewed by cutting out shame and remorse. For all his commendations of an 'organic' view of society as opposed to the atomistic or mechanistic concept, Sidney thought of socialism as modern civilisation minus the recipients of rent and interest, and the irrational and wasteful allocation of resources that their presence entailed. To him 'half-change' seemed both possible and eminently desirable. Thus, in his book on the eight-hour day he concluded:

> If machinery lowers human beings below the level of monkeys in order that they may earn their living we can, at any rate, limit the period of monkeydom. If we cannot make the work manly, we can insist that the workers should have the leisure to become men.[146]

Elsewhere he asserted: 'Prophets nowadays do not found a partial community which adopts the whole faith; they cause rather the partial adoption of their own faith by the whole community.'[147] The belief that this was possible, together with a vision of socialism in terms of the supremacy of the values of the professional stratum and the universalising of their conditions of life, was what separated Webb from Morris and made permeation thinkable to the one and unthinkable to the other. To Morris, a socialism that stopped at abolishing the existing division of labour along with the existing division into classes, which complacently assumed the values of the existing professional strata without seeing how their taste and judgement and style of life were corrupted by their share in privilege and power, was hopelessly unimaginative and unambitious. To Webb, to forego opportunities for enlarging the sphere of social control and provision, in order to retain the purity of your vision of a wholly human society was an act of grotesque inhumanity and folly. Socialism was, he insisted, 'the truest opportunism'.

Beatrice advised Sidney to prepare his deliberate withdrawal from the Fabian Society and to turn his attention – and that of financial supporters, such as Daisy Reeves – to the trade unionists:

> But above all there should be no overt rupture – you should be benign and patient and perfectly without personal feeling, withdrawing your

active help and allowing them to make muddles and feel their own incompetence – without withdrawing yourself … The policy now, I am certain, is to starve the Society so that it shall find its own level. You have been over-feeding it, with the risk of its becoming a dangerous and noxious monster … it cannot be made into a strict 'instrument of progress', its material is too poor.[148]

In fact the rebellion soon blew over. On New Year's Day 1892 Sidney delivered a sermon at the South Place Chapel in which he adopted a reassuringly fierce tone:

Not in Thibet alone do rotatory calabashes satisfy the consciences of the pious; and Roman Catholics have no monopoly of the purchase of indulgences. I am afraid that I must own to an ingrained disbelief in the value of sermons, with or without God.

His text was 'Peace on Earth' but 'the modern commercial world lives in a state of perpetual social war, which was none the less war because the powder used is smokeless and noiseless.' By the bitterest of all ironies, he concluded, 'Peace on Earth' has been caught up and adopted as the precept, not of the poor and the oppressed but as a security to those who profited from it.[149] Undeterred by the Fabian rebellion, he persisted with his candidature and, declaring himself a Fabian, secured the active support of many members of the Society. Indeed he addressed an audience of Fabians who were going to lecture on the LCC elections within a month of Bland's attack on him. This was important, for it was impossible to work a borough like Deptford, which had 100 000 inhabitants and 12 000 electors, within the legally set limit of £100. The procedures and regulations laid down for the LCC had been modelled upon those for a ward of a town council, and were quite inadequate for the colossal magnitudes of London. It was therefore a great help that, well before polling day, he had as many as nine volunteers working for him for nothing.[150]

Presenting himself as 'a Londoner born and bred', and as one who had made London questions the chief study of his life, Sidney mounted a masterly campaign which sent his Conservative opponent down to complete defeat. To begin with he prepared an election address which J.W. Benn, the 'Progressive Whip' and a man not particularly friendly to Webb, recommended as a model.[151] Every point in this succinct document was enlarged upon in his book, *The London Programme*,[152] and a cheap edition of that work was brought out in time for the struggle. The so-called Moderates, declared Sidney, wanted the LCC to be no more than the old Metropolitan Board of Works. But the first task was to enlarge the powers and functions conferred on the LCC by the Local Government Act of 1888, and to make it 'a mighty instrument of the People's will for the social re-generation of this great city'. This meant the abolition of vestrydom and the rule of a miserable oligarchy mostly consisting of small shop-keepers anxious to escape the operation of the sanitary laws.

'I am', said Sidney, 'in favour of replacing private by Democratic own-ership and management, as soon and as far as safely possible.' It was easy enough to sneer at 'gas and water socialism', until one discovered that only half the houses in London had a constant supply of water, and that while this cost less than £700 000 per annum to the water companies, London paid £1 700 000 for it. It was much the same story with gas, and there were private monopolies at the docks and in the markets. But London lay under the shadow of centralised bureaucracy as well as in the grip of private monopolists: it paid for a police force it did not control. Mr Gladstone might pay what compliments he liked to our 'admirable police', yet Trafalgar Square showed that 'the London police will lack the very necessary support from London public opinion until they transferred to the control of the LCC'.

The first care of a London County Councillor must be for his poorer fellow citizens who were daily being crushed down by the 'competitive struggle'. London had 100 000 permanent paupers. 22.3 per cent of London's deaths took place in the workhouse or the public hospital. London had 238 separate hospitals competing with each other without regard to local needs. There was an overwhelming case for supervision; inspection; audit; and systematic co-operation. There must be a Poor Law Council for London, and an end to the inequitable rating of rich and poor districts and the great divergences in the conduct of Boards of Guardians in their treatment of paupers. But beyond all this:

> Some kind of pension scheme for the aged; some means of completely separating our collective provision for the sick and infirm from the Poor Law system; a more humanising nurture of the fifty thousand children to whom the State stands as parent; and some special provision for the technical training of the chronically unemployed unskilled labour class – all these are but the local completing of the great reform of 1834 ... Discrimination by classes must supersede discrimination among indi-viduals, which has been found impossible.[153]

By municipal death duties, by the taxation of ground rents, by the recov-ery of the inheritance which had been filched from London by the City corporations, which spent a fifth of their considerable income on official dinners, an end could be put to paying tramwaymen four shillings for a sixteen-hour day. The example of Liverpool could be followed in the matter of adequately housing the people through public building programmes. 'I am in favour,' declared Webb, 'of trade union wages and an eight-hour day for all persons employed by the Council. I am dead against sub-contracting, and would like to see the Council itself the direct employer of all labour.' He worked hard at organising the trade union vote and, despite a 'dig' at Tom Mann in *The London Programme*, he secured Mann's enthusiastic support.[154] He created a special trade union committee, which included a Tory, to aid his campaign. But he also succeeded in arousing enthusiasm in less likely quarters. At a meeting with the Temperance Party he produced a great effect by exhibiting a map of London with all the public houses marked by red dots. He called it 'London's scarlet fever' and pointed out there were three times as many pubs in the metropolis as there were bakers' shops. (It was not his fault if his audience took such diligent collection of statistics to imply that he was at one with them on the need to close down public houses.)[155] When he went to deliver a sermon on municipal virtue at a Wesleyan Chapel he took good care to prepare an abstract of it which he sent to five religious newspapers.[156] He so far stirred up the Chapel vote that he soon had ministers taking the chair for him at meetings of their own congregations. Such was his ingenuity that he persuaded Miss Orme, a rival of Beatrice's and a most orthodox person, to preside at one of his meetings.[157] Booksellers might fear to exhibit copies of *The London Programme*, but the issue could not be in doubt. Beatrice promised to spend all Sunday consoling him with kisses if he lost,[158] but when the count began it was evident that he was holding his own even in the 'swellest districts' and was leading by two to one everywhere else. Despite a splitting headache he managed a victory speech and then, as he recalled,

was lifted shoulder-high by an excited mob, carried downstairs to the imminent risk of scraping the ceiling with my nose, and so out into the road amid a fearful uproar. I picked up Galton, and took refuge in a hansom, leaving a howling mob parading New Cross Road.

I was *delighted* with the general result elsewhere. It is a simply gorgeous justification of Fabian electioneering, and ought to do something to convince the provincials that our game is the right one – and also to give us the control of London politics for the next three years. I felt inclined to go round by Cannon Street in order, like Jack Cade, to smite London stone with my umbrella and to shout into the night: 'Now is Mortimer Lord of London.' But I went to the Central Telegraph Office instead.[159]

Within a month he found himself on three committees: the Parliamentary, Local Government and Taxation, and the Pubic Health and Housing Committees. These were the ones he particularly wanted to be on, but he was also on the Special Water Committee, which was in virtual evasion of the rule that no one should be on more than three.[160] In May he was appointed chairman of the Technical Education Committee:

> Lord Rosebery who was in the chair to start us was evidently astonished, and rather cast about for an old member, but Lord Hobhouse and Sir T. Farrar pressed for me, and the committee was evidently 2 to 1 on my side (against Hogg). So I was installed in the very high chair which Lord R. vacated ... it was decided that I was to prepare a memo to lay before the committee next time.[161]

At the end of July Beatrice and Sidney married and they went first to Ireland and then to Scotland on their honeymoon. 'The people', so Sidney gaily reported from Ireland to Graham Wallas, 'are charming, but we detest them – as we should the Hottentots – for their very virtues. Home Rule is an absolute necessity in order to depopulate the country of this detestable race!'[162] In Dublin they had a spell of unsuccessful investigation into union records. In Belfast they met peculiarly unpleasant employers, who prided themselves on being able to get 'female flesh and blood and bone for 5/- a week or less'.[163] In Glasgow Sidney complained dreadfully about being sent out in the evenings to collect information in the working-class suburbs,[164] while Beatrice stayed at home. But then they had enjoyed 'two delightful days of real honeymoon in the Wicklow hills'.[165]

If Beatrice was still occasionally touched by doubt, for Sidney 1892 was a year of boundless happiness and triumph. Two years earlier, marriage had appeared to her a form of *felo de se* – fortunately in Sidney the 'death wish' had been strong. The 'partnership' was not only a term which he was the first to coin; it was his love and persistence which had ensured its formation. While she told him: 'However old your coat may be (and that is of no importance) *brush* it! Take care of your voice and pronunciation: it is the chief instrument of influence. Don't talk of "when I am Prime Minister"; it jars on sensitive ears,'[166] he could promise:

> You shall feel my arm under yours whenever you are tired; my strength around you whenever you are weak; my love embracing you whenever you are lonely; my skill and knowledge and facility as a basis whenever your finer taste and insight needs a foundation and a background.[167]

He saw, as other perceptive men and women came to see, that although if you listed Beatrice's characteristics you would say 'what a horrid woman', there was behind the haughty and exacting, imperious and pious, cruel and insensitive displays – a good, loveable and immensely able person. To begin with she brought less to their relationship than he did. He was more knowledgeable. He converted her to socialism, and had already anticipated some of the essential features of her argument about the co-operative movement. Her secure income helped him after he had left the Colonial Office, but he had already resolved upon that step before they became engaged. Yet she had come to share his vision. He had insisted that together they could move the world; recast the map of learning; be inventive of new policies and institutions. She shared that faith and that resolve. Their partnership was to last for fifty years: it required only five before promise turned to achievement.

Part IV
The Early Work of the Partnership 1890–1905

'We are all Socialists now.'

Sir William Harcourt, 1889

'Oh we are all burglars now.'

Sir William Harcourt, 1893

'It will be said of us as it is of Sir Gilbert Parker – in the dead silence of the night you hear a distant but monotonous sound – Sir Gilbert Parker climbing, climbing, climbing.'

Sidney to Beatrice, June 1904

6
Democracy and the Labour Movement 1892–8

Why they wrote the *History of Trade Unionism*—How they wrote it—A measure of their achievement—Towards a re-statement of Democratic Theory—Towards a new political economy—A novel interpretation of the relationship between socialism and the labour movement—The Webbs' influence upon the world of Labour: Mann and Broadhurst: Lenin and Bernstein.

Between 1891 and 1898 the Webbs laid the foundation of labour history and opened the way to the systematic study of labour institutions and of industrial relations. To recall the names of those who might dispute their claim to precedence and pre-eminence is to discover how far the Webbs were from meeting any effective challenge. British industrial conditions had, of course, long aroused the interest and excited the curiosity of foreign observers. Friedrich Engels's *The Condition of the Working Class in England in 1844* had included a sketch of labour movements. The Comte de Paris had published a study of *The Trades Unions of England* in 1869. Two years later Dr Lujo Brentano had produced his *On the History and Development of Gilds and the Origin of Trade Unions*. But Engels's work, so far as workers' organisation was concerned, was necessarily slight. The Comte de Paris derived almost all his material from the Reports of the Royal Commission on Labour which sat from 1867 to 1869, and Brentano, despite his real merits, was badly mistaken about the origins and defining features of trade unionism itself. The English authors who attempted large-scale works on labour made little of the historical component, and what they attempted was subject to the same limitations as those found in the works of foreign scholars. Thus, W.T. Thornton's important book, which helped to discredit the wages fund doctrine, followed the Comte de Paris in its heavy reliance on the evidence given to the Royal Commission.[1] The historical chapters of George Howell's *Conflicts of Labour and Capital* (1878) are simply a plagiarism from Brentano, in which renewed currency is given to the opinion that modern unions are the lineal descendants of the craft guilds. When Beatrice began her investigations into the history of the trade unions the only secondary sources of any value were fragmentary studies of particular unions, of strikes, or of attempts to establish institutions for collective bargaining and the peaceful settlement of disputes. Occasionally there was a short book or monograph that was not to be despised, such as Fynes's *The Miners of Northumberland and Durham*, or the essay in contemporary history by her friends Llewellyn Smith and Nash, *The Story of the Dockers' Strike*. But usually such help came only in the form of a few articles: Brentano's piece on the Engineers, or Beesly's on the Carpenters and Joiners. The English Positivists had indeed produced several pioneering studies and Frederic Harrison, another loyal friend, had once projected a full-scale study of the English wage-earners.[2] They were talented people and Sidney and Beatrice fully acknowledged their helpfulness to them during the nineties, but unlike their master, Auguste Comte, they were intellectually short-distance runners, whose stamina was used up in articles, essays and reviews. When Beatrice was working on the co-operative movement she had at least the benefit of the earlier work by George Jacob Holyoake; there was no Holyoake when it came to writing a general *History of Trade Unionism*.

Yet to establish the Webbs' status as pioneers in the field of labour history in general and trade union history in particular is to do them too little honour. The *History of Trade Unionism* of 1894, with its companion volume, *Industrial Democracy*, still stand as the greatest achievements in the fields of study that they inaugurated. There has been no want of able successors, many of whom the Webbs inspired and encouraged. Yet after fully a century, no one has attempted to supplant their general *History of Trade Unionism*, nor has anyone succeeded in producing a work which could compare in point of originality and comprehensiveness with *Industrial Democracy*, which has been described by a distinguished authority as 'the best single book ever written on the British Trade Unions'.[3] Despite many valuable elaborations and emendations, the terminology and the categories first devised by the Webbs have remained in use. Despite severe criticisms – some of them entirely justified – the chronology they established still organises research. It was not only in the nineteen-fifties that students began to become aware of how far they had taken for granted a conceptual framework which they had received from Sidney and Beatrice. Whitehead, with pardonable exaggeration, described the history of philosophy as 'a footnote to Plato'; with considerably less exaggeration the history of British trade unionism has been a footnote to the Webbs.

Yet the massive and incontestable character of Sidney and Beatrice's achievement as historians has seriously obscured their significance as political theorists. In the eighteen-nineties they were wrestling with the 'problem of democracy'. Their conclusions on this subject have hardly received from historians of political thought the attention they deserve. It will be shown that – far from reiterating the conclusions of John Stuart Mill – they anticipated the discoveries of Anglo-American political scientists and Italian sociologists. Their appreciation of the importance of the permanent civil service in representative government placed them far ahead of Bagehot, as Bagehot's recognition of the crucial importance of the cabinet placed him in front of Mill. Not only did they use trade union experience to draw attention to the place of the salaried officer and professional expert in the formal theory of representative government; they established the basic principles of a sociology of working-class leadership. Long before Roberto Michels demonstrated 'the oligarchical tendencies of modern democracy',[4] the Webbs showed a clear appreciation of many of the administrative and psychological factors which caused officials to acquire powers which the members never intended to confer upon them. They were not inclined to share Michels's pessimism, nor were they tempted to treat tendencies as 'iron laws', but they saw how full-time leadership changed the social status of workmen, and could engender conflicts of outlook and interests between the leaders and those to whom they were formally accountable.

These studies of working-class history and institutions allowed the Webbs to attain new insights into the relationship between socialism and the labour movement. They challenged received opinions about the transition to socialism, and they disturbed the assumptions of the orthodox concerning the character of the future socialist society. Their conclusions lent little support to the view that the working class would spontaneously pass from sectional trade-union consciousness to socialist class consciousness. Socialist ideas were not the peculiar possession of the working class, nor would they be arrived at by the workers' own unaided efforts. And just as socialism was not destined to replace the ameliorative efforts of co-operation or trade unionism during the transition period, so it would not render them redundant after socialism itself had been established. The function of the great voluntary associations of working men and women would certainly change with the progress of social democracy, but it was not to be expected that the need for them would vanish or that their importance would appreciably diminish. This was a perspective which made the socialist presence in the labour movement, and the possibility of a labour alliance, much more acceptable to working-class leaders than the impatience or indifference with which their efforts had hitherto been received by socialist theoreticians. It allowed the Webbs to win, for a time and in a measure, the confidence of the most diverse workers' representatives, and to engage in collaboration not only with Tom Mann but also with Henry Broadhurst. The Webbs made no immediate practical contribution to the formation of the Labour Party, in the guise of the Labour Representation Committee, in 1900, but they did a good deal to contribute to the climate of opinion in which that party could take shape. The origins of the Labour Party have, indeed, been considered much too exclusively in terms of those who were personally or organisationally 'present and correct', to the neglect of modes of thought and feeling that were relevant without being so easily recognised or mustered. Just as Keir Hardie and Ramsay MacDonald were imperfectly representative of the sentimental Walt Whitman–Edward Carpenter–ethical society tendency, so Edward Pease was an inadequate representative of the hard-headed opportunism of the Webbs. These two pervasive tendencies complemented one another within the Labour Party, giving to its dedicated pedestrianism a high moral tone. Nor was the influence of the Webbs' vision of socialism and the labour movement confined to Britain. Bernstein and Lenin helped to introduce their researches to the German and to the Russian publics, and it can be shown that both revisionism and Bolshevism bore considerable traces of a close and critical reading of their work.

These large contentions concerning the Webbs' intellectual achievement in the eighteen-nineties might be thought to supply quite a sufficient basis for detailed discussion and examination. However, Sidney and Beatrice saw themselves as doing more than opening a new field in historical research, or recasting democratic theory, or reinterpreting the relationship between socialism and the labour movement – they aspired to write a work for their own time that would be as influential and definitive as *The Wealth of Nations* – to create a new political economy, to draw anew the map of learning. Where the ancient cartographers had written, 'Here there be savages', they wrote the history of labour. They explored the rainforests that the political economists had defoliated and petrified. But the Webbs did nothing in particular in the 1890s which began to matter half as much to them as what they fancied themselves to be accomplishing in general. This was to be a new way, the assimilation of the social to the natural sciences, a new science of politics which the entire revolutionary tradition acknowledged to be the prerequisite of a new world. Indeed, they were not concerned with a new discipline merely, but a new relation between disciplines; and not with thought only, but with thought in its relations to action: with living as well as with learning. And they tried to create the institutions as well as the conceptual framework of the new third culture. In this they failed, for their ambition outran their daring and perhaps exceeded their time and their chances. They distrusted abstract economics, but they were unable to establish a new political economy. The old political economy was disintegrating thanks to the work of Marshall on the one side and the Webbs on the other. Marshall – proceeding from the general to the particular – from the One to the Many – found it hard to get beyond that theoretically ubiquitous, but socially insignificant being, the 'marginal shepherd'. The Webbs wanted to reverse his procedure. They made the sons of poverty assemble, but only in the end to show them prostrate before the marginal productivity theory of wages. The effectiveness of trade unions, their ability to raise wages, depended upon their contribution to efficiency – although efficiency was conceived in broad and imaginative terms. They saw themselves – in Beatrice's language – doing what the economists had failed to do: comparing the 'order of thought' with the 'order of things'. But however fruitful this may have been, it did not result in the highest kind of achievement: the transformation of the order of thought itself. They created a new school of economics and political science, not a new political economy. In consequence, their theory of the labour movement became excessively institutional, and they failed to supply a theory of economic growth and social accounting adequate to their vision of the social democracy of the future.

During the 1880s Sidney had, in his lectures on trade unions, considered the theoretical possibility that unions might confer upon the workers some of the monopolistic advantages enjoyed by the controllers of the other factors of production. The rise of the new unionism of the unskilled, and in particular the drama of the great strike at the London docks, had compelled socialists to attend to trade union problems. Webb had himself been actively engaged in securing subscriptions to the dockers' strike fund.[5] That great conflict of 1889 had already made inconceivable the indifference which the Fabians, in common with many other socialists, had treated the trade unions only a few months earlier. However, it was certainly Beatrice, rather than Sidney, who first projected a study of trade unionism. Her study of the co-operative movement had obliged her to consider its relation to trade unionism. These relations were, in practice, by no means entirely amicable. Disputes arose over the wages and conditions of co-operative society employees, and there was a disposition on both sides to treat the two great voluntary movements of working men and women as rivals and competitors, rather than as complementary institutions. Beatrice's 'discovery' that the true sphere of co-operation's usefulness lay in the organisation of consumers rather than producers was calculated to reduce rivalry with the unions. In the early nineties both Sidney and she went to great pains to persuade unionists and co-operators that they ought to abandon all pretensions to organise the process of production and look instead to the growth of municipal and state enterprise.[6] If a careful investigation into the history and structure of the co-operative movement could lead to rewarding guides to action, the same lesson might be expected to derive from a comparable study of the unions. The good and evil, scope and limits, of trade unionism were not to be settled by reasoning a priori, but by careful investigation and research. The Webb way was not to present policy recommendations from on high, but to make them proceed – or appear to proceed – from an objective examination of the subject's own success and failure.

Beatrice had first clearly projected a study of trade unionism early in 1891 at the time of her estrangement from Sidney. After their engagement in May she continued to bear the brunt of the work, spending much of her time in the industrial North, interviewing, attending meetings and searching for records. Until March 1892 Sidney was too preoccupied with winding up his civil service career, and developing his new ones in journalism and politics, to give her more than incidental advice and assistance. However in January 1892 they did appoint a joint secretary-cum-research assistant, F.W. Galton, a skilled engraver and metalworker. He was a student at the Working Men's College and was, as Sidney remarked, one of his 'children'.[7] To begin with, all Galton's efforts had to be concentrated in the election campaign at Deptford, but after this had been brought to a successful conclusion he went up to help Beatrice in the North. The fact that she constantly travelled about in the company of a young unmarried man and even stayed in the same public houses with him caused some of her sisters almost as much anxiety and dismay as her impending marriage to Sidney. Galton, for his part, found Beatrice a much more exacting employer than the other one. Every weakness and shortcoming was subjected to merciless criticism. He had, she decided, to be properly trained, and in view of Sidney's fatherly and indulgent attitude towards him this task must largely devolve upon her.

Until the time of their marriage Sidney was continually reproaching himself about 'The Book'. He had insisted that this was to be given the highest priority in their partnership and yet she was doing almost all the work. She was frequently exhausted by the labour of collecting material and distressed by the difficulties of reducing it to order. He swore that after their marriage the main burden should pass from her shoulders to his, and so it did. By the time the first draft of the book was in preparation, around the end of 1892, Beatrice was becoming painfully aware that it was Sidney who was doing most of the work and her complaints about her own 'parasitism' led to their first – not very serious – quarrels. The fact that first Beatrice and then Sidney played a predominant part in the work has to be understood not merely in terms of their temporary circumstances but also of what proved to be their permanent roles. Broadly speaking, Beatrice began their books and Sidney finished them. She was the initiator of this and most of their subsequent works. She had a keen eye for the gaps in learning and was bold and imaginative in her proposals for filling them. She was also pre-eminent with respect to those skills which are most serviceable in the earliest stages of historical and social research. She knew how to gain the confidence of trade union officers, how to get them to talk, part with their records, and let her watch the institution at work. Thus she was by special resolution admitted to the historic rules revision meeting of the Amalgamated Society of Engineers.[8] More than once she attended a conference of the Miners' Federation of Great Britain, to the great astonishment of journalists, all of whom had been excluded. 'Sitting for five or six hours in a stinking room with an open sewer on one side and ill-ventilated urinals on the other is not', she noted, 'an invigorating occupation.' Yet she considered that the experience was fully justified from the research standpoint. 'I am glad I came. These two days debate have made me better appreciate the sagacity, good temper and fair-mindedness of these miners than I could have done by reading endless reports ...'[9] Nor was she any less successful in establishing friendly relations with the first-level leadership in the pit villages than she was with Ben Pickard, whom she privately considered to be a 'cross between a bulldog and a pig'. [10] She was no less studiously attentive at a branch meeting of the Oldham Weavers, than at the Executive Committee of the Cotton Spinners. In chance conversation, and in the ordinary affairs of life, Beatrice was apt to be quick to pride. She could 'quite accidentally' remark to a well-meaning young Tory: 'We shall not wish to convert you, my dear Bill, you are not up to our standard;'[11] but as an investigator she trained herself to be infinitely patient and sympathetic. She endured endless irrelevancies, let error pass uncorrected and prejudice have its head, in the hope that she would earn access to the information she was seeking. And in the content of research, if not always of 'persuasive entertaining', her artfulness did not betray her. She cultivated the old unionists 'because they have the records,'[12] but even a wily and experienced operator like Henry Broadhurst with his 'greasy, unctuous, middle-class, wire-pulling manner' would draw up his chair, look benignly through his 'fat-surrounded eye' and start to confide in her.[13] Her ulterior motives did not tell against her because she was deeply interested in personal character and genuinely enjoyed the gossip. Besides, as she acknowledged, it sometimes helps to be a woman.[14] For example, she noted that Robert Knight, the autocratic leader of the boiler-makers, considered that a woman could not be interested or involved in internal intrigues. At first she would not be taken seriously, but before he knew where he was, an official of this sort could find himself absorbed in the problem she was investigating and which he had never reflected upon before in this way.

Thus Beatrice's strength lay in her unusual success as an interviewer who could win the confidence of her respondents, and persuade them to give her privileged access to research material. She was far less effective when it came to recording and ordering the material and putting it into its final form. She not only found 'serious' writing difficult, she could not even write legibly – a severe drawback to literary collaboration. Moreover she was easily wearied by sustained thought or reading and (like many others) felt humbled by Sidney's apparently unlimited capacity for work. She was vexed by the fact that he appeared to be doing all the solid labour. She used to console herself with the reflection that she was the originator, the architect and the inspirer. She once publicly explained:

> He does the work and I do the inspiration. That I think will be the ultimate position – women to inspire everything and the men to do it. Women have resource and intuition, and more audacity than men, but men have the greater capacity for hard work. My husband and I work together. I bring him the material and he deals with it. As he writes, I sit beside him with my notes. He criticises my plan and I criticise his execution, and so we get on by pulling each other's work to pieces.[15]

The concluding part of this passage is not easily reconciled with the defiant over-simplification of its opening sentence.

If it is broadly correct to say that Beatrice began the *History of Trade Unionism* (and most of their other books) while Sidney finished them, it would also be true to observe that she was the mistress of the 'spoken word' while he was the master of the 'written one'. While she excelled as an interviewer and could in conversation make a fresh interpretation take fire, he knew how to tear the heart out of a document, record it, remember it, and furnish it as an instance or use it as a connecting link. Most of their celebrated notes were made in his swift, legible hand. The first drafts, once they had passed beyond a set of headings or propositions, generally came from him. Because his knowledge was so large, his memory so retentive, his energy so prodigious, it was sometimes assumed that he was insensitive and without the creative spark. Such an assumption has no rational basis, and can be explained by Sidney's special kind of selflessness on the one side and a sharp sense of inferiority on the other. He had no interests or ambitions or even identity of his own which he wished to assert within their partnership or beyond it. She needed to reflect on their respective contributions. He did not. He delighted in her happiness. Admiring her gifts, he objected only if she called them into question. It is unimaginable that he could ever have been brought to protest against any claim, however, extravagant, that might have been made on behalf of her own creative prowess. But just as she did, in fact, contribute to the execution of their work, so was he a great deal more than a willing and exceedingly powerful horse. In their trade union studies some of the most important argument certainly owed more to his experience and to his suggestions than to hers. From the beginning he was ready to make general comments on problems of structure and method. In September 1891 he was questioning whether she ought to spend so long on Tyneside:

> The best knowledge is *comparative* knowledge and, in acquiring it, the first instances studied are studied under the least advantageous circumstances. Hence the argument for not trying to *finish* one district before

having seen some others ... You are obviously right to see the pit village. You need not apologise for that; it is an obvious necessity. 'Ça donne de la physiognomie', as a French official once told me. The work, as you hint, is unlimited in possible extent. But we need not necessarily exhaust our material or terminate our researches on the first publication. We might publish two volumes to begin with (one of material) and *afterwards* go on to deal with other aspects.[16]

Even the Webbs themselves could not have precisely determined the contribution of each partner. The pre-eminence of one or the other with reference to particular skills was never equivalent to a monopoly of them. The *History of Trade Unionism* and *Industrial Democracy* were not, like their *Problems of Modern Industry*, a putting together of separately written chapters. They were the result of a general fusing of minds. Nor should it be forgotten that Galton and others made important contributions to these two books. Had it not been for Galton they would certainly not have been written as quickly as they were. While they were in Netherhall Gardens, Hampstead, during their first months of marriage he used to arrive at 10.00 a.m., and he came earlier after they moved in 1893 to what became the famous workshop and salon, 41 Grosvenor Road. By the time he arrived they had finished breakfast, read the papers and spent an hour or so dealing with correspondence. Over a cigarette they decided on the theme or problem they were going to tackle that morning. Galton went upstairs to sort out the relevant notes. When he came back he might find Beatrice striding about the room, suggesting some hypothesis or other, while Sidney introduced confirmatory or awkward facts and considerations. Then they would sit down, sometimes side by side, on other occasions each at one end of the table, and start to drive through the material. Lunch was at 1.30 and it was unusual for either of the Webbs to touch The Book again that day. Four afternoons a week Sidney would rush off to the London County Council while Beatrice strolled on the Heath, went house-hunting or visited Morris to select furniture or wallpaper. Occasionally she joined Galton for another couple of hours work before Sidney came back for supper. But digging up specific facts, checking references and generally taking charge of everything which could be reduced to a routine fell to the lot of their devoted research assistant. The talk over the simple meat supper was of LCC doings, or of an interview with a cabinet minister, or of some projected reform. Sometimes they would entertain a few working men friends, but more commonly they spent the evening alone in 'peaceful happiness' while he read to her or worked at LCC matters.[17]

This sort of procedure would hardly do when a book was ripening. When this point was reached they went off with Bernard Shaw and Graham Wallas to stay either at the Argoed or else at some cottage in the country. It was at the Argoed in September 1893 that Wallas severely criticised the first chapter of their *History*. In consequence Beatrice reordered it, while Sidney wrote to her draft. Meanwhile Shaw worked almost every morning on the book and largely remodelled the third chapter. 'Sidney certainly has devoted friends,' remarked Beatrice, 'but then it is a common understanding with all these men that they use each other up when necessary – that is the basis of the influence of the Fabian Society in contemporary political thought. The little group are practical communists in all the fruits of their labour.'[18] This 'practical communism' was applied to *Industrial Democracy* as well as to its predecessor. However irritated Beatrice became with Shaw's cruelty and vanity towards women (his cold philandering; what she called his 'sexual vanity – delight in being the candle to the moths'), she was deeply impressed by his generosity towards Sidney and herself. 'With extraordinary good nature he will spend days over some part of our work, and an astute reader will quickly divine these chapters which Shaw has corrected and those which he has not – there is a conciseness and a crispness in parts subjected to his pruning knife, lacking elsewhere.'[19]

Method – the large shadow which the small body of sociological knowledge casts before it – interested the Webbs almost as much as it has preoccupied their successors. However, it left Sidney and Beatrice in a less exhausted condition. They tended to reflect about their methods after, rather than before, they employed them.[20] Just as they were inclined to confuse social studies with sociology, and sociology with the description of social institutions, so they tended to confuse methods with techniques.[21] Their naiveté in these matters has been the subject of much harsh speaking. And if one takes seriously the final account which they offered of their approach to trade union studies there is, indeed, a vision to dizzy and appal. In 1932 they recalled:

When we had actually completed and published our *History of Trade Unionism* (1894) after three years' collection of facts from all industries in all parts of the kingdom, which we had arranged more or less chronologically, we found to our surprise that, apart from the vague generalities in common use, we had no systematic and definite theory or vision of how trade unionism actually operated, or what exactly it effected. It was not till we had completely resorted all our innumerable sheets of paper according to subjects, thus bringing together all the facts relating to each subject, whatever the trade concerned, or the place, or the date – and had shuffled and reshuffled these sheets according to various tentative hypotheses – that a clear, comprehensive and verifiable theory of the working and results of trade unionism emerged in our minds to be embodied, after further researches by way of verification, in our *Industrial Democracy* (1897).[22]

The view that writing history involved collecting all the facts – or at any rate a very large number of them – was an opinion the Webbs shared with Acton, and which E.H. Carr has termed ' the nineteenth-century heresy'.[23] They did repeatedly talk as if there was a 'hard core' of fact in history and a 'surrounding pulp' of disputable interpretation. They evidently imagined that their *History* constituted such a 'hard core', while *Industrial Democracy* corresponded to the 'surrounding pulp' – save that the Webbs were not prepared to allow that there was much room for dispute, and they clearly supposed that writing economics or sociology was a higher order of intellectual activity than doing history:

> With history, [wrote Beatrice] the threads are supplied by the chronological order – you can weave these threads into any pattern; bring one of them to the surface and then another. But with analysis of facts, the threads are hypotheses: to be tested in strength and consistency before you dare weave them into conclusions and illustrate them with facts.[24]

This passage certainly implies a naive realist view of history, in which historical events are considered as pre-existing happenings that occupy a chronological order, which it is the job of historians to come upon. Accordingly interpretation is thought of in the arty-crafty term of 'patterns' to be woven, reduced to an affair of art rather than of science. The Webbs, it has been asserted, were mere narrative historians, indifferent to explanation. They set out to tell a story, and they were negligent when it came to 'the primary economic forces'. Consequently their chronology – although influential – is alleged to be seriously misleading. They were without the analytic tools at the disposal of contemporary historians.[25]

This type of criticism has a limited validity, but it is very much more limited than those who embrace it imagine. When one is entering virgin territory there is generally so much to see that one can return with helpful maps and useful reports without having first deeply pondered what one is going to look for. But there will be neither map nor report if one tries to describe everything. As historians the Webbs would have disappeared without trace had they really supposed that all facts are created equal, and that each fact has an inalienable right to speak for itself. There are occasions when the Webbs saw this quite clearly themselves. Beatrice wrote:

> No doubt the sequence involved in history is as artificial as are the groups involved in classification. How silly it is to suppose that the facts ever tell their own story – it is all a matter of arranging them so that they may tell something – and the arrangement is a purely subjective matter.[26]

Doubtless this observation is as inadequate from one side as the earlier one is from the other. The subtle dialectic between facts and interpretations is not to be described easily or briefly. Yet it shows an awareness of the problem. Those who venture to write for the first time the histories of civilisations or classes or movements cannot but be guided by established schools of historical interpretation and by analogies drawn from other departments of historical learning.

A general *History of Trade Unionism* might have been written from the standpoint of its leaders and heroes. Without organising their work around this theme, the Webbs made important concessions to this Carlyle-like approach. They accorded a disproportionate amount of their space to trade unionism's great men, particularly when they saw in them precursors of their own style of activity. Thus it would be generally agreed that they exaggerated the contribution made by Francis Place to the repeal of the Combination Acts. Then again, trade union history might be written by analogy from military history as a record of battles fought, and the Webbs did not fail to chronicle the bigger and more consequential strikes and lockouts. But it was not in the changing fortunes of the struggle, nor even in the conditions of peace or victory that they found a unifying theme. Theoretically it would have been possible for Sidney and Beatrice to have written their history as social history; to have interpreted trade union development in terms of the 'making of the English working class', to have related the progress of sectional and general movements to the shifting state within the class and to the vicissitudes of class consciousness. They were, of course, alive to the contrasts between the unionism of the artisans, the factory workers and the unskilled. It would have been impossible to neglect these considerations in the early nineties when, at the TUC, the battle was being fought out between the 'old' unionism of the craftsman and the new, general and industrial unionism of the semi-skilled and the unskilled. Yet they made no sustained attempt to work out how changes in the economy, in the organisational structure and in the social attitudes of different strata bore upon the character and the fortune of the trade union movement. They denied that there could be a history of the manners and the customs of the working people. History, they argued, must 'if it is to be history at all, follow the course of continuous organisations.'[27] When the general history of British trade unionism comes to be rewritten it will certainly be done in terms of manners and customs, and of the socio-economic life upon which trade unionism acted and reacted. But there is a sense in which discovery must precede explanation, and until the institutional history of labour had been written it was hardly possible to write that social history which is causally prior to it, for the sufficient reason that the number of facts to be ordered can be multiplied indefinitely. Yet even this proposition has an air of patronising magnanimity. The way in which we write history is not, as some pundits innocently suppose, a mere matter of the analytic tools and instruments that other disciplines have graciously placed at our disposal. When it is said, 'If history is to provide explanations, it must be equivalent to sociological studies of the past,'[28] it is forgotten that it is equally true (and it is not entirely true) that if sociologists are to supply explanations, they must be equivalent to historical studies of the present. In the writing of history the causes we pursue are at least as relevant as the techniques that are to hand. The Webbs wrote the *History of Trade Unionism* as part of the political history of England; they wrote an institutional history, because they hoped and expected that organised labour would transform the world. It is not to belittle the magnificent achievements of some contemporary historians of labour to point out that it is a falling away of faith in the organised labour movement that has accelerated and directed many of their researches. As much as the Webbs – as much as all vital historical work – their effort has been directed by a preoccupation with present rather than past experience. This is not a reproach. This is what distinguishes the historian from the antiquarian.

The Webbs saw trade union history as part of political history. Their chronology was shaped with reference to two major types of political considerations: the changing relations between trade unions and the state, and changes in the government and administration of the unions themselves. Far from setting themselves no higher task than supplying a readable and accurate narrative, they wanted to accustom trade union readers to think about their progress in the past in terms that would condition their programmes in the future. They therefore placed special emphasis upon the struggle for a secure legal status and the method of legislative enactment, along with a careful consideration of the increasing scale of unionism and the growing division of labour and specialisation of function that distinguished its internal government. This did not cause them to neglect entirely other considerations, or to ignore the 'primary economic factors'. Thus, in their account of the origins of trade unionism the Webbs went out of their way to rebut the 'institutionalist' approach of Brentano, who sought to establish their continuity with the craft guilds. The Webbs convincingly demonstrated that there was no direct affiliation between unions and guilds.[29] The presence of certain common features could not be allowed to obscure the profound difference in structure and in function. The differences between these institutions had to be understood in terms of the transformation of the journeyman into a fully fledged wage-labourer, without prospect of personal property in the means of production. They saw that this state of affairs could precede the rise of machine industry. The growth of the division of labour, and an increase in the minimum amount of capital required to establish a business, were, in the Webbs' opinion, the causative factors behind the transformation of occasional meetings of journeymen into settled institutions of wage-earners.[30] They made good use of comparative method to support their conclusion. For example, they showed that the worsted industry in the West Riding produced trade unionism on lines already familiar in the West Country while weavers in the West Riding, where capitalist relations were relatively undeveloped, remained unorganised:

> It is easy to understand how the massing together in factories of regiments of men all engaged in the same trade, facilitated and promoted the formation of journeymen's trade societies. But with the cotton spinners as with the tailors, the rise of permanent trade combinations is to be ascribed, in a final analysis, to the definite separation between the functions of the capitalist entrepreneur and the manual worker.[31]

Having discussed the origins of trade unionism, the Webbs proceeded to divide trade union history into four periods: the struggle for existence (1799–1825); its revolutionary period (1829–1842); the age of the 'New Model' unionism (1843–1875); and the rise of the new unionism of the unskilled in the late eighties. The exact dating suggests that they imagined that one period could be precisely marked off from another. In fact they were well aware that this was not the case, and they tried to explain some of the conflicts within the movement by reference to the presence of vestigial elements left over from earlier times. Moreover, they recognised that they could not do justice to their subject if they neglected important sectional developments which could not always be neatly put away within these big boxes.

The details of this chronology were already coming under some criticism in the Webbs' lifetime, but it is only since their death that a minority of trade union historians have declared that it is structured 'around obvious formal events', and that it is misleading and useless. Yet their cry for a rephasing of history which will 'satisfy the standards of contemporary historians' has not been answered. There has been plenty of detailed criticism, but no large-scale reconstruction.

The Webbs' critics ought to take care before they complain about their alleged attention to 'obvious formal events' lest they betray their own want of the historical imagination. What made these events 'obvious'? To whom did they become obvious and when? How much force has the word 'formal' here?

It is sometimes said that the Combination Acts were not crucial, as is supposedly implied by the Webbs' styling the years 1799–1825 'The Struggle for Existence'. Parliament and the courts had other resources against unionism at this time, and were in no way dependent upon these measures. Nor did they bear down with any uniformly oppressive weight upon organised workmen. On the contrary, numerous instances can be given of trade societies that continued to function openly and undisturbed. Had the Combination Acts been as important as the Webbs imagined, it is hardly possible to understand how they could have been repealed with Parliament scarcely noticing what it was doing. Thus the authors of a work which aspires to bring the Webbs up to date complain that

> This story of legal emancipation, is sometimes written as if the unions depended on the law for their existence, and had wrested every element of their legalisation from an unwilling and hostile legislature, dominated by a class implacably opposed to trade unionism. Both these suppositions are incorrect.[32]

A careful reading of the second chapter of the *History of Trade Unionism* shows that Sidney and Beatrice were well aware of the variety of oppressive instruments which were at the disposal of the state and the employers. They also emphasised that in certain trades and regions unionism enjoyed a comparative immunity from the severities of the law, and pointed out that there were numerous metropolitan craft trades that have 'never been more completely organised' than they were in these years.[33] They placed special emphasis on legal constraints and penalties because they believed that 'it was a change of industrial policy on the part of the Government that brought all trades into line, and for the first time produced what can be properly called a Trade Union Movement.'[34] The point is taken in one full-scale study of the period: 'It was Pitt, who by passing the Combination Acts, unwittingly brought the Jacobin tradition into association with the illegal unions.'[35] The Webbs stressed the immense significance of the state, simultaneously withdrawing all the paternal protection that it had accorded to workmen who had petitioned for their rights while subjecting their associations to a general prohibition. Both Professor Aspinall and E.P. Thompson have made the same observation with immense force and effect.[36] The Webbs' critics have been beside the point here as elsewhere, because they ignore Sidney and Beatrice's avowed intention of writing a general political history of a movement, rather than a detailed account of the industrial vicissitudes of particular trades.

There is a more substantial objection to the Webbs' characterisation of 1829–42 as 'The Revolutionary Period'. They undoubtedly exaggerated the personal role of Robert Owen, and in so far as they equated revolutionary unionism with general unionism, they failed to notice that the first attempts at this came in 1818 not in 1829.

This last correction was clearly made out by G.D.H. Cole.[37] It is also to Cole that the honour belongs of having made the first significant revision of their third period: the age of the new spirit and the new model, the domination of the trade union world by national craft unions based on centralised finance, the principle of high contributions and high benefits; and wage policy based on attempts to control the supply of labour. Despite one defiant charge that the 'new model' must be dismissed as an 'historical fiction',[38] the Webbs' treatment of craft unionism in the third quarter of the nineteenth century is generally allowed to be still the best single exposition of the subject. Cole – wiser than some of his successors – did not question the authoritative account of the characteristics of the 'new model', but confined himself to demonstrating that its writ did not run as widely as the Webbs suggested; that the principle of 'amalgamation' was not necessarily associated with industrial pacifism and that George Potter (a *bête noire* of the Webbs) was a more consequential figure than they were inclined to allow.[39] H.A. Clegg, who is otherwise prone to fall into the trap of considering the Webbs' achievement in terms of his own interests and objectives rather than theirs, makes one further substantial correction when he suggests that Sidney and Beatrice failed to realise how far, in the classic craft unions, central financial controls were compatible with local autonomy in trade policy. In their *History* – as distinct from *Industrial Democracy* – they made light of unilateral regulation by means of which craft unionists, without engaging in collective bargaining, but falling back on out-of-work benefits, imposed their will upon employers in relation to workloads. As Clegg argues, this omission leaves their readers unprepared for the great conflicts which were soon to break out over job control.[40]

If one passed from a consideration of the strengths and weaknesses of their characterisation of periods to their detailed treatment of men and events, one would be struck by the general richness and reliability of the *History* as a source, despite its occasional errors and omissions. Of course they made mistakes, even when they were discussing the mid-Victorian years which they understood so well. Yet Frederic Harrison, who had played a prominent part in the sixties and seventies, could confess to them that he was surprised 'how much it tells me that is new to me, and how fully it explains movements in which I took part, but never till now have understood as a whole and in all their effects.'[41] Thus, they gave particular attention (rightly) to the building trades, but did not so much as notice Richard Harnott, the remarkable leader of the stonemasons.[42] They condemn (rightly, despite attempts at revision) George Potter, the 'strike-jobbing' enemy of the 'Junta', but they do not manage to describe his relationship to the *Bee-hive* newspaper quite correctly.[43] They make Karl Marx read the Inaugural Address to the first meeting of the International, and they left this error substantially uncorrected even after Beesly had told them that Marx's pronunciation of English made it impossible for him to address a large meeting.[44] They overestimated (perhaps deliberately) the role of John Burns and Tom Mann in the rise of the 'new unionism', while they explain the decline of the movement by the onset of a depression that did not begin until after the decline had started.

Matters such as these are the concerns of professional historians. It is more important to consider criticisms of a less technical order. The charge has been made from the Left that the Webbs adopted a 'superior person's' attitude towards the working people, while critics on the Right have argued that they tried to draw the wrong morals from the experience they recorded.

The Webbs would have been surprised by the reproach that they were lacking in a sympathetic insight into their subject. As Beatrice began to find her way through trade union archives she did, indeed, reflect that: 'There is something very pathetic about the records – the struggle with the archaic spirit in every union. The miserable, petty passions which are always threatening to subvert the unions; and the crude economics of the leaders.' Yet she continued:

> But on the whole they have been just as right as the employers in their economics – perhaps righter in their economics than the professors. Does not this arise from the fact that they – the union leaders – have had the right object in view: the making of Man, whereas the econo-mists and the employers have had the making of commodities?

If there were occasions when she privately expressed impatience with workers' representatives (the Derbyshire miners' officials were 'stupid, stupid, stupid, like the men!'),[45] there were many others when she was roused to unqualified admiration and respect. In their *History*, and still more in the companion volume, they showed a profound insight into the problems and attitudes of the organised working class and transcended the narrow horizons of bourgeois respectability. They remarked that

> No discovery is more astounding to the middle-class investigator than the good natured tolerance with which a Trade Union will, year after year, re-elect officers who are well known to be hopeless drunkards. The rooted dislike which working men have to 'do a man out of his job' is strengthened, in the case of a trade union official, by a generous recognition of the fact that his service of his fellows has unfitted him to return to manual labour.[46]

They paid tribute both in public and in private to the high qualities and elements of greatness that they discovered in trade union leaders of the most various types and schools: to Burt, to Burns, to Mann. They pointed out that the trade union officer has to add to personal self-control 'strength and independence of character, a real devotion to the class from which he has sprung, and a sturdy contempt for the luxury and "gentility" of those with whom he will be brought in contact.'[47]

Far from suspecting that they showed too little sympathy and respect for trade unionists, the Webbs were fearful lest the influence of their work would be diminished as a result of the reader detecting the bias in their favour. The criticisms that have subsequently been made of them on this account largely arise from the same source as those concerning the structure and chronology of their book: they showed an excessive respect and regard for stable institutions while adopting a superior and condescending attitude to the relatively unorganised, ephemeral, fitful movements of protest and revolt. When it came to handling these developments the Webbs certainly were prone to the 'superior person' attitude. There can be little doubt that Thompson had Sidney and Beatrice, among others, in mind when, in his *The Making of the English Working Class*, he declared that his purpose was to 'rescue the poor stockinger, the Luddite cropper, the "obsolete" handloom weaver, the "utopian" artisan, and even the deluded follower of Joanna Southcott from the enormous condescension of posterity.'[48] The Webbs understood the tragedy of these people, but they understood it from 'without'. Of men petitioning Parliament against the introduction of new machinery they wrote: 'The artisans had a grievance – perhaps the worst that any class can have – the degradation of their standard of livelihood by circumstances which enormously increased the productivity of their labour. But they mistook the remedy.'[49] They thought the workers 'slow' in seeing how they needed to respond to the break-up of eighteenth-century state regulation of industry.[50] Luddism was an infantile disorder to be dismissed in a sentence. The moderation and restraint of the labour aristocracy was favourably compared with the 'petulant rebellions of hunger strikers',[51] and the 'puerile and sometimes criminal' practice of mystic initiation rites and fearful oaths.[52] They assumed without discussion or serious investigation that machine-breaking was a blind reaction, as irrational as it was ineffectual. Labour historians now recognise that this was a partly mistaken – and wholly inadequate – conclusion.[53] Similarly, when the Webbs discussed Owenism and Chartism there was a tendency to adopt the 'don't-let-it-happen-again' tone of a sententious schoolmaster. Owen and his supporters are marked down for failing to master 'the law of economic rent'; while Chartism, although 'made respectable by sincerity, devotion, and even heroism in the rank and file … was disgraced by the fustian of … its orators and the political and economic quackery of its pretentious and incompetent leaders, whose jealousies and intrigues … finally brought it to naught.'[54]

In short, the Webbs were at their best when they were discussing, not 'the Democracy' of the first half of the nineteenth century with its fierce protests and millenarist expectations, but the institutionalised democracies of the second half, in whose increasing membership and efficiency they saw the measure of trade union progress. They were inclined to explain the passing from one style of movement to the other in excessively intellectualist terms. They thought it had to be understood by 'the spread of education' and 'more practical counsels', and they took 'the effect of economic changes' to be a secondary consideration.[55] This helps to account for their failure to approach the workers responding to the predicaments of the repressive and revolutionary periods with the 'caution and humility' that they might otherwise have done.[56] However the main source of this failure lay deeper – in Beatrice's alarmed distrust of turbulent crowds; in Sidney's scepticism about the practical usefulness of the sacrifice on the Cross; in a profound conviction that social progress must come gradually through and around going institutional concerns.

The charge brought by critics on the Right, that the Webbs drew wrong practical lessons from the experience they described, is most conveniently discussed in relation to *Industrial Democracy,* a companion volume which fully worked out their view on the political and economic implications of trade unionism, and developed the few programmatic suggestions made in the *History* into a coherent body of doctrine.

The Webbs had opened their *History* with a definition of a trade union as 'a continuous association of wage-earners for the purpose of maintaining and improving the conditions of their employment.'[57] In *Industrial Democracy* they set out first to describe how these institutions were governed; how slowly and painfully the workers had discovered how to reconcile administrative efficiency with popular control. Second, they supplied an extremely detailed account of how they functioned, identifying and describing the methods of mutual insurance, collective bargaining (a term which they were the first to coin), legal enactment, and the wide number of restrictions and devices that would now be called 'unilateral' or 'autonomous' job regulations. They showed that these methods had different implications and rested on different assumptions. The first three depended on what they termed 'the device of the Common Rule', and assumed that individual bargaining tended to depress the conditions of the wage-earners' working life to the lowest level. By contrast, the device of the 'restriction of numbers' – the limitation of entry into a particular trade – was not a universal feature of trade unionism. They attempted to disentangle the conflicting policies of trade unionism in reference to three doctrines: of vested interests, of supply and demand, of the living wage. In the third section of their work they tried to evaluate the economic implications of these methods. Here they saw themselves as offering a new, realistic and inductive analysis of the business world. In so far as they succeeded in depicting the economy in terms of a network of bargains, made in imperfect markets, in which the impulse to cheapness was transmitted from one stage of bargaining to the next until – with all its accumulated weight – it settled like an incubus upon the isolated workman's means of subsistence, they advanced understanding. But however salutary their heavy emphasis on market imperfections, they pointed to (rather than anticipated) the work of E.H. Chamberlin and Joan Robinson in the 1930s, and the more recent theory of countervailing power elaborated by J.K. Galbraith. They took the existing conceptual framework of economics into closer relation to the real world, but they did not revolutionise that framework, nor did they even manage to add to it or reorder it. They simply laid hold of the Marshallian marginal productivity theory of wages and related it, not to trade union policy conceived a priori, but to actual policies pursued. In the final part of the book they completed their elaboration of the new theory of democracy, and discussed the place of trade unions in the transition to a future socialist state.

Industrial Democracy is the most original and comprehensive book ever written about the English trade unions. Its riches are such that even more than one hundred years after the first edition it can still suggest fresh lines of research. It was wonderfully architected – always one of the strengths of the Webbs' literary work. By enclosing all their research within a discussion of democracy, they brought the reader back to his starting-point, but at a higher level, and in such a way that everything they had taught him was recalled and effectively deployed in the conclusion. But although they were marvellously successful in organising a vast amount of seemingly disparate material, their arrangements had certain defects and was open to some objections. Thus, by beginning with trade union government and by treating the unions of the miners and the cotton operators as ideal types towards which the whole trade union world was supposed to be tending, the Webbs cut themselves off from certain insights. Professor H.A. Turner has shown how rewarding it can be to relate trade union organisation more closely to function, and to consider carefully the implications of the historical order in which what he terms 'open' and 'closed' unions emerge in a particular industry.[58] But the reader will hardly expect too close, critical examination of *Industrial Democracy* in these pages. He must be content with a discussion of those themes that reveal most about the Webbs, and that bear most directly on their public life.

Whereas the *History* opened with a clear definition of a trade union, the Webbs made no comparable attempt to stipulate what they understood by industrial democracy. They used the term in three different ways. In the first part of the book it simply means the procedures and institutions of trade union government. Elsewhere they made it stand for the extension of public control and ownership to successive branches of economic life so as to confer upon the citizen a similar control over industrial affairs to that which he was supposed to exercise over political ones. In the last part of the volume the term is used in such a way as to incorporate and synthesise these two earlier definitions. It comes to mean a system of industrial relations in which arbitrary and irresponsible power has been replaced by the continual adjustment of interests between the leaders accountable to the workers on the one hand, and the public servants accountable to the community as a whole on the other.

The Webbs introduced their new theory of democracy by accepting the disarmingly familiar proposition of Lincoln's: a government of the people, by the people and for the people. They then demonstrated that if the attempt was made to take this literally and confer on everyone an equal voice in the taking of decisions it was bound to break down. They showed that the early English trade unions had tried to practise such a primitive democracy in which every member was to have an equal say in the taking of every decision. Accordingly business was conducted through general meetings, and the simple offices of chairman, secretary, door-keeper and so forth were allocated by rota. These simple arrangements were found to be incompatible with the requirements of a militant struggle against hostile employers and repressive public authorities. They were also inconsistent with the growth of the organisation. The same logic which associated wage-earners together in a town led them to associate in each region, and nationally, and even internationally. The affairs of the society now required that some civil servant, some one member, should devote himself to the increasing secretarial and organisational work – and that some body should come into being charged with shaping policy for the organisation as a whole. Yet the membership was extremely reluctant to accept the need for increasing the division of labour and the specialisation of function. It had resort to the referendum and the initiative and the device of a rota by which each branch in turn would have responsibility for attending to national administration. The Webbs pointed out that the vestiges of these procedures could still be found in the trade union world, but they held that they were all misconceived. If such arrangements were at all effective in retaining popular control, then they were found to lead to bankruptcy or chaos; more usually they resulted in magnifying the very oligarchical control they were designed to prevent. The salaried officer ran rings round inexperienced lay executives and used referenda to legitimise what were, in reality, his personal decisions.

Thus the workers were brought tardily to an understanding that democracy, in organisations of any size, required representative institutions, and they came to see that a representative must not be confused with a mere delegate: 'a vehicle' by which 'the voices' could be mechanically conveyed. But the construction of an effective representative assembly was no easy matter, particularly for workmen. The Webbs were the first to detect the 'cruel irony' that confronted them.

Whatever may be the natural endowment of the workman selected by his comrades to serve as a representative, he starts unequipped with that special training and that general familiarity with administration which will alone enable him to be a competent critic and director of the expert professional. Before he can place himself on a level with the trained official whom he has to control, he must devote his whole time and thought to his new duties, and must therefore give up his old trade. This unfortunately tends to alter his manner of life, his habit of mind, and usually also his intellectual atmosphere to such an extent that he gradually loses that vivid appreciation of the feelings of the man at the bench or the forge, which it is his function to express. There is a certain cruel irony in the problem which accounts, we think, for some of the unconscious exasperation of the wage-earners all over the world against representative institutions. Directly the working-man representative becomes properly equipped for one half of his duties, he ceases to become specially qualified for the other. If he remains essentially a manual worker, he fails to cope with the brain-working officials; if he takes on the character of the brain-worker, he is apt to get out of touch with the constituents whose desires he has to interpret.[59]

Middle-class observers who still declare themselves perplexed by unofficial strikes, and who complain that the unions cannot control their members, might do worse than to ponder this shrewd account of the members' difficulties in controlling their unions.

However the Webbs were not driven, as Roberto Michels was driven, to the conclusion that there were no intentions so pure, nor rules so perfect, that democracy could be proof against 'the iron law of oligarchy'. They found in the federal parliament of the cotton-spinners and the coal-miners a way of escape between the horns of the dilemma. They noticed that these assemblies implicitly recognised the impossibility of reconciling in any one person the conflicting requirements of a representative. Accordingly they sent *both* rank-and-file members who were still working at their trade and knew where the shoe pinched *and* the salaried officers of the districts. The one type of representative could articulate the wishes of the members at large, and give a democratic legitimacy to decisions arrived at; the other was wise to the way in which rules of procedure and intricate technical matters could be used by other professional experts to secure privileged access to policy-making for themselves, and the Webbs assumed he would be quick to expose such attempts should they be made. Thus:

The specialisation of the executive into a permanent expert civil service was balanced by the specialisation of the legislature, in the establishment of a supreme legislative assembly, itself undertaking the work of direction and control for which the members at large had proved incompetent ... To balance the professional civil servant we have, in fact, the professional representative.[60]

The stress on the importance of federal institutions is less important and novel than the extreme emphasis placed upon professionalism. It must be remembered that the conventional wisdom about representative government in England took no account of the power exercised by professional civil servants. When Beatrice's brother-in-law, Leonard Courtney, published his *The Working Constitution of the United Kingdom* in 1901, he made no reference to the bureaucracy and treated the 'departments' merely as 'offices'. It was not until Lawrence Lowell published his *The Government of England* in 1908 that a more realistic view of the role of the permanent official became current. It is instructive to notice that Lowell found in the Colonial Office (Sidney's old 'department') his most striking examples of departmental power, and the inversion of the formal relationship that was supposed to govern the work of the officials and their Minister.[61] The Webbs had a lively appreciation of the real and growing power of the professional civil servant, and they made it plain that they recognised this power as present in affairs of state and not merely in trade union government. But even more striking was their concept of the 'professional representative' as the indispensable counterweight to the professional administrator. The implications of the distinctions they drew here have still to be thoroughly received into political consciousness. To be a professional representative was – within the trade union movement – to be a salaried official performing a representative function in conjunction with lay colleagues. In the developing industrial democracy of the future – in industrial democracy in its third sense – it was to be someone quite different, an expert *parliamentary* representative: a person quite unlike the amateur politician; an accessible and attentive listener; one able to discern the will of the silent or the inarticulate; a man able to determine precisely the wishes of his constituents. He would need these skills, not because he would be a glorified delegate, but because he would transform the whole etiquette of parliamentary life by actively trying to win his constituents. He would understand that the final command of his constituents would have to be obeyed and he would be ready to obey it but, because this was understood, he would as 'professional debater' conduct 'a propagandist campaign' with the greatest zeal and the greatest educational effect without fear of the consequences. Unlike the amateur politician of the eighteen-nineties, the future professional representative of proletarian constituencies would owe his position not to wealth or prestige or to notoriety. He would not vote as he thought fit in the intervals between the

pursuit of his business or pleasure. He would be 'selected for natural aptitude, deliberately trained for his new work as a special vocation, devoting
his whole time to the discharge of his manifold duties, and actively maintaining an intimate and reciprocal intellectual relationship with his
constituency.' The ultimate tendency of trade union and working-class
democracy must – the Webbs thought – be to exalt the real power of such
a professional representative and to differentiate his functions from those
of the ordinary citizen on the one hand and the otherwise uncontrollable
expert administrator on the other.

Plainly this new statement of democratic theory was not only different,
but in some respects diametrically opposed to the 'primitive' democratic
ideal of 'equal voices' and the absence of any settled differentiation of
function. Sidney and Beatrice did not for one moment attempt to conceal
this transformation. At its best democracy meant a form of government
in which assent and efficiency were mutually reinforcing. In 'primitive
democracy' assent was given to projects; in representative democracy it
was confined to the more substantial matter of results.[62] Democracy, in its
primordial innocence and simplicity, dispensed with leadership, élites
and expertise; representative democracy in its fully developed form
meant 'universal specialisation and delegation';[63] it meant that 'division
of labour must be carried into the very structure of democracy'.[64] Of
course it was paradoxical that in a developed modern democracy, a man
appeared as servant in respect to those matters in which he was most
expert, and as master over what he knew no more about than anyone else.
Yet, in this, there was strength and wisdom. For in our time the best and
most autocratic government is powerless without the support of the 'average sensual man'; while the 'average sensual man' will discover that he is
the subject of a 'terrible engine of oppression' if he allows even the wisest
of men 'the union of knowledge, capacity and opportunity with the
power of untrammelled and ultimate decision'.[65] But in the fully developed political or industrial democracy 'though it is the Citizen who, as
Elector or Consumer, ultimately gives the order, it is the Professional
Expert who advises what the order shall be'.[66]

Yet there was a continuity between 'primitive' and fully perfected
democracy, despite the stark contrast between their structures: a continuity that allowed the individual to sense that he was regaining indirectly
and collectively all that he had lost directly and individually. In all its
forms democracy was distinguished by equality of opportunity and 'acute
consciousness of the interests of the community as a whole'.[67] In the fully
developed industrial democracy there would certainly be intense specialisation of function and everybody would mind everybody else's business,
yet freedom would be greatly enlarged. Democracy was indeed incompatible with liberty, if liberty was understood as every man being his own

master, but that was incompatible with mass society, the division of labour, civilisation itself.

Just as the Webbs' political theory was distinguished from J.S. Mill's by its recognition of the importance of the permanent civil service and the professional expert, so was it quite distinct in its interpretation of freedom. In the *Essay on Liberty* freedom was defined as 'doing what one desired'. In *Industrial Democracy* it was defined as 'such conditions of existence as do, in practice, result in the utmost possible development of faculty in the individual human being'.[68] Mill's definition was intended to be a report on how he took the words liberty or freedom to be currently used: the Webbs confessed that theirs was a persuasive definition framed in accordance with what they took to be socially desirable, but they supposed no other sort of definition was possible. It was consciously and deliberately intended to relate to the laudatory, emotive meaning of freedom, not to the absence of restraint, but to the presence of a particular type of organisation. Whereas Mill feared that democracy might prove inimical to liberty, the Webbs saw democracy as the only way of securing the largest amount of it. They went so far as to cite, with apparent approval, Sir John Seeley's remark that 'liberty, in fact, means just so far as it is realised, the right man in the right place.'[69]

It would be unwise to rush to the familiar conclusions and declare that in truth the Webbs were 'not democrats'; that they were 'antipathetic to the liberal state'; that they neither understood nor valued liberty. Even their most severe critics would have to allow that, as a matter of historical fact, Millite liberalism had been associated with permissiveness towards the encroachments of the rich and the strong upon the poor and weak. As the Webbs remarked: 'What particular individuals, sections or classes usually mean by "freedom or contract", "freedom of association" or "freedom of enterprise" is freedom of opportunity to use the power that they happen to possess: that is to say, to compel other less powerful people to accept their terms.'[70] No one can read Mill's essay without becoming aware of its preoccupation with the freedom of the 'cultivated' person: the person whose faculties have already been relatively highly developed. It is this being who is supposed to be confronted with restraints which may be imposed by some collective: the state, or organised public opinion. The whole tradition of Millite liberalism, which treated freedom as equivalent to doing what one desires, or the absence of restraint, was so vulgarised that it became associated with the ideal of the minimal state. Freedom is the absence of restraint – therefore any increase in the power of the state diminishes freedom. It was not recognised that this proposition was either a tautology or a *non sequitur*: for it is indeed a *non sequitur*, unless freedom means the absence of restraint *by the state*. The Truck Acts, for example, greatly enlarged the freedom of most persons who were affected by them, although they enlarged the powers of the state and restrained employers.

However, the Webbs' critics would hardly be satisfied with this style of apology. It might explain how Sidney and Beatrice came to abandon a common-sense notion of what we mean by freedom; it could not justify the thoroughly pernicious way in which they abused the language. They should have contented themselves with pointing out that the state is not the only agency that imposes restraints; that there are occasions upon which the net result of increased state regulation is to increase the freedom of more people than the number whose freedom it diminishes; that freedom is not the sole good, and that there are circumstances in which it should not be preferred to equality of welfare or security. What cannot be excused is defining freedom in such a way as to make it consistent with forcing people to do what is good for them when they don't want to do it.

It must be conceded at once that no one can properly be said to be acting freely unless he is 'doing as he desires', but although this is a necessary condition for freedom, it is not a sufficient one. The Webbs' search for a more 'positive' conception of liberty was based on sound instinct. If men, in doing what they want to do, act either from desires which have been implanted in them by others, or have been shaped for them within an environment that restricts unduly the development of their critical and other faculties, we hesitate to describe them as exercising a free choice.[71] Moreover as soon as attention is turned to the relative freedom enjoyed by men belonging to different social classes, Mill's simple and obvious criterion suddenly becomes inadequate. No one seriously proposes to discuss the relative freedom of two citizens in terms of the ratio of each man's voluntary actions to all the actions he performs – even if one added the refinement of some sort of weighting system to allow for the varying intensities of the desires that were thwarted or satisfied. One is obliged to take account of different ranges of choice, as well as the number and significance of unimpeded choices made within each range. The citizen who has had much invested in the development of his faculties plainly enjoys more freedom than the one upon whom little has been spent. At the end of the day the factory worker who is released from monotonous toil or the housewife who in no longer chained to the kitchen sink may do what they desire, but it is absurd to contend that they are therefore as free as those who develop their faculties through their work rather than in spite of it. In the exercise of their freedom they are still limited by the experience of their subjection. From the formal standpoint of Millite liberalism they are free to go to the concert hall, the public library or the university extension lecture, and they would experience the pain that is associated with a loss of freedom if they were formally forbidden to do so, but that cannot obscure that they have less chance of so choosing, and that this is a loss of freedom, whether it is felt to be such or not. An adequate account of freedom will be as concerned with the way in which desires are shaped as it is with the extent to which they are satisfied. This in turn discloses a further dimension of the problem which is recognised in the Webbs' approach, but not in that of Mill: freedom is a matter not merely of curbing authority, but of concentrating it in our own hands.

Thus, while it is always dangerous nonsense to talk about freedom being the 'right man in the right place', or to pretend that a man is free when he is being compelled to develop his faculties, it was eminently sensible of Sidney and Beatrice to reject a definition of freedom that made it no more than 'doing what one desires'. By referring to the conditions of existence in their bearing on the development of faculties, they were directing attention to matters that are now habitually – save amongst the most doctrinaire schools – taken into account in the discussion of freedom. As the skills and resources for contriving the wants, and shaping the behaviour, of others become increasingly perfected and concentrated in the hands of a few controllers, complacency about the autonomy and originality of voter or consumer preferences becomes impossible. It is necessary to consider not merely what men want to do, but the opportunities they have had for developing their own tastes, inclinations and powers of discrimination. One can never recognise a free choice from one particular taste or inclination rather than another, but one must never fail to ask how far socio-political arrangements in all reality enlarge on diminish the capacities and faculties upon which the range of choice depends. For the Webbs, freedom was not to be opposed to organisation, but to depend upon a particular form of it.

From the concluding part of their book, where they discuss the place of trade unionism in the industrial democracy of the future, an outline of that organisation emerges.

The Webbs did not use the term 'social democracy', but their whole argument was directed to showing that only within a social-democratic state could trade unions fully develop and attain their maximum usefulness. Autocracies might conceivably accept the objectives of trade unionism, but they could never reconcile themselves to trade union structures and methods. Middle-class republics in which office was monopolised by old-fashioned liberals were bound to disbelieve in the possibility of unionism attaining its aims, and they were certain to dislike its devices. Only in the social-democratic state – a state in which the rulers actively used their political power to promote the efficiency and welfare of the citizens, while being liable to be periodically and peacefully removed from office by those citizens – could trade unionism attain the most favourable conditions for its own development.

This did not mean that trade unionists could expect to carry on in exactly the same ways as they were (1897) accustomed to do, nor did it mean that the relative importance of the several methods which they employed would remain undisturbed. Those methods of unilateral or autonomous job regulation which were associated with the doctrine of vested interests and led to an allocation of resources contrary to public policy must decline in significance. It would be made relatively easy to discard these methods because of the introduction of the state of redundancy and retraining schemes – or, as the Webbs put it,

> Equitable consideration of the interests of existing workers will no doubt be more and more expected, and popular governments may even adopt Mill's suggestion of making some provision for operatives displaced by a new machine. But this consideration and this provision will certainly not take the form of restricting the entrance to a trade, or of recognising any exclusive right to a particular occupation of service. Hence the old trade union conception of a vested interest in an occupation must be entirely given up – a change of front will be the more easy in that, as we have seen, no union is now able to embody this conception in a practical policy.[72]

Likewise the method of mutual insurance was expected to decline in significance:

> Hitherto, the actuarial defects of the Friendly Society side of trade unionism have been far outweighed by the adventitious advantages which it brought to the organisation in attracting recruits, rolling up a great reserve fund, and ensuring discipline.[73]

But the care of the sick and the injured and elderly, along with the burial of the dead, were destined to become a matter of public provision; while the 'complete recognition of Trade Unionism as an essential organ of the Democratic State',[74] to which all workmen would be expected to belong, would mean that the unions would have other ways of attracting and holding members.

Although Sidney and Beatrice referred to trade unionism as the organ of the democratic state, they did not mean to imply that the unions would forfeit their independence, lose their character as voluntary associations and no longer engage in collective bargaining with employers. Trade unions were not just incidental to capitalism but had a permanent function to fulfil in the democratic state. In the course of the transition to that state, they stood as a rampart against social oppression by giant trusts on the one side, and powerful agencies for combating the 'industrial parasitism of sweat-shops and small-scale production on the other'. Under socialism the directors of industry would remain biased in favour of cheapness and of every process that lowered costs of production. Such managerial attitudes were necessary, but they needed to be checked and controlled. What to produce, and how to produce it, were matters for professionally trained experts, not for trade unionists, to decide. But 'if the democratic state is to attain its fullest and finest development, it is essential that the actual needs of the human agents concerned should be the main consideration in determining the conditions of employment.'[75] The unions must be able to offer a real challenge to bureaucratic stupidity or official oppression. In all large-scale organisations there is need to check the malice, caprice and heedlessness of official superiors. The managers and directors of industry, as brain workers, could 'never be personally conscious of the conditions of manual labourers'.[76] The unions must be strong enough to compel public attention and to take strike action if necessary.

Thus the unions would continue to employ the method of collective bargaining. Their continual attempt to raise the level of their own common rules respecting wages, hours and working conditions would still be a dynamic element in the economy and would succeed in so far as it, directly or indirectly, raised the net marginal productivity of labour. However, the unions' attempts at raising the level of their common rules would be checked by the unfettered discretion of management to substitute factors within the productive process, and by the effect upon employment of increases in the price of the product. (The Webbs assumed that out-of-work benefit would be one of the few provisions made by the method of mutual insurance which would retain its importance.)[77] Unlike the 'Doctrine of Vested Interests', the doctrine of 'Supply and Demand' would retain some of its importance, but it would 'manifest itself exclusively in the persistent attempts of each trade to specialise its particular grade of skill, by progressively raising the level of its own Common Rules'.[78] The device of the restriction of numbers would have to be abandoned as contrary to public policy. Collective bargaining would continue, but it would continue subject to increasing concern for the maintenance of the interests of the community. It was not to be expected that the state would stand idly by in the face of serious or repeated instances of industrial dislocation resulting from strike action. It would act by 'authoritative fiat', and supersede free bargaining with some form of compulsory arbitration.[79]

'Democratic public opinion' would also scrutinise the way in which each trade used its strategic position to promote its own interests. It would ask whether its demands were directed to satisfying the appetites of the 'average sensual man', or whether they were conducive to his 'efficiency as a professional, a parent and a citizen'.[80] It would frown upon exalting wage demands to the exclusion of those concerned with hours, holidays, health, comfort and refinement in the conditions of work. This would require more foresight and self-control among the workers, and increased capacity of the civil service of the trade union movement. With the spread of the co-operation and the progressive municipalisation and nationalisation of public services, the unions would come more and more to resemble a professional association:

> The conditions of employment depending on the degree of expert specialisation to which the craft has been carried, and upon public opinion as to needs, each Trade Union will find itself, like the National Union of Teachers, more and more concerned with raising the standard of competency in its occupation, improving the professional equipment of its members, 'educating their masters' as to the best way of carrying on the craft, and endeavouring by every means to increase its status in public estimation.[81]

It was already 'ludicrous' to think of all the manual workers lumped together in a labouring class confronting the capitalist. Already trade unionism had encouraged the infinite grading of the industrial world into separate classes 'each with its own corporate tradition and Standard of Life, its own specialised faculty and distinctive needs, and each therefore exacting its own "Rent of Opportunity" or "Rent of Ability".'[82] The effect of trade unionism was not only to promote a trend to 'professionalism' among the workers; but by the use of common rules it was helping to extinguish the small master and favour the growth of large-scale industry. This meant extending a similar grading to the brain-workers of industry. 'In place of the single figure of the "capitalist entrepreneur", we watch, emerging in each trade, a whole hierarchy of specialised professionals – inventors, designers, chemists, engineers, buyers, managers, foremen and what not – organised in their own professional associations.'[83]

Because of its flexibility and because of the need to check bureaucratic excesses, collective bargaining would retain its place in the trade unionism of the future. But the Webbs were in no doubt that it was the method of legal enactment that had the greatest career of usefulness before it; just as it was the doctrine of the living wage, rather than the doctrines of vested interest or supply and demand, which was destined to become the leading principle of the trade union world. The doctrine of the living wage meant the recognition of a national minimum: 'the deliberate enforcement, by an elaborate labour code, of a definite quota of education, sanitation, leisure and wages for every grade of workers in every industry'. Public opinion would come, not merely to support the unions in making such a demand; it would positively insist upon it. But its insistence would be ineffectual without the active assistance of the trade union movement in embodying it in successive Acts of Parliament, ensuring that it was enforced, and causing it to be promptly and intelligently adapted to changes in industrial conditions.[84] But industrial regulation was not the only matter upon which the fully developed democratic state would require the counsels of working-class organisations. No legislation or administration would meet the needs of manual workers unless it was informed by an understanding of their problems, which only trade unions could supply. This 'service of counsel' was destined to be one of the most important functions of the trade unionism of the future.[85]

To fulfil this and its other functions the new trade unionism would have to be organised by craft, nationalised in its scope, centralised in its administration and served by its own expert official staff. Local branches and lodges would, however, remain 'the local centres of the union's intellectual life' and they would increase their activity. With 'the increasing use which the Democratic State may make of Trade Union machinery', the branch would be expected not only to administer 'the all-important out-of-work donation supplemented, as this may be, by a grant from public funds', but also to conduct technical classes, collect statistics and disseminate information. While there would be rigorous central control of strike funds, the branches would have the task of policing nationally negotiated agreements, and 'constantly considering the particular needs and special opportunities of their own localities.'[86] Through exploitation to the full of the possibilities of federation, the unions would combine the advantages of each specialised section raising the level of its own particular common rules, with the capability of presenting a common front to common employers. Finally, on the federation of craft and occupational unions within each industry, would come a reconstructed TUC – a federation of the whole trade union world energetically lifting the national minimum for the whole wage-earning class.

The political programme of this restructured trade union movement would have two main planks. First to establish and maintain freedom of association: a satisfactory legal status for trade unionism itself. The Webbs sensed the way the wind was blowing, and they stressed the importance of trade unions ensuring that neither parliament nor the courts made anything actionable or criminal, when done by a trade union or its officers, which would not be actionable or criminal when done by a partnership of trades in pursuit of their own gain. The unions had to be perpetually on guard against any 'insidious weakening of their influence' such as would result from 'payments of national insurance funds or employers' benefit societies'.[87] More positively, the TUC must make – and would be inevitably driven to make – the establishing of a national minimum of education, sanitation, leisure and wages the major plank in its programme. This was a principle of crucial importance which, amid all the changes and diversity of industrial life, the unions needed to keep steadily before them: to ingeniously apply, intelligently demand and see sternly enforced.

For the Webbs, the fully developed industrial democracy of the future was necessarily a social democracy in which industries and services were wholly or largely municipalised or nationalised. But it was a remarkable characteristic of their book that they did not see a demand for this as something that would arise simply, uniformly or spontaneously in the trade union world. 'Trade Unionism has no logical connection with any particular form of ownership of land or capital, the members of British trade unions are not drawn as trade unionists unreservedly either towards individualism or towards collectivism.'[88] Poverty no doubt disposed workers in general to favour a more equal sharing of the fruits of their combined labour, but trade unionism was consistent with a very wide variety of attitude towards this 'most momentous issue of modern democracy'. Sectionalism was one of the most deep-rooted characteristics of trade unions, and some unionists calculated – probably rightly – that they would get better terms from a capitalist employer than from a democratically controlled public authority. Sidney and Beatrice believed that there were a large number of issues and interest – ranging from the political and religious to the social and recreational – in which wage earners had neither distinctive purpose nor expert knowledge. The future democracy was not to be thought of in terms of the hegemony of a particular class having some unique vision of life totally reordered in accordance with a comprehensive principle. Rather was it to be considered in terms of the continual adjustment of interests of men as producers, consumers and citizens, where the final accommodation is made in the light of the permanent interests of the community as a whole.

Industrial Democracy was a great book, too great a book to have justice done to it by a summary discussion. Like other great books it was long and demanding. In consequence there has been a pronounced tendency to genuflect before it rather than to reflect about it. It has been commended and condemned on the strength of second-hand accounts, rather than upon the basis of first-hand acquaintance. Its subtleties and qualifications have been drained away in the interests of this or that preconceived and tendentious interpretation of what the Webbs 'really meant'. In fact – subject to certain important qualifications and limitations – the Webbs of the eighteen-nineties emerge as essentially democrats and libertarians who achieved a unique prescience concerning the future of trade union structure and policy. But at every point their opinions are permeated with values and preoccupations peculiar to the new professional stratum of the British middle class.

They were democrats in so far as they insisted that the authority of the decision-makers must depend upon the consent of the governed. They knew how difficult it was to discover the conditions of this dependence and how likely it was to be limited in practice. It was partly for this reason that they insisted that, in a fully developed democratic state, there had to be more than one channel of popular control: that men must be represented not merely as citizens, but also as producers and consumers. Perhaps they were too sanguine about the success of cotton operatives and miners in checking the tendencies to oligarchy. They were certainly hugely optimistic in implying that their federal parliaments supplied a model that could or would be adopted by the entire trade union world. Recognising the role of the professional expert and his indispensable contribution of efficiency, they made a virtue out of necessity and declared the division of labour to be essential to modern democracy. Accordingly they concluded that democratic control must be exercised with reference, not to projects, but to results. They also supposed – with a simplicity characteristic of their time – that since the division of labour was a condition of maximum efficiency for the collective, it would similarly enlarge the all-round development of the individual. There was no evidence for this assumption, and it was against the probabilities. Unless it is accompanied by a policy of deliberate and continual remanning, any division of labour tends to develop skills and dexterities at the expense of 'the utmost possible development of faculty'.

Yet the Webbs were, by intention, libertarians. They criticised the individualist doctrine of liberty, not merely because it could be shown to be incompatible with equality or security or welfare, but because it was largely bogus considered as a doctrine of liberty: it was the flag beneath which the rich and the powerful invaded the liberties of the poor and the weak. Although 'to be able' and 'to be free' are not synonymous expressions, it was the merit of the Webbs to discern the relationship between them; where, thanks to alterable socio-political arrangements, the faculties of men are stunted, they enjoy less freedom than would otherwise be the case, even when they are doing what they desire. They saw that in modern society freedom must be considered in the context of organisation and not in terms of its absence. If they had too little respect for the judgement and discrimination of the 'average sensual man', they knew that puritanism could be the foe of liberty and that it was often 'the vicarious asceticism of a luxurious class – which prefers to give the poor "what is good for them", rather than that in which they can find active enjoyment'.[89] Although they noticed the resemblance between their insistence on the distinction between expert knowledge and ultimate control, and Auguste Comte's proposal to put constitutionally untrammelled authority in the hands of a centralised administration, subject only to the continual moral influence of the spiritual power (made up of a medically qualified secular priesthood supported by workmen and women), they remarked that it was not merely the fantastic form of Comte's projection that separated it from their own. Comte's separation of the powers would not be real or lasting. His administration would be irresistible. The experts, whether in science or administration, were indispensable to democracy, but neither separately nor conjointly could they be entrusted with the power of ultimate decision, if liberty was to be secure.[90] The Webbs had an extravagant confidence in the application of science to human affairs, but they knew perfectly well (when they bothered to think about it) that its findings could not be construed as a code of conduct, and they explicitly rejected the view that there could be a positive science of morals.

The Webbs' precepts and prophecies concerning the future of trade union structure and policy have been the object of severe criticism by conservative and right-wing historians and commentators. In particular their complaint that the TUC failed to give a clear lead to the movement as a whole, that its parliamentary committee failed to function like a cabinet supported by an adequate professional staff, has been taken as showing a real want of insight into the wise prejudices of the practical and capable men who stood at the head of the movement. The historian of the TUC remarks that

> The philosophy of the Webbs was antipathetic to the Liberal State. They held the Trades Union Congress in contempt because it did not sweep away what they regarded as shibboleths and adopt a new 'scientific' basis of organisation. The very things which made the TUC a success were what they despised most: its loose method of organisation, its lack of central control, and the adoption of *ad hoc* policies to meet situations as they arose, instead of a clear-cut plan of campaign to achieve the kind of society they held to be desirable.[91]

Ben Roberts is quite correct when he implies that the Webbs did not regard the mere maintenance of a centre for the promotion of the common interests of trade unionists as something which in itself constituted success. Sidney and Beatrice certainly believed that trade unionism ought to aim at something more than simply responding to events as they arose. While recognising the obstacles to united action which the profound sectionalism within the movement presented, the Webbs believed that it could and should rise to a class programme which would be directed to the causes of working-class hardship and subjection, and would not be confined purely to dealing with the effects that preceded from these causes. The TUC and the entire trade union movement came to occupy much the sort of relationship to the state that the Webbs described. Indeed it is familiarity with a regime in which the government may be committed to the provision of a national minimum standard of life and to continuous consultation with trade union leaders that obscures the novel and radical character of the vision the Webbs attained in the1890s. Whether attention is directed to the growth of legal enactments, or to the decline of the method of mutual insurance, or to the increasing propensity of the state to regulate and control collective bargaining, one is brought to the conclusion that Sidney and Beatrice were uniquely successful in foretelling the shape of things to come. Perhaps they were wrong in imagining that changes in these directions were socially desirable, or perhaps they were mistaken that their advent would have been hastened by a more active and determined campaign on their behalf, but in either case the *onus probandi* lies with their critics. As to their alleged antipathy to the 'liberal state', it would be more to the point to complain of their apparently uncritical and complacent attitude towards its pretence of neutrality and impartiality. The state, as they foretold, has been ready to proceed by 'authoritative fiat' in the face of industrial dislocation, but it has never under any circumstances or in a single instance taken action that strengthened the bargaining power of the workers at the expense of their employers.[92] It has, indeed, used its opportunities as a conciliator to hasten peaceful settlements, but whenever it has acted by 'authoritative fiat' it has been to introduce strike-breakers, or to mobilise public opinion against labour rather than to challenge the position of management. In the concluding part of *Industrial Democracy* the Webbs were true to the spirit of the *Fabian Essays*: the transition to the fully developed industrial democracy of the future is marked, not by the dramatic death-throes of capitalism nor by its impassioned repentance, but rather by ever more shadowy presence until, at last, like the character in O'Casey, it is 'silently seen no more'.

The *History* and *Industrial Democracy* immediately secured the respect and attention of the academic world. But behind the expressions of gratitude and admiration there was frequently a reference to the interested and committed character of the Webbs' book. Geoffrey Drage, secretary to the Royal Commission on Labour, was particularly outspoken, and called into question the disinterested and scholarly nature of the *History of Trade Unionism*. He had been provoked into his outburst by Beatrice, who had written a most severe criticism of the approach adopted by the Commission. She complained about the miscellaneous, long-drawn-out and desultory superficiality that marked the Commission's enquiries. She pointed out that it had failed to discover and verify the facts relating to the several issues it investigated. For example, they had failed to approach the eight-hours question empirically, and, as she triumphantly demonstrated, the facts about the size and distribution of trade union membership were more fully disclosed by Sidney and herself than by the entire Commission with all its assistants. The recommendations of the majority were dismissed by Beatrice as conservative and nondescript. Fifty thousand pounds of public money had been spent so as to allow such cultivated dialecticians as Gerald Balfour and Professor Marshall to score verbal victories over working men and conduct a crusade against social democracy.[93]

Drage took the unusual step of replying to these charges and he did so in highly personal terms. He asserted that Beatrice was aggrieved because she had not been appointed as assistant commissioner, and that Sidney had been humbled by the Commissioners when he had given his evidence before them. He went on to 'expose' *The History of Trade Unionism* as an enormous piece of special pleading on behalf of the new unionism.[94] In the course of his attack, he was guilty, not only of misinterpretations, but of direct misquotation. Beatrice had to be restrained by Sidney, Shaw and Wallas from honouring him with a reply.[95]

There was however one argument in Drage's article that Beatrice was to recall forty years later as having been strangely near the mark.[96] He alleged that

> The so-called Socialist movement in England is an effort on the part of the lower middle class to obtain social recognition, political power and place, by means of the trade union movement which it dislikes and misrepresents. Political power is at present in the hands of what one may call the upper middle class – that is, the class educated at the large public schools. This class Mrs Webb and her friends dislike almost as much as they do the old trade union leaders.
>
> The fact is that the average Eton or Winchester boy [Drage had been to Eton] and the average trade unionist have much the same self-respect and self-reliance, and much the same admiration and capacity for self-denial which is so abhorrent to the advocate of State interference, State pensions, and grandmotherly legislation generally. The average girl from Lady Margaret Hall shares the prejudice of the wives and daughters of trade unionists as to the Socialist doctrine of free love and other extreme views of the new woman as exhibited in the 'new' literature. Neither men nor women of the class above referred to have as yet shown much liking for the Marx-Aveling philosophy, which may be roughly compared to that of the tailless fox of the fable. Advocates of views which involve loss of self-respect and self-reliance generally desire to persuade other men and women that these qualities are despicable.
>
> The strength of the labour movement in England and the reason of its success as compared with foreign movements lies in the fact that the lower middle-class proletariat, who cannot dig yet are not ashamed to beg, have hitherto been unceremoniously pushed aside at the Trade Union Congress.[97]

He concluded:

> What is important is not the high-sounding reforms like old-age pensions, on which the lower middle class expect to ride to power, and in the administration of which they hope to find jobs for their poets, moralists, lawyers and economists, but questions like the testing of weighing machines, and the lack of lifebelts on canal boats, which provoke Mrs Webb's ridicule.[98]

At first sight, Drage's suggestion that the Webbs – these lower-middle-class socialist intellectuals – were distrusted in the trade union world might appear to be justified. In 1893–4 the Webbs were going through a 'left' phase, but they did not appear to be making much headway with the new unionists, or in establishing themselves with the forces which were promoting the rise of an independent working-class party. Disillusionment with the poor performance of the Liberal government and pressure associated with the advent of the Independent Labour Party led Shaw and Sidney to produce their manifesto, 'To Your Tents, O Israel', at the end of 1893,[99] but this document, while saddening Haldane[100] and infuriating Massingham,[101] appears to have made a very limited impression in the world of labour. It appeared to put paid to the policy of permeation without contributing significantly to the development of some new agency of socialist advance. In particular, it did not bring John Burns into closer relations with the Fabians. Beatrice considered that Sidney and Shaw and Wallas needed to add such a popular tribune to their circle if they were to make the greatest impression on public life. They saw a good deal of Burns at Grosvenor Road and noted that he expressed increasing admiration for professional men, but that this was associated with growing contempt for his own class. Beatrice was brought sorrowfully to acknowledge that, despite his magnificent presence and great qualities, Burns was incapable of being a good colleague: his vanity and ambition precluded it.[102]

If the Webbs could not achieve a close working relationship with the biggest figure of the new unionism, how was it to be expected that they would be able to exercise any influence on the representatives of the old? They had now added to their identification with the campaign for the legal eight-hour day, a break with Liberalism which could not endear them to the Lib-Lab leaders at the head of the TUC. In their *History* they had severely criticised the 'front bench' of the Trades Union Congress for its want of ideas and its failure honourably to apply resolutions that were carried against its wishes. In these circumstances Drage appeared to be on safe ground when he dismissed the Webbs as isolated figures without influence in any quarter of the labour world. In fact he knew better.

He had been present when Sidney gave his evidence to the Royal Commission and he knew, or at least strongly suspected, that Webb was the author of the minority report formally attributed to Tom Mann.

Sidney gave his evidence to the commission in June 1893, just about the time when his 'left' phase was beginning. His remarks were generally distinguished by a bold and aggressive tone. He did not hide his irritation with the way the Commissioners appeared to him to be misunderstanding their task. He showed a marked impatience with Leonard Courtney's loaded questions, and with the manner in which Alfred Marshall confused enquiry by a Royal Commission with a *viva voce* examination at Cambridge. After the first day, Beatrice took him to task for his rudeness and he subsequently made a gracious apology for any discourtesy he had shown.[103] But if Beatrice was embarrassed by Sidney's plain speaking, the working-class Commissioners were grateful for a display of the kind of impatience which they themselves were coming to feel. Although he expected to be asked about matters of fact rather than opinion, Sidney used the opportunity to elaborate his proposals for the extension of 'collective philanthropy' and municipal enterprise. These proposals caused Sir Michael Hicks Beach to speculate about the consequences for the rates:

> If the rates increased what would happen then?
> Webb: I think in all probability the amount received by the owners of rent in London would be diminished.
> Sir Michael: Supposing it had to go as far as 20/- in the £. What then?
> Webb: That is a consummation I should view without any alarm whatsoever.
> Sir Michael: The municipality would then have rated the owners out of existence?
> Webb: That is so.[104]

Gerald Balfour asked Sidney whether he did not think it might be perfectly sound to regard neither socialism nor individualism as absolute principles:

> Webb: I seldom, I think, use the word 'absolute' myself. I never know what it means.
> Balfour: Let us put it this way: Do you not think it might be perfectly sound in logic and in practice, to regard both individualism and socialism as essential elements in any constitution of human society to which we can look forward?
> Webb: I think that view will always commend itself to Englishmen.
> Balfour: Does it commend itself to you?
> Webb: No.[105]

Once the Webbs were persuaded that the Commission was at best an academic exercise, at worst part of a campaign to discredit social-democracy, they began to take active steps to counteract its influence. They arranged, through Massingham, for the *Morning Chronicle* 'to run down the Commission and show up the futility of its investigations.'[106] They opened up communications with Tom Mann so as to secure a minority report. Tom was delighted to have the assistance of 'Lord Sidney' or 'father Sidney' or 'Uncle Sidney' as he variously addressed him.[107] In fact from Mann's point of view there were only two difficulties: first, Sidney's draft of the minority report was inclined to be rather too extremist. He told Webb:

> While I endorse all you have just forwarded, I do think it has been written when you were in a somewhat different mood to that in which the previous portions were prepared. This on women workers and arbitration is a slashing into the capitalist system on lines that I often indulge in on the platform but which are not of the staid, dignified character of the early portions and which I understood you to say was a necessary style to achieve success and with which I agreed. The first is S.W. the second is T.M. – as regards style, though it may be S.W. in specific recommendations.

He added: 'Don't alter it if you think it is not too stiff,' but went on to reiterate his main point, that while some of these passages were 'all right from a bouncing trade unionist … don't forget how damned respectable and considerate I am for others' feelings, eh?'[108]

The second difficulty was how to persuade the other workers' leaders on the Commission to sign such a minority report. Tom Burt was the father of Lib-Lab parliamentarians and there was no prospect of winning his support. The chances of getting Mawdsley, the most prominent of all the Tory trade union leaders, seemed equally remote. Not long since he had told Webb and Shaw to take their 'frenchified' looks and 'Cockney' impertinences elsewhere. Lancashire operatives understood their own interest on the eight-hour question and all else quite well enough. They were not going to be 'led into a pitfall by the London school of inexperienced would-be leaders of trade unionism who arrogate to themselves the power to rectify all the evils pertaining to our social life'. When Beatrice had told him she was going to marry Sidney, he had sworn and cursed, declaring that he had always thought that she had belonged to 'them'. He would rather she had married Auberon Herbert.[109] Nevertheless, Mawdsley saw that it would be difficult for him to accept the do-nothing position of the majority of his fellow commissioners, and he was as weary as Tom Mann with the logic-chopping of Leonard Courtney and the circumlocutions of Professor Marshall. He duly arrived at 41 Grosvenor Road.

Sidney stood in front of the fire and read out the parts of the report which would affect him most. Tom Mann played up by making advanced criticisms which allowed Sidney to endorse Mawdsley's expressions of dissent. Soon the cotton workers' leader was treating the document as his own and expressing his profound satisfaction with its practical and detailed proposals. With Mann and Mawdsley agreed, the assent of two further labour leaders on the Commission – Austin and Abraham – was easily secured.

Mawdsley did insist that the word 'socialism' should be struck out of the report, but it otherwise remained in all its essentials as Sidney had drafted it. It began by criticising the methods of the majority and the paucity of their recommendations. It declared that the fundamental cause of industrial disputes was to be found in the poverty and subjection of the wage-labourers, many of whom were overworked, in overcrowded and unhealthy conditions, for wages that were inadequate to keep body and soul together. One in three of them ended his days in receipt of poor relief and died in the workhouse or the workhouse infirmary. This state of affairs could not be understood except in relation to the fact that two-thirds of the annual product of the community was absorbed by one-fourth of its members:

> The social and economic progress of the workers depends in our judgement, mainly upon the systematic development of democratic public activity in its three principal forms – the national or municipal administration of such industries as can conveniently be managed socially, the regulation of private enterprise in industries not yet taken over by the community, and the public provision – through the taxation of rent and similarly unearned income – of educational and other facilities necessary for the mental and moral development of all classes of the community.

This was followed by a series of specific recommendations for the reform of the sweated trades; the prevention of excessive hours of labour; and the promotion of regularity of employment. The report concluded:

> The whole force of democratic statesmanship must, in our opinion, henceforth be directed to the substitution as far as possible of public for capitalist enterprise, and where this substitution is not yet practicable, to the strict and detailed regulation of all industrial operations, so as to secure to every worker the conditions of efficient citizenship.[110]

This report was soon circulating as a cheap pamphlet in thousands of copies. Beatrice was surely entitled to congratulate herself on a triumph over the Labour Commission which had tried to shut her out, and tried to deny socialists' belligerent rights.

Dear old Leonard [Courtney] who told us with pompous superiority that they were all agreed; and that there was no prospect of any Minority Report – and we had it all the time, lying on our table, and had been putting the last touches to it that very morning. Certainly persons with brains and independent means may have a rare good time in the part of permeator or fly on the wheel.[111]

But it was not only a personal triumph: it was an event of great social and political significance that four trade union leaders of such high standing and diverse opinions, could be brought together on the basis of what was – in all but name – a socialist programme.

It demonstrated the practical possibilities of the conception of the relationship between socialism and the labour movement that the Webbs were elaborating in their own great books of the eighteen-nineties. Socialists were not necessarily doctrinaire enthusiasts setting up in competition with trade unionism for the loyalty of the working class. They accepted that trade unionism had a permanent, if changing, sphere of usefulness. They could be professional experts, ready and able to assume the role of clerks to the trade union movement. Close and respectful students of the long, spontaneous efforts of working men to limit competition and raise their standard of life, they could be inventive and pragmatic when it came to drafting those distinctive programmes for labour which more and more working men were coming to respect and demand from their leaders. Even Henry Broadhurst was not above turning to the Webbs, and Sidney wrote his minority report for the Royal Commission on the Aged Poor.[112]

Thus, the suggestion made by Drage and accepted by a number of historians, that the Webbs were isolated from the trade union leadership and distrusted by them, is not in close accord with the facts as they stood in the early 1880s. If labour leaders did show some reserve towards them, it must be remembered that the workers' leaders habitually showed a great deal towards each other. As the 'new unionism' receded – leaving a permanent deposit of organisation and principle behind it – conflicts over policy were overshadowed by conflicts between personalities. In March 1894 when the Webbs were seeing a good deal of Burns and Broadhurst, Mann and Mawdsley, Beatrice sketched a depressing picture of the condition of the TUC:

From all accounts the Parliamentary Committee is torn asunder by jealousy and suspicion of leading members. Fenwick [miner, Lib-Lab MP and secretary to the Parliamentary Committee after the retirement of Broadhurst in 1890] resolutely refused to move, indolent and reactionary. Burns – not over certain that the Parliamentary Committee should get the credit of his work. Broadhurst – trying to out-Herod Herod in order to get back to his position as paid secretary. Mawdsley and other officials, preoccupied in their own society's work, generally go to sleep at sittings, and arouse themselves when awake in getting Tillett against Burns, and Broadhurst against Fenwick.[113]

This was not a situation in which anyone, either directly or indirectly, stood much chance of doing consistent, purposeful work. Although in terms of character and intelligence they greatly preferred Burns to Broadhurst, the Webbs found themselves trying to help the latter when Burns engineered the famous coup by which the TUC standing orders were overturned, block voting introduced, and the trades councils and 'unattached' socialists excluded from Congress. Broadhurst came to them for help because he found himself in danger of exclusion. He asked Sidney to draft alternative standing orders, but it was too late.[114] Burns who, a few months earlier, had seemed 'excessively friendly' and 'relying a good deal on the Fabians for advice', had cut off his nose to spite his face, and there was nothing to be done about it.

In the course of writing their two books the Webbs had been brought into contact with all the leaders of the trade union world, and had come into service as the clerks of organised labour. They aspired to be the tutors in general to the trade union world and, although this was an ambition bound to inspire resentment, they succeeded to a certain extent, to be measured by the immediate access which they gained to the ruling councils. Modesty is becoming to historians, but the fact remains that he who interprets the past of a nation or a class or a movement must powerfully shape its future. The Webbs informed the British labour movement with a Fabian sense of destiny, and in theory and in practice contributed to a special order of trade union–socialist collaboration.

Nor was their influence confined to Britain. When Shaw addressed the International Socialist Congress held in London in 1896 his paper reflected in its details, as well as in its general spirit, the results of the Webbs' trade union studies. This was particularly evident in the section of his speech concerned with 'Fabian democracy' and his eleventh resolution which repudiated the referendum and direct democracy as likely to 'place the organised, intelligent and class-conscious Socialist minority at the mercy of the unorganised and apathetic mass of routine toilers, imposed upon by the prestige of the aristocratic, plutocratic and clerical forces of reaction'.[115]

By a paradox there were two men in the Socialist International who were particularly influenced by the Webbs' work, and who were responsible for introducing them to the German and Russian publics: Eduard Bernstein, the prophet of revisionism, and V.I. Lenin, the founder of

Bolshevism. In his old age Sidney was to give an inaccurate and muddled account of the matter. He made Bernstein the translator of *Industrial Democracy*, and Lenin the translator of the *History of Trade Unionism*.[116] In fact, the Russian translation of the *History* was supplied by a Menshevik, the Mensheviks deriving particular encouragement from the story of the legal emancipation of the British unions.[117] Lenin and Krupskaya, in exile in Siberia, translated *Industrial Democracy*. The Webbs, being ill-informed about the essential facts of the matter, can hardly have understood what the Russian Marxist valued in their work. Indeed, even today there is an element of conjecture in the answer. However, it is in Lenin's classic monograph *What is to be Done?* (1902), which was concerned with the organisational principles of a revolutionary workers' party, that one discovers most of the direct and indirect evidence of the Webbs' influence.

Lenin appears to have drawn on the Webbs' work at several crucial points. First, he refers directly to their book in the course of his polemic against the 'primitiveness of the Economist' – the 'economists' being those who wanted the Russian working class to subordinate the political to the economic struggle, and who called for a broad, democratic form of organisation. Referring to the Webbs' 'interesting chapter'[118] on primitive democracy in English trade unionism, Lenin argued that even apart from the requirements of the struggle against absolutism, his opponents were adopting an unrealistic position. Second, Lenin was concerned to discredit the theory of 'spontaneity': the view that the working class will come to socialism of its own accord, and as a result of its own experience. The 'economists' argued that it was wrong to think in terms of the political struggle, but necessary to give the economic struggle a political character. 'Read the works of the thoroughly scientific (and thoroughly opportunist) Mr and Mrs Webb,' replied Lenin, 'and you will find that the British trade unions long ago recognised and have long carried out the task of giving the economic struggle itself a political character.'[119] The Webbs had shown this, but they had also shown that trade union politics did not lead spontaneously or inevitably to socialist politics. Third, Lenin, in insisting 'that the history of all countries shows that the working class exclusively by its own effort, is able to develop only trade union consciousness,' went on to argue that modern economic science is as much a condition for socialist production as modern technology, and that 'the vehicles of science are not the proletariat, but the bourgeois intelligentsia'.[120] Leaving their differences about the exact nature of economic science on one side, the Webbs' work fully supported this conclusion. Indeed, the Fabians and the Bolsheviks were unique in the Socialist International in the candour and persistence with which they made this point. Fourth, Lenin, in waging war upon 'primitiveness', laid as much stress as the Webbs did upon the need for professionalism. If Sidney and Beatrice demonstrated for the

English labour movement that the professional expert, whether civil servant or representative, was of decisive importance, Lenin demonstrated that for Russia only a party of professional revolutionaries who utterly rejected amateurism would be of any effect. Fifth, the Webbs' concept of the place of the professional representative in democratic organisation is strikingly similar to the Leninist conception of the role of the professional revolutionary within 'democratic centralism'. Both the Webbs and Lenin transcend the traditional distinction between the delegate and the representative. The new professional leader is to be accorded an active and creative role denied to the delegate without enjoying the autonomous judgement and independence of his constituents associated with the classic notion of a representative.

It is not being suggested that Lenin derived his conceptions from the Webbs; it is being conjectured that he made use of their material and that he critically worked through some of their theoretical ideas in the course of arriving at his own standpoint. Upon Bernstein on the other hand, the Webbs exerted an influence that was formative and persuasive. This was denied by Bernstein himself,[121] because he was anxious to insist upon the originality of his revisionism and to establish its source in the Marxist tradition. He got to know the Webbs during his 'years of exile' in England, and formed a high opinion of them (particularly of Sidney) despite the fact that he was unaccustomed to their matter-of-fact and unashamedly middle-class way of addressing socialist meetings.[122]

In his old age Sidney was under the impression that Bernstein had translated *Industrial Democracy* into German. According to Webb, Bernstein was 'severely' blamed for introducing such heretical ideas to the socialist flock; he narrowly escaped dismissal from his party offices. But these very ideas presently became the basis of much of the 'revisionism' which, he thought, had – unfortunately very tardily – since transformed the programme of the German Social Democratic Party.[123] In fact, it was R. Bernstein – not Eduard – who translated *Industrial Democracy*. Eduard's contribution was limited to writing an afterword to the first German edition of the *History of Trade Unionism*.[124]

By 1895 the German trade unions had funds and members enough to make themselves heard in the councils of the Social Democratic Party, 'and the Party did not always like to hear what the unions had to say.'[125] In this situation Bernstein took from the Webbs a sense of the invincible, primary and permanent character of trade union organisation and consciousness. He declared that the unions were 'indispensable as organs of democracy and not merely as temporary coalitions'. The revisionist perspective of social reform – itself partly shaped by Bernstein's acquaintance with England and with the Fabians – offered a prospect of a much better rapport between the unions and the party. (Both would be concerned with making the most of immediate opportunities, and the unions would not be required to subordinate their everyday work and struggle to the long-range revolutionary objectives of the party.) But while Bernstein associated himself with the Webbs' conception of the trade unions' large sphere of independence and practical usefulness, he fully subscribed to their view that they were not qualified to take the management of the economy into their own hands. Bernstein's famous and fatal utterance: 'I have extraordinarily little interest or taste for what is generally called "the final goal of socialism". This aim, whatever it is, is nothing to me, the movement everything,'[126] was anticipated almost word for word by Sidney a few years earlier: 'My view of Socialism is not that it is a kind of heaven, a kind of stationary state, but a principle of action.'[127]

Lenin and Bernstein were both interested in the Webbs' books because of the light cast upon the problem of 'trade union consciousness' versus 'socialist consciousness', upon the problem of the correct relationship between trade union organisation and political organisation. The answers that were supplied to these challenges had to vary according to national circumstances – to the level of development of the labour movement at a particular time besides such other differences as might arise from conflicting concepts of 'class' and 'state', 'capitalism' and 'socialism'. In the infant Russian labour movement of the 1890s, to accord primary importance to the economic struggle and to trade union organisation was equivalent at best to surrendering the political initiative to the bourgeoisie; at worst, surrendering to absolutism. Therefore, Lenin used the Webbs to reinforce his attack on spontaneity and to reinforce his case for the leading role of a disciplined party of professional revolutionaries. In Russia one could believe in the imminent revolutionary crisis and the duty of subordinating all else in order to prepare for it; but in Germany a crisis appeared more and more distant. Instead of increasing immiseration, the German working class experienced the continual expansion of capitalist production combined with improved social security, thanks to the provisions made by Bismarck and maintained by his successors. In these circumstances it was bound to appear that the socialist party, if it was to maintain its hold on the trade unions, could do so only by slackening it. The unions had to be accorded parity of esteem with their elder and better – the party. Therefore Bernstein used the Webbs to make out what amounted to be a case for the sufficiency of trade union consciousness within modern capitalism.

In England the Webbs, in common with other socialists, were obliged to take as their starting-point the primacy – in point of time and mass loyalties – of the trade union movement – a movement that was 'outside' politics and independent of all parties, with the partial exception of the Great Liberal Party. They saw that the trade unions could be won for socialism only if it was presented to them as a more favourable environment in which they could continue to pursue their familiar policies and procedures, and which did not seriously modify their independence. Socialism was accordingly presented as the fullest and most perfect form of democracy: a mere logical extension of modern radicalism and an elaboration of some of the implications of trade unionism itself. In short, the conflict between the short-run aims of the unions and the long-run goal of socialism tended to be obscured when it was not obliterated altogether. The primacy of trade union consciousness was taken for granted, whether one thought of socialism being promoted through a reconstructed Liberal Party or – as the Webbs occasionally did – through the creation of a new party into which the unions would enter as an important component. As has already been pointed out, the Webbs' systematic and thorough development and popularisation of the past and future of organised labour needs to be taken into account in interpreting the origins of the Labour alliance. But while Sidney and Beatrice helped to prepare the climate in which trade unionist-socialist association became possible, they did not prepare opinion for the shocks that were bound to disturb it. In their brilliant projection of the advance to a fuller and more perfect democracy they failed to discuss the implications of a mixed economy, and they failed to envisage a situation in which the national minimum would extend beyond a definite quota of education, sanitation, leisure and income to the right to work, to full employment. Once this happens, the conflict between trade union consciousness and socialist consciousness can no longer be concealed. If the unions carry on with sectional, competitive collective bargaining, then the state will be driven to take coercive measures against them to check inflationary pressure. In doing so the state turns the wages question from an industrial into a political, from a sectional into a class issue. If the unions recognise this situation for what it is, then they are obliged to exchange mere trade union consciousness for socialist consciousness; they are compelled to stop thinking in terms of partial and limited responses made in relation to one class of economic decisions (wages) and to see that their priorities can be achieved only if they are able to exert control over the determination of other categories of decision bearing upon other incomes, investment and prices. To the extent that the English labour movement has been imbued with mere trade union consciousness it is ill-prepared for such a challenge. Whether it will be surmounted and the English working class will go forward to industrial democracy is one of those questions which, as Sidney and Beatrice used to say, 'make the future interesting'.[128]

7

Heroic Opportunism: Towards a Third Culture and Education in London 1893–1905

Webb's odd 'silence' about education in 1892—The Technical Education Board and the machinery of 'capacity-catching'—Foundation of the LSE and the 'profession' of social science—The reorganisation of London University—The battle over the Education Acts of 1902 and 1903—The third culture and the balance sheet of a heroic opportunism.

When Sidney Webb conducted his campaign in Deptford in 1892 as one of the two 'Progressive' candidates seeking election to the London County Council, he had next to nothing to say about educational policy or provision. If this was ironical in view of how much he himself owed to further-educational institutions in the metropolis, it was still more so in relation to his future career. For if Webb made his influence felt in relation to many departments of London government, it was in the field of educational provision that he made his mark. Indeed, within the next ten years he became the most important single influence upon learning in London and a man to be reckoned with when it came to the shaping of great national measures.

Webb's failure to make education an issue in Deptford is not to be understood in terms of any concessions to that 'tadpole philosophy' of which some authors suspected him and which so frequently attracts self-made men. Despite much harsh speaking he never felt the temptation to play the part of a frog, croaking out a mock encouragement to the less fortunate of the species to follow his example. Neither to shed their tails, nor to distend their mouths and stomachs and hop, as he had done, nimbly on to dry land. He never argued that because he had got out of the pond, it could be left stagnant. Men might resemble tadpoles in being unequal in terms of their natural endowment, but that never became a reason for treating men like tadpoles – certainly not if they were Londoners.[1]

Nor was this strange and ironic silence to be understood as the result of a paucity of ideas. By 1892 the Fabians had quite overtaken the Social Democratic Federation as the carriers of the most advanced socialist programme in relation to education. It is arguable that in 1888 Sidney had helped to involve the Fabians in the Democratic Committee for the School Board more in the interests of improving them as electioneers than in the interests of London education as such, but no such uncertainty can be attached to his subsequent activities. In the same year, he had tried to impress upon the Liberal Party's managers the importance of the subject. He had argued that they ought to be committed to enabling all the children of London, 'even the poorest', to obtain the best education that they were able to assimilate. What that meant in practice, so he maintained, was the abolition of all fees whether in board or voluntary schools. In turn, that required an increase in the government grant and the formation of a proper Ministry of Education. Moreover, after children had concluded their elementary education on a full-time basis there ought to be provision for its universal continuation in evening schools 'in all cases' together with 'abundant scholarships' to secondary schools for those capable of benefiting from them. This implied, for Sidney, the registration and inspection of all private educational establishments.[2]

As for the higher learning, in the late eighties Sidney was giving public voice to the long-standing and deeply felt contempt which he had for Oxford and Cambridge. He saw them as the spoilt children of higher education. They were centres of social prestige rather than of learning. He insisted that they shut out strenuous effort in favour of a well-mannered indolence. They had long lost any claim to consideration as leaders of advanced thought – as anyone with the smallest concern with the progress of biology or sociology must be aware. If they had importance, it lay in their role as preparatory schools for the ruling class – or *'classe dirigeante'*, as he preferred to call it. He viewed them as preparatory schools in which idlers were prepared for mockeries of careers as religious instructors, defenders of the Empire or, worst of all, in what they insolently and shamelessly described as 'public administration'. At every point Sidney's concern for the under-advantaged children of London was matched by his derision for the pampered youths and maidens who inhabited the colleges and halls of the ancient universities. As for their teachers, he fancied that even the best of them suffered from the cardinal vice of traditional university life – the separation of thought and action. They deserved their undergraduates: seven out of every ten of whom he considered to belong to that 'unthinking "Junkerthum"' which, in such an inquiry, counts for no more than the "pigs and philesters" whom Heine excluded from the population of Göttingen'.[3]

However, Sidney was always more interested in the waste attendant upon neglect than he was in the waste attendant in extravagance. He cared more for the potentialities lost through under-expenditure upon the talented poor than he did about the cost of cultivating the undistinguished children of the rich. He never valued justice as much as opportunity. He frequently imagined that the best way of approximating to the former would be found through an extension of the latter. Justice was easily confused with envy and malice; by avoiding that confusion one increased the chances of passing off a concession to equity as a contribution to efficiency.

This is not the spirit normally associated with rallying cries. Yet Sidney had powerfully contributed to such a cry several months before he went to Deptford. He had helped to frame a statement of educational policy, which became recognised as 'a landmark in the educational history of the labour movement' and 'a mine of ideas for socialist and Labour candidates during the following decade'.[4] In Fabian Tract No. 25 Sidney began by following faithfully in the footsteps of the Social Democratic Federation – free school meals and trade union conditions for school board employees. These were demands that had been made familiar already by Annie Besant and others. Nor was the Tract breaking new ground when it reiterated the Nonconformist demand for the discontinuation of public money to church schools and the secularist call for an end to Bible lessons and prayers. But it went on to effectively occupy the greater part of the territory that lay between these proposals and the claim to secondary education for all. It called for an enormous increase in expenditure. It wanted improved school buildings with better-decorated classrooms and more ample playgrounds. It required more teachers, smaller classes and more higher-grade and evening schools. Then it raised the whole issue of special schools for the physically handicapped and the mentally retarded. It demanded the provision of crèches in every infant school and a vast extension of kindergarten. It advocated – in one and the same breath – a great development in the provision of manual education and the raising of the school leaving age to fourteen. Teachers and women were to be made eligible to serve as school inspectors and there were to be unsectarian training colleges. Board Schools were to be empowered to finance scholarships to secondary schools out of public funds. It was impossible to go further without making the imaginative leap involved in the demand for 'Secondary Education for ALL!': a slogan still some ten years ahead of the labour movement's consciousness.

The obvious, but not entirely adequate, answer to the question, 'Why did Webb fail to make these points at Deptford in 1892?' is that they were not what his old master, Jeremy Bentham, would have called 'agenda'. To give them prominence would have been to choose the wrong issue and the wrong election. Deptford was one of the most depressed parts of

London. Its population had doubled in twenty years while employment had been reduced as a result of the closing of its dockyard and foreign cattle market. Consequently, it had more than its fair proportion of the 100 000 families dwelling in the metropolis and less than its fair proportion of jobs. Accordingly, Sidney concentrated on housing, sanitation and securing an adequate water supply together with a proposal for the reorganisation of the docks under public management. The first plank in his platform was the need to secure further powers for the LCC to ensure the efficient government of London.[5] If Sidney already knew that this would mean encroaching upon the powers of the London School Board, he took care not to enlarge upon that subject. For the time being, Fabian Tract No. 25 could be regarded as addressed to the school board, rather than county council electors, and it was soon to exercise a 'very great influence' in that quarter.[6] Webb behaved as if anything but silence on educational matters could only confuse and divide the voters. The Deptford parent of a child of an age below twelve or thirteen was not helpless when it came to promoting his or her educational opportunity. He was an elector and he had only himself to blame if the London School Board fell into the hands of religious obscurantists like the Revd J.R. Diggle. He could prefer the infinitely more enlightened administration associated with T.H. Huxley or Annie Besant, as many Londoners did. In theory, the power was there to be exercised if the electors chose to use it. There were few other aspects of metropolitan life of which the same could be said.

The parent who strolled past the board school might console himself with the thought that his son or daughter was receiving the elements of knowledge: being kept off the streets, and not being indoctrinated with one particular creed or faith. He might equally well curse and fume at the expense he was being put to as a ratepayer. Or complain of being deprived of the earnings, which he might otherwise expect his children to contribute to household income, or shake his head over the godlessness and infidelity to which he imagined the youngsters were being exposed. But whether the board school aroused his approval or disapproval, the sight of it could not occasion the same sense of powerlessness as the pavement along which he was walking. If it was badly paved, ill-lit and dirty, he hardly knew how to call anyone to account. This elementary matter was not the responsibility of some clearly identifiable body of men, such as those who sat on the school board or the county council. It was, rather, the preserve of vestrymen about whose hole-in-corner proceedings he could know little and about whose jobbing or cheese-paring policies he could do less. If he left the pavement to enter one of London's great markets, boarded a tram to go home, turned on the tap, lit the gas, each of these four simple operations was associated with the payment of a tribute to a monopolist.

At the summit of this mountain of traditional privileges and impudent extortion there were to be found, so he was told, the great London livery companies. If there was an honest member of the 'Court of Assistants' he was to be discounted as mere protective covering for his turkey-guzzling and champagne-swilling colleagues: the misappropriation of the inheritance of the greatest city in the world. The presence of such people at the centre of London's life was a hateful anachronism wholly at odds with the development of civic pride and public duty.

Placed in this context, the 'silence' of Sidney and most other Progressive candidates about educational matters becomes rather more intelligible. What they wanted was a London County Council that would be able to be more democratic and more effective than the old Metropolitan Board of Works; a council which would be able to make war on the abuses, ancient and modern, of the 'monopolists'. The presence of the London School Board, despite its limited jurisdiction, meant that at least a part of metropolitan life was managed in accord with the requirements of modernity, efficiency and accountability. Accordingly, education was not 'agenda'.

However, matters were more complicated than this. During the election campaign a body describing itself as the National Association for the Promotion of Technical and Secondary Education addressed an appeal to the electors. It drew attention to the fact that county councils had been empowered to act as providing bodies under the Technical Instruction Act of 1889. It pointed out that under the Local Taxation Act of 1890, county and county-borough councils in England and Wales might appropriate the proceeds of beer and spirits duties for the purpose of technical education within the meaning of the Technical Instruction Act. It complained that only Middlesex and London were failing to do so. It deplored the argument that the money was wanted for the relief of the rates. It dismissed with contempt the objection that this 'whisky money' might only be available for a limited period. It exposed as little better than humbug the suggestion that the only proper fund for financing educational expansion, beyond the elementary level, was to be found in the coffers of the city companies and guilds. It cited with approval the judgment of the *Trade Unionist* that

> it ought not to be possible for a body like the LCC to vote away its share of the grant, amounting to no less than £163,000 in relief of the rates, as it did last year ... To wait until the City Guilds can be made to disgorge is a fantastic and perfectly preposterous attitude.[7]

Sidney was a contributor to the *Trade Unionist* and he wrote signed articles for it throughout the period of the election campaign.[8] Beatrice's old friend, Hubert Llewellyn Smith, was the Secretary of the National

Association for the Promotion of Technical and Secondary Education. H.D. Acland MP, another associate of the Webbs and the nearest thing to an Education Minister in Gladstone's last administration, was also heavily involved. The right hand knew what the left was doing. As a Progressive candidate Sidney was hardly in a position to scold his colleagues and predecessors for failing to do their duty: but he could rejoice when others did so. He neither inspired nor dictated the London Programme, but he did succeed in writing it, popularising it, and occasionally – as the Progressives' licensed 'dreamer of dreams' – introducing one or two 'premonitions' into it. Thus, the most attentive reader could find nothing about education if he consulted the table of contents or referred to the index, but if he read it – and it was eminently readable – he would have come across Webb playing at being the chairman of the Finance Committee. In his 'budget' speech Sidney referred to the cost of a new teaching university for London: the extension of evening classes: the establishment of a small public library in each ward and the provision of free breakfasts for needy children. He concluded this section of his imaginary speech with a genuflection to the independence of the School Board, but followed it immediately with a clear statement of intent, ten years ahead of its time, to supersede it through a single educational authority for the whole of the metropolis:

> As the School Board, like the Poor Law Council, is formed by independent election, I have, in this Council, no further comment to make upon its work. But I may observe that the decision to place under the control of a single administrative authority the whole of the educational work of the metropolis, from the infant school to the University, and from the crèche to the technical college, bids fair to make the 'educational ladder' really open to all London's children, and to do something, in one city at any rate, to make up for the lamentable want of a genuine Minister of National Education.[9]

Most New Liberals and Progressives would never have stood for this if they had thought for a moment that it was 'serious politics'. The New Liberalism proudly insisted on its continuity with the old when it came to a defence of liberty against monolithic administrative projects. The proposal that there should be 'a single administrative authority for the whole of the educational work of the metropolis' was as likely to have aroused its fears of 'Bonapartism' as one for the establishment of a Ministry of Justice.[10] Nor did it favour a steep increase in public expenditure on education or anything else. It was the misappropriation of public money rather than socialistic proposals for altering the proportions as between public and private expenditure that served as the Progressives' rallying point. The 'moderates' might accuse them of planning to raise the rates, but they could sincerely reject that charge and point out that they had no designs on the hard-earned income of the middle classes as such. Their target was only the rent rolls of ground landlords, the extortionate profits of monopolists, and the property and income of those city companies that had wrongfully expropriated the inheritance of London.

The expression 'New Liberalism' was first coined in 1889[11] – the year of the new unionism's greatest triumphs. As the new unionism made its biggest impact upon London so the New Liberalism was first made flesh in the shape of London's Progressive Party. But the Progressives were as much a response to the 'backward' as to the 'advanced' character of metropolitan life. London was not only a place which had more than its due proportion of socialists and new unionists, but was also a provincial backwater at the heart of an empire: the last fortress of Old Corruption left standing sixty years after the passing of the Great Reform Act. It was a place where the Old Liberalism still had useful work to do, but it could do it only by harnessing the support of new social and political forces. The slogan: 'Home Rule for London!' nicely expressed an attachment for Mr Gladstone while making a discreet protest against treating the Grand Old Man's obsession as if it was an adequate substitute for an order of political priorities. But that slogan also suggested continuity with the traditional liberal concern for political and administrative, rather than social, reform. Sidney believed that they could be made to pass from the one to the other. If he could teach them expediency they would learn principle. Indeed, it was one of the distinctive features of Fabianism to treat expediency – not as the point of departure from 'principle' – but as a way of arriving at it. However, this required that Webb should follow one course of action as lobbyist, another as draughtsman and yet another as candidate. Thus, in the matter of educational policy he could be demanding, imaginative or discreetly silent as circumstances required.

When Sidney went to the offices of the LCC at Spring Gardens in mid-March 1892 he was – according to the *Daily News* – one of the first to arrive and he took his seat high up in the chamber. In fact, he was one of the last to arrive and took his seat low down. As he remarked to Beatrice: 'Thus is history written.'[12] In fact, the history of the LCC was to be neither made nor written in the council chamber, but in committees. Webb rejoiced in the LCC's 'discovery' of government by committee. Committees were his natural habitat. He was on the Progressive Party Committee and on seven others before the first council meeting ratified these appointments. It was the function of the Progressive Party Committee to resolve all key decisions on policy and personnel in advance. Prodded by John Burns who was mindful, no doubt, of the old adage concerning idle hands and the Devil and wanted no interference in his own sphere of activity, Sidney was immediately placed on several committees and soon on more! The list comprised seven committees by the end of 1892. In addition to the four previously noted – Parliamentary, Local Government and Taxation, Public Health and Housing, and the Water committee – he also joined two more; the Appeals committee and the Establishment committee. He was made vice-chairman of Local Government and Taxation.

Even the first four committees would have been an evasion of a convention, which ruled that no one should be on more than three. Yet one more was to be added to the six. At the beginning of March 1892, Sidney had an important conference with Sir Thomas Farrer, who had been first chairman of the 'Progressist' Party and had become vice-chairman of the Council in 1890. Farrer 'spontaneously suggested' that Webb should become chairman of the Technical Education committee. Sidney had already reckoned that he would have to spend nearly twenty hours a week on Council business, but he showed no hesitation in accepting the proposal. His only regret was that he was not on the Highways committee![13]

By 4 March he was discussing with Llewellyn Smith how best to enlist his help and advice. The following day he was reporting to Beatrice that he had been making arrangements with Quintin Hogg, an alderman and principal patron of the Regent Street Polytechnic, as to how best to get the 'technical education question brought on next Thursday when the estimate comes up'.[14] (He had, of course, also had a word with Evan Spicer, who was chairman of the Finance committee.) 'It so happened' – as Beatrice charmingly remarked – 'that SW's first motion on the Council was one proposing that a committee should be appointed to consider whether the Council should not proceed under the [Technical Instruction] Act.'[15] There is no proposal in politics that it is harder to resist than a call for an inquiry. This is the magic wand that unites all and sundry since those who imagine it will prepare the way for change are joined by others who notice that it will defer it. Sidney's first motion was carried *nem. con.* Moreover, he was left to choose the committee – always subject to maintaining the exact party balance on the Council. In latter years Sidney often explained how, in his anxiety to put on the ablest members from the various sections, he found he had not provided for a chairman, as practically all his nominees proved to be chairmen of other committees. He was virtually driven 'to preside himself.'[16]

Such tales magnified the Webb reputation for both modesty and cunning. In fact, the 'Polytechnique men' on the Council did not relish the prospect of a full inquiry. No matter how hard Sidney looked to preparing the ground and reassuring everyone that it was safe to proceed, those who were already associated with great and established institutions of technical education were uneasy. When Webb's committee met Lord Rosebery was in the chair and called for nominations. Although Sidney

was proposed, Rosebery cast around for older members. Hogg, head of
the 'Polytechnique party', secured a nomination and only retired in
Webb's favour after Lord Hobhouse and Sir T. Farrer had spoken in
favour of the Fabian. That evidently much astonished his lordship, who
hastily vacated the (embarrassingly high!) chair in favour of Sidney. Webb
promptly undertook to prepare a memorandum for the next meeting,
which would lay down the scope of the inquiry. The decision as to
who was to be employed to conduct it was postponed.[17] Sidney himself appears to have been undecided between two outstanding candidates:
Dr William Garnett and Hubert Llewellyn Smith. In the end he resolved
the difficulty in a characteristic manner by securing the services of them
both. While Smith prepared the report on the state of technical education
in London, Garnett was recruited as permanent secretary to what became
the London Technical Education Board.

For the purpose of the inquiry, Llewellyn Smith had everything to recommend him. He was respected as a scholarly authority on economics
and as a contemporary historian. He was, through Beatrice, a friend.
Above all, he was already exceedingly well informed about the subject
and a determined advocate of increased educational provision. His
approach was marked by a serious historical perspective and a lively
appreciation of social needs. He believed that Victorian England had
inherited not one educational tradition, but two. The first he identified
with the Renaissance and the scholastic and classical tradition of the
grammar school; the second he associated with the Reformation and the
customary apprenticeship of the workshop. He saw both traditions as
defective in so far as they identified learning with mere instruction and
sacrificed the development of faculty to the acquisition of knowledge. He
shared Matthew Arnold's concern about 'the immense social loss to the
country in an age of social and political change and upheaval, caused by
the inferior training of the mass of the middle class, on whom so much
depended.'[18] Secondary education was a class question and, in the first
instance, a middle-class one. Like Bryce, he inclined to see secondary education as something to be devised for those not wholly absorbed in daily
toll. Such a conception corresponded to existing social reality in London
where he found that the institutions of higher day and evening schools
catered for that small minority that continued their education beyond the
age of twelve or thirteen. The secondary schools, whether they were
'endowed' or 'proprietary' or 'private adventure', were reaching barely 3
per cent of the population outside the City and Westminster. They were
schools attended by the sons of clerks, tradesmen, manufacturers and professional men. The working-class contribution to the secondary school
population was small and drawn almost entirely from 'the upper stratum'. In Bethnal Green there were 47 working-class children in secondary

schools and in Poplar there were 27, but of these only 3 in Bethnal Green and 1 in Poplar were the sons of labourers.[19]

From these facts Llewellyn Smith drew the conclusion – a surprising one for us – that it was middle-class education that was the most neglected. He argued that

> it is the development of universal primary education that has brought with it the need for some capacity-catching machinery for selecting the most promising boys from the elementary schools, and carrying their education to a higher point. Whether in turn this – the modern – idea will give place to the idea of universal secondary education, is a question for the future. The present problem is to devise the best machinery for selection.[20]

On existing evidence he was persuaded that the social class of the majority of boys selected by scholarship did not, and would not, greatly differ from that of the other pupils of secondary schools. Only the fringe of the working class could be or would be touched. However, it was at this point that the distinction, such as it was, between secondary education in general and technical education came in. He wanted to catch the brightest children and to improve the chances of working-class boys by lowering the age of selection for scholarship to ten or eleven while introducing maintenance grants which would rise with each year that a child was kept at school. Yet he feared that what this would do no more than

> take a few boys from one class, and place them among a number of boys of another class, coming from a different kind of home and aiming at a different kind of career. The newcomers must assimilate themselves to their new surroundings under the penalty of miserable isolation during their school career … In other words such sons of artisans as secure scholarships tend to receive in the higher school the stamp of middle-class ideas, and an almost irresistible bias towards a middle-class trade or profession … [If the workmen's children were not to aspire beyond their station in life] some powerful corrective must be applied … a larger infusion of some form of manual or practical instruction … a more practical and modern curriculum.[21]

Clara Collet made the same point with respect to working-class girls:

> The domestic needs and habits of different classes vary considerably, and there may be a danger that in promoting the secondary education of girls of the working classes along the same lines as those pursued by the girls of the middle classes, their domestic happiness may be sacrificed to a theoretical equality.[22]

Yet despite these anxieties the National Association for the Promotion of Technical and Secondary Education came to the conclusion that

> the most urgent need of our time is to provide facilities for the secondary education of workmen's children, and in the interests of all classes, it is highly desirable that this education should be given as far as possible in the same schools as those attended by the middle class.[23]

But while Llewellyn Smith and his collaborators were far from consistent about class priorities in education and about the distribution, if any, between secondary and technical education, they were well informed about the inadequacies of the system and of the provisions for post-elementary education in London so far as the lower middle and upper working classes were concerned.

Llewellyn Smith's reports showed those existing provisions for secondary and technical education to be woefully inadequate. He reckoned that there were probably under a thousand scholarships in the whole of London leading from elementary to secondary schools. In the largest single category of secondary school – the private venture school conducted for the profit of the master – there was an immense and damaging turnover. (There were approximately 450 of them and in 1889–90, 71 had disappeared and 38 new ones had arisen.[24]) Even in the endowed and proprietary secondary schools there was little attempt to break with the old tradition of purely literary training. It was a tradition, which was not appropriate to the 'neglected' middle class and perhaps worse than useless for the fringe of the working class that entered secondary education.

By 1893 Sidney was armed with the facts and fortified by expert opinion. Even so he was obliged to be both cautious and inventive. If there were few who were prepared to oppose technical education outright, there were many that were uncertain about what it was or else fearful about certain ways of promoting it. Thus, the SDF while favouring 'industrial education' as the best education for all classes, echoed the old slogan of the Socialist League according to which technical education was 'a capital idea for the capitalist'.[25] William Morris took the sense of these objections. While insisting that education was a dangerous gift to give slaves he feared that technical education would deaden the spirit of artistic life. Trade union opinion was also characterised by divisions and equivocations. The 'old' unionists attempted a novel distinction between technical education, of which they approved, and 'trade teaching', of which they did not. The new unionists tended to argue that all workers, not just the labour aristocracy, ought to have a chance to acquire skills and improve them. Yet they were not free from misgivings, and suggested that ends would be promoted that were unwelcome and non-educational.

Employers were necessarily influenced by the characteristics of the particular labour markets with which they were confronted. Nor were representatives of secondary and higher educational institutions much less wary. Their attitude was bound to be affected by how any increased expenditure was to be channelled and controlled. Finally, within the LCC itself there were men, like John Benn, who had taken an active interest in providing scientific and technical instruction in various trades, who felt that it was the duty of the city companies to meet the bill. They were zealous defenders of the interests of voluntary organisations already in the field. They were conscious of the need to keep down rates. They were set to take offence at any innovation that they had not thought of themselves or that might be construed as exposing a tardiness on their part to accept responsibility.

Accordingly Webb was content to wait nearly a year in order to unite his Technical Education committee behind agreed proposals. On 29 January 1893 the committee asked the council to accept responsibility for seeing that every district in London was adequately provided with technical education from workshop to university level, taking account of local occupational structure. Opportunity was to be enlarged. Yet as much emphasis was placed upon preventing wasteful overlapping in provision as upon closing gaps in it. The committee asked for little financially and for much administratively. It requested the council for no new rates, but only for one-third of the funds received from the beer and spirits duties. On the other hand, it asked the council to share its responsibility with other parties. It called for the creation of a Technical Education Board, upon which only twenty places would be reserved for councillors while fifteen went to outside interests. Webb saw no future in the LCC setting up new institutions in rivalry to the polytechnics or other established bodies. His committee wanted to add to them and to coordinate their work; not to supplant them. To be sure, this would have to be conditioned upon certain rights of scrutiny and representation. If the claim to scrutiny and representation was to be acceptable it needed to be matched by according to the school board, the City and Guilds Institute, the Head Masters' and the Head Mistresses' Associations and certain other bodies, representation upon the new Technical Education Board itself.[26]

Thus, Sidney took to the council a report which was carefully researched and well informed: an economical response to a great challenge upon ingenious and yet balanced lines to a profound administrative problem. These qualities were not, however, sufficient to ensure an easy passage for the report. Webb anticipated the difficulty, and took pains anonymously to mobilise pressure on his fellow councillors before the crucial debate occurred.[27] He was not entirely successful. Benn wanted to make the council acceptance conditional upon the City livery companies contributing for the same purpose one-tenth of their corporate income. He pointed out that Webb had asked the companies what they were doing and had found that it was disturbingly little. Was it good enough to chalk on the walls of the City Halls 'Pay What You Owe' and then to run away?[28] Sidney disposed of this 'wrecking' amendment by expressing his sympathy with its intention and suggesting that it should be modified in the sense that the companies should be 'invited' to contribute their fair proportion to the cost.[29] If he had himself asked for all the 'whisky money' he might have had a great deal more trouble in negotiating this obstacle. Nor was this the only difficulty that had to be surmounted. Many councillors were uneasy about the notion of setting up a board in which the LCC was to share power with other bodies. Even when Sidney had managed to subdue the anxieties about this as a matter of principle, he had to deal with detailed objections that this body had not been invited or that one had been over-represented. Why was London University not represented? Webb replied that it should be once it had become a teaching institution and not merely an examining one. He successfully resisted that amendment, but he was unsuccessful when it came to proposals from 'Labour' councillors that the London Trades Council should have extra places at the expense of the London School Board. If Sidney was privately not too disturbed by being defeated on this issue, he took good care to keep his opinion to himself.[30] More important, he took steps to ensure that the council would never again meddle with his committee to such effect. He secured agreement that the Technical Education Board should not have to report to the council every week, but only once a quarter. He also saw that it was released from the usual obligation of a committee to expend no more than £50 at a time without the council's consent. Thus while the TEB required powers of inspection and control over other bodies, it succeeded in releasing itself from customary forms of scrutiny. To further enlarge the effective independence of the committee, Sidney developed the habit of not only drawing up the agenda but of drafting, in advance, the conclusions he wished it to arrive at. If there was a contentious point he included it twice so that if it was struck out in the first instance it might survive in the second. Moreover, if he negotiated a contentious issue through the board he avoided contention occurring in the council by circulating notes to all councillors in advance explaining the grounds of the board's decision. Nine times out of ten such proposals went through without debate.[31]

The Technical Education Board met for the first time on 28 April 1893. Quintin Hogg, Sidney's rival of a year earlier, proposed that Webb be elected chairman and this was carried unanimously.[32] He served in this capacity until 1898 and during the first two years of the board's life he also belonged to seven of its key sub-committees. But it was not Webb's way, for all his phenomenal energy, to take all the work on his shoulders. He fully appreciated the importance of delegation, and never feared to enlist the collaboration of gifted and independent colleagues. Thus, Garnett came in as secretary, but Llewellyn Smith's services were retained by inducing the council to nominate him a member of board. He subsequently became a member of the Royal Commission on Secondary Education (the Bryce Commission). Sidney and Garnett were among those who gave evidence and they all played into each other's hands in the most accomplished manner.[33] Meanwhile, close contact was maintained with Acland so that the board might lawfully construe technical education to cover virtually everything save ancient languages and theology.[34] Beatrice's old friend and collaborator Ella Pycroft was placed in change of the domestic economy classes for girls, expanding existing provision, training teachers and giving to the work a special relevance for working-class rather than middle-class households. For example, the girls were taught how to cook for a meal for an entire family using a single saucepan.[35]

Nor did Webb neglect public relations. He did not rely only on the representative character of the board to ensure that all concerned knew about its work. In the first year no fewer than four major conferences were convened with interested groups of trade unionists. Thus, on 4 July 1894 there was a conference of the book, paper and printing trades held at County Hall. Fears were very forcibly expressed that technical education was tending to lower the price of labour by increasing its supply. Webb could use his unique knowledge of the trade union movement to show insight into these anxieties. Indeed, he entirely removed them by promising that the board would give instruction only to those actually engaged in the trade.[36] From the beginning he used the press to publicise the board's work, making particular use of *London*, the journal of the Reform Union. On 22 October 1894 a new monthly, *The London Technical Education Gazette*, appeared. It was intended to be an organ of communication between the board and all interested in technical education. It survived until March 1904 when the Education Committee under the London Education Act of 1903 superseded the board.

The expenditure of all this political energy and intelligence resulted in achievements in which Sidney always took special pride. First, the board extended educational opportunity in several ways, but principally through its scholarship ladder. When he presented his first report to the council in January 1893 Webb drew a shameful comparison:

Six times as many people attended evening classes in Manchester as in London, and Manchester would not make a sixth of London. Every year 100 000 children leave our Board Schools. Their education should be continued for at least three years afterwards, that is, there ought to be between 300 000 and 400 000 young persons in evening classes. They number less than 30 000 taking the students at all classes of science, art or technology.[37]

Four years later he was boasting that London's capacity-catching machine was 'the greatest the world had ever seen'.[38] In its first year the board established 500 junior county scholarships for children from households in which earnings did not exceed £3 per week or £150 a year. These covered fees and a small sum intended as compensation for loss of earnings. Above the junior scholarship there were intermediate and senior ones sharply tapering off in number, while competition was enlarged by making children from higher-income groups eligible. But in 1894 the board devoted only a tenth of its total expenditure of £80 000 to scholarships.[39] It asked a host of secondary and higher-grade schools, polytechnics and commercial colleges to expand their provision in exchange for grants. Thus, when it came to training Ella Pycroft's 'little housewives', the board offered money to each of the recognised London polytechnics on condition that a school of domestic economy was established where girls who had completed their elementary education could be trained to become homemakers. These classes should involve at least six months' full-time work. The scholarship girls were to have free food and clothing made by themselves, other pupils paying a 'moderate fee'. Battersea Polytechnic was to get a grant in exchange for establishing a college for the teachers with a view to a continuous extension of the movement.[40]

Second – and hardly less important – the board raised standards. In 1893 it issued a circular to technical institutes offering grants upon conditions intended to ensure: (a) the invariable performance of practical, experimental or laboratory work by the students themselves; (b) discouragement of mere lecturing, or book work, in physical science; (c) abandonment of 'farming' classes to the teachers; (d) freedom to teachers to substitute other courses or methods from those proscribed by the department; (f) greater regularity of attendance; and (g) reduction of the high fees hitherto charged for certain subjects.[41] Arrangements were immediately made for the proper inspection of grant-aided institutions of secondary education.

Third, in the same circular the board made it plain that it wanted greater co-ordination of the educational institutions with which it dealt and that it was determined, not only to help in filling gaps, but also to eliminate wasteful overlapping. In general it encouraged existing institutions to take fresh initiatives, but occasionally, as with the establishment of a new technical school in Hoxton, it took matters directly in hand. By 1894–5 it had begun to promote the higher education of clerks in London by organising a course specifically designed to bring them up to the level of their 'German rivals'.[42] When 'others' took important initiatives, as with the foundation of the London School of Economics, the board was at hand to give its aid. Finally, the TEB by skilfully publicising these activities powerfully contributed to preparing educational and governmental opinion to regard the county councils as the appropriate *de facto* authorities for all secondary education. Thus Garnett and Webb – with Sidney taking the lion's share of the questioning – induced the Bryce Commission to look to the county councils as the proper bodies to be entrusted with secondary education. This is not to imply that Bryce's recommendations were entirely welcome to Webb. The Royal Commission proposed that the distinction between 'secondary' and 'technical' education should be maintained; elementary education was to be left to the school boards, technical to the TEB, and a new authority, which might be modelled on the TEB, was to take charge of 'secondary' education. In his evidence, Sidney, in the interests of removing all restrictions on the work of the TEB, had tried to diminish to vanishing point the distinction to which the Commissioners were so attached. This led to some entertaining exchanges:

'You spoke' [remarked Dr. Fairburn, one of the Commissioners] 'about secondary education proper. May I ask you what you meant by that?'
'I should be very loath to give a definition unless that of all education between the elementary standards and the University.'
'This is evidence on technical education?'
'I should be sorry to define technical education as exclusive of secondary education, or secondary education as exclusive of technical.'
'Then do we understand that the Committee you represent has the whole field of technical education for its own?'
'The functions of the Board are of course limited by its powers, and its powers are only those that are given by the Technical Instruction Acts. I understand therefore that we could not aid the teaching of Greek, unless Modern Greek, nor the teaching of Latin, nor History, and probably literature. But I do not know quite what other subjects would fall outside the definition in the Technical Instruction Acts.'
'Still, an education which excludes the subjects which you have just alluded to can hardly be recognised as secondary?'
'That is a matter of opinion upon which I should not like to express myself. It is simply a matter of definition.'
'It does not cover the whole field that lies between the elementary schools and the Universities?'
'Certainly it does not.'[43]

Llewellyn Smith intervened:

'With reference to that, is it not the case that the Technical Instruction Acts do not exclude the Board from aiding schools which are giving instruction in the subjects you named, provided they also give instruction in the subjects falling within the Technical Instruction Acts?'

'That is so and as I shall have occasion to show we have aided schools which call themselves Secondary Schools and which do teach the subjects.'

Sir John Hubert asked: 'Have you aided any Grammar Schools?' When Sidney affirmed that the board had done so, the Dean of Manchester quickly observed: 'So your Secondary Education after all is "proper"?'

To this Sidney cheerfully replied: 'I had not suggested that it was not.' As he made clear in subsequent answers:

> It is not within our function to take care that the study of literature, for instance, does not suffer; but one cannot ignore the fact that by being able to endow the teaching of science, languages, commercial subjects, economics, and numerous other things under the definition of technical education, and not being able to endow the teaching of some other subjects, so long as there is no other body which is able to supply any makeweight, it is impossible but that those other subjects should not somewhat tend to be neglected. Consequently, speaking as a citizen and without reference to technical education, one cannot help feeling that the inequality must somehow or other be redressed.[44]

It was not, in his view, to be redressed by establishing some other body responsible for part of the post-elementary education: it was 'almost inconceivable' that it should be done. Bryce wanted to attempt it, but Sidney had administrative convenience and history on his side. As with the distinction between technical and secondary education, there was little to choose between having history and having administrative convenience on one's side.

Yet if the work of the TEB was 'hardly ever criticised', it did have its critics. If Sidney was responsible for enlarging the educational opportunities of Londoners he did not enlarge them by so much. If the cost of his 'capacity-catching machinery' ran to £80 000 at the outset, and rose to £120 000 by 1896, throughout its entire lifetime the TEB never had recourse to raising the rate that the Technical Instruction Act of 1889 had made permissible.[45] Moderates and Progressives might view that with satisfaction, but was it not a proper subject of discontent among socialists or among educationalists who knew the extent of London's untrained ability?

Then, again, as 'Labour' critics were bold enough to point out, 'opportunity' was enlarged far faster than 'equality' was approached. The TEB might insist that it was promoting the education of the poorest of London's children, but its own statistics hardly bore out that conclusion. The *Technical Education Gazette* might notice, ever and anon, that the majority of scholarships went to the children of the 'working class'. But that majority was never large, never grew at a dramatic rate and was always achieved by amalgamating the impressive achievements of journeymen's offspring with the distressingly poor results achieved by the sons and daughters of unskilled labourers.[46] John Burns, Ben Tillett, Will Crooks and Keir Hardie found plenty to grumble about. They did not stop grumbling after Webb had been forced to increase the representation of the London Trades Council at the expense of the London School Board, nor when the minimum scholarship was raised from £5 to £10 so as to make the sacrifice relatively easier for working-class parents to bear. The petite bourgeoisie was the main beneficiary. The poorer districts were being neglected. Working-class children were being imbued with middle-class standards, as exemplified by that worthless character the University Man. (As Will Crooks pointed out, 'there never was a university man yet who built a ship or a house, or rendered any service to the community … He wanted education extended to the poorest of the poor, and it would do no harm to society, he imagined, if they had educated scavengers.')[47] Keir Hardie complained that the scholarships inculcated the worst type of middle-class competitiveness.[48] Nor was it the workers' leaders alone who discovered that the work of the TEB was deformed by the values of existing society. Feminists pointed out only a third of the scholarships were for girls and that many of these were devoted to courses of study which confirmed them in their role of 'little housewives'.

Sidney met these objections as best he could. He reminded the feminists that there simply was not the same demand for education for girls. If girls had had to be adjudged by equal standards they would hardly have gained one-quarter of the scholarships never mind one-third. Similarly, with respect to the 'bad districts' he pointed out that thirty scholarships were reserved for the least successful schools. Yet the success of the TEB was undoubtedly purchased at the price of accommodation to the requirements of the existing order. The method of averting hostility by befriending all and sundry had its costs. If it was silly to complain that the TEB saved the endowed schools by giving them conditional aid, Sidney himself drew the line at subsidising private venture schools. By 1900 he had got himself into the ridiculous position of attacking the livery companies in print while he was defending them in the council and committee as indispensable participants in the TEB. He was dismissing John Benn's statements about their extravagance and waste even when they were based on his own *Facts for Londoners*.[49]

An important reproach against Sidney during the formation and fertile years of his leadership in technical education (1892–5) is that he held a constant ideal before him – but that it was administrative rather than educational. He knew, in other words, how London education should be organised, but he had not asked himself what it was to be for. It might be argued – and very plausibly – that he dismissed theory and was impatient with definition because he was anxious to get things done and like most men who care to get things done did not care too much about what it was that he was doing. This is nearer the mark than the objection that he was an incorrigible elitist whose deepest commitment was to building capacity-catching machinery rather than to a concern for the children of London taken as whole. He wanted every Londoner to have an educational opportunity that would be at least equal to that enjoyed by the children of the superior artisan.[50] If he believed, as he certainly did, in the unequal endowment of capacity, he affirmed his faith that even the dullest razor ought to be given the sharpest possible edge.[51] He never deluded himself that the capacity he was catching began to approximate to all the capacity that needed to be caught. But he declined to defend inertia behind the walls of principle or postpone the elevation of some children out of a misplaced sense of justice towards the rest. He had made it plain that he was not going to be detained by protests to the effect that he was giving inequality a protective colouring. Nor could he understand the objection that the 'do something' policies of today might become the mothers and fathers of the 'do nothing' policies of tomorrow. How could he, when he was already so ambitious for tomorrow?

On Monday, 13 August 1894 Sidney was in Oxford reading a paper on the economic heresies of the LCC to the Economic Section of the British Association. It will be remembered that his activities on the council were by no means confined to the pioneering work of the TEB. His subject on this occasion was the employment policies of the council and he defended it in a long, heavily documented argument. He successfully conveyed the impression that he was spokesman for the Progressive majority while implying that progressive policies were 'socialist' and anathema to those who fancied themselves to be the defenders of economic orthodoxy. The heresies were three in number. First, the LCC followed the practice of the London School Board in insisting that not less than the standard rate of wages should be paid. This meant paying the union rate in each trade and never paying less than sixpence an hour to adult males or less than eighteen shillings per week to women. As recently as November 1892 Lord Farrer himself had declared that the council in adopting the standard rate would 'lose its independence ... Be run by trade unions ... be bound hand and foot to obey their orders.' Sidney suggested that Lord Farrer himself would now recognise that that was 'alarmist'. It meant paying a moral minimum wage to the unskilled, keeping them above Booth's poverty line and paying the negotiated rate for skilled men. Nobody would recommend that county councils should buy engineers or medical officers in the cheapest market, but 'owing to the extraordinary ignorance of the middle and upper class' it was wrongly thought to be another matter when it came to 'common workmen'. Second, the council imposed these policies upon private contractors, thus, allegedly, diminishing the contractors' freedom and raising costs. But this, Sidney argued, was to confuse the contractors' expenses with the community's costs. The council was not abolishing competition, but shifting its plane from mere cheapness to industrial efficiency and ingenuity. Finally, the council had encouraged the heresy of getting rid of the contractor altogether by executing its own works directly. Sidney demonstrated, with a wealth of detail, that some contractors had conspired together not to compete with each other, and so to induce the council to abandon its fair wages clause. 'The Council preferred to abandon the contractor' – at least once it found that it could effect a net saving of nearly 50 per cent by doing the work itself. Sidney concluded that the integration of productive processes under the direct control of salaried managers accountable to the consumers had been the way forward in British business history for the last twenty years and if it was economic heresy it was increasingly industrial orthodoxy.[52]

The delivery of this paper at Oxford confirmed Sidney in his status not only as a recognised leader of the Progressive Party but also as a recognised economist. He had got in – if only just – upon the right side of the professionalising process that had been going on in British economics since about 1890. A profession requires a definitive text and a recognised corpus of theory. Marshall had met this need with his *Principles*. When this book appeared many had the experience – so indispensable to professionalism – that 'this is what I have been saying' or that ' this is what I should have said'. This was true in Sidney's case. But professionalism requires more than a minimum agreement about scope, methods and conclusions: it presupposes organisation strong enough to include all the 'recognised practitioners' while excluding the rest. It is a painful, tension-ridden process. In 1889, Sidney had written defiantly to Marshall: 'If I am wrong in my economics I shall be glad to be corrected.'[53] He was admitted in the following year as one of the founding members of the British Economic Association, along with five other Fabians.[54] Yet there was an active distrust on both sides. Webb feared that the *Economic Journal* was going to be a mere individualist organ and that it was being established to queer the pitch for the *Oxford Economic Review*.[55] If he was happy to join the Economic Association he was also a member of Professor James Bonar's Economic Club, which was founded about the same time and which admitted only those who were able to 'furnish satisfactory evidence of Economic Training'. In 1894 it had 56 members. It was exclusive. Yet it combined an old mixture of established academics like Marshall,

Cunningham, Edgeworth, Foxwell and L.L. Price with civil servants like H. Llewellyn Smith and influential investigators such as Sidney and Beatrice, Ella Pycroft and Charles Booth. Then there were publicists, such as Schloss, and charity organisers like C.S. Loch. In short, the early 1890s represented the formative years of English economics, a period marked by rival journals and competing attempts at organisation, an age distinguished by halting steps away from mere amateurism. It was a time in which conflicting ambitions met in terms of a drive to shut out the negligible, while admitting all those who had a legitimate claim to attention.

One of the critical moments in this long professionalising process occurred in Oxford on the very day after Sidney delivered his paper on the economic heresies of the LCC. (It may safely be presumed that he was present.) A number of reports were delivered by members of a committee, which Professor W. Cunningham of Cambridge presided over. The topic was 'Methods of Economic Training in This and Other Countries'. A tone of anxiety and of the most profound gloom pervaded the discussion. In the United States economics was supported by an enthusiastic public opinion and in universities it escaped relegation to the position of a subject outside the usual curriculum. In England, if it appeared in the curriculum at all, it was as a subordinate and narrow subject:

> In the University of London, Economics holds no position but the somewhat unfortunate one of a subject for candidates proceeding from the BA to the MA degree in Moral Science, a position which at once restricts the number of students likely to study it and prevents its study from exhibiting much beyond the knowledge of general theory. It is not a subject, either optional or obligatory, at any other examination.

At Oxford it related to little more than certain prescribed passages in Adam Smith and Walker. At University College, Nottingham, the same professor taught history, literature and economics. Only at Cambridge, under Marshall, was the position markedly better, since economics entered examinations for three degrees. But feelings about Marshall were equivocal. After the appearance of his *Principles* in 1890 British economists felt that little more needed to be done on the general theory of value. But the standing and growth of the profession required that it should change the popular impression of the economist as 'a compound of text-book theory and ignorance of fact'. Perhaps Marshall for all his talk about the Cambridge method of finding the One in the Many and the Many in the One was not the man for that. Others besides Sidney might have written, 'I *do* feel a sort of reverence for Marshall as our leader in economics and I always uphold him as such. But I wish he would lead a little.'[56] Perhaps Cambridge was not the best place for leadership. The people who stood in most need of a training in economics belonged to a *'nouvelle couche sociale'* to whom that place was closed.

As Marshall himself noted, the study of economics did not lead to high financial rewards. If the prevailing indifference was to be overcome then economics would have become part of the professional qualification of lawyers and civil servants, as was the case in many other European countries, notably in Austria, Germany and to a lesser extent France. In England it was not regarded as a necessary part of any professional curriculum.

At Oxford on 14 August 1894 a clear consensus was arrived at. If economics was to become an influential profession then some regular system of teaching had to emerge. This teaching had to have a character, which made the subject realistic and useful as well as intellectually elegant. The influence of foreign, chiefly German, economists had to be recognised, and the subject had to come to terms with the 'peaceful political revolution by which power had been transferred to the working classes', while thought had been more and more impressed by the doctrine of evolution. Economics must become part of any professional curriculum and no longer left as a cinderella subject within universities. The responsibility for encouragement rested entirely with educational bodies.

It is a fair conjecture – although no more than that – that Sidney Webb left this meeting to go to Borough Farm, a couple of miles south-west of Godalming, where Beatrice, Wallas and GBS were staying. In his pocket he had a letter dated 2 August 1894 from a Derby solicitor, W.H. Whiston, enclosing a copy of the last will and testament of H.H. Hutchinson. This eccentric old gentleman had been an enthusiastic supporter of the Fabian Society. However, he took the decidedly un-Fabian step of blowing his brains out. He left an estate to the total value of some £20 000, of which about half was absorbed by bequests and legacy duty. The balance went to a trust to be administered by his daughter, Constance, and by Webb. He had never met Sidney, but he made him chairman of the trustees who were to be five in number. The other three were the Fabians De Mattos, William Clarke and E.R. Pease. The trustees were directed to apply the money 'at once, gradually and at all events within ten years to the propaganda and other purposes of the said [Fabian] Society and its Socialism, and towards advancing its objects in any way they deem advisable'.[57] According to Graham Wallas, the London School of Economics – unlike most important institutions – was born at a precise time and place: 'a certain day in August 1894' at the Borough Farm. Sidney and Beatrice 'woke up early, had a long discussion, and at breakfast told us that part of the money would be used to found a school in London on the lines of the École Libre des Sciences Politiques in Paris.'

Beatrice first referred to these events 'a few weeks' after they occurred. Sidney had already been warned by Whiston that, as 'Old Hutch' was undoubtedly of unsound mind, he had taken steps to improve the widow's position under the will. (She had been left only £100 a year, which Webb suggested should be immediately doubled.) 'The question', wrote Beatrice in late September, after the Hutchinson family had shown no intention of disputing the will,

is how to spend the money. It might be placed to the credit of the Fabian Society and spent in the ordinary work of propaganda. Or a big political splash might be made with it – all the Fabian executive might stand for Parliament! and ILP candidates might be subsidised in their constituencies. But neither of these ways seems to us equal to the occasion. If it is mainly used for the ordinary work of the FS, then it will merely save the pockets of the ordinary subscribers or inflate the common work of the organization for a few years beyond its normal growth. Moreover, mere propaganda of the shibboleths of collectivism is going on at a rapid rate throughout the ILP – the ball has been set running and it is rolling down the hill at a fair pace. It looks as if the great bulk of working men will be collectivists before the end of the century. But reform will not be brought about by shouting. What is needed is *hard thinking*. And the same objection applies to sending nondescript Socialists into Parliament. The Radical members are quite sufficiently compliant in their views: what is lacking in them is the leaven of knowledge. So Sidney has been planning to persuade the other trustees to devote the greater part of the money to encouraging *research* and economic study. His vision is to found, slowly and quietly, a London School of Economics and Political Science – a centre not only of lectures on special subjects, but an association of students who would be directed and supported in doing original work.[58]

It is easy enough to draw together the considerations that brought forth this proposed line of action. Not least in importance was Beatrice's preference for research as opposed to mere politics. Then there was Sidney's hostility to Oxford and Cambridge, his admiration for the laboratory method in economics, exemplified by the MIT. He was aware of the failure, hitherto, of the TEB to meet that need for higher commercial education which Llewellyn Smith had identified in his initial report. These considerations must have added to the impact of the discussion at the British Association on the unhappy state of economics teaching in Britain. It is more difficult to grasp how the Webbs proposed to surmount the extraordinary difficulties that stood in their path. Could the Fabian be induced to believe that the founding of an academic institution was consistent with the terms of the Hutchinson Trust? Would it be found to be so if it were tested in a court of law? How was the Fabian to be reassured without arousing the suspicions of the TEB, the Chamber of Commerce or the railway companies whose support would be indispensable? After all, the Hutchinson money could be used for little more than pump priming. Where was an adequate staff to be found or suitable buildings secured?

Hutchinson's choice of trustees was extremely fortunate from Webb's point of view. Once Sidney had made it clear that he wanted to behave generously towards her mother, Constance Hutchinson gave her unqualified support to the proposal to use most of the money for educational purposes. On 2 September 1894 she warned that Whiston, the family lawyer, 'has no sympathy with father's wishes'. Characteristically, Webb immediately persuaded him to act on behalf of the executors. Pease, Webb's most devoted admirer, could be relied upon under all imaginable circumstances. The remaining Fabians were manageable, although they probably required to be managed in opposed ways. W.B. De Mattos was the lecture secretary of the Society. In proposing that a substantial portion of the Hutchinson money should be used to fund a lecture in the provinces, Webb effectively diminished the likelihood of any resistance from that quarter. Indeed, the notion of a 'London School' might be presented as but a more permanent and institutionalised expression of the concept that informed the lecture programme. Moreover, De Mattos's advocacy of 'free love' and his habit of ravishing the daughters of Fabian worthies made it difficult for him to be too quarrelsome. William Clarke was a much more considerable figure. Somewhat austere, aggressive and made irritable through ill health and overwork, he might have offered a formidable challenge. However in 1893, in a discussion of the 'Limits of Collectivism', he had gone on record that

> The Universities and higher colleges should be left a good deal to themselves … The special schools which are now arising over England and America for imparting higher education through the best teachers indicate what the best of the future will be like. They will far more closely resemble the University of Paris in the Middle Ages than the aristocratic English collegiate system of later times.[59]

(Clarke had been one of the first non-collegiate students admitted into Cambridge. His purse not being long enough to pay college bills, it had been a blow to him until he concluded that a college was only a glorified public school). Thus he shared with Webb a resentment against an ideal of a university which reduced itself to a device for giving the youths and maidens of the upper classes a 'ripping time', while subscribing to the view that learning and research would either make socialists of their own accord or else not at all. Thus, contrary to received opinion, Webb was fortunate in his Fabians.

This became apparent as soon as the trustees decided that they had better consult the Fabian executive regarding their proposal to improve the settlement so far as the widow was concerned. There was something uncommonly like nervous insecurity in the terms that Sidney – on behalf of the trustees – addressed the executive when it met on 28 September. He absented himself from the meeting, preferring to communicate by letter. Hubert Bland immediately noticed the contradiction between Webb's insistence that the executive must not encroach upon the prerogative of the trustees and his request that it should approve of what they intended to do on behalf of the widow! Olivier held that the executive was the sole arbiter as to what were and what were not the purposes of the Fabian Society. It was only after a prolonged debate that it was decided *nem. con.* not to take any steps to upset the arrangement. Shaw, who had represented Webb at the meeting, advised that Bland must be given 'a proprietary interest in our projects'. Webb attended to this by making Bland a member of an administrative committee, which took over some of the functions of the trustees so far as the government of the new school was concerned, rather than a trustee. Olivier was brought on at the same time. It was of course now far too late for them to affect the crucial decisions about how to dispose of the Hutchinson money. Indeed, it was too late for Shaw himself. He had quite taken Webb's point that the money would be wasted if it was publicised in such a way as to persuade Fabians that they had no need to make the same calls upon their pockets, as they had done before. He evidently did not realise until too late that 'the acquiescence of the Fabian Executive went a long way towards freeing the Trustees from any obligation to consult the Fabian Society'. Within a year Shaw himself was sending vain and brilliant protests to Beatrice about Sidney's 'atrocious malversation' of the bequest. The great entertainer showed an entertaining *naiveté* when he complained that Sidney, in treating of 'Hutchinson business' at executive discussions, exhibited 'an appalling want of sense of the situation'. He attained to the highest reaches of absurdity when he insisted that 'the Collectivist flag must be waved and the Marsellaise played if necessary in order to attract fresh bequests.' If Sidney was outwitting businessmen and was found out it would be declared an 'uncommonly smart thing'; but if, on the other hand, he was to be discovered outwitting Fabians, including George Bernard Shaw, it would be a very great outrage!

All that is necessary [so Shaw assured Beatrice] is to avoid shocking the common sense of the public and the ILP or Fabian critic by talking about academic abstraction and impartiality. Even if such a thing were possible its foundation out of Hutchinson's money would be as flagrant a breach of trust as handing it over to the Liberty and Property Defence

League since it was expressly left to endow Socialism. Further, the Fabian executive must not be told that it has nothing to do with it ... My dismay when Webb did not even understand why the subject had been put on the agenda paper was acute. Please show him this letter and allow it to rankle.[60]

The time had passed when it might rankle. Sidney had already received an 'opinion' from Haldane, which confirmed that the trustees had an unfettered discretion when it came to deploying the Hutchinson money. Whether this was 'bad law' is as unimportant as whether Sidney also asked Haldane whether he would be in order in endowing a disinterested and unbiased educational institution, so long as he believed that such an institution would tend to support and promote the findings of Fabian socialism. The law knows no trespass unless it would be found to be such in the courts, nor can ordinary moral principles be brought to bear upon omniscience – especially when assumed so simply and felt so sincerely. As for Shaw – within a few weeks of receiving his letter Beatrice had made the acquaintance of Charlotte Payne Townshend:

We, knowing she was wealthy and hearing she was socialistic, interested her in the London School of Economics. She subscribed £1000 to the library, endowed a woman's scholarship and has now [September 1896] taken the rooms over the School at Adelphi Terrace, paying us £300 a year for rent and service. It was on account of her generosity to our projects and 'for the good of the cause' that I first made friends with her. To bring her more directly into our little set of comrades I suggested that we should take a house together in the country and entertain our friends ... Graham Wallas bored her with his morality and learning. In a few days she and Bernard Shaw were constant companions.[61]

Miss Townshend had succeeded Constance Hutchinson as a trustee in November 1895. She married Bernard Shaw three years later.

As for other leading Fabians, Sidney was at pains to consult them. Moreover, members of the Fabian Society might enroll as students at the school at half price – the balance being made up out of the Hutchinson Trust. In the first year of the school's life one out of every six students was a Fabian.[62] Had Graham Wallas been appointed as first director of the school as Webb had intended he should, its socialist bona fides might have been above suspicion. In the event Wallas declined that honour.[63] Confronted with so much cleverness it is understandable that some historians have questioned whether Webb ever seriously intended that this invitation should have been accepted. If Webb knew that Wallas had little capacity for what he called 'business', he must also have suspected that Wallas had little taste for it. By offering his leadership he may have contrived to disarm real or imagined critics without risking being lumbered with a republican and an infidel who was *persona non grata* with some members of the educational establishment in London.[64] However, Sidney appears to have taken Wallas's refusal of the appointment as a genuine setback. He described it in these terms in a private letter to Pease, a quarter in which deceitfulness would appear to have been nearly unnecessary.[65]

In any event the selection of W.A.S. Hewins as first director was – given that the Fabian hash had been settled – greatly to be preferred. Sidney and Beatrice had first met him while visiting the Bodleian in pursuit of their trade union studies. They had not been well received by the librarian but Hewins, a tutor at Pembroke College, had come to their aid. He was accordingly a man of some academic standing. He had been a serious, if unsuccessful, contender for the chair of economics at King's College London. Although not a socialist in any serious sense of the term he had been a member of the Christian Socialist Guild of St Matthew and addressed reproaches to unregulated capitalism half out of nostalgia for the Middle Ages and half out of regard to the requirements of imperialism. In economics he favoured historical and applied studies to 'abstract theory'.[66] (It was not until 1897 that, through Cannan, the LSE offered a course which went beyond 'descriptive economics', to one dealing with 'the leading principles of economic history'.) Although he grew impatient with students and with teaching in ways Wallas was not to do, Hewins was emphatically a man with a taste for great enterprises. He was free, as Wallas was not, to go along to the Chamber of Commerce and try to solicit funds with the assurance that 'the School would not deal with political matters and nothing of a socialist tendency would be introduced.'[67] And it was perfectly plain that if original research projects were to be carried out and more and more students enlisted in three-year coursework, the funds would have to come from more regular and more assured sources than the Hutchinson Trustees or Charlotte Payne Townshend. Sidney set out to secure a regular income from the Technical Education Board. His request was for £500 a year in respect of higher commercial education, 'on the understanding that the proposed subjects and lecturers be submitted for the approval of the Board in consultation with the London Chamber of Commerce and that the Board's grant be restricted to such lecturers and subjects.'[68] He succeeded and – with the most active help from Beatrice – went on to secure endowments and gifts from great financial and industrial institutions, as well as from such rich men as Rothschild and Passmore Edwards. By the turn of the century the LSE had the most swell board of directors of any educational institution in the metropolis. It enjoyed the active support of the Earl of Kimberley and Lord Rosebery, and the blessing of the chairman of the LCC and of the Bishop of London – Dr Mandell Creighton, who laid the School's foundation stone on 2 July 1900 and became president of the Court of Governors.

There were, to be sure, a number of dissatisfied and ill-disposed persons who did their best to make trouble. For example, James Ramsay MacDonald found it decidedly unsatisfactory that no part of the Hutchinson money was employed to make him either a Member of Parliament or a university lecturer. (Sidney and Beatrice doubted his qualifications for the first of these positions and were confident that he would prove entirely inadequate in relation to the requirements for the second. MacDonald retaliated by complaining first that it was improper that the Hutchinson money should be used for purely academic purposes and subsequently that it was improper that public money should be used to advance the interests of Fabian socialism! Outmanoeuvred by Webb and bewildered and perplexed by Sidney's obscure opinion concerning the relationship between learning and politics, MacDonald gave Pease some advanced notice of his own priorities. 'Golf', he remarked, 'is better than Socialism.')[69]

Was the LSE the fruit of bad faith on the part of the Webbs or was it, as one of its principal apologists has contended, the offspring of 'dual inspiration' rather than of 'double think'? Webb's admirers find it perfectly natural that when he was speaking to socialists he drew attention to one side of the school's activity and when he was dealing with businessmen or public authorities he attended to another. The presence of Graham Wallas, the lectures on German social democracy by Bertrand Russell, the teaching undertaken by Sidney and Beatrice themselves, together with the preferential treatment accorded to Fabians who enrolled as students, might all be taken as evidence of respect paid to Hutchinson's purpose. On the other hand, when dealing with the Chamber of Commerce or the TEB it was useful to refer to Hubert Hall's course on palaeography and diplomatics, not to mention the lecture on railways by W. H. Ackworth – a subject upon which good Fabians considered him to be 'hopelessly wrong and invincibly stupid'. Certainly, the majority of teachers either were non-socialist or actively opposed to socialism. Throughout their lifetime the Webbs exercised the decisive influence over the choice of director and until after the First World War every director was identified with imperialism. Undoubtedly Sidney and Beatrice imagined that this ensured respectability while shutting out the main enemy: the backward elements who still championed abstract deductive methods, individualism and *laissez-faire*.

If University College, 'the infidel institution in Gower Street', aroused a strong initial hostility, there is no doubt that the LSE was for long the subject of uneasiness and mistrust.[70] The Webbs' accomplishments, their energy, devotion, capacity for research and their personal disinterestedness generally protected them from crude reproaches about bad faith. However, not even the most plausible and sophisticated account of the 'dual inspiration' of their enterprise could shield them from the charge of self-deception and 'double-think'. The belief that the advancement of learning in the social sciences must promote the advance of Fabian Socialism was absurd, since it required knowledge of conclusions as yet unknown. Of course Sidney would have denied that he was pretending to this omniscience. He would have brushed such logic-chopping aside and confessed that he was acting on a well-educated hunch. He who gets things done is to be detained by neither timidity nor by pedantry.

But the trouble with 'the man who gets things done' is that he rarely knows what he is doing! It seems more than likely that Webb was acquainted with the essential history of University College and that the example of that institution, as much in their different ways as MIT or Columbia College, or the École Libre des Sciences Politiques in Paris, contributed to the idea of the school. Yet the problem of starting with £10 000 rather than £160 000 merely symbolises the differences in the degree of difficulty. It was not only that the utilitarians had a stronger material base.[71] They came to protest against religious tests, and other forms of exclusion. They had all the self-confidence that comes from a sense of the perfect match between their wider economic and social ideals and their educational activity: the most perfect freedom and independence ought to distinguish human experience in all the departments of life. The Fabians did not begin by searching out the limits of these contentions, nor did they attempt a restatement of the relationship between learning and living. The LSE was never thought of as a workers' educational institution. If Sidney and Beatrice began by drawing up a list of researchable questions, they were in no position to design a new map of learning, although they made an immense contribution to the development of labour studies and of public administration. It was with the founding of the school that the difficulties of opportunism first became apparent. It was an exciting place, but it was never to be entirely free from a sense of *mauvaise foi*. All Sidney's skill at manipulating and evading was required to reassure this eminence and that interest. He was even forced to withdraw for a time from the government of the place when certain railway directors proved to be less complacent and easy-going about 'dual inspiration' than he was himself.

With the school established, Sidney became more than ever anxious to see the formation of a teaching university in London. Plainly the standing of the LSE would be enhanced and its future secured if it could be incorporated within such an institution.[72] Unfortunately the proposals of the so-called Gresham Commission of 1894, while recommending this development, failed to reassure and placate all the interested parties. As Webb had sought Richard Burdon Haldane's opinion concerning the legality of his administration of the Hutchinson trust, so he now sought his collaboration in the interests of this great undertaking. 'What', inquired Haldane, 'is your idea of a University?' 'I have', replied Sidney, 'no idea of a University, but here are the facts.' There is no reason to suppose that the report of this exchange is apocryphal.[73] Since Haldane had been educated in Göttingen it was only to be expected that he would begin with 'the Idea'. Sidney's impatience with this manner of proceeding was soon to become a matter of public record. When Lord Milner admonished him before a Royal Commission on University Education, remarking, 'I thought the state and the university were absolutely incompatible terms,' Webb answered: 'Again I suggest that we had better throw overboard the idea of a university and the idea of the state; it does not help us at all.'[74]

To give short shrift to metaphysical enquiries is no proof of mindlessness. If Webb was unable or unwilling to supply an abstract idea of a university, he had an exceptionally clear and distinct vision of what the University of London should be like. It became a compelling vision because it was not plucked out of the air but appeared to issue from a keen appreciation of the realities of social geography and the possibilities of public administration. It joined a subdued and mild-mannered criticism of 'ancient places' to the enthusiasm of civic pride, democracy and imperialism. It accommodated existing interests even as it transcended them. It conveyed both the difficulty and the elegance to be expected of a new and hard way of thinking about the structure, function and purposes of public institutions. It was a style of argument that outraged the traditional intellectuals to begin with but left them nonplussed or more than halfway persuaded by the end.

London University should not compete with Oxford or Cambridge at undergraduate level. It should have its own standards of excellence, which were to be worked out in relation to the needs and opportunities of the metropolis:

> It may be at the outset be admitted that for any university of the Oxford or Cambridge type the metropolis is perhaps more unfit than any other spot that could be chosen. By no possible expenditure could we create at South Kensington, in the Strand or at Gower Street, the tradition, the atmosphere, the charm, or the grace of collegiate life on the Isis or the Cam. Nor is it possible to secure, amid the heterogeneous crowds of London and all its distractions, either the class selection or the careful supervision required by the parents of boys fresh from Eton and Harrow, with two or three hundred a year to spend in pocket-money …

Now that Oxford and Cambridge are open to students of all creeds and all races, no parent, living himself away from London, wishing to place a boy of eighteen amid safe and advantageous social surroundings, would willingly send him to live as an undergraduate in London lodgings.

The typical undergraduate would be Londoner living at home and coming from a household sustained by an income of under £1500 a year.

These limitations had to govern the curriculum and the character and the geographical distribution of the teaching. On the other hand there was practically no limitation on size.[75] The whole of Scotland maintained four successful universities for a population which was only two-thirds of the size of this place, which was better thought of as a province than as a city. If Paris and Berlin could successfully compete with scores of other universities and yet enroll in their universities 12000 students each, London might easily expect 20000:

> Exactly as the "middle-class" origin of the typical London undergraduate by opening up a clientele of enormous extent, makes possible a large university so his professional needs compel an intensive culture of each subject unknown at the older seats of learning.

This new race of students had to make their way in the world. They needed a 'technical school for all the brain-working professions', albeit one that would encourage the 'subtle cultivation of the imagination and generosity of aim'.

However, the very practical and humdrum character of London University meant that its teachers must excel in their specialisms, even if they fell short of men of a large and general culture. And this meant that a rightly organised and adequately endowed London University must become 'the foremost post-graduate centre of the intellectual world.' Above and beyond the bread-and-butter democracy of undergraduate studies there must arise 'a new aristocracy of advanced students' drawn from London and from all over the world by the prospect of a 'post-graduate life unattainable in the more leisurely cloistered homes of university culture'. (Here Sidney's argument was informed by a correct appreciation of developments in the United States, which has – as yet – received little notice or understanding in England.) The highest function of a university lay in the *production* rather than in the distribution of learning. And for Webb the advancement of learning was not mainly a matter of *culture* – a knowledge of the past and present achievements of mankind – but of *science*. What Bacon meant by the advancement of learning had come to mean

> costly laboratories and experimental workshops in physics and chemistry, hospitals and asylums for medicine and surgery, schools for

pedagogy, documents and social institutions actually at work for economics and political science ... It was by no mere accident that Davy and Faraday, Huxley and Tyndall, Sir Joseph Hooker and Mr. Herbert Spencer, all worked in London.

It followed that the constitution of the new university should fearlessly face these limitations the better to make the most of these advantages. Organisation ought to be by faculties, not by colleges. Unicellular organisation, as in the provincial universities, or multicellular replicas of the same elementary types as at Oxford and Cambridge, must give place to a more highly organised structure: highly differentiated faculties capable of dealing with all the appropriate teaching and research from one end of London to the other. Professorial megalomania must be redirected away from the disruptive work of raising the prestige of each collegiate unit and brought into the service of the faculty so as to enhance the reputation of the whole university. Extreme local dispersion of 'mere undergraduate teaching' had to be coupled with a centralised and highly organised intercourse between all the teachers in any given subject. For properly qualified undergraduates, the university must offer an open door at approved courses at polytechnics or adequate institutions in such 'unacademic places as Tottenham or West Ham'. For the hundreds of post-graduates, it would supply, at centrally located institutions, care by the ablest and most distinguished of professors for whom undergraduate teaching had become of strictly secondary and subordinate importance. Thus, the teaching staff should exhibit 'multiplicity of grade and diversity of type'. Within each faculty the many professors would each concentrate on particular aspects of their subject rather than pretend to do justice to it as a whole:

> The principal professors, on whom mainly we depend for research, should, of course, have life tenures, high salaries, and abundant leisure, whilst the bulk of the university teachers required by so extensive an undergraduate population as that of London will necessarily be engaged for short terms, earn only modest salaries, and work at times and seasons convenient to those whom they serve.

Each faculty having a central college as the headquarters of its particular kind of learning would need not only its own specialist library, but its own business manager or secretary. His business should be not to teach or investigate but to attend to the multifarious administrative work. His duty would be to ensure the faculty attended to the requirements of the senate, that those engaged in teaching and research had the resources they required, and to make sure that in every district of London the sort of learning associated with the particular faculty was adequately provided for. He would try to raise additional funds. In short, he would undertake all the work for which teachers had neither the time nor the training. (Sidney never ceased to be astonished that while no university administrator imagined that he was competent to be a professor of Arabic, every professor of Arabic fancied himself to be a first-class university administrator.)[76]

But if organisation had to be by faculty rather than by college, the pivot had to be the senate. Only through a powerful senate could unity be given to the whole university. This meant that the senate must wield the power of the purse. It had to be able to appoint and pay all the principal professors and be in the position to find the money for the appointment of additional staff and so to determine where they would be most serviceable. Such a body must be no mere academic council or professorial board. Beside some of the leading professors it should number among its members 'eminent doctors and lawyers, engineers and business men'. Not only the professoriate and the graduates should be represented on the senate but also 'the Inns of Court, the City Companies, the City Corporation and' – obviously – 'the London County Council.'

Webb concluded by specifying what was wanted in each of the main faculties and by costing it. With respect to the arts, 'the characteristic need of and special opportunity of London is a great school of languages.' At least fifty languages from Annamese to Zulu were taught in other European universities. To match this required a new income of £30000 or £40000. In science and engineering, University College should become a great centre of original investigation in pure science (£250000), but in addition there should be a British Charlottenburg – an extensive and fully equipped institute of technology (£500000). The Faculty of Medicine would require the most radical reorganisation so as to release the great hospitals from the duty of teaching raw students and allow them to engage in more systematically organised research into cancer and phthisis (£250000 for a school of preliminary medical studies). The faculty of economics and political science – centred in the LSE – needed a capital sum of a quarter of a million to supply, not more buildings, but more professorships. In the Faculty of Law, £10000 a year from 'the great and wealthy lawyers' would suffice to make a start with those advanced studies in legal history and scientific jurisprudence, and comparative legislation and international law that were so much wanted. Webb concluded that the new university could get off to good start for an overall expenditure of about five million pounds, half of which would come from individual donors and half from the rates:

It may be that we must forego in London University the culture born of classic scholarship and learned leisure. But if we can show that there is no incompatibility between the widespread instruction of an under-graduate democracy and the most effective provision for the discovery of new truth; between the most practical professional training and gen-uine cultivation of the mind; between the plain living of hard working students of limited means and high intellectual achievements, we shall not, I venture to believe, appeal in vain. London University must take its own line. They are futile dreamers who seek to fit new circumstances to the old ideals; rather must we strive, by developing to the utmost the opportunities that the present affords us, to create out of twentieth cen-tury conditions new kinds of perfection.

From 1895 until well after 1900 the Webbs tirelessly reiterated both in public and in private this lucid argument. But it had no easy triumph. There were powerful interests that felt either threatened or ignored. In 1896 and again in the following year the bishops took the lead in inducing the House of Lords to throw out private members' bills based upon the recommendations of the Gresham Report. These reactionaries were aided and abetted by the staff at University College and similar institutions who insisted that the supreme power in any new university must be in acade-mic – that is, professorial – hands. At University College these impossi-bilists were so intransigent that they declared themselves in favour of a second university with no external examinees at all. This was bound to be opposed by the existing graduates through Convocation and in Parliament by their representative Sir John Lubbock. More in sorrow than in anger, Haldane felt that he had no choice but to resign from the govern-ing body of University College.[77] Meanwhile, within the LCC, it was slowly dawning on John Burns and other labour representatives that when Sidney talked about combining in this new university 'a sane and patriotic Imperialism with the largest minded Internationalism' the empire in question was not so much the British as his own. The TEB; the LSE; a whole new university! Then indeed might 'Uncle Sid', the learned, self-effacing friend of labour, strike his umbrella against London stone and cry out into the night: 'Now is Mortimer Lord of London.'[78] What was all this clever comparison of the boy going to Oxbridge from Eton and Harrow with £300 in the way of pocket-money with the typical Londoner coming from a household with less than £1500 a year to live on, but so much eye-wash? It is doubtful whether there was a single house-hold dependent upon wage-derived incomes that could marshall £500 a year, never mind three times that sum. The suspicion was bound to arise that Webb was looking after his own: that this great 'undergraduate democracy' of his had a decidedly lower-middle-class character.

Such were the impediments the Webbs and Haldane had to remove from their path. They began their joint operation in good earnest after the second defeat in the Lords in 1897. At first sight it is difficult to make out how they managed to co-operate to such effect. They had all been friends for some years. Sidney and Haldane were both learned in the law. And they were both able to think about university education without forever harking back to the unrivalled excellence of Oxford and Cambridge. But Haldane was a metaphysician and a sensualist. When he wasn't engaged in high thinking and lusting after first principles he was in pursuit of high living, being exceedingly fond of what Beatrice called 'choice edibles'. He consumed them to the accompaniment of 'portions and potions of nicotine and alcohol, also of select quality'.[79] He thoroughly enjoyed high society provided it had – as with the 'Souls' – some literary interests and artistic pretensions. Beatrice fancied that he had been converted, 'in a sort of vague metaphysical way to the principles of Collectivism'. But it was necessary to keep dinning it into him. In moments of impatience she told him: 'what *we* think today, *you* will think tomorrow.'[80] In fact it appears to have taken about a month. It took Beatrice rather longer than a month to recognise that Haldane himself was a dab hand himself at public-spirited conspiracies and adept at manipulating 'influential persons into becoming followers of Rosebery and members of the *clique*. Be it said to his credit, that he has some extent manipulated us into this position.'[81] Webb and Haldane were both essentially 'behind-the-scenes' men. Neither had any strong identification with Party. Together they brought chivalry and high-mindedness into plotting and intrigue.

Haldane recalled how they laid siege to the citadel:

> We went round to person after person who was prominent in the administration of the existing university. Some listened, but others would not do so and even refused to see us. In the end we worked out what was in substance the scheme of the London University Act of 1898.[82]

It would leave Convocation unduly powerful but it was the best that could be managed given the existing balance of forces and state of opinion.

Haldane then went to see Balfour – soon to be Prime Minister and to play at playing the philanderer – with Beatrice. After consultation with his colleagues, he informed Haldane that the government, without staking its life on the matter, was prepared to adopt the measure as its own.[83] Sir John Gorst introduced it into the House of Commons. Haldane himself made the greatest speech of his parliamentary career on its behalf. Afterwards both Chamberlain and Asquith assured him that it was one of the very few occasions in which a single contribution to debate had converted a hostile or indifferent House.[84]

This was a decisive moment of triumph, but it did not put an end to the struggle to establish the new university on sound lines. The Act set up a commission to devise a detailed constitution. Fortunately, Dr Mandell Creighton, Bishop of London and an old friend of the Webbs and of the LSE, was a member of it while Lord Davey, who was counted by Beatrice as an 'old acquaintance', became chairman.[85] Despite his growing difficulties with the members of the LCC and with Ramsay MacDonald in particular, Sidney was able to get financial support from that quarter. Accordingly, he appeared on the governing body not only 'mentally on the spot' long before his fellow senators had arrived there, but with a considerable power of the purse in his own hands. Nevertheless the chancellor, vice-chancellor and registrar, whom Beatrice described as representing respectively 'apathy, stupidity and ill will, each carried to its nth', often vexed him.[86] The endless little dinners for senators were not always successful. As late as May 1902 Sidney was overstretched and had to ask Beatrice to help with the latest article on London University. He muttered plaintively: 'I am not a big man. I could not manage any larger undertakings.' Beatrice comforted him. She told him that it was commendable to be so aware of one's own limitation.[87]

For the greater part of 1898 the Webbs went away on a tour of the English-speaking world. On the way home Sidney was already beginning to turn his mind to the great educational muddle and the way out. Lord Salisbury's administration had already made on abortive attempt at an Education Act in 1896. This attempt to conserve the traditions of the past while supplying the needs of the future, to protect the interests of the Church while acknowledging the claims of economy and efficiency, aroused more hostility than support. A.J. Balfour apparently regarded the government's setback with a gentlemanly complacency. He reputedly observed, 'In these matters I am a child.' This infuriated Beatrice, who observed:

> We do not want clever school boys at the head of our great departments … Who would trust the building of a bridge to a man who started with such an infinitesimal knowledge of engineering as Balfour or Gorst have of national education and its machinery?[88]

However, if the Tories were incapable of designing new machinery some of them were perfectly capable of putting a spanner in the works. Gorst, vice-president of the Privy Council Committee on Education, appears to have conspired with some of his officials to multiply difficulties so as to undermine the *status quo* and make possible changes of the sort that he favoured. After the failure of the 1896 Bill, he chaired a committee that examined the method whereby the Science and Art Department distributed its grants. It found against the school boards, some of the best and bright-est of which had been developing higher elementary work for children who stayed on until the ages of fifteen, sixteen or more, and had pio-neered evening classes for adults. Adopting Gorst's advice, the Department resolved that from 1897 the counties and the county bor-oughs should be recognised as the authorities for secondary education. Through further administrative steps Gorst went on to diminish the school boards and to reduce their opportunities for promoting advanced work. Finally in June 1899 a school of art in London – backed by members of the Cecil family – brought an action against the London School Board in which it complained of competition it was suffering from evening classes run by the Board. The district auditor, Cockerton, disallowed expenditure from the rates by the LSB towards the running of science or art schools.[89] Here were or were to be administrative steps, quasi-judicial decisions and judicial ones and interim legislative measures which desta-bilised, every bit as much as they stabilised, all preparatory to accom-plishing in 1902 what could not be done in 1896. A conspiracy blessed by the Cecils and the Duke of Devonshire, designed by Gorst, worked out by his lieutenant Robert Morant? And of Webb? Where did he stand? Was he numbered among the conspirators?

Initially, almost certainly not. It was not his style. 'What I like about you, Webb,' said Graham Wallas to Sidney having watched him rush towards a moving railway compartment, 'is that you don't care about style.' In fact, it was a feature of Webb's style as social engineer that he hated the demolition work. If he was devious it was always in the inter-ests of construction. It was not until Sidney and Beatrice had left the coun-try that his successor as chairman of the TEB, a moderate, applied under the revised education code to be recognised as the sole recipient in London of grants from the Science and Art Department.[90] William Garnett subsequently claimed that he was responsible for this initiative, as he claimed the credit for encouraging the action that culminated in the Cockerton judgement which made a new Education Act imperative.[91] Perhaps he was too proud to allow that he was merely Sidney's cat's-paw in all this, but there is no evidence to support such a conclusion. Webb was impatient with nonentities. One of the costs of declining to employ them is that those who are appointed may act off their own bat. On the other hand, it may be doubted whether Garnett would have dared to act as he did if he had anticipated that he would arouse Webb's active hostil-ity. Moreover, in the original statement of his vision of London education the place accorded to the school board is anomalous. It is deferred to as an established democratic power, but how it is to be accommodated within the new comprehensive system is left unclear. Finally, it was certainly con-venient that Sidney could come before the Fabian Society as one who was entirely innocent of spilling the board's life blood and who came rather to bind up its wounds and to secure its future. The proposals that he laid before the Society in 16 May 1899 expressly defended the schools boards in London and in the larger provincial centres. Sidney began by exposing the reality of the existing 'muddle', went on to identify the possible responses to it and then cleverly suggested that there was one – and only one – way out that would be acceptable to intelligent, practical and progressive minds. It was not perfect, but he was subsequently to demonstrate the ways of making the best of it. The muddle lay in having ten cabinet ministers who shared some responsibility for various kinds of educational provision but who gave little or no evidence of trying to thrash out some concerted policy. But if the position at the centre was bad enough, it was far worse locally. There were some districts that could barely supply the most minimal needs. However, if there were some places where rent and rates were hardly being spent at all, there were others where the school boards were responsible for one sort of school and the county, borough and urban district councils for others. The boards had – in theory at least – no restriction on the size of the resources at their command, but only upon which they might expend them. Their rival authorities suffered no restriction upon the upward reaches of the educational world, which they might aid, but had restricted rating powers. This division of labour – one that was still most imperfectly achieved in practice – led to rivalry, prejudice and unbalanced estimates of real needs. Chaos, arbitrary separation of one part of education from another, stupendous inequalities and 'a policy of drift' prevented administrative unity and coherent schemes.

One response would be to adopt the Nonconformist and Liberal cry, 'school boards everywhere and for everything'. But to this there were – so Sidney maintained – insuperable objections. To begin with, over one third of England there were no school boards. To set them up where they were not wanted or petitioned for or where they were not absolutely required by the failure of the 'voluntary' or Church schools would be 'politically impossible'. Second, the great majority of school boards – 2085 out of the total of 2527 – had populations of less than 5000. The notion that they could supply a comprehensive educational service was plainly absurd. Accordingly, to make the school board the sole authority for all education would involve scrapping nine-tenths of them and reconstituting them on a much larger basis. But even were it possible, which person would want to infect secondary and technical education with the deplorable strife that surrounded the boards' provision of the purely elementary sort?

Another possibility would be to abolish all the existing responsible bodies and to replace them with a new educational authority, which would take responsibility for freshly drawn districts. This project would be revolutionary enough to mobilise the 2527 school boards and the 1200 county,

borough and urban district councils against it without removing the theological differences and sectarian passions that constituted such a large
part of the difficulty. Besides, 'We have, in fact, ceased to believe in the
need for *ad hoc* authorities. During the last sixty years they have been as
far as possible absorbed and abolished.'

Webb concluded – leaving the Poor Law on one side for his present
purpose – that the way out lay in trying to concentrate in a single, elected
body for each locality all the public business that ought to be entrusted to
localities. This meant that outside London and the county boroughs, the
county councils should take over the functions of the school boards and
become responsible for every kind and grade of education within their
area. By a statutory requirement to appoint special educational committees, the county and borough councils should ensure that they could co-
opt educational experts and, in particular, overcome the disability that
women could be members of school boards but not of councils. The
admitted problem of hugeness could be dealt with by a limited delegation
of powers to local committees. As to the great problem of existing voluntary schools, this should be dealt with by allowing the council to offer
substantial grants in aid. The grants would be to improve efficiency and
raise teachers' salaries in exchange for rights of inspection and audit, exercise ultimate control of appointments and dismissals, and obtain a general
right of surveillance and report.

As to the case of London and the 62 county boroughs, there the school
boards would be left 'for the most part' untouched. The LCC's spending
powers – outside the powers of the School Board – should henceforth be
unlimited. The School Board should have the power 'to terminate its own
existence' if it so wished on transfer of those powers to the municipality.

For the rest, the new Board of Education (established by an Act of 1899)
should have far-reaching powers of inspection, criticism and audit of all
types of educational provision that depended upon any degree of public
funding. Without striving after 'rigid uniformity', it ought to have the
means of providing for both 'the highest specialist efficiency' and for 'the
national minimum'.

Webb concluded that to provide a ladder whereby a few could climb
from elementary school to university required an administrative unity,
which would ensure that every rung on it was kept in good repair. His
critics – at the time and subsequently – ignored or dismissed his insistence
that this ladder was *not* the democratic ideal. In highlighting him as an
apostle of 'National Efficiency' they wholly discounted his remark that:
'What the national well-being demands, and what we must insist upon,
is that every child, dull or clever, rich or poor, should receive all the education requisite for the full development of its faculties.'[92] His adversaries evidently assumed – rightly or wrongly – that Webb himself was

uninterested in what he really took to be 'sentimental twaddle'.[93] Doubtless they suspected him of equally disgraceful insincerity when he observed, 'Our plan is to extend popular control and popular assistance to every branch of education.'[94]

Sidney's opinions occasioned the most bitter conflict within the Fabian Society itself. Two of its most admirable eccentrics, Stewart Headlam and Graham Wallas, were leading members of the London School Board. Between them they marshalled a searing passion and a searching scepticism against Webb to such good effect that it was not until January 1901 that Tract 106 went to the printers. Its claim to being the most famous and influential of all Fabian Tracts rests upon the assertion that Gorst asked for 50 advance copies and that the government's measure corresponded to it closely save for the fact that all the school boards outside London were abolished.[95]

The debate within the Fabian Society anticipated the larger and still stormier one that was developing without. Sidney was not merely impatient for what he termed a 'Truce of God' in the schools: he was incapable of understanding the passionate indignation of Nonconformists at having their money – or worse still, their children – taken from them and delivered into the hands of the parson. He correctly sensed that these excitements had more to do with the nineteenth century than with the twentieth. Convinced that his complacency concerning the Almighty would come to be widely shared, he made little effort to understand the holy passions that were now aroused. Even if he had tried it is doubtful whether he would have managed it. But whereas Sidney made light of subsidising religion out of the rates, pointing out how little of the child's time would be occupied by it, Beatrice was rather in favour. She assumed that a purely secular education would be equivalent to making 'pure materialism' into the 'national metaphysic'. The lie of materialism was worse than the untruths of Christian doctrine. Presumably, the pernicious nature of 'materialism' consisted in its supposed contempt for awe and wonder about the origins and nature of the human condition; in its failure to recognise how transient were all the greatest interests of the hour, and how important it was to occasionally distance oneself and to purify oneself through sacred music and through prayer. Besides, most Englishmen, if they thought about it at all, thought of themselves as Christians.

Beatrice wrote:

> I see no way out of the dilemma, but the largest variety possible of denominational schools, so that there may be the utmost possible choice for parents and children, and, let me add, the widest range of experiment as to the results of particular kinds of teaching on the character of the child and its conduct of life.[96]

Sidney saw his own and the Tory government's proposals as a way, not of propping up the Church, but of gaining control over its educational work in the interests of the children. So far as London was concerned there was overwhelming evidence of the higher attainments of those who went to the board schools rather than to the 'voluntary' ones. Why then abolish the school boards? The Nonconformists, the Liberals, the Progressives, the TUC and the great majority within the labour movement saw them as instruments of democratic control which had shown themselves to be capable of a progressive extension of their functions through higher-grade work and evening classes for adults.

It must be remembered that the Webbs and the Fabians were taken by surprise when Robert Morant succeeded in getting the abolition of all school boards outside London written into the government bill. Nevertheless they had certainly favoured a great reduction in their number. As against their defenders, Sidney and Beatrice insisted that the boards' achievements had been patchy and that they afforded no sure escape route from the power of squires, parsons and cheeseparers. Even in London the Revd J.R. Diggle had held power for considerable periods, and Diggleism had stood for economy in everything and obscurantism.[97] So when the government finally turned its attention to the greater deferred issue of educational authority in the metropolis Sidney surpassed himself in the energy of his wire-pulling on behalf of the LCC. The school board was now so isolated that it was virtually doomed. The main danger was the fear and loathing with which many senior Conservatives approached London and its government. They felt for it almost as much as the men of Versailles had dreaded the Commune of Paris thirty years earlier. There was a project for emasculating the LCC by making the new educational authority depend upon the metropolitan boroughs which had been established as a result of the London Government Act of 1899. There was talk of creating a vast new, *ad hoc* authority. After the full strength of Nonconformist outrage began to disclose itself at the polls through by-election results there were even rumours that school boards had to be retained. At this critical juncture the Webbs got little help from Robert Morant, who declined to co-operate with them, making excuses to the effect that he was overworked and that his 'rotten' staff was not fit for anything.[98]

The Webbs' response to this situation was to entertain the Prime Minister; to pass days and nights in conversation with Members of Parliament; and to try their powers of persuasion on Anglican and Catholic dignitaries. The churchmen had to be persuaded that if power passed to the boroughs they would be faced with the power of the elementary school teachers and that the LCC would be more considerate. But this in turn required that the Progressives – by now thoroughly alert to Fabian intrigue and manoeuvring – had to be persuaded to ignore the clamour of many of their own supporters and accept the need to extend their powers. The press had to be tuned and worked as never before.[99] But when the government unveiled its proposals in the summer of 1903 all this effort appeared to have gone for nothing. The Conservatives resolved to take something from each of the distinct schemes that had been under consideration. The new authority was to have 97 members, of which 36 were to be appointed by the LCC, 36 by the metropolitan borough councils and 25 co-opted, plus 5 more from the old school board.

This curiously ramshackle construction rather confirmed Morant's gloomy account of how matters stood within the administration. It pleased hardly anybody. While the school board condemned it, the LCC announced that it would prefer the school board to it. It did nothing to stop the majority of Progressives complaining about the anomaly of paying teachers' salaries out of public money while continuing to subject them to religious tests. The Fabian executive condemned the Bill as practically unworkable and the society went on to demand complete administrative control under the LCC. Thirteen resolutions were adopted, framed as definite amendments to the bill. In June 1903 *Fabian News* was able to demonstrate that eleven and a half of these were accepted by the government and they duly became law.

This was a great triumph from the Webbs' point of view. Far more clearly than in the case of the 1902 Act, the London Education Act of 1903 was inspired by them. If Beatrice was growing tired, Sidney was still bursting with energy and determination when all his adversaries were running out of steam. It only remained for him to point out how to make the best of the new measure and to sum up twelve years of achievement in his book *London Education*. As he observed with satisfaction: 'the London County Council can now (with the help of new and increased Government grants) equip London with a complete educational system, as efficient in its own way as the fire brigade'.[100]

In 1892 Sidney Webb had set out on his career as educational reformer with little more than a vision.[101] Twelve years later the vision had been realised in all its essential administrative and institutional respects. Moreover, the vision as amended in practice had become larger rather than smaller. The history of English education can show no comparable achievement by one man, neither before nor since – at any rate, not within such a limited span of time and to the accompaniment of much else besides. With patience and intelligence each advance was made into the stepping-stone for the next. Each lucky chance and each authentic improvisation was kept in place in relation to a governing purpose and a steady ideal. But this heroic opportunism had its costs in personal and social relationships. And over the record of it hang questions about its own ultimate nature and essential worth.

He who pulls himself up by his own bootstraps would do well to ponder the fate of Antaeus. As Sidney mounted his own 'educational ladder'
he distanced himself from the earth in which he had his roots and from
which he drew his strengths. His disinterestedness became open to question. His closest friends reproached him with malpractice. Labour men
came to agree with Old Etonians who pronounced him to be a mere
intriguer for the lower middle class, while Nonconformists and Progressives discovered him to be a Tory. Over the future of the London
School Board and the Education Act of 1902 he came into conflict with one
of his oldest and closest friends, Graham Wallas. Graham Wallas charged
Webb with double-dealing, while Sidney dismissed Wallas's insistence
that education must be primarily concerned with the fullest development
of the faculties of all children by a conventional reference to the demand
side – by a reminder that most boys and girls would have to go into
menial employment.[102] By 1904 Sidney and Beatrice were secretly looking
forward to the defeat of their own Progressive Party at the approaching
LCC elections. They went to the length of drawing up a list of their 'enemies' whose political ruin they would welcome.[103] Although the Fabian
Society had affiliated to the Labour Representation Committee at the time
of its formation in 1900, the Webbs ignored it. Thanks to them the Fabian
Society appeared to have cut itself off from the labour movement.[104] It
was isolated and distrusted. This was in no small measure due to the fact
that it was identified with an educational policy that seemed far more
conventional and far less ambitious than that of the Trades Union
Congress. (Despite some backsliding, the TUC had committed itself to a
programme of secondary education for all through a common school.)[105]

Thus, if the Webbs' achievement was undeniable it was certainly purchased at a considerable cost. Moreover, the question arose as to whether
the achievement was not merely a matter of administrative tidiness rather
than of cultural innovation. Webb had a keen sense for the two cultures,
but had he any inkling of the possibilities of a third? He certainly had a
keen eye for the limitations of that classical, literary and aristocratic culture whose twin summits rose at Oxford and Cambridge. He knew it had
been in retreat, but he did not imagine that it had been reformed out of
existence. The gentlemanly, leisurely, socially exclusive, complacent and
still theology-tainted learning that flourished by the Cam and by the Isis
had not become a merely vestigial presence because it was obliged to
make some concession to modern mathematics, to economics and to
mechanical engineering. It remained a fit object for progressively informed
aggression. As for provincial bourgeois culture, which had been nourished
by the Scottish experience of the democratic intellect and by a number of
literary philosophical and lunar societies; long before it took a shape – in
Gower Street – it is not clear that Sidney had thought through his attitude

towards it. It found favour with him in so far as it arose out of protest against the old cultural hegemony and in so far as it stood for an open, practical, useful and scientific style of learning. Did he imagine that all that was wrong with it was that it was inadequately endowed and insufficiently specialised and differentiated? In educational policy, were the new utilitarians obliged to be nothing but the old ones writ large?

At his best the Fabian came forward as the genuine protagonist of a third culture. This was not – and never could be – a matter of designing new maps of learning as distinct from planning new expeditions: it was concerned with proposing fresh problems, not imposing new conclusions. The third culture could no more quarrel with the second than it could with the first over the merits of different sorts of mathematics or physics, or even perhaps French. It could and – to the eternal credit of Sidney and Beatrice – it did suggest that history should be extended to allow for the annals of toil and to make ready for the advent of the democracy by reflecting about the rules of democratic public administration. (The conspicuous failure to enquire how the democracy would distribute scarce resources between competing wants, once the 'democracy of the market place' had been dispensed with, was explicable, but not excusable.) The inhibitions of the new utilitarians – their silences and their propensity to be devious and to hush things up – were all related to the discontinuities between their socio-economic position and that of their predecessors.

The Benthamites had a prosperous 'material base'. They had to go cap-in-hand to no one but themselves or their own supporters. In the 1820s the bourgeois Radical had much that he could identify as his own and which he could declare himself ready to defend and fortify. Their socialist successors enjoyed no such prosperity. In the 1890s what little they had by way of a party of their own was in decline. When that party recovered in the following decade the experience of Ruskin College suggested how difficult it was for the third culture to emulate the second. The new professionalism had come to reinforce mere wealth, to ensure that every educational institution was limited. In default of a labour or socialist treasure, the Webbs drew upon imperialism. They assumed, without discussion or reflection, that its power and interest could be substituted for the power and interest that they wanted – just as they assumed that if they were presently enlarging the opportunities for children of the lower middle class then that must lead on to the emancipation of the proletarian child, rather than to delay that happy advent. No evaluation of the Webbs' heroic opportunism would be adequate that failed to take a full and searching account of its squalid, imperialistic side.

Unlike William Morris's, the Webbs' concept of socialism did not extend to a notion of New Man. For example, they were reconciled to the fact that for the foreseeable future vast numbers of men and women would have to endure the 'monkeydom' of factory, mine and mill. All that socialism could offer these unfortunate beings was a prospect of shorter hours and improved wages and conditions. It could also supply them with a governing elite, which would be fully imbued with the values and standards of the best professional men. These expert administrators would put as much time and effort into perfecting their own training as good medical men put into theirs and they would serve the citizenry with a similar sense of proper priorities. The Webbs were certainly alert to an unresolved conflict within provincial bourgeois culture: its celebration of individuality and its cultivation of a professionalism that exalted service and discipline above self and beyond personal aggrandizement. Sooner or later this third culture, with its stern lesson for the rich and its solace for the poor, would use the resources of public authority to displace the wealth and power of land and capital. In the meantime there was nothing for it but to exploit the craze for imperialism and to bring it into the service of social reform. The legacy of Rome and the example of the Japanese had to be employed against the traditions of Manchester. The purpose of the democracy had to be cultivated beneath the protective shade of empire. Nonconformity had to be beaten into submission by the state while the state succumbed to the claims of society.

Socialism and imperialism were beating on the same drum. They sent the same message to individualism: the greatest object in life is not the highest cultivation of the self: 'Renounce, renounce, renounce.' In the end it was into the service of this confusion that so much of the Webbs' clarity went.

8

Squalid Opportunism: Fabianism and Empire 1893–1903

Burns and the coup against the socialists at the TUC—The Webbs' alienation from organised labour—The accommodation to imperialism—Travels in the United States, New Zealand and Australasia—The Boer War—The absence from the LRC foundation meeting—Intrigues with the Liberals—The Co-efficients—The measure of the Webbs' social imperialism.

In November 1893 Shaw and Webb published 'To Your Tents, O Israel'. It announced their disillusion with the Liberals and all their works (or rather want of them) and proclaimed the need for a Labour Party rooted in the trade unions. In the *History of Trade Unionism* and still more clearly in the companion volume of 1897 the Webbs clearly gave to Labourism its historical perspective and its line of march. Clearly, a Labour Party was needed to complete the tripartite institutional world of labour in which man must be represented as a citizen as well as a producer and a consumer. In 1900 they were still as impressed as ever with the deficiencies of the existing party system. Yet they were not numbered among those who met at the Memorial Hall, Farringdon Street, London, on Tuesday, 27 February 1900 to set up the Labour Representation Committee. The Fabian Society was represented and it went there with the Webbs' blessing, but it was a blessing of a very perfunctory sort. They were making their escape from Labourism at the very moment when the Labour Party was being born. They were in the course of exchanging that 'small world' so wanting in big men for high political society which was so wanting in realignments and rejuvenation. They believed that the future of socialism lay in encouraging the small, turning movements of imperialism rather than in the mindless rhetoric and half-hearted effrontery of Keir Hardie and James Ramsay MacDonald. With the single exception of the LSE the Webbs showed little enduring parental feeling for their offspring. They were inclined to abandon them as soon as they could

308

walk. In this instance they escaped the squalid proceedings in the maternity ward altogether.

In measuring the stages of their escape from Labourism one must take the measure of their starting. 'To Your Tents' was a decidedly 'trendy' document. It was about the challenge of the ILP from without and the dissidents' voices within the Fabian Society. These were the imperatives that it answered as much, or more, than those arising from the indulgent and delinquent behaviour of Gladstone's last great Liberal administration. This is the context in which complaints about its over-hasty fault-finding with ministers who were doing their best need to be considered. Beatrice never cared for it. She was unsurprised when it turned out to be one of the divisive rallying cries of the 1890s. She deplored the sorrow of Haldane along with the anger of Massingham. She plainly believed that her boy and 'the Sprite' (George Bernard Shaw) ought not to have gone in to this enterprise without the aid of a man of true political stature. 'What the [Fabian] Junta needs to make it a great power', she mused, on the eve of publication, 'are one or two personalities of weight, men of wide experience and sagacity, able to play a long hand, and to master the movements.'[1] Tom Mann was too fickle: too given to 'light-headed changes of front on all questions human and divine.'[2] Keir Hardie was a token Fabian whom she neither liked nor understood. The best bet appeared to be John Burns. She saw him quite frequently in the autumn of 1893. Sidney had a high opinion of him. Beatrice knew of no one else who could

> so complete the Fabian trio [of Wallace, Shaw and Webb] and make it thoroughly effective. If Burns would come in and give himself away to the other three as they do to each other – the Fabians could dominate the reform movement. Burns is, in some respects, the strongest man of the four.[3]

But even if Beatrice did not ponder the conceptual difficulty inherent in the notion of a self-effacing strong man, she was quite clear that Burns suffered from 'an instinctive fear of comradeship'. After spending a morning with him, she summed up:

> A man of splendid physique, fine and strong intelligence, human sympathy, practical capacity, he is unfitted for a really great position by his utter inability to be a constant and loyal comrade. He stands absolutely alone. He is intensely jealous of other labour men, acutely suspicious of all middle-class sympathisers; whilst his hatred of Keir Hardie reaches the dimensions of mania.[4]

The validity and importance of these insights was demonstrated a year later when Burns played a central role in the TUC coup. After the 1894 congress the Parliamentary Committee, to which Burns belonged, changed the basis of representation. The 1895 congress was convened upon the basis of fresh rules, which its predecessors had had no opportunity to consider. From this time forwards only those employed at their trade or the professional officers of affiliated organisations could attend as delegates. The trades councils were excluded. Block voting was introduced. The effect of these changes was to exclude Keir Hardie and to diminish socialist representation. The Webbs found the way in which these alterations had been brought about distasteful but they persuaded themselves that their own influence would remain as strong as ever. Still understandably elated by their success in uniting the minority of the Royal Commission on Labour behind their own proposals, they believed that 41 Grosvenor Road might remain the intellectual HQ of the entire movement. At the Cardiff TUC they entertained Mawdsley, the Tory leader of the cotton workers, to dinner after he had got the coup ratified by a congress that could hardly do otherwise without condemning itself. Beatrice marked the occasion in her diary with a magnificent phrase: a muddled thought and an absurd expectation. She decided that Mawdsley was 'far too cynical to be suspicious'. She went on to conclude: 'Whether or not we use Mawdsley, we may rest assured that he will use us: which after all is all we desire.' Finally she remarked: 'Poor Burns, to have ousted Keir Hardie from the Congress and let in Sidney Webb to the Parliamentary Committee!'[5] It is doubtful whether Sidney himself was as optimistic about the implications of Coal and Cotton collaring congress. It is certain that his socialist commitments were firmer than hers and that he saw it as indispensable to the unions that they should assume a general political role. (Beatrice doubted the wisdom of such a development.)

In the event the coup did not tend to increase the number of proletarian leaders who visited Grosvenor Road. Coinciding as it did with the departure of the failed Liberal government, it tended to the estrangement of the Webbs from organised labour. The Liberals were brought down not because they were inattentive to the requirements of the national minimum in relation to health, education or housing but rather in the matter of cordite for the army. Under these circumstances Keir Hardie and his supporters became the Liberals' companions in disaster rather than their supplanters. The Webbs were quicker to learn 'the lesson' than other socialists were and Hardie was quicker to brand them for it as 'the worst enemies of the Social Revolution'. Indeed, he did so before the event. Beatrice had it that it was Sidney, rather than the pair of them, who held a little dinner for Hardie and Mann from the ILP and Pease and Shaw from the Fabians, with MacDonald and Frank Smith as conciliators, late in January 1895. Anyway, Beatrice was by no means unhappy with Hardie's characterisation. For her part, she saw in Hardie's insistence on a clear separation from the Liberals only a design that would allow him to boss the movement. He was a lower type than Tom Mann, who was possessed with a genuine religious zeal worthy of a secular church. She concluded: 'No great transformation is possible in a free democratic state like England unless *you alter the opinions of all classes of the community* and, even if it were possible, it would not be desirable. That is the crux between us.'[6] Accordingly, Beatrice took the results of the election in her stride. Four days before the country went to the polls she attended a meeting of the London Trades Council at which there was hardly an allusion to that approaching event. It was but another proof of the political incapacity of the trade union world. She was unsurprised and almost satisfied by the defeat of Keir Hardie and the other Labour men. The ILP would no longer be able to advance its futile and absurd policy of abstention and wrecking to block 'the more reasonable policy of permeation and levelling up'. Like the official Liberals, who had given 'numberless signs that our opinions were discounted', the election ought to have been a salutary lesson. Having held aloof from both the ILP and the Liberals, the Webbs could conclude, 'The rout of both, therefore, is no defeat for us. It leaves us free, indeed, to begin afresh on the old lines – of building up a new party on the basis of collectivism.'[7]

The international socialist congress which was held in London the following year (1896) merely confirmed Beatrice in her opinion that the important distinction in politics was not that between workmen and non-workmen, but between thinkers and non-thinkers:

The rank and file of Socialists – especially English Socialists – are unusually silly folk (for the most part featherhead failures) and heaped together in one hall with the consciousness that their every word would be reported by the world's press, they approached raving imbecility. The confusion of tongues, of procedure, the grotesque absurdity of masquerading as 'nations', and you have the factors for a hideous fiasco from the point of view of public opinion. The Fabians sat silent taking notes as reporters for the capitalist press...The Fabians at any rate write history if they do not make it.[8]

The prominence that this congress gave to the problem of anarchism and the anarchists could not but appear to the Webbs to make it absurdly *passé*. They longed for 'a quiet exchange of thought and experience between the cultivated and intellectual socialists of all countries'. They could endure the company of Kautsky and Adler since for all their Marxism they were men of established political position, which set them above the 'frothy irresponsibility of our English movement'. As for the Belgian leader, Vandervelde, he was 'a man of quite exceptional charm and distinction – a scholar and a gentleman'.[9] But for the rest, the Fabians could only go out of their way to distance themselves as far as possible from the deplorable tone of the entire proceedings. Shaw warned the congress against the absurdity of 'Socialists denouncing the very class from which socialism has sprung as specifically hostile to it.' This characteristic confusion between the characterisation of a class and of a small, unrepresentative contingent recruited from within it was followed by a most unfamiliar preoccupation with war and foreign policy. It was decidedly a straw in the wind that these matters which had hitherto been dismissed as being as irrelevant to the Fabian as metaphysics or the institution of marriage should suddenly be elevated into by far the longest section of the report.[10]

The section began with a peculiarly traditional, ritualistic and un-Fabian denunciation of standing armies, as having more bearing on the war of classes than that of nations. It then affirmed that huge armaments spread universal fear and paralysis to the advantage of only the smallest states. It went on to protest that it was capitalist concern for the vested interests of chartered companies that prevented 'order and public responsibility in the colonisation and settlement of new colonies'. The great European states, unable to undertake the world of colonisation themselves, were being brought to war, 'not only with barbarous races, but with one another, in defence of enterprise over which they have no control'. The Fabians concluded by warning the workers against an appeal to national pride and explaining that it was only capital that stopped the army being an instrument of 'national greatness and honour'.

It is unclear as to whether Beatrice put this down to the account of 'the thinkers' or the 'non-thinkers'. However, in the same year Sidney himself was revamping his *The Difficulties of Individualism* so as to take account of the newly discovered importance of adequate supplies of cordite. The references to a new feudalism, 'based upon the tenure of capital ... against which the democracy sullenly revolts' and to the 'irresponsible personal authority over the actions of others – expelled from the throne, the castle and the altar – [which] still reigns almost unchecked, in the factory and the mine', were retained. But the pursuit of personal gain was newly found to present 'its most serious difficulty [in] its effect upon the position of the community in the race struggle. The lesson of evolution seems to be that international competition is really more momentous in its consequences than the struggle between individuals.'

Thus in 1896 there was a shift in emphasis away from what democracy compelled to what the interests of the race required. One discerns the introduction of that strange Fabian dialectic in which competition is to be superseded at home in the interests of its better pursuit abroad. The sentiment that

> We dined, as a rule, on each other.
> What matter? The toughest survived

was being brought under the sway of 'the negation of the negation'.

It is doubtful whether in 1896, in distancing themselves from organised labour while beginning to accommodate themselves to imperialism, the Webbs were consciously subordinating themselves to the requirements of the 'School', but they were certainly serving them. It was one thing for Sidney to give a sermon in a Congregational chapel in the North on the morality of the child labour laws and another for him to be associated with the failed endeavours of the class warriors on the national stage. Under any circumstances it is doubtful whether he would have thought it suitable to expend the Hutchinson bequest in helping James Ramsay MacDonald to set up ILP branches, but when such activities could be funded only at the expense of the LSE it made him more disinclined to favour it. Similarly the Webbs would have been likely to have welcomed collaboration with Haldane under most circumstances, but the aid he was able and willing to afford them as educationalists made it all the more imperative to cultivate him. It was not until 1903 that the Webbs consciously recognised that they would have to pick their public political opinions in the interests of maintaining the school's reputation. But long before poor Hutchinson's intentions had been thus turned inside out they had an instinct for those associations that would protect their young and those that would work to a reverse effect. It was better that the arch permeators should themselves be permeated by one wily fat Scotsman than that they should be emasculated by the enthusiasm of one thin one.

In 1897 the Webbs had completed *Industrial Democracy* and felt themselves to have done with their major contribution to labour historiography and to labour studies. They were already contemplating their next great intellectual undertaking – the history of English local government. They were planning their tour of the English-speaking world, a sort of busman's holiday which was to take them to the United States and Australasia. If they were still engaged by the concerns of labour, labour's engagements were no longer favoured by fortune as they had been some ten years earlier. Then both Sidney and Beatrice had been aroused from their dogmatic slumbers by 'the full, round orb of the dockers' tanner'. In 1897–8 one of the longest and best established of British trade unions was going down to defeat before the employers. Sidney fully involved himself in playing the adviser to Barnes, the leader of the Amalgamated Society of Engineers. But he was powerless to save them from defeat: from selling the pass, as he saw it, of national collective bargaining for the 51-hour week. In truth, this was a critically important moment in the great, triumphant 'employers' offensive' that marked the turn of the century. Threatened by increasing international competition, armed with the new American lathe, supplied with a sufficiently versatile class of machine-minders, the employers resolved to be masters in their own shops. They were determined to devise the division of labour and introduce their own mode of remuneration or in agreement only with specific groups of work-men. In vain did Sidney insist upon the union putting itself right with public opinion. In vain did he urge a full commitment to the utmost possible efficiency in exchange for assurances respecting national collective bargaining and the defence of the minimum standard. In vain did he champion the authority of the centre against the claims of rebellious voices from below. When the Webbs left for America the employers appeared to be well on the way to the old ascendancy which had seemed to be in jeopardy ten years earlier.

In the six years since their marriage Sidney had gradually been accepted into the family. But in the households of Beatrice's sisters there was little evidence to be found to suggest that the perspective of altering the opinions of all classes of opinion offered a better prospect for collectivism than an exclusive reliance upon labour. Leonard Courtney remained as impervious to the difficulties of individualism as ever. Henry Hobhouse, who 'alone among my brothers-in-law ... welcomed Sidney with grave courtesy into the family', remained an incorrigible mugwump. But it was Alfred Cripps who displayed attitudes that most clearly threatened Beatrice's perspective. Starting with him at Parmoor she noticed that there was

No nonsense about enlightenment, or any impartial study of the common weal ... He is of course, far too clever not to compromise – but his compromise will always be the best compromise for his class and not the best of the community ... Sharp wits are all that are required to perceive an attack upon the fundamental principles of 'private property and the growth of the Empire' – sharp wits, and physical force are all that is needed to defend them ... Having decided to stand by his class, being honestly (and no doubt justly) convinced that that class has everything to lose and nothing to gain by an alteration in the status quo, the one thing needful is to appeal to the popular suspicion, fear, prejudices and fallacies to keep back any further reforms. I do not mean this as a moral indictment [*sic*]. Alfred's original conviction that it is desirable that an upper class, owning most of the property and keeping the control of the nation, should exist is a proposition which can be perfectly well defended. But it is a proposition which, in face of a political democracy, it is impossible to state overtly and equally useless to attempt to prove ... Alfred Cripps is far too clever not to perceive that the real interest of the people is hostile to that of the classes – to meander about like Henry Hobhouse attempting to discover the common weal argues simply, to his mind, a lack of capacity. There is no common weal – there is a solution which will suit the 'haves', and a solution which will suit the 'have-nots', and there is, of course, a compromise ....

Alfred's temperament and intellectual position is interesting because I think it is typical of the intellectual tone of the genuine conservative.[11]

Yet whatever the deficiencies of the brothers-in-law in relation to facts and reasoning, and however inconsiderate it was of them to leave the whole onus of economic discovery and political education to be borne by those who valued complete social democracy, they had their uses. An example was when it came to securing a charmingly fitted cabin for a voyage across the Atlantic; cried R.D. Holt:

> Come and look at your cabin, you will see what an advantage it is to be connected with the commercial aristocracy. The White Star Line has treated you as well as a Duke: could not have done better if you were HRH himself. Come along, come along, this way: we'll show them, Betty, what we have done for them.[12]

They did nothing for Sidney, who soon became a wreck from seasickness. But Beatrice spent the time walking the decks enchanting the Yorkshireman who had turned revolutionary adventurer in Brazil.

The Webbs left England towards the end of March 1898. They spent three and a half months in the United States visiting New York, Washington, Baltimore, Philadelphia, Ithaca, Harvard, Boston, Pittsburgh, Cincinnati, Chicago, Denver, Leadville, Salt Lake City and San Francisco.[13] On 10 July they were aboard the *Coptic* bound for New Zealand via Honolulu. They arrived in Auckland on 3 August. They left Wellington for Sydney on 2 September. They spent a couple of months in Australia before returning to England in December.[14] The young C.P. Trevelyan accompanied them. His family connections were useful, although Sidney and Beatrice were already overloaded with introductions. For the rest, Charles was not too interesting. He was inclined to be stingy and Sidney had to supply the tips, which he forgot to leave. In New Zealand he went in for a lot of singing which Beatrice found of uncertain quality. It was there that he alarmed his elders by swinging himself across the flooded river at the loss of his baggage. He was to be a life-long friend, but at this stage he was found unworthy of one of Beatrice's celebrated portraits.

The Webbs were never at their best when observing societies other than their own. As on this occasion they usually compromised their discipline as social investigators in the interests of a holiday, which they needed, but which they were temperamentally incapable of taking. They were armed with introductions, which took them into the society of all manner of men and women, including two future presidents of the United States, the prime minister of New Zealand and countless eminencies in Australia.

But they had no intention of making the English-speaking world into one of their 'subjects'. Accordingly, they attempted no extensive or systematic background reading. Their special interest was to be in the institutions of local government, but they appear to have been unacquainted with J.P. Goodhow's work and they did not seek him out in Columbia. They were equally ill-prepared for their Australian visit. They were very ready to learn, but more in the sense of picking things up than in coming to understand. They did not expect to be surprised nor did they intend to carefully compare. They protected themselves from over-exertion by considering academics in terms of their appearance and manners and politicians by their intellectual powers.

This is not to suggest that the Webbs were incapable of shrewd insights or that their self-assurance invariably expressed itself in terms of supercilious judgements. Beatrice complained about the American distrust of representative assemblies, found the House of Representatives extravagantly absurd and looked forward with an almost misanthropic satisfaction to the prospect of the total submission of these amateurs to the rule of professional bureaucrats. Yet she also anticipated Lincoln Steffens in her understanding of the shallowness of the good government reformers and in her appreciation of how Tammany Hall performed social functions that helped to maintain it in power. Her distaste for the vulgarity and corruption of much in United States political life did not prevent her from recognising the good manners and the vitality of American social life.

This nine-month tour of the English-speaking world ought to have accelerated the Webbs' progress away from Labourism towards imperialism, but there is hardly any evidence that it did so. Certainly they took little interest in American labour or labour conditions. They did not seek out trade union organisers or socialist leaders, although they visited Jane Addams at Hull House, Chicago, a rough equivalent of Toynbee Hall. In noticing the highly effective business organisation and productivity of the Carnegie works in Pittsburgh, they did not fail to notice too that the employers were the worst kind of sweaters. When Haldane suggested that they should approach Carnegie on behalf of London University, Beatrice declined to have any doings with that 'reptile'. The Webbs failed to consider the extent to which the Carnegie men were simply unable to gain acceptance into the older upper-class structure of Pittsburgh.[15] However, her leading complaint against him was not so much that he had smashed trade unionism, but that he and his associates took no responsibility for the municipal government of the city, which they disfigured and polluted. In Australasia, on the other hand, they took the most energetic interest in the experiments in conciliation, arbitration and labour legislation generally. In New Zealand, the family association with Richard Oliver, Otago businessman and leader of the opposition, did not prevent them from recognising in R.J. Seddon, the Liberal leader and Prime Minister, an archetypal representative of a labourist political culture. He might introduce his daughters as 'The Honourable Miss Seddons', and in the presence of a gang of workmen shout to his Minister of Public Works, 'Take that bloody excrescence down.' But the Webbs saw clearly that these deplorable vulgarities did not warrant his critics' charges of corruption and that it was absurd to talk of Tammany in connection with New Zealand. Of all the countries they visited they understood and enjoyed New Zealand best precisely because of the then absence of millionaires, the employers' fear of the law and the approach to social democracy. Although Sidney, referring to the immediate political scene, found the explanation of the whole position in Seddon's personality, Beatrice saw that he had been selected by a new political culture:

> Most of his impulses are vulgar, none of them are distinguished. For all that, I still believe that his dominant desire and most permanent impulse is to conduct the business of government so as to obtain the greatest advantage for the majority of the people, with the expectation that, if he does so, he will be kept in office. That the great advantage is, to his mind, always material and immediate, is another way of saying that he is no philosopher and cannot be ranked as a great statesman. But what chance is there in a political democracy, of ousting such men from power when the leaders of the Opposition, however well mannered and scrupulous in their transaction of public business, are consciously or unconsciously impelled by one directing motive – the immediate and material interests of the minority of property-owners.[16]

Of course, this keen appreciation of the realities of class did not prevent her from keeping her distance, everywhere she went, from the 'SDF types' whose ugly jaws and low foreheads signalled a mindless ferocity. She even managed to discern their presence as a faction within the Democratic Party in the House of Representatives:

> ci-devant workmen with rough clothes and awkward manner, undeveloped young men with narrow chests, low foreheads and red ties – what we should call SDF youths – whose occupation in the House seems to be heckling and disturbing the speaker of the other side.

She compared them with the Senators – 'large headed fine featured men with grave and dignified manners; almost punctilious in their behaviour.' Towards the end of their Australian tour the Webbs were actually taken prisoner by the SDF types. They had done their best to keep off platforms, although they had both addressed the Wellington Trades Council on their last night in New Zealand. In Melbourne Sidney refused to give the Victorian Socialists a lecture, but a public reception was advertised all the same:

> In an out of the way, dirty and badly ventilated place we met our poor relations, the believers in socialist shibboleths: a nondescript body of no particular class, and with a strong infusion of foreigners; a Polish Jew as secretary and various other nationalities, (among them black) being scattered among the audience. The chairman was the usual SDF young man, with narrow forehead, retreating chin and dirty coat, and the inevitable red tie.

After Beatrice had skilfully evaded the issue of women's suffrage, 'Sidney in a wily address tried to explain the Fabian policy of permeation.' As a result the chairman, in his concluding remarks, recommended the meeting to adopt 'Mr Webb's suggestion of taking the capitalist down a back street and then knocking him on the head!' Only the Webbs' enforced visit to the Melbourne Cup afforded a comparable instance of total mutual incomprehension.

Long before 1898 Beatrice had been in the habit of passing judgement on national character and racial disposition with a complete disregard for the need for verification and the other canons of social investigation upon which she normally insisted. Having taken care to remind any future reader of her travel log that these were but the jottings of a tourist, she felt free to pronounce upon the blacks at the Howard University for 'coloured folk'. These young victims of mechanical drilling in classics, mathematics and theology were

> of all degrees of blackness (some of the coal black, with animal features, other quite white and refined looking, but with some hidden trait of negro, forbidding them intercourse, on equal terms, with the surrounding population) gathered together to take part in a sniffling little religious service. They were all so anxious to learn their lessons, so docile and modest, so naively anxious not to be physically repulsive – in a word so painfully conscious of their inferiority of race. In their wistful expressions – deprecating repulsion – one thought one could read past and future tragedies of feeling.

At least this had some redeeming ambiguities of feeling and understanding as compared with other assurances concerning 'Jewish intelligence' or the 'base' Irish. Without making a single reference to the central importance of ethnicity in American society she concluded that the Americans were 'the most intelligent and the least intellectual of the white races'.

As for the Hawaiians, the difficulty was to decide whether their troubles were more due to their fatalism or to their 'ever present and urgent lasciviousness'. Perhaps the New Zealanders, 'an easy-going race', had 'just a suspicion of the Polynesian!' Before she got to Australasia Beatrice came near to setting up what might have been a researchable problem. Noticing that 'the Chinese are great favourites with the ruling class of the ruling race' in Honolulu, and that 'the Jew and the Chinaman' resembled one another 'in combining a low standard of life with ambition and persistent industry', Beatrice minded herself to ask about the relative rent-producing faculty of various races and the bearing it might have upon the standard of life. But one is reminded of the essential casual character of all these references to race and race relations by the total indifference shown by the Webbs to the contrasting positions of the Maoris in New Zealand and the Aborigines in Australia. Perhaps Sidney lost his patience with this chatter and gently reminded his beloved that the whole notion of 'Race' was unscientific, atavistic, a mere vestige of tribal superstitions and to be employed only in the interests of manipulating imperialist silly-billies. Yet if reflections on racialism were avoidable, a consideration of militarism and imperialism must have appeared inescapable. The United States was going to war with Spain. Australia was on the point of federation, which meant rethinking internal relations between the states and redefining the relation with the Crown. In fact, as was to prove the case with the Chinese revolution of 1911 and forced collectivisation in Russia in 1932, the Webbs regretted that their arrival should have coincided with such disturbances. It was decidedly tiresome that that Americans were obsessed about Cuba when they had come to investigate local government. It was some consolation to have some meetings with Theodore Roosevelt. His deliciously racy conversation made Beatrice excited and prim. 'B (a Senator) came up to me and said that he was in favour of going to war but did not agree with my reasons', Roosevelt reported to her. 'Go to war because you don't like god, if you please, but go to war', she excitedly noted the great man as replying! Beatrice found it unedifying that accusations of stock exchange corruption should be bandied about as motives for or against peace.

Sidney took the trouble to give his account of the issues in a special report to the *Echo* – a journal in which the Webbs had acquired a small financial interest. He found the predisposing causes in 'The financial interests… Cuban Bonds… the Sugar Trust… needy American carpetbaggers.' But this was a 'newspaper war', for the 'money power' on balance had preferred to maintain peace. While allowing that there was genuine sympathy for the Cuban freedom fighters and while noticing Roosevelt on the ennobling influence of war in offsetting a sordid commercialism, Webb predicted that the American people 'might be chastened by defeat, but it will never be improved by victory'. Witnesses to the annexation of

Hawaii, the Webbs were of the opinion that it would bring untold millions to the resident capitalists by ridding them of the United States import duty on refined sugar while 'the whole American people took a childish delight in the new militarism.'

Of course a knowing and disparaging attitude to others' imperialism may coexist with a more indulgent one towards one's own. This possibility lurked in Beatrice's insistence upon the 'French' character of American patriotic sentiment. She was referring to the nation's sense of property in the universal principles of human deliverance as formulated in the second half of the eighteenth century. But she did not go on to propose the case for the sleepier and more pragmatic style of empire-building any more than she welcomed the occasional invitation to herald the approaching advent of Anglo-Saxondom around the globe. On an October evening in Melbourne the Webbs dined with Isaac Isaacs, destined to become the first native-born governor-general of Australia. 'He was an imperialist and the night he dined with us he began by a rhapsody over the Empire; when he saw, however, that we were not impressed he went on to explain his new bill against Usury.' Sidney and Beatrice returned to England via the Red Sea. Even if they had gone back around the Cape it is doubtful whether they would have been any more imperialist than they had been when they set out nine months earlier.

Upon returning to 41 Grosvenor Road, the Webbs lost no time in immersing themselves in their old concerns. In relation to the LCC, Sidney was more inclined than ever to make clear the limited character of his ambitions, in exchange for having his own way in all that pertained to the Technical Education Board. At the school he was soon busying himself again about everything, from getting economics acknowledged as a science within the new university to the provision of linoleum. Beatrice visited her sisters and went down to see Herbert Spencer, who had invested everything in the Linotype Company in the interests of breaking the power of the compositors. By the middle of 1899 the Liberals, in pathetic disarray and aware that they were short of talent, had Sidney at Lord Tweedmouth's, dining off gorgeous plate in the hope of inducing him to stand for Parliament. They made a 'dead set' at him, but he would have nothing of it. His only regret, so he assured Beatrice, was that he had failed to impress upon his host and upon the other guests what had to be done if they were to win London.

Beatrice noticed that Sidney was as energetic as ever, but 'his energy is perpetually seeking the line of least resistance for the cause he believes in – and the line of least resistance for his cause is the line of least advancement for himself.[17] If it at least occurred to Sidney that he might go for the Liberals, it never occurred to him at this time that he might identify himself with 'Labour'. By the second half of 1899 the leading political issues had become the future of secondary education and the Boer War. On both these issues the Webbs were either totally opposed to the direction in which Labour was moving or out of sympathy with its temper. In the same month in which J.R. MacDonald was elected secretary of the Labour Representation Committee, he resigned from the Fabian Society – formally because it refused to make any pronouncement on the war, in practice because it was in the hand of a pro-war majority. Sidney belonged to that majority despite the fact that in his heart of hearts he was pro-Boer by sentiment, thought the war would have been avoidable up to the point at which the South Africa Company had been granted its charter and distrusted Chamberlain and Milner. However, the war having begun, all the recrimination was useless. Henceforth the Transvaal and the Orange Free State must be within the British Empire. As the war dragged on far longer than anyone had expected, he resisted all Beatrice's suggestions that he should read the Blue Books. Loathing the whole business, he resolved to practice what Auguste Comte called 'mental hygiene'. In other words, he 'carefully avoided anything on the subject'.[18] Beatrice's own position was less agonised. In 1895 she had not only greeted the advent of Tory government with some complacency, but had indulged in some conventional banalities. She had written:

> The whole mind of the country is at present [8 October 1895] absorbed in foreign politics. There has been a dramatic interest in the Transvaal events. Secrecy in international matters has, I think, been finally discredited so far as England is concerned. And the occasion has found the man. Joe Chamberlain is today the national hero... In these troubled times, with every nation secretly disliking us, it is a comfortable thought that we have a Government of strong, resolute men – not given either to bluster or vacillation – but prompt in taking every measure to keep us out of a war and to make us successful should we be forced in it.

Five years later the doings in the Transvaal were acknowledged to be 'an underbred business' and even the 'national hero' was accused of 'vulgarly provocative talk'.[19]

Yet Chamberlain was still allowed to have convictions 'and he expresses them honestly and forcibly – qualities at present rare in the political world'. Beatrice concluded: 'To my mind, given the fact that the Boers were fully armed, confident in their strength, and convinced of our weaknesses, war was inevitable.'[20] At best Beatrice too came to occupy a kind of middle ground from which she tried to placate and correct – if not to mediate – between the conflicting views of her sisters and her brothers-in-law. One month she would wring her hands over the fact that 'The Boers are man for man, our superiors in dignity, devotion and capacity – yes in *capacity*', and ask herself whether it would not be good for the British as a 'ruling race' to take a beating. Then a month or two later she would tease her sister Kate Courtney, whose husband had sacrificed everything for his pro-Boer convictions, by agreeing with her that 'Kruger really believes in God, and God's Government of this world.' Having cheerfully admitted as much Beatrice added: 'Which proves to me he is an impossible person for the rest of this wicked world to treat with.' In *Fabianism and Empire* Bernard Shaw gave the Society the edge on all disputants by drawing attention to the way in which the interests of the vast black majority were disregarded by both the white imperialists and the white colonialists. Long after the war was over Beatrice took pleasure in recalling this sensitivity which the Fabian was almost alone in displaying. But it had been little more than a characteristic Shavian debating point. The neglected claims of five or six million 'Kaffirs' were of incidental and quite subordinate importance in relation to the main thrust of the argument. Progress consisted in the submission of the more backward to the more advanced civilisation. It was a nice matter to determine whether one had to be more of a cosmopolitan or more of an Irishman in order to entertain, without a qualm, this sort of historicism.

In trying to account for the Webbs' absence from the Memorial Hall meeting it would be a mistake to attach too much importance to the mutual distrust between themselves and J.R. MacDonald. All the recognised Labour leaders were pro-Boer and all of them were equally inclined to side with democracy and Nonconformity in the emerging debate on education. The Webbs were unequalled in their grasp of history and the historical possibilities of labour at an institutional level, but they had long ceased to begin to think about the organisation of class power. Besides, in the case of the Labour Party this appeared as a baffled instinct that had been reduced to the narrowest and most precarious party ambitions: a party without members, without leaders and without principles. Such a nondescript institution hardly held out the prospect of becoming institutional. Perhaps, among its founders, there was an awareness of spiritual possibilities, which were not the subjects of bargains or the spatchcock organisational arguments. If so that was what the Webbs understood and cared for least. They knew the labour movement but they were disinclined to enter into communion with it. The religion of socialism was a tiresome irrelevance to such an irreligious person as Sidney. As for Beatrice, if a religion of socialism was possible at all, it was far too arduous a project to be effected by the likes of Keir Hardie or Ramsay MacDonald. So great were these difficulties that she herself was reduced to assigning religion and socialism to quite distinct compartments of her personal life, religion belonging to the most exclusive and inaccessibly personal part of it. She valued loving kindness and respected fellowship, but found a summons to 'fraternity' impossibly indiscriminate. As for moral indignation, which was so much in demand within the Labour Party during the Boer War and after it was over, Beatrice found it profoundly distrustful:

> Well, rightly or wrongly we don't believe in moral indignation … Don't believe in publicly expressing dislike of conduct about which we don't *know* more than the ordinary man. Moral indignation is self-righteous and often perilously near hatred, and is apt to take you into dangerous places – I mean dangerous from the standpoint of public welfare. It may be your duty to intervene, either with words or deeds, to prevent wrong happening, but why be indignant? We are all of us miserable sinners and mental defectives – that is the fate of the human being, and is not a fate which he has brought on himself. One must assume free will in oneself – but in so far as the conduct of others is concerned I am a 'determinist'.[21]

With this sort of lofty austerity and high-minded mumbo jumbo the British Labour Party had nothing to do. Whatever the disadvantages of too much moral indignation they must be small compared with those of spiritual pride. Within it the deliverance of the Nonconformist conscience might be sloppy, but it was not to be confused with the sins of the intellectual pride found among Unitarians, spiritual pride found among Quakers or with the insolence of high-minded social investigators.

Apart from the fact that the Webbs' grasp of the institutional world of labour outdistanced their comprehension of the social and cultural history of the British working class, they preferred the cultivation of going political concerns to the heavy work of pioneering fresh ones. A successful intrigue was more attractive than the joy of the battle. So it was while Labour was beginning its long and hesitant march away from Liberalism that Sidney Webb was busy encouraging Lord Rosebery's 'Escape from Houndsditch.' (see p. 325) It was a measure of the witlessness of the 'recognised Labour Leaders' that not one of them pointed out that it was he, Webb, who was trading in the second-hand clothes market and that Lord Rosebery could be made to serve as nothing – not even a tailor's dummy!

The Tory khaki election of 1900 was a foregone conclusion. In retrospect, it seems more remarkable for the limited character of the Tory gains rather than anything else. Beatrice regarded it with a certain grim satisfaction. She concluded that the electors had shown common sense. The Liberals were plainly too divided to govern. The pro-Boers, under the leadership of Lloyd George, took up what Beatrice regarded as a 'hopelessly unpopular cause'. They acted in the tradition of the Victorian moral reformer: people who cared less for outcomes than the public articulation of right thinking and good feeling. The Liberal Imperialists (the Limps), Asquith, Haldane and Grey, egged on by the Tory press, supported the war. From across the floor of the House, Joe Chamberlain was regarded with a jealous malevolence. His imperialism of industrial capital had not by 1900 found its expression in protectionism, but considerations of party were underpinned by differences of economic interest and social connection. He might well have subscribed to Beatrice's account of the Limps: 'They are so desperately in awe of the City, consider the opinions of *The Times*, and have their eye of the goodwill of the manufacturers – even on that of the brewers. Intellectually, they are more with us than the more Radical section; but they have no pluck and no faith.'[22]

They also had no leader, despite the fact that they were ready to play the devoted lieutenants to Lord Rosebery, if only that vain, perverse and aloof figure would allow them to do so. The unfortunate Henry Campbell-Bannerman presided over this shambles and did his best to avoid being captured by either side. However, in the summer of 1901, commenting on how the British Army tried to cope with guerrilla war by establishing concentration camps, he let slip the fatal words – that these were 'the methods of barbarism'.

The Liberal leader's words were first spoken in June 1901 at a dinner in the Holborn restaurant. This aroused a 'Liberal taste for dispute by public banquet' or 'war to the knife and fork', with which Sidney found himself involved.[23] Under the influence of another Balliol man, Lord Milner, Asquith took his differences with his leader to the vote. The Liberal Imperialists determined to celebrate this defiance with a dinner in Asquith's honour. 'We are fighting for our lives,' Haldane explained to Beatrice, 'both Asquith and I would attach much importance to Sidney being present at the dinner; we do not like to press it, because the whole movement may be a failure.' Webb agreed to go, insisting that he attached no importance to it and even less to his own presence at it. He would do it because he had no strong convictions about the immediate issue and it might be a duty to friends who were at least not hostile to 'our views' as others were. 'And now that he has agreed to go', wrote Beatrice:

I am worrying about it. First and foremost, I know he loathes the war; he thinks the whole episode of the Rand and the Chamberlain negotiations a disgrace to this country (though he attributes the inevitability of the war to the granting of the Charter to the SA Co, and the discovery of gold on the Rand); he distrusts Milner; above all he feels uncertain as to his own opinions; having carefully avoided reading anything on the subject. 'It is not my show,' he has often said when I have suggested he should read blue-books. From a more selfish point of view, it suits him not to be on either side so as to get what he can from both for his own projects.[24]

In the event, the dinner went off all right. Beatrice in the company of her sister Margaret Hobhouse viewed it from the gallery. Sidney, she noticed, 'Was amongst the most distinguished of the guests.' Asquith did well but suffered by comparison with Rosebery's 'artistically sensational utterance'. With Rosebery there still remained a problem, not of art, but of substance. Haldane and Shaw now pressed Sidney to supply Rosebery with a domestic policy that would allow him to systematically destroy Gladstonianism, rid the Liberal Party of its old-fashioned image and challenge the Tories, whose conduct of the war had been so deficient, from the standpoint of national efficiency. Webb undertook the task. The result appeared in the September issue of *Nineteenth Century*, improved by an occasional suggestion from his wife and a dash of literary genius from Shaw, under the title of 'Lord Rosebery's Escape from Houndsditch'. It proved to be the most 'social' of all the manifestos of 'social imperialism'.

Webb argued that Lord Rosebery could not possibly waste his time patching up the old clothes of Gladstonian Liberalism: he must needs lead a regenerate Opposition – which was not necessarily one with the Liberal Party. Liberalism had done good work in the past – but it had done it. In the new century, men were thinking, and would continue to think, in terms of communities rather than of individuals. Obsolete hypotheses about people rightly struggling to be free and the principle of nationality were nothing but 'Fenian abstractions'. These abstractions were but individualism writ large. According to this outmoded dogma, each distinct race (there were no distinct races) had an inalienable right to self-government irrespective of its consequences for the world at large.

It was wrong to think of the South Africa War as being to blame for the Liberals' misfortunes. They had been in decline since 1874. The war had merely changed indifference into unpopularity. What was wrong with them was not so much their Little Englandism as their administrative nihilism. The Gladstonians were incorrigible destructives and moralists, blind to the fact that the state, that greatest of co-operative societies, required our first loyalty. As to the socialists, their 'boom' during 1885–92 had collapsed because they had nothing to say for themselves on the great rising issue of imperialism. Keir Hardie, by out-Morleying Morley, had put the ILP out of the running. What agitated the electors was shame: shame at the slackness of merchants and traders. What was wanted was a full-scale assault upon the sources of national inefficiency. A war against industrial parasitism would, by extending the Factory Acts, lead to the creation of that material and moral minimum indispensable to the rearing of an Imperial Race. The submerged one-fifth must not be housed, washed and watered worse than horses. The Public Health Acts had to be enforced and three rooms and a scullery made to take the place of the neglect of local government. The severity of the workhouse and the withholding of all aid to the able-bodied were applauded, but the vast majority of paupers did not belong in that category. There must be humane treatment for the aged, scientific provision for the sick, and the best possible rearing of the children of the state. (Not a single pauper child in all London had ever won a junior scholarship.) An end had to be put to 'parsimonious thriftlessness. The 50 000 indoor pauper children and the 100 000 pauper sick constitute no trivial part of the human material out of which our Empire had to be built.'

Similarly in education, where the law was held to be in advance of its administration, the national minimum had to be enforced. 'It is in the class-rooms of these schools that the future battles of the Empire for com-mercial prosperity are being already lost.' These things were every bit as much great imperial needs and great imperial questions as the want of a 'system of scientific fighting [in place of] our present romantic and inca-pable soldiering'. What were wanted were not jingoism but virility in government. Sidney assured his readers that 'Jingoism is going the way of all rowdy fashions when they have been slept on.'

A month later Beatrice was carrying this message to Oxford. A month after that Sidney had tarted it up for the Fabians in the shape of Tract 108 on *Twentieth Century Politics*. And a month after that Lord Rosebery at Chesterfield, after doing something to placate the pro-Boers, explained that the Liberals must abandon their old shibboleths and go for national efficiency. Campbell-Bannerman was not alone in detecting Sidney as the *eminence grise*. He told Herbert Gladstone that the Chesterfield speech was an affront to Liberalism. 'Efficiency as a watchword! Who is against it? This is all mere réchauffé of Mr Sidney Webb, who is evidently the chief instructor of the whole faction.'[25] Rosebery himself had, indeed, been delighted with Webb's offering. He wrote to Beatrice advising her to keep her husband out of London or have him protected by the police, 'for his life can hardly be safe since the publication of his article in the *Nineteenth Century* – the most brilliant article that I have ever read for many a day.'

Haldane and Asquith were equally enthusiastic and were all for getting Sidney into the House. But even if Beatrice would have stood for it – and she would not have been prepared to do so in the short run – the time for that was already passing or past. The Rosebery–Webb combination was most imaginable in terms of some profound realignment in party politics. As Chamberlain made his peace with Balfour and as the Boer War drew to an end the old party lines became more secure.[26]

In 1902, organisations such as the Liberal Union and Beatrice's dining club, the Coefficients, came into being, but they were born too late for whatever chances they might have had. The Coefficients was established in November 1902 as a sort of shadow Ministry of All the Talents, except that it was more talented and more bizarre than such ministries tend to be and had no prospect of becoming a ministry. Beatrice carefully omitted all reference to it in *Our Partnership* and all the other participants came to be inclined to a comparable reticence or forgetfulness. Sidney Webb wrote to H.G. Wells in September 1902:

Dear Wells, The Dining Club takes shape; and I am asked by the half a dozen members who have nominated themselves the first members to invite you pressingly to join. It is proposed to restrict the number to ten or twelve; to arrange for about eight dinners a year, mostly at a restaurant at the members' own expense; that the subject of all discussions should be the aims, policy and methods of Imperial Efficiency at home and abroad; that the Club is to be kept carefully unconnected with any person's name or party allegiance; and, in particular, it is not to be talked about – prematurely.

The first step is to meet at dinner at 41 Grosvenor Road on Thursday 6 November at 7.45 p.m. to discuss final membership and all arrangements. Kindly book this date at once, and fail not.

The printed minutes of the Coefficients record that

On 6 November 1902 at a dinner given by Mr and Mrs Sidney Webb, it was resolved to found a dining club to be known as the Coefficients. The original members were Mr L.S. Amery; Lieut. Carlyon Bellairs, RN; Sir Clinton Dawkins, KCB; Rt. Hon. Sir Edward Grey, Bart. MP; Prof. W.A.S. Hewins; Mr H.J. Mackinder; Mr L.J. Maxse; Hon. W.P. Reeves; Hon. Bertrand Russell [who resigned on 15 June 1903]; Mr Sidney Webb and Mr H.G. Wells.

The founder members were the main participants, but Bernard Shaw was among those who participated from time to time.

The Coefficients achieved nothing in any direct or immediate sense. Yet the record of their proceedings is unrivalled as a source for studying social imperialism and the state of mind of some of the most eminent British politicians and intellectuals at the start of the twentieth century.

They began by asking: 'How far and on what lines are closer political relations within the Empire possible?' They had no difficulty in agreeing that there ought to be periodical conferences between imperial ministers and the ministers of the self-governing colonies. They all followed Reeves in this as they all concurred in the view that a community of sentiment needed to be kept up. They had much more difficulty with the management of imperial commerce and defence than with the merely political question.

Accordingly they went on, under Hewins's leadership, to look at what was shortly to become an issue of the first importance. How far and upon what conditions, is preferential trade within the empire attainable or desirable? Doubtless Hewins, who was shortly to become Chamberlain's right-hand man rather than Sidney's, took the 'radical' view that former markets were being 'narrowed down'. Flourishing industries were shrinking and there was a period of relative decline. Under these circumstances, armaments could only be maintained if we looked to the markets and sources of supply within the empire. But against this and against appeals to the historic example of the Zollverein, and the contemporary example of imperial self-sufficiency supplied by the United States, the 'conservatives' disputed even relative decline. They insisted that if revenue presented any difficulty it would be because of the political difficulty of squeezing enough out of the propertied classes. This was followed by a couple of meetings in which the relationship between the United Kingdom and the United States was the main issue. Only mass emigration from the United Kingdom to Canada could avert starvation in the event of war. Sir Clinton Dawkins thought that to avert such a war the British would have, among other things, to dispose of the Irish Question and resentment concerning their pretensions to commercial supremacy. The suggestion that America would be more sympathetic if Britain were to further republicanise its institutions elicited no permanent support (only Wells thought that the monarchy was expendable).

In historical retrospect, the fifth meeting of the Coefficients on 27 April 1903 was one of the most important. Upon that occasion Sir Edward Grey attempted to deal with the question 'What should be the relations of Britain to the great European powers?' He argued that hitherto it had been wise for Britain to back the Triple Alliance, since this had been in the interests of peace and had given us a free hand against in the French in Egypt. However, Germany, rather than France, was becoming suspect and restless. Our difficulty was that we could secure the friendship of France only by arriving at some far-reaching agreement with Russia. Thereupon the Coefficients divided as between those who held that we should compromise with Russia (at Germany's expense), those who felt that Russia was never to be trusted, and those who believed that Germany indubitably aimed 'to take our place in the trade and shipping of the world'. While all present agreed that Russian expansionism in Asia raised the most fundamental problems, there were still some who felt that we ought not to be pushed into the forefront to oppose the one or the other.

At its sixth meeting the Coefficients abandoned such diverse and difficult problems as to whether hostilities with Russia should be postponed in the interests of checking German ambitions. They addressed the delightful question, 'For what end is a British Empire desirable?' The minutes record that, after Amery's opening address,

> There was a general agreement among members that in practice the Empire was for them an object in itself, an ideal that had gradually grown up in their minds, which it did not occur to them to refer to any standard, but which was to them in itself a principal standard by which they judged political issues. To use the words of one member, he 'no more asked himself why he became an imperialist than he asked why he fell in love'.

(This was the point at which Russell, for all the fact that he had been keen on the war, decided to resign.) The others – or some of them – tried to supply their reasons for this infatuation. They found them in the impotence of small states, the dialectic through which the colonies democratised England while England delivered the colonies from parochialism, and the preparation that the empire supplied for the union of Anglo-Saxondom. As for 'Oriental or Uncivilised people', some members thought our rule over them a subordinate or even an objectionable part of our political condition. Fortunately,

> it was generally agreed that one's rule over subject races was a duty which we could not abandon and which conferred considerable advantages. It provided a large field for our commerce, it contributed to our military strength and it afforded scope for the development of a very high type of individual whose existence tended to react upon and stimulate our democracy at home.

Besides, we were very considerate to our subject races:

> It was also further suggested that if these people were not directly ruled by a higher race, they would acquire some of the powers conferred by modern civilisation, such as the use of arms and machinery, without absorbing the moral and political elements of civilisation, and thus become a menace to the civilised world.

It was not until their seventh meeting, held almost exactly a year after their foundation, that the Coefficients turned to the question 'How far is it possible by legislative regulation to maintain a minimum standard of National well-being?' As opener, Sidney rehearsed the arguments that were familiar from the 'Escape' and earlier writings. But he broke new ground in suggesting that the notion of the national minimum could be extended to cover 'the prevention of marriages of persons diseased or otherwise physically below a certain standard', while proposing that education to the ages of 18 or 21 might be made to incorporate a 'system of physical and military training'. Evidently the discussion turned largely upon the problem of how far a protective tariff was a logical complement to the systematic application of the national minimum:

> It was urged that just as it was necessary to have legislation in order to enable the individual to maintain a higher standard, so a State which endeavoured to set up a higher standard required to be protected ... It was suggested that just as there could be an 'abyss' of casual work population in a great city, so there might be an 'abyss' nation ... picking up whatever casual work circumstances brought it.

At the next meeting H.G. Wells attempted to answer the question, 'What is the proper scope of municipal enterprise?' He demonstrated, to general satisfaction, that the existing scale of local government areas was 'an inconvenient anachronism'. Sir Clinton Dawkins followed, on 'What form, if any, of compulsory service is possible and desirable?' On this matter there 'was a remarkable degree of unanimity among members'. A great physical improvement and a consequent prolongation of working life would compensate for the immediate loss of working time. But the great point was that National Service should be seen as a measure of insurance:

> The enormous fabric of British credit now rested on a very slender and delicate basis, and anything like a successful raid on England, or even the mere fancy that such a raid was possible, might create a terrible panic, and finally shift the world's centre of capital to some other country.

Moreover, it was noticed that progressive taxation 'involved considerable danger in the creation of a large irresponsible community. This would be counteracted by the imposition of the personal tax of service'. In subsequent meetings Mackinder argued that higher education should be made free to all qualified to benefit from it, while Haldane argued for devolution of powers to local government aided and partially controlled by the device of grants in aid. After Maxse had offered some reflections on *savoir-faire*, Birchenough made some suggestions about the linguistic unity of the empire. Newbolt defended the monarch (H.G. Wells dissenting) while L.S. Amery addressed himself to the problem, 'How far is it possible to evolve a system of national ethics for the British Empire?' He began by giving short shrift to the competing notion of the brotherhood of man. It was evident that that would not do at all, since it

> involved the sacrifice of all those virtues which had developed under the influence of the ideal of patriotism. Moreover, it did not provide to a

sufficient extent for the element of a community of conflict. It provided no element outside to be resisted and overcome.

On the other hand, the empire preserved that good thing, an enemy – powers of darkness and oppression, anarchy and outer chaos – requiring to be set in order to be kept out. At the same time it was an ideal almost as wide as the ideal of humanity, from which it differed 'quantitatively rather than qualitatively'. The British Empire was to be the new religion, which meant for Amery submission to an intense feeling of overmastering purpose. Despite some hesitation and confusion at this point there was general agreement that 'Prussian efficiency and Japanese bushido required to be engrafted on English justice, English public spirit, and English patriotic idealism, to produce the desired end.'

In the light of this it is hardly surprising that H.G. Wells found himself in some difficulty when at the next meeting he tried, *à propos* of the future of the coloured races, to define civilisation in terms of the conditions of internal and external peace. The majority of Coefficients were evidently agreed that this would not do at all. After all, the Australian 'blackfellows' were peaceful while 'almost all the great civilising nations have been war-like'. They concluded that civilisation was about efficiency and powers of organisation. However, they could find no justification for the view that the lowest races should be exterminated or even permanently enslaved. They were, so it was thought, capable of elevation.

Similarly, when Pember Reeves suggested that militarism had no redeeming features, his fellow Coefficients disputed his use of terms. No one had anything to say in favour of Prussian militarism (the military domination of civilian life) but devotion to efficiency in all matters, including military ones, was no evil. Conscription was not more brutalising or more deadening than the division of labour within modern industry and might lance 'the cyst of individualism'. On 17 April 1905 Webb gave what appears to have been a rather boring paper on 'The Future Revolution in English Local Government'. A couple of months later the regular meetings of the Coefficients appear to have come to an end. Haldane had warned Webb that social reform could come only in association with imperialism and only by slow turning movements. After four years' experience in courting Rosebery and the Limps and acting as convenor to the Coefficients, it must have become apparent to Sidney that these turning movements were wondrous slow and far from sure. Of course his patience would be more explicable if he was an imperialist *per se*. But was he?

Towards the end of his life W.A.S. Hewins had a chance meeting with Beatrice Webb in London. Recalling their happy association in the founding of the LSE, he extended the area of nostalgia to include their commitment to imperialism. He was astonished when Beatrice laughingly rebuked him. 'We were', she assured him, 'never imperialists.' He was being asked to believe that the Webbs had used him. That his successors as directors of the LSE, Reeves and Mackinder – all imperialists and all Coefficients – had been used also to compromise the claims of learning and respectability with those of socialism. The Webbs escaped the reproach of having been imperialists by insisting that it had never been anything more than hypocrisy and trickery.

There was 'something in it'. Undoubtedly the New Machiavelli bore a striking resemblance to one of the Babes in the Wood - but to which one? It must not be imagined that in these great matters of war, race and empire, Sidney and Beatrice were entirely of one mind. Beatrice confessed in 1900 that 'we don't *quite* agree. Sidney is on the anti-war side of the line, I am on the 'war was inevitable' side, but we are both of us so close to the dividing line that we can still go on holding hands!' Similarly, if both of them occasionally used the vocabulary of racism, Sidney was ready to caution against it, while Beatrice was ready to dwell upon its immense, if yet to be determined, importance. The commonplaces about the national and imperial interest came more readily to her lips than to his. On the other hand, it was Sidney, with his indifference to large state-ments of principle, who showed no scruple in latching on to them. As he explained to Herbert Samuel, what mattered in political thought were the axiomata media which connected the fundamental principle to the partic-ular project. Without these middle axioms such as 'collective regulation of all matters of common concern', the principles were but hot air and the projects 'merely empirical'. As already noted (p. 63), when he told Bertrand Russell that he liked to draw his own conclusions from other men's premises' and the philosopher replied, that then the conclusions followed anyway and were either not to be thought of as his or he was guilty of sophistry, Sidney doubtless thought that provided he had control of the axiomata media that objection fell.

However, the central difficulty of the social imperialist project was whether the major premise, the duty to advance the interests of empire, was consistent with the minor premise, the need to develop an imperial race, so that they might be made together to yield the conclusion that the interests of empire required us to elevate, compulsorily, the standard of life. The majority of politically conscious workmen believed that imperial-ism, far from making for social reform, did exactly the opposite. This has been taken to be the distinctively proletarian ground of opposition to the Boer War. If one looked at the excuses made for deferring the introduction of old-age pensions, for example, the priority to be given to defence had had a high place. Curiously enough, the Webbs never appear to have reflected about this question. They never decided whether J.A. Hobson was correct in maintaining that empire was at the cost of the metropolitan working class, or whether Cecil Rhodes was right in believing that it could be made to buy off the social revolution. They approached the problem in an exclusively intellectualist way. Since John Morley and other champions of the minimal state were Little Englanders, it followed that the imperialists who were already thinking in communities must incline to do so at home as well. Sidney was neither a Jingo nor a Little Englander: he was a Greater Londoner. If the highest object of public policy was the prosperity of the London School of Economics or the progress of the new Charlottenburg, then doubtless the imperialists were the best bet. To insist that this was the decisive consideration may seem preposterous. But when Hewins decided to throw in his lot with Chamberlain and go for an imperial tariff, the Webbs were agreed that whatever his own opinion might have been, Sidney would have to have opposed this project in the interests of maintaining the school's reputation for detachment. (Fortunately, he was, on balance, hostile to Chamberlain's proposals. He had been a better Fabian and Fabianism was essentially about socialism in one country. He would have had to come closer to Shaw, who recognised the absurdity of worshipping at the altar of free trade.) There was more to the Webbs' imperialism than an unheroic and rather mindless opportunism – but not much more. They were deeply persuaded of the futility of turning one's back on on-going institutional concerns, such as the Church or the empire. No doubt Sidney sincerely believed that the empire had to be the 'unit of consideration'. Any mere revulsion against it would simply play into the hands of irresponsible adventurers:

> Our own duty with the British Empire is, not to 'run' it for our own profit, or with any idea of imposing Anglo-Saxondom on a reluctant world, but to put our best brains into the task of so ordering it as (consistently with the paramount aim of its maintaining as a whole [*sic*]) to promote the maximum individual development of each geographical unit within its bounds.

Within this benign framework the non-adult races were to be improved out of existence. Simultaneously, by properly attending to the task of averting race deterioration at home, the prospect of the country falling into the hands of the Irish, the Jews or the Chinese was to be avoided . Not all these demagogic appeals or paranoid anxieties found full expression during the period 1901 to 1903, but it was within these years that the foundation for them was laid.

To take the proper measure of the Webbs' social imperialism it is necessary to understand the profound transformation that took place in their location within the family circle and the wider social world during this period. They did, indeed, drift into imperialism. Their relatively moderate or detached attitude towards the Boer War facilitated this process since 41 Grosvenor Road became a haven open to the warmongering and the pacifist brother-in-law alike. From Sister Kate, Beatrice learned at first hand what it was like to be completely out of it, for Leonard Courtney was made to pay very heavily for his principled opposition to British imperialism. For the first time the Webbs were free from all taint and fully acknowledged as distinguished members of the family. This could hardly be otherwise, for 1901 to 1905 might be characterised as their prime-ministerial years. Their circle was dominated by Prime Ministers past, present and future, together with those who aspired to that office or who were connected with it in one way or another.

First, there was the former premier, to whom they were introduced in the interests of one of Haldane's fantasies or intrigues. Beatrice had been utterly done up after a week of dissipation. Dining with Alfred Cripps in a private room in the House of Commons – 'a veritable hole of Calcutta' which had proved too much for Margaret Hobhouse – she struggled on chatting with Carson, 'a clever, cynical and superficial Irishman'. Then there had been a little dinner on Friday. On Sunday she had supped with Willie Cripps. On Monday she had debated in the Chelsea Town Hall with an anti-regulationist. On Tuesday she had dined with the Creightons and Professor Ramsay to talk London University. Then on Wednesday

> we dined with Haldane to meet a select party of Roseberites including the great man himself. Haldane sat me down next to Lord Rosebery against the will of the latter who tried his best to avoid me as neighbour, but all to no purpose. Haldane insisting on his changing places. At first he avoided speaking to me. But, feeling that our host would be mortified if his little scheme failed utterly, I laid myself out to be pleasant to my neighbour, though he aggravated and annoyed me by his ridiculous airs: he might be a great statesman, a Royal Prince, a beautiful woman and an artistic star, all rolled into one. 'Edward', called out Lord Rosebery to Sir Edward Grey as the latter, arrayed in Court dress, hurried away to the Speaker's Party, 'don't tell the world of this new intrigue of Haldane's.'
>
> And I believe Lord Rosebery winked as he glanced at me sitting by him.[27]

As she subsequently noted:

> Unmarried, living a luxurious physical but a strenuous mental life, Haldane's vital energies are divided between highly skilled legal work and the processes of digestion – for he is a Herculean eater. He finds his relaxation in bad metaphysics and in political intrigue – that is, trying

to manipulate influential persons into becoming followers of Rosebery and members of his *clique*. Be it said to his credit, that he has to some extent manipulated us into this position.[28]

Two years later she was taking the Prime Minister himself into dinner. 'I say 'took' because he was so obviously delivered over into my hands by my kindly hostess who wished me to make as much use as possible of the one and a quarter hours he had free from the House.' She found Balfour modest, unselfconscious and intellectually serious in a way in which Rosebery was not:

I set myself to amuse and interest him, but seized every opportunity to insinuate sound doctrine and information as to the position of London education…Three dinner parties and two evenings at one's house in eight days is severe! But it seemed desirable to give a Conservative-LCC dinner and a London University reception; and also a Limp dinner, and a Limp reception. Then there was a dinner to Lady Elcho to acknowledge her kindness to us in Gloucestershire and our introduction to Balfour, an introduction which may have good results. So I asked her to meet John Burns, the Shaws, H.G. Wells, and Asquith… Asquith was simply dull. He is disheartened with politics, has no feeling of independent initiative, and is baffled by Rosebery, shuns and is snubbed by Campbell-Bannerman. He has worked himself into an unreal opposition to the Education Bill. He is not really convinced of the iniquity or unwisdom of the Bill he is denouncing. He eats and drinks too much and lives in a too enervating social atmosphere to have either strenuousness or spontaneity. Clearly he is looking to the money-making Bar for his occupation in life. As a lawyer he is essentially common quality; [with] no interest in, or understanding of, legal principles; no ingenuity or originality in making new influences or adapting old rules to new conditions. However, he is under no delusion about himself; he has resigned himself to missing leadership.[29]

Other future Prime Ministers who had not yet made the mistake of crossing the Webbs fared rather – if not much – better. 'For three days I have been off with strained eyes', Beatrice recorded in July 1903:

Strained not with work, but with dissipation of strength at four dinners last week…My diet saves me from worse ills than mere fatigue. Unfortunately I don't always stick to my regime – specially when I am bored.

We went to dinner with Winston Churchill. First impression: restless – almost intolerably so, without capacity for sustained and unexciting labour – egotistical, bumptious, shallow-minded and reactionary, but with a certain personal magnetism, great pluck and some originality – not of intellect but of character.[30]

Quite a little Joe in fact, had it not been for his being a Little Englander at heart and for his penchant of looking 'to haute finance to keep the peace'.

As for he who lusted most for office and who was never entirely absent from her thought, he who was most powerfully called but never managed to be chosen, she had to get on with his daughter and she met him now and again with diminishing emotional perturbation. His great physique, like that of the nation's as a whole, was deteriorating. But she was just in time to offer a last salute to the slipping monocle and the dropping orchid. 'We lunched at Chamberlain's,' she recorded on 17 June 1904. 'I sat on one side of my old friend' – this obsession with the details of processioning and positioning is characteristic – 'and we talked without constraint.' This is extremely doubtful. 'He is obsessed with the fiscal question – has lost his judgement over it – refuses to think or talk of anything else.' Under the circumstances this was wholly understandable. 'He looks desperately unhealthy, rather thin too; a restless look in his eyes' - under the circumstances this must be allowed to be forgivable – 'bad colour, and general aspect of "falling in".' What does this mean? 'But I should imagine that there is plenty of force in the man yet; an almost mechanical savage persistence in steaming ahead.' Good gracious me! He had been the Colonial Secretary, not the First Lord of the Admiralty! 'I tried to suggest the "national minimum" as a complementary policy to export duties.' Good try, girl! 'I have no prejudice against it', he answered, 'but it would not do for me to suggest it – it would be said that I was trying to bribe the working class.' Game, set and match to Mr Chamberlain? Game and first set to Mr Chamberlain! It would have been the match as well had he not gone on to remark: 'If I had been Prime Minister, you would not have had the Education Act.' 'The one and only reason', said Beatrice sweetly, 'for my not regretting that you are *not* Prime Minister.' And with that she went off to comfort Mrs Chamberlain. 'There must be times when the great personage with his irritability, one-sidedness, pitiful unhealthiness and egotism and vulgarity, is rather a heavy handful for that refined and charming little lady.'[31]

Bonar Law was present at this lunch, but apart from noting the fact Beatrice paid no further attention. However, this neglect was more forgivable than the Webbs' dismissive attitude towards Campbell-Bannerman; their failure to even consider Lloyd George's importance for popular politics; and their failure to restore relations with J.R. MacDonald. MacDonald would hardly have declined if they had invited him to join them in high political society. However, he was busy spreading tales about Sidney and

Beatrice making money out of the 'School': a particularly unpleasant fabrication which was made into a grotesque one by the Webbs' gifts to that institution and their practice of teaching there without payment.

Of course there was relief from 'dissipation' in going off together to study prisons or sewers or some other aspect of the history of local government. In particular there was the pleasure of long stays with Bertrand and Alys Russell at their home at Friday's Hill or as companions on a cycling holiday in Normandy. Beatrice had some difficulty in categorising Bertie. Since he was a grandson of Lord John – 'Finality Jack' – Russell he too had the prime-ministerial connection, but Beatrice decided that despite the incomprehensible nature of his enquiries he was an expert: 'an expert in the art of reasoning, quite independently of the subject matter'.[32] She also decided that the Russells were the most attractive married couple she knew. When they became more and more estranged she made every effort to comfort Alys and to help them to repair their relationship. She also tried to help the philosopher in his career: 'Can you and Alys come to lunch on *Thursday* 10th and meet Mr Balfour? I am taking him to Bernard Shaw's play. Could you not take tickets for that afternoon? It will be well for you to know Mr Balfour – in case of Regius Professorships and the like!'

The Russells were coming to be preferred even to the Shaws. As early as 1899 when the Webbs used to dine sumptuously in Charlotte's flat above the LSE, Beatrice watched George Bernard Shaw in his 'fitful struggles out of the social complacency natural to an environment of charm and plenty' and asked herself: 'How can atmosphere be resisted?'[33] Five years later she found the smart world tumbling over one another in the worship of Shaw. Even the Webbs had a sort of reflected glory as his intimate friends. If his self-conceit was proof against flattery, that hardly made the transformation scene less remarkable: 'the scathing bitter opponent of wealth and leisure – and now! the adored one of the smartest and most cynical set of English Society.'[34] (Not let it be noted of the electorate. Sidney was a good deal of time puffing Shaw in the *Daily Mail* and otherwise trying to get him elected to the LCC in 1904. He was above having anything to do with such orthodox devices as election addresses or polling cards. His own invention insisted that he was an atheist and though a teetotaller would force every citizen to imbibe a quarter of rum to cure any tendency to intoxication. He laughed at the Nonconformist conscience, chaffed the Catholics about transubstantiation, abused the Liberals and contemptuously patronised the Conservatives.)

Beatrice was intermittently aware that she and Sidney were themselves at risk of becoming a supporting act in these performances in which the smartest and most cynical set of English society enjoyed being so safely outraged. Between meeting Prime Ministers she sometimes suspected that entertaining the Webbs – as persons with a special kind of chic – was becoming a requirement in parts of fashionable society.[35] Her old friend and teacher, Frederic Harrison, had observed long ago that a little playful radicalism went down very well in the highest circles of the aristocracy. Occasionally, she noticed that it was unwholesome, but she was very reluctant to allow that it was futile. Incapable of distinguishing between the ruling class and the governing oligarchy, she deluded herself into supposing that it was all in a good cause, and anyway it did not do any harm to Sidney. All power resided, so she persuaded herself, in the hands of a ruling clique. Thus, in the London educational world, no one could resist Sidney because he was in the little clique at the centre of things and had the LCC power of making grants.[36] Government by cliques might not be quite wholesome if the hidden hand was less efficient and less beneficent. But then politics, so she told herself, was a by-product of their lives. 'If we came to throw our main stream of energy into political life, we should have to choose our comrades more carefully.'[37] In that case she could never have allowed Haldane to suggest that they should work with such 'a loathsome person' as 'Imperial Perks': 'a combination of Gradgrind, Pecksniff and Jabez Balfour.'[38] It would have been intolerable to feel that one was becoming so near to being 'both a spy and a traitor'.[39] Although she periodically remembered that she would look to a different social base than that considered by the Limps, her prevailing mood for most of the time was one which inclined her to

> detach the *great employer*, whose profits are too large to feel the immediate pressure of regulation and who stands to gain by the increased efficiency of the factors of production, from the ruck of small employers or stupid ones. What seems clear is that we shall get no further instalments of reforms unless we gain the consent of an influential minority of the threatened interest.[40]

Sidney was fully party to the politics of permeating the ruling cliques. But since those distant days when Beatrice had cured him of his habit of starting sentences with the words 'when I am Prime Minister', he had passed beyond the reach of personal and social ambition:

> Sidney is simply unconscious of all the little meanness which turns social intercourse sour: he is sometimes tired, occasionally bored, but never unkindly or anxious to shine, or be admired, and wholly unaware of the absence of, or presence of, social consideration. I verily believe that if he were thrown, by chance, into a company of persons all of whom wanted to snub him, he would take up the first book and become absorbed in it, with a sort of feeling that they were

good-natured enough not to claim his attention, or that they did not perceive that he was reading on the sly. And the greater personages they happened to be, the more fully satisfied he would be at the arrangement; since it would relieve him of any haunting fear that he was neglecting his social duty and making others uncomfortable. On the other hand, whether in his own house or in another's, if some person is neglected or out of it, Sidney will quite unconsciously drift to them and be seen eagerly talking to them.[41]

One day Beatrice found three separate entertainments which she would like to have gone to – Lady Wimborne's, Arthur Balfour's and the Duchess of Sutherland's evening parties. Having spent a great deal of money on a new dress, she wanted to parade herself. But Sidney was obdurate. He told her:

> You won't be able to work the next morning, and I don't think it is desirable that we should be seen in the houses of great people. Know them privately if you like, but don't go to their miscellaneous gatherings. If you do, it will be said of us as it is of Sir Gilbert Parker – in the dead silence of the night you hear a distant but monotonous sound – Sir Gilbert Parker climbing, climbing, climbing.[42]

Nor did Sidney, for all his marvellous simplicity and wonderful self-deadness, manage to work the ruling cliques in the way in which he intended without losing the confidence of his old friends. Wells, an acquaintance refreshingly plebeian and made perceptive by envy and malice, warned that Sidney appeared too 'foxy' and that 'he had better fall back on being an enthusiast'. Besides, was he not in the end the junior partner who would finish up serving his wife's reactionary and anti-radical purposes?[43]

By the end of 1905 Mr Balfour no longer felt that he needed to be Prime Minister in order to complete the picture of 'the really charming man'.[44] On 22 November the Webbs were dining with Lord Lucas in his great mansion in St James's Square and Beatrice was feeling a bit ashamed of herself for dissipating her energies in this 'smart but futile world' when in came the PM to 'dissipate' her regrets. 'It is always worthwhile, I thought, to meet those who really have power to alter things… He was looking excited and fagged on the eve of resignation.' The Webbs lunched with him six days later before going off to see *Major Barbara*. On the way to the theatre the Prime Minister apologetically explained to her why he could not supply her with better colleagues on the Royal Commission on the Poor Law, to which she had just been appointed.

At least both the Webbs could point to places on Royal Commissions as some reward from these prime-ministerial years. Even the cultivation of

Rosebery had been worth £5000 or more to the School. But as to rest there was little to show for it all. Those whom they had cultivated least had been swept back to office over a divided and exhausted Tory government by trade unionists and Nonconformists raving about peace and liberty, Chinese coolies and untaxed breakfast tables. Beatrice ought to have counted herself jolly lucky that John Burns, newly appointed as president of the Local Government Board, went straight to 41 Grosvenor Road from congratulating 'Sir Enry the new Premier' on this his 'most popular appointment'. Instead, she grew weary of his boasting. 'Don't be too doctrinaire about the unemployed, Mr Burns,' said she. To which he replied, 'Economise your great force of honesty, Mrs Webb.'

A record of failed intrigue is not improved by a want of diplomacy. The question of whether 41 Grosvenor Road was occupied by the New Machiavelli or by the Babes in the Wood has already been raised. There were times when it was difficult to determine the answer.

It is difficult to class the Webbs as racists. They did not employ the vocabulary of biology, but of education. The division was not between peoples of different colour, but of different opportunity and experience. The distinction was between the 'adult' and 'the non-adult races'. It was condescending and patronising and opportunist. It was not a concession to the prejudices of Gobineau or to those that were to become identified with Adolf Hitler.

Part V
Epilogue

And we are, as I said in my diary when we were first engaged, 'second rate minds – neither of us are outstandingly gifted – it is the "combinat" that is remarkable'. And this brings me to the criticism of the Webbs which seems to me simply funny: we are said to lack 'humanity', to be strangely inhuman. Why? Because we have continued to be devoted to each other and have worked together ceaselessly, without friction! Why should an unblemished monogamy be considered 'inhuman'?

(D, 25 September 1933)

Beatrice Webb: 'Marriage is the waste-paper basket of the emotions.'
Virginia Woolf: 'Wouldn't an old servant do as well?'
Beatrice: 'Yes, I dare say an old family servant would do as well'.
The conversation took place in September 1918, but this characterisation of marriage was well established as one of Beatrice's stock remarks.

See L. Woolf, Beginning Again, 1964, pp. 116–17

9

An Ideal Marriage?

Beatrice's attitude of superiority—The marriage as a business relationship—Beatrice's sexual impulses and 'relapses'—Sidney's attitude—The
achievements.

The Webbs always had at least two domestic servants. Had it been otherwise, Sidney would have had to do the washing-up. He would have done
it uncomplainingly, even joyfully. Meanwhile, Beatrice (who was over
eighty before it first dawned upon her that she could not boil an egg),
would have sat upstairs smoking a cigarette, her feet on a stool, reflecting
about the unanticipated and wasteful implications of social equality.

Beatrice distanced herself from the organised feminist movement,
showing towards it indifference, standoffishness or hostility. But her most
characteristic attitude was one of superiority. This proceeded from her
sense of being a successful feminist in her own practice. She had achieved
equality and, perhaps, something more. When she joined with other eminent women – most of them merely the wives of eminent men – in opposing the extension of the suffrage on the grounds that power corrupted
women's nature, she was already indulging in the most ruthless type of
sexual politics at the expense of every vulnerable male in sight.[1] When she
refused to follow Alfred Marshall's advice and specialise in the study of
women in industry, she knew that she would never achieve full parity of
esteem with male social investigators by going along that road.[2] When she
provoked the 'screeching sisterhood' by declaring: 'I never saw a man, the
most inferior, but I felt him to be my superior,'[3] she had already concluded a contract in which the most perfect intellectual equality had been
conceded and a good deal more besides. In disassociating herself from the
individualist ladies crying out for rights which they had no notion of how
to exercise – unless it was at the expense of their proletarian sisters – she
left herself free to campaign in the Westminster Vestry for more public
lavatories for women – something which required more daring than many
'a more advanced' woman could have managed.[4] Having got herself
involved with the essentially timid and woolly-headed International

Congress of Women she suddenly discovered the importance of principle
and withdrew from the executive because it would not abandon the practice of morning prayers. She found this proceeding wanting in consideration of the claims of Jewesses and religious-minded agnostics like herself.[5]
Until she made her very dignified and qualified repentance in 1906,[6]
Beatrice's persistence in these attitudes was related to her own success in
turning the tables on the opposite sex.

This did not mean that Beatrice identified with other emancipated
women who lived their feminism out in the practice of life. She saw herself as superior to them as well. Thanks to the benign influence of her
father and Herbert Spencer she had not had 'to struggle against the prejudice and oppression of bigoted and conventional relations to gain her
freedom', a struggle which might demoralise those who were forced to
engage in it. Such a woman as Maggie Harkness had 'never been disciplined by a Public Opinion which expects a woman to work with the masculine standard of honour and integrity'.[7]

In *Our Partnership* Beatrice concealed the extent to which her marriage
was thought of quite literally as a business arrangement. As she admitted
on her side (and she had the whip hand economically) it was a cold-
blooded calculation. 'To the well trained commercial mind there is charm,'
she wrote, 'in making the ideal bargain, the best possible to both partners.'[8] As to the nature of the bargain: the woman was to take the unimportant decisions. The man was to take the important ones. And she
(Beatrice) was to determine which was which![9] (It does not matter if the
story is apocryphal; it supplies an excellent first approximation to reality.)

Few ideal marriages are childless, but there were to be no children.
Sidney would have liked to father Beatrice's child, but he would certainly
not insist upon it. In any case she was over thirty and childbirth in the
1890s carried far greater risks than was to be the case a hundred years
later. Chamberlain's first two wives had died in childbirth. A family
would inevitably hinder her in the pursuit of her professional career and
have costs for both their research and public life. From the standpoint of
the British race it was obviously deplorable that the Shaws, the Webbs
and (before 1921) the Russells had no offspring. She sometimes suspected
that it might be damaging, even to the quality of the existing elite, never
mind the future generations. But, on balance, it was a necessary decision
and a right one – at least for her. In politics she would accept the subordinate role of the wife. However, her conception of that role involved initiatives, which hardly conformed to conventional expectations on that subject.
(She rejoiced in providing Sidney with an entry into circles that he would
have otherwise found inaccessible. But she would have been insulted if
anybody had ever suggested that *she* thereafter displayed the customary
political and educational passivity of the woman.) However, the main

thing was that politics was to be treated as secondary to research. Sidney was not to accept any invitation to a station in public life that would prevent this or seriously hinder it. Despite the fact that he contributed far more to their joint work – at least to the drudgery of it – than she did, here she was to be treated as fully equal. He was not to get ill. He was not to get tired. Nor was he ever to complain about the austerities of their domestic regime even if he was to be spared the full rigour of her own more Spartan excesses. Fortunately for Beatrice, she found, in Sidney, a man who was able to accept these arrangements – one who was ready (in exchange for a delightful companionship or an occasional 'interval for human nature') to accept that reversal of conventional marriage roles which she was looking for. For him the yoke was paradise – even while she still indulged in occasional fantasies concerning the monocle and the orchid.

These fantasies did recur. In recording them and in reflecting about them Beatrice's working feminism was revealed at its fullest extent and confronted with its ultimate predicament. Beyond the transitory joys of vengeance and atonement; beyond the happiness of creative work together; the bargain had sentenced what she often took to be the deepest (as well as the worst) side of her to a state of internal exile.

Her strong sexual impulses were not fully satisfied. In acknowledging their strength she put herself in advance of Olive Schreiner and the vast majority of emancipated women of her time. In sensing the relationship between these impulses and the highest and most ephemeral side of her experience, she entertained a shamefully radical prospectus. In facing that her passion for Chamberlain was related to a desire to submit to the most masterful figure of the time, she brought herself to the conundrum that was to confront succeeding generations. If full sexual realisation comes only in submission, how is that to be reconciled with liberty and equality in every other department of life? How was the woman who ought always to be sought to be reconciled with the woman who was bound to assert herself?

It is difficult to be sure when Beatrice first discovered the difficulties of the working feminist who simply reverses the established terms of sexual chauvinism. Probably she was more aware of the improvement in Sidney before she fully realised the limitations of her own happiness. Staying with the Trevelyans over Christmas 1895, she rejoiced in the way in which her husband listened to G.M.'s historical essays and gave hints: drawing out, appreciating, criticising. 'The perfect happiness of his own life has cured his old defects of manner – he has lost the aggressive, self-assertive tone, the slight touch of insolence which was only another form of shyness – and has gained immeasurably in persuasiveness'.[10] She concluded that: 'All ties should be made secure – to be broken only by mutual consent and for very sufficient reasons...How I hate Anarchism in all its forms.'[11] Yet in relation to Chamberlain she herself was still subject to what she called 'relapses', despite the fact that she could assure herself that 'I am absolutely happy with Sidney – our life is one long and close companionship; so close it is almost a joint existence.'[12] Even at the beginning of the Boer War she was mortified to find that she was striving, rather unavailingly, to meet criticisms of 'Joe' from Sidney and Leonard; and that she was 'prey to an involved combination of bias and counterbias...'[13] Then, in the spring of 1900,

> The last three months have not been satisfactory. My work has not had my best thought and feeling, foolish day-dreams based on self-consciousness and personal vanity, foolish worrying over an invest-ment in the *Echo*, which is likely to be a dead loss and may involve us in legal complications – a certain physical revulsion to intellectual effort – have all combined to make my work half-hearted and unreal. Sidney is free from all these defects and every day I live with him the more I love and honour the single-mindedness of his public career and his single-hearted devotion to his wife. And every year I appreciate more fully the extraordinary good luck which led me to throw in my lot with him. (So much, one might remark for 'the well-trained commercial mind'!) Just as it was the worst part of my nature that led me into my passionate feeling for Chamberlain so it was the best part of my nature which led me to accept Sidney after so much doubt and delay. And certainly, just as I was well punished for the one, I have been richly rewarded for the other course of feeling and conduct. And yet, not withstanding the con-viction, I find my thoughts constantly wandering to the great man... Sometimes I think I should like to meet him again. At other times I reject the thought as a needless expenditure of feeling.[14]

Two months later, after a large dinner party of Haldane's, the Webbs were walking along the terrace of the House when the 'Great Man' appeared. She introduced him to her husband. 'I think you were in my Office, Mr. Webb,' said the Colonial Secretary. 'That is hardly correct,' replied Sidney. 'When I was there you were not.'

The return of the old aggression was accidental; quite unintended. He had meant to say that he had not had the honour of serving under Chamberlain. Beatrice was sure of that. She was equally sure that there was still a bond, 'a bond of sentiment between us – I for the man I loved – loved but could not follow'.[15] By the end of the year rumours of Chamberlain's separation from his wife led Beatrice to experience

> a whole month of suspense...And then a morbid consciousness that owing to that most unfortunate meeting on the terrace in the

summer there are some persons who are going about attributing to me the separation, *I* who have never met her, and *I* who have only seen him once in thirteen years... *I* must turn my thoughts away. All *I* want to feel certain of, in my own conduct, is that if ever *I* meet him again my whole influence, if *I* have any, shall be devoted towards their reconciliation.

And to think that I am over forty and he is over sixty! What an absurdity![16]

On New Year's day 1901 Beatrice attempted a long retrospect:

Possibly I owe a debt to Chamberlain. He absorbed the whole of my sexual feeling, but I saw him at rare intervals and loved him through the imagination, in his absence more than his presence. This emotional preoccupation made my companionship with other men free from personal preferences and deliberately controlled with a view to ends.

As to Sidney:

His lack of social position, even his lack of personal attractiveness gave him, in relation to me, the odd charm of being in every respect the exact contrary to Chamberlain and my ill-fated emotion for that great personage ... The fact that neither my physical passion nor my social ambition were stimulated by the relationship seemed in itself an element of restfulness and stability. Then again my pity was appealed to. I felt his love for me was so overpowering that his life and work might be wrecked if I withdrew myself. Added to all these thoughts and feelings there was a curious strain of altruistic utilitarianism. I had a competence, more than enough to sustain one intellectual worker. I had social position of a kind, I had knowledge of men and affairs; all these Sidney lacked to be successful. Why not invest my different kinds of capital where it would yield the best results from the standpoint of the community? And so we pledged our words at the Co-operative Congress, May 1901 ... We are still on our honeymoon and every year makes our relationship more tender and complete. Rightly or wrongly we decided against having children. I was no longer young, he had been overworking from childhood ... Our means though ample for ourselves and our work, would not have allowed a family and continued expenditure upon investigation and public life. But perhaps the finally conclusive reason was that I had laboriously and with many sacrifices transformed my intellect into an instrument for research. Child bearing would destroy it, at any rate for a time, probably altogether ... On the whole I do not regret the decision, still less does Sidney ...[17]

Even before her reunion with Chamberlain it had occurred to Beatrice that women might relinquish the bonds of unblemished monogamous love in favour of having one man for one purpose and another man for another.[18] She discussed polygyny without embarrassment and noticed that despite the enormously disproportionate profligacy of the male, 'scientific breeding' could hardly be confined to the selection of the man. Moreover she discerned that 'women's sexual feeling towards the man is, in many cases, indistinguishable from her reverence towards and obedience to the Priest; religious sentiment being related to sexual instincts.'[19] However, in view of contemporary ignorance about the importance of genetics in the history of society and her own revulsion at the prospect of 'anarchy' she briskly turned her back on these conjectures and insights and closed the door firmly behind her.

Of course Sidney shared neither Beatrice's sexual discontents nor her propensity to romanticise nor her religiosity.[20] He was unable to conceal from her that he thought of her preoccupation with 'prayer' and the rest of it as 'neurotic'.[21] He would have nothing to do with it, save as the loving companion who patiently reintroduced her to the therapy of everyday life. Yet these differences between them in point of mind and temperament were certainly far more important than their differences of opinion over feminism, socialism or the Boer War, or the occasional 'tiffs' which occurred in the course of their joint research. These were all minimal and marginal. It is hardly surprising that the perfect harmony of their research, in which Beatrice would throw in a problem or a hypothesis and Sidney would torment it with his learning, occasionally broke down. She confessed:

> Sometimes I am a bit irritated because ... he will not listen to what seems to me a brilliant suggestion – dismisses it with 'that is not new' or with a slightly disparaging 'hmm'. But I generally smile at my own irritation and take back any idea to clear up or elaborate or correct with other thoughts or to reject as worthless. Sometimes I flare up and scold – then he is all penitence and we kiss away the misunderstanding.[22]

These small differences did not diminish the most fruitful partnership in the history of the British intellect. Even by 1905 it had done enough to fulfil the promise which Sidney had insisted that it would realise – together they had 'moved the world' – if but a little way and not always just as they intended. They had completed one immense research project and had advanced into another. They had played a great part in the reshaping of educational institutions in London, creating an environment in which they hoped that the new learning might take root and grow. Fabianism had become the most characteristically English form of socialism and they had managed, with varying degrees of success, to expound and apply it to astonishingly large and varied audiences. Yet, however wonderful the achievements of the 'combinat', it was flawed by a persistent evasiveness: a failure to identify and confront certain crucial issues. Thus, the failure to examine the arithmetic of imperialism or ask what were the cultural possibilities of publicly funded education or to examine how ruling cliques were related to ruling classes may be related to a failure of communication within the partnership itself. As it was, a dangerously large number of unexamined assumptions and neglected major premises were allowed to occupy the territory which lay between Beatrice's excursions into metaphysics and Sidney's world of the axiomata media.

Revolutionaries may object that these evasions relate to matters of very different degrees of difficulty and importance. They may complain that it is part of the very nature of reformism to be impatient with every question that might get in the way of its practice and to pretend that it is only through practice that they can be answered. But the Webbs were not merely practitioners within the English reformist tradition; they must be numbered among the makers of it. However late in the day, they did contemplate alternative possibilities. *'And what'* asked Beatrice, *'exactly is the daily life you ought to live if you wish to be, and to be thought to be, a genuine revolutionary?'* Characteristically, Sidney dismissed this as a quite unrealistic question, which could have no consequence for the Webbs who had no intention of so ordering their lives as to be, and to be thought to be, revolutionaries.

Conservatives may object that it was of very little consequence that Beatrice's propensity to interest herself in the big questions was never brought into a complete relationship to Sidney's capacity for supplying answers, since the pursuit of progress, whether in one way or another, is always a mistaken enterprise. They might recall the words of Goethe: 'To think is easy: to act is difficult: to act in accordance with one's thoughts is the most difficult thing in the world.' But Sidney and Beatrice both knew their Goethe. They would have pointed out that his remark should be read, not merely as a note of caution, but as a word of consolation and hope.

Halfway through their lives the Webbs had accomplished much. Fabianism had become the most distinctive and influential mode of socialism in England. Sidney and Beatrice had laid the foundations of modern labour historiography. They had begun an equally distinguished, multi-volume study of English local government. They had enlarged technical education in London. Sidney had gone on to enlarge educational opportunity more generally. With Beatrice he had founded the LSE and with Haldane helped to make the Imperial College of Science and Technology the new Charlottenburg near the head of a great new *teaching* university. These accomplishments would have been enough in themselves to ensure the Webbs' enduring fame and importance. However from 1906 to 1947 they did much more: they discovered one of the few great principles of public administration as they set about the abolition of the Poor Law and the prevention of destitution. (Beatrice assumed the leading role in this campaign.) They came back from the Orient to engage with syndicalism and to mount a formidable critique of it. Beatrice could hardly face the horrors of the Great War. Sidney urged her to follow the example of the French peasants and to continue to cultivate their fields directly behind the line of fire. This meant immersing himself in the activities of the War Emergency Workers National Committee and the Campaign for the Conscription of Riches. This in turn led to the new constitution of the Labour Party and the formulation by Webb, with Henderson, of the 'infamous' Clause IV.

With the peace Sidney went on to the Sankey Commission on the Coal Industry. This led on to his adoption as Labour candidate for Seaham Harbour. He became a member of the first Labour government in 1924. The Webbs had then to confront the experience of the General Strike. While Sidney did his best to cope with the realities of cabinet and parliament, Beatrice devoted herself to cultivating friendly and productive relations with the women of Seaham Harbour and attending to mending the manners of the ladies who came into the social life of the House of Commons. As Colonial Secretary in the second Labour administration, Sidney appeared to switch his support away from the settlers in Palestine and Kenya in favour of the indigenous population.

With the Great Slump came the downfall of the second Labour government. Beatrice dismissed the 'flies on the wheel of world welter' while Sidney cursed the 'pigs' at Transport House as well as the American bankers. The turn towards Soviet Communism had begun. It continued as they visited Russia. Was it continuous or discontinuous with earlier efforts? Was it as simple and uncomplicated as Ernest Gellner took it to be or was it far more complicated than he and others allowed?[23]

'The strangest couple since Adam and Eve.' 'Two typewriters beating as one.' The witticisms about the Webbs are stale and inadequate. Their individual characteristics need to be rediscovered. For example, Beatrice's tendency to believe that manners maketh man inclined her to celebrate good ones in a way which could be rather hard and vulgar, while Sidney was inclined to confuse the art of the possible with the possibility of being artful. They both tended to underestimate the costs of their childless marriage. Beatrice was astonished that a child should confuse her style with that of a princess. Russell's daughter Kate recalled that when the Webbs were staying with her family in Cornwall she bumped into Sidney in one of the darker corridors. 'Lend me your eyes,' said he to the terrified child. No doubt Bertrand gave his daughter a clear and correct account of

Sidney's intended meaning. The intention was to value and reassure, not to frighten and dismay.

In looking forward to the second part of their lives and concluding this account of the formative years we leave the Webbs as observed by Mildred Minturn at Friday's Hill in late June 1901:

The Russells and Logan [Pearsall Smith] have a sort of confession they put their friends through – a series of questions which if answered truthfully bring out practically all a person's character. I shall never forget Mrs Webb laying bare her soul before us all, looking awfully handsome, her dark face flushed with excitement, slouched back in a big chair by the fire, smoking cigarette after cigarette, her bright black eyes snapping as she brought out one surprising confession after another. She had only married her husband because she wished to write her [*sic*] Trade Union book with him. The devotion for which they are notorious came after. She thought one of her principal faults was cruelty and she knew she was not quite a lady! That almost finished us all – for sheer audacity and indecency of self-revelation one could hardly go further.[24]

When Beatrice advised Sidney that she was embarking on a second autobiographical volume, he responded, 'yes, but no personalities please'.

Notes and References

1 The Shaping of a Professional Man 1859–85

1. Notes on Sidney Webb supplied to Barbara Drake by Sidney's brother Charles, n.d. (1948?); hereinafter referred to as CWN (R.H. Tawney Coll. LSE). See also B. Webb, *Our Partnership*, 1948, p. 2; hereinafter referred to as *OP*. The spelling of the street name has been variable, but the modern practice, which is followed from this point forwards, is to drop the 'e'.
2. Enumerator's Return; Census 1861, Public Record Office.
3. Marriage certificate, Somerset House.
4. Enumerators' Returns, Peckham; Census 1851 and 1861. Will of James Webb; Passfield Papers (hereinafter PAS).
5. CWN.
6. M.I. Cole, *The Story of Fabian Socialism*, 1961, p. 28.
7. *Daily News*, 31 May 1865, where some 400 names are listed in alphabetical order.
8. GBS to SW, 26 March 1946.
9. SW to S. Olivier, 7 July 1885.
10. Ibid.
11. Enumerator's Return, 44 and 45 Cranbourn Street; Census 1861, Public Record Office.
12. Poor Rate Book, Westminster City Archives, acc. no. 938, class no. A883/A13.
13. S. Webb, *The Way Out*, March 1885; (PAS VI/19).
14. S. Webb, 'Reminiscences No. 1 Trade Unionism', *St Martin's Review*, October 1928, pp. 478–81.
15. Ibid., and CWN.
16. S. Webb, *The Ethics of Existence*, 1880–1 (A talk to the Zetetical Society; see the abridged prospectus of October 1881); PAS VI/3–4.
17. Webb, 'Reminiscences …'
18. CWN.
19. S. Webb (unsigned), 'Banks of Today' (review of P. Kropotkin, *In Russian and French Prisons*), *International Review*, 3 September 1889.
20. Ibid.
21. CWN.
22. Webb, 'Reminiscences …'
23. CWN and G. Wallas, Note on meeting with S. Webb etc.; Wallas Coll., LSE, Box 11, Biographical material.
24. CWN. (She won the Society of Arts Gold Medal – open to all England – for the greatest number of first-class certificates in one year.)
25. Wallas, Note.
26. For useful discussion see J.A. Banks, 'The Challenge of Popular Culture', in P. Applean, W.A. Madden and M. Wolff (eds), *1859: Entering an Age of Crisis*, Indiana, 1959.
27. *City of London College, 1848–1948* (1948?).
28. Educational Awards; PAS 111/21.

29. Representations of the Birkbeck student committee (S. Webb, secretary), 8 January 1880. Minutes of the Committee of the Birkbeck Literary and Scientific Institution, 1880.
30. Wallas, Note.
31. S. Olivier, 'Not Much', in M. Olivier (ed.) *Sydney Olivier: Letters and Selected Writings*, 1948, pp. 31 et seq. and p. 227.
32. SW to GW, 14 June 1887.
33. Educational Awards; PAS 111/21.
34. 'I *do* see much of myself in Pattison': SW to GW, 8 June 1885.
35. M. Pattison, *Memoirs* [edited by Mrs Pattison], Macmillan, London, 1885.
36. S. Webb, 'The Factors of National Wealth' (April 1889?) (notes for series of lectures on Capital to City of London College); PAS VI/38–39.
37. VI/1 (n.d., but delivered in June 1876 since it refers to an article by Gladstone on the Courses of Modern Religious Thought having appeared in 'this month'. The article was published as 'The Courses of Religious Thought,' vol. 28, in the *Contemporary Review* June 1876, pp. 1–26.)
38. Ibid. (written on the back of the above).
39. SW to GW, 24 December 1885.
40. 'Theological influence has been used to direct a portion of the surplus value to "Spiritual Uses", nourishing (like the meats offered to idols) whole classes of non-producers.' S. Webb, 'The Economic Basis of Socialism and Its Political Programme' – address to Hampstead Society for the Study of Socialism, December 1887; PAS VI/33.
41. G.A. Williams, *Rowland Detrosier: A Working Class Infidel*, Borthwick Paper No. 28, York, 1965.
42. Zetetical Society, Abridged Prospectus, October 1881; PAS VI/4.
43. N.E. Himes, *Medical History of Contraception*, New York, 1963, pp. 243–59.
44. J.M. Davidson, *Eminent Radicals In and Out of Parliament*, 1880, pp. 191–9.
45. R.J. Harrison, 'The Positivists: A Study of Labour's Intellectuals', in his *Before the Socialists*, 1965, pp. 251–342.
46. PAS VI/3.
47. J.S. Mill, *Autobiography*, 1873, pp. 133–4.
48. Ibid., p. 142.
49. Witness, for example, F.L. Lehman, 'Pessimism, Positivism and Socialism', *Today*, n.s. vol. II, no. 2, August 1884, pp. 263–74.
50. S. Webb, 'The New Learning of Nineteenth Century: Its Influence on Philosophy' (n.d., 1880?); PAS VI/2.
51. PAS VI/5.
52. C. Darwin, *Variation of Animals and Plants under Domestication*, vol. II, 1868.
53. Anthropometric test of SW by Francis Galton, 13 September 1884.
54. *The Star*, 1889?; newspaper cutting PAS VI/95/xiv.
55. Bertrand Russell's recollection, in an interview with the author, January 1967.
56. E. Brooke, *Transition*, 1895, pp. 100 et seq. (Miss Brooke was secretary to the Hampstead Historic Club and was a member of Argosy, which Sidney joined in November 1882. Sidney appears as Philip Sherridan.)
57. Lady Simon of Wythenshaw's recollection in an interview with the author in 1966.
58. G.B. Shaw, *Sixteen Self-Sketches*, 1949, p. 65.
59. Ibid.
60. GBS to SW, 23 March 1946.
61. GBS to SW, 31 January 1934, cited by BW, D, 1 February 1934.

62. St John Ervine, *Bernard Shaw*, 1956, pp. 68–9.
63. S. Webb, 'The Works of George Eliot' (n.d., 1881?); PAS VI/6.
64. Wallas, Note.
65. Ibid.
66. Sir J. Stamp and others, Graham Wallas, 1858–1932: Memorial Address 1932. Contribution by Lord Passfield, pp. 9–10.
67. SW to GW, 29 January 1886.
68. SW to GW, 24 December 1885.
69. Ibid.
70. H. Sidgwick, 'The Theory of Classical Education', in F.W. Farrer (ed.), *Essays on a Liberal Education*, 1868, pp. 81 et seq.
71. *The Debater*, 11 October, 10 November and 22 December 1883; and 8 March and 26 April 1884.
72. Ibid., 2 February 1884.
73. SW to GBS, 11 August 1883; Shaw Coll. BM Add MSS.
74. SW to GBS, 4 November (1884? 1883); Shaw Coll. BM Add MSS. 1884 according to BM but almost certainly 1883 since SW refers in this letter to being off tonight to explain to his confiding students why feudalism collapsed. SW lectured on the 'Rise and Fall of Feudalism' (VI/10), and on the following Sunday on the 'Growth of Industrialism' (VI/11). Between 1883 and 1887, 4 November fell on a Sunday only in 1883.
75. SW to GBS, 5 August 1885; Shaw Coll. BM Add MSS.
76. SW to GW, 17 August 1885.
77. S. Webb, 'Rent, Interest & Wages: Being a Criticism of Karl Marx and a Statement of Economic Theory', 1886; PAS VII/4.
78. S. Webb, 'The Economic Function of the Middle Class', lecture to the Argosy Society, 6 February 1885; PAS VI/20. First given to the London Dialectical Society, 2 April 1884, and published in the *Church Reformer*, 16 June 1884, with slight variations in form.
79. [1885?]; PAS VI/25.
80. Webb, 'Rent, Interest & Wages: Being...'.
81. Leaflet, Working Men's College, '8 lectures on Economic History of England'; PAS VI/16. (PAS VI/17 appears to be notes for the last part of this course.)
82. Working Men's College, 1883–4 (leaflet advertising SW on Political Economy). Recommended books; PAS VI/8.
83. Webb, 'Rent, Interest & Wages: Being...'.
84. Marx's account of the managerial expropriation of this old function of the capitalist did not appear until the third volume of *Capital* was published. Accordingly Webb could not have been familiar with it in 1886.
85. Ibid.
86. Webb, 'The Economic Function...'.
87. Ibid.
88. Ibid.
89. Ibid.
90. Ibid.
91. Ibid.
92. Ibid.
93. 20 March 1885; PAS VI/19.
94. S. Webb, 'Rome: a Sociological Sermon', *Our Corner*, vol. XII, 1888, pp. 53–60 and 79–89.
95. E.S. Beesly, *Catiline, Clodius and Tiberius*, 1878.

2 The Prevailing Fabian 1885–90

1. E.R. Pease, *History of the Fabian Society*, 2nd edn, 1925, pp. 46 and 52.
2. R.C.K. Ensor, *England, 1870–1914*, Oxford, 1936, p. 99.
3. G.D.H. Cole, *British Working Class Politics 1832–1914*, 1941, p. 80.
4. G.B. Shaw, 'What's in a Name? How an Anarchist Might Put It', *The Anarchist*, March 1885.
5. *The Anarchist*, July 1885.
6. 'Propagandist Fund', ibid., March 1885.
7. SW to GW, 30 November 1885 (they do not appear to have been published).
8. S. Webb, 'Considerations on Anarchism', 1885?; PAS VI/18.
9. S. Webb, 'What Socialism Is', *Practical Socialist*, June 1886, p. 116.
10. SW to GBS, 5 August 1885 (GBS/BM).
11. SW to GW, 28 May 1885.
12. A.S. Hardy, *But Yet A Woman*, Boston, 1883.
13. J.P. Smith, *The Unrepentant Pilgrim*, 1966, pp. 170–1.
14. SW to GW, 21 June 1885.
15. Ibid., 8 June 1885.
16. Ibid., 2 July 1885.
17. SW to S. Olivier, 7 July 1885.
18. E. Bellamy, *Dr Heidenhoff's Process*, New York, 1880.
19. SW to GW, 2 July 1885.
20. Ibid., 26 July 1885.
21. Ibid., 17 August 1885.
22. Ibid., 30 November 1885.
23. Ibid., 29 January 1886.
24. G.B. Shaw, *A Manifesto*, Fabian Society Tract No.2, 1884.
25. For an account of the success of the socialists and Radicals in asserting the right to free speech in Dod Street, Limehouse, see for example: G. Elton, *England Arise*, 1931, pp. 119 et seq.
26. Pease, *History*, pp. 49–52.
27. Ibid., p. 52.
28. SW to GW, 30 November 1885.
29. G.D.H. Cole, *History of Socialist Thought*, vol. II, 1954, *passim*.
30. Report of the Proceedings of the Three Day Conference, June 1886 (MSS, LSE). Also *Practical Socialist*, July 1886.
31. PAS VI/28.
32. S. Webb, 'Economics of a Positivist Community', *Practical Socialist*, February 1886. Abstract of the paper together with the discussion and Podmore's criticisms.
33. Pease, *History*, pp. 57 et seq.
34. SW to GW, 7 August 1886.
35. SW to S. Olivier, 7 July 1885.
36. E.P. Thompson, *William Morris*, 1955, chapter 6.
37. G.B. Shaw, *The Fabian Society: Its Early History*, Fabian Tract No. 41 (originally published in 1892 and under this title in 1909), Fabian Society, 1984 (published as Tract 493 in a facsimile edition of the 1909 reprint).
38. SW to GW, 7 August 1886.
39. *Practical Socialist*, February to June 1887.
40. C. Tsuzuki, *H.M. Hyndman and British Socialism*, Oxford, 1961, p. 55.
41. *Practical Socialist*, vol. II, no. 14, February 1887.

42. *Our Corner*, June 1887.
43. 22 November 1887; in D.H. Laurence (ed.), *Bernard Shaw: Collected Letters 1874–97*, 1965, p. 177.
44. Cited in Thompson, *William Morris*, p. 585.
45. *The Times*, 16 August 1887.
46. SW to GW, 17 August 1887.
47. *Our Corner*, July, August and September 1887.
48. See 'Income Tax Rates and Yields 1798–1939', in B.R. Mitchell and P. Deane, *Abstract of British Historical Statistics*, Cambridge, 1962, pp. 427–9.
49. Notes for lectures to Working Men's College, 1884–85; PAS VI/17.
50. PAS VI/33.
51. Argosy: Annual Report of the Society, July 1883.
52. SW to Mr Meade, 18–21 April 1888, with notes by his superiors in the Colonial Office.
53. GW to SW (n.d. but 'probably written in May 1888' according to a note in Wallas's hand) and with replies added or attached by SW, S. Olivier and GBS; Wallas Coll, LSE, Box 10.
54. See the review of *Fabian Essays* by William Morris, *Commonweal*, 25 January 1890.
55. These words were taken directly from his *Rome: A Sociological Sermon*, to which reference has already been made above. Webb frequently cribbed from his own work.
56. G.B. Shaw (ed.), *Fabian Essays in Socialism*, 1889. The 6th edition appeared with an Introduction by Asa Briggs in 1962.
57. Russell's recollection, given to the author in January 1967.
58. SW to Herbert Samuel, 20 March 1902; Samuel Collection A/15, House of Lords Record Office.
59. J. Hamburger, *Intellectuals in Politics: John Stuart Mill and the Philosophic Radicals*, Yale, 1965; and R.J. Harrison, 'Intellectuals in Nineteenth Century Politics', *Government and Opposition*, vol. 1, no. 4, 1966, pp. 563–7.
60. S. Webb, 'The Historic Basis of Socialism', in Shaw (ed.), *Fabian Essays*, p. 45.
61. A. Comte, *A General View of Positivism*, 1848, translated by J.H. Bridges, 1865, p. 136.
62. E.J. Hobsbawm, 'The Fabians Reconsidered', in *Labouring Men*, 1964, pp. 250–71.
63. G. Wallas, *Francis Place*, 1898, p. 65.
64. J. Hamburger, *James Mill and the Art of Revolution*, Yale, 1963.
65. S.E. Finer, *Sir Edwin Chadwick*, 1952, p. 14.
66. R.J. Harrison, 'E.S. Beesly and Karl Marx', *International Review of Social History*, vol. IV, parts 1 and 2, 1959, pp. 22–58; 208–38.
67. See pp. 62–3.
68. GW to E.R. Pease, 4 February 1916; Wallas Coll.
69. This is a proposition which has the form of a large empirical generalisation, but which functions as a category through which evidence is collected and organised, rather than as a proposition to be tested by the evidence itself.
70. Ibid., 8 June 1885.
71. K. Marx and F. Engels, *The Communist Manifesto*, 1848.
72. K. Marx, *Inaugural Address to the International Working Men's Association*, 1864.
73. H. Collins and C. Abramsky, *Karl Marx and the British Labour Movement*, 1965, p. 118.
74. See Chapter 4: 'The Formation of the Partnership'.

75. F. Engels to V. Sorge, 18 January 1893; *Karl Marx and Frederick Engels on Britain*, Moscow, 1962, p. 576.

76. E.R. Pease, 'Recollections for My Sons', unpublished MS begun 10 March 1930; Pease Coll., Nuffield College.

77. *Quarterly Journal of Economics*, April 1887 and *QJE* 11, 1888, cited in A.M. McBriar, *Fabian Socialism and English Politics 1884–1918*, Cambridge, 1962, p. 40.

78. SW to GW, c/o Kennedy, Todd & Co, 63 William Street, New York, 13 October 1888.

79. SW to GW, 17 September 1888.

80. E.R. Pease, 'Recollections …'

81. F. Harrison, *Autobiographic Memoirs*, I, 1911, p. 255.

82. Membership List, 1891; Fabian Archives, Nuffield College, Oxford.

83. Sunday Lecture Society, *Proceedings 1869–90*, 1890. SW lectured on 'The Progress of Socialism: Its Effect on Social Welfare' on 22 January 1888.

84. See, for example, the Sunday Lectures advertised in *Reynolds* between 8 January and 3 June 1888. (Thus on 8 January 1888 SW spoke to the Socialist League at Kelmscott House on 'The Irish National Movement and Its Bearing on Socialism', and on 3 June 1888 to the Chelsea Branch of the Social Democratic Federation on 'Socialism on the School Board'.)

85. Lecture course begun at City of London College, 14 January 1889; PAS VI/37.

86. PAS VI/37, begun on 14 October 1889.

87. *Star*, about October 1889.

88. PAS 95/XIV.

89. SW to Sir H.B. Brown, 5 August 1888.

90. E.R. Pease, *History*, p. 59.

91. *Practical Socialist*, February 1886.

92. SW to Jane Burdon Sanderson (photocopy), National Library of Scotland.

93. *Star* [?], n.d., 1889; PAS VI/95/xiv.

94. *Daily News*, 5 September 1888 (correspondence between SW as secretary of Holborn Liberal and Radical Association and Mr Gladstone).

95. Letters of J.L. Mahon to F. Engels concerning the Central Democratic Club, 17 April 1889 and 22 May 1889, in Thompson, *William Morris*, pp. 872–4.

96. *Star* [?], June 1889; PAS VI/xi.

97. Pease Coll., LSE.

98. Everyone else found Pease remarkably stiff and difficult to approach!

99. L. Woolf, 'Political Thought and the Webbs', in M. Cole (ed.), *The Webbs and Their Work*, 1949, pp. 251–64.

100. *Star*, 7 May 1889 ('The Great Eastern Question: Mr Charles Booth's Terrible Numbering of the People').

101. Sometimes surprise is expressed that Webb, Olivier and other civil servants were able to engage so often and so actively in politics. It must be remembered that to begin with the Fabian Society, before the publication of *Fabian Essays* in 1889, was not regarded as a serious political organisation or much of a party until it affiliated to the Labour Party in 1900. That professional civil servants would join working men's clubs was hardly considered possible. The local parliaments at Charing Cross or Lambeth were not worth worrying about. Curtailment of the party political life of civil servants occurred more usually after 1900. Sydney Olivier after 1900, rather than Sidney Webb before, ran into serious difficulties. See A. Lawrence Lowell, *The Government of England*, vol. 1, 1908.

3 The Making of a Gilded Spinster 1858–85

1. See below, p. 178.
2. G. Meinertzhagen, *From Ploughshare to Parliament: A Short Memoir of the Potters of Tadcaster*, 1908, p. 266.
3. Ibid., p. 264.
4. S.A. Tooley, 'The Growth of a Socialist: An Interview with Mrs Sidney Webb', *The Young Woman*, February 1895. ('I am afraid I was a revolting daughter', laughed Mrs Webb, 'for both my father and mother were Conservative and Church people, having left Liberalism over the proposed extension of town suffrage in 1867.')
5. B. Webb, *MA*, p. 49.
6. Ibid., p. 72.
7. Ibid., pp. 175–6.
8. D, 15 October 1882.
9. B. Webb, *MA*, p. 146.
10. D, 22 January 1881.
11. D, 20 September 1882.
12. D, 24 July 1882.
13. D, 12 March 1887.
14. D, 30 September 1889.
15. Ibid.
16. Ibid.
17. 'The Glorified Spinster', *Macmillan's Magazine*, vol. VIII, 1888, pp. 371–6; M. Harkness's letters to Beatrice, 1878–90; E. Pycroft's letters to Beatrice, 1885–90.
18. C.S. Hadland, *Occupations of Women Other than Teaching*, paper read to the Oxford Conference of the Head Mistresses' Association, 1886, pp. 14.
19. E. Pycroft to BP, 6 July 1886.
20. M. Harkness to BP, n.d. [1878?].
21. E. Pycroft to BP, 21 September 1888.
22. Harkness, op. cit.
23. Ibid.
24. D, 13 November 1889 (Maggie claimed to have paid Keir Hardie's election expenses, acting as a go-between for the 'underground Labour party' of Champion, Burns and Mann. She insisted that she was indifferent to their cause and only wanted to observe for the purposes of research. One day she would bring it all out in a book. Beatrice did not approve of this kind of participant observation. The rising social investigator looked at the aspirant political reporter with 'blank amazement, in face of such utter deficiency of honour'. She put it all down to the requirements of the struggle, or rather the habits of mind that the struggle had occasioned).
25. E. Pycroft to BP, 14 August and 12 September 1886.
26. J.E. Carpenter, *Life of Mary Carpenter*, 1879, for a leading example before the rise of the Glorified Spinster.
27. D, 1 November 1887.
28. D, 6 May 1887. (This was the custom with some London dockers. The haddock was first dried in the chimney.)
29. See below, pp. 113, 155–6.
30. D, 8 March 1885 and 8 November 1886 ('The bright side of East End Life is the sociability and generous sharing of small means … ').

31. D, 22 February 1888.
32. D, 24 May 1883.
33. D, 27 November 1887.
34. D, 8 June 1933.
35. As already noted, Bertrand Russell affirmed that Webb had a cockney accent. However he considered that 'almost all Englishmen had cockney accents' – an opinion which rather diminishes the value of his testimony; but, see below, p. 179, for stronger evidence.
36. The young Beatrice found the Germans: 'dirty, slovenly looking creatures. So underbred and rowdy looking'; D, 15 June 1877. She was not favourably impressed by the Magyars; D, 5 October 1877. The French were ingratiating but she found something 'curiously agreeable' in the ugliness of the Dutch; D, 27 June 1882. At least they did not make her 'shudder' as the proximity of 'John Chinaman' had done when she visited San Francisco; D, 7 November 1873. She never admired any of the Chinese before Mao Tse-Tung. However she always had admiration and affection for Jewish genius and vitality; D, 19 September and 1 November 1875, 12 October 1878.
37. B. Webb, *MA*, p. 60.
38. 'I am simply ridiculously stupid with arithmetic – a sort of paralysis taking place in my brain when I look at numbers'; D, 13 August 1882.
39. Lawrencina Potter's Diary cited by B. Webb, *MA*, p. 11.
40. D, September 1875.
41. D, 15 June 1887.
42. For example: D, September 1874 or D, 14 September 1882.
43. D, 22 June 1881.
44. D, 27 August 1882.
45. D, 14 September 1882.
46. D, 1877.
47. D, 14 May 1881.
48. Apart from Spencer's own works, see J.D.Y. Peel, *Herbert Spencer: The Evolution of a Sociologist*, 1971, and the useful volume of extracts from S. Andrewski (ed.), *Herbert Spencer: Structure, Function and Evolution*, 1971.
49. H. Spencer, *Social Statics*, cited in Andrewski, *Herbert Spencer*, p. 218.
50. Ibid., p. 217.
51. Ibid., p. 219.
52. Ibid., p. 233.
53. H. Spencer, *First Principles*, 1863, section 57.
54. T.P. Kirkman, *Philosophy Without Assumptions*, 1876, p. 292.
55. H. Spencer, *Social Statics*, cited in Andrewski, *Herbert Spencer*, p. 250.
56. B. Webb, *MA*, p. 25.
57. Ibid., p. 26.
58. Ibid., p. 26.
59. Ibid., p. 38.
60. Ibid., p. 29.
61. Lawrencina Potter's Diary, January 1865. Beatrice's references to her relationship with her little brother are distinguished by being both perceptive and austere. *MA*, p. 11. The earliest of Beatrice's known letters (reproduced on the accompanying page) assures her mother that 'I love little Dicky very, very much'. The last of the three brief references to him in *My Apprenticeship* is interestingly indirect: Beatrice's earliest memory was of being hurled out naked into a corridor by his nurse; *MA*, p. 58.
62. D, 27 December 1883.

63. D, Autumn 1872.
64. D, 27 March 1875.
65. D, 16 March 1876.
66. D, Autumn 1877.
67. D, 14 September 1880.
68. D, 23 February or 6 May 1882.
69. D, 14 September 1882.
70. D, 2 July 1882.
71. Ibid.
72. D, 5 May 1883.
73. D, 8 December 1903.
74. H. Spencer, *The Man Versus the State*, 1884.
75. G. Lichtheim, *A Short History of Socialism*, 1970, pp. 173–4.
76. Beatrice recalled that it was Frederic Harrison, the leading English Comtist, who first 'explained to me the economic validity of trade unionism and factory legislation.' *MA*, 1926, p. 145. Unfortunately she does not state when he first offered this explanation (which might have been at any time from the late seventies onwards), nor when she first found it persuasive. She saw a lot of Harrison in 1886: D, 28 May 1886; but while she would have been more receptive to his arguments at this time than in earlier years she was certainly not swiftly converted by them.
77. 'Probably no one – not even Dr Marx himself (his works being inaccessible in English) has done so much to promote the spread of socialistic ideas as Mr Spencer…'. F. Fairman, *Herbert Spencer on Socialism*, 1884, p. 16. Among other socialist writings that found contradictions in Spencer and which attempted to show that 'logically' he was making for socialism, see H.M. Hyndman, *Socialism and Slavery*, 1884; E. Ferri, *Socialismo e Scienza Positiva*, Rome, 1894; G. Lacy, *Liberty and Law: An Attempt at the Refutation of the Individualism of Mr Herbert Spencer*, 1888.
78. B. Webb, *MA*, p. 38.
79. B. Potter, *The Co-operative Movement in Great Britain*, 1891. The central theme was the contrast between the intentions and purposes of the co-operators and the functional adaptation of the movement independently of these intentions to the work of retail distribution.
80. T.H. Huxley, 'Administrative Nihilism', *Fortnightly Review*, vol. X (n.s.), 1871.
81. Both Spencer and his critics tended to forget that argument from analogy is never conclusive. Mrs Sarah Howard has drawn attention to a distinction made by Spencer but forgotten by the socialists and subsequent commentators, between inner and outer regulatory systems in the higher animals and higher societies. The inner regulatory system was concerned with sustenance and requires no centralised reponse: the outer regulatory system is concerned with the environment and aggression. Spencer thought that this distinction supported the division of societies into lower 'militant' and 'higher' industrial types.
82. Compare H. Spencer, *The Man Versus the State*, 1969, p. 107, with S. Webb in G.B. Shaw (ed.), *Fabian Essays*, 1908, pp. 147–8.
83. B. Webb, *MA*, 1826, p. 23.
84. D, 14 and 22 February 1883.
85. D, 23 April 1883, 2 May 1883.
86. D, 1 February 1883.
87. D, 31 March 1883.

88. D, 22 February 1883.
89. D, 1 March and 11 March 1883.
90. D, 31 March 1883.
91. Ibid.
92. D, 15 May 1883.
93. D, 20 March 1883.
94. D, 24 March 1883.
95. D, 30 April 1883.
96. C.L. Mowat, *The Charity Organisation Society, 1869–1913*, 1961.
97. D, 20 May 1883.
98. D, 18 May 1883.
99. E. Pycroft to BP, 15 July 1886. (They first met in January 1885 (D, 16 January 1885.) It is not certain – merely probable – that Pavey was the man in question; nor is it possible to discover exactly how Beatrice contributed to his death.)
100. D, 10 September 1883.
101. C.L. Mowat, *The Charity Organisation Society*, p. 117.
102. S.A. Barnett, 'Practicable Socialism', *Nineteenth Century*, vol. XIII, April 1883, p. 554–60.
103. D, 3 June and 27 June 1883.
104. D, 18 July 1883.
105. J.L. Garvin, *Life of Joseph Chamberlain, I*, 1932, p. 385.
106. Ibid., chapter XVIII.
107. Ibid., p. 392.
108. Ibid., p. 393.
109. T. Maguire, 'Chamberlain and Socialism', *Progress*, vol. V, July 1885, pp. 316–20.
110. D, 27 July 1883.
111. D, 17 September 1883.
112. D, 26 September 1883.
113. Ibid.
114. This also seems to relate to 26 September 1883.
115. B. Webb, *MA*, 1926, pp. 152–4; D, 31 October 1886.
116. Ibid., pp. 154–62.
117. [A. Mearns], *The Bitter Cry of Outcast London*, 1883. Its publication is generally accepted as crucial to the 'rediscovery' of poverty in the 1880s. The original attribution to Mearns has been challenged in recent years: see the more recent attribution to William C. Preston in the Leicester University Press, Victorian Library edition, 1970, edited and introduced by Anthony S. Wohl.
118. D, 31 December 1883.
119. D, 27 December 1883.
120. D, 12 January 1884.
121. Ibid.
122. D, 16 March 1884.
123. Ibid.
124. D, 22 April 1884.
125. Ibid.
126. See the terms of his tribute to his second wife; Garvin, *Life of Joseph Chamberlain*, p. 207.
127. D, 9 May 1884.
128. Ibid.

129. D, 15 October 1884.
130. D, 16 January 1885.
131. D, 14 February 1885.
132. D, 12 May 1886 (retrospective entry).
133. L. Courtney to BP, 28 July 1885.
134. K. Courtney to BP, 23 July 1885.
135. J.L. Garvin, *Life of Joseph Chamberlain*, p. 549.
136. Ibid., p. 551.
137. Ibid., p. 564.
138. *Punch*, 14 February 1885.
139. D, 7 August 1885.
140. D, 'Sunday' 1885 (between 29 January and 14 February 1885).
141. D, 6 March 1886 (retrospective entry).
142. Ibid.
143. This contention about heavy rural immigration is not supported by modern social historians; see G. Stedman Jones, *Outcast London*, Oxford, 1971, p. 148.
144. B. Potter, 'A Lady's View of the Unemployed at the East', *Pall Mall Gazette*, 18 February 1886, p. 11.
145. J. Chamberlain to BP, 28 February 1886.
146. For the initial letter of uncertain date, but attributed by Peter Fraser (*Joseph Chamberlain: Radicalism and Empire, 1886–1914*, Cassell, 1996, p. 123), probably correctly, to 4 March 1886, see JC 5/59/1, Chamberlain Papers Birmingham University Library. For the subsequent letter, which Chamberlain apparently did indeed destroy, see D, 6 March 1886.
147. D, 19 December 1885.
148. Beatrice Potter, Last Will and Testament, 1 January [1886?]. (She bequeathed all her cash to Leonard Courtney 'towards the achievement of his political causes'. She 'earnestly begged' that her diary be destroyed. 'I should prefer that no one should have looked at them. If death comes it will be welcome for life has always been distasteful to me... (PAS).')
149. J. Chamberlain to BP, 5 March 1886.
150. Local Government Board Circular, 15 March 1886, cited in S and B. Webb, *English Poor Law History*, II, 1929, pp. 646–7.
151. J. Harris, *Unemployment and Politics*, Oxford, 1972, p. 76, argues that the Webbs and other students have exaggerated the importance of this circular. Yet despite the fact that some local authorities had anticipated the circular and despite the fact that Chamberlain sought to strengthen rather than to supersede the Poor Law, the problem of the unemployed did appear in a new light by central authority.
152. D, 12 April 1886.
153. D, 4 April 1886.
154. Ibid.
155. BP to Anna Swanwick, n.d. (July?) 1884 reprinted in *MA*, pp. 191–3. She begins by declaring herself agnostic on all questions 'divine and human'. Goes on to question democratic theory and enthusiasm and the wisdom and capacity of the masses and their leaders. But then she questions Spencer's 'materialism': that is, his alleged attempt to reduce the higher to the lower sciences and makes cogent criticisms of his organic analogy. She rejects Spencer's misuse of theory, but she supports his resistance to programmes for state intervention. If she 'were a man, and had an intellect' she would be a sociologist and independent of both Spencer and Chamberlain.
156. D, 1 January 1886.

157. D, 15 September 1885.
158. D, 8 November 1886 (partly retrospective).
159. D, 15 September 1885.
160. D, 8 November 1886.
161. Ibid.
162. E. Pycroft to BP, 9 February 1886.
163. Beatrice to her father, n.d. [August 1885].
164. E. Pycroft to BP, 19 February 1886.
165. Ibid.
166. E. Pycroft to BP, 26 February 1886. (Edward Bond, a fellow of Queen's and a Director of the East End Dwellings Co that owned the Buildings, became Conservative MP for East Nottingham 1895 to 1906.)
167. When the Whitechapel Mansion House Relief Committee offered street sweeping at 2/- per day to 130 men, only 13 accepted and half of them threw down their brooms and left. The less skilled men in the Buildings wanted such work, but skilled furniture workers considered they would never get work in their trade again if they accepted it. E. Pycroft to BP, 4 March 1886.
168. Joseph Aarons to BP, n.d.
169. E. Pycroft to BP, 4 March 1886.
170. D, 8 November 1886.
171. E. Pycroft to BP, 6 July 1886.
172. E. Pycroft to BP, 15 July 1886.
173. E. Pycroft to BP, 14 August 1886.
174. E. Pycroft to BP, 4 September 1886.
175. E. Pycroft to BP, 15 July 1886.
176. E. Pycroft to BP, 21 August 1886.
177. Ibid.
178. E. Pycroft to BP, 4 September 1886.
179. E. Pycroft to BP, 26 February 1886.
180. E. Pycroft to BP, 12 September 1886.
181. D, 12 May 1886.
182. S. Barnett to BP, 26 February 1886.
183. T.S. and M.B. Simey, *Charles Booth: Social Scientist*, Oxford, 1960; B. Norman-Butler, *Victorian Aspirations: The Life and Labour of Charles and Mary Booth*, 1972; E. Yeo, 'Social Science and Social Change', unpublished DPhil thesis, University of Sussex, 1972.
184. D, 28 May 1886.
185. B. Webb, *MA*, p. 247.
186. D, 29 August 1887.
187. T.S. and M.B. Simey, *Charles Booth*, p. 248, draw attention to this difference. They remark that if Booth had had the gift for imaginative hypotheses, which Beatrice wanted, 'objectivity might have been sacrificed to theorising.' The risk is undeniable. However, the question is whether sociology would have been advanced or retarded by running it.
188. D, 2 July 1886.
189. D, 18 July 1886.
190. B. Potter, 'The Rise and Growth of English Economics', 1886, unpublished.
191. H. Spencer to BP, 2 October 1886.
192. D, 4 October 1886.
193. B. Webb, *MA*, p. 445. This improves the language of her unpublished 'The Economic Theory of Karl Marx' without disturbing its sense.

194. B. Webb, *MA,* pp. 43–5.
195. However, there is a suggestion that it was Booth who borrowed from Beatrice; M. Paul to BP, 15 September 1886: 'You had better be quick with your idea or Booth will forestall you … I was chuckling as I came home in the train last night when I was talking to him about the labour-market and heard him using almost the same ideas as yours though not in quite the same learned phraseology about "faculties" and "desires". I know you don't mind me making fun of you – it is all good humoured.'
196. C. Booth to BP, 21 September 1886; D, 20 March 1887.
197. D, 31 October 1886.
198. D, 8 November 1886.
199. D, 13 April 1887.
200. B. Potter, 'The Dock Life of East London', *Nineteenth Century,* vol. XXII, October 1887, pp. 496–7.
201. D, 6 May 1887.
202. D, 24 March 1887.
203. D, 6 May 1887.
204. D, 24 March and 13 April 1887.
205. D, 10 December 1886.
206. J. Chamberlain to BP, 19 May 1887.
207. D, 8 August 1887.
208. D, 9 June 1887.
209. D, 8 August 1887.
210. J. Chamberlain to BP, 1[?] August 1887.
211. D, 8 May 1890 (inserted at the end of vol. 14).
212. D, 26 April 1888.
213. D, 18 September 1889.
214. See above pp. 28–9.
215. D, 4 June 1889. Also Beatrice's note on an undated letter to her from Edgeworth.
216. D, 8 August 1887.
217. D, 11 February 1889.
218. M. Booth to BP, 20 June 1889.
219. D, 7 March 1889.

4   From Social Investigator to Socialist 1885–90

1. B. Webb, MA, pp. 391–3.
2. P.G. Hall, *The Industries of London Since 1861,* 1962, p. 55.
3. B. Potter, 'The Dock Life of East London', *Nineteenth Century,* vol. XXII, October 1887, pp. 494.
4. Ibid., p. 496.
5. Ibid., p. 498. Leonard Courtney was greatly distressed by the reference to the consumer as spoilt child. See his letter to Beatrice, 14 August 1887.
6. D, 27 November 1887.
7. B. Potter, 'The Dock Life of East London', p. 499.
8. Ibid., p. 487.
9. M. Booth to BP, n.d. [1887], for Charlie's delight in East End food and the way the life relaxed him after his business concerns.
10. J. Lovell, *Stevedores and Dockers,* 1969, p. 36.

11. B. Potter, 'The Sweating System', *Charity Organisation Review*, no. 37, January 1888, p. 15.
12. D, 18 October 1887. Burnett seemed 'hard-headed', humourless, good mannered and dignified. He was impressed by the progress of socialism and sympathetic to it, while dismissing the socialists as 'loungers'.
13. B. Potter, 'The Sweating System', referring to a report by Burnett.
14. D, 11 April 1888.
15. B. Potter, 'Pages from a Work Girl's Diary', *Nineteenth Century*, vol. XXIV, September 1888, pp. 301–14. Reprinted as 'The Diary of an Investigator', in S. and B. Webb, *Problems of Modern Industry*, 1898, pp. 1–2.
16. D, 11 April 1888.
17. S. and B. Webb, *Problems*, p. 19.
18. First report from the Select Committee of the House of Lords on the Sweating System, 30 July 1888. Beatrice's evidence, 11 May 1888: questions 3246–3415, pp. 319–33.
19. Ibid., questions 3348–9.
20. Ibid., question 3292.
21. Ibid., questions 3390–2.
22. Ibid., questions 3303–4.
23. Ibid., question 3339.
24. D, 12, 16 and 25 May 1888.
25. D, 27 August 1888.
26. First report from the Select Committee, questions 3411–13.
27. B. Webb, MA, p. 324.
28. B. Potter's draft letter of the summer of 1888 to editors; included in a section of the Passfield Papers and entitled, 'B. Potter to Friends 1884–1892'.
29. H. Spencer to BP, 21 November 1887.
30. 'The Peers and the Sweaters: A Day in the House of Lords', [unsigned] *Pall Mall Gazette*, 12 May 1888, pp. 2–3.
31. Lord Thring to BP, 8 June 1888.
32. D, 21 August 1888.
33. B. Potter, 'East London Labour', *Nineteenth Century*, vol. XXIV, August 1888, p. 176.
34. Ibid., p. 181.
35. Ibid., p. 183.
36. D, 11 February 1889.
37. A. White, 'The Invasion of Pauper Foreigners', *Nineteenth Century*, vol. XXIII, March 1888, pp. 414–22.
38. B. Potter, 'The Jewish Community', in C. Booth (ed.), *Life and Labour*, 1889.
39. Ibid., p. 574.
40. B. Potter, 'East London Labour', p. 176.
41. B. Potter, 'The Jewish Community', p. 598.
42. K. Marx, 'On the Jewish Question', in *Karl Marx, 1818–1883. Early Writings*, translated and edited by T.B. Bottomore, 1963, pp. 1–40. This is the most accessible source for Marx's review of Bruno Bauer, *'Die Judenfrage'* (1843) which was published in the *Deutsch-Französische Jahrbücher* (1844).
43. B. Potter, 'The Jewish Community', p. 590.
44. *Life and Labour*, p. 590.
45. J. Brown, 'Charles Booth and Labour Colonies', *Economic History Review*, 2nd ser., vol. XXI, no. 2, 1968, pp. 349–61.

46. D, 15 March 1887.
47. B. Potter, 'The Lords and the Sweating System', *Nineteenth Century*, vol. XXVII, June 1890, pp. 885–905.
48. D, 8 March 1889.
49. D, 15 March 1889.
50. D, 30 October 1889. H. Collins was an executor of Spencer's.
51. D, 29 August 1889.
52. Ibid.
53. D, 1 September 1889.
54. D, 28 May 1886.
55. 'An Appeal Against Female Suffrage', *Nineteenth Century*, vol. XXV, June 1889, pp. 781–8. Mrs Broadhurst signed this 'appeal' along with Beatrice, Mrs Huxley, Mrs Humphrey Ward, Mrs Lynn Linton, Mrs Beesly, Mrs Bagehot, Mrs Asquith, Mrs Matthew Arnold and many others.
56. D, 'Tuesday' [first week September 1889].
57. Ibid.
58. D, 18 September 1889.
59. D, 11 February 1889.
60. D, 13 March 1889.
61. D, 19 November 1889.
62. D, 22 September 1889. (However, her contribution was to be confined to working out the plot and providing the characters while he supplied the reformed world on individualist lines.)
63. B. Potter to J.C. Grey [November 1889?].
64. D, 1 February 1890.
65. Ibid.
66. Author's interview with Bertrand Russell, 19 January 1967.
67. For example, Dame Margaret Cole.
68. R.D. Laing, *The Divided Self*, 1960.
69. B. Webb, MA, pp. XIII–XIV.
70. Ibid., p. 279. In the discussion of her 'dead point' she hints at the deeper levels of her 'divided personality'.
71. Ibid., pp. 11 et seq.
72. D, 10 December 1886.
73. D, 14 September 1880.
74. See the Appendix to this chapter.
75. B. Webb, MA, p. 43.
76. D, 17 November 1889.
77. M. Harkness to BP, 24 August 1879. 'I wonder very much if you will ever fall in love with anyone. I suppose you will live above the herd and never do anything so vulgar. I do not mean fall foolishly in love, so as to injure your prospects in life, but I wonder if you will care for any man more than you do for yourself. Anyway, if I live long enough, I shall have the satisfaction of seeing you in love ten years after marriage. I fancy that it will be a mild and amiable passion.' D, 11 February 1889, for Beatrice's expression of continued love for this false friend.
78. B. Webb, *MA*, 1926, pp. XIV, 2.
79. Ibid., 'Why I became a Socialist', pp. 346–415.
80. *MA*, p. 392.
81. D, 1 February 1890.
82. Ibid., 20 August 1886.
83. R. Harrison, 'Bertrand Russell and the Webbs', *Russell*, n.s., vol. 5, no. 1, summer 1985, pp. 44–9.

5 The Formation of the Partnership 1890–2

1. J. Bowle, *Politics and Opinion in the Nineteenth Century*, 1954, p. 227.
2. B. Potter, *The Co-operative Movement in Great Britain*, 10th impression with a new preface, 1930, pp. 149 et seq.
3. SW to BP, 12 December 1891.
4. L. Woolf, *Sowing 1880–1904*, 1960, p. 68: 'Sidney's façade was no façade at all'; p. 71: 'I have never known anyone who had no carapace or façade at all, but I have known people who had extraordinarily little, who seemed wonderfully direct, simple, spiritually unveiled.'
5. BP to SW, 22 June 1890.
6. BP to SW, n.d. [22 August 1890?] (item 10).
7. SW to BP, 21 September 1890.
8. D, 14 August 1891.
9. D, 13 January 1891.
10. S. Webb, 'The Economic Limitations of Co-operation', *Co-operative News*, 12 January 1889.
11. Herbert, First Viscount Samuel: Notes on a Visit to Passfield, 22 August 1944 (Samuel Collection A/119/9).
12. SW to BP, 4 January 1892.
13. BP to SW, 3 January 1892.
14. D, 14 February 1890.
15. D, 26 April 1890.
16. SW to BP, 30 April 1890.
17. Ibid., 14 May 1890.
18. Ibid.
19. SW to BP, 30 April 1890.
20. SW to BP, 14 May 1890.
21. D, 'First Day Congress', 24 May 1890.
22. 'Fabian Society Lectures', *Co-operative News*, 27 September 1890. SW's letters appeared in the issues for 30 August and 4 October 1890, Holyoake's in the issue for 1 November, and Greening's in that for 22 November 1890.
23. D, 'The Glasgow Congress', 23 May 1890.
24. BP to SW, n.d. [28 May 1890?] (Item 3).
25. SW to BP, 30 May 1890.
26. BP to SW, 31 May 1890.
27. D, 31 May 1890.
28. D, 1 June 1890.
29. D, 27 July 1890.
30. SW to BP (day after his thirty-first birthday).
31. SW to BP, 16 June 1890.
32. SW to BP, 24 June 1890.
33. SW to BP, 19 June 1890.
34. SW to BP, 29 July 1890.
35. SW to BP, 2 August 1890.
36. BP to SW, n.d., [about 7 August] (Item 13).
37. SW to BP, 11 August 1890.
38. SW to BP, 26 August 1890.
39. Ibid.
40. Ibid.
41. SW to BP, n.d. [13 August 1890?].

42. BP to SW, 23 August 1890.
43. GBS to BP, 6 October 1890.
44. D, 7 September 1890.
45. Ibid.
46. SW to BP, 15 October 1890.
47. D, 22 October 1890.
48. D, 1 December 1890.
49. SW to BP, 12 October 1890.
50. SW to BP, 11 October 1890.
51. SW to BP, 30 November 1890.
52. SW to BP, ibid.
53. BP to SW, n.d. [2nd week December 1890?] (Item 29) and also [3rd week December 1890?] (Item 31).
54. SW to BP, letters of 4, 5 and 6 December 1890.
55. BP to SW, n.d. [end December 1890?] (Item 31).
56. SW to BP, 30 December 1890 (returning her letters); on Auguste and Clothilde, 14 December 1890.
57. SW to BP, 14 December 1890.
58. BP to SW, n.d. [2nd week December 1890?] (Item 29).
59. SW to BP, 27 January 1891.
60. Ibid.
61. BP to SW, 13 January 1891.
62. SW to BP, 19 January 1891.
63. BP to SW, 21 January 1891.
64. SW to BP, 22 January 1891.
65. SW to BP, 3 March 1891.
66. SW to BP, 14 March 1891.
67. SW to BP, 6 April 1891.
68. SW to BP, 14 March 1891.
69. D, 11 April 1891.
70. D, 21 April 1891.
71. D, 22 May 1891.
72. SW to BP, 30 May 1891.
73. SW to BP, 23 June 1892.
74. SW to BP, 25 May 1891.
75. D, 20 June 1891.
76. SW to BP, 3 November 1891.
77. BP to SW, about 21 August 1891 but n.d. (Item 43).
78. BP to SW, n.d. [mid-October 1891?] (Item 63).
79. SW to BP, 23 September 1891.
80. SW to BP, 'Wednesday' [23 October 1890?].
81. D, 13 January 1891.
82. BP to SW, 11 December 1891.
83. SW to BP, 9 December 1891.
84. BP to SW, n.d. [mid-November 1891?] (Item 79).
85. SW to BP, 20 November 1891.
86. SW to BP, 21 November 1891.
87. SW to BP, 31 December 1891.
88. BP to SW, 'Last day of Newcastle Congress', 12 September 1891?
89. D, 11 August 1891.
90. Ibid.
91. D, 17 December 1891.

92. BP to SW, n.d. [late October 1891?] (Item 67).
93. E. Pycroft to BP, 10 January 1892.
94. D, 4 May 1892.
95. SW to BP, 7 January 1892.
96. BP to SW, n.d. [29 May 1892?] (Item 34).
97. SW to BP, 3 May 1892.
98. D, 21 January 1892.
99. D, 15 July 1891.
100. D, 21 September 1892.
101. SW to BP, 24 March 1892.
102. SW to BP, 22 March 1892.
103. SW to BP, 21 May 1892.
104. SW to BP, 24 March 1892.
105. SW to BP, 6 March 1892.
106. B. Potter, *The Co-operative Movement in Great Britain*, 1930, pp. 225 et seq. (But SW gave her particular help with this chapter; see p. xxi.)
107. S. Webb, 'The Best Method of Bringing Co-operation within the Reach of the Poorest of the Population', Manchester, n.d. [1891?] A paper presented to the Lincoln Congress of 1891.
108. B. Potter, *The Co-operative Movement*, p. ix.
109. Sir James Stuart (1843–1913), Professor of Mechanics at Cambridge and Liberal MP for Hoxton 1885–1900; for Sunderland 1906–10.
110. SW to BP, 16 June 1890.
111. GBS to T. Wemyss Reid, 14 January 1890; in D.H. Laurence (ed.), *Bernard Shaw: Collected Letters 1874–97*, 1965, pp. 234–5.
112. SW to BP, 31 October 1891.
113. SW to BP, 13 September 1891.
114. SW to BP, 1 April 1892.
115. SW to BP, 15 September 1891.
116. D, 7 July 1891.
117. SW to BP, 9 December 1891.
118. GBS to Sydney Olivier, 16 December 1890; Wallas Coll., LSE.
119. SW to BP, 12 December 1891.
120. SW to BP, 9 October 1890.
121. SW to BP, 12 December 1891.
122. SW to BP, 16 June 1890.
123. SW to BP, 21 September 1890.
124. SW to BP, 16 November 1891.
125. SW to BP, 25 November 1891.
126. SW to BP, 12 December 1891.
127. S. Webb, 'John Burns', [*Political World*, 1889?] (Album of Press Cuttings 95/xiii).
128. S. Webb and H. Cox, *The Eight Hours Day*, 1891.
129. Ibid.
130. SW to BP, 7 September 1891.
131. SW to BP, 9 September 1891.
132. SW's notes of his speech enclosed with his letter to BP of 12 December 1891.
133. S. Webb, *Wanted, a Programme, An Appeal to the Liberal Party* for private circulation only (August 1888), p. 16.
134. S. Webb, *Socialism in England*, 1890, p. 131.
135. SW to BP, 17 September 1891.

136. SW to BP, 25 October 1891.
137. SW to BP, 'Wednesday' (23 October 1890?).
138. SW to BP, 23 September 1891.
139. SW to BP, n.d., May 1892? (end sheet only). See also GBS to Jim Connell
      8 June 1892 in Laurence (ed.), *Collected Letters*, p. 341. See also G. Wallas to
      Sir Charles Russell, 18 June? 1892 in which GW wants help in getting out of
      a very ugly business resulting from Hyndman's charge that the Fabians
      were going to the Home Office behind the backs of other socialists.
140. H.W. Hyndman to SW, 25 May (1890?).
141. SW to BP, 5 December 1891.
142. *Financial Reform Almanack*, Liverpool, 1892.
143. SW to 'my dear Fenton', 3 March 1891, asking if he might get adopted for
      West Islington. 'Of course, I should in that case stand by Lough and back
      him for Parliament.'
144. SW to BP, 16 November 1891.
145. W. Morris, *Commonweal*, V, no. 180, 22 June 1889, cited in A.E. Morgan,
      Edward Bellamy, New York, 1944, pp. 401 et seq.
146. S. Webb and H. Cox, *The Eight Hours Day*, 1891, p. 243.
147. S. Webb, *Socialism in England*, 1890, p. 7.
148. BP to SW, n.d., December 1891 (Item 89).
149. SW, Peace on Earth, 1891; PAS VI/52.
150. SW to BP, 6 February 1892.
151. SW to BP, 25 January 1892. (His election address was sent to BP with a letter
      on the back of it, 11 February 1892.)
152. S. Webb, *The London Programme*, 1891.
153. S. Webb, *The London Programme*, pp. 99 et seq.
154. SW to BP, 30 January 1892.
155. Ibid.
156. SW to BP, 14 February 1892.
157. BP to SW, 1 January 1892, and SW to BP, 4 January 1892 (Miss Orme not
      cordial) and SW to BP, n.d. [1 January 1892?] (Miss Orme takes chair at one
      of his meetings).
158. BP to SW, n.d. [February 1892?] (Item 18).
159. SW to Graham Wallas, 6 March 1892; Wallas Coll., LSE.
160. SW to BP, 23 March 1892.
161. SW to BP, n.d. (end sheet) between 7 and 10 May 1892.
162. SW to G. Wallas, 29 July 1892.
163. D, 16 August 1892.
164. BP to G. Wallas, n.d., from Glasgow [August or September 1892?].
165. D, 16 August 1892.
166. BP to SW, n.d. [August 1890?] (Item 13).
167. SW to BP, 28 December 1891.

6 Democracy and the Labour Movement 1892–8

1. *On Labour*, 1869; the second edition of 1870 was reprinted in facsimile in
    1971 by the Irish University Press.
2. R.J. Harrison, *Before the Socialists*, 1965, p. 341.
3. E.J. Hobsbawm, *Labouring Men*, 1964, p. 255 fn.
4. R. Michels, *Political Parties*, 1915. (First English edition; translated from the
    Italian by Eden and Cedar Paul.)

5.	*Daily News*, September 1889; PAS VI (the Spoken Word)/95: album of press cuttings.
6.	B. Potter (Mrs S. Webb), *The Relationship Between Co-operation and Trade Unionism*, Manchester, n.d. [1893]. Being a lecture to a conference of trade union officials and co-operators at Tynemouth, 15 August 1892.
7.	SW to BP, 2 November 1891.
8.	D, 2 July 1892.
9.	D, 16 January 1896.
10.	D, 17 January 1896.
11.	BP to SW, n.d. [summer 1891?], Item 42.
12.	BP to SW, n.d. [24 October 1891?], Item 66.
13.	D, 14 February 1890.
14.	BP to SW, 24 January 1892.
15.	*The Gentlewoman* [!], 12 March 1904.
16.	SW to BP, 18 September 1891.
17.	F.W. Galton, 'Investigating with the Webbs', in M. Cole (ed.), *The Webbs and Their Work*, 1949, pp. 29–40; also D, 21 June 1893.
18.	D, 17 September 1893.
19.	D, 24 May 1897.
20.	D, 19 October 1897. She had been reading Sach's *Botany* and Darwin's *Prefaces* to prepare the introduction to *Industrial Democracy*.
21.	S. and B. Webb, *Methods of Social Study*, Longmans, 1932, p. 94.
22.	Ibid.
23.	E.H. Carr, *What is History?*, 1961, p. 9; 2nd edition, 1987, p. 15.
24.	B. Webb, *Our Partnership*, 1948, p. 47; hereinafter *OP*. *OP* here reproduces a *Diary* entry at the Argoed for 8 August 1895.
25.	V.L. Allen, 'Valuation and Historical Interpretation', *British Journal of Sociology*, vol. XIV, no. 1, March 1963, pp. 48–58.
26.	B. Webb, *OP*, p. 44; D, 10 July 1894.
27.	S. and B. Webb, *The History of Trade Unionism*, 1911, p. lxi; hereinafter referred to as *TU*. All references are to the 1911 edition.
28.	V.L. Allen, 'Valuation' p. 51.
29.	*TU*, pp. 12 et seq.
30.	V.L. Allen's account of the Webbs' opinions on this subject is particularly inaccurate and misleading, and his own version of the 'economic pressures' responsible for the change is vague and unsatisfactory. 'Valuation', pp. 55–6.
31.	*TU*, p. 35.
32.	H.A. Clegg, A. Fox, and A.F. Thompson, *A History of British Trade Unions Since 1889, vol. I, 1889–1910*, Oxford, 1964, p. 46.
33.	*TU*, p. 75.
34.	Ibid., p. 41.
35.	E.P. Thompson, *The Making of the English Working Class*, 1963, p. 500.
36.	A. Aspinall, *The Early English Trade Unions*, 1949.
37.	G.D.H. Cole, *Attempts at General Union*, 1953 (in its original form this appeared in 1939).
38.	V.L. Allen, 'Valuation', p. 54 (Clegg *et al.; A History*, p. 7, offers a much more moderate criticism).
39.	G.D.H. Cole, 'Some Notes on British Trade Unionism in the Third Quarter of the Nineteenth Century', *International Review of Social History*, vol. 2, 1937, pp. 1–23.
40.	H.A. Clegg *et al.*, *A History*, p. 38. See also Clegg's contribution, 'The Webbs as Historians of Trade Unionism 1874–94', *Bulletin of the Society for the Study of Labour History*, no. 4, 1962, pp. 8–9.

41. F. Harrison to BW, 5 May 1894.
42. R.W. Postgate, *The Builders' History*, 1923. (While making those and other criticisms, the author found that his own research 'merely served to confirm and heighten my opinion of the learning, good sense and industry which have gone to the making of that [a reference to *TU*] remarkable book'; p. xvii.)
43. S. Coltham, 'The Bee-hive Newspaper: Its Origin and Early Struggles', in A. Briggs and J. Saville (eds), *Essays in Labour History*, 1960, pp. 174–204.
44. E.S. Beesly to BW, 8 May 1894.
45. D, 12 November 1893. She was staying at the Angel, Chesterfield: 'a stupid, stolid lot of men characterised by fairmindedness and kindliness – but oh! how dense! The officials are of the ordinary good type, hard-working, narrow-minded, whisky-drinking, self-complacent persons: excellent speakers on the one question of Miners' Trade Unionism, and competent negotiators, but stupid, stupid, stupid, like the men! Is it the (?) quality of the whisky these good fellows drink – without being drunk – or is it brain work carried on by an uncultivated and untrained mind? How can anyone fear anything but unmitigated conservatism from the English democracy.'
46. *TU*, p. 455.
47. Ibid., p. 458.
48. Thompson, *The Making*, p. 12.
49. *TU*, p. 47.
50. Ibid., p. 56.
51. Ibid., p. 77.
52. Ibid., p. 79.
53. E.J. Hobsbawm, 'The Machine-Breakers', in his *Labouring Men*, 1964, pp. 5–22.
54. Thompson, *The Making*, p. 158.
55. Ibid., p. 169.
56. Ibid., p. 592.
57. In deference to socialist criticisms they amended this definition in the 1920 edition: replacing the words 'of their employment' by the expression 'of their working lives'.
58. H.A. Turner, *Trade Union Growth, Structure and Policy*, 1962.
59. S. and B. Webb, *Industrial Democracy*, first published 1897; hereinafter referred to as *ID*. Unless otherwise stated, this and all further references are to the 1911 edition.
60. *ID*, pp. 59–60 [in edition of 1902].
61. A.L. Lowell, *The Government of England*, 1910, vol. I, pp. 177 et seq.
62. *ID*, pp. 60–1.
63. Ibid., p. 848.
64. Ibid., p. 843.
65. Ibid., pp. 844–5.
66. Ibid., p. 845.
67. Ibid., p. 809.
68. Ibid., p. 847.
69. Ibid., p. 847.
70. Ibid., p. 847.
71. The reader may recall that at the end of the Korean War the prisoners on both sides exercised a free choice which appeared to entirely satisfy the Millite requirements, but provided a universal (and probably justifiable) scepticism.

72. *ID*, pp. 809–10.
73. Ibid., p. 828.
74. Ibid., p. 828.
75. Ibid., p. 821.
76. Ibid., p. 824.
77. Ibid., pp. 828–9.
78. Ibid., p. 825.
79. Ibid., p. 814.
80. Ibid., p. 816.
81. Ibid., p. 826.
82. Ibid., p. 843.
83. Ibid., p. 843.
84. Ibid., p. 817.
85. Ibid., p. 830.
86. Ibid., p. 848.
87. Ibid., p. 840.
88. Ibid., p. 832.
89. Ibid., pp. 362–3.
90. Ibid., pp. 845–6.
91. Cited in R.J. Harrison, 'Practical, Capable Men,' review of Ben Roberts on the history of the TUC, *New Reasoner*, VI, 1958, p. 104.
92. See the authentic, authoritative work by V.L. Allen, *Trade Unions and the Government*, 1960.
93. B. Webb, 'The Failure of the Labour Commission', *The Nineteenth Century*, vol. XXXVI, July 1894, pp. 2–22.
94. G. Drage, 'Mrs Sidney Webb's Attack on the Labour Commission', ibid., pp. 452–67.
95. D, 21 September 1894.
96. D, 9 August 1932. It is presumed that this entry related to Drage: BW was musing over the death of Graham Wallas. ('The purpose of the Fabian Society', wrote an angry Tory journalist in 1894 'is to substitute for the present governing class of public school and university (Oxford and Cambridge) men, lower middle class men like Sidney Webb'. Well, well, if we examine the personnel of the two Labour Cabinets and reflect on J.R.M.'s premiership and Snowden's presence in the National Government of 1932, the Tory sneer of 1894 has proved to be an accurate forecast. But this reflection cannot be cast on Graham Wallas …')
97. G. Drage, 'Mrs Sidney Webb's Attack', p. 455.
98. Ibid., p. 460.
99. Originally: Symposium – 'What Mr Gladstone Ought To Do', *Fortnightly Review*, 53, 1893, pp. 276–87; parts by Shaw and Webb.
100. R.B. Haldane to SW, 2 November n.d. [1893?].
101. H.W. Massingham to SW, 3 January 1893 ('utmost sorrow … measureless regret').
102. D, 17 September 1893.
103. B. Webb, *OP*, p. 40; D, 24 December 1893.
104. Minutes of Evidence, Royal Commission on Labour (June 1893), 17 November 1892, Q. 3886–88.
105. Ibid., Q. 3918 and 3921–2.
106. D, 21 September 1894.
107. T. Mann to SW, 9 November 1893, and eight other letters to 27 April 1894.
108. T. Mann to SW, 9 November 1893.

109. BP to SW, 21 January 1892.
110. RCL, Final Report (Minority), 1894, vol. xxxv, pp. 127 et seq.
111. D, 25 December 1893.
112. D, 2 March 1894.
113. Ibid., 2 March 1894.
114. Ibid., 15 January 1895.
115. Fabian Tract No. 70, 1896, p. 14.
116. S. Webb, 'Reminiscences No. 1, Trade Unionism', *St Martin's Review*, October 1928, pp. 478–81.
117. Ex-ambassador Ivan Maisky in an interview with the author in Moscow, July 1966.
118. V.I. Lenin, *What is to be Done?*, Selected Works, vol. 2, 1936, p. 156.
119. Ibid.
120. Ibid., p. 61 (citing Karl Kautsky).
121. P. Gay, *The Dilemma of Democratic Socialism: Eduard Bernstein's Challenge to Marx*, New York, 1962, p. 108.
122. E. Bernstein, *My Years of Exile: Reminiscences of a Socialist* (Tr. Edward Miall) 1921.
123. S. Webb, 'Reminiscences'.
124. S. and B. Webb, *Die Geschichte des Britischen Trade Unionism*, Dietz, Stuttgart, 1895. E. Bernstein's *'nachwort'* was omitted from the second edition, published in 1906.
125. P. Gay, op. cit., p. 133.
126. Ibid., p. 74.
127. Minutes of Evidence, Royal Commission on Labour, op. cit., Q. 3931.
128. *ID*, p. 71.

7 Heroic Opportunism: Towards a Third Culture and Education in London 1893–1905

1. R.H. Tawney, *Equality*, 1931. It should be noted that this work was dedicated 'with gratitude and affection' to Sidney and Beatrice Webb.
2. S. Webb, *Wanted a Programme*, An Appeal to the Liberal Party for private circulation only (August 1888), pp. 14–15.
3. S. Webb, *Socialism in England*, 1890, ch. v
4. W.P. McCann, 'Trade Unionist, Co-operative and Socialist Organizations in Relation to Popular Education, 1870–1902', PhD thesis, University of Manchester, 1960. This is a first-class piece of scholarship and the author's judgement commands respect.
5. *Kentish Mercury*, 21 January 1892.
6. McCann, 'Trade Unionist, Co-operative and Socialist Organizations', p. 23, where it is argued that Tract No. 25 had little effect upon the school board elections of 1891 but that a slightly revised edition of 1894 had 'very great' influence in that year.
7. National Association for the Promotion of Technical and Secondary Education, *The LCC and Technical Education: An Appeal to the Electors*, n.d. [1892].
8. S. Webb, 'The Labour Interest in the County Council Election', *Trade Unionist*, 23 and 30 January; 13 and 20 February; 5 March 1892.
9. S. Webb, *The London Programme*, 1891, pp. 175–6.
10. In fact Webb proposed to deprive the Home Secretary of control of the Metropolitan Police: ibid., p. 137 et seq.

11. P.F. Clarke, 'The Progressive Movement in England', *Transactions of the Royal Historical Society*, 5th series, vol. 24, p. 166.
12. SW to BP, 16 March 1892.
13. SW to BP, 4 and 23 March 1892.
14. SW to BP, 5 March 1892.
15. *OP*, p. 78.
16. Ibid.
17. SW to BP, n.d., but between 7 and 10 May 1892.
18. Arthur H.D. Acland and H. Llewellyn Smith (eds), *Studies in Secondary Education*, 1892, p. 11.
19. Ibid., p. 162.
20. Ibid., p. 179.
21. Ibid., p. 187.
22. Ibid., p. 207.
23. Ibid., p. 302.
24. Ibid., pp. 162 et seq.
25. McCann, 'Trade Unionist, Co-operative and Socialist Organizations', ch. IV, 'The Labour Movement and Technical Education'.
26. *London*, 16 February 1895.
27. *London News*, January 1895. Reference is made to this article by E.J.T. Brennan, 'The Influence of Sidney and Beatrice Webb on English Education', MA thesis, University of Sheffield, 1959. This is a work of outstanding excellence and I am indebted to it at many points in this chapter.
28. A.G. Gardiner, *John Benn and the Progressive Movement*, 1925, p. 172.
29. Ibid.
30. *London*, 16 February 1895.
31. *London*, 22 August 1895.
32. TEB Minutes, 28 April 1894.
33. Royal Commission on Secondary Education, vol. XLIV, 1895. See in particular evidence given by Webb and Garnett on 29 May 1894: Questions 2537–2858. Hereinafter referred to as 'Bryce'.
34. B. Webb, *OP*, p. 80, but this is rather too complacent. See W. Garnett, 'A Retrospect', *Educational Record*, April 1929. Beatrice herself described this as 'an authoritative account of the TEB': *OP*, p. 81, fn. 1.
35. *London*, 5 October 1893.
36. *London*, 24 June 1897.
37. *London*, 2 February 1893.
38. *London Technical Education Gazette*, February 1897.
39. Brennan, 'The Influence of Sidney and Beatrice Webb on English Education', pp. 82–3.
40. *London*, 26 October 1893.
41. Ibid.
42. Ibid., 22 August 1895.
43. Bryce, Q. 2568–76.
44. Ibid., Q. 2644.
45. Brennan, 'The Influence of Sidney and Beatrice Webb on English Education', p. 117.
46. The *London Technical Education Gazette* published tables giving the occupations of the parents of all candidates for scholarships, both successful and unsuccessful. Unfortunately these tables appeared only intermittently and the classification of occupations was changed from one year to another. However, in the last of these returns made in 1903, workers took 370 of the

607 scholarships, or 60.9 per cent. Out of the total, general labourers took only 44 scholarships; carpenters and joiners alone accounted for 22; compositors 19, and other skilled workers in printing and publishing a further 27. Journeymen tailors took 10. Over the years the children of widows did particularly well and the sons and daughters of schoolmasters peculiarly badly. In the first three competitive examinations, for instance, schoolmasters' children accounted for 46 candidates but only four were successful.

47.   *London*, 16 February 1893. For John Burns's allegation, that 'the work lads had not that access to the funds of the Board which the lower middle classes were securing', see *London*, 25 February 1897. Webb's rejoinder was that 'at least 5% of the scholarships went to the children of unskilled labourers'!

48.   *The Times*, 1 August 1896.

49.   Brennan, 'The Influence of Sidney and Beatrice Webb on English Education', p. 117.

50.   *London*, 12 October 1893.

51.   F.E. Willard, 'A Scientific Socialist', *British Weekly*, 29 June 1893. Sidney's observation was made in the context of a discussion in which Beatrice maintained, 'I never saw a man the most inferior, but I felt him to be my superior.'

52.   S. Webb, *The Economic Heresies of the LCC*, 1895.

53.   SW to A. Marshall, 28 February 1889.

54.   *Economic Journal*, vol. 1, 1891.

55.   SW to BW, 23 February 1891.

56.   Ibid., 30 October 1890.

57.   S. Caine, *The History of the Foundation of the London School of Economics*, 1963.

58.   B. Webb, *OP*, pp. 85–6; D, 21 September 1894.

59.   H. Burrows and J.A. Hobson (eds), *William Clarke: A Collection of His Writings*, 1908, p. 42 (the article first appeared in the *Contemporary Review*, February 1893).

60.   G.B Shaw to BW, 1 July 1895, Burrows and Hobson, *William Clarke*, pp. 45–7.

61.   D, 16 September 1896.

62.   W.A.S Hewins to E.R. Pease, 19 October 1895; Fabian Collection (FC), Nuffield College.

63.   SW to W.A.S Hewins, 24 March 1895: 'Graham Wallas now decides after all that he cannot undertake the Directorship! This is an unexpected blow.' Five days later Webb wrote again: 'The Hutchinson Trustees decided yesterday to go ahead with the proposal of a London School of Economics and Political Science on the lines which you and I worked out together. They attach great important to securing your cordial assistance and, indeed, unless you can undertake the Directorship and carry out the scheme it will probably have to be abandoned.' (Hewins Papers, University of Sheffield)

64.   SW to BP, 4 January 1892.

65.   SW to E.R. Pease, 25 March 1895; FC, Nuffield College.

66.   W.A.S. Hewins, *The Apologia of an Imperialist*, 1929, and his papers at the University of Sheffield.

67.   Lady Beveridge, *An Epic of Clare Market*, 1961, cited in Caine, *The History of the Foundation of the London School of Economics*, p. 43.

68.   Caine, *The History of the Foundation of the London School of Economics*, p. 42, being a recommendation of the TEB, 6 May 1895.

69.   J.R. MacDonald to E.R. Pease, 1 July 1897. (FC, Nuffield College)

70.   It was almost equally likely to arouse socialist hopes, particularly from abroad. As early as 23 July 1895 Lily Von Gizycki wrote to Beatrice from Berlin urging the claims of Tonnies: '[H]e is one of our best representatives

of Scientific Socialism [*sic*] and consequently denied a University post in Germany.' She thought that the LSE would be 'a high school for Socialism'.

71. L. Stephen, *The English Utilitarians*, vol. II, 1900, pp. 32–3.

72. SW to E.R. Pease, 17 July 1907, reporting that Hewins had been appointed Professor of Political Economy at King's College and that this was an honour for the School. Webb added that it also 'increases his claim to the future Professorship in the New University – and almost ensures what we have been playing for, viz. The inclusion of the School in the future University and thus our virtual command of the Economic Faculty...'; FC, Nuffield College.

73. E.J.T. Brennan, *Education for National Efficiency: the Contribution of Sidney and Beatrice Webb*, 1975, p. 139. As the following note suggests, there is no need to consign this episode to the category of 'Webbian folklore'.

74. Royal Commission on University Education (The 'Haldane Commission') – 6 vols., 1910–13. Appendix to the 1st Report, Minutes of Evidence, July 1909–April 1910. SW gave evidence on 18–19 November: see Questions 395–607. For Milner's exchanges with Webb see particularly pp. 34–6. This is the hard evidence for Webb's response to requests for his idea of a university. The objection that it is not evidence of what transpired in a private conversation between Haldane and Webb some ten years earlier is valid, but it makes it more likely that it did. There is no evidence that Webb ever sympathised with that way of proceeding. There is remarkable consistency in the progress of his opinions on the subject of London University from 1892 to 1909. Thus a lot of his evidence to the Haldane Commission in 1909 was taken from his *London Education* of 1904, much of which drew on his 'The making of a University', *Cornhill Magazine*, vol. XIV, April 1903, pp. 530–40. This, in turn, contained expressions as well as ideas lifted from his own contributions to the *Nineteenth Century*, June 1902, and to *The Times* in June 1901. If Webb's position develops it does so only in becoming more detailed and precise, bolder and more self-confident. If he told Haldane that he had no idea of a university, but here are the facts; he certainly advised Milner: 'it does not help us at all. If you go far enough back the University and State were coincident; they were both *Universitates* and I think you need not be troubled by either the etymology or the history ... If the State gives a Degree, it will be only doing what the Pope of Rome has done.' The nearest Sidney came to satisfying those who required his idea of a university was to point out that his proposals conformed to the Spencerian notion that progress was marked by a growing differentiation and specialisation of function. Spencer's maxim was congenial rather than formative. Indeed, it is hard to see how it could have been formative. In practice Sidney was working up the principles of a new discipline – that of public administration. He was applying them – or in Brennan's admirable phrase 'teasing them out' – in relation to the specific problem of the case for a teaching university in London. It will be argued that he was doing so in relation to some premonition – however vague – of the deficiencies of the two cultures and the need for a third. There is no intention to conceal the fact that his approach to this great undertaking was sometimes preposterous or naive. Thus, when Milner protested that his proposals would place too much power in the hands of state officials; he replied: 'But I never object to the tramcar that I go home in being in the hands of officials.' 'I want to suggest', interjected Sir Robert Morant, 'that that was just the point. Education is different from providing trams ...' (p. 37) (On Sidney's propensity for confusing education with other public

services including the fire brigade see also p. 60). All quotations from Webb in this note come from his contribution to the *Cornhill Magazine*, unless otherwise stated.

75. This was an aspect of the matter about which Sidney did become more aggressive and expansionist as time passed. Asked by Milner at the Haldane Commission whether it would not be best to confine the University of London to the area of the LCC, while trying to establish other Universities at Brighton and Colchester, Webb replied: 'No I think it would be disadvantageous to Brighton and Colchester not to be included in a larger entity and I do not think it is at all disadvantageous to London to include so large an area.' He drew the line at including Oxford and Cambridge with their 'malarial marshes' and thought that a University for all England would preclude competition, emulation and differentiation, which were good things in this context. Ibid., p. 47.

76. '[T]he Professor of Arabic is as much an amateur, when it comes to administering, as the administrator is when it comes to professing Arabic, and with this further drawback that the Professor of Arabic thinks he understands administration, whereas the administrator knows that he does not understand Arabic.' Ibid. Sidney became a Professor of Public Administration.

77. R.B Haldane, *An Autobiography*, 1929, p. 125.

78. See Chapter 5, p. 212.

79. B. Webb, *OP*, p. 96.

80. D, 3 May 1897.

81. D, 28 February 1902; *OP*, pp. 227–8.

82. R.B Haldane, op.cit., p. 125.

83. Ibid., p. 124, and R.B. Haldane to A.J. Balfour, 16 October 1897; Haldane papers, National Library of Scotland.

84. R.B Haldane, *Autobiography*, pp. 127–8.

85. B. Webb, *OP*, p. 102.

86. D, December 1900.

87. D, 4 May 1902.

88. D, Whitsun 1896.

89. Brennan, 'The Influence of Sidney and Beatrice Webb on English Education', pp. 50–1.

90. Ibid.

91. Education Reform Council, Education Reform: Being the Report of the Education Reform Council (Published for the Teachers' Guild of Great Britain and Ireland), 1917. Foreword by William Garnett, chairman of the Education Reform Council, pp. ix–xxxii.

92. Fabian Society, *The Education Muddle and the Way Out*, Tract No. 106, 1901. Pease's attribution of authorship to Sidney is supported by a letter to him from SW, 3 May 1899: 'Here is the (that is, my) gospel on the Education muddle … If we publish this it will enhance our practical reputation.' Pease's qualification to all his attributions – 'they were probably amended by the Society', E.R. Pease, *History of the Fabian Society*, 2nd edition, 1925, p. 289 – is supported by some references. Thus, about a year later Sidney complained in a letter to Pease, 17 May 1900, that the Tract was all right in substance, but did not 'lap to the eye'. The Executive would not, he thought, accept it without much discussion. However, on 28 December 1900 Sidney wrote to Pease, remarking, 'Here is the Education Tract'. It was an urgent matter since its publication ought to precede the possible announcement by the government

of its Bill on 14 February (FC, Nuffield College). It is clear that Sidney took the initiative, that he 'prevailed' in all essential respects and that he had the last word. It is not certain that he made no concessions on minor questions or verbal ones to meet the requirements of 'sentimental twaddle'.

93.   'The idea that education is valuable for its own sake he clearly regarded as no more that sentimental twaddle.' – B. Simon, *Education and the Labour Movement 1870–1920*, 1965, p. 204.

94.   Fabian Society, *The Education Muddle*, p. 20.

95.   E.R. Pease, op. cit., p. 144. On 8 May 1901 SW wrote to Pease that Gorst's speech on the Government's Education Bill was full of echoes of the Tract. SW wrote to BW, 7 May 1891: 'Gorst is even now introducing his Bill about which we know nothing yet.' (This letter is not reproduced in MacKenzie.) Thus, the extent of the liaison between Webb and the Fabians and Gorst and the government ought not to be overestimated.

96.   Brennan, 'The Influence of Sidney and Beatrice Webb on English Education', p. 53.

97.   Ibid., p. 56.

98.   R. Morant to SW, 16 January 1903; PAS.

99.   D, 1 February 1903: 'Harmsworth … handed over the direction of the campaign in the *Daily Mail* to Sidney'; and *OP*, pp. 257–8 and footnote.

100.   Fabian Society [SW], *The London Education Act 1903: How to Make the Best of It*, Tract No. 117, February 1904, p. 2.

101.   In her old age Beatrice wondered whether there had been a vision or a grand design from the beginning. Brennan, 'The Influence of Sidney and Beatrice Webb on English Education', discounts it. However he mistakenly asserts: 'there is no mention of the subject of education in … [t]he important *London Programme*', p. 6.

102.   SW to G. Wallas, 4 December 1902.

103.   D, 15 June 1903 and 7 March 1904.

104.   Beatrice did, however, press Pease to take a more active interest; FC, Nuffield College.

105.   B. Simon, *Education and the Labour Movement*, pp. 196–207.

8 Squalid Opportunism: Fabianism and Empire 1893–1903

1.   D, 17 September 1893.

2.   A. D. 12 October 1893.

3.   D, 17 September 1893.

4.   D, 12 October 1893.

5.   D, 9 September 1895.

6.   B. Webb, *OP*, p. 123.

7.   *OP*, p. 127.

8.   *OP*, p. 134.

9.   Ibid.

10.   *Report on Fabian Policy*, Tract No. 70, 1896.

11.   *OP*, p. 130–1.

12.   Cf. the reference to this incident in the published version of the Diary, vol. 2, p. 138.

13.   See David Shannon (ed.), *Beatrice Webb's American Diary*, Madison, 1963.

14.   See A.G. Austin (ed.), *The Webbs' Australian Diary*, Melbourne, 1965.

15.   J.N. Ingham, *The Iron Barons*, 1978, p. 37.

16. *Visit to New Zealand in 1898: Beatrice Webb's Diary with Entries by Sidney E. Webb*, Prince Milburn, Wellington N.Z., 1959, p. 31.
17. D, 15 May 1899.
18. D, 1 July 1901.
19. D, 10 October 1899.
20. D, December 1899.
21. D, 25 September 1933.
22. D, 9 July 1901.
23. R. Jenkins, *Asquith*, 1967 edition, p. 136.
24. D, 9 July 1901.
25. G.R. Searle, *The Quest for National Efficiency*, 1971, p. 132.
26. Ibid., p. 139.
27. D, 16 March 1900; B. Webb, *OP*, p. 198.
28. D, 28 February 1902; B. Webb, *OP*, pp. 227–8.
29. D, 28 November 1902; B. Webb, *OP*, pp. 248–9.
30. D, 8 July 1903; B. Webb, *OP*, p. 269.
31. B. Webb, *OP*, pp. 292–3.
32. Ibid., p. 216.
33. D, 30 October 1899.
34. D, 14 October 1905.
35. B. Webb, *OP*, p. 275.
36. Ibid., p. 225.
37. Ibid., p. 229.
38. Ibid., p. 231.
39. *OP*, p. 227.
40. Ibid., p. 205.
41. Ibid., pp. 304–5.
42. Ibid., p. 294.
43. Ibid., p. 289.
44. D, 23 July 1903; B. Webb, *OP*, pp. 270–1, sets this on 24 July.

9 An Ideal Marriage?

1. 'An Appeal Against Female Suffrage', *Nineteenth Century*, vol. xxv, June 1889, pp. 781–8.
2. Ibid.
3. F.E. Willard, 'A Scientific Socialist', *British Weekly*, 29 June 1893.
4. 'Mrs Webb pointed out that Westminster...had failed to provide lavatory accommodation for women. Mrs Webb strongly repudiated the suggestion that there was a prejudice among women against patronising these public institutions. "That", she said, "was purely a man's notion which influenced some vestries..."' Beatrice added that there should be more lavatories for each sex and that they should be free. She explained that she was not in favour of women going on vestries as women, but as citizens who sometimes had specialised qualifications and leisure not possessed by men. Women were fully equal to men in point of administrative capacity; *London*, 13 December 1894.
5. The International Congress met in London in July 1899 (D, 3 July 1899). Since within two years Beatrice was showing the most perfect indifference to the claims of the Nonconformist conscience in relation to the Education Bill, it seems proper to interpret her gesture as a mere pretext for distancing herself from the pious 'do-gooders' whom she felt would do no good.

Contents

Illustrations

'Academy Ratio'. The expanse beyond that reveals how the proportions of the CinemaScope screen image allowed filmmakers to introduce more on-screen observers to the central action, offering plausible visual vantage points for audiences to imagine they too could 'be there'. Even intimate moments between Marcellus and Diane (top) are open to public viewing, taking place in the slave market.

General Editor's Introduction

This is the first serious and sustained analysis of the depiction of history in Hollywood films of the 1950s and it is a superb achievement. It is based on a systematic viewing of 300 films, the analysis of 147 scripts, 550 pressbooks and 300 production code files, and an investigation of the private papers of two dozen leading Hollywood figures involved in the making of historical films. This massive amount of primary research has been backed up by the mastering of and engagement with the secondary literature. The critical analysis is throughout carefully contextualised and the choice of historical subjects by filmmakers is persuasively related to the political and cultural history of the United States in the 1950s.

Eldridge has discovered that history films, broadly defined, constituted around 40 percent of total film production in that decade. He analyses the various industry motives lying behind this: box-office returns, perceived audience preference, the impact of technological change (in particular the introduction of widescreen processes) and the importance of overseas markets. He looks at the production of individual films in the context of the Cold War, the HUAC hearings and the Hollywood blacklist, showing how costume dramas like *Ivanhoe* contained coded attacks on McCarthyism, how biblical epics like *Quo Vadis* indicted current totalitarian regimes such as Soviet Russia, and how the studios expressed considerable anxiety about the depiction of revolutions in such films as *Scaramouche* and *Viva Zapata*. He explores the problems and pitfalls associated with the filming of the lives of recently deceased celebrities: the nature and function of popular memory, the conventions of the biopic and the demands and interventions of the friends and relatives of the deceased.

Eldridge gives us the first systematic account of the role of the historical advisor in films and examines the quest for authenticity which almost invariably clashed with the demands of the drama. He also charts the largely negative depiction of historians in films, attributing it to the growing distance between academic and popular history, the McCarthyite attack on intellectuals and the contemporary reputation of historians. Thorough, perceptive and authoritative, this book opens up a hitherto under-explored area of cultural history and represents a major contribution to our understanding of the nature, role and function of historical films in society.

Jeffrey Richards

Acknowledgements

While the stars and supporting actors that receive credit for this production may not quite amount to a DeMille style 'cast of thousands', they deserve even more accolades than *The Ten Commandments*. The producer of this little epic therefore wishes to express his gratitude to: the Arts and Humanities Research Board of the British Academy, the Sara Norton Fund and Jesus College, Cambridge, for their financial support; the University of Hull for granting me leave for edits and retakes; Ned Comstock at the University of Southern California School of Cinema-Television in Los Angeles; Haden Guest and Noele Carter at the USC Warner Bros. Archives; Al Willis and Jeannie Foreman at the Theatre Arts Library of the University of California, Los Angeles; the staffs of the Wisconsin Center for Film and Theater Research in Madison and the British Film Institute in London; with a standing ovation for Barbara Hall, Val Almendarez and Sandra Archer at the Margaret Herrick Library of the Academy of Motion Pictures Arts and Sciences in Beverley Hills.

The supporting cast also includes the many students at the University of Hull who have taken my courses, and my colleagues, especially Jenel Virden, Neil Sinyard and Sylvia Tynan. In order of appearance, I also credit: Ted Westervelt, Jaap Kooijman, Richard Coxon, Tony Badger, Kaele Stokes, Edward Meek, John Thompson, Jonathan Bell, Amy Davis, Nick Cull, Ed Countryman, Lynn Dumenil, Lary May, Loli Tsan, David Culbert, Ken Short, Jeffrey Richards and Phillipa Brewster. And finally, Academy Awards go to Steve Spackman, Rich McBain, Martin and Leslie Eldridge, and Tony Dean.

Introduction

The people of hoary antiquity and their many accomplishments are not just matters to be read about in books, nor are the artefacts they fashioned to be left untouched and only looked at from a distance through protective glass in a museum.

Henry S. Noerdlinger on *The Ten Commandments*, 1956

American intellectual history suggests that during the early years of the Cold War thinking about the past was dominated by a 'consensus' school of history – one that affirmed the 'rightness' of America in its confrontation with Communist ideology, while downplaying dissent and political conflict within the history of the nation itself. This characterisation, formulated in 1959 by John Higham, has been subject to substantial debate – from the suggestion that the paradigm would be better described as 'counter-Progressive', to the detailed study of individual texts and the historians who produced them.[1] But, turned in on academia itself, this discussion has commonly overlooked one of the most important qualifications: that these historians did not have a monopoly on thinking about the past.

Between 1950 and 1959, Hollywood released over 1200 films that engaged with history, at the very least by virtue of being set in it. Over 40 percent of all films made in the Fifties were set in the past. Generating a huge and frequently challenging discourse about history and how it could be represented, the production of these movies involved over 300 directors, 400 producers, at least 700 credited scriptwriters and innumerable researchers, designers and actors. Filmmakers developed interests in specific periods, which studios presented in particular styles; the representation of the past in one movie would influence and reinforce the way history was handled in other films; and a wide variety of narrative strategies were employed to interpret the past and its meaning. It was a level of historical interest unprecedented in the industry.

Yet, while there have been detailed studies of contemporary academic historiography – the most magisterial analysis of the American historical profession being Peter Novick's *That Noble Dream* – Hollywood's comparable, if less academically inclined, 'school' of history has been largely ignored or dismissed.[2] Historian Michael Kammen, for instance, has led the study of the nation's historical consciousness, with *Mystic Chords of Memory* (1991) and *In the Past Lane* (1997) exploring the way in the which popular understanding of the past has been shaped by historians, politicians, artists, museum curators and so forth – but filmmakers get no mention.[3] This was true in post-war analyses as well. As C. Vann Woodward suggested in 1955, contemporary historians were clearly interested in 'American Attitudes Toward History', noting that 'the American Clio has been placed in the role of a sacred oracle from which the meaning of events and the pathway of the future are periodically sought'.[4] But while critical that 'this quest for the American past' was being carried out through 'historical novels, fictionalised biographies, collections of pictures and cartoons', academic commentators persisted in leaving the movies out of the equation.[5]

Obviously this book seeks to address this absence, and does so by providing an intellectual history of Hollywood's historiography at a particular moment in time. This is not to argue that many period-set movies made in the Fifties were not overly reliant 'on the most trite version of history', nor that they would impart an enhanced understanding of historical reality.[6] One can hardly make great claims towards reassessing the pedagogical value of a decade of films that gave us Hannibal crossing the Alps on rainbow-coloured elephants, Wyatt Earp teaming up with Butch Cassidy and Buffalo Bill, Robin Hood forcing King John to sign the Magna Carta, or John Wayne playing Genghis Khan as a medieval gunslinger.[7] But no matter how idiotic the end result might have been, even these films were the product of the industry's historical consciousness. As cultural historian Warren Susman observed, 'the idea of history itself, special kinds of historical studies and various attitudes towards history always play – whether intelligently conceived or not – a major role within a culture'.[8] My exploration of the 'attitudes toward history' in the culture of 1950s Hollywood proceeds on this premise.

In doing so, it both draws upon and contests recent studies of historical films. Scholars have certainly challenged the simplistic assessment of 'how true a work remains to the facts', apparent in the comments on individual films in *Past Imperfect* or *Hollywood Faction*.[9] As Robert Rosenstone points out, 'you do not have to see many films to know that such an approach is ridiculous'.[10] Most films simply are not 'accurate' in terms that a traditional historian would accept, and rarely even attempt to be so. Instead, as demonstrated by texts such as Robert Brent Toplin's *History by Hollywood* and the essays collected in *The Historical Film*, the identification of embellishment and distortion is only the starting point for an analysis, which ought to appreciate the context of the medium itself.[11] Toplin's most recent study, *Reel History*, responded to a research agenda that he himself set out a decade ago, when he commented that 'few historians…are looking into the trail of evidence regarding specific films in order to ask: How and why were the films made? Who made them, and which ideas influenced the filmmakers? How did the films interpret history, and what biases affected the interpretation?'[12] Robert Sklar proposed an even more flexible approach, arguing that the necessary task was to analyse how the filmmaker has interacted with professional historiography, public attitudes, political utilisation of history and the convention of the historical film genre to craft a narrative and style that convey a perspective on the past through cinematic means.[13]

Yet, this positive approach to treating filmmakers as historians – or rather as people who draw on the materials of history to construct their narratives – has been almost exclusively applied to modern movies, rather than the products of 'classic' Hollywood. In recent discourse, there has been a notable effort to define a 'New History Film' – first evident in a 1995 volume edited by Rosenstone, entitled *Revisioning History*, which presented a selection of international works such as *Walker* (1988), *Sans Soleil* (1985) and *Distant Voices, Still Lives* (1988) as 'postmodern' in their approach to the past. Less esoteric films such as Oliver Stone's *JFK* (1991) have generated similar in-depth discussion for problematising knowledge and questioning 'official' versions of history, while many movies like *Reds* (1981), *Malcolm X* (1992), *Schindler's List* (1993) and *Black Hawk Down* (2001) have been judged according to their conscious sense of the 'integrity' of the past. This more tolerant attitude has even benefited *Titanic* (1997) and *Gladiator* (2000), both the subject of anthologies by historians and film scholars despite neither film being especially 'new' in its approach.[14] But no similar analysis has been applied – in a sustained or systematic manner – to the precursors of these films. Indeed, earlier films have often been presented as embarrassments. Pierre Sorlin evoked this when trying to establish the legitimacy of studying history films, claiming that professional historians were 'wary' of Hollywood movies because 'Robin Hood and his fellows have disappointed them'. Noting that techniques had 'evolved' and films now paid 'more attention' to historical documents, he assured his readers 'that films and filmmaking have changed since the 1960s'.[15] From this perspective the 'New Wave' had made history films of the 1950s anachronisms of both cinema and history.

Sorlin's comments suggest how this drive to categorise was engendered by an effort to establish a canon of 'worthy' history films that would challenge academic prejudice against film studies. But this perpetuates a subjective instinct to judge films according to the seriousness with which they present the past. Even *Reel History* continues to do this, in Toplin's awarding of the 'Herodotus' prize to 'significant' history films, and the 'Brooks' to films which 'fail to communicate a thoughtful picture of the past'.[16] In consequence, not only have films made before the 1960s been routinely excluded from analysis, but so too have whole approaches to depicting the past. Rosenstone was not alone in elevating the 'New History Film' by disparaging the 'costume drama that uses the past solely as a setting for romance and adventure'.[17] Sorlin similarly excused himself from considering 'those pictures which are basically costume comedies or dramas and which only use the past as a colorful background'; while Leger Grindon sought to define the 'historical fiction film' as a genre by 'setting aside…the costume picture that adopts a period setting but fails to engage historical issues'.[18] However, in accepting these definitions, the devaluing of films lumped together as 'costume dramas', ignores a vast amount of material which is shot through with ideas of history and which tells us a great deal about the historical consciousness of the people who made them. The very simple fact that the majority of films set in the past *do not* take history seriously has apparently struck few academics of actually being of significance itself.

Of all those interested in cinematic historiography, to my knowledge, only Sue Harper has explicitly insisted that 'it is inadequate to deal only with films which represent historical events'.[19] Rehabilitating the British costume drama, she extended the definition to encompass movies that use 'the mythical and symbolic aspects of the past as a means of providing pleasure, rather than instruction'.[20] A far more productive and expansive perspective from which to begin analysis, Harper's definition also suggests that westerns, swashbucklers, Arabian Nights adventures, musical-comedies, and indeed any film set in the past, merits investigation on these terms.

Indeed, writers on the western have long accepted this, hardly ignoring the genre because it does not take the past seriously enough. While the western rarely pretends to be reality, it typically depicts and interrogates 'a living legend of frontier history'. Lee Clark Mitchell, for instance, makes the case that while few Americans at the time 'attached more than passing significance to Indian wars, railroad extensions, mining and lumber operations' and so forth, the western turned these 'prosaic events' into myths and legends. Indeed, argues Mitchell, writers and filmmakers were able to use this material in 'mythmaking' so readily precisely because most Americans viewed the facts of frontier history as rather inconsequential – and therefore did not mind it being turned into fiction.[21] Richard Maltby takes this further, suggesting that the most consequential element of these historical events and actors was the very fact that they became encapsulated in legend. In this analysis, the history exists because the legend exists. Maltby notes, for example, that fictional accounts of the gunfight at the OK Corral were read by the public – and entered their historical consciousness – long before it entered the history books.[22] Thus when a filmmaker like John Sturges made *Gunfight at the OK Corral* in 1957, his engagement with myth was as central to the project as his engagement with history. In respect of such thought-provoking analyses of how the past is configured, and their import for discussing the film industry's understanding of that past, it seems ludicrous to restrict ourselves to particular genres or styles of film.

The investigation that follows is therefore deliberately inclusive – embracing westerns, romances, biopics, biblical epics, comedies, musicals, colonial adventures, pirate films and more besides – acknowledging all the work on history that was done in Hollywood. As long as the setting of the film's action predates the year in which it was released by more than five years, it has been counted as a 'History Film'. This label is founded on the hypothesis that all films which utilise the past contain and reflect ideas about history, whether or not they are explicitly conceived of as 'historical'. A director who uses the past purely to indulge a passion for 'colourful' costumes, may not be thinking 'historically', but it suggests an intuitive conception of history as pageant. Or the use of historical locations as 'no more than...an exotic setting for romance and adventure', might reflect a notion of the past as a 'different country', which implicitly (and mistakenly) conceptualises the past as somewhere that can be visited.[23] As the wide variety of case studies in this book indicate, each film is a product of the historical consciousness of the individuals who made it, and the industry and culture in which it was developed, no matter how 'trite' that consciousness might appear. There is, in this analysis, no 'waste heap' to which films that 'grossly simplify history, trivialize it, or bend it to shape the needs of the artist' might be consigned.[24]

In consequence, this book embraces the full cross-section of films produced between January 1950 and December 1959. The artificiality of this decading is deliberate, avoiding the connotations of other ways of defining 'the Fifties'. A study of 'Cold War' history films, for instance, might set the parameters between 1945 and 1960, or the 'Eisenhower Years' of 1952 to 1960, but this would tie the analysis too tightly to political interpretations of the past. The impact of McCarthyism on Hollywood in the form of the investigations of the House Un-American Activities Committee was certainly severe but, as will be demonstrated, a much broader viewpoint is needed to understand the contours of the industry's turn to history. Parameters defined by genre, too, would be counterproductive in their reductivity. Obviously the vogue for epics such as *The Ten Commandments* (1956) and non-biblicals like *Knights of the Round Table* (1953), draws particular attention when looking at the Fifties, but to survey the range of films made between *Samson and Delilah* (1949) and *Cleopatra* (1963), for instance, would falsely imply that an epic film was more representative of Hollywood's historical consciousness than a period comedy. Films from the late 1940s and early 1960s are considered where they illuminate patterns of production, but the cross-section of 1950–59 enables an evaluation of crucial influences without privileging any one factor or genre.

The commentary is shaped largely by factors which were specific to the film industry in the 1950s, such as the burst of innovation and experimentation in widescreen technologies, the economic crisis that prompted it, and the effect of the McCarthyite blacklist. But other considerations emerged directly from the 'trail of evidence' uncovered in the archives, such as the neglected area of the work of historical advisors and researchers; cases in which living 'historical figures' interfered with the production of history films; and the appearance in publicity materials of concepts such as 'thrill history'. Grounded in production documents, this study presents a reconstruction of how filmmakers themselves understood their treatment of the past – which, it is hoped, will better inform future work on the importance of Hollywood histories in influencing 'collective memories'.

This analysis of Hollywood's particular brand of historiography begins with *The Story of Mankind* (1957), demonstrating from the outset that even the most unintelligently conceived versions of the past can reveal the role of history in a culture's 'world view'. Providing the perfect vehicle for detailing Hollywood's unprecedented retrospection, Irwin Allen's rapid gallop through world history (courtesy of clips from other Warner Bros. movies), spotlights the eras that most interested contemporary filmmakers, and suggests how different periods were perceived. Moreover, in accord with Vann Woodward's assertion that contemporary Americans used the past as 'a sacred oracle', *The Story of Mankind* offered a reckoning with history that could renew one's faith in the future of humanity, when the threat of nuclear apocalypse was hanging overhead.

Chapters 2 through 5 examine the less ethereal anxieties motivating the embrace of the historical, focusing on factors that affected filmmaking as an industry. While studio finances, for example, are too often ignored in film studies, *Economic History* demonstrates that movies with historical settings were consistently more profitable that those set in contemporary times – and examines how filmmmaker's interpreted such box-office trends. Chapter 3, *Thrill History*, develops this to look at a specific response to the economic crisis, namely the industry's turn to technology in the search for a potential saviour to stave off a box-office implosion. This raises a fact previously unexplored – that the innovations of 3-D, CinemaScope, Todd-AO, Technirama and so forth, were all wedded to history films, with period-set movies used to showcase each 'advance'.

The fourth chapter *Political History*, deals directly with the impact of Cold War politics. History was used – and rewritten – by filmmakers of a variety of political persuasions to advance anti-Communist propaganda, to promote America's diplomatic goals, and to criticise the tactics of HUAC and McCarthy. It also looks at the blacklist's effect in muting criticism, an issue developed in the parallel Chapter 5, *Social History*, which explores how filmmakers approached contentious subjects, such as race-relations, using the distancing effect of a historical setting as a 'cloak'. Focusing on 'real' historical moments and events in *Political History*, and the generic period setting of the western in *Social History*, these two chapters explore the cultural resonances of different historical settings, to suggest the opportunities they provided and the limits they imposed on filmmakers who wanted to develop analogies with the present day.

Having established the value of the past to Hollywood and its film-makers, the final three chapters examine the effect that the production of so many history films had on the industry's historical consciousness. One obvious, but overlooked, factor is that filmmakers came into more frequent contact with historians and historical advisors. To some of these advisors, this presented an opportunity to educate Hollywood about history, and Chapter 6, *Researching History*, looks at the nature of this interaction and its limitations. In doing so, it works to establish what 'authenticity' meant to filmmakers, and the context in which they were confronted with 'real' history and material evidence. These confrontations took on a different edge too, as Hollywood became more interested in the recent past, especially in the biographies of near-contemporary public figures. While filmmakers rarely employed academic historians in the development of their history films, they could not avoid the involvement of the subject him- or herself, if they were still alive, or of relatives if the subject were recently deceased. As the chapter on *Living History* reveals, those who had personal memories of the past wanted to ensure that it was shown in a particular light, and either fought or collaborated with filmmakers to ensure that this happened. In the process, filmmakers became increasingly aware that historical 'truth' was far from fixed, but contested, interpretative and conjectural.

Thus as filmmakers increasingly explored a 'usable' past – relevant to the present-day needs of both the industry and the audience – they were simultaneously confronted with questions of historical understanding and interpretation, and with a heightened (but partial) awareness about the generation of historical evidence. The final chapter, *Intellectual History*, draws these strands together, in an analysis of the industry's image of itself as a purveyor of popular and relevant history. Reflected in the disparaging picture of 'what historians do' – evident in films like *Blackboard Jungle* (1955), *The Left-Handed Gun* (1958) and *The Bad and the Beautiful* (1952) – the 1950s witnessed a growing awareness in Hollywood that the work of professional historians also involved fictional construction and imagination. Naïve as the insight might have been, it further encouraged filmmakers to pose as 'public historians', who could displace 'dry and dusty' academics.

Addressing many films which, until now, have been unanalysed, it becomes very clear that the academic discipline of history was just one component of Hollywood's understanding of the past – incorporated into a consciousness which also valued legends, myths, literature, memories, and a myriad of other forms of public history. It cannot be dismissed, and it should not be reduced. The multiple viewpoints offered in this book – from perspectives that are economic, political, social, historiographical and intellectual – all worked to define the terms in which filmmakers engaged with the materials of the past and thought about representing them. If we understand that, we can better understand the essential role that Hollywood has played in the nation's historical consciousness, and the influence that many of these films continue to exert on our collective memory.

1

The Story of Mankind

If there is no tomorrow and no men of tomorrow, all the yesterdays will have had no meaning.

The Spirit of Man, *The Story of Mankind* (1957)

Audiences in 1957 generally ignored the release of Irwin Allen's *The Story of Mankind*, and film historians have continued to do so, with some justification given its absurd plot device of a celestial High Tribunal summoned to determine whether or not to save humanity from a final nuclear apocalypse. Yet, as a history film it is unique, for as the Devil and the Spirit of Man draw their evidence for prosecution and defence from the 'entire span of human history', it offers the cinematic equivalent of a Western Civilization survey course, from ancient Egypt through to the end of World War II. A direct result of a culture of production that was preoccupied with the past, Allen's film represented a reductive version of the other, collective, 'story of mankind' that Hollywood offered through the 1202 history films produced in the Fifties.

Indeed, *The Story of Mankind*'s relationship to Hollywood's interest in history could hardly have been more explicit, since much of the 'evidence' used in the trial was simply a selection of clips from earlier history films. Thus the building of the pyramids was included because unused scenes from Howard Hawks' *Land of the Pharaohs* (1955) were available. Similarly, the siege of Troy was lifted from Warner's 1955 production of *Helen of Troy* (1956), with library footage of *Captain Horatio Hornblower* (1951) and

10

King Richard and the Crusaders (1954) also informing which events were shown as 'representative' of human history.[1] And when *Story* featured new material, the reconstructions were ones already familiar to moviegoers: Hedy Lamarr's scene as the Maid of Orleans recalled Ingrid Bergman's *Joan of Arc* (1948); while Peter Lorre's histrionic performance as Nero played to

Storyboarding Mankind: Hedy Lamarr consults the costume design for her portrayal of Joan of Arc, as producer-director Irwin Allen shows her what goes into the telling of *The Story of Mankind* (1957). (Courtesy of the British Film Institute)

audiences well-acquainted with the maniacal Roman emperors of *Quo Vadis* (1951), *The Robe* (1953) and *The Silver Chalice* (1954).

This dependence on Hollywood's pre-existing versions of the past also created an imbalance in the film's trial. With his focus on villains and despots, cruelty and war, the Devil had the industry on his side, with much more visual material to make his case. In the 1950s alone, Hollywood produced ten films featuring tyrants from pre-Christian history, 23 starring blood-thirsty pirates, some five hundred western gunfights, and over one hundred accounts of brutal death in World War II. The Spirit of Man, seeking to emphasise the human capacity for faith, enlightenment and progress, could do little but draw on the Old and New Testaments (15 films in the 1950s), the age of chivalry (14 films) and the American Revolution (just five movies). Reviewers were concerned that 'much of what is good is only talked about, never shown' – but the film's construction itself suggests that this charge could readily be levelled at Hollywood's history films as a whole.[2]

Offering some preliminary observations about the attitudes and pre-conceptions that shaped Hollywood's use of particular pasts, what follows is an account of how the industry's more expansive 'story' was construed in the Fifties. *The Story of Mankind*'s 100-minute survey of history certainly embodied key aspects of contemporary Hollywood's imaging of the past, but there were major points of divergence too. This is immediately apparent in the weighting of interest in certain periods. *The Story of Mankind* devoted 20 minutes of its screen time to pre-Christian history, 12 minutes to the Age of Discovery, 15 minutes to the eighteenth and nineteenth centuries, but only 180 seconds to the last 50 years. However, as **Figure 1.1** demonstrates, Hollywood, overall, offered a very different temporal emphasis.

Derived from dates given on the screen and the settings recorded in scripts and production materials, **Figure 1.1** represents the number of history films set in particular time periods.[3] Ancient history received notable attention in the first half of the decade, although production of films using this setting was always relatively small in numbers. Interest in the Early Modern period was also greatest at the beginning of the decade. Overall, only 11 percent of history films were set before the nineteenth century, but this is distorted by the dominance of westerns set in the 25 years following the American Civil War; only 29 movies set between 1865 and 1890 defy classification as westerns. However, the preponderance of westerns should not distract from the emphasis placed on the twentieth century, with interest in the most recent history increasing (at the expense of films set early in the century) as the 1950s progressed.

In further contrast to *The Story of Mankind*'s approach it is also important to note that cinema's conception of history was defined frequently more by genre than by chronology. Taking the 45 films set in the eighteenth century, for example, films such as *Mohawk* (1956) and *Daniel Boone, Trailblazer* (1956) owe as much, if not more, to the conventions of westerns usually set in the mid-nineteenth century. The dozen or so films that concern piracy, including *Treasure Island* (1950) or *The Crimson Pirate* (1952) were clearly conceived as generic sea-faring swashbucklers, with little to distinguish them from pirate adventures set in the seventeenth century, except that it was more common for the latter to feature genuine historical characters such as Captain Kidd (*Captain Kidd and the Slave Girl*, 1954) or Captain Edward Teach (*Blackbeard the Pirate*, 1952). And *Prisoners of the Casbah* (1953) took the plasticity of periodisation to an extreme in relocating a typical Arabian Nights adventure, complete with scheming grand vizier, from the usual setting of ninth-century Persia, to eighteenth-century Algiers. However, as Richard Slotkin suggests, such genres are defined by 'a powerful association between particular kinds of setting and particular story forms'.[4] Historical settings thus function as the 'mythic spaces' of

Figure 1.1: Chronological Distribution of History Films, 1950–1959

	1950	1951	1952	1953	1954	1955	1956	1957	1958	1959	Total
BCE	1	1	1	4	3	3	2			1	16
0-500		1	1	2	4					3	11
501-1000	1	2	3	3	2			2	2	1	16
1001-1500	3	3	3		4	4	4	2			23
1501-1600		1	1	6		2	1				11
1601-1700	3	4	4	3		1					15
1701-1800	3	4	10	8	6	5	2	2	1	4	45
1801-1859	12	13	21	17	12	14	12	7	5	7	120
1860-1865	7	9	4	8	3	3	5	6	1	3	49
1866-1890	84	69	72	53	50	39	58	56	45	24	550
1891-1910	14	13	19	13	9	12	8	8	9	3	108
1911-1920	2	3	5	7	1	3	3	3	3	4	34
1921-1930	2	5	8	3		3	5	8	3	5	42
1931-1940	3	2	6	3	3	7	3	4	5	6	42
1941-1945	6	15	7	14	3	3	10	11	22	11	102
post-1945		1		3	1	1	3	2	3	4	18
Totals	141	146	165	147	101	100	116	111	99	76	1202

particular genres, with a specific historical moment commonly identified 'with the fictions created about it'.[5] Although this attitude towards history is certainly different to a historian's way of thinking about the past, it was a product of the industry's particular needs and practices, and meant too that each 'mythic space' evoked an authentic time and place, with film-makers well aware of an era's cultural resonances.

THE ANCIENT WORLD: 'THE EPIC STRUGGLE BETWEEN FAITH AND PAGANISM'

This perspective was present from the outset of *The Story of Mankind* as it characterised 'the ancient world' as a temporal space in which 'mythology and history become interwoven'. It was certainly true of Hollywood's treatment of Homeric epic as history in *Helen of Troy,* and of the historical validity accredited to biblical stories such as the plagues on Egypt and the Exodus in *The Ten Commandments* (1956).[6] Allen's construction of ancient history encompassed both Helen and Moses, along with the building of the pyramids, the 'Golden Age' of Greek civilization, the reign of Cleopatra, the Roman Empire, and the advent of Christ. Hollywood reflected all of this directly in *Land of the Pharaohs, Alexander the Great* (1956), *Serpent of the Nile* (1953), *Julius Caesar* (1953) and the 'New Testament' epics that began with *Quo Vadis.*

The dominance of this history in *The Story of Mankind* certainly over-emphasised the small number of films actually set in ancient times. It was arguably justified, however, by the fact that the majority of these films were large-scale epics, showcasing spectacular visual production values and sold with a corresponding level of showmanship that gave them a unique stature among history films. The prestige accorded to *The Ten Commandments* or *Ben Hur* (1959) freighted the films with profoundly elevated significance, commensurate with the history they depicted. Indeed, this was an era conceived in terms of nothing less than the rise and fall of civilizations, and 'Western man's spiritual beginnings'.[7]

These themes were encapsulated in the first evidence presented by the Devil, calling as a witness the Pharaoh Khufu, for whom the Great Pyramid of Gizeh was built (and rebuilt in *Land of the Pharaohs*). Holding up Khufu as a tyrant who enslaved the souls of men to ensure his own deification, *Story* emulated the characteristic way in which Hollywood's biblical films overlaid questions of faith and paganism with the theme of freedom versus tyranny. 'Man in his confusion worshipped many false Gods,' confessed the Spirit of Man, 'and as a result people were enslaved and oppressed.' *The Ten Commandments*, for one, was explicit in this, setting the God of Moses against the dictatorial Rameses, who made slaves of the Hebrews while worshipping animal-headed idols. This was repeated in the narratives of New Testament films as well, which depicted the persecution of the early Christians by despotic Roman emperors who set themselves up as gods (as in *Quo Vadis, The Robe*, or *Androcles and the Lion* (1953)). The effect of this narrative continuity was to construe ancient history as a prelude to the coming of Christ, a 'turbulent era of pagan worship' over which the 'true faith' in one God would triumph.[8]

The influence of this conception extended beyond the biblical films. *The Egyptian* (1954), set in 1300 BC, presented the monotheistic beliefs of Pharaoh Akhnaton as 'a prevision of a Christian-like God'.[9] The militaristic dictator who overthrows Akhnaton and slays his disciples, is associated with the pagan beliefs of priests who fear this new religion will mean the end of their hold over the populace. Even *Alexander the Great* did not quite escape this mindset, drawing attention to Alexander's insistence that the Greeks deify him. When his attitude changes to a realisation that 'We are all alike under God – the father of all', his imperial ambitions become tempered and his 'tyranny' is immediately diminished.

There were, of course, efforts to present a different perspective. *Alexander* for instance, sought a psychological interpretation of its protagonist, influenced by the 1950s preoccupation with troubled and alienated youth. Robert Rossen depicted the conqueror as the scion of a dysfunctional family, whose determination to surpass the victories of his father, Philip of Macedonia, is encouraged by his power-hungry mother, Olympias. William Wyler also sought to stake out new ground with *Ben Hur* as a 'thinking man's epic', reacting against the melodramatics of Cecil B. DeMille's productions. Audiences were hardly short-changed in the spectacle of the chariot race or the great sea battle, and publicity still defined the period in terms of 'the epic struggle between faith and paganism' – but the real conflict originates in the political differences between Judah Ben Hur and Messala, with the focus as much on Ben Hur shaking off his apathy to challenge the power of Rome, as on his spiritual realisations.[10] However, the pertinence of ancient history was still primarily in terms of providing a context of oppression, tyranny, and the corruption of power – while Christianity, as the Spirit of Man put it, then brought 'new hope into a world where hope was dead'.

THE OLD WORLD: 'TURMOIL AND ADVENTURE'

Attempting to continue this line of reasoning, *The Story of Mankind* proceeded to present medieval history in terms of men 'fighting and dying for their faiths'. However, films like *King Richard and the Crusaders* (1954) undercut this interpretation, suppressing religious conflict so that the commanders of the Christian and Islamic forces (Richard and Saladin respectively) could unite in defeating a common foe of renegade knights. It was also in this period, rather than the pre-Christian era, that the interweaving of mythology and history was most evident in Hollywood's historical consciousness. *Knights of the Round Table* (1953) and *The Vikings* (1958) presented their legends and sagas with aplomb. Yet, when Camelot faced down threats first from Vikings in *Prince Valiant* (1954), then Saracens in *The Black Knight* (1954), it was evident that filmmakers blurred it all into one mythic space.

Indeed, movies directly concerned with medieval history consistently defined the period 'when knighthood flowered' through the filter of Sir Walter Scott's imagination. Direct adaptations of Scott's serials were presented in *Ivanhoe* (1952), *King Richard and the Crusaders* and *Quentin Durward* (1955), but his fictional accounts of hostility between oppressed Saxons and tyrannical Norman overlords informed almost every other medieval film Hollywood released. *Lady Godiva* (1955) depicted the roots of conflict in the reign of Edward the Confessor, while the foreword to *The Black Rose* (1950) even insisted that 'the bitterness between the Norman conqueror and the Saxon conquered lay still unhealed' more than two centuries after the Battle of Hastings.[11] This questionable context allowed filmmakers to present Saxon heroes as righteous 'freedom fighters' – kin to Robin Hood (who himself turned up in three films) – and contributed to the 'current vogue', noted by one industry observer in 1954, 'for historical pictures to just let the audience have a hell of a lot of entertainment'.[12]

While it is certainly true that these cinematic versions of British medieval history 'recuperated the period as a celebration of an energetic and classless masculinity', the same description can be applied to Hollywood's depiction of the preceding Dark Ages, of the subsequent history of modern Europe through to the Napoleonic era, and also the peculiar Middle East of Arabian

Nights fantasies.[13] This is evident, for example, in Tony Curtis crossing class barriers in ninth-century Tangiers in *The Prince Who Was a Thief* (1951), discovering he is not really a peasant but a member of King Henry IV's nobility in *The Black Shield of Falworth* (1954), and rescuing aristocrats from the French Revolution's guillotine in *The Purple Mask* (1955). The 'historical indeterminacy' of masculine heroics in historical adventure films, which Brian Taves documents in *The Romance of Adventure*, was in part a consequence of the studio system. While historians associated the Arabian Nights stories with the Abbasid Caliphates of the ninth century, the film industry explicitly conceived of them as a 'distinct but shortlived branch of the swashbuckler' and assigned them to production units such as Sam Katzman's at Columbia – where he also supervised adventures set during the Crusades (*The Saracen Blade*, 1954), on the high seas of piracy (*The Golden Hawk*, 1954), during the reign of George I (*The Iron Glove*, 1954), and even in colonial India (*The Flame of Calcutta*, 1953), alongside 16 westerns.[14] The generic conventions of action adventures united a range of disparate pasts.

Yet, as Taves suggests, history was integral to such adventures, since the stories contrive to endow their heroes with 'a sense of meaning and purpose' by suggesting that without their participation the past would have taken a different course. Even imaginary heroes gained stature from historical settings, as in the fictitious Prince Roland in Katzman's *Prince of Pirates* (1953), whose adventures contribute to the defeat of 'Spain's dream' of conquering Western Europe in the early sixteenth century. Moreover, despite the fact that adventure stories were 'conceded a wide degree of poetic license', specific temporal settings still retained some pertinence.[15] Each age was presented with its own 'code'. Medieval adventures combined the possibility of an individual affecting the flow of history with a code of honour and chivalry that made their motives 'pure'. And as this 'golden age' was eclipsed by the rise of modern politics – a process gently satirised in *Quentin Durward* – swashbucklers set in later periods adapted the rules. Films set in seventeenth- and eighteenth-century Europe tended to uphold the code of the Musketeers – 'All for one and one for all' – to maintain collective honour in a Machiavellian world of self-interest: *The King's Thief* (1955), for example, transposed it to the English Restoration court of Charles II. The 'pirate code' became such a cliché that it was parodied in *The Crimson Pirate* – but it also allowed the genre to present heroes who were more ambiguous in their morality, while the isolating expanses of the high seas enabled them to act with greater freedom and a pronounced relish for any action that came their way.[16]

An alternative frame of reference for European history did exist in depictions of courtly romance. Taking audiences 'behind closed doors' to explore the interplay of personality and politics, filmmakers entered the palaces of Philip II of Spain in *That Lady* (1955), Henri II of France in *Diane* (1955), and England's Henry VIII in *The Sword and the Rose* (1953) and *Young Bess* (1953) each concerned with the love lives of royal youth. The formula was also applied to later periods, as in *The Naked Maja* (1959) and its version of the relationship between the Duchess of Alba and the artist Francisco Goya, or the account of Napoleon's rise and fall seen through the eyes of a woman who loved him in *Desiree* (1954). *Beau Brummell* (1954) offered an interesting take by depicting the relationship at court between two men – George Brummell and the Prince of Wales.

Yet, even in this framework, swashbuckling adventure was not entirely escapable. When *The Virgin Queen* (1955) sought to emulate the success of 1939's *The Private Lives of Elizabeth and Essex*, it made sure to establish the masculine credentials of Sir Walter Raleigh by opening with a swordfight replete with up-turned tables, agile leaps on to balconies, candles sliced in two, and women screaming in fear and admiration. In many cases too, there was often little to distinguish the courts of Europe from the palaces of Hollywood's Arabian Caliphs – with both providing opulent settings against which filmmakers could conjure 'sharp contrasts between lavish luxury and cruel horrors'.[17] This was particularly true when it came to French history, with the stories of Alexander Dumas and Rafael Sabatini inspiring the continued clash of rapiers, from Louis XIII's Musketeers (and their offspring in *At Sword's Point* (1952)) to the post-Napoleonic *Sword of Monte Cristo* (1951).[18]

The Napoleonic Wars did allow for more thoughtful treatments of historical drama, as Italian producer Dino DeLaurentiis released *War and Peace* (1956) and *Tempest* (1959) in America and demonstrated the epic potential of the period. Stanley Kramer emulated this scale and scope with *The Pride and the Passion* (1957), celebrating Spanish opposition to Napoleon's ambitions. But Hollywood provided little space for the Spirit of Man's perception of European history as a 'great and endless flow of human expression', of man discovering 'the sacredness of human rights'. Something was presented of the 'free thought of the individual beautifully expressed' by artists such as Goya, Vincent Van Gogh (in *Lust for Life*

(1956)) and Toulouse Lautrec (in *Moulin Rouge* (1952)). But William Shakespeare and Leonardo Da Vinci only appeared in *The Story of Mankind* itself, and only *Martin Luther* (1955) dealt seriously with the social, religious and political realities of the Reformation – and that semi-documentary was made outside of the studio system, sponsored by an organisation of Lutheran Churches. As the Devil's testimony asserted, Hollywood took it for granted that there was greater drama in 'homicidal mania and unmitigated villainy' – or in what *Casanova's Big Night* (1954) parodied as 'an era of turmoil and adventure; murder for revenge; passion for the sport of it'.[19]

THE NEW WORLD: 'A FIERCE DESIRE FOR INDEPENDENCE'

Spirit of Man: The spirit of adventure, exploration and discovery fought for and experienced by Columbus, opened a new territory, half again as large as the world already known. Columbus showed the way and mankind followed.

The Devil: … But to what ends? Murder, pillage, rape? … The violent pattern set by the blood-thirsty Cortez turned out to be one of my better jobs. The slaughter of the New World was endless but delightful. Was this what they called a high road to a better world?

Despite the importance accorded Christopher Columbus by the Spirit of Man, the discovery and colonization of America barely registered in other films. Only two contemplated the Spanish conquests: a low-budget quest for the Fountain of Youth in *Hurricane Island* (1951), and *Seven Cities of Gold* (1955), a more serious consideration of the eighteenth-century expeditions into California and Father Junipero Serra's establishment of Franciscan missions. The latter film does acknowledge the Devil's description of the savagery of the conquistadors; when one young soldier tells stories of the 'glory days' of Cortez, Serra furiously sets the record straight, stating the conquest of Mexico was 'ungodly', and that 'your grandfather's grandfather walked in blood up to his ankles'. However, in depicting Serra's peaceful conversion of native peoples, the film also agreed with the Spirit of Man's qualification, that 'the slaughter wasn't quite endless because there were others [who] didn't believe in these methods of forceful submission'.

The settlement of the Eastern colonies was also considered in just two films. Again, one was minor (United Artists' release of *Captain John Smith and Pocahontas* (1953)), and the other a prestige production from MGM, entitled *Plymouth Adventure* (1952), which told the story of the Mayflower Compact through the eyes of the ship's captain. Otherwise colonial America was confined to ten films about clashes between settlers and natives, and the French-Indian Wars, taking a lead from James Fenimore Cooper's novels – with a focus on 'frontier history' that cast films like *When The Redskins Rode* (1952) or *Fort Ti* (1953) as precursors to nineteenth-century westerns.

Disney's *Johnny Tremain* (1957) came closest to capturing what the Spirit of Man saw in the American Revolution, that 'mankind will neither be dominated nor misled for any great period of time; and that under the shackles of oppression, spirited heroes are created'. Showing the Boston Tea Party and the Battle of Lexington, *Tremain* depicted the heroic leadership of Patrick Henry, Paul Revere, Sam Adams and James Otis, but also demonstrated that 'a fierce desire for independence burning in the hearts' of unsung patriots like the fictional young Johnny, 'made the deeds of our great men possible'.[20] However, only three other films used the War of Independence as background: MGM released *The Scarlet Coat* in 1955, using the treachery of Benedict Arnold to shape a spy story; Warners used naval hero *John Paul Jones* (1959) to construct a swashbuckler; and George Bernard Shaw's *The Devil's Disciple* was adapted to reunite Burt Lancaster and Kirk Douglas in 1959 after their successful pairing in *Gunfight at the OK Corral* (1957). DeMille redeemed things somewhat in *The Buccaneer* (his final film which, due to illness, he 'supervised' rather than directed in 1958). Although set in 1815, dealing with the contribution of outlaw privateer Jean Lafitte to Andrew Jackson's victory over the British at the Battle of New Orleans, it captured a sense of the historical significance of Revolution in having Lafitte enamoured of the 'inalienable rights' defined in the Declaration of Independence. 'If they are not just words on paper,' asserts Lafitte, clearly stirred, 'they might be worth fighting for.'[21]

Several filmmakers were more engaged by the history and characters of the post-Revolution period. The Alamo was the subject of six films in the early 1950s, when the 'story of Texas' was held to 'symbolize the spirit of independence so close to the heart of all Americans'.[22] Other events committed to film included the exploration of the continent by Lewis and Clark in *The Far Horizons* (1955); the election of Andrew Jackson in *The President's Lady* (1953); Polk's dispute with Britain in *The Oregon Trail* (1959); and the opening of diplomatic relations between America and Japan in 1856 in *The Barbarian and the Geisha* (1958). However, reticence returned again when it came to the Civil War. At least 40 of the 50 films set against the Civil War might best be described as westerns – and only a handful of these had explicit historical content. Even *The Story of Mankind* skirted around the conflict, with the Devil suggesting how difficult it was for man to 'talk his way out of that one'.

The Spirit of Man did point to the Emancipation Proclamation as evidence of the good that came out of the Civil War – though Hollywood's treatment of the abolitionist movement was limited to *Seven Angry Men* (1955), focusing on John Brown's raid on Harper's Ferry. *Band of Angels* (1957) was unusual in its attention to the war's racial politics, casting Sidney Poitier as a proud black man raised by slave-trader Clark Gable. However, while the title referred to the short life expectancy of freed slaves who fought with Union troops, the film was more concerned with the love story between the trader and his half-caste mistress. Moreover, publicity from Warner Bros., specifically reassured audiences that 'though laid in the Civil War era', the film would 'underplay the North-South military struggle' and 'instead emphasise the love-theme'.[23]

The fact that studios thought that such a promise was necessary reflects the poor reception accorded to movies which did deal directly with the 'military struggle'. John Huston tried a deliberate approach in his 1951 adaptation of Stephen Crane's *The Red Badge of Courage*, evoking the war through the eyes of a young farm boy turned solider, who loses his courage in the heat of battle. A self-consciously poignant meditation on heroism, it was heavily edited by a nervous MGM and fared badly at the box office, encouraging Hollywood to regard the war as unreliable material. Aside from the *Gone With the Wind* model of epic costume-melodrama, followed by *Band of Angels* and *Raintree County* (1956), the other strategy was to depict the conflict as an adventure, with daring incursions into enemy territory forming the dramatic basis for *The Raid* (1954), *The Great Locomotive Chase* (1956), *Drums in the Deep South* (1951) and *The Horse Soldiers* (1959). *The Horse Soldiers* represented John Ford's only full-scale feature on the Civil War and, for the most part, it avoids the war's sectionalism to instead manufacture a conflict *within* the Union forces between

Colonel Marlowe and the unit's army doctor. The fate of the South is represented metaphorically through the experience of a high-spirited Southern belle, who endures hardship and humiliation at the hand of Marlowe; but ultimately respect and even love emerges from their antagonism. However, one of the strongest moments in the film comes when boys from the military academy, none older than 16, march out to delay the Union raiders. Based on an incident from the 1864 Battle of New Market, in which over fifty cadets from the Virginia Military Institute were killed or wounded, Ford rewrote history to celebrate the bravery and gallantry of both sides, with Marlowe's men refusing to fight, falling back as they pretend to be routed by the youngsters. The sequence manages to provide a 'heartbreaking image of the war's sacrifice of the young', without making it an unbearable tragedy – but that this required a change to history is indicative of the difficulties experienced in handling the Civil War.[24]

THE AMERICAN WEST: 'YOU'RE LIABLE TO GET KILLED!'

The generic conventions of the western were so well established by the 1950s that there were few such problems in presenting the history of the American West. Westerns accounted for almost 60 percent of the decade's history films, with over 700 released. The dramatic possibilities of greedy land-grabbing, gunfights, lawlessness, and both 'red' and 'white' man 'fighting for his very survival', were identified by the Devil and every western filmmaker. Yet, even in its most formulaic presentation, history remained central to the genre, not necessarily as a source of specific events or people, but rather for the fact that Will Wright perceived: that on the frontier, 'for a brief time' between 1860 and 1895, 'many ways of life were available, each of which contained its own element of adventure'.[25]

'Farmers, cowboys, cavalrymen, miners, Indian fighters, gamblers, gunfighters, railroad builders', and so on, may have 'had little contact with each other' in reality, but they were all 'out West' at the same time, and offered themselves to screenwriters as a 'source of narrative inspiration'. Indeed, western narratives represent the almost endless permutations of bringing such types together and generating 'clear-cut conflicts of interest and values'. Moreover, the 'real but limited' use of gunplay to settle differences on the frontier, provided scenarists with a simple way to end the conflicts with 'abrupt, clear resolutions'.[26]

As presented in the 1950s, the western made full use of these 'situational antagonisms' inherent in frontier development. The US cavalry fought spies in the Civil War (*Springfield Rifle*, 1952), carpetbaggers during Reconstruction (*Thunder Over the Plains*, 1953), and outlaws afterwards (*Slaughter Trail*, 1951), along with the expected battles against marauding Indians (*Thunder Pass* (1954) being a typical example). Outlaws fought Native Americans too (*Ambush at Tomahawk Gap*, 1953), when not in conflict with lawmen (such as *Oklahoma Justice*, 1951), or even the occasional female rancher (*Cattle Queen*, 1950). Towns competed for the coming of the railroad (*Overland Pacific*, 1954), while riverboat tycoons and stagecoach owners tried to stop it altogether (*Rock Island Trail* (1950) and *A Ticket to Tomahawk* (1950) respectively). Itinerant preachers got involved with quarrels between settlers and ranchers (*The Peacemaker*, 1954), and Quakers came up against timber barons (*The Big Trees*, 1952). Homesteaders fought with cattle barons (as in *The Marauders* (1955)), cattlemen feuded with miners (*Hills of Utah*, 1951), and miners killed each other (*Duel At Silver Creek*, 1952). With all the blood shed, it was hardly surprising when *Curse of the Undead* (1959) suggested that the West had been popular with vampires!

Different periods in the development of the West did have particular virtues and narrative resonance. The background of the Civil War and its immediate aftermath provided an excuse for introducing 'many types of people who would not under normal circumstances be there, such as sons of former plantation owners, ex-Confederate officers', Union agents and the like.[27] Many post-Civil War plots required veterans to put right the wrong done by unscrupulous men who had taken advantage of the conflict to grab land or political power. In other films, veterans – like Ethan Edwards in *The Searchers* (1956) – were displaced, unable to settle. As Richard Maltby notes, 'one cultural function of the post-Civil War western was to provide a meeting ground for Southern Codes of chivalry and Northern, commercial versions of Manifest Destiny'.[28] *Vera Cruz* (1954) was a prime example, contrasting the values of a former Confederate colonel and a horse thief entangled in the Mexican revolution against emperor Maximilian. Or, as in the case of *Sugarfoot* (1951), Southern refugees mellowed their aristocratic attitudes and learned the 'Code of the West'.

Over the following twenty-five years or so, 'American civilization surged westward in a tidal wave'.[29] Vignettes of the lives of settlers, such as *The Missourians* (1950), and pioneer westerns like *Wagonmaster* (1950),

Westward the Women (1951) or *A Perilous Journey* (1951), allowed filmmakers to repeatedly make the point 'that people, men and women, grow in proportion to their determination and the difficulties they faced'.[30] Many were concerned with the development of early settlements into viable communities – and made heroes out of crusading newspaper editors, doctors, spiritual leaders and tough lawmen who challenged the 'feudal' interests of men who stood in the way of society's progress.[31] Others, such as the romanticised accounts of *The Pony Express* (1953) and railroad building in *Denver and the Rio Grande* (1952), concerned themselves with the ways in which the settled West became integrated into the nation, with the achieving of statehood at stake in movies like *Montana Territory* (1952).

Westerns set nearer the turn of the century, however, tended to be darker, depicting the period with considerable concern about 'the passing of the Old World into the modern society, and the western hero's increasingly complex and ambiguous relationship to that process'.[32] This tone was apparent at the very start of the decade in *The Gunfighter* (1950), and then in *High Noon* (1952). Though neither film provides a specific date, they are clearly set at the moment identified in 1890 as the 'closing of the American frontier' – a historical setting which enhances the sense of time running out for their protagonists. *High Noon*'s Sheriff Will Kane cannot persuade the people of his town to help him defeat a vengeful killer because they are too concerned that violence will scare off Northern investors who promise to bring stores and factories to their isolated community. Johnny Ringo, the eponymous gunfighter, is the victim of his own western 'legend', unable to make the transition to a safe, domestic life, because callow youths challenge him to take over his title as 'the fastest gun in the west'.

In films such as these, as Andre Bazin suggested in his contemporary study of 'The Evolution of the Western', history became more than just the 'material' of the genre in the Fifties; it 'often became its subject'.[33] A resurgence of 'A-feature' westerns reached new heights with prestigious projects like George Stevens' *Shane* (1953), John Ford's *The Searchers* (1956) and William Wyler's *The Big Country*. Each of these self-consciously explored 'themes' of western history: violence, racism, masculinity and social transition. Others followed *The Gunfighter* to interrogate the mythology of real life western legends, including Billy the Kid in *The Left-Handed Gun* (1958), Doc Holliday and Wyatt Earp in *Gunfight at the OK Corral* (1957), and *The True Story of Jesse James* (1957).[34] Even in lower-budget productions, there was a 'collapse of fantasy', and a critical examination of the psychology of frontier characters, typified in the works of Anthony Mann and Budd Boetticher such as *Bend of the River* (1952) and *The Tall T* (1957).[35] Filmmakers then used moments such as the end of the Civil War or the closing of the frontier to add poignancy and significance to the hero's personal transition.

The Story of Mankind's history of the American West, however, made little of any of this, stressing instead 'the outrageous stealing of land from the Indians', and the white man's use of 'the foulest of methods' to suppress the native population. In this, Allen's film responded to a change in historical consciousness evident in a number of Fifties' westerns, beginning with *Broken Arrow* (1950), which sought to portray Native Americans with sympathy. The Chirachau Apache tribe in Delmer Daves' seminal film was presented as honourable and civilised, in direct contrast to the greed, intolerance and hatred displayed by the whites who encroached upon their land.

Certainly many films continued to express the view voiced by Peter Minuit in *Story*, that 'You're crazy to go West. The whole West is full of Indians – you're liable to get killed.' Westerns set in the eighteenth century, such as *Many Rivers to Cross* (1955), gained drama from the fact that frontiersmen had to face the threat on their own, with no possibility of the cavalry riding to their rescue in the final frames. Civil War westerns like *Escape from Fort Bravo* (1953), and *Revolt at Fort Laramie* (1957), depicted Native Americans 'slaying Northerner and Southerner indiscriminately', thus compelling soldiers of the Union and Confederacy to reunite in common cause.[36] And post-war films such as *Massacre Canyon* (1954) and *Ambush at Cimarron Pass* (1958) continued to treat Indians as savages, as nothing more than 'an immediate physical threat to the hero and his charges'.[37]

However, *Story* itself satirised this attitude by having Groucho Marx play Minuit – with his comment about being 'crazy' directed at the Lenape Indian Chief he conned out of Manhattan. And following *Broken Arrow*, a series of westerns revisited the Indian Wars, showing them to have been provoked by trespassing gold-rushers breaking treaties, by murders committed by racist white men, and by bandits stirring up violence for their own ends. *Comanche Territory* (1950), for instance, had Jim Bowie treat with Native Americans on behalf of the government for access to the silver ore on their lands – and then lead the Comanche in repelling local settlers who try to claim the wealth for themselves. Films such as *Tomahawk* (1951) and *Fort Massacre* (1958) cast over-zealous cavalry officers as the villains, with Disney's *Tonka* (1958) presenting General Custer as an obsessive white supremacist. Isolating individual bad guys did allow filmmakers to absolve the federal government, and 'the white man' as a whole, of blame for atrocities – but even this historical interpretation came under scrutiny in *Davy Crockett, King of the Wild Frontier* (1955), when it depicted the Indian Resettlement Act of 1830 as a product of 'the corrupt nature of Jacksonian politics'.[38]

More realistic pictures of historical Native Americans – particularly Geronimo, Cochise and Chief Crazy Horse – were also sought, rather than continue depicting Indians as nameless savages or victims. Most filmmakers chose to mediate their stories through the eyes of white men, just as *Broken Arrow* was narrated by 'Tom Jeffords' (who indeed had helped to end the Apache Wars in 1872). Audiences in 1956 were told about *Walk the Proud Land*'s Geronimo by Indian agent John P. Clum, while *Conquest of Cochise* (1953) related Indian history through the story of a cavalry officer's efforts to keep a lid on further conflict. *Chief Crazy Horse* (1955) also seemed to start the same way, with a fictional Major Twist narrating the story. However, the film soon sidelined him in favour of a more direct presentation of the Lakota Sioux war chief. Indeed, this biopic explicitly dealt with Crazy Horse as 'one of America's greatest generals', devoting time and respect to his strategy and tactics at the Rosebud and Little Big Horn. The impulse to present the 'other side' of history was not entirely altruistic; the director of *Chief Crazy Horse* admitted that 'letting the Indians win for a change is a great boost at the box office'.[39] But it did result in a much broader depiction of Native American experience, from figures such as Lance Poole, who won a Medal of Honor at Gettysburg (*Devil's Doorway*, 1951), to sports star Jim Thorpe, who dominated the 1912 Olympics (*Jim Thorpe – All American*, 1951). In contrast, the black absence in Hollywood's story of the American West remained to be addressed.

THE TWENTIETH CENTURY: 'DANCE OF DEATH'

The Spirit of Man sought to counter 'the madness' of the western's 'greed, pestilence and murder', with reference to progress in technology and culture achieved since the Civil War. But while he emphasised the 'accomplishments of great inventors', including Alexander Graham Bell, Thomas Edison and the Wright Brothers, the rest of Hollywood demonstrated no such interest.[40] *Excuse My Dust* (1951) did depict an amateur inventor of early automobiles, but purely as a light-hearted fiction that pit the car in a race against a horse. It was akin to *Fireman, Save My Child* (1954), which turned the modernisation of a San Francisco firehouse into slapstick comedy, with both films employing the 'turn of the century' background as a 'safe' moment of historical transition. Indeed, the turn of the century setting presented an opportunity for films to share the western's sense of an era giving way to inexorable progress, but with nostalgic grace and humour instead of violent resistance. Reflecting this, filmmakers generally preferred to associate the social transformations of the 1890s and 1900s with personal, rather than technological, development – as in 'the forging of manly individualism' at the heart of *Old Yeller* (1957), or a 'gawky young girl's blossoming into a glamorous woman' in *Gigi* (1958).[41]

Attention was paid to the Wright Brothers' invention, even if Wilbur and Orville themselves were ignored. The airplane's contribution to Allied victory in World War I was evident in *Lafayette Escadrille*'s (1958) account of the American pilots who flew with the French Air Corps, while *The Court Martial of Billy Mitchell* (1955) examined the arguments for America developing its own air force in the 1920s, and *The Spirit of St Louis* (1957) depicted Charles Lindbergh's epic trans-Atlantic flight of 1927. However, *Spirit* possessed little sense of Lindbergh's impact on modern aviation, and *Billy Mitchell* showed that while the General had been right in his predictions about the centrality of aircraft in modern warfare, military bureaucracy had prevented his vision from being acted upon. In contrast to *The Virgin Queen*, for instance, in which Sir Walter Raleigh personally persuades Elizabeth I to finance a new kind of ship to ensure England's dominance over the seas, twentieth-century biopics seemed less convinced that any individual could exercise such a decisive influence over the course of modern history. Thus individual inventors, in modern, corporate society, seemed to be of less significance. Or, if their inventions were of great importance, it was no longer clear that this constituted unqualified progress – especially, as the Devil noted, since mankind had ultimately 'used his greatest intellectual invention of the airplane' to drop the bomb on Hiroshima and Nagasaki.[42]

The Spirit's evidence of man's cultural development was also compromised by the way in which Hollywood depicted biographical history. *The Story of Mankind* referred to great composers such as Beethoven, Brahms and Verdi – but while Richard Wagner briefly featured in the industry's historical consciousness (*Magic Fire*, 1956), filmmakers gave pre-eminence to popular songwriters of the twentieth century, such as Bert Kalmar, Harry Ruby and Gus Kahn, and bandleaders like Glenn Miller and Benny Goodman. These films celebrated the development of mass culture as the democratisation of the arts, as talented individuals defied elitist cultural prejudices. *The Great Caruso* (1951), for example, depicted the emotional and unrefined tenor Enrico Caruso challenging the patrician patrons of the New York Metropolitan Opera and widening the appeal of the art form. *I'll See You in My Dreams* (1951) presents Gus Kahn's Tin Pan Alley lyrics as a modern equivalent of the love poems of Elizabeth Barrett Browning, perhaps even more relevant in their expression of emotion. And *St Louis Blues* (1958) acknowledged the accomplishment of African-American blues composer W.C. Handy, culminating in the 'ultimate' symbol of cultural acceptance when his work is performed as a symphony at Carnegie Hall.

Such biopics of performers and celebrities offered a 'justification of the legitimacy of popular entertainment', which in itself shored up Hollywood's own self-image at the very moment it felt threatened by television.[43] The industry reflected its own history in biopics of Buster Keaton, Lon Chaney, Rudolph Valentino and Will Rogers, and celebrated its ability to adapt in *Singin' in the Rain*'s account of the early days of talking pictures.[44] Other films, such as *Jeanne Eagels* (1957), suggested that the time that their protagonist had spent working in the movies had been the highlight of their career. However, the makers of biopics also responded and contributed to the contemporary trend for 'adult' and 'psychological' drama – and so in films like *I'll Cry Tomorrow* (1955), *Love Me or Leave Me* (1955), *The Joker Is Wild* (1957) and *Too Much Too Soon* (1958), alcoholism, violence and abusive relationships blighted the lives of Lillian Roth, Ruth Etting, Joe E. Lewis and Diana Barrymore respectively. Presenting their problems as internal and psychological, the context of history became less relevant to the narratives. In *Love Me or Leave Me*, for example, the setting is referred to only once – even though Etting's rise to fame depended on her manager's connections to Chicago's gangster underworld. In *I'll See You in My Dreams*, Kahn is only directly affected by history when the Wall Street Crash is internalised as a 'symbol' of personal failure.

Like the newspaper headlines and newsreel clips that accompanied the Devil's 'record' of twentieth-century history, these biopics represented the past in terms of sensational gossip and private tragedy rendered public. The 1920s were particularly associated with scandal, with films outside the world of entertainment depicting this through the adultery and financial corruption of New York mayor Jimmy Walker in *Beau James* (1957), or the Leopold-Loeb murder case in *Compulsion* (1959). A mock-up of a newsreel in *Beau James* itself described the Twenties as 'The Decade of Delirium', mirroring the Devil's dizzying montage. These films, and other biopics like *Fear Strikes Out* (1957) and *The Gene Krupa Story* (1959), suggested a self-destructiveness in modern man in accord with the Devil's accusation that the twentieth century reached new 'depths of greed, immorality and self-indulgence'. The perception of the last fifty years as a 'dance of death' was one that the Spirit of Man was unable to challenge, and one that Hollywood also seemed to be leaning towards. A cycle of a dozen gangster pictures defined the interwar years in terms of violence, beginning in 1955 with *Pete Kelly's Blues*, and moving on to the lives of historical gangsters and psychopaths. *Baby Face Nelson* (1957), *Machine Gun Kelly* (1958) and *Al Capone* (1959) were noted for their 'coldly realistic' portrayal of 'slaughter, blood-lust and machine gunning' – with only *Some Like It Hot* (1959) helping to relieve the tension.[45]

According to *The Story of Mankind*, however, all of this was a sideshow, a distraction from the fact that Adolf Hitler, one of the Devil's 'most brilliant creations, was creeping out of the woodwork'. Yet, if Hitler's threat had been realised too late, Hollywood was certainly concerned with him in retrospect. Over one hundred movies were made about World War II – more than ten times as many as were set against the First World War. While only Stanley Kubrick's *Paths of Glory* (1959) directly depicted World War I's 'grisly years of trench warfare' and the arrogance of officers who sacrificed their troops for no significant gain, it was clear that filmmakers found World War II much more 'usable' for its image as a victorious and edifying 'good war'.[46] This was particularly true at the start of the decade, when two years of stalemate in Korea generated a cycle of war films that attempted to provide inspiration through the clearer aims and achievements of World War II.

Thus in 1951, 15 war movies were released, including two John Wayne vehicles that traded in the clichés of the combat movies made during the Second World War itself. In *Flying Leathernecks* Wayne played a harsh leader of aviators, whose tough methods are questioned until the demands of real warfare prove him right; while in *Operation Pacific* he took charge of a submarine after the commander sacrificed his life for the safety of his crew. Both presented their stories as 'unmistakeable evidence that our country – then as always – would fight against the aggression and all the aggressors that challenged the rights of free men'.[47] Similar 'guts-and-glory' scenarios were depicted in *The Tanks Are Coming* (publicised as 'The Happy, Scrappy Story of those Hit-'Em-First Heroes!') and *Go For Broke!* (which more originally presented the 'double victory' of Japanese-American soldiers overcoming racial prejudice and Nazi Germany).

While production of war films lulled between 1954 and 1955, Hollywood eventually covered the war from almost every angle in which American lives had been at stake. The war before America's official entry in 1941 was the subject of only two movies (*Sea Chase* (1955) and *Timbuktu* (1959)), but after Pearl Harbor (depicted in *From Here to Eternity* (1953)), the gloves were off. Seven movies about submarine warfare were released, beginning with *The Enemy Below* (1957) which deftly demonstrated the claustrophobic potential of the setting. Six were set in North Africa – including the battle of *El Alamein* (1953) and Rommel's assault on Tobruk in *The Desert Rats* (1953). Another 38 films depicted the war in Europe, from the Italian front in *The Bold and the Brave* (1956), the Battle of the Bulge in *Attack!* (1956), and the Normandy landings in *D-Day, the Sixth of June* (1956). The war in the Pacific received marginally more coverage, with over fifty movies devoted to the conflict with the Japanese, from *Okinawa* (1952) to *The Battle of the Coral Sea* (1959). Some were biopics of real war heroes – including the stories of Commander Frank Wead, USN (*Wings of Eagles*, 1956), Commander Francis Fasne's Caribbean demolition team (*Underwater Warrior*, 1958), and the most decorated US soldier of the war, Audie Murphy (*To Hell and Back*, 1955). Many more derived their stories from memoirs and novels written by veterans – with subjects that ranged across the problems of conscience besetting pacifists in wartime (*Deep Six*, 1958), the contribution of female espionage agents (*I Was an American Spy*, 1951), and even the morale boosting USO shows (*Purple Heart Diary*, 1951).

Twenty-two war films were released in 1958, the year in which Hollywood's interest reached its peak. But, when contrasted with the films released in 1951, combat missions were presented in a much darker vein, especially when depicting military command. *Tarawa Beachhead*, for example, concerned a platoon leader shooting one of his men for personal gain. *The Naked and the Dead*, adapting Norman Mailer's novel, depicted an amoral, kill-happy army sergeant, sent on a suicide mission by an arrogant general who sees war as a game and soldiers as expendable pawns. The submarine commanders of both *Torpedo Run* and *Run Silent, Run Deep* were also fixated in their goals, driven by a desire for vengeance, and consequently endangered their crews. In the former, Commander Doyle's obsession with sinking an aircraft carrier that took part in Pearl Harbor, leads him to launch torpedoes against ships carrying prisoners of war, which the Japanese are using as a 'human shield'. As the 1950s progressed, the morality of warfare and the question of sacrifices made for the 'greater good' became altogether murkier.

This was also evident in a reassessment of the enemy – at least presenting things from the German perspective, if not the Japanese. This began in 1951 when *The Desert Fox* broke new ground in crediting the military genius of Field Marshal Erwin Rommel; but again a more 'tragic' tone coloured the 1958 releases of Edward Dmytryk's *The Young Lions* and Douglas Sirk's *A Time To Live and a Time to Die*, both of which concerned the disillusionment of German soldiers who come to see the evil that men do in the name of patriotism. Indeed, *The Young Lions* culminates with Christian Diestl's discovery of a concentration camp, and his stunned horror at uncovering the Final Solution. This was unusual because, with the notable exception of George Stevens' *The Diary of Anne Frank* (1959), Fifties' film-makers either took the Holocaust for granted, or turned a blind eye to it. Even *The Story of Mankind* was guilty of ignoring it with the Devil preferring to proclaim the dropping of the atomic bomb as his 'greatest, boldest, most spectacular triumph'.

And there *Story*'s survey of human history ended. Likewise, very few Fifties' films set after V-J Day can really be considered as 'history films'. The Cold War itself was the subject of numerous contemporary films, but few looked back to actual events. *I Was a Communist for the FBI* (1951) did, in presenting Matt Cvetic's service as an informant in the early 1940s, but the elaboration of his testimony before HUAC was more a product of the Red Scare than a representation of 'real' history. The same can be said for the majority of the 52 films set against the Korean War. Half of them were released while the conflict was still in progress, with most of the remainder made during the last year of the war and released shortly thereafter. Not until five years after the 1953 cease-fire can Hollywood be judged to have cast a retrospective eye over the Korean quagmire, most notably in the account of *Pork Chop Hill* (1959). A sense of futility hangs over the film's mission, as 110 out of 135 American marines sacrifice their lives for little but a demonstration of national resolve. Filmed as a memorial to the soldiers who died, director Lewis Milestone sought to remind audiences that

'Pork Chop Hill was held, bought, and paid for at the same price that we commemorate in monuments at Bunker Hill and Gettysburg' – suggesting how Korea had already become 'the forgotten war'. 'History,' mused the film's foreword, 'does not linger long in our century.'[48]

EPILOGUE: 'TO BRING AN END TO MANKIND'

The sense of unease underlying the introduction to *Pork Chop Hill* raises a fundamental point about Hollywood's collective 'story of mankind'. In stressing the need to reflect on the past when the present is moving at too fast and disturbing a pace, it corresponded with the Devil's frenetic presentation of the last few decades as a mad rush towards Armageddon. *Story*'s tribunal, sitting in judgment on man's record, made explicit the imperative behind Hollywood's unprecedented retrospection – the product of an equally unprecedented nuclear threat which had the potential to bring an end to history.

Richard Hofstadter similarly noted a 'keen sense of insecurity' driving the 'overpowering nostalgia' he saw at work in postwar American culture. He also suggested that this preoccupation with the past was conducted in a tone of ahistorical escapism; 'If the future seems dark,' he wrote, 'the past by contrast looks rosier than ever.'[49] However, Hollywood's depiction of history was not so straightforward. Certainly particular periods could be treated as 'rosy', such as when harking back to biblical times when simple faith could sustain a man, to chivalric codes ordering a moral life, or to World War II as a moment when men fought for a cause that was clearly necessary and just. However, few history films were really 'escapist', and the challenges of the past were usually depicted as being as dangerous as the present day. Especially as the decade progressed, war films and biopics became pessimistic about the effectiveness of individual agency in the modern world; faith resulted in martyrdom; and in the retrospective science fiction of *20,000 Leagues Under the Sea* (1954) and *From the Earth to the Moon* (1958), it was even suggested that nuclear technology had been a threat since the nineteenth century.[50]

In the end, the final decision of *Story*'s celestial tribunal was highly ambivalent. Having weighed the evidence – itself derived from the demonstration in Hollywood's history films that man's capacity for violence and destruction always existed alongside his capacity for heroism and regeneration – the God-like judge determined that 'mankind is as evil as he is good. His holiness has been equalled by his tyranny, his nobility by his lack of faith.' And while the explosion of the Super H-Bomb is deferred 'to allow man more time to set his house in order', nuclear anxiety was not alleviated when 'God' effectively abdicated responsibility: 'The fate of man is now laid at the doorstep of man himself. By the villains you encourage, by the heroes you create, you shall soon achieve eternal life or oblivion.' Forced to come to their own conclusions, wisecracking reviewers commented: 'Whether it proves mankind should survive is open to question. This department's vote is, not if pictures like this have to be endured!'[51]

Yet, however weak the film and its ending, it matched an aspect of contemporary historical consciousness that had been proclaimed to the nation at large by *Time* magazine in March 1947. 'Our Civilization Is Not Inexorably Doomed' was the headlined 'prophecy' that made British historian Arnold J. Toynbee the toast of the American media. The article in *Time* was occasioned by the publication of an abridgement of the first six volumes of *A Study in History* – the vehicle for Toynbee's grand historical conception of the rise and fall of civilizations. The section of the thesis which really grabbed the public attention was that of 'Challenge and Response', in which Toynbee argued that common challenges called societies into being, and the response to such challenges determined how a civilization would develop. In summarising (and thus interpreting) the work, *Time* chose to emphasise that although historically all civilizations had eventually fallen, there was no reason why 'history' should end for America if it remained alert and flexible:

> One hopeful meaning stands out... The real drama unfolds within the mind of man. It is determined by his response to the challenges of life; and since his capacity for response is infinitely varied, no civilization, including our own, is inexorably doomed.[52]

In March of 1947, of course, the challenge facing the United States was the start of the Cold War, and the perceived need to 'contain' Communism. Whittaker Chambers, author of the *Time* profile, asserted that *A Study in History* had 'surpassed and supplanted' *Das Kapital*, providing an ideological counter-offensive to Marx's materialist model of history.[53] Published the same year that Hofstadter noted the popular use of history 'to give reassurance', Toynbee's work became a massive bestseller. Irwin Allen's own monumental survey of history was much less successful, but *The Story of Mankind* did demonstrate that the notion that history was 'escapable' had resonance throughout the Fifties. Allen's hope 'to show that good will always win out in the end' was fully consistent with Hollywood's formulae – but he also appeared to have Toynbee in mind when he then declared that even 'if this is the hope that is left for our civilization, it is at least something tangible to grasp when there aren't any more straws left in the wind'.[54]

The shadow of the nuclear bomb, however, was far from being the only anxiety affecting filmmakers. *The Story of Mankind* itself suffered from an insecurity much more particular to Hollywood, as original plans for a three-hour documentary shot in 18 countries, and utilising an advisory board of 'the world's most eminent historians, theologians, and philosophers', came to nought when the filmmakers began to assess its box-office potential. As Allen began to worry that 'a history lesson is not the solution to entertainment', the script was eventually whittled down to just 100 minutes 'of names and places familiar to the layman's memory' – which had already been lodged in the public consciousness by previously successful history films.[55] Nuclear anxiety may have prompted the turn to the past, but the box office determined which histories were made.

Economic History

> Combining history with semi-fictional story lines has been one of filmdom's most lucrative accomplishments.
>
> *Sign of the Pagan* Press Release

The past was indeed one of Hollywood's 'most lucrative' gold mines, and history films were only made because producers expected them to make money. Yet, acknowledgements of this simple fact, as in the admission in a 1954 press release for Universal's *Sign of the Pagan*, were very rare.[1] More typically, filmmakers expressed scepticism, and seemed to assume that audiences were drawn to history films *in spite* of their historical content. When Fox publicists prepared to promote *Prince of Players* (1955), the film's writer and director, Philip Dunne, warned them not to stress that the film was 'a period picture'. In Dunne's opinion, his biopic of nineteenth-century actor Edwin Booth was 'completely modern', and he insisted that 'the story would play just as well in modern dress'. He seemed convinced that emphasising the film's historical content would alienate potential audiences, and that the period was only an 'asset' in so far as it added 'flavor'.[2] Dunne's doubts about history's appeal at the box office were quite widely shared, but it was an opinion which was maintained in the face of overwhelming evidence to the contrary – a paradox which is central to understanding the industry's attitudes towards the past.

Reliable financial data on films produced within the studio system has always been difficult to find. Film producers and studios simply did not make these statistics available. As anthropologist Hortense Powdermaker discovered when she studied the Hollywood community in 1947: 'In all fieldwork there is usually one piece of esoteric data which is hidden by the natives. Among the Melanesians in the Southwest Pacific it is black magic. Among the Hollywood executives it is net profits.'[3] In the 1990s, however, researchers gained access to two ledgers which do provide financial profiles for MGM and Warner Bros., breaking down the production costs, domestic and international revenues, and (for MGM) profit margins for every film.[4] MGM's ledger, kept by vice-president Edgar 'Eddie' Mannix, indicates that the 105 history films released by the studio between 1950 and 1959, generated a total revenue of over $430 million. At Warner Bros., according to the statistics compiled by Jack Warner's executive secretary William Schaefer, the 109 history films they released earned just under $360 million. Over the course of the decade then, the average history film could earn over $4 million at MGM, and almost $3.5 million for Warners – at a time when the average film *not* set in the past was earning each studio just over $2 million.[5]

While of course masking some variation in individual years, this does correspond with the usual (and more generalised) indications of box-office performance given by trade papers such as *Variety*, or the data in texts such as Joel Finler's *The Hollywood Story*. The six highest-grossing films of the decade were all history films – *Ben Hur, The Ten Commandments, Around the World in 80 Days, The Robe, South Pacific* and *Bridge on the River Kwai*. According to Finler, the top 25 films of the 1950s generated $329m at the domestic box-office – and 16 history films accounted for $237 million of this.[6] Moreover, history's dominance at the box office increases in significance when one weighs the unparalleled economic uncertainty that the studio system faced in the 1950s against the consistency with which producers continued to invest in history films.

The breakup of the studio system through the late 1940s and 50s is a familiar story to film historians. As the majors lost control of their cinema chains, production costs rocketed and audiences stayed at home to watch television, MGM head Dore Schary acknowledged that the industry had 'lost a huge segment of the public who used to go to pictures merely to be occupied'.[7] Between 1946 and 1960 the average weekly attendance at American cinemas fell from 90 to 40 million patrons, and by 1959 Hollywood could only count on receiving 5.5 percent of the average American's 'recreational expenditure', as compared to 20 percent in 1946.[8] Factors such as suburban growth took audiences away from downtown cinemas, while alternative pursuits, especially sports, competed for leisure dollars after the war. Television's impact can be gauged from the fact that by 1956, it had penetrated over 35 million homes, with the average American household glued to the set for five hours a day.[9] Even President Eisenhower reflected, 'if a citizen has to be bored to death' it was at least 'cheaper and more comfortable to sit at home and look at television than to go outside and pay a dollar for a ticket'.[10]

The effects of the end of the 'intense love affair between the mass of the American public and their movies' were exacerbated by the Supreme Court ruling in *United States v. Paramount Pictures* in 1948.[11] This ordered the major film studios to divorce their production and distribution activities from the chains of cinema theatres that they owned. While the 'Big Five' only owned 17 percent of cinemas in America, they accounted for the majority of the highly profitable first-run theatres.[12] Runs in these theatres were necessary to establish a film with good reviews and publicity, creating a public awareness that would then compel independent cinema owners to book that movie. With the industry practice of 'block-booking' too, independent cinemas had had to buy a package of unseen movies in order to get the ones that their customers would really want. Declared an illegal constraint of trade by the Court, the industry was compelled to gradually bring an end to block-booking, and as this way of doing business came to an end, company profits fell dramatically. When Paramount complied with the decrees, its profits dropped from almost $21 million in 1949, to just $6.6 million the following year. MGM delayed its compliance the longest, waiting until 1956 – but still profits fell from $4.6 million to a loss of $0.5 million.[13] The economic assumptions that had sustained the studio system for 20 years had come to a crashing end.

THE SPOILS OF HISTORY

The impact of this on history films, however, seems at first glance to have been minimal. **Figure 2.1** provides a breakdown of the number of films released annually by each studio, and how many of these were period-set movies. Television had a particular impact in reducing the number of B-westerns produced for the cinema. The process began in 1948 when William Boyd's Hopalong Cassidy pictures made the transition from the big screen to little, and culminated, in 1954, when Vincent Fennelly made the last cinematically released B-western, Monogram's *Two Guns and a Badge*. Fennelly himself then moved to television to produce the legendary *Rawhide* series. B-movie westerns constituted 155 of the history films released between 1950 and 1953, and the end of this format therefore accounts for the subsequent drop in 'history film' production at Columbia, Republic and Monogram. But when such B-westerns are factored out, the uniformity with which studios devoted resources to history films is very

Figure 2.1: Studio Production of History Films, 1950–1959

		1950	1951	1952	1953	1954	1955	1956	1957	1958	1959	Total
MGM	Total Features	37	40	37	43	22	23	24	27	24	20	297
	History Films	11	17	15	9	8	11	11	8	11	4	105
Fox	Total Features	31	39	38	35	26	23	26	47	34	31	329
	History Films	14	11	19	16	15	11	15	18	17	13	149
Paramount	Total Features	22	25	20	26	17	15	17	18	23	16	199
	History Films	9	8	7	13	6	4	8	8	6	7	76
Warner	Total Features	28	26	27	27	19	21	18	19	22	16	223
	History Films	10	14	14	15	9	10	8	8	13	8	109
Columbia	Total Features	61	58	49	45	30	35	28	31	27	27	391
	History Films	20	29	25	26	16	13	11	13	11	10	174
Universal	Total Features	30	35	34	32	26	33	34	36	30	12	302
	History Films	11	15	20	17	17	16	11	9	9	6	131
United Artists	Total Features	16	24	21	30	28	26	41	53	39	34	312
	History Films	4	4	10	11	12	8	18	22	14	15	118
RKO	Total Features	30	32	28	15	12	12	13	-	-	-	142
	History Films	10	12	12	5	4	5	5	-	-	-	53
Republic	Total Features	43	34	25	23	13	20	18	19	14	2	211
	History Films	18	10	16	14	4	8	7	8	1	1	87
Buena Vista	Total Features	-	-	-	-	1	3	3	2	5	5	19
	History Films	-	-	-	-	1	2	3	2	4	4	16
Allied Artists/ Monogram	Total Features	37	38	34	33	23	25	26	32	29	14	291
	History Films	14	18	20	15	6	6	8	11	8	4	110
Other	Total Features	59	36	22	24	14	19	36	25	34	34	304
	History Films	20	7	8	6	3	6	11	4	5	4	74
Total Output	Features	394	387	335	333	231	255	284	309	281	211	3020
	History Films	141	145	166	147	101	100	116	111	99	76	1202

apparent. B-movie companies such as Eagle Lion and Roger Corman's American-International may have only made the occasional period movie, but at the major studios history films consistently represented between a third and a half of their output. Moreover, it is apparent that when the beleaguered studios cut production, as most did after 1954, the release of history films remained in proportion.

Given MGM's association with 'prestige' pictures, it is perhaps surprising that history films were a smaller percentage of its output (35 percent overall) than any of the other major studios, but this was mainly because Metro produced fewer westerns than the others. Warner Bros., which had had great success with costume dramas and swashbucklers in the 1930s, led the studios in the 1950s in setting 49 percent of its releases in the past – although, by the middle of the decade, it was co-financing and distributing more independent productions than its own films. The divestiture decrees and the end of block-booking created a more level playing field, on which Columbia, Universal and United Artists, in particular, found they could compete – and all invested in history films to match the majors. As United Artists gained from the rise of independent production that accompanied the end of the studios' contract system, so its involvement in history films grew, coming to represent a 40 percent share of the releases it financed and distributed. Walt Disney's Buena-Vista also established itself after 1954, and rarely released anything other than films set in the past. This consistency relates to the strategies that each studio pursued in the context of financial difficulties – strategies that proved to privilege particular types of history film.

In his analysis of the Schaefer ledger up to 1951, Mark Glancy suggests that the health of Warner Bros. relied on a large number of low-budget films, which could provide good returns.[14] In 1950, Randolph Scott's *Colt. 45* provided the highest rate of return on investment, costing only $635,000, but bringing in over $3 million. In the same year, two other westerns – *Barricade* and *Return of the Frontiersman* – each brought in revenues of almost $1.5 million, more than three times what they had cost to produce. The reliability of these returns then allowed the studio to continue to invest in lavish costume-adventure films, such as *Captain Horatio Hornblower* (1951), which cost almost $2.5 million, and generated just over twice as much. However, as the decade progressed this pattern of production was undermined by increased costs, and an additional raising of budgets in an effort to further distinguish movies from television. Thus while Scott's next five westerns continued to generate revenues of $2 million, by 1953 they were now costing the studio over $1 million each, greatly reducing the profit margin.

Yet, the removal of this safety net did not diminish investment in the more expensive history films. In 1952, *The Crimson Pirate* cost Warner $1.9 million, while the most costly films of 1954 were *King Richard and the Crusaders* ($2.6 million) and the biblical epic of *The Silver Chalice* ($3.2 million). With films like *Giant* (costing $5.6 million) and *The Spirit of St Louis* (over $7 million), period productions accounted for three-quarters of the studio's most expensive productions.[15] This was equally apparent at MGM and at Fox (according to the incomplete data collated in Aubrey Solomon's 'corporate history' of the latter studio).[16] In 1951, MGM's most expensive films were *Quo Vadis, Showboat* and *Westward the Women*; in 1952, seven of the eight costliest productions were also historical – including the adventures of *Scaramouche* and *Ivanhoe*, the melodrama of *Plymouth Adventure*, and the period musicals of *The Merry Widow, The Belle of New York* and *Singin' in the Rain*. By 1954 at Fox, following the introduction of CinemaScope technology, the average history film was consistently given a budget in excess of $2 million, while films without a period setting cost the studio less than $1.5 million on average.

These figures obviously reflect the increased costs of costumes, settings and research associated with period films, but they also reflect a change in strategy which saw the majors concentrating on fewer, but bigger pictures. With the end of block-booking, the studios had to 'sell' their films to exhibitors on a picture-by-picture basis – and exhibitors clearly wanted movies that were likely to generate big revenues. Thus films which were most likely to be booked, and which could be sold at higher prices, were those which exploited popular stars, known directors, stories derived from best-sellers, and featured lavish spectacle that could not be seen on television.

Filmmakers certainly did not think of historical settings *per se* as being a 'key element' in box-office success, but the pursuit of 'single, one-off successes' placed emphasis on genres that were commonly set in the past. Biopics, costume adventures, period musicals, war films and epics were all regularly given budgets in excess of $2 million by MGM, Fox and Warner. MGM gave such budgets to 69 films in the 1950s, 43 of which were history films.[17] When a western like *Shane* generated revenues of $8 million for Paramount in 1953, the typical budget of an A-feature western increased considerably – Fox first approved $2 million budgets for *Garden of Evil* and

River of No Return in 1954, and Warner Bros. did the same for *Strange Lady in Town* in 1955 and *The Searchers* in 1956. MGM followed with almost $3 million for *Tribute to a Bad Man* in 1956.

Of course, this was a risky gamble. *Tribute to a Bad Man* made receipts of only $1.2 million at the domestic box-office, and *Strange Lady in Town* only $1.3 million. Even when *The Searchers* took $4 million, the increased costs certainly reduced the return on investment, in contrast to an earlier John Wayne western like *Hondo* (1953), which had generated a similar revenue but had cost $1.2 million less. Details of actual *profits* are recorded in the ledger for MGM, and the Mannix data certainly demonstrates that not all top-grossers were ultimately profitable. The romantic and mannered comedy of *The Swan* was MGM's highest-grossing film for 1956, taking $3.8 million worldwide, but it had cost $3.1 million to make and, after the studio's accounting, a net loss of $0.8 million was calculated. Even more strikingly, *Raintree County* (1957) grossed over $9 million, having cost $5.5 million, yet was recorded as making a loss of almost half a million dollars. Costs beyond production such as distribution, publicity and the striking of prints were taken into account before profits were calculated, along with studio overheads and 'miscellaneous' costs (which may have given room for considerable 'phony accounting'). Clearly though, high production costs ate into profit margins, and history films were therefore often the most expensive risks. Among the ten most disastrous movies from MGM during the decade were six history films: *Plymouth Adventure, The Barretts of Wimpole Street, Lust for Life, Diane, Jupiter's Darling* and *Kismet*, which lost over $12 million between them.

However, the Mannix ledger does show that, despite the risk, history films accounted for a much larger share of MGM's profits than non-history films. In 1951, for instance, the studio released 16 history films, which made a combined profit of $8.7 million. In contrast, the 21 non-history films produced that year lost MGM almost $5 million. Historical productions did make big losses in 1955 and 1956, but even when they are included, history films had made the studio an aggregated profit of $31 million by the end of the decade, while films without historical settings lost a total of $19 million. Half of MGM's history films made a profit, making them a safer bet than non-history films, of which just 36 percent were profitable. According to *Fortune* magazine, by 1955, studio heads were gambling that 'the way to gross big money is to spend it', balancing the risk by including in the picture 'all the built-in insurance' they could find.[18] A historical setting certainly appears to have been one such element of security.

Indeed, the profitability of history films ensured their continued production even as the studio system collapsed. Period movies were embraced by independent filmmakers, even though they lacked the research departments and the expertise with costumes, props and sets that studios had long invested in to support their production. Thirty-eight percent of films released through United Artists were history films, ranging from westerns like *High Noon* (1951), through war films like Robert Aldrich's *Attack!* (1956), to prestige pictures such as Stanley Kramer's *The Pride and the Passion* (1957) and the biblical epic of *Solomon and Sheba* (1959). This was only slightly less a percentage than Paramount, and slightly more than MGM's releases.

In part, this consistency was because many independent producers had once been under contract to the studios – and while they had been let go when the majors released their contract personnel in order to cut overheads, many had prior experience in making history films. Pandro Berman, for instance, having produced many of MGM's costume adventures, made *The Brothers Karamazov* through his own production company, Avon, in 1958, which Metro then released. MGM's prime producer of period-set musicals, Arthur Freed, also went 'independent' with *Gigi* in 1958. Western and B-movie producer Leonard Goldstein worked for Universal until 1954, when he made a deal with Fox to finance and distribute his independent westerns, *Siege at Red River, Gambler of Natchez* and *Three Young Texans*. As a result, in combination with the financial rationale for making history films, the significant changes in the system of production hardly seemed to affect the overall volume of period movies on release.

THE AUDIENCE FOR HISTORY FILMS

The figures in themselves do not explain why particular history films were made, nor why some filmmakers still doubted the appeal of history. Yet, understanding how producers responded to the feedback they were getting from the box office is rendered problematic, partly because the industry remained largely indifferent towards consumer research, despite the problems it faced. In the late 1940s, Eric Johnston, as president of the Motion Picture Association, sought to generate sound statistical data through an inter-industry research committee – but a distinct lack of enthusiasm on the part of the studios made the committee ineffectual and it was soon abandoned. By the late 1950s, more 'scientific' survey data was being commissioned, but the Opinion Research Corporation data that Garth Jowett has reproduced in *Film: The Democratic Art*, gives no indication that the industry was analysing audience preferences by film type.[19]

Box-office grosses did, however, drive production decisions 'at least to the extent of apportioning the numbers of each broad generic category'. Studio sales departments monitored the patterns of receipts, especially in the domestic market, and responded to the comments of exhibitors. Through annual conventions or via the New York executive offices, they would then inform the heads of production in general terms that profit could be maximised by producing a programme of 'so many Westerns, so many rough-stuff melos, so many comedies with real snappy kick in them, so many this, that and the other'.[20] Producers additionally kept a close eye on the competition, and then analysed successes and failures through the prism of their own perception of what audiences wanted.

The studio system had itself encouraged the production of certain cycles of history films, as particular producers operated in-house units that would specialise in specific genres. Arthur Freed's musical production unit at MGM was the prime example, but low-budget versions at Columbia and Universal, for instance, ensured a steady stream of Arabian Nights adventures while this system lasted. Before going independent, Goldstein had regularly presented Universal with orientalist swashbucklers such as *The Desert Hawk* (1950), *The Prince Who Was a Thief* (1951) and *The Golden Blade* (1953), while Sam Katzman supervised a similar cycle (which included *The Magic Carpet* (1951) and *Siren of Bagdad* (1953)) at Columbia. However, the process by which economic considerations influenced production is perhaps best illustrated by the cycle of historical adventure films initiated by MGM.

The trade press considered 'swashbucklers' and 'adventures' to be a subset of what it termed the 'general action market', for which there was a guaranteed audience of 'action fans'.[21] However, MGM expanded that audience greatly with a cycle of big budget swashbucklers that included *Ivanhoe, Scaramouche* and *The Prisoner of Zenda*. These recaptured the spirit of humorous high adventure that had earlier characterised Errol Flynn's escapades for Warner Bros., in *The Adventures of Robin Hood* (1938) and *The Sea Hawk* (1940). Warner had tried to develop a post-war comeback film for their ageing star in *The Adventures of Don Juan* (1948), intended to capitalise on Flynn's association with heroic roles and his by-then notorious womanising, but the film was not a hit. However, the same year at MGM saw the massive success of Pandro Berman's production of *The Three Musketeers*, which encouraged Metro to target the audience that had once belonged to Warner. By 1955, MGM's 11 historical action adventures (which also included *King Solomon's Mines, Knights of the Round Table* and *Kim*) had taken combined receipts of over $57 million. All were identified by *Variety* as 'box office naturals' with 'all the ingredients to capture public fancy'.[22]

At 20th Century-Fox, Darryl Zanuck analysed his rival's success and asserted his own interpretation of what those ingredients were. Hoping that *The Black Rose* – which concerned the adventures of a Saxon fighting with Genghis Khan in Mongolia – would be able to tap into this market, Zanuck insisted that movement and excitement had to be the keynotes of the production:

> An adventure story should be an adventure story and it should be resolved in the terms of action, suspense and excitement... *King Solomon's Mines* will do splendid business because it is not ashamed of what it is. It is not afraid of physical action and excitement even though it may be deemed hokey... There is no law that says you have to make this kind of picture - but if we make it we must go all out.[23]

Zanuck was right about *King Solomon's Mines* – it was MGM's most profitable film of 1950, grossing just under $10 million. The same year, Warner Bros. found a replacement for Flynn in Burt Lancaster, whose *The Flame and the Arrow* brought in over $5 million – which also expressly presented its action as 'obvious hokum – broad, carefree, candid circus stuff' that went 'all out' to entertain.[24] However, *The Black Rose* failed in its efforts. Costing Fox in excess of $3.7 million, it recouped a million dollars less than that in the domestic box-office, earning less than half the takings for *King Solomon's Mines*.

It therefore took the receipts of almost $11 million for MGM's *Ivanhoe* to pique Zanuck's interest in the genre once more. His immediate response was to begin production on *Prince Valiant* in November 1952, intended for audiences 'who dote on fanciful derring-do'.[25] However, the lessons Zanuck drew from *Ivanhoe* were filtered through his own experience of successful filmmaking, notably his personal production of *Gentleman's Agreement* (1947) as an exposé of American anti-Semitism:

> In analyzing *Ivanhoe* I realize why they had a fine success. Their picture was a *combination* of adventure, pageantry and story. They had the very good Semitic angle which one does not find frequently in adventure stories. This gave a sense of character and *depth* to the personal story. It *seemed* to be about something more important than it actually was.

Acknowledging that 'we have no such device' in their adaptation of Harold Foster's comic strips, Zanuck advised his writers to 'devote a little more time to the *character* of Prince Valiant' in order to 'give the appearance of telling solid story and still not lose any of the best physical episodes'.[26] In fact, as production developed, Zanuck's interpretation of *Ivanhoe*'s success led to the issue of 'Christianity versus Paganism' being brought to the forefront of *Valiant*'s plot, in order to 'give us a kind of depth and roots'.[27]

Because of scripting problems and the introduction of CinemaScope in 1953, *Prince Valiant* was not released until 1954, when it was overshadowed by MGM's *Knights of the Round Table*. The latter grossed $4.5 million in America alone (over $8 million worldwide), compared to *Valiant*'s $2.6 million domestic take. At Warner Bros. too, the effort to emulate *Ivanhoe*, in adapting Sir Walter Scott's *The Talisman*, went awry when the resultant film – *King Richard and the Crusaders* – grossed only $3.7 million world-wide, having cost almost $3 million to make. Both studios steered clear of such productions in the future. MGM though sought to continue mining the vein – until, in 1955, both John Houseman's *Moonfleet* and Berman's *Quentin Durward* lost $1.2 million each. *Durward* grossed just $2.2 million, less than one-fifth of what *Ivanhoe* had taken three years before. Berman realised that *Durward* had been 'one too many', and while the cycle had made the studio profits of over $8 million, executives brought it quickly to an end.[28]

In contrast, MGM tended to follow, rather than lead, in the production of war films. Instead, Fox exploited the genre the most, releasing ten war movies between 1950 and 1953 and a further 12 between 1956 and 1959 – figures which reflect two different cycles of films set against World War II. **Figure 2.2** demonstrates this, indicating each studio's releases.

The first cycle coincided with the Korean War, and film historians have suggested that Hollywood responded to the quagmire in Korea by producing films that celebrated the heroics of World War II instead – as a conflict with a clear enemy, an apparent black-and-white morality, and with a definite victory for the USA. This proved to be a successful strategy, in 1950 and 1951 at least, with *Halls of Montezuma, An American Guerilla in the*

Philippines and *The Frogmen* generating consistent grosses of more than $2 million at the American box-office for Fox. For Warner Bros., the same was true of *Breakthrough* (1950) and *Operation Pacific* (1951). MGM tested the water too, with *Go For Broke!* (1951), and similarly generated takings of

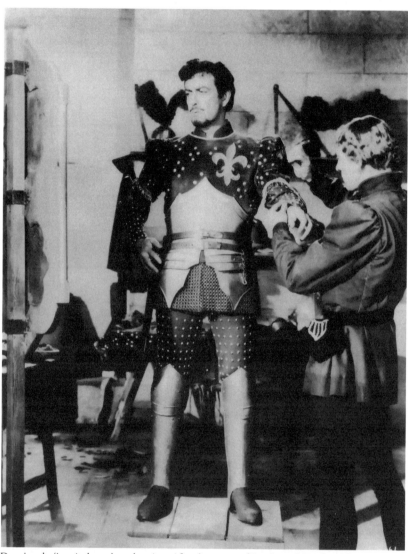

Donning the 'iron jockstrap' one last time: After the success of *Ivanhoe* and *Knights of the Round Table*, Robert Taylor is dressed for medieval action for the final time in *The Adventures of Quentin Durward* (1955). With decreasing box-office returns, MGM producer Pandro S. Berman realised *Durward* had been 'one too many' and brought the cycle to a swift conclusion. (Courtesy of the British Film Institute)

$2.6 million. Stories with an emphasis on combat, directed at the 'masculine action fan', seemed to generate a very dependable revenue.[29]

Therefore, when making *The Desert Rats* and *Destination Gobi* for release in 1953, Zanuck warned against tampering with a successful formula. When director Robert Wise suggested making *The Desert Rats* in a semi-documentary style, Zanuck was convinced that this would 'destroy the commercial value of this project'. He instead insisted that they should 'follow the successful pattern of *Twelve O'Clock High, Sands of Iwo Jima* and *Halls of Montezuma*' in emphasising 'certain exploits' of a 'small group of leading characters and one in particular', rather than try to 'recreate historically the entire Siege of Tobruk'.[30] Similarly, the making of *Destination Gobi* was influenced by Zanuck's analysis of why *The Frogmen*, while profitable, had not quite made it into 'the hit category of *Halls of Montezuma*'.[31] However, despite this analysis, the American audience for *Gobi* and *Rats* was apparently no longer there. Each took less than $1.2 million, not enough to recoup their costs. This may have been the result of 'war fatigue', and certainly the drop off in production after 1953 mirrors the decline in war films that had followed V-J Day. Fred Zinnemann, however, recalled that when trying to adapt Irwin Shaw's *The Young Lions* in 1952, he was discouraged by the 'considerable apathy' of executives who told him 'that the audience now is only interested in the Korean War'.[32] In fact, returns on Korean War films were usually only on a par with World War II films at this point, with Warner's *Retreat, Hell!* (1952) and MGM's *Battle Circus* (1953) generating $1.6 million each from American audiences.

Perceived as a melodrama, the $12 million success of Zinnemann's alternative project, *From Here to Eternity* (1953), did not really change executive coolness towards war films. However, attitudes were very much

Figure 2.2: Production of World War II Films, 1950–59

	1950	1951	1952	1953	1954	1955	1956	1957	1958	1959	Total
Columbia		2	2	4	1		1	2	4	1	17
MGM		1	1		1		1	3	3	2	12
Paramount	1			2			1		2	1	7
RKO		2					1				3
Fox	4	3	1	2			2	5	3	2	22
Univ		2	1			1	1		1	1	7
Warner	1	3		2		3	1		4	1	15
UA			1	2	1		1	1	3		9
Other		2	1	2			1		2	4	12
Totals	6	15	7	14	3	4	10	11	22	12	104

affected by the fact that while only seven war films were produced in 1954–55, four of them grossed over $6 million dollars each. Of these, only Audie Murphy's autobiographical picture, *To Hell and Back* (1955) emphasised combat experience. Warner's comedy, *Mr Roberts* (1955) generated $8 million and, like *Battle Cry* (1955) which took $7.7 million, was more concerned with the frustrations of non-combat assignments. Topped by Columbia's *The Caine Mutiny* (1954), which gained domestic receipts of $8.7 million, these films prompted and shaped the second cycle of war films which peaked in 1958 with 22 movies in cinemas.

However, unlike the earlier cycle, audience reaction was far less predictable, and the production decisions seemed to be far more haphazard. The success stories of mid-decade certainly informed MGM's production schedule, and a successful effort was made to tap the market made apparent by *Mr Roberts*, with two wartime comedies, *Don't Go Near the Water* (1957) and *Imitation General* (1958), both making over $1 million in profit. However, its efforts to emulate *Battle Cry* in its narrative of wartime romances were far less remunerative, as *Gaby* (1956) and *Until They Sail* (1957) both lost over $1 million. *To Hell and Back* presumably helped to greenlight John Ford's biopic of Navy flyer Frank 'Spig' Wead, *Wings of Eagles* (1957), but that too made a substantial loss. Yet, with comedy seemingly the only reliable way to go to win an audience, MGM instead chose to release three serious combat dramas, each with an explicitly masculine edge: *Torpedo Run* (1958), *The Angry Hills* (1959) and *Never So Few* (1959). All of these lost money, suggesting serious errors in judgement.

In 1950, writer Al Hine had predicted that it would be 'from war novels and war plays that most future war movies will be taken'. The second cycle proved him right, when the successful adaptations of James Jones' *From Here to Eternity* and Herman Wouk's *The Caine Mutiny* led to Hollywood 'following a public demand proved by someone else'.[33] All four of the war films released in 1955 were based on books and plays, while nine novels were adapted in the peak year of 1958. With versions of Charles Shaw's *Heaven Knows Mr Allison* and Irwin Shaw's *The Young Lions*, Fox secured properties that grossed over $4 million each in 1957 and 1958 respectively, while Anton Myer's *In Love and War* also brought in another $2.5 million at the US box-office. In 1958, this was triumphantly surpassed, at $17.5 million, by the screen version of the smash Broadway musical *South Pacific*, itself adapted from *Tales of the South Pacific* by James Michener. Fox thereby continued to have its hit war films, but these were driven less by Zanuck's analysis of successful formulae (for Zanuck had left in 1956), than by gauging audience tastes from the bestseller lists.

Thus the second cycle of war films was dominated by efforts (usually unsuccessful) to copy the hits of rival studios, and by a demonstrable reliance on war stories already embraced by the American public. Moreover, returns on war films became increasingly uncertain, as budgets varied from less than $1 million for *The Naked and the Dead* to $3.5 million for *Young Lions* or *Never So Few*. During the first cycle, profits were at least more predictable when the costs of a war film had always hovered around $1.5 million. The contrast in the two cycles rather points to the lack of direction as the studio system began to unravel, and to less assurance about what would attract audiences.

In part, this loss of confidence was a consequence of changes in personnel. Dore Schary had joined MGM as Vice-President in Charge of Production in 1948, with Louis B. Mayer eventually ousted in June of 1951, after 27 years as chief executive. Schary improved the studio's efficiency and centralised production, and initially had great success with the hit war film, *Battleground* (1949). However, the history films he championed in the 1950s did not repeat this accomplishment. *The Red Badge of Courage* (1951) became a notorious symbol of the different visions of Schary and Mayer, and though Schary prevailed in getting John Huston's take on the Civil War made, it lost the studio over a million dollars. His subsequent forays into the past fared little better. Aside from his second war film, *Go For Broke*, the other historical productions he personally oversaw were failures, including *The Swan* and *The Last Hunt* (1956), and *Plymouth Adventure*'s loss of $1.9 million in 1952.

At Fox, Zanuck resigned as head of production in 1956, despairing that the changes in Hollywood had reduced him from a 'cultural impresario' to 'a negotiator, an executive, a peacemaker'.[34] Since everyone else in the industry seemed to be making their fortunes as independent producers, he joined them. Buddy Adler succeeded him, and certainly had much more success with history films than Schary did. His four personal productions – *Inn of the Sixth Happiness*, *South Pacific*, *Heaven Knows Mr Allison* and *Anastasia* – were all highly profitable movies. However, Adler was relying heavily on what he thought was 'sure-sell' material and 'announced month after month the heavy purchase of novels and plays'.[35] It was a strategy that alarmed the New York head office, because even successes like *South Pacific* could not guarantee a large enough, sustainable audience to justify the expense of Adler's programme as a whole. Moreover, Adler's approach to developing prestige blockbusters was not based on the confident knowledge of his audience that Zanuck had displayed in the past.

Zanuck had certainly advocated the purchase of what he termed 'presold' material, but he also made 'great efforts in developing original material at the same time'.[36] His assurance in doing so, though, had been strongest in the late 1930s and early 1940s. Before World War II, four out of ten residents of Los Angeles had migrated to the city from the Midwest – and Zanuck himself had been one of them, born in Wahoo, Nebraska. As George Custen suggests, Zanuck felt attuned to this audience, and anticipating their interests was a sound commercial strategy since the far west accounted for 90 percent of Fox's theatres.[37] However, when Fox complied with the *Paramount* decision, Zanuck could no longer rely on the profits from this sector, and could no longer fully trust his intuitive sense of gauging what the public wanted.

With the audience changing too, this had a particular impact on period films depicting small town Americana. Like the Andy Hardy pictures of Mayer's MGM, the characteristic Zanuck picture of the late 1930s had been a 'romanticized look at American history: the building of a city, the founding of a religion, the finding of a musical sound...'.[38] With musicals, biopics and comedies set in an idealised middle America at the turn of the century, Zanuck had successfully tapped into nostalgia for the 'values of the small town life' that his target audience had left behind.[39] At the beginning of the 1950s, *Variety* reviewers had continued to welcome 'heartwarming' films such as *Has Anybody Seen My Gal* (1952), *Wabash Avenue* (1950) or *Cheaper By the Dozen* (1950), as 'pleasant, homey entertainment' that sat 'particularly well with family audiences'.[40] Yet they no longer sat well enough. The four nostalgic comedies produced at MGM between 1950 and 1953 each proved to be a reasonable attraction, taking average receipts of $2.1 million, but this was not adequate to return a profit. Zanuck did better, with *Cheaper By the Dozen* grossing $4.3 million in 1950, and his biopic of John Philip Sousa taking $3 million at the American box-office in 1952. But 1952 was the year when the *Paramount* decision first affected Fox, and when Zanuck's personal exercise in rural nostalgia, *Wait Til the Sun Shines Nellie,* took only $1.3 million domestically. *The Farmer Takes a Wife* was the last of such films produced at Fox in 1953, while nostalgic vaudeville musicals, which had long been associated with the studio, also vanished from the programme after *Tonight We Sing* (1953) and *There's No Business Like Showbusiness*

(1954) struggled to cover their costs. This once popular style of period movie therefore came to an end, with two key factors apparent in its declining fortunes. First, the 'family audience' was splintering. Second, profitable filmmaking was becoming ever dependent on attracting an international audience.

One of the most striking elements of *Variety* reviews as the 1950s progressed was the acknowledgement that the 'traditional' family audience was no longer the norm. In reviews such as that for Disney's *Darby O'Gill and the Little People* (1957), the trade press thought it necessary to point out that 'juves, teeners, adults and oldsters' would find 'something to get excited about'.[41] The existence of a generation gap was acknowledged when *Variety* opined that *Showboat* needed to be sold on two levels, targeting either 'oldsters out for a nostalgic treat or new generation viewers', and that *The Barretts of Wimpole Street* would only appeal to 'old lovers, not the young'.[42] The box-office failure of *The Barretts* indicated that catering to a more elderly audience segment was a mistake. Indeed, surveys suggested that by 1957, over half of motion picture audiences were under 20 years old, and almost three-quarters were under 30. This was a demographic that lacked any reason to regard the turn of the century as fondly as Mayer or Zanuck did.

Foreign audiences also failed to relate to nostalgic Americana. In the international market in the early 1950s, the least successful of MGM's films were *The Happy Years* (a comedy about life in a New England prep school at the turn of the century), *Stars in My Crown* (concerning the life of a nineteenth-century southern rural clergyman), and *Magnificent Yankee* (a biopic of Supreme Court justice Oliver Wendell Holmes). *Stars in My Crown*, for example, grossed $2 million in the American box-office, but only $184,000 abroad. Filmmakers could not afford to ignore this fact. Before 1948, the domestic American audience had normally been great enough to ensure that a film broke even, with foreign markets often regarded as 'dumping grounds for films that had already made their profits'.[43] Any revenue a film made abroad simply put it further in the black. However, as the domestic market shrank, foreign revenues became increasingly important. By 1960, more than half of Hollywood's revenues came from foreign sales – making them now essential for a movie just to break even.[44] The Mannix ledger illustrates the issue: only 42 percent of MGM's films managed to cover their costs at the domestic box-office before they were released worldwide, but foreign revenues enabled a further 36 percent to break even.[45] Predicting the tastes of a much more disparate international audience was therefore essential, but not something to which American filmmakers were very accustomed.

In determining how history films could operate within these new audience conditions, it took some time for the major studios to decide if period settings could attract the attention of younger picturegoers. Until the success of MGM's *Blackboard Jungle* in 1955, teenage audiences were associated with 'exploitation' films made by independents – typically low-budget fodder for drive-in audiences, with elements of sex or horror that could be exploited by publicists (what *Variety* termed 'the ballyhoo market').[46] Mostly contemporary or futuristic in setting, only a few movies like *Untamed Women, Prehistoric Women* or *The Viking Women and the Sea Serpent* were located in the past – and each of these used the setting as an excuse to display pneumatic young girls in fur bikinis.

Thus when the major studios did make history films directed at young audiences, the feeling was that they had to instil 'a contemporary flavor in the presentation'.[47] Shortly after Zanuck left Fox, this was achieved when Elvis Presley made his film debut in a Civil War western, *Love Me Tender* – which proved itself a 'natural for the screaming set' by grossing $4.5 million in America.[48] *Burning Hills* (1956) similarly cast Tab Hunter and *Rebel Without a Cause*'s Natalie Wood in a western, in order to appeal to their 'teenage fans' – and at a low-budget cost of $870,000, it made $1.4 million. Likewise, Pat Boone, in Fox's *Journey to the Center of the Earth* (1959) was heralded as a 'built-in teenage attraction…who draws the non-delinquent elements of the teen trade'.[49] The comments of the trade press certainly imply that youth audiences were thought of as ahistorical, being interested primarily in attractive young stars, and requiring a greater incentive than other audiences to watch period-set films. However, historical subject matter was occasionally still considered to be an attraction, with youthful 'rebels' such as Jesse James and Billy the Kid featuring in *The True Story of Jesse James* (1957) and *The Left-Handed Gun* (1958) respectively. Other filmmakers capitalised on troubled characters from the more recent past – as in the bandleader's drug addiction in *The Gene Krupa Story* (1959), or Rocky Graziano's delinquent youth in *Somebody Up There Likes Me* (1956).

In comparison, filmmakers were always rather more confident that foreign audiences would respond well to history films, especially historical spectacles. At MGM, the average history film could expect to return

$1.9 million from abroad, compared to just $863,000 for films without period settings. The story at Warner Bros. was just the same, with history films making average international revenues of $1.3 million and the rest only averaging $848,000. These revenues were particularly important, as 'epic' films like *Quo Vadis, Helen of Troy, Land of the Pharaohs* and so on, simply had to reach a global audience if they were to ever cover the inflated costs of their extravagant production values. In August 1953, just before the launch of *The Robe*, Zanuck listed the projects then in preparation – *Prince Valiant, King of the Khyber Rifles, Demetrius and the Gladiators, Hell and High Water, Garden of Evil, The Virgin Queen, The Egyptian* and *Prince of Players*. With the exception of *Hell and High Water*, all were large-scale and historical. This over-specialisation, with a notable absence of the more meditative and controversial projects he had made in the 1940s, was not typical of Zanuck – who acknowledged that 'it might appear that perhaps I have put too much emphasis on big-scale action and adventure stories and outdoor spectacles'. It was, however, a policy driven by economics, and he assured his producers that 'when we consider the entire world as one market, our decision to emphasize action and scope will prove a wise decision'.[50]

However, Zanuck did not demonstrate such certainty when it came to applying his analysis of the global audience to the development of specific history films. When scriptwriter Daniel Taradash came to adapt *Desiree* in the summer of 1953, the first advice Zanuck gave him was the warning that 'under our new program we have to be careful to try to get not only *good* pictures whose subject matter is interesting, but we have to try for pictures with *world wide* appeal'.[51] He therefore insisted on changes that he thought would better secure this audience. In developing the story of Desiree Clary, a woman who marries Napoleon's marshal, but remains infatuated with the Emperor, Taradash had wanted to emphasise the character of her husband, Jean-Baptiste Bernadotte, who became the king of Sweden and ultimately led an army against Napoleon after the retreat from Moscow. As Zanuck perceived it, however, an international audience would be drawn to the story because of their knowledge of Napoleon.

Taradash therefore had to rework his script so that the diminutive dictator was at the forefront, with the film's central attraction being one of telling a 'strange and practically unknown love story in the life of Napoleon'. Napoleon's career would be illustrated by showing the moments at which it intersected with Desiree's life. Yet, Zanuck's analysis started to flounder at this point. While telling Taradash that 'each picture we make must be a success in the world market', in the very next breath he claimed that 'what I am concerned about mostly is the chances in this country'. The new strategy had been imposed upon him by the financial concerns of the New York office, but what Zanuck really understood was the 'chances' of a film's success with American audiences. Zanuck knew from experience and instinct that 'audiences – *American audiences, at least* – don't care how Napoleon got to be emperor, or how Bernadotte got to be King of Sweden; …they don't care to listen to a discussion of the political aspects or backgrounds'.[52] But he was less sure that foreign filmgoers would feel the same way.

It was therefore against this background of unfamiliar audiences that filmmakers worried about the prospects of their films, and how well history would serve them at the box office – even though the actual figures should have suggested less cause for concern. Philip Dunne's *Prince of Players*, dealing with an actor not really known outside of America, seemed to have little appeal abroad, and also did not seem to be a subject which would attract a younger audience at home. And just as Dunne expressed his concerns on the matter to Fox's publicists, so Stan Margulies, who handled public relations for Kirk Douglas, warned United Artists not to use 'photographs and sketches of the players in costume' in publicity for *Paths of Glory* (1957). If Stanley Kubrick's film was too closely associated with its World War I setting, Margulies feared that 'we may face a problem in convincing audiences that this is a modern, hard-hitting, up-to-date film about men at war. They may just take one look at the World War I costumes and decide that this is an old fashioned film.'[53] Similarly concerned about the demographics of audiences and their interest in the Great War, David O. Selznick ordered director John Huston to cut much of the 'war material' he had filmed for *A Farewell to Arms*, on the assumption that audiences were 'not much concerned with a war they don't know about and don't care about'.[54]

However, despite such concerns, the production of history films continued apace because, like Adler, filmmakers responded to economic uncertainty by accelerating their search for 'pre-sold names' and properties that would automatically attract attention. As in the case of the second cycle of war films, the popularity of historical novels in post-war America ensured that the public's appetite for period fiction was translated into cinematic form. Six of the top ten best-selling books of 1948, for example, were historical – including *The Big Fisherman*, *The Naked and the Dead*, *The Golden*

Hawk, Raintree County and *The Young Lions* – and each of them was made into a film during the next ten years. The ten best-sellers of 1952 alone resulted in a further six history films: *The Silver Chalice, The Caine Mutiny, East of Eden, My Cousin Rachel, Giant* and *The Saracen Blade*.[55]

Moreover, the past itself was a prime source of 'pre-sold names'. Napoleon was evidently the pre-sold property in *Desiree,* which is why Zanuck wanted Taradash to emphasise the emperor and not his marshal. Robert Rossen made the safe assumption that Alexander the Great was a figure that the 'whole world knows of', when launching his 1956 movie, while other films like *The Story of Robin Hood, Knights of the Round Table* and *The Vikings* based their appeal to audiences on traditional conceptions of mythical and historical figures.[56] For the same reason, independent producers with lower budgets were drawn to exploit the notoriety of gangsters like Al Capone and Baby Face Nelson. Indeed, the highest-grossing films commonly reflected the instant recognition that historical characters and events possessed – from *Helen of Troy* to *Salome*, from *The Glenn Miller Story* to *The Great Caruso*. Trade reviewers agreed, one acknowledging that while Universal's *Lady Godiva* would probably bore audiences with its references to the politics of pre-Norman Conquest Britain, the film itself would undoubtedly find an audience because 'everybody is interested in Lady Godiva' for an altogther different reason.[57] As Zanuck affirmed, by adapting material that audiences already knew a little about 'you immediately ring a bell…You don't have to go around explaining the picture. They already know about it, and when they know about it half the battle is won.' Reflecting on the economic troubles, he also asserted that 'today, when business has boiled down to weekend business at the theaters, the value of a pre-sold property has doubled'.[58] As the ledgers suggest, if a historical subject was considered to be a 'pre-sold property', Zanuck's calculation proved to be very accurate indeed.

As the next chapter demonstrates, Hollywood's economic troubles also shaped the presentation of the past by associating history with its potential for scope, action, fighting, spectacle and exotic locations – epic production values which, it was hoped, would win back the 'lost audience'. However, many filmmakers still had intentions that went beyond commercial success. Economic circumstances enabled certain types of history films to get made (and discouraged the production of others), but how filmmakers then depicted or used the past was an issue that was influenced by very different attitudes and experiences.

3

Thrill History

If Ava Gardner played Godiva, riding in the bare
The public wouldn't pay a cent and they wouldn't even care
Unless she had glorious Technicolor, breathtaking CinemaScope,
And Stereophonic Sound!

Cole Porter's lyrics to 'Stereophonic Sound', *Silk Stockings* (1957)

In May 1953, publicists at Warner Bros. introduced a new term to the lexicon of historiography. Conceived in the campaign to distinguish the 3-D (stereoscopic) western, *The Charge at Feather River*, from the multitude of 'flat' horse-operas that had preceded it, this 'New 3-D THRILL HISTORY' promised audiences 'the flaming color and vast pageantry of the Great American West as no living person has ever seen it before!'[1] Unsurprisingly, 'Thrill History' was a neologism that never caught on, but it reflected an important side to the industry's attitude towards history, representing a connection in the minds of filmmakers between depicting the past, the psychology of audiences, and the technological developments that Hollywood hoped would fend off box-office meltdown.

Film historians have extensively covered the development and introduction of a huge variety of film processes, lenses, screen sizes and sounds systems that the industry tried out in the 1950s, in an effort to entice audiences back to the cinema. Each invention sought to diminish the impact of television, with widescreen technologies in particular reminding Americans how puny their small black-and-white TV sets were. The expansion of the screen size was most dramatically demonstrated in

56

September 1952 by Cinerama – a system of projecting a composite picture from three synchronised reels onto screens that arched 146 degrees around the audience. The phenomenal popularity of *This Is Cinerama* spurred a rush among Hollywood studios to find a comparable system more suited for regular cinema theatres. The next few years saw a contest between the processes of CinemaScope, VistaVision, Technirama and Todd-AO, with 20th Century-Fox's aggressive and successful campaign to have Cinema-Scope adopted as the industry standard also undercutting the development of 3-D.[2] Writing in March 1953, producer John Houseman complained that 'confusion reigns' with 'three-dimension, wide-screen and a whole lot of other thirty-year-old inventions being hailed with greater excitement than the Last Trump on Judgment Day'.[3]

Yet, one aspect of the intense competition has been overlooked. All of these technological advances and gimmicks, so characteristic of 1950s cinema, were launched with one foot firmly in the past – heralded by history films. CinemaScope was unveiled in 1953 with the biblical epic *The Robe*. When MGM licensed 'Scope from Fox, it similarly first used the process on a history film, *Knights of the Round Table* – and then made *Raintree County* and *Ben Hur* the first beneficiaries of its own MGM Camera 65 process. *Oklahoma!* and *Around the World in 80 Days* were the first films

'You're There!': Advertising for Warner's *Charge at Feather River* (1953) promised direct engagement with history in all its dimensions. (Courtesy of the British Film Institute)

thought suitable for introducing Todd-AO to the public. SuperScope was unleashed with a Universal western, *Vera Cruz*, in 1954, and *The Big Country* showcased Technirama in 1958. Paramount planned to showcase VistaVision with *The Ten Commandments*, with the process promoted as bringing 'glory' to 'the motion picture that the whole world is waiting for'. Due to production delays *White Christmas* actually was the first VistaVision release – but even that film opened with images of World War II.[4] The partnership of history and technological innovation continued with each new tweaking of the screen, with CinemaScope 55 (*The King and I*), SuperTechnirama 70 (*Solomon and Sheba*), and into the Sixties with Ultra-Panavision (*Mutiny on the Bounty*) and the eventual marriage of Cinerama and narrative film in *The Wonderful World of the Brothers Grimm* and *How The West Was Won* in 1962.

Likewise, the first films in 3-D used historical settings. Arch Oboler's independent *Bwana Devil* was laid in British East Africa at the turn of the century, while Warner Bros. brought 3-D in the studio system with *House of Wax*, set in 1902. When Spyros Skouras first considered making *The Robe* in Milton Gunzberg's 'Natural Vision' stereoscopic process, he was critical of the small scale of Gunzberg's promotional pilot, *Sweet Chariot*. 'You don't open it with this sort of thing on the screen, you don't open with a little picture!' Skouras told him. '*Cleopatra!* That's the sort of thing for this!'[5]

The connection was no coincidence. Five of the first seven CinemaScope films released in 1953 were history films, as were 21 out of the 35 released in 1954. Over time, filmmakers became less concerned about finding 'appropriate' subjects for the medium, and applied CinemaScope to all types of films, but it is clear that the initial use of CinemaScope on historical subjects was a deliberate decision. As Skouras' remarks reveal, filmmakers were instinctively drawn towards history when looking for subject matter which would do 'proper justice' to the new techniques and capture the public imagination.

On one level, the roots of this instinct are quite obvious. It was Cecil B. DeMille's 1934 account of the Queen of Egypt that was at the forefront of Skouras' mind 23 years later, because of the way in which DeMille (and D.W. Griffith before him) had inexorably linked history to epic films of spectacle, pageantry and excess. The lavish production values of epic movies would demonstrate the potential of the new processes, especially as directors felt challenged to find ways of filling the new visual expanse. Following the patterning of excess as historical spectacle in pre-CinemaScope epics like *Quo Vadis*, *The Robe* filled a screen three times as large with 'movie murals of slave markets, imperial cities, grandiose palaces and panoramic landscapes'.[6] Howard Hawks, who directed *Land of the Pharaohs* in CinemaScope, dismissed it as 'good only for showing great masses of movement', but critic Andre Bazin appreciated Cinema-Scope's 'affinity with genres like the western whose specific framing is the establishing shot, exposing the landscape as far as the horizon'.[7] Darryl Zanuck agreed, suggesting that CinemaScope was best suited to 'big-scale action and adventure stories and outdoor spectacles' – an emphasis which favoured historical genre films such as epics, swashbucklers, war films and westerns.[8]

Moreover, the marriage between history and widescreen went further than demonstrating the dimensions of the screen. As John Belton suggests, CinemaScope and the other processes 'introduced a level of visual spectacle that often threatened to overwhelm the narrative'. Historical epics, though, could 'contain' this threat – presenting visual excess in an appropriate narrative context, where audiences were already accustomed to (and expected) such extravagance. The imperial Rome of *The Robe* had been established in the public mind (largely through earlier films) as a site of grandeur and decadence. In consequence, the production of historical spectacles functioned to 'naturalise pictorial splendor', providing a rationale for excessive display.[9] However, in turn, the new technology expanded the filmmaker's conception of history as an extravagant pageant.

A NEW ERA OF MOTION PICTURES

Vivian Sobchack has suggested that pioneers of this technology embraced epics because they told stories which were endowed with a sense of 'general historical eventfulness', which could then be reflected back on to the film itself.[10] Since the studios wanted the launch of a new process to be seen as an 'event', the epic offered opportunities to suggest that the technology being showcased was itself as historically significant as the events being re-enacted. Howard Hughes' production of *The Conqueror* was heralded as being as 'Mighty in Scope' as the conquests of its hero, Genghis Khan, while posters advertising *Knights of the Round Table* were deliberately obscure as to whether 'The Biggest Event in History!' referred to Arthur's founding of Camelot or the release of the film itself.[11] Moreover, marketing sought to enhance the stature of widescreen formats in suggesting only they could convey history as it *should* be seen:

> *Knights of the Round Table*, it might almost seem, had waited for CinemaScope so that it could be offered in all its majestic splendor. And CinemaScope, it could be said, had waited for *Knights of the Round Table* so that the potentialities of the technique could be realized.[12]

In its concern with 'splendor', 'dramatic scenes of conquest', 'exciting sequences of sport' and 'romantic episodes of love and courtly intrigue', the publicity for *Knights* supports Sobchack's contention that generating an impression of 'historical eventfulness' was seen as more important than really representing history. However, the specific choice of historical setting or event often had more deliberate significance. Michael Todd, for instance, associated himself with the visionary Jules Verne and qualities of Victorian gentlemen adventurers in his decision to film *Around the World in 80 Days* in Todd-AO. Having sunk his personal fortune into the development of the system, to challenge CinemaScope's grasp over first run audiences, Todd was pictured as a reincarnation of Phileas Fogg, 'a man who bets everything he has against heavy odds that he can pull off an improbable feat'.[13] Likewise, but with greater audacity, the producers of *The Robe* used the film's subject matter to comment on CinemaScope itself. Casting publicity in New Testament rhetoric, the industry was encouraged to welcome the 'good news' of the 'new era' that would dawn with the 'modern miracle' of CinemaScope. Jack Warner took particular umbrage at Fox's purposeful 'Bible-stumping' campaign to present 'Scope as 'the savior' of Hollywood, but the technology was explicitly promoted as history-making in its own right, on a scale commensurate with the resurrection of Christ![14]

The talk of salvation reveals the insecurity behind all this bluster. Hollywood was inflating the significance of movies as historical events, at a time when its biggest fear was of being reduced to cultural *insignificance* by television. *Singin' in the Rain* (1952) notably used history to offer reassurance, noting that the industry had faced challenges before, but that exploiting technological advances (as in the adoption of sound in 1927) could presage a revival of fortunes. Other history films also demonstrated resilience in the entertainment industry, including *There's No Business Like Showbusiness* (filmed in CinemaScope in 1954), detailing the struggles of a vaudevillian family who continue to entertain even though the heyday of their theatre has passed by. Neither show change as easy, but optimism about the ability to adapt and thrive under adverse conditions was a message that had much appeal in the beleaguered studios.

In that context, *House of Wax* – the first film to be produced within the Hollywood studio system for 3-D release – takes on a different dimension, for it too is concerned with cultural displacement, and had something specific to say about the role that representations of history could play. Producer Bryan Foy was sensitive to change in the entertainment industry, having been part of a famous vaudeville act, the Seven Little Foys, before moving into the film industry as vaudeville became obsolete. He had also helped oversee Hollywood's transition to sound in the late 1920s, prepping Warner Bros. 'First 100% All Talking Picture', *Lights of New York* (1928). With *House of Wax*, Warner Bros. was trying to reinvigorate the studio's pioneering reputation by touting 3-D as the greatest catalyst for change in the industry since sound.[15]

House of Wax is set, according to its script, in 1902. This is a deliberate change from its source, a 1933 Warner film, *Mystery of the Wax Museum*, which had a contemporary setting. In part, this was because a period setting lent a little extra prestige to the picture, even though, as a horror film, it was still not an 'A' feature. However, when one considers wax sculpture as part of Hollywood's heritage as a cultural form, the specificity of the date becomes significant.[16] The film makes reference to New York City's Eden Musee which, in 1902, was America's leading centre for waxwork exhibition, just as Madame Tussaud's was in London. In 1903, however, the Eden Musee introduced audiences to a new form of artistic entertainment, premiering Edwin S. Porter's *The Great Train Robbery*, the first American narrative film.[17] *House of Wax* thus depicts the wax museum at the very moment it was about to be displaced by cinema.

In order to turn his fortunes around and survive this transition, sculptor Henry Jarrod (Vincent Price) is forced to change the way he presents history to the public. From the outset, it is evident that Jarrod specialises in sculpting historical figures, with exhibits of Mark Antony and Cleopatra, Joan of Arc, Marie Antoinette, Lincoln and John Wilkes Booth and others, staged in tableaux recreated with detailed authenticity. (Intriguingly each of these subjects are associated with filmmakers considered to be masters of historical cinema – D.W. Griffith (*Birth of a Nation*), DeMille (*Cleopatra* and *Joan the Woman*) and Irving Thalberg, who died during the production of *Marie Antoinette* (1938).) Jarrod's business partner, Matthew Burke, however, is convinced that his beautiful exhibits are no longer commercially viable. He dismisses the Jarrod's work as a 'historic peepshow', asking 'Who cares a hang about history in wax?' By implication, 'lifeless' history might generate prestige, but not cash.

After Burke destroys the exhibition (and mutilates Jarrod in the process), Jarrod has no choice but to adapt, and Burke's assessment is proved right. When Jarrod rebuilds his museum, he makes much greater profit catering for the 'morbidly curious', fashioning a chamber of horrors that will 'send them out into the streets to tell their friends how wonderful it is to be scared to death'. At first Jarrod suggests that he will be far more concerned with depicting contemporary events, 'crimes of violence' which are 'still fresh in the public mind'. But the actual exhibition in his new museum remains dominated by historical subjects, including Anne Boleyn on the execution block, Charlotte Corday knifing Marat in the bath, wife-murderer Bluebeard, and William Kemmler, the first man executed by electric chair in 1890. The only notable concession to modernity is Matthew Burke himself, murdered by Jarrod and put on public display. Even Jarrod's

'Who cares a hang about history in wax?': About to destroy a lifetime's work, Matthew Burke (Roy Roberts) taunts sculptor Henry Jarrod (Vincent Price). Jarrod's waxwork tableaux may have great artistic merits, but lifeless models can't compete with the sensationalistic past represented in 3-D glory in *House of Wax* (1953). (Courtesy of the British Film Institute)

intention to recreate his model of Marie Antoinette as his 'leading lady' continues the association of history with death and violent crime, since his plan is to kill a real woman, whom he will then cover in wax to represent the French queen consort. Taking Burke's way of thinking to an extreme, Jarrod embraces the morbidity of his audience, suggesting that 'the historic figures I am about to show you will be *much more interesting* when I tell you that their faces were molded from the original death masks'. History therefore remains central to Jarrod's art, but is approached and promoted with a very different set of priorities.

As William Paul has noticed, the script frequently presents the wax works as a 'metaphor for 3-D' itself.[18] Burke's insistence that Jarrod needs to cater for a public that seeks 'sensationalism' and 'shock', was precisely the thinking behind the marketing of *House of Wax* itself. Critics had already commented on the exceptional impact of *Bwana Devil*, whose box office far surpassed the actual quality of the movie, 'with people going out of the theatre with headaches and eyestrain plus a poor picture and telling this to the neighbors, only to have those neighbors rush to get the same treatment'.[19] Elaborating on the success that *Bwana Devil* had in making viewers jump through putting 'a lion in your lap', Foy went one better and engulfed them in a tide of boiling wax!

Moreover, *House of Wax* implicitly affirms that audiences could be won back by construing the past in sensationalist ways – a belief many 3-D filmmakers seemed to share. Of the 46 3-D films released between November 1952 and May 1955, 22 were set in the past (most either westerns or gothic horrors), with each publicised in the style of 'exploitation' movies. *Devil's Canyon*, for example, promised 'Relentless Heat! Savage Nights! 500 Desperate Men! Caged Up With One Woman!' *The Nebraskan*'s image of sultry Roberta Haynes and a sturdy Phil Carey told audiences that 'If the Indians Didn't Get Them… They'd Get Each Other!!' The films were not necessarily of low quality, but they were 'designed for immediate appeal and quick payoff'.[20]

There is, however, a measure of regret in the *House of Wax*'s acknowledgement that history had to be exploited, in its awareness of artistry being sacrificed to the demands of the market. Art critic Sidney Wallace greatly admires Jarrod's original sculptures, crafted with real sensitivity and presented in a realistic and unembellished context. It is apparent, from the comments of Burke, and Wallace too, that this way of representing history is a tough sell, yet it is also far more edifying than the cynical attitude towards exploiting the past that Jarrod adopts subsequently – and given that his new method of recreating the past involves encasing corpses in wax, it is clearly both warped and superficial. Moreover, director Andre De Toth wanted to show that 'the loss of his art hurt more than his disfigurement', and Jarrod's longing to recreate his masterpiece of Marie Antoinette suggests a real dissatisfaction with the heartless but commercially successful nature of his new approach.[21] Ultimately, this suggests integrity (both artistic and historical) would have to be comprised to capture an audience.

Yet, in Jarrod's wax-coated cadavers there is also a new level of physical realism which, as his comments about the death masks suggest, holds a fascination of its own. This was the principal appeal of 3-D, in making the movies appear more 'real', of purportedly creating a more realistic experience. 3-D was supposed to engage audiences in the action on the screen, prompting a visceral reaction akin to being part of the film. Advertisements for *The Charge at Feather River* made out that

> with spears, tomahawks and arrows whizzing by the theater patron's heads and with the realistic sound of advancing horses and the ricochet of bullets, the paying customers are virtually fighting for their lives every second along with star Guy Madison.[22]

This, in part, explains the affinity between 3-D and the past in minds of filmmakers. Contemporary settings were perhaps felt less suited to the process because audiences could then compare the filmic experience to their own fully dimensional existence. But the use of the past (as well as the future, since six of the films released in 3-D were science fiction) could be sold as revealing something that was beyond their physical experience; and 3-D could, it was sensed, make the past feel more tangible. Indeed, as publicity for *The Charge at Feather River* suggested: 'Only 3-D could reach back into history and bring it so close to you!'

However, this idea of creating a 'realistic' experience of the past was undermined by the 3-D effects themselves. Studios apparently perceived it as 'bringing the screen closer to reality', 'dissolving the barriers' between the frame of the screen and the audience. However, the way in which 3-D films relied on rocks, fists, arrows, charging horses and severed heads apparently emerging from the screen, as well as the special glasses that viewers had to wear, continually reminded audiences that they were watching a 3-D movie. As Michael Kerbel argues, 'while 3-D is undeniably realistic, it is at least equally anti-realistic' because 'the tension involved in almost all movie-going – between believing that the screen image is a record of something that actually happened and recognising that it's a staged, manipulated piece of artifice – is accentuated with 3-D'.[23] In the end, 3-D movies quickly lost their novelty value, but filmmakers continued to hold on to the idea that audiences wanted to feel that they were 'experiencing' the past.

PARTICIPATING IN THE PAST

The concept of participation lay at the heart of the technologies that Hollywood chose to explore. Although evidently considering television to be its prime enemy, Hollywood also knew that other changes in popular tastes in entertainment and leisure had contributed to the decline in cinema audiences. In 1955, *Fortune* magazine surveyed the recreational market, and discerned that Americans increasingly 'demanded more engagement from their diversion'. The film industry partially tapped into this with the craze for drive-in movies, but *Fortune* noted that 'the sharpest fact about the post-war leisure market is the growing preference for active fun rather than mere onlooking'.[24] It was a conclusion that Darryl Zanuck had reached two years before, warning his industry peers that 'the public is more participation-minded than ever before', and that Hollywood had to shift from providing passive 'entertainment' to offering 'recreation' – 'something in which you participate'.[25]

A key function of the new screen technologies in the early Fifties was therefore to redefine the meaning of 'spectatorship', to sell the cinematic experience as a participatory event. The initial promotion material for each system categorically invited the spectator to join in the action on the screen. Cinerama began this, with advertising that declared 'you won't be gazing at a movie screen – you'll find yourself swept right *into* the picture, surrounded with sight and sound'.[26] Following suit, Jack Warner proposed that 3-D 'literally enables us to give the spectator the thrilling experience of actually being a participant in the dramatic action'.[27] Of course, there was nothing 'literal' about this – in practical terms, widescreen images and 3-D projectiles could only give the experience of 'heightened physiological stimulation'.[28] But three years later, when Todd-AO made its debut with *Oklahoma!*, filmmakers still made the promise that it would turn 'passive appreciation into living participation'.[29]

The explicit use of 'participation' to describe the sensory experience of the new formats went into overdrive in the promotion of history films. As might be expected, spectacle was a major issue, with publicity for *The Robe* stressing that the film would 'encompass you in all its awe-inspiring splendor and breathtaking grandeur'. But it was the suggestion that technology could put you right in the heart of historical events that really dominated the hype: 'Now, through the magic of CinemaScope, you become part of the miracle of *The Robe* – you share each moment of this wondrous drama – as the imperial might of Rome crashes against the word of God!'[30] *Knights of the Round Table* stressed that 'Scope would make 'the spectator feel as though he is actually enveloped in the action' of Arthurian legend, while Paramount introduced its first VistaVision western, *Run For Cover* with that claim that: 'The limitless range and incredible clarity of the new process have added the final dimension needed to make you completely a part of every charged moment of a gripping story.'[31]

This was the 'Thrill History' that *The Charge at Feather River* had promised, but ultimately the audience remained observers. Since things seemed to come *out* of the screen in stereoscope, 3D filmmakers could not even suggest that audiences would be swept into the screen. Over time then, the language used to describe the experiences became slightly more nuanced. William Paul notes that the concept of participation only makes sense 'if we could give "participate" more of a passive meaning', by which the audience 'give themselves up to the image that has taken over our field of vision'.[32] Thus the notion of 'witnessing' the past, rather than actively taking part in it, also entered the industry's discourse. Illustrations on posters and press advertisements showed an exaggerated expanse of the widescreen encircling the audience to suggest that 'the feeling of engulfment makes the viewer lose awareness of the screen's frame'.[33] According to this, the spectator's field of vision would be filled with the action on the screen and the physical presence of the theatre itself would not be registered. In effect, as cinematographer Leon Shamroy claimed, 'with the lack of consciousness of a framework imprisoning the action, you feel as if you were actually witnessing an event, rather than watching a picture of it'.[34]

In the context of this discourse, the use of history films to demonstrate the value of an augmented cinema possessed a deliberate logic. While widescreen responded to the challenge of television, its use of historical settings responded to one of the other key, outdoor recreational vogues of the post-war decade – the 'Living History' museum. With more time and money to spend, Americans headed to attractions such as Colonial Williamsburg, Old Sturbridge Village, and Henry Ford's Greenfield Village in record numbers. In 1954, an estimated 48 million tourists visited 1000 historic sites in the United States. Greenfield and Williamsburg had both opened in the 1930s, but the Fifties saw their greatest expansion. Visitors to Williamsburg increased from 166,000 in 1946 to 341,000 in 1956, and Greenfield experienced year-on-year increases in customers as high as 30 percent in 1956–57.[35] Both sites increased their holdings and exhibits, reinvigorated their educational programmes, and were duly emulated by a rash of new ventures. Old Sturbridge had opened in 1946, intended to 'preserve the ever-good things of New England's past in a manner that will teach their usefulness to the people of the present', recreating the daily work activities and community celebrations of a nineteenth-century rural town.[36] In 1950, Walter Knott bought and restored Calico, in the Mojave Desert, recreating 'the spirit of the Old West' in an 'authentic silver mining town'.[37] And in 1951, John D. Rockefeller expanded his patronage of Williamsburg to include 'Sleepy Hollow Restorations' in the Hudson River Valley. Walt Disney's nostalgic representations of 'Main Street USA', 'Liberty Square' and 'Frontierland' in 1955's opening of Disneyland, also demonstrated the influence of this thinking in Hollywood.

These museums stressed that they were more than exhibitions, that they enabled patrons to engage with the past. Visitors were certainly aware that what they were witnessing was essentially a theatrical display, with actors playing roles against authentically reconstructed settings, but they also were encouraged to believe that they were bearing witness to past ways of life. Assessing their popularity, Michael Kammen suggests that the context of the Cold War lent these museums the 'character of inspirational shrines, which enhance very powerful feelings of national pride and patriotism'.[38] To Hollywood, however, they clearly demonstrated a vigorous public interest in 'experiencing' the past, which could be exploited if cinema could produce or convey a similar sensation through its new cinematic technology. Filmmakers were thus encouraged to favour historical settings in demonstrating the illusion of participation.

Furthermore, Hollywood had keen advantages. While a site like Williamsburg was tied to its specific location and the actual moments of colonial history that gave it its significance, cinema could suggest participation in any number of historical events. *The Robe* could intimate the physical recreation of ancient Rome in a way that a tourist visiting the ruins of the city could never experience, and then appear to populate the palaces and arenas in a far more plausibly 'life-like' manner than a few tour guides in costume. Living history museums would always have tourists in modern clothes breaking the illusion, representing an intrusion of the modern world. In cinema, however, it was the sight of masses of people, seemingly at home in the expansive settings, with no such intrusion apparent, which enabled a film to convey the sense of being an eye-witness to it all.

However, this drive to create the illusion of participation had consequences for the way in which the past was presented. It certainly exacerbated the tendency of filmmakers to emphasise spectacle. Audiences could only be made to feel as if they could conceivably have 'been there', if they could merge with the crowd and become one of the 'cast of thousands' in the battle scenes or pageants. History on film therefore needed to be spectacular for that sensation to be sustained. Depiction of intimate and private moments in history would risk disrupting this by reminding audiences that they were 'voyeurs' rather than participants. Sudden awareness of one's status as an interloper on history to which no one could have been privy, would reinstate the boundary between film and spectator which widescreen developments were supposed to dissolve.

This becomes apparent when comparing the visual structure of *The Robe* with that of *David and Bathsheba*. Both films were biblical epics, scripted by Philip Dunne and photographed by Leon Shamroy. However, *David and Bathsheba* was released in 1951, two years before the introduction of CinemaScope, and was notably more intimate in both its visual and narrative construction than its successor. Of the 38 principal scenes of *The Robe*, 11 are played out against large crowds of people – at the slave market, outside the gates of Jerusalem, in busy taverns and baths, on Calvary, and in the streets of Cana. The openness of these settings enables almost all of the key dramatic action to be filmed with bystanders and witnesses evident on screen. The slave market, for example, is 'crowded because the old Emperor's heir and regent, the young Caligula is coming to buy gladiators'. As Marcellus wanders through the market, the film regales the audience with the sights and sounds they might plausibly have experienced if they were part of that crowd. When Marcellus collides with the Greek slave Demetrius, onlookers encircle the men while Demetrius' fate is discussed. However, the circle remains open at the front, inviting the audience to adopt the position that the camera maintains, as a member of that group of interested spectators.

Bearing Witness: In these screen-captures from *The Robe* (1953), the lightened area represents what would have been seen in the old 'Academy Ratio'. The expanse beyond that reveals how the proportions of the CinemaScope screen image allowed filmmakers to introduce more on-screen observers to the central action, offering plausible visual vantage points for audiences to imagine they too could 'be there'. Even intimate moments between Marcellus and Diane (top) are open to public viewing, taking place in the slave market.

Similarly, the crucifixion of Christ takes place with the audience encouraged to identify with the witnesses on the screen. The camera pans across an array of saddened faces, stressing the presence of many people. With the exception of one shot taken from behind and above Christ's head, looking down on Marcellus, the *mise-en-scène* does not challenge the audience's sense of being subjective spectators. Other sequences explicitly depict contemporary audiences 'present' at these historical events: sitting around listening to Miriam relate the story of the resurrection, preparing to hear the gospel from the apostle Peter, or attending with 'the entire court' the judging of Marcellus by Caligula. In that final trial scene, the court is lined up in tiers, and the cameras are positioned to show the events from three angles – from the perspective of the crowd on the floor, from the gallery, or sometimes from the right hand side of Caligula, as if from the perspective of the Praetorian guard. From all angles, the audience could imagine themselves in the position of one of those shown to be present.

In contrast only four different public gatherings were presented in *David and Bathsheba*: the army encampment at the film's opening; the Hebrews outside Jerusalem awaiting the arrival of the Ark of the Covenant; the courtiers at the royal wedding; and the angry mob that confronts David over his adultery with Bathsheba and follows him out to his supplication before the Ark. The camera does not stay with these crowds though – it continually cuts away to personal and private scenes that take place out of sight of the people. Moreover, unlike the panning shots of *The Robe,* the camera does not specifically emphasise their presence. The wedding scene, for example, begins in extravagant style with Bathsheba walking past the dignitaries gathered in the open court, but then abruptly cuts away from the anticipated spectacle to show instead the beginnings of a sandstorm outside. In consequence, only 29 minutes of the running time of *David and Bathsheba* (26 percent of the film) is spent on these public scenes, in contrast to the 54 minutes of action played against public gatherings in *The Robe* (41 percent of its length). Moreover, even when *The Robe* is not showing crowds and attention is focused on the principals, audiences can still see figures in the background. When, for example, Marcellus puts on the robe and is struck with madness, he is ignored by the many people hurrying into Jerusalem for shelter. The audience, however, becomes a viewer that tarries with him.

The Robe is therefore staged in a way that is far more open to audience 'participation' than *David and Bathsheba*. Even in ostensibly private moments, *The Robe* offers audiences with a credible location from which to be an eye-witness to the action. The Emperor Tiberius dismisses his courtiers to engage in an ostensibly confidential conversation with Marcellus – yet it is still visually made clear that guards are present in the background, and at one point a slave steps into shot from the near right hand side of the camera, as if we have been standing alongside him witnessing the discussion. When Diana and Marcellus first confess their love for one another, they do so out in the open, on the dockside, with the camera initially positioned to suggest that the viewer is watching them from the deck of Marcellus' ship. In *David and Bathsheba*, however, intimate moments exclude such possible vantage points, generally taking place in the enclosed set of King David's private chambers. Rather than being given an optically plausible position, members of the audience are turned into hidden voyeurs. Indeed, the film itself seems to acknowledge this, repeatedly depicting voyeurs intruding on such private moments, including a scene in which David and Bathsheba are making love, only to realise that a lone

In contrast to *The Robe*'s visual openness, in the pre-CinemaScope *David and Bathsheba* (1951) the camera is always intruding on private moments, putting the audience (like director Henry King) in the position of an unlikely voyeur. (Courtesy of the British Film Institute)

shepherd boy has been watching them (which only leaves the audience to identify with the sheep!).

The implication of this is that widescreen encouraged filmmakers to exploit the 'illusion' of drawing the audience into events by construing history in terms of public display. The lateral proportions of the screen engendered new visual patterns, allowing for people to cross scenes in the background or at the sides, while principal dialogue and action occurred in the centre and foreground. As Charles Barr asserts, this changed cinema's depiction of events (whether historical or otherwise): 'Before Scope it was difficult to show the "event" lucidly, with each detail given its appropriate weight… On the whole, the tendency was to split up the event into its component parts.'[39] When CinemaScope and widescreen reduced the need to cut from one perspective to another to show action and reaction, it was easier to make audiences feel as if they, rather than a series of cameras, were witnessing the event.

In an ironic twist, the living history museums that encouraged this thinking, in turn looked to Hollywood. In 1956, Colonial Williamsburg commissioned Paramount studios to make a half-hour film, entitled *Williamsburg: The Story of a Patriot*, for their visitors' centre. Constructing a special cinema to project the film in VistaVision format, Rockefeller and the managers of Williamsburg had evidently fallen for the hype too, conceding that Hollywood's new technology was more capable than their costumed re-enactors and restored buildings of creating an illusion that 'would enable the viewer to feel that he was "at the scene" and participating in past events'.[40]

TIME TRAVELLING

Hollywood's competition for the dollars of historically minded tourists found a further advantage in the panoramic possibilities of widescreen. The launch of Cinerama had openly exploited increased interest among Americans in domestic and international travel and sightseeing.[41] The first half of *This is Cinerama* took audiences to Niagara Falls, the canals of Venice, the Edinburgh Tattoo and a bullfight in Spain. Its second half, entitled 'America The Beautiful', showed them the 'scenic wonders' of the nation as seen from the nose of a low-flying B-25. *Cinerama Holiday* (1955) depicted a European couple touring America, taking in Las Vegas, Chicago and a Fourth of July parade in New Hampshire, while *The Seven Wonders of the World* (1956) included the Taj Mahal, the Parthenon, Mount Sinai and the Grand Canyon.

Seeking to replicate the experience of Cinerama, studios similarly turned to displays of domestic and foreign vistas as another form of spectacular excess. At a time when television drama was studio-bound, it was anticipated that exotic locations would prove a further enticement. The effect of Fox's stress on 'big outdoor films' on using history films to showcase Cinema-Scope has already been noted, but as Zanuck informed Philip Dunne, in composing the production schedule for 1953 he also 'tried to select varied foreign locales as a plus value'.[42]

Script notes for *Garden of Evil*, a post-Civil War western, dating from June 1953, indicate how effective exploitation of widescreen was at the forefront of Zanuck's thinking about history films. 'As I told you,' he informed the writers, 'we need, particularly for CinemaScope, a new and startling locale.'

> I do not see why we cannot transfer the locale of the story to Mexico – about 1870 or 1880. By using a volcano background for the locale of the hidden mine we can get something fresh and new in CinemaScope – and our trek to and from the mine can lead us through some very fresh and picturesque sections of Southern Mexico.[43]

For the new formats to make their greatest impact, filmmakers wanted to present audiences with things they had not seen before, and the 'past as a foreign country' *in* a foreign country offered double the opportunities.

Some of the most spectacular examples of Hollywood's history films did just this. *Ben Hur, Helen of Troy* and *A Farewell to Arms*, among others, used studios and locations in Italy. *Gigi* filmed in Paris. Locations in Norway and Brittany provided the background for *The Vikings*, while *Land of the Pharaohs* and parts of *The Ten Commandments* were filmed in Egypt. Film-makers also impressed on audiences (and apparently themselves believed) that this 'authenticity' of the location added to the accuracy of the history being depicted. Stanley Kramer's Napoleonic-era epic, *The Pride and the Passion*, was shot in Castilla-La Mancha, to 'insure a quality of authenticity' as well as to 'glorify the grandeur of Spain', while *Knights of the Round Table* utilised locations around Tintagel in Cornwall, 'the actual site where King Arthur's castle is supposed to have stood for centuries'.[44] Even when filming in America, it was implied that the setting could actually contribute to a better understanding of the subject matter, as suggested by publicity for *Run For Cover*: 'Never before have the natural backgrounds that are, after all, so much part of the very make-up of our western heroes, been so real, so full of true impact.'[45] Location was at once part of the historical context, as well as the spectacle.

Since Europe was the 'Old World', there was a natural predisposition for films made abroad to be set in the past. However, this was not especially driven by the exploitation of widescreen. The need to use up frozen funds in European countries, and the incentive of lower costs for extras and technicians, had already encouraged studios to film abroad before Cinerama and CinemaScope arrived on the scene. *Quo Vadis*, for example, was filmed in Cinecittà studios outside Rome, without the benefit of CinemaScope, in exactly the same manner that *Helen of Troy* was shot there in the process five years later.

One film, however, that did explicitly and extravagantly develop the connection of technology, history and location, was *Around the World in 80 Days*. Michael Todd was a leading Broadway stage producer, who had hoped to cash in on the development of Cinerama. However, during the making of *This is Cinerama*, he soon realised that the format's potential was limited by the problems of projecting three strips of film simultaneously and by the fact that its sheer size made it difficult to tell a conventional narrative. He therefore approached American Optical to develop a system that would simulate Cinerama, yet be suited to regular methods of filming and motion picture storytelling. The resulting Todd-AO system contained a 'bug-eye' lens which could achieve spectacular long-shots, but also allowed cameramen to switch to lenses with narrower angles for medium-shots and closeups. The quality and definition of the 70mm stock helped Todd-AO establish itself in a niche market as a 'high-class' format. It consolidated this with the 'most highly sought-after theatrical property of the decade', Richard Rodgers and Oscar Hammerstein's musical, *Oklahoma!* This 'treasured item of Americana' exploited the process's ability to imitate Cinerama by opening on the vast expanse of a 16-feet high field of corn, then taking audiences on a ride through the mid-western landscape, in the 'surrey with a fringe on top'.[46]

Forced to take a back seat during the production of *Oklahoma!*, Todd considered other historical material with which to make his mark – including versions of *Richard III* and *War and Peace* – before settling on Verne's 1872 novel. Making a success of *Around the World in 80 Days* represented a personal challenge, since Todd had already sponsored a failed stage version of the story, starring Orson Welles, in 1946. The movie became a showcase for Todd-AO, with the story of global travel in the past used to spectacular visual advantage, and publicity stressed the excesses that the production team went to in following the footsteps of Phileas Fogg. Filming occurred in 13 different countries, including substantial sequences in Spain and India; 68,894 people were filmed, representing 'the most people ever photographed in separate world-wide locations'; the 'most sets ever' were used, in '140 actual locations'; and over '4 million air passenger miles' were travelled by the cast to make the film. In reality, locations in America stood in for many foreign settings, such as the Alabama Hills in California doubling as the Pyrenees; but it was consistently publicised as an authentic travelogue, flitting through England, France, Spain, Egypt, Japan, China, and across the United States and other countries besides. According to Todd, it was a 'show' rather than a movie – 'a wonderful adventure story which is also a great documentary, a romantic legend which is a breathtaking travel picture with a world-wide expanse of beautiful scenery'.[47] Even to critics, it was a 'trip on a magic carpet to the most exotic and novel places all over the world'.[48]

The emphasis on locations tended to underplay the historical setting of the film, yet this came back into focus when Todd sought to position Todd-AO in the pantheon of major scientific advances in an on-screen preface to the movie. Edward R. Murrow introduced *80 Days* with excerpts from George Méliès' silent, monochrome version of Verne's *Trip to the Moon*, made in 1902 – including the famous effects shot of the rocket ship jutting out from one of the eye sockets of the man in the moon. Audiences saw this projected in the standard 35mm Academy ratio. Then the Todd-AO camera took over and the screen was seen to expand to its massive 56 feet wide capacity, with shots of a guided missile being launched in New Mexico. From a camera in that missile, the screen depicts 'never-before-seen color films' of the curved surface of the Earth, viewed from space. As Murrow's voiceover refers to the 'stretching fingertips of science', technological progress in rocket science, transportation and new photographic processes are equated, boosting Todd-AO's significance. Moreover, the subsequent film demonstrates that the technology which is capable of showing man what the world looks like from space, is just as able to show viewers what it would have been like to circumnavigate the globe 80 years ago. Indeed, by associating this technology with an allegedly 'authentic portrait of the era of 1872', Todd-AO was aligned not only with progress in cinematography, but with a technical achievement that science-fiction authors like Verne and H.G. Wells had only imagined: the creation of a Time Machine. 'Few men,' asserted Todd's own publicity, could have 'turned back the clock with as much daring and imagination.'[49]

The narrative itself compounds this attitude, celebrating technological progress in Fogg's race against time. In Verne's novel, the use of 'modern' methods of transportation and communication conveyed a sense that the 'distances between the world's civilizations' were shrinking. The film visualises the ships and intercontinental railroad systems that were responsible for this, as symbols of primitive, but rapidly advancing technology, from balloon, to ship to train. Moreover, the film presents America as being well in advance of other nations. In India, Fogg is delayed by the fact that the cross-continental railroad is incomplete; and the English refuse to push the matter, since it 'just isn't done' to interfere in native affairs. In contrast, the American railroad from San Francisco is already complete and heralded as a symbol of 'American determination and tenacity'.[50] Implicit is the message that America leads the way, and has done for decades – a reputation confirmed by both the nineteenth-century technologies in the film, and the twentieth-century Todd-AO process that presented them.

This sense of America's historical lead in scientific and industrial progress had great resonance in the Fifties, as the nation's unprecedented economic growth and rising standard of living was seen to be the product of technological achievement. New industries – electronics and electrical firms such as IBM, airline companies, chemical engineers, pharmaceutical and plastic manufacturers – became the leading lights of the American economy, and their products affected the everyday lives of Americans. This gave the nation a particular sense of pride and strength in the Cold War too, as Vice-President Nixon famously made clear in 1959, when boasting to Kruschev about 'gleaming American kitchen conveniences' at a trade show in Moscow. America's competitive advantage over the postwar economies of Europe and Asia was heightened by 'ever-larger investment in research and development, which in turn spurred impressive advances in science and technology, keys to leaps in productivity and per capita income'.[51]

This optimism was often undercut by the atomic bomb as an ever present reminder that scientific advances did not always signify progress. Yet like much of 1950s culture, Todd's film circumvented that anxiety. Murrow's introduction, and the image of a missile being launched, did remind audiences that 'man has devised a method of destroying most of humanity'. But unlike the doom-laden ambivalence of *The Story of Mankind*, Todd's optimism – and faith in his own success – rested in embracing new technologies. If atomic and rocket science had the capability to lift humanity 'up to a higher plateaux of prosperity and progress never dreamed of by the boldest dreamer', then cinema's 'boldest dreamer' implied that Todd-AO could similarly lift Hollywood's fortunes to unprecedented heights.

A strange symbiosis thus existed, whereby history films celebrated film technology, and film technology was used to celebrate the past. The belief that technological development was beneficial and progressive was central to the studios establishing their cinematic innovations as 'the way forward' for the industry – but they constantly looked back to the past to demonstrate this. They also used historical settings as a platform from which to point out the necessity of adapting and embracing change. Those responsible for the new screen processes used the past to reflect historic glory on to themselves and their product. They depicted themselves as pioneers, and suggested that they were not only representing history, but making it.

This affected the presentation of history in turn, putting a premium on spectacle, excess and sensation. According to their publicity, any spectacle that past civilizations had been capable of creating, Hollywood was now capable of matching. Widescreen and 3-D were what history had been waiting for! Yet, underlying all this hype was an attitude towards the past that would disturb historians. As *House of Wax* suggested, the entertainment industry could not value historical representation as an admirable artistic achievement in its own right, unless it stimulated a reaction that would generate a profit. The new technologies and processes of the screen were therefore considered a success if they could make *even* history seem exciting.

4

Political History

History is creating a new sort of world. Cruel, political, thoughtful, violent.

Lord Malcolm, *Quentin Durward* (1955)

For many in Hollywood at the start of the decade, the past was a problem. When the House Un-American Activities Committee came, first in 1947 and then in 1951, to ask the question, 'Are you now, or have you ever been, a member of the Communist Party?' hundreds of filmmakers were forced to scrutinise their personal histories, and proclaim or deny their actions and beliefs. In the fervent anti-Communism of the early Cold War, denouncing one's past became a ritual of redemption. Those who refused to accept that their earlier political affiliations and sympathies had been 'sinful', found themselves 'blacklisted' and unable to work, beginning with the Hollywood Ten whose refusal to acknowledge HUAC's authority confirmed them, in the public mind, as recalcitrant Stalinists. Although HUAC's focus was concentrated on Hollywood for only two years, consistent pressure to maintain 'ideological correctness' was applied from without by groups such as the American Legion, and from within by the Motion Picture Alliance for the Preservation of American Ideals, dedicated to fighting 'any effort' to 'divert the loyalty of the screen from the free America that gave it birth'.[1]

The ensuing political and intellectual climate was one that profoundly affected history films. Voicing a common opinion that HUAC's investigations had been more about stifling social criticism than rooting out genuine Communist subversives, blacklisted screenwriter Walter Bernstein

78

presented Hollywood's turn to costume pictures as key evidence of an industry beaten into submission. According to Bernstein, 'bland and timid' biographies and period musicals in the Fifties 'achieved a stupefying dullness that the old movies rarely approached'. As he saw it, filmmakers embraced history as a source of 'safe' escapist entertainment, a way of withdrawing from the controversies of contemporary politics.[2]

Bernstein credibly pointed out that *The Glenn Miller Story*'s concern with the 'search for a sound' was far removed from the narratives of men dedicated to the betterment of humanity seen in earlier film biographies of Abraham Lincoln, Thomas Edison or Louis Pasteur. However, his argument flies in the face of an increasing body of scholarship that has explored the ways in which Fifties films engaged with Cold War politics. Moreover, studies of various individual movies and genres frequently demonstrate how filmmakers made imaginative use of historical settings to achieve their political statements. Although Pierre Sorlin's assertion, that history on film is 'nothing more than a useful device to speak of the present time' requires considerable qualification, it is certainly true that many filmmakers – across the political spectrum – found that history could provide them with some very 'usable' pasts.[3]

Indeed, it is striking that both critics and defenders of McCarthyist anti-Communism repeatedly turned to three particular periods as sites for presenting relevant allegories – namely biblical history, the medieval past and the history of the American West. Reading criticism of HUAC into *Quo Vadis*, Maria Wyke argues that the suicide of the intellectual Petronius mirrors the severe consequences of the witch hunts inaugurated by the committee; while Bruce Babington and Peter Evans find condemnation of political pressure to 'name names' in *The Robe*'s account of Roman persecution of early Christians.[4] John Lenihan has commented on the way in which *Ivanhoe*'s writers Waldo Salt and Marguerite Roberts – then anticipating their subpoenas – evoked medieval witch hunts to present their opinion of HUAC's hearings as orchestrated and anti-Semitic. The trial of Rebecca, the daughter of Isaac the Jew, is presented as only a pretext for Prince John's plot to discredit King Richard and seize power for himself.[5] In the guise of a western, the scenario of *Johnny Guitar* also sought to disparage the self-righteous fanaticism of McCarthyist red-baiters who 'threaten, bully, and make empty promises to the innocent victims'.[6] *Broken Arrow* too, has been interpreted as encouraging sympathy for suspected subversives. In the accusations of treachery that Tom Jeffords faces when he befriends the leader of the Apaches, film historians have found echoes of what writer Alvah Bessie endured, as one of the Hollywood Ten, for his own belief in peaceful co-existence for modern-day 'reds' and 'whites'.[7]

Supporters of HUAC's anti-Communist zeal, however, used just the same pasts to advance their own perspectives. DeMille's introduction to *The Ten Commandments* compelled an anti-Communist reading of its story of 'two great opposing forces…forces which still – at this very moment – are engaged in mortal combat for the future of all mankind'.[8] Readings advanced by Steve Cohan and Alan Nadel make the allegory even more specific, relating it to the Suez Crisis which was indeed raging at the 'very moment' the film was released in October 1956.[9] Similarly Wyke notes that the makers of *Quo Vadis* introduced Imperial Rome to audiences as they imagined life in the Soviet bloc to be: where 'no man is sure of his life; the individual is at the mercy of the state; [and] murder replaces justice'.[10] Among medieval adventures *The Black Knight* offers a version of Arthurian mythology which only makes sense when read as 'an allegory for the triumph of American values over a Communist threat'. With high-placed traitors making Camelot vulnerable to the Saracen 'infidel', *The Black Knight* referenced and exploited anti-Communist anxieties about Fifth Columnists weakening nations in preparation for a full-scale invasion.[11] And in western settings, such international conspiracies threatened America itself, with Russian agents trying to break up the Union in *California Conquest*.[12] Richard Slotkin's masterful analysis of the western genre in *Gunfighter Nation* further relates *Rio Grande* to the Korean War, *The Gunfighter* and *High Noon* to conservative assessments of American preparedness for the Cold War, and *Vera Cruz* to counter-insurgency strategies for confronting the Communist threat in the Third World.[13]

However, as Toplin notes, many of these allegorical readings have been 'highly speculative', lacking in any basis in the production experiences of filmmakers.[14] Take *High Noon*, for example, as probably the most frequently referenced western of the McCarthy era. Harry Schein read the narrative as analogous to America's foreign policy in Korea. Marshal Will Kane thus represents America, wishing to 'retire' from the international stage after World War II, but compelled to resist the external threat posed by Communism, represented by the violent Frank Miller gang. Schein interpreted the unwillingness of the townspeople to support Kane as symbolic of 'other nations content to let the US go it alone in Korea'. This reading, among others, posits the film as explicitly anti-Communist in tenor.[15] But others informed by the film's production context, tend to see it as a parable about Hollywood and McCarthyism. Summoned before the Committee in the middle of production, scenarist Carl Foreman refused to co-operate and took the Fifth Amendment to avoid testifying. Despite previous assurances to the contrary, producer Stanley Kramer promptly broke off their partnership. Foreman himself has since argued that he fashioned the screenplay in anticipation of his blacklisting, watching Hollywood 'beginning to crumble around the edges as these high powered politicians came in':

> They were either capitulating to the...political gangsters from out of town – or they were being executed by them there. I could see my time was coming sooner or later...and I wanted to write about that. I wanted to write about the death of Hollywood.[16]

Accordingly, the Miller gang represents HUAC returning to Hollywood in 1951, with the film community reflected in the 'the craven townspeople [who] find a variety of reasons why they cannot stand up to this threat', leaving Kane/Foreman to his fate.[17]

What evidence from 'production experiences' really shows is that fully developed allegories were actually few and far between. The periods of western history and medieval/Arthurian history were particularly amenable to allegory because Hollywood had long constructed and understood them more as 'mythic spaces' than as moments in real history. In films that operated within a framework of historical fact, and were thus constrained by specific factual detail, allegories were much less sustainable. Even biblical epics found this – the story of Moses did not especially lend itself to a Cold War reading, which is why DeMille himself chose to appear on screen before the start of *The Ten Commandments* to assert its relevancy. Therefore, rather than constructing allegories, makers of history films who wanted to reflect on Cold War realities more commonly perceived of 'related moments in time'.

This was a phrase used by Dore Schary in promoting MGM's production of *Julius Caesar* in 1953. Schary acknowledged that it was 'not literally true that history repeats itself', but that 'today's frame of historical reference' encouraged people to find patterns in the past which appeared 'strikingly familiar'.[18] The importance of mythic spaces in defining the historical consciousness of filmmakers is not to be overlooked, as Chapter 5 makes clear. However, it is in looking at how real 'related moments in time' were identified, treated and contested that we can best understand the effect of the Cold War on Hollywood's sense of the past.

'HE'S ENTITLED TO TELL HIS STORY'

Experience with HUAC tended to dominate the film industry's impressions of the anti-Communist crusade – whether that was a positive assessment from the members of the conservative Motion Picture Alliance, ambivalence from Hollywood's liberals, or a profoundly negative one from those on the left who felt victimised. It is important to remember that anti-Communism was not simply dominated by right-wing demagogues like Joseph McCarthy, but that many strains co-existed with aspects embraced by evangelical Protestants and Catholic priests, union leaders and business executives, liberal internationalists and staunch American Legion patriots. While the right presented Communism as 'the embodiment of a mythological evil' engaged in a 'satanic conspiracy to take over the world and enslave all mankind', liberal anti-Communists at least could agree that there were 'deadly threats to democracy coming from the left as well as the right, requiring difficult decisions between greater and lesser evils'.[19] Within these conceptions, a loose consensus thereby existed – and within that, a wide variety of perspectives defined the 'related moments' that filmmakers perceived.

Schary's own sense of 44 BC being such a point in time was defined by a whole range of Cold War concerns: 'Dictatorship versus a free society, political violence, demagoguery, mob action, partisan purges.'[20] It reflected the perspective of a liberal anti-Communist, albeit generalised enough to avoid any controversy. However, the makers of *Julius Caesar* felt more specifically embattled by the threat to civil liberties and liberal democracy that they saw in the hyperbole and the methods of countersubversive red-baiters. Director Joseph Mankiewicz had himself been targeted in 1950, when DeMille tried to force his resignation as president of the Screen Directors Guild. Having opposed moves to compel members to sign loyalty oaths, Mankiewicz was subjected to 'smear and abuse' – culminating in DeMille's tirade against him in front of the Guild, which began with a paraphrase of Mark Antony's funeral oration: 'I have come before you neither to praise Caesar nor to bury him…'[21] When it came to that moment in making the film adaptation two years later, Mankiewicz subtly reworked it into an image of self-serving demagoguery, staging the scene so that Antony (played by Marlon Brando) is shown building the crowd into a frenzied mob. Then when Antony pauses 'as if overcome by grief', the director cut to a shot of Brando, 'who, with his back to the crowd, exhibits not grief, but a look of cold calculation' and a 'sardonic smile that spells out clearly his demagogic intentions'.[22]

It was in this frame of mind that those who had been cowed by HUAC and the Red Scare looked to history for opportunities to remind (or educate) audiences about the dangers of politically induced intolerance. A strong example of undistorted history providing pertinent lessons came in the re-counting of the Dreyfus affair in MGM's *I Accuse!* (1958). Writer Gore Vidal and director-actor Jose Ferrer were inspired by Nicholas Halasz's work on the subject, published in 1955, which was tellingly entitled *Captain Dreyfus: A Story of Mass Hysteria*. Both book and film reflected the imme-diate 'post-mortem' on McCarthyism that followed the senator's censure in 1954. Contributors to 1955's *The New American Right* advanced the argument that McCarthyism had been a 'popular insurgency' of genuine anti-Communism, agitated into a phenomenon of mass hysteria by irra-tional anxieties.[23] Working together on their script, Vidal and Ferrer saw parallels between the 'extremely spy conscious' French public of 1894, and the fears induced in post-war America by the threat of internal espionage, at moments when both countries were 'just becoming aware' of their place 'in the dangerous international situation'.[24]

These fears had a genuine basis, demonstrated in the prosecutions of Klaus Fuchs and Julius and Ethel Rosenberg, and the implication of Alger Hiss having betrayed State Department secrets to the Soviets – just as the Dreyfus case had begun when Major Esterhazy sold military secrets of the French Army to the Germans. But the subsequent climate of 'hysteria and unreason' had – from the perspective of liberals – hurt 'innocent victims' instead of exposing real Communists.[25] Both Vidal and Ferrer had actively campaigned for the abolition of HUAC in 1948, opposing the committee on constitutional and moral grounds, seeing the intimidation of socially conscious filmmakers as a form of censorship. Vidal was sensitive to the way in which homosexuals in public office had been targeted and hounded as security risks.[26] Ferrer's experience was more direct. Accused of Communist associations by the Motion Picture Alliance's Ward Bond, Ferrer was sub-poenaed by HUAC just as the Academy was deciding whether to award him an Oscar for *Cyrano de Bergerac* (1950). By this time, the Supreme Court had refused to review the case of the Hollywood Ten, rejecting the argument that the First Amendment militated against them being compelled to con-fess their membership of the Communist Party or any other political group. The alternative strategy of refusing to answer on the grounds of the Fifth

Amendment, avoiding self-incrimination, had also proved ill-advised for those in Hollywood who wanted to continue their careers, since their guilt was then automatically assumed. Ferrer therefore pursued a different approach, instead hiring 'a whole battery of lawyers' to prove that each and every charge of affiliation was unjustified.[27] His involvement in anti-fascist groups, opposition to Franco in the Spanish Civil War, support of the Civil Rights Congress, and his friendship with Paul Robeson, were considered as evidence against him. He was repeatedly forced to explain how his name had been 'unwittingly' used by organisations that were now believed to be 'fronts' for the Communist Party.[28]

With Ferrer himself playing Alfred Dreyfus, *I Accuse!* found parallels in the 'twisting about' of 'perfectly innocent actions' to suggest that a loyal man had undermined national security. Dreyfus had been arrested and condemned as a traitor on the basis of evidence that he was not permitted to see or refute – and although Ferrer had refuted the charges against him, he was one of the first to have had that opportunity, and continued to voice disapproval of the way in which previous hearings had been conducted. He also identified with the fact that Dreyfus, being of Alsatian birth, had been regarded by the French military as an 'outsider'; Ferrer himself had been born in Puerto Rico, and his cooperation with HUAC was partly predicated on the need to protect his citizenship as well as his career.

Dreyfus' case had already been linked with the cause of the Hollywood Ten. One of them, Dalton Trumbo, had derived the title of his attack on the committee – *The Time of the Toad* (1949) – from 'a rhetorical conceit employed by Emile Zola in his pamphleteering on behalf of Dreyfus'. Zola had claimed that only by swallowing a poisonous toad every morning could he stomach the lies of the French press, and Trumbo suggested that the 'compulsive madness' of the Red Scare necessitated a similar diet.[29] *I Accuse!* concurred, and specifically drew attention to the anti-Semitism of the French media which had fomented the public hysteria. Vidal followed Halasz in suggesting that Dreyfus' loyalty had only ever been in doubt because of the prejudices of the French General Staff, who regarded 'all Jews as security risks'.[30] Similar strains of 'Jew-baiting' had long been associated with HUAC, most notably emanating from the 'godfather' of the Committee, John Rankin, whose virulent attacks on the film industry were based on an outspoken belief that 'Russian Jews control too much of Hollywood propaganda'. This – along with the fact that the majority of the Hollywood Ten were Jewish – had 'stiffened the backbone of Hollywood's liberal conscience' in their opposition to HUAC, and clearly still had resonance in 1958.[31] By then, however, the Red Scare had subsided and Vidal and Ferrer did not feel the need to over-work the analogies. Rather they presented *I Accuse!* as a case study of how such a 'poisonous' atmosphere had developed in the past. Thus, just as the Dreyfusards had chosen to argue their case in terms of universal justice, so the 'true meaning the dark scandal', as Vidal saw it, was that 'injustice to one is injustice to all' – and history did not need to be rewritten to make that point.[32]

A rather more conflicted view emerged in the questions of justice in *The Court Martial of Billy Mitchell* (1955), which concerned General William Mitchell, a pioneering crusader for the army's fledgling air corps in the early twentieth century. In spite of an impressive performance during World War I, the commanders of America's armed forces had continued to think of the airplane as little more than a carnival attraction. Even after using his planes to destroy an 'unsinkable' captured German battleship, Mitchell saw funds dry up and friends killed because of poor and outdated equipment.

The Time of the Toad: Subpoenaed by HUAC in 1951, and questioned about his loyalty to America, Jose Ferrer revisited the experience as Captain Alfred Dreyfus in *I Accuse!* (1958). (Courtesy of the British Film Institute)

Vigorously campaigning for air defence, his court-martial came when he issued statements in 1925 that attacked the War Department and Navy Department for allowing the air service to deteriorate to dangerous levels. Found guilty, it was not until the attack on Pearl Harbor that his earlier statements, about the necessity of an American airforce and the potential threat of Japan, made Mitchell appear to have been uncannily prescient. Marking the 30th anniversary in 1955, screenwriter Emmett Lavery was given the task of presenting Mitchell as something of a seer, forced by his far-sighted concern for national security to challenge a blinkered establishment.

In 1947, Lavery had been president of the Screen Writers Guild. If anywhere in Hollywood was perceived as a hotbed for left-wing radicals, it was the SWG, and many saw this as a liability. At the beginning of the Red Scare, the Guild was consequently in the throes of an internecine conflict in which moderate members were seeking to purge the leftists, to protect themselves from the attention of HUAC. Lavery was a Catholic moderate liberal, and in his electioneering for the presidency he argued that the writers among the Hollywood Ten had 'knowingly harmed Guild interests by linking the writers' union with Communism in the public mind'.[33] When he appeared before HUAC in his official capacity in October, he strongly disputed accusations that the SWG was 'under Communist domination' and made it clear that he intended only to defend 'the reputation of the Guild', not the radical members who had just been cited for contempt of Congress. Indeed, he even suggested that HUAC should support his efforts to reform the SWG and not provoke a backlash:

> My only concern with respect to this whole proceeding, Mr Chairman, is merely that people might go back home and think that they [the Hollywood Ten] have been political martyrs. An election in November which is coming up in our Screen Writers Guild might be seriously affected, and not for the better, if people thought that Government had interfered more than was necessary in the normal operations of the guild.[34]

Lavery's testimony cost him the election and many friends, but in taking on *The Court Martial of Billy Mitchell* eight years later he appeared to be justifying the stance he had taken. In developing his ideas about the project, Lavery described Mitchell's position as 'an impossible dilemma'. To say what he felt was necessary for the sake of national security, Mitchell had been compelled to 'discredit the service he loved and the friends he loved'. Arguing that sometimes 'you have to sacrifice your friends as well as your enemies – but in a good cause it's all worth it', the screenplay presented Lavery with an opportunity to show that his decision to put the wider interests of the Guild first had been principled and far-sighted, and to associate himself with Mitchell's moral courage.[35]

Lavery did inject a moment of liberal criticism into the script during the court-martial scenes; when the generals hearing the case retire to consider whether Mitchell should be allowed to justify his disobedience. Until this juncture, any attempt to introduce supporting evidence had been overruled as 'irrelevant' – a scenario familiar to HUAC witnesses, whose efforts to read prepared statements had been silenced by the gavel of Chairman Parnell Thomas. In the film, however, General Douglas MacArthur (played by Dayton Loomis) makes an appeal to his fellow judges:

MacArthur: The whole foundation of our legal system, and of our country for that matter, rests on the right of a man to defend himself and his right to use every means to defend himself. He may be wrong, but at least he's entitled to tell his story. And the minute we forget that we're in very grave danger.

Unlike the majority of the dialogue, which was based on transcripts of the actual court-martial, this scene was entirely Lavery's invention – and it reflected common criticism of HUAC's methods. But, by putting the sentiment in the mouth of a military hero revered by the Republican right, Lavery covered his tracks, and maintained his sense of irony.

However, in identifying Mitchell as a man who had been vilified but eventually vindicated by the course of history, Lavery was also rationalising his strain of liberal anti-Communism. Prior to Pearl Harbor, Mitchell had been dismissed as a scaremonger. Lavery had shared a similar opinion of HUAC, critical in his 1947 testimony of what he saw as the Committee's efforts to scare the American public by exaggerating the Communist threat.[36] However, such attitudes had subsequently been shaken by the Communist victory in the civil war in China, Russia's testing of its own atomic bomb, and the Korean War, which all seemed to affirm the worst fears of militant anti-Communists. *Court Martial* reflected this changed perspective, with the audience encouraged to support Mitchell's alarmism on the grounds of national security. As the film suggests, Mitchell sought to scare the public out of their complacency, in order to build a strong force that would act as a deterrent in future wars.

Indeed, the arguments presented in Mitchell's defence were very much related to contemporary debates. As Lavery demonstrated, Mitchell had predicted that 'in the future, air battles taking place miles away from the frontiers will be so decisive…that the nation losing them will be willing to capitulate without resorting to a further contest on land or water'. He had warned that 'if a nation ambitious for universal conquest gets off to a "flying start" in a war of the future, it may be able to control the whole world'.[37] When witnesses such as Eddie Rickenbacker and Carl Spaatz gave Mitchell their support, they shocked the courtroom and the public by revealing that America had slipped to eighth place in aviation ranking in the world, and that, despite the official claims that the War Department had 1800 planes, only nine aircraft were ready for combat purposes. These arguments for deterrence and the urgent need to respond to a 'gap' in America's military capabilities corresponded strongly with views advanced in the mid-1950s, that the United States should 'not meet the enemy gun for gun but instead rely on those forms of power, above all atomic and aerial, at which it excelled and which might provide quick victory' in event of a superpower confrontation.[38] This was the perspective that informed Eisenhower's 'New Look' policy, announced in 1954, and which *The Court Martial of Billy Mitchell* implicitly endorsed just as America was about to plunge into the next phase of the arms race.

In the scripting of *The Court Martial of Billy Mitchell* (1955), Emmett Lavery identified parallels between his own 'friendly' testimony before HUAC and Mitchell's decision to take an unpopular stand in the interests of national security in the 1920s. Director Otto Preminger seemed to appreciate this, securing permission to film in the Senate offices in Washington DC where Joseph McCarthy had earlier held his committee hearings. (Courtesy of the British Film Institute)

Left-wing filmmakers, who were largely excluded from Hollywood by the blacklist, viewed this Cold War militarism from the outside, and saw it as a 'tactical mission' to 'inculcate a martial spirit' in the American people. Michael Wilson, one of the most prominent blacklisted scenarists, noted both the high volume of war films released in the early 1950s and that the vast majority were set in the Second World War rather than the Korean conflict. 'If skilfully revised, combat stories of Normandy and Okinawa could play upon patriotic memories of a middle-ageing generation,' wrote Wilson, 'while feeding the glory dreams of a younger generation born too late to take part in the crusade against German and Japanese fascism.'[39] John Howard Lawson saw such attitudes projected even further back into the past in *The Red Badge of Courage*, which, according to his analysis, had much in common with Korean War movies like *Steel Helmet*. MGM's adaptation of Stephen Crane's story, Lawson maintained, 'makes a comment on history which is extremely valuable to today's war-makers… In transferring the education-of-a-killer theme to a Civil War background, it attempts to justify the Korean aggression by saying that it is no better, and no worse' than the 'warfare to preserve the Union.'[40] Since John Huston had been a founding member of the Committee for the First Amendment that had sought to defend the Ten, Lawson was prepared to give the director the benefit of the doubt, and instead blamed the studio bosses for the alleged 'propaganda' of *The Red Badge of Courage*. However, as the making of *The Court Martial of Billy Mitchell* suggests, an anti-Communist consensus had been forged by the early 1950s and liberal filmmakers were often contributing to projects that supported America's Cold War policies.

'AN EVIL SCHEME TO DESTROY THE EARTH'

The dominant political rhetoric of the post-war years encouraged this attitude, as – courtesy of J. Edgar Hoover – Communism was rebranded as 'Red Fascism'.[41] Obliterating any substantive distinction between Stalinist Russia and Nazi Germany, this made for an 'easy transition in public perceptions' between the enemy forces of World War II and the ideological enemy of the Cold War.[42] The post-war image of the Communist Party of America as a 'fifth column' for the Soviet Union, for instance, drew upon knowledge of subversive Nazi activity, including Hitler's use of sympathisers in Austria, Czechoslovakia and Norway to pave the way for annexation.[43] This defined the new conflict in familiar terms and insisted upon the aggressiveness of Communist Party doctrine by reminding Americans of Nazi and Japanese ambitions. The Cold War could then be presented readily – as it was by President Truman in the announcement of his foreign policy doctrine – as a war of 'freedom against tyranny', reconstituting a far-reaching struggle between 'free' and 'totalitarian' ways of life.[44] And just in case anyone in Hollywood remained oblivious, the Motion Picture Alliance spelled it out once again, insisting that 'the whole world is torn by a great political issue – Freedom or Slavery, which means Americanism or Totalitarianism'.[45]

This kind of rhetoric found particular favour in history films set in 'mythic spaces'. Publicity for swashbucklers of all varieties frequently described the villains as 'tyrants', 'dictators' and 'despots', suggesting that history could provide an abundance of precursors to Stalin and Mao. Encompassing the feudal settings of *The Black Shield of Falworth* and *The Court Jester*, the Persian fantasies of *The Siren of Bagdad* or *The Thief of Damascus*, and the eighteenth century of *The Purple Mask* and *Captain Scarlett*, each of these films was promoted as concerning young individuals banding together to 'challenge the tyrant's reign of terror', 'thwarting the dictator' and breaking his 'tyrannical grip' on an oppressed population.[46] Moreover, the production of other history films emulated the conflation of Communism and Nazism. MGM's adaptation of Rudyard Kipling's *Kim*, for example, was conceived in 1942 with the villains cast as German spies; by the time of the film's release in 1950, it was a simple matter to transform them into proto-Soviet emissaries, Fifth columnists working for the Russian Tsar to stir native uprisings against the British Raj.[47] Biblical epics reflected the same perception. Producer Frank Ross had acquired the rights to Lloyd C. Douglas' *The Robe* in 1942, thinking to 'present a parallel to political history in the making' which 'would show those who caused the death of Our Lord upon the Cross as prototypes of the modern dictators then identified as Hitler and Mussolini'. In 1953, however, 'modern parallels' seemed even more acute to anti-Communists, 'for at last the great struggle between Christ and the anti-Christ had been joined, not merely upon political levels but upon the fundamental level of religion also'.[48]

The last point was crucial to American perceptions of the Cold War enemy, for rigid atheism and 'ungodliness' were developed into features that made Stalinism an even greater evil than Nazism. Communism was demonised as a conspiracy against God as well as democracy, while evangelical crusader Billy Graham made his name by aggressively preaching that

Communism was 'masterminded by Satan himself', and devoted many sermons to the 'death duel between Christian America and atheistic Russia'.[49] Binarisms thereby abounded and reinforced one another – democracy vs. totalitarianism, freedom vs. slavery, and faith vs. atheism. DeMille, for one, brought them all together in *The Ten Commandments*, defining the 'theme of this picture [as] whether men are to be ruled by God's law or whether they are to be ruled by the whims of a dictator like Rameses. Are men the property of the state or are they free souls under God?'[50]

Related moments in history, beyond the generic spaces of the swashbuckler and the biblical epic, were found to parallel these perceptions. One noteworthy example was *The Miracle of Our Lady of Fatima* (1952), an account of events in Portugal in 1917, when three young children claimed to have seen a vision of the Virgin Mary near their home at Cova da Iria. Pressure from sceptical family, friends and, significantly, from anti-religious government officials failed to shake their conviction in their story. Indeed, the visions allegedly came to them again, the Virgin appearing six times to Lucia dos Santos, Francisco Martos and Jacinta Martos – and they soon attracted vast gatherings of pilgrims from the surrounding countryside, even though only the children could see the apparition. However, after the final visitation, the crowds themselves witnessed a sight that convinced them: as the sun changed colour, it seemed to fall towards the earth and then spun in the sky 'like a wheel of fire'.[51]

This was a well-documented story, accepted as a miracle by many Catholics and endorsed by the Vatican in 1930, but what made it more significant in the Cold War context were the warnings given by the apparition. According to the reports of the Catholic Church, the third time the children saw the Lady, she prophesised both an end to World War I and the coming of a Second World War during the 'pontificate of Pius XI'. Moreover, God would 'punish the world for its crimes, by war, famine, and by persecution of the Church and of the Holy Father':

> To prevent this I ask for the consecration of Russia to my Immaculate heart... If my request is attended to, Russia will be converted and there will be peace; if not, her errors will spread throughout the world, causing wars and persecution of the Church, good people will be martyred...[and] various nations will be destroyed.[52]

The specificity of this 'Fatima Message', given just at the time of the Bolshevik Revolution, now seemed uncannily relevant, and contributed to a great revival of interest in the prophesy.[53]

Capitalising on this, Warner Bros. assigned the project to producer Bryan Foy and writer Crane Wilbur as soon as they had completed work on *I Was a Communist for the FBI*, strongly suggesting the anti-Communist vein in which the *Miracle* screenplay was conceived. Indeed, as producers of *Mission to Moscow* (1943), and having been strongly committed to the New Deal and anti-fascism in the 1930s, Warner Bros., had a lot to repent for in the eyes of the anti-Communist right – and did so fervently. In their original script, Foy and Wilbur rewrote history in order to emphasise the Cold War message, moving the reference to Russia from the third visitation to the final appearance of Our Lady, to make the warning the climax of their picture. They also suggested that the miracle occurred at the 'exact time and day' that 'Lenin entered Moscow', and dialogue was simplified from the accepted text to make the connection absolutely clear: 'In Russia there is an evil scheme to destroy the peace of the earth. To prevent this, I ask that she be consecrated to the Virgin Mary.' In the end though, the message was moved back to the third visitation of July 13, 1917, when the Production Code Administration warned the filmmakers 'to adhere scrupulously to the many chronicles available on the subject' to avoid offending 'the religious sensibilities of many millions of people to whom the story of Fatima is intimately known'.[54]

The Production Code, however, did not prevent Foy and Wilbur from rewriting the history of Portugal to suit their purposes. They opted instead to heighten the film's anti-Communism by opening with scenes of a 'rabble-rouser' speaking to a 'hysterical mob of citizens' and proclaiming the success of the Portuguese revolution of 1910 as 'the birth of the People's Socialist Republic'. The revolution was explicitly described as a 'swift and sudden uprising, planned and executed by a Socialist minority, its purpose to overthrow the government and establish a police state'. Further, the narrator intoned, this was 'an early pattern of what was to happen time and again in many countries of Europe'. In contrast, historians contend that Portuguese revolutionaries had strongly dissociated themselves from the 'socialist element' since the 1870s, promoting instead the principles of political democracy and appealing to the bourgeoisie. Rather than the revolution of a 'socialist minority', it had been sparked by a *coup d'etat* of junior army officers belonging to the secret society of the *carbonari*, and was then sustained by the professional classes of Lisbon.[55]

Lacking the facts to support their presentation of a socialist revolution, the filmmakers seized upon the revolutionaries' anti-clericalism to associate them more closely with the Bolsheviks. The Republican government had been stridently anti-clerical, separating Church and State in 1911, and the film presented the 'savage persecution of all religious orders' within Portugal as a parallel to the execution of priests, monks and nuns in Lenin's regime. However, in Portugal, this attitude had not been inspired by Marxism, but by the Freemasonry of the Republican leaders and their reaction to the alliance between their Royalist opponents and the Catholic Church. District Administrator Artur de Oliveira Santos, who had terrorised Lucia, Francisco and Jacinta in an effort to discredit their visions, was himself a Freemason, and believed that the Church had 'prepared' the apparitions in order to stimulate a religious revival.[56] The film, however, having aligned the Republican government with socialism, presented Santos as an *apparatchik* following the orders of a fictionalised 'Ministry of Police'. His hostility to the public display of faith is depicted as an ideologically conditioned reflex, with no explanation. Moreover, the assault of 'the

Rewriting history for political point-scoring, the Portuguese revolution of 1910 was turned into a warning about 'Godless Communism' by the makers of *The Miracle of Our Lady of Fatima* (1952). District Administrator Artur de Oliveira Santos (Frank Silvera, left) was transformed into a socialist apparatchik, threatening innocent children to further his government's attack on the Church. (Courtesy of the British Film Institute)

People's Socialist Republic' on the Church was explicitly characterised as 'anti-religious', rather than 'anti-Catholic', so that the revolution becomes as an undiscriminating threat to ecumenical faith and spirituality.

The Miracle of Our Lady of Fatima was one of the top-grossing films of the year, in contrast to the poor performance of *I Was a Communist for the FBI.*[57] Audiences were obviously far more receptive to anti-Communism embedded in a 'simple story of faith' than to the 'agit-prop' of explicitly anti-Communist movies. After all, it offered a more positive message than the notion that spies were abroad in the population. Milton Luban, writing in the *Hollywood Reporter*, correctly anticipated that the film would 'strike a responsive chord with audiences everywhere, regardless of creed, if only because in these troublesome war-threatening times it seems that only Divine intercession in the form of another miracle can halt man's wild rush to destroy himself'.[58] Being set in the past also added to the film's sense of hope, since the Portuguese Republic had been overthrown in 1926 in a military coup – replaced with the increasingly pro-American regime of Antonio Salazar. A coda to the movie showed footage of thousands of pilgrims worshipping at the basilica in Fatima in 1951, demonstrating that it was possible for 'socialist' gains to be overturned. But in the absence of any reference to Salazar's dictatorial police-state, the film simply implied that it was all down to the power of prayer and devotion.

Indeed in searching for historical parallels that would indict the goals and methods of contemporary Communism, filmmakers seemed to change or suppress far more historical facts than did those who sought to critique American anti-Communism. Barre Lyndon, for instance, initially founded his script for *Omar Khayyam* (1957) in valid historical sources, including the eleventh-century *Political Will of Nizam al-Mulk*. This text recounts the childhood friendship between the Nizam, Omar Khayyam, and Hassan Ben Sabbah, and the services that in later life they provided to the Sultans of Persia, Alp Arslan and Malik Shah. It is also documented, as the film depicts, that Hassan Ben Sabbah, 'plunged into the maze of intrigue of an oriental court', set himself up as the head of the fanatical sect of Ismailians – better known as the Assassins – and became the legendary 'old man of the mountain'.[59] Nizam al-Mulk himself was one of his countless victims.

In making this relevant in the Cold War, however, Lyndon departed from history to make Hassan the secret head of the Assassins from the start. The film's 'Hussani' uses the connections of his friends to get himself appointed as the Sultan's Keeper of the Seal, so as to conspire against the

Persian empire from within. Lyndon's notes prove he knew that Hassan only became the 'old man of the mountain' years after he was forced to leave the court in disgrace; but the movie makes him far more cunning and subversive, the kind of 'traitor in government' that McCarthy could only dream of.[60] Depicting his assassins as 'the underground movement that all but conquered the world' – 'a monstrous conspiracy dedicated to world domination' – the film's publicity encouraged this reading.[61] The intimation that the assassins ought to be seen as proto-Communist conspirators was furthered by identifying them through distinctive red caps, red cloaks, and red-handled daggers, explicitly making them a 'Red Menace'. Moreover, those who join the cult are turned into 'human weapons' through a process of brainwashing, expedited with hashish:

> *Hussani:*   When life-long beliefs have been shattered and all faith is gone, we tell them what to believe. Any who still have moral scruples are condemned to death… They deliver themselves to us, body and soul. A perfect weapon – and one that is never idle!

Devoid of religious faith, and fanatically devoted to their cause, the assassins are thus presented as embodiments of Hoover's definition of a Communist 'dupe' as an 'individual who unknowingly is under Communist thought control and does the work of the Party'.[62] Following the Korean War, the concept of brainwashing had become something of a cultural obsession, when it was claimed that one in six American prisoners of war had collaborated with their captors after being subjected to a 're-education process'.[63] Hollywood had only just explicitly considered the question of Communist mind-control and indoctrination in *The Rack* (1956), when Lyndon co-opted it for his own screenplay.

Ironically, the film's assassins are intent on subverting an imperialist power, with the audience therefore asked to support an absolute monarch – rather bringing to mind America's support of undemocratic rulers in Iran, Indochina and Guatemala during the 1950s. However, Lyndon avoids this connotation through his characterisation of Khayyam, emphasising his individualism, and crediting him with an explicitly 'modern' philosophy that embraces the search for truth, equality for women, the setting free of slaves, and the pursuit of scientific knowledge for the betterment of mankind. Anachronistically casting Khayyam as prefiguring the Enlightenment, and hence as more 'Western' than Oriental, we are explicitly told at the start of the film that his is a 'philosophy that has conquered the hearts of men and women' since that time.

This is contrasted with the materialist philosophy of Hussani, whose dreams of global domination are scorned by Omar, who claims that while 'such men as you have risen in every generation, from the dawn of man to our times, each with another form of the ancient conspiracy to rule this earth', none have ever succeeded. But when the poet claims that 'millions of men have died to prove you wrong' he can only be speaking to the modern-day audience, for in the context of the film itself only a handful of characters had been killed. Still, *Omar Khayyam* presented an opportunity to raise contemporary fears about Communist subversion, and then reassure audiences that their predecessors had always failed in the past. However, assurances of this nature only worked when filmmakers rewrote history.

'I GUESS THE WESTERN CLOAK FOOLED HIM'

As Hollywood's anti-Communists stressed the need for 'eternal vigilance' to win the Cold War, they too looked for signs of subversion. Luigi Luraschi, head of Domestic and Foreign Censorship at Paramount, certainly recognised the criticisms of American society that Carl Foreman had advanced in his script for *High Noon* and put pressure on the Academy of Motion Picture Arts and Sciences to prevent the film being honoured with an Oscar. Luraschi was particularly alert, having been asked by the Central Intelligence Agency in 1953 to inform them of film content which might present an unfavourable picture of America. His critique of *High Noon* featured strongly in one of his first reports, but warned that 'the plea will be made that this is just a Western and anybody finding fault with it must be a fanatic':

> Actually, the period is Western and one of the situations is, but the types and the basic plot line are not Western, but dressed in Western clothes to appear so. The *good* people of the town are a bunch of weak-spined individuals, who haven't the guts to support the Sheriff (Cooper) in keeping a criminal from returning to town.

Thus, Luraschi argued, when Kane defeats Miller's gang, 'takes his badge off and throws it disdainfully into the dust', we 'can't help but agree with him, since our American Western town is made up of a pretty worthless lot of people'. Luraschi further pondered why Gary Cooper, who had co-operated fully with HUAC, had 'got sucked in' by such an 'un-American' project. 'He's a savvy guy,' he concluded, 'but I guess the Western cloak fooled him.'[64]

Because of his day-to-day involvement in questions of censorship, Luraschi was probably more sensitive than most to the subversive potential of historical settings, but he was not alone, and other anti-Communists were ready to pounce whenever they thought they saw 'Marxist' history creeping on to the screen. Dore Schary's production of *Plymouth Adventure* should have been an uncontroversial use of history to celebrate the origins of Americanism in the Mayflower Compact. Schary was convinced that the strength of the film lay in depicting the Pilgrims as 'real people', as 'men and women of courage, spirit, faith and humanity – 3-dimensional and, I think, true'.[65] Admittedly in presenting this, Schary, director Clarence Brown and scenarist Helen Deutsch did think it was 'high time to revise' the classic image of the Pilgrim as a 'stiff-collared fellow, wandering through the snow with a dead turkey slung over his shoulder, and a blunderbuss in his hand – a bloodless man, one-dimensional, dull and dry'.[66] However, when their intentions were paraphrased by *Time* magazine, it was implied that MGM was engaged in baseless revisionism that would 'shock' those schooled in the 'popular tradition of the Pilgrim Fathers'.[67] Already a target for red-baiters, as the most liberal of the studio bosses, Schary soon came under fire for 'debunking' the national heritage.

Writing in the *National Republic*, Marian Strack savaged the film as 'Marxist propaganda' designed to 'cheapen, deride and to satirize persons and events held in reverence by those who take pride in this country's origins and in the priceless heritage from which stem its laws and its parliamentary procedures'. Schary and Deutsch had included some of the conclusions of then-recent historiography, demonstrating that only 40 of the *Mayflower*'s passengers were separatists from the Church of England, and that many of the others had seen the colonial enterprise in economic terms. But to Strack, the depiction of some of the Pilgrims as shopkeepers 'who saw a money-making opportunity' was a 'Marxist gibe' – and part of a 'conspiracy to slander the founders of this country'.[68]

This was a familiar line of attack in Hollywood during the Red Scare, ever since the Motion Picture Alliance's 1950 publication, *Screen Guide for Americans*, stressed the need to weed out 'Marxist' interpretations of history. Written by Ayn Rand, one of the few HUAC witnesses to contend that Communist propaganda actually had reached the screen, this text warned filmmakers not to 'smear the free enterprise system', 'wealth', 'industrialists' or 'success', and not to 'deify the common man'.[69] The 'robber baron' version of the past which Progressive historians had developed in the 1930s had no place in the cinema. The implication that Schary was trying to 'smear' the Pilgrim Fathers by associating them with imperialist greed clearly put him in breach of these guidelines. Strack directly encouraged the descendants of the *Mayflower* to 'inaugurate a campaign to expose its various ramifications', which led to the Society of Mayflower Descendants threatening a boycott of the film – and undoubtedly contributed to *Plymouth Adventure* becoming MGM's least successful film that year.[70] The care and extensive research that had been put into the production meant that the film's version of history could be defended, but the experience made it plain that the past was not always the safe refuge that Walter Bernstein had thought it to be.

Under such scrutiny, films about progressive historical subjects did become fewer, especially in the early years of the decade when studios demonstrated almost paranoiac caution. Colin Shindler records that Monogram Pictures 'cancelled a projected biopic on Henry Wadsworth Longfellow, on the grounds that Hiawatha's peace activities might be construed as propaganda for a Communist peace initiative'.[71] In 1950, production of *John Paul Jones* was postponed for nine years, because Warner Bros. executives worried that the hero's escapades in the War of 1812 might be 'exploited by enemy propaganda in England...as a means of dividing the British and American people'.[72] A remake of *Scaramouche* in 1952 cut the storming of the Bastille and other aspects of the French Revolution, which had been central to Rafael Sabatini's original novel and the 1923 film version. The reason for the change, as *Variety*'s reviewer realised, was that 'were the hero allowed to spout the 1789 theme' of 'Liberty, Equality, Fraternity', reactionary critics would have drawn an 'inevitable Red analogy'.[73]

Such anxiety was particularly notable during the production of *Viva Zapata!* When John Steinbeck and Elia Kazan developed the life story of Mexican revolutionary Emiliano Zapata for 20th Century-Fox, Steinbeck argued that they should address America's 'misconception of the forces in back of Mexican outbursts'. Chief among these misconceptions – as Steinbeck saw it in 1949 – was the belief that Zapata intended to establish a 'Communistic' economic system.[74] Zapata's rebellion had been instigated when the regime of dictator Porfirio Diaz had supported landholders in appropriating public grazing lands for themselves, and advisors at the

Production Code Administration warned 'that Zapata was, and could easily still be considered by many, if not a Communist, at least an extreme agrarian radical'.[75] The screenplay, however, sought to present Zapata as a 'land-reformer' rather than a radical, with Steinbeck asserting that his agenda was 'communal…in a pre-Marx sense, but Communistic it was not'. He further characterised Zapata as 'a symbol of the individual standing out against collectivisation' from both the 'extreme left and the extreme right'.[76]

Darryl Zanuck insisted that Steinbeck and Kazan 'make this very clear'. 'In the present script,' he observed, 'there is inadvertently a peculiar air about certain speeches which might be interpreted by the Communists to claim that we are subtly working for them.' Of course, it was not really socialist reviews of the film that worried Zanuck. *Viva Zapata!* was prepared and realised in the interim between the 1947 and 1951 HUAC hearings, and executives did not want to give the Committee an excuse to return. Evidently panicking a little in December 1950, Zanuck raised the question: 'Is this the right time to make the picture?'[77]

His nervousness proved justified when Kazan was subpoenaed by HUAC the next year and made his now notorious decision to co-operate – for in the course of his testimony Kazan was called upon to defend *Viva Zapata!* Fortunately, in responding to Zanuck's concerns, he and Steinbeck had injected the character of Fernando Aguirre, a sinister opportunist who attaches himself to the rebels' cause, and who represents the 'voice of ideology' in the film. Fernando's ideology insists on the 'systematic use of force and violence to win and hold power' – and his true colours as an 'opportunistic totalitarian' are revealed when he turns against Zapata to instead serve a military regime that is unscrupulous in the exercise of such power.[78] The contrast allowed Steinbeck to more readily align Zapata's rebellion with liberal grass-roots democracy, and to reject revolutionary ideologies. And in consequence, Kazan was actually able go before HUAC and argue that *Viva Zapata!* was an 'anti-Communist picture'.

This was not simply a case of self-censorship, but reflected changing political attitudes as the Korean War prompted a reconsideration of what was at stake in the Cold War. 'Seventeen years of watching the Soviet Union turn into an imperialist power' led Kazan, among many others, to revise his analysis of Communism and turn away from leftist politics.[79] HUAC often only compelled them to make the final decision about where they stood, at a time of increasing evidence about the Soviet Union's aggressive ambitions. Nevertheless, voices of dissent were further marginalised and excluded by the blacklist, which did reinforce a turn to more conservative interpretations of history. Lester Cole, for instance, had already advanced his own interpretation of Zapata's life – but his script for *Zapata the Unconquerable* was dismissed as 'radical' when Cole became one of the 19 Hollywood Communists subpoenaed in 1947.[80] Only then did Kazan's 'anti-Communist' version get made.

Some on the blacklist sought a way of countering this, getting their work on the screen by writing under pseudonyms or having friends 'front' for them. Michael Wilson and Carl Foreman, for example, injected their critique of American militarism into the screenplay of *The Bridge on the River Kwai*, changing the ending from the novel so that the bridge is destroyed, to signify the irrationality and futility of war. Wilson also developed the character of Shears (William Holden) to express his own cynicism about the 'high price of military values', his 'distrust of heroics', and his 'explicit distaste for the wastefulness' of war.[81] Dalton Trumbo tried to interest Kirk Douglas' company in his script for *Montezuma*, which emphasised the brutality of imperialism, and suggested parallels between the Red Scare and the Spanish Inquisition.[82] Although this remained unproduced, Trumbo eventually became the one who 'broke the blacklist' – and did so with another history film, receiving his screen-credit for *Spartacus* in 1960, based on a novel by fellow ex-Communist, Howard Fast.

For the most part, however, former members of the Hollywood left had to turn to television to advance a progressive alternative to Hollywood's versions of history. Indeed, blacklisted scenarists were the driving forces behind many of television's historical projects such as the British series of *Robin Hood* (1955–60) and *Ivanhoe* (1958–59) or the CBS series of *You Are There* (1953–57). As producer Hannah Weinstein explained, she conceived of *Robin Hood* as a way of providing 'socially edifying entertainment... while at the same time providing work for those whom the witch-hunters back home were trying to outlaw and starve into despair'.[83] Having herself moved to England to avoid HUAC's subpoena in 1952, the outlaw band who joined Weinstein in transplanting their experiences into Sherwood Forest included Hollywood Ten members Ring Lardner, Jr. and Adrian Scott, blacklisted writers Waldo Salt, Ian McLellan Hunter, Robert Lees and Howard Dimsdale, and fugitive directors Joseph Losey, John Berry and Cy Endfield.[84] *You Are There* provided similar work for Abraham Polonsky, Walter Bernstein and Arnold Manoff, engaging them to write 'dramatic recreations' of 'authentic and specific' moments in history, which were then presented as if television news reporters had been on hand to film them. As John Schulteiss points out, the trio frequently chose topics which touched on political and religious intolerance and other 'challenges to moral and intellectual freedom', from 'The Crisis of Galileo' to 'The Scopes Trial', from 'The Execution of Joan of Arc' to 'The Trial of Susan B. Anthony'. Bernstein even wrote an episode about 'The Dreyfus Case', aired in May 1953, five years before Jose Ferrer persuaded Hollywood to revisit it in a similar frame of mind. And Polonsky succeeded where Trumbo failed, in getting the story of Montezuma to the screen in the April 1953 episode of 'The Conquest of Mexico by Cortez', providing a strong indictment of religious bigotry, racial prejudice and imperialism.[85]

These blacklistees congratulated themselves on 'conducting guerrilla warfare' in their use of the past.[86] As Bernstein noted, 'in that shameful time of McCarthyite terror, of know-nothing attempts to deform and defile history, to kill any kind of dissent, we were able to do shows about civil liberties, civil rights [and] artistic freedoms'.[87] They also applauded themselves for not rewriting history in making their point, and distinguished their approach from political propaganda by arguing that any 'message' flowed naturally from the facts of historical conflicts. By selecting subjects that they believed had 'bearing on what was happening in the world today', they attested that history would speak for itself 'if treated with accuracy as best as we could research it and find it'.[88] Thus, while the right sought to tar the left with the 'crime' of 'Stalinist' revisionism, the left found less need to reinvent history to serve their cause than the anti-Communists in Hollywood.

Ultimately though, both sides shared a common attitude which consciously sought to use the past in the present. The notion of constructing a 'usable past' had been popular among progressive historians in the 1930s, who saw history as the key to a world view that would shape and reorient political programmes and action. The overall effect of the anti-Communist crusade was to make filmmakers acutely aware of this perspective – even as academic historians themselves were retreating from it. This made Hollywood ever more conscious of the malleability of the past. The industry was long accustomed to changing facts for the sake of entertainment, but now greater attention than ever before was paid to the ideologies underpinning accounts of history.

5

Social History

Ed:	What's eating you?
Little Boy:	American history!
Ed:	What's wrong with it?
Little Boy:	White man lick Indian, he win great battle. Indian lick white man…massacre!

Jim Thorpe – All American (1952)

It is a commonplace assumption in writing on the western that the HUAC investigations prompted filmmakers to find refuge in its 'mythic space'. Philip French's musings on the genre in 1973 took it for granted that the volume and complexity of post-war westerns was, in large part, due to Hollywood's loss of 'nerve' and the search for 'a framework in which controversial issues could be handled in a less obviously contentious fashion'.[1] John Lenihan's *Showdown* provides dozens of examples in which directors and writers continued to address contemporary politics, race relations and social concerns, while using the distancing conventions of the genre as a cover.[2] And as Luigi Luraschi's letters to the CIA demonstrate, this is not simply a retrospective reading – filmmakers in the 1950s were well aware of how this 'western cloak' operated in practice.

This analysis is buttressed by the observation that HUAC's return to Hollywood in 1951 heralded the end of a postwar cycle of contemporary 'social problem' films. In her study of the blacklist, Dorothy Jones records that at the peak of the cycle in 1947, 28 percent of American films dealt with 'social themes'.[3] Producers like Zanuck had returned from World War II, inspired to make films which would 'espouse the things we know to be right' and help 'guide mankind to more peaceful and orderly ways'.[4] Consequently, they developed films that drew attention to the problems of rehabilitating war veterans (*The Best Years of Our Lives* (1946), *The Men* (1950)), the pervasiveness of anti-Semitism (*Gentleman's Agreement* and *Crossfire* in 1947), the treatment of the mentally ill (*The Snake Pit*, 1948), and racial prejudice (*Lost Boundaries* (1949), *Pinky* (1949), *No Way Out* (1950)). As the release dates suggest, the round of congressional investigations in 1947 did not initially stifle Hollywood's social conscience, and the unexpected re-election of President Harry Truman in 1948 – whose platform included a commitment to civil rights legislation and the promise of a 'Fair Deal' to continue the work of FDR – rather boosted liberal morale and encouraged the 'race' films of 1949. But following HUAC's subsequent sortie at the height of McCarthyism and the Korean War, Jones notes that the proportion of films dealing with social problems dropped to just 9 percent by 1954.[5]

HUAC and McCarthyism were certainly not the only factors involved in this decline; moreover some substantial critiques of American society continued to be advanced in movies set in the present day. Yet there is clear evidence that filmmakers did use the western to go 'underground' when responding to the particularly controversial questions of race relations and the emergent civil rights movement. As conservative Southerners presented any agitation against racial segregation as part of a Communist plot to discredit the United States, so the risk of being branded 'un-American' for even raising the issue was greater than that associated with any other social problem. Hollywood was already sensitive about alienating its audiences and so, after *No Way Out* distinguished itself as the first film to depict a race riot, consideration of the 'race problem' between whites and African-Americans all but vanished from the screen until the end of the decade. However, many filmmakers realised that black-white relations in middle of the twentieth century could readily be transposed to the conflict between reds and whites on the nineteenth-century frontier.

Indeed, this had been demonstrated at the height of Hollywood's interest in race films by *Broken Arrow* (1950). With Michael Blankfort fronting for him, the script was written by Albert Maltz, one of the Hollywood Ten, and was applauded by Fox executives for its 'theme of racial brotherhood, mutual respect and tolerance'.[6] When Caucasian Tom Jeffords befriends Apache leader Cochise, and eventually marries an Apache princess, he confronts the hatred of a racist white community – and their animosity and greed results in the murder of his bride. Jeffords' efforts at reconciliation and encouraging mutual understanding do not directly challenge racial segregation (in terms of the reservation system), but his marriage breaks the 'taboo' of miscegenation, and substantiates his insistence that 'each race must change its thinking and conduct so as to accommodate the other'. *Broken Arrow* has often been criticised for having harnessed the sympathies of the contemporary audience by 'transforming its Indians into model white men instead of doing justice to the Indian's distinctive character'.[7] At the time though it mirrored the position of the National Association for the Advancement of Colored People, and later Martin Luther King, Jr., which held that if they were to challenge white prejudices African-Americans similarly needed to present themselves as model citizens, worthy of acceptance and integration.

Subsequent lessons in racial tolerance and the destructiveness of race hatred have been noted in westerns as varied as *The Great Sioux Uprising* (1953), *Broken Lance* (1954), *White Feather* (1955), *Reprisal* (1956), *Walk The Proud Land* (1956), *The Last Hunt* (1956), *The Tin Star* (1957) and *Tonka* (1958). Caution does need to be exercised in simply reducing all Native Americans in post-war westerns to simple 'stand-ins' for African-Americans (as Thomas Cripps once claimed).[8] *Apache* (1954), for instance, depicts real-life warrior Massai (played by Burt Lancaster) waging a one-man war against the American military in a scenario that definitely indicts white racism, but otherwise offers few parallels to modern black-white relations. However, film historians agree that certain westerns did offer 'related moments in time' – with John Ford's production of *The Searchers* (1956) acclaimed as a prime example, produced amid the political fallout from the Supreme Court's ruling against segregated schools in the case of *Brown vs. the Topeka Board of Education*.

Cited as one of the genre's 'most powerful explorations of miscegenation', *The Searchers* presents audiences with an unreconstructed white supremacist as the protagonist, in the form of John Wayne's Ethan Edwards.[9] As Arthur Eckstein observes, the film superficially fits the bill as a 'white triumphalist' western, with Ethan and his companion, Martin Pauley, rescuing Debbie (Ethan's niece and Martin's adopted sister) from the Indians who killed her parents. In the end, 'the Indian who dared to violate her sexual and racial purity – the Comanche war chief Scar – is killed. So too is the Comanche girl Look, who attempts to marry Martin.' Martin is then free 'to marry his 100 percent white girlfriend Laurie Jorgenson – who is herself a virulent racist'.[10] Seen from this perspective, *The Searchers* mirrored the fear and loathing of miscegenation that was then being angrily voiced by Southerners intent on rendering the *Brown* decision dead in the water.

Racial politics in the South had practically polarised overnight when school segregation was declared unconstitutional in May 1954. Voices of moderation collapsed in the face of the sheer determination of a white minority not to let segregation go without a fight. The first Citizens Councils, established in July, represented the supposedly 'respectable' face of white supremacy, yet shared much the same ideology as the Ku Klux Klan – that blacks were hereditarily inferior to Caucasians, and were thus rendered unsuitable for free association with white society. Segregation, in the view of the Councils, was a system that defined and controlled the black man's interaction with the white world (as slavery once had done), and thereby made tolerable the black presence in America. That fear of miscegenation lay at the heart of this was evident in the Councils' express determination to 'preserve the white stock'.[11] White supremacist discourse repeatedly stressed the belief that 'school desegregation would lead inexorably to interracial breeding', with Southern politicians accusing the NAACP of pursuing *Brown* simply 'to open the bedroom doors of our white women to Negro men'.[12]

The Searchers was scripted as this backlash took centre stage, and was released just as Southern congressmen formally endorsed the pro-segregation campaign of 'Massive Resistance' and signed the Southern Manifesto. Ethan is directly aligned with this attitude in his refusal to recognise the South's surrender in the Civil War, in keeping with the white supremacists of the 1950s who were again unfurling their Confederate battle flags. Moreover, even before the Comanches attack, Ethan's deep-seated racism is apparent – and specifically directed against miscegenation – when he rejects Martin as a 'half breed' (on account of one of his great-grandparents having been a Cherokee), even though Martin has been adopted and clearly loved by Ethan's brother and sister-in-law. It is in this moment that Ford actually establishes *The Searchers* as a condemnation of white supremacy. Martin's racial status deliberately departed from the source novel by Alan LeMay, in which he was fully white. In the film, however, it is Martin's 'mixed ancestry' that 'introduces us to Ethan's tragic racist flaw'.[13]

The development of this flaw into a characterisation of brutal racist hatred has been discussed at length by Brian Henderson and Douglas Pye.[14] In brief summary of their points, it gradually becomes apparent that Ethan's determination in hunting for Debbie 'is not to rescue her, but to kill her as he believes she has been hopelessly "defiled" by living among the Indians'.[15] Even though she is his last surviving blood relative, the fact that she has become one of Scar's wives ('living with a buck') is too much for Ethan to tolerate. He explicitly denies that she is 'blood kin', and is only prevented from shooting her when Marty gets in the way. He is pleased to think that she will be killed when the cavalry attack Scar's camp. Yet, the irrationality of Ethan's fear is pointed up by Ford's decision to depict Debbie, assimilated into Comanche culture, as a beautiful Indian princess, neither 'unhinged' nor 'impure'. Moreover, in contrast to Ethan, Marty 'grows ever stronger both morally and even physically, so that by the end of The Searchers he is a far more attractive and dependable figure (even though the product of miscegenation) than Ethan can ever be'.[16] Though Debbie is not actually Marty's 'blood kin', he shows far greater familial feeling than Ethan, constantly determined to save her, even from her own uncle.

Ford certainly did not idealise Indian culture in the way Broken Arrow did. The Indians function only as symbols (often of savagery) in his dissection of white racism, and the presentation of Look as comic relief is jarring. But the film goes further than simply presenting racial tension as a problem caused by extremists on both sides – which had been Eisenhower's judgement on the post-Brown situation. White society at large shares in Ethan's race hatred – even Laurie Jorgenson, whose engagement to Martin might suggest greater tolerance, declares that Debbie would be better off with 'a bullet in her brain' now that she is nothing more than 'the leavings of a Comanche buck'. Moreover, the audience itself is made to regret laughing at Look (as Ethan does) in the wake of her tragic death at the hands of the US cavalry – itself an example of institutionalised racism.[17]

Ford's use of the western setting in presenting these issues reflected his command of the genre. The period setting makes it clear that America's racial problems are perennial ones, while also suggesting that such racism is best left in the past. As David Grimstead notes, The Searchers also uses the conventions of the genre to present a western hero 'with whom the audience could identify, while strongly feeling his racist excess' and realising 'the sad necessity of his exclusion' from the re-integrated family at the conclusion of the film. Ford additionally exploited the fact that audiences for westerns, as demonstrated by *Broken Arrow*, were already favourably disposed to seeing relationships between Indians and whites (in contrast to their accepting of unions between whites and African-Americans), which further encouraged a perception of Ethan's obsessive hatred as unnecessary and irrationally destructive. While present-day 'message pictures' necessarily wore their hearts on their sleeves in order to 'espouse what we know to be right', Ford could make audiences see that Ethan goes too far in upholding his standard of white supremacy without ever becoming preachy. The western setting enables *The Searchers* to show 'pride in the core' of the American tradition and its inclusiveness, while remaining strongly critical of 'the racism now seen as the severest threat to it'.[18]

In contrast, only after 1957 were filmmakers emboldened to advance their views on race relations in a contemporary setting. This followed the televising of images of violent, hate-filled white supremacists rioting in Little Rock, Arkansas, which had compelled Eisenhower to intervene and protect African-American schoolchildren; and it came after the liberal imagination had been captured by black activism and King's exemplary leadership in the Montgomery Bus Boycott. As both events validated the 'messages' evident in the subtexts of *The Searchers* and *Broken Arrow*, they encouraged a new wave of modern-day 'race problem' films, including *Edge of the City* (1957) and *The Defiant Ones* (1958).

Yet, filmmakers also incorporated into the western a wide range of contemporary concerns which, ostensibly at least, were nowhere near as controversial as civil rights. Unlike the race problem, filmmakers had been willing and able to deal up-front with the anxieties over juvenile delinquency, the emasculation of working men in a faceless 'corporate society', or the 'trap' of suburban domesticity, in a whole variety of films set in the present day – as *Rebel Without a Cause* (1955), *Man in the Gray Flannel Suit* (1956), *All That Heaven Allows* (1955) and many others attest. This in itself casts some doubt on the 'cloak' thesis. Indeed, the transposition of these concerns to a western setting seems particularly redundant when a movie like *The Big Country* (1958) can be described as 'The Man in the Gray Flannel Suit Goes West', or when *The True Story of Jesse James* (1957) is dismissed as nothing more than 'a replay of the conflicts and tensions' apparent in *Rebel*.[19]

THE YOUNG GUNS

It is particularly tempting to see *The True Story of Jesse James* as an opportunistic leap onto the bandwagon of America's post-war obsession with troubled and violent youth. In Nicholas Ray it had the same director as *Rebel Without a Cause,* and publicity promoted him as the 'standout choice' for a film described as 'essentially a story of juvenile delinquency'.[20] Biographers of Ray have also regarded it as 'the product of a brief period…when he was marking time', noting that he made *True Story* only to fulfil his contractual obligations to Fox, and that it obviously 'borrowed' from his earlier considerations of delinquency in *Rebel, They Live by Night* (1948) and *Knock on Any Door* (1949).[21] There is certainly reason to see Ray's depiction of Jesse James as a revisiting, in western guise, of themes he had already exhausted. Yet, when the film is read closely, and in its specific context, it soon becomes apparent that Ray's use of the western setting was much more controlled and deliberative.

On one hand, Hollywood's fears of controversy were more of an issue than the success of *Blackboard Jungle* (1955) and *Rebel Without a Cause* might at first suggest. Though both movies established the problems of youth as a fitting and extremely profitable subject for filmmakers, there had also been a substantial backlash. *Blackboard Jungle* was denounced by the National Congress of Parents and Teachers, voted the film 'that hurt America the most in foreign countries in 1955' by the American Legion, and was withdrawn from the Venice Film Festival after pressure from ambassador Claire Booth Luce and the State Department, worried about the impression given by its depiction of vicious, alienated youth. It had also been singled out for mention by Senator Estes Kefauver's investigating committee in March 1956, with Congress suggesting that the movies themselves might be contributing to delinquency. *Rebel,* too, was 'the focus of furious reaction', banned in Milwaukee, accused of being the inspiration for various 'copycat crimes' and knife fights, and subjected to censorship cuts abroad.[22]

Wanting to avoid such controversy, but still tap the $8 million that *Blackboard* had made, Hollywood proceeded to 'reduce the dosage of realism'. Subsequent 'teen pics', set in the present day – such as *Teenage Thunder* (1957), *Juvenile Jungle* (1958) and *High School Confidential* (1958) – simply 'sampled' delinquent stereotypes from the serious films, maximised profits with substandard production values, and offered no new analysis of the problem.[23] Some western filmmakers clearly tried to cash in too. *The Burning Hills* (1956), for example, was promoted with 'lurid ads' that featured Warner's teenage stars in an animalistic embrace: Tab Hunter with his chest bared, and Natalie Wood powerless to resist him. Taglines promised that 'this was the night' when 'young Trace Jordan met the mixed-up teenage girl' – and that 'after tonight they'd have to start running'.[24] Yet, the film itself featured no such scene of requited teenage lust. 'Shucks,' wrote one reviewer, 'you never saw two nicer kids... Why, they only kiss twice; he steals one, grinning boyishly, halfway thru the film, and they co-operate on a triumphant but circumspect embrace after the bad guys have been vanquished.'[25] In contrast to these films, *The True Story of Jesse James* not only reveals itself as another retreat into the western past to avoid controversy, but also one in which Ray could avoid the degeneration into the prevalent stereotyping of modern youth culture, and continue to make a serious commentary on delinquency.

It needs to be acknowledged that Ray was not simply 'marking time'. Ray had produced *Rebel* at the height of national anxiety over delinquency, when 'frightening apparitions of adolescents gone awry' had dominated the media and political discourse.[26] As juvenile arrests rose by 45 percent between 1948 and 1953, *Life* reported on 'Teen-Age Terror on New York Streets', and J. Edgar Hoover ranked 'the juvenile jungle' as dangerous a threat to American freedom as Communism. The Senate investigations into the problem were launched in 1953, and reached their height of activity in 1955, which in itself lent 'credence to the impression of a mounting youth crime wave'. As James Gilbert's *Cycle of Outrage* demonstrates, the threat was greatly exaggerated, with more arrests made (and hence more coverage generated) simply because more attention was being paid to the issue. But whatever the facts, a large portion of the public believed that 'a whole generation stood on a moral precipice' and 'clamoured to understand how and why this was happening'.[27] *Rebel* itself was part of Hollywood's reaction to this 'clamour' – reflecting on the fact that vandalism, joy-riding and various 'crimes of behaviour' had crossed into middle-class suburbia as well. Yet, when making *True Story* in 1957, the hysteria had calmed, and Ray was able to look back on these explanations from a distance.

The over-determined 'legend' of Jesse James provided rich material for this purpose. Ray exploited the flashbacks conventionally used in historical biopics to 'explain' a person's life, with each flashback presenting the perspective of a different member of Jesse's family.[28] In turn, his mother, his wife Zee, and his brother Frank, each offer an answer to the film's guiding question – posed by a newspaperman who prepares to write Jesse's obituary – 'what makes him Jesse James?' Presenting the narrative as a process of inquiry, with multiple and subjective explanations given for Jesse's criminal behaviour, *True Story* thus mirrored 'the casting about for answers' to the problem of juvenile delinquency that had characterised debate in the middle of the decade.[29]

Apparently, Ray's first idea had been to use Jesse's involvement in the Civil War as a 'period study' of 'the effects of war on the behaviour of young people'.[30] This was informed by analyses of modern delinquency that suggested 'the viciousness of mankind in the past few decades [had] taken its toll'.[31] The western setting easily conveyed a parallel age 'that treasured violence and rewarded brutality', and Ma's flashback in particular represented this perspective, constantly blaming 'the Yankees' for brutalising her 'gentle boy'.[32] Russell Hughes' first draft of the script was even more specific: 'When [Jesse] left he was an eager youngster – going away to a glorious war. He had returned a restless, wild spirit – and hardened by the familiarity with danger and violent death.'[33] Ray, however, came to question this interpretation, and undercut Ma's explanation by having the obituary writer dismiss it from the outset. 'You and I were in the war too,' he reminds his assistant, and neither of them were 'brutalised'. Rather more credence is given to suggestions that delinquent youth had 'turned to total violence to solve their own problems', because they had grown up in a culture that 'accepted the premise that total violence could be a solution to world problems'.[34] Jesse's success in persuading his brother and friends to embark on bank robberies is predicated on that basis – what worked for them as Quantrill's Raiders during the war, will solve their post-war problems too.

Zee's flashback embodies the theory that the crisis of American youth stemmed from the fact that their lives were 'characterised by premature adulthood'.[35] As young Americans in the 1950s married at a higher rate and at a younger age than at any other point in the twentieth century, so Zee tells Jesse that 'friends my age are married, some have children'. Jesse is certainly no older than 18 at this point in the film, and Zee is younger still – and she begins the conversation by unwittingly admitting how 'premature' this is, by saying 'we'll soon be grown-ups ourselves'. Moreover, this pressure to 'grow up' fast – *Growing Up Absurd* as Paul Goodman put it in 1960 – directly encourages Jesse's criminal delinquency, as he first steals to raise a sufficient dowry to marry Zee, and then continues to do so to finance her aspirations of having 'a home of our own'. Robert Merton's analysis of delinquency suggested that criminal behaviour 'filled the gap between the American ideology of success and plenty, and the failure of many young people to achieve that'.[36] Jesse's crimes certainly allow him to achieve the 'American Dream' after society has closed off the more conventional route – for when the James brothers' attempt to make an honest living as farmers, their efforts are wrecked by hate-filled neighbours.

However, what the audience sees of Jesse somewhat conflicts with Zee's vision. Lenihan claims Jesse is like Jim Stark in *Rebel*, and that his setting up of a home with Zee suggests that, despite his alienation, he 'rebels not against middle-class values, but against the failure of adults to live honestly by those values'.[37] The house they rent in St Josephs is certainly emblematic of 1950s suburbia, representing a 'stable' place in middle-class society, fully furnished with striped wallpaper, ornate lamps, a decorative fireplace and 'tasteful' works of art. The real-estate agent is pleased to think of them as a 'nice genteel couple', who will 'help keep property values high'. But, contrary to Lenihan's reading, it becomes apparent that Jesse does 'reject' this middle-class culture by making a mockery of it. Passing himself off as a 'respectable' businessman – and slyly noting that his money is in 'railroads and banking' – he parodies the conservative morality expected of such men. Pompously declaring that a print of Rubens' *Venus and Mars* is 'obscene', he insists that Zee pick out something 'more uplifting instead'. At first it is not clear if he is serious, but the end of the sequence makes it clear that while Zee wants to be part of this society, Jesse sees it as a subterfuge. After briefly indulging her fantasies of sitting at home 'singing hymns and read [ing] Mr Dickens', Jesse reveals that settling down is the last thing on his mind, for rather than joining his wife in bed on their first night in their new home, he runs out to join his gang 'on business'. The hurt on Zee's face in visible, as she realises that this ostensible embrace of middle-class virtue is only a cover for his continued anti-social pathology.

As Jesse says early in Zee's flashback, 'I don't care much for the way grown-ups think'. His leaving her and the trappings of domesticity, in order to meet his gang corresponds with Albert Cohen's theory that delinquent gangs reinforced 'an alternative mode of behaviour for children who…could not or refused to accept the predominant (middle class) values of the core culture'.[38] In *Delinquent Boys*, Cohen also argued that this behaviour was encouraged when youth discovers that, in its particular social context, 'individual responsibility and control of physical aggression produced negative results'. Jesse and Frank discover this in post-Civil War Missouri when their efforts to become farmers culminate with their farmhand being lynched and, later in the film, their mother being injured and their younger brother killed. The 'product' of this situation, according to Cohen, was a 'rogue male' whose conduct 'attack[ed] and derogat[ed] the respectable culture' and raised 'untrammelled masculinity' as its norm.[39]

Jesse's existence as just such a 'rogue male' is dissected in Frank's flash-back which also suggests, as an alternative explanation, that Jesse is pre-disposed to criminality by virtue of 'an almost psychotic personality'.[40] Confronting his brother after the disastrous raid on Northfield, Minnesota, Frank realises that while they may have begun their crime wave 'for Zee, Ma, and protecting the farm', Jesse is now only robbing and killing because it 'satisfies some twisted urge within'.[41] Internalising the problem as one of psychology, Jesse's response suggests this 'urge' is part of an identity crisis – as he asserts that he is 'proud' of his killings because now the name of 'Jesse James' 'means something'. With this, Ray invoked Erik Erikson's

Revisiting *Rebel:* Middle-class respectability in a suburban home is a dream come true for Zee (Hope Lange), but for Jesse James (Robert Wagner), it is just a façade for continuing his juvenile crime wave, in Nicholas Ray's *The True Story of Jesse James* (1957). (Courtesy of the British Film Institute)

'identity theory' of delinquency, advanced in 1955. Defining adolescence as a crucial period of experiment and role-playing, in which a youth tried to find his 'adult' identity, Erikson's theory was that delinquency was one 'distorted' path which a young male might choose as a way to resolve questions of 'identity diffusion'.[42]

Indeed, questions of Jesse's identity and what it 'means' are repeated throughout the film. Reverend Bailey ironically tells us that the name Jesse signifies 'God's Grace', even as he claims Jesse really has 'the devil in his heart'; detective Remington cannot get positive identification of Jesse's body, since no law officer has ever seen him and lived; and when the posse capture Cole Younger and ask where the gangleader can be found, his only response is to laugh and ask, 'Who's Jesse James?' With no sure or fixed identity, the importance of making a 'name' for himself becomes Jesse's driving force – and, in accord with Erikson's theory, he tries on various 'roles' for size, including his false identity as the respectable 'Mr Howard', or using his ill-gotten gains to pay a widow's mortgage so as to live up to the 'Robin Hood' label that a dime novel gives him. Ray reinforces this interpretation by depicting Bob Ford as another adolescent with an identity crisis. Constantly referred to by the diminutive 'Robbie' – except when Bailey mistakenly calls him 'Charlie' (much to his annoyance) – it is only when he murders Jesse at the end of the film that he 'becomes' 'Bob Ford'. Indeed, this violent, adult identity is one that he proclaims for himself, running into the street shouting so that everyone will know 'It's me – Bob Ford! *I* shot Jesse James!' With measured irony, however, the ballad singer who closes the film denies both men their identities, simply referring to 'the dirty little coward who shot Mr Howard'.

Various other 'theories' were also briefly raised. The lack of a father figure corresponds with Walter Miller's examination of delinquency among lower-class female-centred families.[43] 'Pillars of society' such as the Church are shown to be weak, with Reverend Bailey offering no help to Zee, just fire-and-brimstone platitudes.[44] And Frederic Wertham's fear about 'the harmful influence' exerted on children by violence in popular culture is evident when Jesse finds his own children (who do not know their father's true identity) playfully 'shooting' one another in emulation of the dime novel 'Jesse James'.[45] While Ray seemed to favour Erikson's theory – in tune with his own observation that 'for all those adolescents from "ordinary families", delinquency was a way of drawing attention to themselves' – he studiously avoided accepting any reductive explanation.[46] In this, he mirrored too, the rejection by the Kefauver Committee and the Children's Bureau of 'single cause' theories of delinquency. Ray had subscribed to these before – presenting an 'attenuated Thirties perspective' on the problem in *Knock on Any Door*, in which Nick Romano is the product of a blighted urban environment.[47] Compelled to rethink this in *Rebel*, as delinquency began to affect prosperous suburban communities, he spent considerable time at juvenile detention centres and with police and criminologists in an effort to understand the change. However, even *Rebel* was accused of being too simplistic in its explanation – *Nation*'s reviewer, for one, remarking that 'it is easy to explain delinquency if you assume that parents are howling idiots; but the assumption is neither true nor very interesting'.[48] But with *The True Story* detached from a contemporary setting that would have demanded an 'answer', Ray had nothing to prove and a lot more to say. Thus while Ray may have originally accepted the assignment because it was 'the most promising thing' on offer at Fox, he quickly grasped the opportunity to interrogate the 'myth' of Jesse James to the full, and reflected on delinquency with far greater breadth than he had achieved before.[49]

A MAN ALONE

In comparison with the real, if exaggerated, problem of delinquent youth and the serious racial tensions in the South, the concern that sociologists expressed about 'the changing American character' in the 1950s seems nebulous and rather feeble. Yet, David Riesman's 1949 study of this development in *The Lonely Crowd* validated the perception of a 'crisis of masculinity' which permeated culture throughout the following decade.[50] It was largely a matter of heightened apprehension about the complacent materialism, homogeneity and conformity that American intellectuals identified and dissected in studies like *The Affluent Society, The Organization Man, The Hidden Persuaders* and *The Power Elite*.[51] However, the general media expanded on this theme too, in various assertions that, after the militarism of World War II, men had been 'feminized' by marrying early and settling down in suburbia, by working in white-collar corporate environments, and by a society that expected them to adopt a 'docile persona' which was fundamentally at odds with their 'natural' masculine instincts.[52]

Sloan Wilson's 1955 novel, *The Man in the Gray Flannel Suit* struck this particular nerve, the title itself suggesting 'someone who was sacrificing his individuality to become a part of the new, more faceless middle class'.[53] Tom and Betsy Rath are placed firmly in this context, when Tom starts work as a 'public relations man' at the United Broadcasting Company. Yet Tom confesses (to himself at least) to 'detesting' UBC 'with all its soap operas, commercials and yammering studio audiences', and knows that 'the only reason I'm willing to spend my life in such a ridiculous enterprise is that I want to buy a more expensive house and a better brand of gin'.[54] Wilson's novel personalised and dramatised the idea of C. Wright Mills' *White Collar*: that while the standard of living had increased dramatically for many Americans, 'the new white-collar life was turning into something of a trap' and 'the greater material benefits it promised and delivered were being exchanged for freedom and individuality'.[55] It was further popularised in 1956, when Zanuck produced *The Man in the Gray Flannel Suit* as a film starring Gregory Peck. By then, as Steve Cohan points out, the title had become an iconic shorthand for describing the 'typical American Male' – thereby identifying both the national character and the 'crisis in masculinity' with the white, middle-class domesticated breadwinner.[56]

Since intellectuals, novelists and filmmakers were fully capable of treating the 'crisis of masculinity' in its contemporary manifestations, Michael Coyne's description of William Wyler's epic western, *The Big Country*, as 'The Man in the Gray Flannel Suit Goes West' certainly suggests a redundancy in transposing the issue onto the past.[57] But it should be obvious that the western had a particular edge in allowing for nostalgic depictions of unbridled masculine action. Nicholas Ray pointedly presented Jesse's gang as the outlaw's way of 'escaping' middle-class domesticity and the civilising influence of Zee. In addition, when *True Story*'s Northfield raid ends in disaster, it is largely due to the fact that the other gang members have used their loot to settle down and have become too comfortable; as Jesse notes with disgust and concern, 'they've gotten soft'. Likewise, in *Gunfight at the OK Corral* (1957), Wyatt Earp is only free to act decisively because he is not restrained by ties to any woman or home – unlike his brother who is unable to help him clean up Tombstone, because his wife has asked him to 'quit marshalling'.[58] Conceived as a male action genre, the western typically made a cult of masculinity and individualism.

Many post-war westerns, however, used this nostalgia to (often regretfully) acknowledge that there was no longer a place for old-style, unrestrained masculinity in modern, civilised society. Fiercely independent trapper Bushrod Gentry eventually succumbs to the 'tender trap' of marriage in *Many Rivers to Cross* (1955). Howard Hawks' *Red River* (1948), suggests how a post-war setting requires a more humane, and indeed 'feminised', style of male leadership – in the form of Montgomery Clift's Matthew – instead of the bullying, brutal individualism of John Wayne's Dunson. Director Anthony Mann repeatedly presented his western heroes – in films such as *The Naked Spur* (1953), *The Man from Laramie* (1955) and *Man of the West* (1958) – as men in an 'untenable position', torn between 'competing images of masculinity: on the one hand, the claims of settlement, civilization, and social responsibility, and on the other of wandering, wilderness and independence'.[59] In doing so, Mann gave dramatic voice to analyses by sociologists such as Helen Mayer Hacker, who argued that 'competing demands on men to be passive *and* aggressive, emotional *and* stoic' in contemporary culture had engendered the 'crisis' by making 'masculinity a site of contradiction'.[60] And if the 'typical American Male' in the 1950s was conflicted, the heroes of Mann's films were driven to extremes of mental anguish by their problems. But as Douglas Pye points out, characters such as Glyn McLyntock in *Bend of the River* (1952), or Link Jones in *Man of the West* (1958) do not really have a choice – there is no real alternative to settlement. As in the case of Jeff Webster in *The Far Country* (1954), the 'traditional' western hero's drive for independence is presented as self-destructive. To relieve his anguish, he must ultimately return to the community 'if he is to know any meaningful happiness and fulfillment'.[61] Yet Mann also undercuts the 'fantasy' that settling down presents a 'happy ending' for such men – since in settling they cannot keep their identity and strength as westerners.

In contrast, *The Big Country* stands apart from this in its ability to dissect the western's 'cult' of normative masculinity in a way that actually reinforces the hero's identity as an individual. It certainly shares with *The Man in the Gray Flannel Suit* – along with the starring presence of Gregory Peck – the narrative of a man seeking to assert his individualism against social pressures to conform. But what consistently distinguishes *The Big Country*'s Jim McKay from Tom Rath is that while the latter's sense of self is in a state of flux, McKay never once doubts a masculinity that he defines entirely on his own terms.

Indeed, McKay is presented as the epitome of David Riesman's 'inner-directed' man.[62] The 'inner-directed' character type, according to *The Lonely Crowd*, possessed 'the capacity to go it alone', directed by steadfast principles and a 'set of goals' that he had internalised early in life. This social character – who, asserts Riesman, had been prominent in nineteenth-century society – had been displaced in modern America by the 'other-directed' type, 'whose conformity is insured by their tendency to be sensitised to the expectations and preference of others'.[63] Tom Rath fears this 'other-directed' conformity lies for him in corporate society, aware that his career goals have been defined by his wife, and that he may lose all trace of individuality if he does not stop himself becoming another 'cheap, cynical yes-man'.[64] There is a hint too, in *The Big Country*, that McKay's interest in moving to Texas is spurred by such concerns; as he tells his prospective father-in-law, Major Terrill, a career in the family shipping business in Baltimore is beckoning, but 'I just can't get interested in boilers and board meetings'. The frontier, he assumes, will allow him the greater freedoms he had earlier valued when a sea captain.

But the American West, as Wyler constructs it, also expects men to conform, especially to 'codes' of honour. This is most evident when McKay 'goes it alone' to ride out of Terrill's Ladder Ranch and explore the territory, navigating with his compass. On his return, he is confronted by the Major's foreman, Steve Leech, who publicly accuses McKay of lying when he insists he was never lost. McKay's refusal to respond to this affront to his honour costs him the respect of the Major, the Ladder ranch hands, and his fiancée Pat, who 'cannot believe that a man, any man, could turn down such a challenge'.[65] In their minds, it confirms earlier doubts about his masculinity, raised when McKay failed to protect himself when he and Pat were harassed by the Hannassey clan, and when he backed out of Leech's challenge to break-in Old Thunder, a wild stallion used to 'initiate' new ranchers. However, McKay is no coward. He soon demonstrates his ability to master Old Thunder, and beats Leech to a standstill – but only when nobody else is there to see him do so. He simply refuses to be goaded into action by worrying about what others may think of him. As Riesman described, while the goals of other-directed men are defined by their 'need to be liked by their peers', the inner-directed person displays 'relative impermeability to the needs and wishes of his peers'. McKay clearly remains 'impermeable' to the expectations of the people of Ladder and displays his ability 'to steel himself against their indifference or hostility'.[66] As he tells Pat when she questions his masculinity, 'I'm not responsible for what people think – only for what I am'.

The 'Way of the West' he refuses to conform to is one where 'bluster and sheer physical violence have been the hallmark of a man'.[67] All the other characters, save for school teacher Julie Maragon, and Mexican ranch hand

Ramon, have a very blinkered vision of masculinity, exclusively defined by the feuding patriarchs of Major Terrill and Rufus Hannassey. Pat and Leech both idealise the Major and unquestioningly accept his assertion that 'a man's honour and his good name are his finest possessions', as their definition of 'normative masculinity'. Leech is described in script notes as 'a man who justifies his conduct on the basis of a western "code" of honor', and when Pat is angry with McKay, the strongest insult she can muster is that he will never be 'half the man Major Henry Terrill is'.[68] Rufus too is determined to 'make a man' of his son Buck, who consequently brags, bullies and shoots – and even tries to rape Julie – in an doomed effort to be as 'manly' as his father wants him to be.

Buck, Leech and Pat are certainly 'other-directed' characters, but the film's indictment of patriarchy also serves to put McKay in conflict with a 'tradition-oriented' society – the stage that Riesman suggested preceded 'inner-directed' cultures. This becomes evident when he further challenges the 'Way of the West', as represented by the long-standing feud between the Terrills and the Hannasseys over the waters of Big Muddy. While this replays the typical western plot of a range war, McKay defies convention by refusing to endorse the feud at all, let alone take sides. Indeed, his decision to buy Big Muddy himself so as to ensure water is available to everyone is, more than any other action, crucial to McKay's self-definition. At first Julie, who originally owns Big Muddy, refuses to sell it to him, noting that since he is engaged to Pat, 'that would be the same as selling it to the Terrills'. Rufus has also accused him of being 'a Terrill man'. However, as Jim's actions have proved throughout, he is no one's man but his own – and his response to Julie is simple: 'The name is McKay, James McKay...'

McKay's refusal to be identified as a 'Terrill man' mirrors Tom Rath's anxiety about subsuming his identity to the corporation, of becoming a 'company man'. But in the present-day setting, *The Man in the Gray Flannel Suit* had to cheat by allowing Rath to have it both ways. In the end, Rath asserts his 'integrity' to stop himself getting too caught up in the rat race, but it also concludes with him happily conforming to the role of domestic breadwinner, working nine-to-five to support his family. Wyler's use of the western's mythic space, however, meant that McKay did not have to compromise in his non-conformity. Unlike Mann's westerners, McKay is not torn by the 'conflicting terms' by which society defines a man; rather his rejection of the western codes of conduct actually serves to change society itself. The partiarchs are dead and Leech sees an alternative way of 'being a man'. As Peck himself saw it, by the end of the film, McKay 'has taken over and established a new way of life based on decency and morality'.[69] While clearly unrealistic in modern society, it was much more plausible in a western setting, given the frontier's cultural resonance as a place of transition. And even if Wyler's critique was really directed against

The Man in the Gray Flannel Suit Goes West: When Jim McKay (Gregory Peck) rejects the 'Code' of the West, traditional gender roles are disrupted and Patricia Terrill (Carroll Baker) possesses the gun-phallus – until McKay presents *The Big Country* (1958) with a new definition of masculinity. (Courtesy of the British Film Institute)

modern society, the sense that McKay was challenging an ingrained histor-ical 'tradition' made his inner-directedness seem all the more heroic.

THE SECOND GREATEST SEX

Given the masculinity and virility associated with the genre, it is hardly surprising to note that few westerns identified a comparable 'crisis of femininity'. But then, neither did contemporary social commentators. It was only in the early 1960s that magazines such as *Newsweek* acknowledged how many American women suffered from a 'deep' and 'pervasive' malaise of discontent, and television documentaries reported on 'The Trapped Housewife' – part of a slowly growing awareness which culminated in 1963, when Betty Friedan looked back on the Fifties to identify 'the problem with no name'.[70] As Friedan's *The Feminine Mystique* described it, the female counterpart to the masculine crisis was similarly rooted in the cultural exaltation of domesticity, which gave white, middle-class women few options beyond the roles of homemaker, housewife and mother, and prevented them from 'grow[ing] to their full capacities'.[71] The 'image of feminine fulfilment in the form of husband, babies and suburbia' had, she argued, been so pervasive that women had been stifled by it, made to feel inadequate if they 'did not feel this mysterious fulfilment waxing the kitchen floor'.[72]

Film melodramas of the decade, made with a female audience in mind (in contrast to the western), had demonstrated some awareness of this situation. This was most notable in Douglas Sirk's *All That Heaven Allows* (1955), wherein Cary Scott feels disoriented when faced with the chance to explore her own identity and her own desires after her husband dies and her children leave home. There was occasional recognition of such 'discontent' in westerns too: in *Shane*, for example, with Marian Starrett torn between her desire for the adventurous romance that Shane represents, and her de-votion to her kind, if dull, husband and their homestead. But the dominant pattern of the western genre was to depict women as embodiments of the civilising virtues of femininity. *Seven Brides for Seven Brothers* (1954) for example, presents this in the way Milly civilises the wild, rough-hewn Pontipee boys and her husband Adam, by exposing them to culture and teaching them 'etiquette' so that they can be 'suitable matches for refined ladies in town'. Peter Biskind notes the contrast between the feminine influence and the masculine during the wonderful barn-raising dance sequence. Milly has warned the Pontipees to be on their best behaviour, and when the men of the town trip them up, push them down and hit them with planks, they 'turn the other cheek' and get on with building the barn. Only when Adam taunts them with 'momma's boys' do they fight back, and then the walls they have raised come crashing down. 'In this film,' observes Biskind, 'it is momma's boys who build civilization; when they listen to dad (or big brother), they destroy it.'[73]

Seven Brides also bears out Friedan's argument that, while the nurturing of civilised values was always part of a 'traditional' imaging of femininity, the cultural trend of the 1950s was to promote the 'feminine mystique' to the exclusion of anything else. The filmmakers specifically rewrote the character of Milly, from Stephen Vincent Benet's 1938 story 'Sobbin' Women', to excessively idealise her influence. Benet depicted Milly in a much more manipulative vein, for when she finds herself overworked by the brothers, Milly is the one who tells them the story of the Sabine Women and plants the idea that they should kidnap girls from the town. She then pretends to be upset at what they have done, while subtly conditioning the abducted girls into seeing that the Pontipees actually are good marriage material.[74] However, by changing the story to make sure that Adam is the one inspired by Plutarch in the film, and making Milly genuinely aghast at the subsequent abductions, MGM deliberately reduced Benet's Milly to a one-dimensional idealisation of civilising virtue. It was this type of reductivism that Friedan found repressive.

However, recognising the importance of female pioneers to western development did require filmmakers to acknowledge their strength, courage and endurance, and a number of westerns did put strong women at centre stage. This was true of star vehicles such as *Rancho Notorious* (1952) for Marlene Dietrich, *Johnny Guitar* (1954) for Joan Crawford, and *The River of No Return* (1954) for Marilyn Monroe. While *The River of No Return* is often dismissed for exploiting Monroe as a sex object, Molly Haskell notes that Monroe's dance-hall entertainer fundamentally challenges Robert Mitchum's preconceived notions by proving that 'she can not only pull her own weight in a trek through the wilds, but can act with more generosity and moral freedom because she is concerned with saving skin rather than saving face'.[75] *Westward the Women* (1951) also subverted expectations, presenting a whole 'cavalcade of virgins, whores, tomboys, matrons and good/bad and bad/good girls' embarking on a perilous journey that allows them, temporarily at least, to 'break free of their imprisoning stereotypes'.

Yet even this well-intentioned effort to address the experience of female pioneers, was based on the premise that they were going West to marry into 'a community of eager, female-starved pioneers and thereby convert the wilderness into a garden'.[76]

Calamity Jane (1953) provides one of the best illustrations of the feminine mystique at work, and the limits of the American West as a mythic space for challenging it. As a musical comedy set within an obviously fictionalised 'Wild West', the conventions of the western could have been relaxed, but the notion of the West as an inherently masculine enterprise is evident from the start, as Jane herself feels the need to be overtly masculine in order to fit in. The legend of the real Martha Jane Canary and the evident scarcity of women in Deadwood serve to 'explain' and naturalise her transgression of gender roles, as Doris Day dresses in buckskin, shoots better than any man save Wild Bill Hickok, and turns genre convention totally on its head by rescuing an Army Lieutenant from the Indians. But while Calamity is well liked, and even feared at little, her efforts as a masculine woman do not command much respect. She remains a parody of manliness, and when Hickok punctures her insistence on bragging and exaggerating her exploits, the men of Deadwood readily mock her. This laughter certainly relieves the threat to their own masculinity that her skills represent, but here *Calamity Jane* was also in accord with the reactionary concerns about the 'masculinization of women' infamously expressed by psychiatrist Marynia Farnham in *Modern Women: The Lost Sex* (1947).

Regarding feminism as a psychological illness, Farnham argued that women – particularly working women – were acquiring 'unfeminine' characteristics of aggressiveness and competitiveness that threatened men, and left women resentful and unfulfilled. Instead, 'the woman who is to find true gratification must love and accept her own womanhood'.[77] Calamity fails to win the heart of the man she loves, Lieutenant Dan, even when she rescues him, because her actions undermine his own masculinity. Moreover, according the dictates of contemporary self-help guides, such as *Win Your Man and Keep Him* (1948), she is too aggressive in her pursuit – since women should never 'give a man the idea you are running after him'.[78] Eventually, Hickok himself falls in love with Jane, but she has not been chasing him, and it only happens when she has abandoned her masculine pretence and followed the lead of the film's 'ideal' lady, Katie Brown (Allyn McLerie). Farnham's insistence that 'no matter how great a woman's masculine strivings, her basic needs make themselves felt', is also borne out when

Calamity finally admits to Bill her 'hankering' for a husband, a home and children.[79] Then, rather than experiencing the mood swings, anger, jealousy and irrational behaviour that characterised her when she was trying to be like a man, Jane is instantly serene and in tune with 'nature', expressing her 'Secret Love' to the golden daffodils.

Calamity Jane also reflected the advice bombarding women, about how best to cultivate their femininity. A psychologist writing for *Ladies Home Journal* told readers that girls who were not getting dates were guilty of careless grooming, unsuitable clothes, poor dancing and aggressive behaviour – which is precisely what renders Calamity unsuitable for marriage.[80] As Bill tells Calamity early in the film, 'if you only crawled out from that deerhide and dolled up a bit, I've a hunch you'd be a pretty passable gal'. The film thus endorsed the advice given to 'any girl who reaches her middle twenties without a proposal': that she should 'take steps to make herself more interesting and attractive'.[81] Katie Brown's shock at the state of Calamity's shabby cabin begins the makeover – making Calamity conscious for the first time that it's 'not fit fer a dog, let alone a lady', and undermining her self-confidence. The song routine that follows transforms the cabin into a Fifties-style suburban home, while also employing Katie's 'wardrobe, cosmetics and accessories' to 'evolve' Calamity into a 'beautiful young lady'.[82] Having changed out of a man's check shirt and jeans into a yellow dress, Calamity finally understands what 'A Woman's Touch' can achieve. The merging of the two transformations into one also underlines the message that homemaking itself 'makes' a woman – with her subsequent desirability reiterated in the lyric's claim that 'the pies and cakes a woman bakes, can make a fella tell her that he loves her very much'.

There is an element of subversion in the film's implicit acknowledgement that gender identity is a matter of role-playing for both sexes, and that the 'ideal' woman herself is a social construct. Not only does Calamity impersonate a man, but Hickok is 'humiliated' by having to dress as an Indian squaw, and song-and-dance man Francis Fryer appears as a chorus girl. Even Katie Brown herself is a 'female impersonator' at first, when she passes herself off as the popular vaudeville diva, Adelaide Adams. The characters who first see through each other's masquerades are performers themselves: Francis realises Katie is not Adelaide, Calamity is the first to see that Francis is really a man in drag, and laughs loudest and longest at Hickok's moment in a dress. Suggestively it is Hickok who sees through all of Calamity's stories, hinting perhaps that his 'Wild Bill' moniker connotes a 'false' identity of excessive masculinity too. Moreover, *Calamity Jane*'s narrative of a butch tomboy heading to the city to bring back a pretty girl, who then moves into Jane's cabin where they live together in domestic bliss, has, to say the least, left itself open to queer readings. It is Calamity's idea that they should cohabit because 'there ain't many women in town', and when Katie flees the town in distress – following a phallic contest of marksmanship between them – Calamity rides out to bring her back home, just as earlier she had chased after Dan. As the reunited women cuddle inside the returning stagecoach, the driver looks in to mutter 'Females! Two females!' In the end, however, the feminisation of Calamity (defined as her 'natural' state), and the double-wedding of Jane and Bill, Katie and Dan, ultimately reinforced the normative gender roles of the feminine mystique.

Publicity material surrounding the film did the same – albeit in implicit acknowledgement of *Calamity Jane*'s transgressions. As Joanne Meyerowitz observed in her analysis of 'true stories' in Fifties women's magazines, even publicly successful women were depicted with an emphasis on their femininity, to assure readers that 'conventional gender distinctions and heterosexuality remained intact', while seeming to cloak 'a submerged fear of lesbian, mannish or man-hating women'.[83] Warner's press releases mirrored this, explicitly 'feminising' Doris Day's masculine costumes by noting that '*her* buckskin pants are doeskin and tailormade'. Likewise Francis Fryer's cross-dressing was rendered as a heterosexual joke, by having actor Dick Wesson warn readers not to 'let anyone tell you that impersonating a woman is a gay lark'. More substantially, Allyn McLerie and Doris Day were offered as 'role models' for women who might identify too greatly with the masculine side of Calamity. In one interview, McLerie confessed to having been 'something of a tomboy' herself when young – but that she too 'transformed' when her mother 'called a halt to her offspring's baseball and basketball games with the neighborhood boys and suggested that she devote her attention to more ladylike pursuits'. Having consequently taken up ballet, McLerie's femininity was now self-evident in her possession of 'two of the shapeliest legs in these forty-eight states'. Best of all was a piece ghostwritten for 'feminine tomboy' Doris herself, which claimed that it was a 'healthy thing for a woman at times to give free rein to pent up tomboyish inclinations'. Day was even alleged to have said that the 'average woman' should 'once a week, at least, don an old pair of dungarees, ride horseback, climb a tree, leap over a fence'. But this advice was advanced purely in better service of femininity, since – having dispelled all that manliness in one energetic burst – the 'normal woman' would 'be twice as feminine after such spells'![84]

Unwittingly imbedded in this article was a recognition that the 'feminine mystique' was a construct that repressed the 'tomboy traits' of every 'normal woman'. However, the western setting meant that Calamity Jane's behaviour would be identified as 'exceptional' rather than normal. The frontier context provided opportunities for self-expression and excitement outside of the home, which female audiences in the 1950s might have envied – but the conjunction of the narrative and the period setting discouraged them from thinking that something *better* than married life might now be available. There may have been once, but that was in the past – and even then the women who had exercised such freedoms had been isolated and unhappy, and did not know any better. Once she was exposed to the modernity of Chicago and realised 'how far from being a lady' she was, even Calamity Jane desired to be more like a 'modern' woman.

In commenting on the social concerns expressed in the western, Philip French rightly described it as 'a hungry cuckoo of a genre, a voracious bastard of a form, equally open to visionaries and opportunists ready to seize anything that's in the air from juvenile delinquency to ecology'.[85] As a 'cuckoo' the western truly was a hybrid genre: *Calamity Jane*'s humorous discussion of gender identity was possible because the setting could absorb both comedy and the performative excesses of the musical; *True Story* imposed the flashback structure of biopics to interrogate the motives of a western legend; and *The Big Country* gained additional stature as an 'epic Western' by transposing from the biblical epic a narrative about a new personal 'faith' challenging an established patriarchal tyranny.

As it was constructed in the 1950s, however, the mythic space of the genre was only conducive to particular forms of social analysis. As the 'crucible' in which the American character was shaped, at least according to Frederick Jackson Turner's theory, the frontier setting was ideal for isolating and replaying contemporary challenges to the 'national character'. The resonance of the frontier as a place of transition allowed filmmakers to suggest which values should be embraced in the future and which should be left in the past. Associated with mythmaking, as real people such as Calamity Jane and Jesse James became legends during their lifetimes, the American West was also an ideal setting for exploring the construction of identity. But constructed as a white, male, imperialist enterprise – as it was in the 1950s – the genre was rather less suited to exploring the problems faced by women and racial minorities – except in terms of depicting misogynistic, patriarchal or racist white men whose prejudices are then challenged.

However, if the West was heavily weighted with normative definitions of sex roles, the Roaring Twenties proved much more amenable to the gender-bending of Billy Wilder's *Some Like It Hot* (1959). Using the era's gangsters as a reason to get Jack Lemmon and Tony Curtis into frocks, and exploiting the androgynous aesthetic of the decade's flappers to avoid sexualising their transvestism, Wilder got away with a lot more than *Calamity Jane* ever could in deconstructing sexual identity. If a filmmaker wanted a 'cloak' for presenting ideas that might be too controversial in a contemporary setting, there were always other pasts available.

6

Researching History

We did research
Authenticity was a must
Zooks! Did we search
And what did we find?
A lot of dust!

Lyrics from title song of *The Court Jester* (1956)

That Hollywood's desire for 'authenticity' could be parodied in the title sequence of a spoof of medieval costume adventures is testament to the term's pervasiveness in the discourse surrounding history films. A third of the 550 pressbooks examined for this book made explicit mention of authenticity, most frequently associating it with the costumes, props and characters of the film, but also often asserting that filmmakers had based their narratives 'upon fully authenticated material'.[1] Films as diverse as *David and Bathsheba* and *The Great Missouri Raid* competed to achieve 'the ultimate in authenticity'.[2] Indeed, even as the film itself mocked the notion, publicity for *The Court Jester* proudly claimed that the castle in the movie had been 'reproduced down to the last, intricate ornate detail'.[3] The insistence that 'authenticity was a must' was no joke.

Of course, as historians have rightly pointed out, 'a movie may feature numerous authentic-looking props yet still communicate poor history'.[4] Natalie Zemon Davis argues that 'the usual marks of historical authenticity in films' – period costumes, props, locations and so forth – only add 'to the credibility and genuine historicity of the film' when these details are

127

'connected to the values and habits of a period and are used with some discernment about their truth status'.[5] However, many filmmakers, thinking in visual terms, seemed to replicate costumes and settings in the belief that 'a movie that *looks* like the past *is* like the past'.[6] Studio publicity in the 1950s frequently implied that props, costumes and locations imbued a film with *automatic* historicity, in terms which often reduced history to a mere patina of authenticity, present only in the period details. The industry's common conception of historical authenticity rarely matched a professional historian's sense of the term.

Yet, no matter how inadequately conceived, authenticity was – and remains – a highly valued commodity in Hollywood's history films. Indeed, it acquired even greater importance during the Fifties. First, if audiences were to be persuaded of the capacity for widescreen and 3-D to enable them to 'witness' history, the recreation of physical environments of a period became ever more crucial. Production values had to be sufficiently high for audiences to suspend disbelief and be 'convinced' that they were 'reliving' genuine experiences. Obvious anachronisms and inaccuracies would undermine their credulity and jar audiences out of the sense of immersion and participation that the filmmakers sought to engender. Second, filmmakers who used history to critique contemporary society, found it important to be able to stress that their work was supported by 'fully authenticated material'. No one could afford to leave themselves open to charges of distorting history for propagandist purposes, and claims of authenticity associated their films with the image of 'disinterested' objectivity and neutrality possessed by academic histories. This was also part of a wider Cold War phenomenon. In a climate of distrust, 'veracity' became a crucial issue – with Dwight Macdonald detecting a contemporary 'fetish' for 'concrete details' in, among other things, the cultural weight given to the 'numbers' of subversives that Joseph McCarthy claimed to have identified.[7] Moreover, as Peter Novick observes, the intellectual culture of the Cold War was dominated by the 'celebration of objectivity as the hallmark of thought in the Free World', in contrast to the disdain for objective truth demonstrated by totalitarian regimes.[8] Hollywood's focus on authenticity thus both stemmed from and contributed to this desire for verifiable 'facts'.

However, this cult of authenticity existed in tension with an equally ubiquitous perception of history (also acknowledged in *The Court Jester*'s lyrics) as 'dusty', anathema to the dramatic priorities of filmmakers.

This was epitomised in the opening of Sam Goldwyn's *Hans Christian Andersen* (1952), in which the Danish storyteller is seen entertaining a crowd of schoolchildren with his fable of the Emperor's New Clothes. When the schoolmaster arrives to find his truant charges, he berates Andersen for having the audacity to tether the string of a kite to volumes of the history of Denmark. Disarmingly, the storyteller responds that 'the history of any country can always stand a little fresh air! Do you know the story of the history book that took a vacation and came back a much better history?' This whimsical statement effectively offered a justification for the movie itself, which eschewed the factual biopic format, and instead presented Andersen's life 'as he might have written it', as a 'fairy tale about this great spinner of fairy tales'.[9] The film not only describes stories and myths as a different way of learning, but also suggests that they ought to be privileged above history as vehicles for imparting lessons to young audiences. Hans' allegorical stories (and, by self-reflexive implication, similar history films) are more beguiling and enchanting than the weighty narrative of the history textbook, yet still embody 'truths' about the human condition that may

'A little fresh air': Weighty volumes of history are put to better use as a tether for Danny Kaye's kite in *Hans Christian Andersen* (1952). (Courtesy of the British Film Institute)

even be more meaningful to his audience. History, it is implied, functions best as an anchor, a point in objective reality, from which more imaginative fantasies can soar in a Technicolor sky.

Most history films resolved Hollywood's paradoxical positions by demanding authenticity in the visual details while privileging imagination in the narrative drama. This was a fudge, moreover, that was often compounded by the very people whom historians might have hoped knew better. In the Research Departments of the major studios, filmmakers had access to a potentially excellent range of historical sources and materials, and advisors who knew these holdings inside out. And yet, rarely was a filmmaker's understanding of the value and meaning of historical authenticity challenged. When discussing her work in 1954, the head of the Research Department at 20th Century-Fox, Frances Richardson, argued that 'the big challenge is to discover the trimmings, the filigree of an epoch', while, by comparison, contending that 'the straight line of historic events is easy enough to establish'.[10] This is hardly a claim that anyone who has actually tried to write history would make, but since Richardson was employed to advise filmmakers on questions of historical content, it is little wonder that this attitude would be reflected in their movies. In short, the merit of history films was contingent on the quality of the dialogue between filmmaker and advisor. Yet, this crucial dialectic has been almost totally ignored by film historians.

FURTHER AND FASTER THAN A PHD

The first studio research department was formed in 1914, when Elizabeth McGaffey, a 'newspaper woman with stage ambitions', persuaded Paramount's Jesse Lasky 'to give her a dictionary, the *National Geographic* magazine and a public library card', so that she could advise production staff on dressing sets to fit the story.[11] At first reliant on the Los Angeles Public Library, the research department gradually developed its own identity, as publications were acquired to meet the demands of successive films. How this innovation spread to other studios is uncertain, but McGaffey's move to RKO in 1933 indicates the expansion of interest in her work. Fox had its own department by 1928, while Warner Bros. followed suit in 1936. Rapid expansion of personnel occurred in the late 1930s, supporting an increasing number of historical pictures, and by 1941 all studios were employing research staff.[12] By the 1950s, therefore, these departments were an established part of the industry's culture of production, and had played a central role in defining the ways in which Hollywood thought about history.

Central to this was the fact that research departments were reactive and service-oriented, rather than pro-active and critical. Moreover, McGaffey's policy had been to recruit librarians rather than historians or 'people with extensive training in academic research'. One researcher explained this by arguing that academics 'know *too much*':

> If you ask them something they pop right up with the answer, and at least once out of every ten times they're wrong. A good researcher always says, 'I don't know, but I'll find out.'[13]

Whatever the actual justification of this statement, by the Fifties it had become a rationalisation for the status quo. A 1953 guide to careers in Hollywood advised prospective research assistants that the 'best training' for the job was to 'get on the library staff of your school or college'. The 'perfect' experience would be 'with any of the museum libraries', such as the Huntingdon Library in Pasadena. Director Mervyn LeRoy (responsible for history films such as *Anthony Adverse* (1936), *Madame Curie* (1943) and *Quo Vadis* (1951)) devoted two pages to explaining why 'mature, preferably unmarried' women were ideal candidates. He also insisted that knowledge of a second language was a must. But when it came to familiarity with history, all he had to say was that a major in the subject *might* be 'a help'.[14]

Within the studio system, researchers were usually assigned to particular productions in the early stages of development. They would start work reading the outline, or the source story of the screenplay, 'and begin to reconstruct the culture of the historical period in which the story is set':

> From periodicals she clips pictures or articles treating of the period. From books, both contemporary and current, she finds pictures and descriptive material which she reproduces photographically for the clipping file... By the time the research department receives a script or screenplay, much of the spadework may have been completed, and the researcher can begin relating materials directly to the production requirements.[15]

When the script arrived, every detail of costume, architecture, scenery and props would be broken down under various headings to anticipate the inquiries of every other department. Records of the Warner Bros. Research Department illustrate the typical volume and nature of questions researchers could expect. A. Adler, for example, was assigned to *King Richard and the*

Crusaders, based on Sir Walter Scott's *The Talisman*, and started receiving requests from writer John Twist and producer Henry Blanke in September 1952. In response to requests for 'background material for the Crusades' and 'books about the Middle Ages', the department could supply them with texts ranging from Henry Davis' *Mediaeval England* (1924) to George Coulton's *Medieval Panorama* (1949), while Adler also acquired Kate Norgate's 1884 account of *England Under the Angevin Kings* from the LA Public Library. Heavily illustrated works were clearly favoured: E.L Cutts' *Scenes and Characters of the Middle Ages* (1886) had a copiously illustrated chapter on 'Knights of the Middle Ages', while Paul Lacroix's *Military and Religious Life in the Middle Ages* had over 400 engravings and woodcuts from the period.[16]

Over the next year, as the script was drafted and reworked, Adler responded to a variety of questions from Twist, such as 'What is the landscape like near Acre?'; 'Were pen and ink used in the 12th century?'; 'Was chess invented before 1100?' *Encyclopedia Britannica, National Geographic* and Lacrousse's *Art au Moyen Age et l'epoque de la Renaissance* provided most of the answers. Following approval of the screenplay in September 1953, Adler started to receive production-related questions. The Prop Department wanted pictures of 'flags and banners, all of period 1190', 'Wedding Rings of the 12. Century', and illustrations of Saracen lances and trumpets. Bill Peck wanted examples of 'charms' in order to develop his design for the Talisman itself, while Joe McLaughlin wanted to find inspiration in the 'songs and music for the Crusades'. And once filming was underway, the Publicity Department required more literary material for use in writing press releases (such as biographies of Sir Walter Scott), or simple fact-checking (as in the correct form of address for Richard I).[17]

Research directors boasted that they went 'further and faster than most PhDs preparing a thesis – often several million words further'.[18] However, they were rarely expected to interpret the information they accumulated. Researchers were 'nonselective' in gathering materials, collecting all pertinent pictorial material, unless it was 'a ridiculously obvious misrepresentation'. It would be actually more appropriate to see studio research units as reference departments. The 'bibles' they produced were compilations of raw material, with no evaluation of the sources' reliability. The purpose was not to provide 'authenticated history', but rather to 'stimulate the creative thinking that goes into the making of a picture'.[19] Unlike the historian, a film researcher's work was essentially done once the material had been gathered together. Yet, as the PhD comparison suggests, researchers had a tendency to rate their work as superior to that of historians.

This attitude was often compounded by the way in which 'technical advisors' were employed in the research process. These were individuals who specialised in particular areas of knowledge, brought in to supplement research assistants or, in the case of independent productions, as substitutes. Research departments maintained card-indexes of hundreds of experts in a diverse range of subjects, whom they could call upon for quick answers to a producer's questions. The index at Warner Bros. contained everyone from botanists to psychologists, from a Canadian Mounted Policeman to a waiter who had worked at Delmonico's in 1890.[20] However, if more in-depth consultation was required, advisors could be invited to liaise directly with the production company.

A small body of a dozen or so professional advisors, living in Los Angeles, had established themselves as respected authorities – although none of them appeared to possess specific academic qualifications. Hilda Grenier, for instance, provided detailed technical notes for MGM's *Diane* in 1955, as their expert on royal protocol, having once been a dresser to Queen Mary of England.[21] Charles B. Beard was consulted as 'an expert on armor, weapons and costumes of the 18th and 19th centuries' – which oddly was qualification enough to advise on *St Joan* and *The Story of Robin Hood*.[22] Most is known about Louis Van den Ecker, referred to as the 'dean' of this coterie of advisors. Originally from Belgium, he served as a government archivist before coming to Hollywood in 1923. In the words of industry publicists, Van den Ecker had then become 'world renowned for his comprehensive knowledge of historical material', and advised on more than forty features, including *The Adventures of Robin Hood* (1938), *Beau Geste* (1939) and, during the 1950s, *Lady Godiva, The Black Shield of Falworth* and *The Vagabond King*.[23]

In 1950, Van den Ecker published an article that was evidently intended as a guide of 'good practice' in employing technical advisors. He wrote that the 'best of them are not merely specialists in a single field, but men who have built up their own libraries of books and field material'. (That he had his own such library was not without relevance.) More particularly, he stressed that technical advisors were not 'outside' academics, but were part of the culture of Hollywood and understood the demands of drama. 'The best' had absorbed 'enough of the dramatic instinct to sacrifice absolute authenticity when it is in conflict with the values of the scene.'[24] When the respected biblical historian and interpreter of the Dead Sea Scrolls, Professor Moshe H. Gottstein, was asked to comment on the script of *Ben Hur*, he told director William Wyler that the scene of census-taking was 'impossible' because 'no Census would have involved long serpents of people and thousands of human beings going along'.[25] In contrast, 'impossible' was not in Van den Ecker's vocabulary. 'As long as the action seems logical and effective,' he insisted, 'license should be taken and a compromise established.' While this flexibility certainly pleased directors, it also meant that technical advisors remained supplemental, rather than integral to history film production. Van den Ecker did urge scenarists to use his services during script development, so as to draw inspiration from 'the environment and the period', but acknowledged that typically he was consulted only when shooting was about to begin, with only an opportunity to 'correct some of the grossest script blunders'.[26]

With research departments already primed for that particular task, filmmakers more often turned to technical advisors for other reasons. Budget-conscious producers of war films, for example, courted senior members of the military establishment in the hope that they might grant access to genuine military hardware and other facilities. Jerry Wald, producer of shore-leave comedy *Kiss Them For Me*, revealed this directly in asking Fox executives to find him 'a good technical advisor', because 'our basic problem will be to warm up and win the Navy over so that we can use the Almeda Naval Station for the picture'.[27] Similarly, when films were set abroad, Hollywood found it expedient to involve international advisors. The script for *Kim*, for example, was scrutinised by the Indian government before they would permit filming in Rajasthan – but approval was eased considerably by appointing I.A. Hafesjee as technical advisor, who just happened to be a member of India's board of film censors.[28] For films dealing with religious subjects, the Production Code Administration also encouraged filmmakers to submit draft screenplays to interested theologians, most commonly Monsignor John Devlin (whose involvement often signified that the Catholic Legion of Decency would approve of the film), and John Stone of the Los Angeles Jewish Community Council (who 'carried great weight with the Jewish press'). Specialist knowledge was therefore commonly sought and employed in ways that turned research into a public relations exercise.

The involvement of academic advisors was infrequent. Filmmakers were far more concerned about offending military, religious and ethnic sensibilities than they were about crimes against history. Outraged historians, after all, were unlikely to withhold valuable resources, boycott a film or press for greater censorship. Research departments did cultivate some contacts within universities, but archaeologists were more sought after than historians. Thus, the makers of *Helen of Troy* consulted Cesare D'Onoforio, as professor of the Institute of Archaeology in Rome; while *David and Bathsheba* benefited from the advice of Chester Charlton McCown, former director of the American School of Oriental Research in Jerusalem, who provided information about the construction of the king's palace, the gates of Jerusalem and the Tabernacle housing the Ark of the Covenant. Description and confirmation of visual details, rather than argument or interpretation, were the priorities.

Since films necessarily had to depict the visual, research departments and most advisors took it for granted that the historical elements of a screenplay could, and should, be considered as a series of component facts. Standard practice meant that what was 'real' and 'tangible' about the past had to be identified and classified, with the 'facts' subsequently considered more or less in isolation. In consequence, the process of research itself became a substitute for actually thinking about history. This gives some justification to Pierre Sorlin's characterisation of the history film as a 'dissertation about history which…establishes relationships between facts and offers a more or less superficial view of them'.[29] Few challenged this because advisors who did come into conflict with filmmakers were unlikely to be re-employed, and the careers of studio research staff similarly depended on them working within the boundaries of their defined role. However, there were occasions in the 1950s when historically minded individuals did maintain a more independent and critical stance.

Carl Milliken

Any flexibility in the remit of researchers rested entirely on the judgement of individual filmmakers. In spring of 1954, director Elia Kazan, 'hot' from the success of *On The Waterfront*, came to Warner Bros. to make *East of Eden*. The movie was concerned only with the final quarter of John Steinbeck's 600 page novel, located in northern California during the First World War – and while the town of Mendocino provided some exteriors, Kazan wanted to 'recreate' the Salinas of 1917 on the studio lot, with 'authenticity and verisimilitude'.[30] Of particular concern was the staging of an actual historical occasion – a war recruitment parade. As head of Warner's research department, Carl Milliken assigned himself to the project.[31]

Wanting details about specific parades, rather than the general information history books might contain, Milliken travelled north and spent a couple of weeks in Salinas collecting photographs and interviewing citizens about their town's history. Using the resources of the town historical society, Milliken found contemporary descriptions of the 'Loyalty Day' pageant of June 1, 1917, which enabled Kazan to determine the precise form of the parade – including fire trucks, Spanish war veterans, floats depicting California and Uncle Sam, the Elks Lodge and Prohibitionists. Further, when screenwriter Paul Osborn suggested that people in the parade should march carrying 'brooms, mops, etc., in lieu of guns', Milliken warned Kazan that 'the buffoonery implicit in the mop business' would have been out of character for the people of Salinas.[32] Respecting his knowledge, Kazan altered the script accordingly.

Most significantly, Milliken's presence in Salinas gave him a unique opportunity to follow up his research. Reading through the *Monterey Daily Cypress*, Milliken came across accounts of anti-German sentiments at such parades boiling over into racist violence.[33] In his autobiographical novel, Steinbeck had made brief mention of a German tailor, Mr Fenchel, being attacked by a mob that tore down his 'white picket fence and burned the front out of his house'.[34] Kazan intended to film this incident, but Milliken spoke to residents about the actual occurrences. Robert Green had already proved helpful in digging up many pictures from the period, and his father's photographic studio had been situated next to the shop of William Schuman, a German Jewish tailor who was evidently the inspiration for Steinbeck's Mr Fenchel. Green recalled that Schuman's 'feelings and sympathies were primarily American' and that the tailor had tried to display this by 'making a very large American Flag of silk and teaching his boys the Salute to the American Flag'. But during a Liberty Bond drive in May 1918

> an English Army Officer, who was touring the United States, gave a speech to the crowd, telling of the atrocities the Germans were doing to the women and children of Belgium and France. Mr Schuman...listened for some time and finally could no longer control his anger and shouted in his German accent, 'You are a damned liar' and other things of that nature. The crowd immediately turned on him and he might have been seriously hurt but for the intervention of the police.[35]

Going far beyond the usual practice of gathering reference material, Milliken was generating new historical sources. Indeed, he took his interview with Green even further and paid townspeople $50 each for their written reminiscences, which then informed the performances and nuances Kazan captured on screen. Moreover, Kazan directly adapted Green's oral history into an emotional scene in the movie, with a British officer inciting the crowd, and James Dean's Cal (rather than the police) intervening to protect his German neighbour.[36]

Milliken's research thereby made a central contribution to the historicity of the film, which was now adapting history rather than just the book. The effort was appreciated by critics too, who, while divided on the merits of James Dean's performance, had little but praise for the setting:

> Nobody who was around at the time will deny that it reproduces with compelling fidelity the small-town United States of 1917 – the patriotic parades, the draft boards, the hysteria and the heroism, manners and customs of the people, old and young, rich and poor, at work, at play, at living... The 1917 of *East of Eden* is the period to the life.[37]

However, the situation went to the other extreme when Milliken had to deal with producer Milton Sperling the following year. Sperling forwarded a script of *The Court Martial of Billy Mitchell* to the department in June 1955 – but this was the final draft, for a production that had to go into rehearsals by the end of the month. It was an independent film, part-financed by Warner Bros., and writer Emmett Lavery had already undertaken substantial research of his own. Sperling evidently decided only to use the studio's resources at the last minute, expecting them simply to verify the screenplay and then advise the designers. Milliken voiced his resentment in no uncertain terms, angry that the 'impossible task' Sperling expected was putting the reputation of his department on the line. Without the opportunity to prepare as usual, 'we are left with a whole mass of research minutiae which we are simply unable to provide and which will necessarily be faked by the various production departments'.[38]

East of Eden was now clearly a touchstone for Milliken. When he warned Sperling that the success of *Billy Mitchell* would 'hang on a sense of realism', he also pointed out that Kazan would be 'the first to tell you that a considerable factor' in the acclaim for *Eden* 'was the care which went into the authentic Salinas background'. Recalling his earlier efforts, Milliken also tried to convince the producer that the 'closest possible adherence to the facts' could, of itself, produce the 'highly dramatic elements' needed in a screenplay. However, he neither described what these elements might be, nor suggested how 'the facts' could improve the script. He did suggest the producer 're-examine the dramatic necessity' of some of the changes that Lavery had made to Mitchell's life (including the writing-out of his wife), and predicted that audiences would recognise that they were being short-changed. But rather than developing an alternative framework, Milliken was basically venting a great deal of pent-up frustration – evident when he impressed upon Sperling that 'I'm sure you will understand that this department is firmly convinced that the words "dramatic license" are over-worked in this town'.[39]

Yet, part of the reason why 'dramatic license' was so overused in Hollywood was that research department staff (including Milliken himself for the most part) were rarely so pro-active. Accepting that their role was to provide visual reference material and draw attention to matters of inaccuracy and anachronism, they did not effectively demonstrate how history could be interpreted in dramatic terms. Relying on the rare opportunities prof-fered by sensitive filmmakers to flex their intellectual muscles – and the occasional outburst against the insensitive ones – studio researchers did not encourage filmmakers to think differently about the past. Most significantly, there was no effort to explain, nor even much recognition, that history could be comprised of anything more than 'facts'.

Two men, however, did try to challenge this. One was Hugh Gray, who developed a role for himself as a script doctor on historical films; the other was Henry Noerdlinger, Cecil B. DeMille's personal research con-sultant. The institutionalised research culture did constrain their efforts to a great extent, but – through different approaches – both forged relation-ships with filmmakers and tried to encourage a rather more sophisticated understanding of history.

Hugh Gray

Hugh Gray, surprisingly, was unique in combining the roles of technical advisor and screenwriter. He was an English-born scholar, with a degree in Classics from Oxford, and though he originally intended to pursue an academic career, he instead became a playwright and theatre critic. Exposed to filmmaking through his friendship with Alfred Hitchcock, he came to write screenplays for Zoltan Korda – including *Forget Me Not* (1936) and *The Drum* (1938) – as well as cinema criticism for *The Listener*. During

World War II, the RAF film unit sent Gray to Hollywood to assist John Boulting in preparing films intended to promote stronger Allied cooperation. After the war he accepted an offer from MGM, moved to Los Angeles, and began work on developing *Quo Vadis*.[40]

Although Gray only received screen credit for penning the lyrics that Nero sings while Rome burns, he actually developed an extensively researched screenplay in conjunction with director John Huston. Based on

Script doctor for several history films, classicist Hugh Gray was repeatedly frustrated by the 'intellectual spirit' in 1950s Hollywood. (Courtesy of the UCLA University Archives)

the novel by Henryk Sienkiewicz, the project had been in development at MGM since the late 1930s. When Huston and producer Arthur Hornblow, Jr., revived the project in 1948, they brought in Gray to advise on an existing script. He soon compiled an immense research bible – three books of illustrations for costume, makeup, sets and props, and a descriptive volume that contained a 'scene by scene analysis of the script, giving the fullest available period information on the characters of our story, and the atmosphere and action of the scenes'.[41] Sharp enough to observe such things as the correct number of guests at a Roman dinner party, and that a reference to ambassadors was 'out of key with the time', the index to this volume alone was 34 pages long.[42] Grabbing Huston's attention, the director immediately requested that the 'exceptionally cultivated' Gray be allowed to collaborate with him.[43]

Together they produced a screenplay that was replete with historical allusions. In one instance, Gray scripted a conversation between the world-weary Petronius and the story's hero, Marcus Vinicius, which referred to the conflict with Boadicea in Britain. Gray recalled the claim of ancient historian Cassius Dio, that the revolt had been fuelled when Seneca called in loans he had made to British chieftains. Asking about Boadicea's fate, Petronius was told 'she preferred death by poison for herself and her daughters'. 'So,' mused Petronius, 'she surrendered her entire inheritance to Nero and made Roman Britain safe once more for the usuries of our moralist, money-lending friend Seneca. Like tutor, like prince!'[44] This dialogue was imaginative but, against the typical Hollywood style, Gray did not load it with specific historical significance. Instead it was presented merely as the sort of incidental gossip which would have amused a cynical Roman. Audiences may not have fully understood the references, but this did not worry Gray. As he later explained, he deliberately wanted to avoid period dialogue which constantly sought to 'explain' history to audiences – since, he believed, this 'destroyed the illusion' that audiences were seeing the past unfold before them as if 'for the first time'.[45]

The opportunity to advance this different perspective, however, was shortlived. Louis B. Mayer was highly critical of the material that Gray and Huston developed, accusing Gray of 'arguing with Christianity'.[46] Gray had sought to better define Rome's pagan theology, to present Nero's persecution of the Christians in an accurate context – and developed scenes of elaborate tributes to the gods Juno, Minerva, Apollo et al, with the intention of contrasting pagan grandiosity with the simpler virtues of the

Christian faith. The cruelty of the massacre of the Christians was also emphasised, making a spectacle of 'the arena [as] a forest of crucifixes', with the implication that they were sacrificed as further tribute to the Roman deities.[47] Claiming that Huston's only idea was to 'throw the Christians to the lions', Mayer took advantage of production problems to shelve the film for a year, and then passed it into other hands.[48] The script was taken over by John Lee Mahin, and Gray's involvement was cut back to producing a guide to the pronunciation of Greek and Latin words, and writing Nero's songs. However, Sam Zimbalist, the new producer of *Quo Vadis*, was as impressed with Gray's research as Huston had been, and gave him another chance on *Beau Brummell*.

While Gray's work on *Beau Brummell* was confined to research, the 'bible' he produced was full of examples of how Zimbalist's writers could develop effective drama from a process of historical interpretation. In one key instance, Gray knew full well that the filmmakers needed a love interest for George Brummell, which was difficult to reconcile with the fact that the dandy never married, never mind the imputations of homosexuality. However, Gray's research uncovered 'undisputed evidence that women idolized him', as well as a letter written by Brummell late in his life, which showed him to have been 'deeply in love' with at least one 'unknown woman'. Given that the recipient of the letter was not identified, Gray suggested that the filmmakers could justifiably create a composite lover from the known facts about his affections for Lady Hester Stanhope and the Duchesses of York, Devonshire and Rutland. 'Substitute for them one person unknown to history,' he advised, 'to whom he could write in the terms of the very emotional letter that dates from his days in exile.'[49] The writers did exactly this, creating the character of Lady Patricia for Elizabeth Taylor – with Gray having demonstrated that the conventions of period films could be maintained without destroying the integrity of existing evidence.

He sought to do the same for the film's central dramatic relationship, between Brummell and the Prince of Wales. It was through this friendship that the dandy had risen to public prominence and become the epitome of style in Regency England. According to Gray's reading of history, when their friendship ended and Brummell was ostracised from court, both he and the Prince declined in fortune.[50] However, because the break was a personal matter, there was little concrete evidence and much dispute among historians about its cause. The near-contemporary memoirs of Captain Rees Gronow suggested that the Prince of Wales was 'offended' when

'Brummell warmly espoused the cause of Mrs Fitzherbert', and Gray took his lead from this.[51] A devout Catholic, Maria Fitzherbert had been secretly married to the Prince of Wales in 1785, in defiance of the Royal Marriages Act, but Parliament insisted that George marry the Princess Caroline of Brunswick instead before he became Prince Regent. In 1811 a great party was thrown to celebrate his Regency, and Mrs Fitzherbert was invited. However, 'instead of sitting at the head of the Prince's table as his wife, which he had always insisted upon in the past...[she was] seated at the foot of the table as a commoner', signifying the end of their relationship.[52] Gray found evidence in a parody letter written in 1812 by Irish poet Thomas Moore, which suggested that Brummell's quarrel with the Prince also dated from 1811 – and so inferred that Brummell might have taken his friend to task for his display of bad manners. He then developed the thesis that this quarrel continued because of the machinations of the Prince's mistress, Lady Hertford, and that Brummell's own arrogance prevented any reconciliation.[53] Interpreting genuine evidence, in its historical context – and then developing drama from that – Gray acknowledged that historians themselves used imagination in constructing a narrative, but showed how they worked with the evidence, not against it.

Unfortunately, the Production Code Administration insisted on a different version, refusing to allow a positive depiction of the 'adulterous' relationship between the Prince and Mrs Fitzherbert that continued during his 'official' marriage to Princess Caroline.[54] This ended up requiring changes that made nonsense of the real chronology.[55] But Gray's impact was still felt in the characterisation of the Prince himself. Challenging the 'smug hypocrisy of Victorian writers' such as William Thackeray, who 'dismissed' George IV 'finally and irrevocably as a worthless waster and a bad king', Gray argued that the filmmakers should return to contemporary observations. In particular, he quoted the Duke of Wellington, who pictured the king as 'the most extraordinary compound of talent, wit, buffoonery, obstinacy and good-feeling – a medley of the most opposite qualities with a great preponderance of the good'.[56] It was precisely this 'touching' and 'charming misfit' that Peter Ustinov translated to the screen.[57]

In 1952, Gray moved to Warner Bros., returning to his classicist roots and writing the screenplay for *Helen of Troy*. However, the experience was almost identical to that of *Quo Vadis*, as he was soon replaced by more conventional studio scenarists. Gray's requests to the research department demonstrate the level at which his approach was pitched – consisting of Euripides' *Helena, Trojan Women* and *Iphigenia in Aulis*, Seneca's *Trojan Women* and *Agamemnon*, Shakespeare's *Troilus and Cressida* and Juvenal's *Satires* (in Latin). In contrast, his replacement, John Twist, asked only for a 'condensed' copy of the *Iliad* and a 'book about Greek customs'.[58]

Gray solved many of the problems in bringing credibility to the threads of mythology in Homer's epic. This included plausible explanations of why Helen ran away with Paris (with Menelaus portrayed as an abusive husband), and of why the Trojans would bring the wooden horse into their city only hours after the siege had been lifted. (In Gray's version, Odysseus convinces the Trojans that it is a totem for Greek victory, and two Trojan princes determine to capture it in order to break Greek morale.)[59] But while these elements remained in the final film, the ahistorical attitudes of his colleagues grated. Producer-director Robert Wise once came to him and said, 'Could we get someone to prophesy the coming of Christ?'![60] In another instance, Gray made considerable effort to create 'fresh' dialogue, deliberately avoiding the cliché about 'the face that launched a thousand ships'. Still embodying the sentiment, his script expressed Menelaus' declaration of war in unmistakably Homeric terms:

> Such an expedition shall be mustered as never before has sailed the wine-colored Aegean waters. Not 200 – not 500 – but 1000 ships shall be launched upon them! Troy shall see what store we put on the lovely face of Helen, and seeing that vast panoply of war – shall tremble![61]

Yet, when John Twist inherited the script, he was astonished to find that the famous phrase had been omitted. Gray knew that the lines had been written by Christopher Marlowe in the sixteenth century, and had no place in the mouths of Homeric characters; but Twist asked the research department where in the *Iliad* he could find the quotation. Despite being informed by an amused researcher that it actually came from *Dr Faustus*, he used it anyway.[62]

To a disillusioned Gray, this summed up the 'atmosphere and intellectual spirit' he had to work with.[63] He stayed with Warner Bros. for a further year, retained principally as a script doctor, although he was given the opportunity in January 1953 to suggest 'promising' subjects for history films. He sought to introduce studio producers to a range of historical literature wider than the current bestseller lists, from the thirteenth-century courtly romance of *Chatelaine de Vergy* by Charles Bedier, to *The Song of Roland* which offered 'romantic and colorful' possibilities, with 'its chivalry, its Roland-Oliver friendship, its lusty-warrior-bishop Turpin, its story of treachery, its imposing figure of Charlemagne, and the echoing music of Roland's horn down the pass at Roncevalles'. He drew attention to Boadicea (evidently a figure who inspired him), and characters like Sir John Hawkwood, 'the leader of the English mercenaries known as the White Company', who could be set against the 'background of fourteenth century Italy with Popes and Princes thrown in for good measure'; the Holy Roman Emperor Frederick I, 'probably the most fantastic character of the middle ages, far in advance of his time'; or 'the dark and brooding figure of Savanorola as he scourged with his tongue the Florence of the Medicis'. Since none of these were produced, Gray evidently failed to ignite the imaginations of Jack Warner's producers. Interestingly, though, he did anticipate history films released in the 1960s, recommending the 'color and excitement' of El Cid, and the 'last stand of Spartacus' as 'one of the most exciting battles of history'.[64]

Gray left the industry in 1954 to pursue, at last, an academic career. Remaining in Los Angeles, he became a professor of theatre studies and screenwriting at UCLA, translated Andre Bazin's seminal *What Is Cinema?*, and received an honorary doctorate from the Sorbonne. He did, however, make a brief return to Hollywood at the end of the Fifties, working for Sam Zimbalist one last time, in an advisory capacity on *Ben Hur*. Apparently influenced by his earlier experience with Gray, Zimbalist had engaged playwright Christopher Fry to rewrite the scripts with an ear for capturing the ancient idiom. Fry's work greatly improved *Ben Hur*, vindicating the style of dialogue that Gray had always tried to promote. Indeed, when asked for his opinion, Gray was impressed by the epic, noting a real change in the filmmaker's approach to history. He was particularly pleased that the film presented 'a truly human conflict' in its characterisations of Judah Ben Hur and Messala, rather than the dispute between 'two apparently rival but never clearly defined schools of theology' common in biblicals like *Quo Vadis*.[65]

Now able to speak as a well-respected critic, Gray also took the opportunity to identify and challenge the sources of 'orthodoxy and pedantry' in Hollywood's history films. While praising *Ben Hur*, he implicitly attacked over-reliance on the materials provided by research departments, which filmmakers unquestioningly accepted as 'accurate'. Filmmakers were not exposed to the interpretative or analytical side of history, and assumed that because facts were immutable, they were automatically of significance.

These facts, translated into visual details, on-screen prologues and unnatural dialogue, were therefore pushed to the forefront of the history film in an effort to make the film itself appear significant – continually demanding the attention of audiences, saying, 'Pay attention – this is History!'

Noting that 'the public may know certain things' about any given historical subject, Gray appreciated that 'a number will check to see if these things are there in they way they know them...[and] want to see their particular version...confirmed in detail'. He warned, however, that the 'danger' was that filmmakers anticipated this too much, and so simply went 'through all the recognised motions known to those of moderate education' – subsequently producing period films that were 'just a record of some traditional story'. Too often actors were 'held at arm's length to be observed self-consciously performing deeds of historical, textbook significance'.[66] Filmmakers instead, he suggested, should learn that historians too used imagination, but developed their narratives from the 'latent' drama that was inherent in the facts.[67] Making drama out of the facts, instead of seeing them simply as 'manifest' signifiers of history, would, in Gray's opinion, result in the ideal history film – one which would 'create the effect on an audience that must have been created in those who saw these very things happen'.[68] This was the most sustained analysis offered by any historical advisor, but, coming at the very end of the 1950s, only director William Wyler was exposed to it.

Henry Noerdlinger

Henry S. Noerdlinger had greater success in influencing production than Gray, though the way that Cecil B. DeMille used his abilities was just as revealing of the industry's perception of historical research. Noerdlinger had been a researcher at MGM for 11 years when he replied to DeMille's advertisement for a private research consultant in 1945. Following his appointment, Noerdlinger coordinated the research for *Unconquered* (1947), which dealt with the French-Indian wars and the seige of Fort Pitt in 1763, and *Samson and Delilah* (1949), the biblical epic which set the pattern for the post-war cycle. DeMille's first movie of the 1950s – the Oscar-winning circus story, *The Greatest Show on Earth* (1952) – had a present-day background, but in 1952 he began work on the last film he directed, the gargantuan remake of *The Ten Commandments*.[69] Thus while

Noerdlinger researched only one history film in the 1950s, it happened to be the biggest of the decade.

Educated in Switzerland, Noerdlinger had travelled extensively through Europe before crossing to America in 1929. It was his knowledge of foreign languages that secured his position at MGM, rather than any training in history. However, by the time he went to work for DeMille, he had substantial experience of working on 'pictures of a historical nature', having

Henry Noerdlinger – posed here with a selection of texts used to research *The Ten Commandments* (1956) – had a position 'unique in the entire industry' as Cecil B. DeMille's personal research consultant. (Courtesy of the Academy of Motion Pictures Arts and Sciences)

often advised on two or three pictures at once. Under DeMille, he was able to concentrate on one epic subject at a time, and began his work long before writers were assigned to the project, so that when engaged they could immediately be supplied with historical background. Moreover, since DeMille usually employed a team of writers working simultaneously, Noerdlinger's influence in guiding the story was greater than that of any one screenwriter, and he was present at all the daily script conferences. It was, as he noted, a 'position unique in the entire industry'.[70]

DeMille approached *The Ten Commandments* from the perspective that, since Judaism and Christianity were historical religions, this was to be a history film as well as an inspirational biblical story. Authenticity in the historical background would imbue the religious/supernatural elements with an aura of authority and veracity – conflating religious beliefs with historical truth. Moreover, in dealing with a text that was sacred to both Christians and Jews, DeMille realised that extensive research would also assure audiences that he was approaching the Bible 'with sincerity, integrity and intelligence'.[71]

Noerdlinger's research therefore played an essential role in establishing the integrity of the film and its director. This was particularly important because the first half of the film necessarily involved considerable dramatic invention. The Bible story did not explain what happened to Moses during the 30 years that followed his adoption into the Pharaoh's court, having been discovered as a baby in the bulrushes. Much of Noerdlinger's research was centred on constructing a plausible and documentable account of the young Moses' life, in a manner which would logically conform to the narrative which had to follow – his confrontation with the Pharaoh, the plagues, and the Exodus of the Hebrews. This had to be established 'to the effect that the final result [would] rise above the possible criticism of any one religious group'.[72]

DeMille's strategy for anticipating and disarming this criticism was to lay out Noerdlinger's research for scrutiny, incorporating it into a massive public relations campaign that simultaneously promoted the film. Indeed, given that the producer's name had long been synonymous with spectacular showmanship and extravagant production, DeMille purposefully employed Noerdlinger to enhance this reputation. Noerdlinger, for instance, kept track of the number of books, periodicals, clipping files, maps and prints that he consulted, and appended a list of the libraries and museums he drew upon – ranging from the Beverley Hills Public Library to institutes in

Melbourne and Cairo. This tally was then used to produce a 'Comparison of Amount of Research Material', contrasting *The Ten Commandments* with previous DeMille epics – 1644 publications exceeding the 1113 used for *Samson and Delilah*; 30,390 photographs dwarfing the 11,593 Noerdlinger collected for *Unconquered*.[73] This list then promoted the degree to which the film had been 'authenticated'. In a genre that put a premium on excess, the unprecedented quantity of research on *The Ten Commandments* was raised as a unique selling point.

This, of course, was not a new notion. Publicity departments often produced press releases that highlighted a filmmaker's dedication to authenticity. Publicists at Universal, for example, had considered that *The Black Shield of Falworth* (1954) presented a 'chance to dig up a good feature on the man-hours a…research department will spend on authenticity'.[74] Technical advisors had long been seen to have value in public relations – and Noerdlinger fully understood that he had been employed with an 'overall view of the making and *exploitation* of a motion picture'.[75] However, his association with DeMille and the sheer scale of *The Ten Command-ments* meant that Noerdlinger's pronouncements would have a far greater impact on public consciousness than was usual.

Indeed, the film's research 'bible' itself was published, through the University of Southern California Press, as *Moses and Egypt: The Documen-tation to the Motion Picture 'The Ten Commandments'*. Alan Nadel has rightly described this book as an 'outstanding example of pseudo-history', which 'gathered every possible source without any attempt to authenticate one over the other, to discover points of corroboration, or to reconcile points of contradiction'.[76] But, in fairness to Noerdlinger, he knew it was not a 'history'. As Noerdlinger admitted, DeMille paid for the publication so that it could be distributed 'among the educated clergy, Sunday school teachers, newspaper and magazine editors', and any others who could be expected to lead local public opinion about the movie. *Moses and Egypt* was not designed 'to give full justice to any given subject, but rather to point out what we did in the picture and with what justification'.[77] DeMille's screenwriters had constructed their narrative by drawing on Noerdlinger's research – but *Moses and Egypt* turned the process around, presenting first the script and then detailing, scene by scene, the evidence that now supported the film. In doing so, though, it inadvertently emphasised the constructed nature of the supposedly 'historical' narrative.

Along with *Moses and Egypt*, Noerdlinger put his research to use in defending and publicising *The Ten Commandments* in debates and interviews, scripting speeches for DeMille, and writing letters in response to critical reviews – all the time drawing attention to the research process. The purpose was to impress upon readers and audiences that, while DeMille and his writers '*could* have filled in the missing years of Moses' life with their gifted imagination', their drama was, instead, inferred from valid historical sources. *Moses and Egypt* pointed to sources such as the Midrash Rabbah (an ancient compilation of rabbinic commentaries), the Qu'ran, Philo's *Life of Moses* and the writings of Josephus and Eusebius. Noerdlinger referred to some of these texts – written centuries after the Exodus itself – as 'traditions' rather than 'histories', but argued that they still constituted valid evidence. Josephus and Eusebius in particular suggested that Moses had been made a prince of Egypt who 'conducted a successful campaign…against Ethiopia', and told of court intrigues which might explain the biblical reference to him 'killing the Egyptian'.[78] DeMille's writers used this to set up Moses and Rameses as rival princes, and developed Rameses' jealous hatred of his adopted brother as the root of the later confrontations detailed in Scripture. This was similar to the plot of Dorothy Clarke's romance novel, *The Prince of Egypt*, published in 1949, which already appealed to DeMille. However, when Noerdlinger read Clarke's book, he quickly informed the producer that 'all the elements in it can be established in ancient sources'.[79] Rather than relying on an explicitly fictional text, DeMille was able – and hence encouraged – to infer his drama from the historical record.

With DeMille receptive to this way of thinking, Noerdlinger's ideas further shaped the historical discourse surrounding the film. At an address following the New York premiere, DeMille took the chance to show off his knowledge, explaining how, by process of inference, they had concluded that Moses' adoptive Egyptian mother, Bithiah, must have accompanied him on the Exodus.[80] Carrying the implication that Hollywood's usual standards for historical invention were lacking by comparison, this address was made before the most important members of the film industry establishment. Audiences around the world were also exposed to these arguments, when DeMille appeared on screen at the very beginning of the movie to explain how it had been necessary to 'fill in' the areas of the life of Moses that 'the Holy Bible omits'. The film's trailer highlighted the methodology used to fill these gaps in historical knowledge – making visible the research materials themselves, including copies of Josephus, the Midrash, the Dead

Sea Scrolls and volumes from Chicago's Oriental Institute displayed on DeMille's desk. The trailer went on to raise a multitude of questions: 'Did Sethi find out the Prince of Egypt was a Hebrew slave?'; 'What did Moses do when he learned the truth about himself – that he – a rich and powerful prince was less than the dust beneath the wheels of Pharaoh's chariot?'; 'How did he escape from Egypt – and who gave him sanctuary from Pharaoh's sentence of death.'[81] Of course, the movie itself provided 'the answers'; but by raising these questions, and referring directly to the texts that had been consulted, audiences were made aware of the way in which the narrative was conjectural, and constructed from a variety of sources.

In one of his most pompous pronouncements on the subject, DeMille declared that 'Research does help to bring out of the majesty of the Lawgiver and the eternal verity of the Law'.[82] Yet the detailed promotion of the making of *The Ten Commandments* worked to undermine the notion of 'eternal verity' – at least for History, if not for holy Law. The man most associated in the public mind with Hollywood history had been loudly asserting that history did not simply consist of 'manifest' facts, but was instead something that had to be inferred and constructed from an incomplete factual record. Using Noerdlinger's words, DeMille likened the producer 'to the restorer of a broken mosaic':

> Some parts of the mosaic can be supplied by the historians. The missing parts, the gaps and lacunae...the producer must supply; but the integrity of the whole work demands that what the producer supplies must fit in with what history knows.[83]

While DeMille may only have been paying lip-service to historical integrity, Professor Keith Seele of the Oriental Institute at Chicago (who had given Noerdlinger much advice) recognised that, nevertheless, the processes of historical interpretation had been 'placed before the eyes of millions'.[84] Since Hollywood so consistently presented history as a 'given', Noerdlinger's achievement was all the more important. Most historians would instinctively be more sympathetic towards Gray than Noerdlinger. While Gray resisted efforts to compromise historical evidence, Noerdlinger's public display of his research materials did not really result in a model history film. *The Ten Commandments* is, in contrast to Gray's efforts, full of dialogue that sounds either falsely archaic and portentous, or else laughably modern. It uses costumes and sets that none of the characters appear to have lived in, and retains the constant sense of DeMille showing off his ability to fill the screen with excessive production values that are supposed to signify 'the past'. But Noerdlinger had actually come to conclusions very similar to Gray's about the nature of turning history into drama and, having convinced DeMille of the advantages of being seen to be historically aware, made considerable efforts to improve his understanding. With the help of Professor Seele, he challenged the prevalent idea that one source was as good as another, and persuaded DeMille to appreciate that the 'truth status' of texts was varied.[85] He also railed against Hollywood's misuse of the word 'authenticity', arguing that detailed costumes and props were not, of themselves, authentic, but simply 'adaptations' based on available relics and survivals from the past.[86] Authenticity, he impressed on DeMille, was a goal to strive towards, not something that could be reproduced, especially when 'embellished' by filmmakers who possessed the mind 'of a dramatist and not a scholar'.[87]

As Gray knew from experience, filmmakers who reduced the historical content of films to reproduced detail – 'the filigree of an epoch' – were bound to think of history as dry and dusty in comparison to imagination and fantasy. With encouragement though, some filmmakers – including Kazan, Zimbalist, and even DeMille – could appreciate the dramatic potential in real history when it was made apparent to them. Despite the limitations of his approach, Noerdlinger made a wider audience aware of that potential. For writers and producers who were inspired to think about history in a similar fashion to Gray, Noerdlinger provided proof that, with the right kind of showmanship, they could have historical integrity and still make a profit.

7

Living History

Ah yes! I remember it well.

Honore Lachaille, *Gigi* (MGM, 1958)

In 1952, *The I Don't Care Girl* purported to take audiences behind the scenes of a Hollywood biopic. Producer George Jessel played himself on screen, frustrated by his writers' inability to find a way to tell the story of vaudeville star Eva Tanguay. Sent to interview people who knew and worked with the 'boisterous performer', the scriptwriters gain information about her life from three men, whose reminiscences are presented as flashbacks. Although each man claims that her success began when she met him, they each knew Eva at different stages in her career, and taken together their memories add up to a consistent picture of her rise to stardom.

Despite its obvious self-reflexivity, this was a disingenuous portrait that suppressed the real difficulties faced by Jessel and his writers in explaining Tanguay's life. Since her death in 1947, they had tried a variety of strategies, from the usual 'rags-to-riches' formula, through a focus on her formative years, to Darryl Zanuck's suggestion that, after 11 months of abortive efforts, maybe they actually ought to 'investigate the real true life story'.[1] This revealing comment eventually inspired the treatment by Arthur Ceasar that shaped the final movie. Caesar's original idea was that when the writers conducted their interviews, each of the three men should reject the others' accounts, and claim that they were telling the story 'the way it really was'.[2] However, Zanuck firmly vetoed the showing of 'the same episode told in three different ways, from the viewpoint of three different men'.[3] Despite the precedent of Orson Welles' *Citizen Kane* (1941), Zanuck did not believe that audiences would readily accept the idea that multiple and contradictory perspectives on the past could, and did, co-exist. Rather than question the validity of personal memories or the authority of biography as historical 'truth', the film continued to suggest that the various perspectives of participants would easily add up to a coherent whole.

Biographical history came to play an increasingly important role in Hollywood's thinking about the past – especially when it concerned celebrities like Eva Tanguay whose fame had occurred within living memory. In the 1930s, more than three-quarters of biopics had been concerned with figures separated from audiences and filmmakers by at least a generation – characteristically depicting such historical luminaries as Queen Victoria, Cardinal Richelieu and Marco Polo. In the 1950s, however, Elizabeth I and Joan of Arc found themselves sharing sound stages with the likes of Lon Chaney, Rocky Graziano and Jane Froman, personalities much closer, temporally, to contemporary audiences. Indeed, stories about individuals of recent note came to account for 60 percent of the decade's biographical pictures.[4]

Various factors informed this greater attentiveness to twentieth-century lives. During World War II, filmmakers had turned to combat heroes, such as Alvin York and Eddie Rickenbacker to provide inspirational propaganda. The positive response of audiences ensured that recent military figures continued to exercise a hold on filmmakers' imaginations during the Cold War, resulting in such films as *The Wings of Eagles, The McConnell Story* and *To Hell and Back*.[5] Likewise, a cycle of gangster biopics, including *Al Capone* and *The Bonnie Parker Story*, emphasised the interwar years. But most importantly, George Custen observes that the type of person commemorated in biopics had undergone a change, as 'the entertainer rather than the political leader became the paradigmatic famous figure'.[6] Almost half the decade's biopics featured stars of stage and screen, musicians and athletes – from silent film idol Rudolph Valentino to contemporary golf legend Ben Hogan – which Custen presents as an effort by an insecure industry to promote 'a worldview which justified Hollywood's place' within American popular culture.[7] This gave prominence to modern cultural figures, with 24 out of the 31 popular entertainers commemorated on film having had their original moment of fame within the previous 30 years.

The success of scurrilous scandal sheet *Confidential* was also influential. Its publisher, Robert Harrison, claimed that the televised hearings of the Senate Crime Commission of 1951 had educated Americans 'to the fact that there was excitement and interest in the lives of people in the headlines', and revealed to him how much the public relished stories of contemporary vice. Launched the following year, his magazine spawned dozens of imitators, such as *Behind the Scenes, Uncensored* and *Hush-Hush,* producing an 'endless proliferation of exposé stories' and scandals, many of which related the addictions and sexual peccadilloes of the stars.[8] Hollywood had been using the *chronique scandaleuse* formula for a long time, but primarily to depict the intimacies and intrigues of earlier centuries – *Catherine the Great* (1934), *The Affairs of Cellini* (1934) and *The Private Lives of Elizabeth and Essex* (1939) being prime examples. But when *Confidential*'s circulation reached four million in 1955, Hollywood had turned to depicting recent public figures in a similar tabloid style. Alcoholism blighted the lives of Lillian Roth in *I'll Cry Tomorrow* (1955) and F. Scott Fitzgerald in *Beloved Infidel* (1959). Sex scandals embroiled New York mayor Jimmy Walker in *Beau James* (1957), and Evelyn Nesbit's charms provoked the murder of a leading architect in *The Girl in the Red Velvet Swing*. Drugs (*The Gene Krupa Story*, 1959), abusive relationships (*Love Me or Leave Me*, 1955), delinquency (*Somebody Up There Likes Me*, 1956), and mental breakdown (*Fear Strikes Out*, 1957), all became features of screen lives. And the popularity of these movies only encouraged filmmakers to buy the rights to ever more revelatory biographies.

Whatever the reasons for Hollywood's turn to recent lives, it had an important consequence for the historical consciousness of the industry. More than ever before, filmmakers were compelled to engage with the historical memories of living people. This included the recollections of audiences. The figures in Fifties' biopics were not simply distant characters recalled from vaguely remembered history lessons or books, but were now part of the living memories of many members of the audience. Studios, of course, were counting on this to generate interest in the film. But it also meant that the representation of history in these movies would be tested against personal memories. Moreover, producers, directors and writers now had to work closely with people who had been intimately involved in the events they sought to portray – and who had their own accounts of what happened and why. As David Thelen has observed, 'since people's memories provide security, legitimacy and finally identity in the present, struggle over the possession and interpretation of memories are deep, frequent and bitter'.[9] Many filmmakers were to discover this first-hand.

MEMORY AND HISTORY

Contemporary intellectual analysis of the workings of memory and its relationship to biographical history was deepened in 1950, with the posthumous publication of the work of French sociologist Maurice Halbwachs. Halbwachs argued against Sigmund Freud's assumption that individual memories are inherently personal, suggesting instead that memories are social constructs – reminiscences shaped by, and woven into, an understanding of the past which itself is socially constructed and interpreted.[10] Biography and autobiography commonly demonstrate such a process, wherein an individual's development is related to the historical moments in which their life unfolded.[11] The moments that are recollected, and the forms these memories take, are affected by a sense of their significance, which is itself determined in reference to external signifiers – the way in which an individual memory is recalled depends on the contexts in which we find ourselves and the groups to which we belong.

Halbwach's concept of 'collective memory' built on this observation, to suggest that all individuals carry a 'baggage load of historical remembrances' about events which they never actually witnessed (and never could have done). Consciousness of these events is a 'borrowed' memory, for the historical events have not been personally experienced, but have been read about or heard about, or seen in representational paintings, photographs, newsreels and movies. Occupying part of one's cultural milieu, collective memories remain a vital component of an individual's identity, but need to be affirmed and 'recalled' by others to be sustained, and constantly undergo redescription as the socio-cultural context in which they are recalled continues to change.[12] In this regard, Hollywood's history films both contribute to and draw upon the cultural reservoir of collective memory, representing a moment for 'collective recollection' of the events they supposedly depict.

Unlikely as it is that any filmmaker read Halbwachs, they instinctively understood something of the difficulties and opportunities posed by the contours of collective memory. Director Jean Negulesco used it in trying to sell Zanuck on his cherished ambition to produce *Lust for Life*, by stressing that Vincent Van Gogh 'has become a legend – a popular one', and that his art 'appeals to the masses in every country'.[13] However, in Zanuck's assessment, the collective memory of Van Gogh's life consisted of the artist going mad, cutting off his ear, and committing suicide – which was not, to his way of thinking, a good basis for an effective marketing strategy. In contrast, Zanuck found John Philip Sousa to be a much more promising subject, because American audiences knew the bandleader's compositions but were less aware that Sousa was really 'a rather sedate, dignified, humorless man'. Thus, the makers of *Stars and Stripes Forever* (1952) could get away with rewriting him entirely, provided they included enough familiar marches. Sousa's daughters did not particularly mind either, pleased that Hollywood had made the man as entertaining as his music, thereby retrospectively fashioning a positive collective memory of their late father.[14]

Yet, while this aspect of Halbwach's analysis corresponded with the film industry's experience, the cinematic depiction of historical lives remained wedded to Freud. Given the off-screen obsession with psychoanalysis in Hollywood, this was hardly surprising. It was certainly apparent on screen, for example, in the oedipal analyses offered of *Alexander the Great* by Robert Rossen, and of Billy the Kid in Arthur Penn's *The Left-Handed Gun*; while Nicholas Ray interpreted Jesse James as acting out a death wish. More intriguingly, when it came to questions of memory and biography, Freud's ideas were imbedded in, of all places, the opening scenes of *Singin' in the Rain*.

At the glamorous 1927 premiere of Don Lockwood's silent swashbuckler, the star (played by Gene Kelly) is interviewed by gossip columnist Dora Bailey. When Bailey mentions that 'the story of your success is an inspiration to people all over the world', Lockwood takes the opportunity to recount his stellar career. However, the verbal account that he gives is distinctly at odds with the accompanying visuals. While Lockwood speaks of his immersion in the high culture of dramatic academies and music conservatories, with offers 'pouring in' from film studios, the images depict a far less illustrious ascendancy rooted in vaudeville, burlesque houses and B-movie stuntwork. The disparity between images and words in this sequence apparently confused studio editors, who allegedly spent several weeks 'trying to make the sound and image coincide'.[15] Even if this story is apocryphal, director Stanley Donen evidently expected the visual evidence to be read as the *real* story of Don's rise to stardom, ironically rendering his purported motto – 'Dignity, always dignity' – as vacuous as Bailey's questions. Yet this presumed that audiences would instinctively award greater authenticity to the visual 'recollections', rather than the conscious verbal report.

Freud had explicitly attributed such authenticity to 'recovered memories' – and Don's flashbacks epitomise this idea. According to Freud, the unconscious mind preserves all of life's memories intact, which is why analytical introspection should be able to recover unconscious memories of the past as it was experienced. This unconscious record of memory exists in contrast to the often 'false' memories of the conscious mind, which are partial and continuously revised by the individual to serve present-day needs. In this sense, Don's verbal account is what Freud termed a 'screen memory' – a fictive memory 'projected backward to fill the gaps created by the repression of memories of actual experience'.[16] As Barry Allen suggests, memories recovered from the unconscious possess a 'flashback quality' and 'enjoy a special authenticity as hints at a hidden truth', precisely because they disrupt the conscious version of the past that the individual has constructed as a self-serving narrative.[17] Lockwood's flashbacks perform just such a disruption, and thus acquire a 'truth value' which the audience takes seriously. Moreover, the truth status of the flashback memories is confirmed when they – rather than the phoney 'life story' – prove central to Lockwood's behaviour later in the film. It is Lockwood's background as a song-and-dance vaudevillian that means he is capable of surviving Hollywood's transition to sound, and become a successful musical star; while the fact that he had to work his way up from the bottom provides common ground with Kathy Selden, the aspiring actress whom he comes to love. This corresponds to the presumption of Freudian therapeutic practice that retrieved memories constitute one's real identity, and knowledge of this increases 'one's power to act effectively in the world'.[18]

However, the false memory which Don recounts is not really a recollection from his own consciousness. Just before he begins to speak, a fan is shown clutching a copy of *Screen Digest* magazine, with the headline: 'Lockwood and Lamont: Real-Life or Reel-Life Romance?' His story is one that the studio has invented for him, just as they have fabricated the romance between Don and Lina Lamont to generate publicity. Thus it becomes more than just a contrast between retrieved memory and conscious recollection, but raises questions about the historical record too. The introduction of *Singin' in the Rain* implicitly privileges personal memory over 'official' versions of history which are distorted by present-day concerns. The publicity for the film invoked a similar perspective, stressing that it was 'true' because it was a 'musical born in the reminiscences of producer Arthur Freed'.[19] Freed's first job in Hollywood had been in developing one of the earliest musicals, *Broadway Melody* (1929), and the script for *Singin' in the Rain* was constructed by Betty Comden and Adolph Green from his memories. Moreover, with MGM stalwarts such as costume designer Walter Plunkett, set decorator Edwin Willis and art director Cedric Gibbons working on the film, Comden and Green 'could grill people on their memories and search for relics of those so recent long-gone days'.[20]

Both the film's narrative and its publicity thereby held recovered memory up as a guarantor of historical veracity. Of course, this creates the ironic situation of MGM expecting audiences to believe that the memories it is disseminating within *Singin' in the Rain* are authoritative and 'real', when the memories constructed by the fictional studio within the film itself are shown to be false and expedient. But, however light-heartedly it was treated, the notion that a past reconstructed from living, retrieved, memory is more honest than 'official' written histories was evidently taken for granted by the makers of this film. Yet, at the time *Singin' in the Rain* was being made, this perception was being undermined by the experiences of filmmakers engaged in modern-day biopics.

THIS IS YOUR LIFE

Historians could hardly sue studios over the misrepresentation of Napoleon or Joan of Arc; and in this respect filmmakers were relatively free to ignore historical advisors. But the still-living subjects of modern-day biopics were able to exercise much greater control over the way in which they were remembered. Individuals who had already published autobiographies had, in effect, preselected the elements of their lives deemed 'open' for public consumption. Lillian Roth, for example, had not only exposed in best-selling print her trouble with drink, her four marriages and her suicide attempt, but had also further bared her soul on *This Is Your Life*. This served the filmmakers well on a financial level since public interest in Roth was already engaged and sympathetic. In terms of narrative, however, Roth's multiple marriages caused problems with the Production Code Administration, and also resulted in a highly repetitive script. Yet, the relationships had to be portrayed, because her successful biography also represented a 'subsurface reef' of cultural memory which filmmakers could not challenge.[21] Moreover, any autobiographer had a strong interest in ensuring that Hollywood did not diverge too far from what had already been accepted by the public as his or her 'authentic' life story.

Frequently, therefore, the personalities themselves were intimately involved in the production. Ruth Gordon adapted her own autobiography for George Cukor to film as *The Actress*. Sheila Graham was on set during the production of *Beloved Infidel*, based on her account of her relationship with F. Scott Fitzgerald. Audie Murphy, Jackie Robinson and Bob Mathias went even further, starring as themselves in the movie versions of their lives.[22] Charles Lindbergh, on the other hand, felt secure enough to take a back seat in the making of *The Spirit of St Louis*, because he had sold the rights to the titular book alone, not to his life story. Director Billy Wilder was thus confined to the facts of the historic trans-Atlantic flight and a few flashbacks to Lindbergh's early obsession with flying. Since Lindbergh did not meet his future wife until after the flight, this meant a story without a love interest, and restricted Wilder from referring to the subsequent kidnapping of the 'Lindbergh baby' or the aviator's notorious fascination with the Third Reich. The limits of Lindbergh's published autobiography preserved the 'Lucky Lindy' image he wanted the public to remember, but left Wilder to conjure with only the story of 'a man, sitting alone in a cockpit for thirty-three hours'.[23]

If Wilder found Lindbergh a 'very difficult man to make into a movie hero', it was nothing compared to the problems MGM experienced in telling the story of *Carbine Williams* (1952). While serving a 30-year sentence for the murder of a deputy sheriff who raided one of his moonshine stills in 1921, David Marshall ('Marsh') Williams invented the lightweight M-1 carbine rifle, which was subsequently adopted by the American military for use in World War II. Granted a pardon in 1929, Williams was employed in turn by Winchester, Colt and Remington, and his designs 'revolutionised the munitions industry'.[24] In March 1951, Williams' story had been published in *Reader's Digest*, recounted by the prison governor who had permitted him to build his gun models. Enjoying his subsequent celebrity, Williams sold his own 'true story', describing himself as 'a man who, starting out wrong, paid heavily for a crime he did not commit, and yet had the fortitude to lift himself out of despair and hopelessness and win freedom with his inventive genius'. The gun he created was heralded as 'the handiest little weapon in the world for the close-in fighting our men saw so much of in the South Pacific jungles' – suggesting that in the process of winning his own freedom, Williams had also helped win it for the democratic world.[25] MGM saw cinematic potential in this interpretation of Williams' historical significance and they sent screenwriter William Bowers to Fayetteville, North Carolina, to interview him, his family and friends.

Biographers frequently note the importance of building 'a tie between biographer and source' which 'encourages the flow of feeling and fact'.[26] However, when Bowers met Williams face-to-face, he found it impossible to establish such a rapport. When 'Marsh' defended his illegal activities as

Real Meets Reel: Jean Hagen, Jimmy Stewart and Bobby Hyatt – the stars of *Carbine Williams* (1952) – encounter the real family who inspired the film. David 'Marsh' Williams (centre back) keeps a close an eye on the script, no doubt intrigued to see just what the writers did with his life story. (Courtesy of the British Film Institute)

'merely exercising a right to protection of his private property', and painted himself as 'a pioneer in upholding the civil rights of the people' during Prohibition, Bowers felt disconcerted.[27] At first he believed Williams when he claimed he had not killed the deputy. But then he discovered that Marsh had only been in prison for three months when he and four other inmates plotted to kill another prisoner for 'talking too much'. Bowers came to the conclusion that Williams was a man 'of complete black and whites': 'There are no shadings in his evaluations of events or people. Where the ordinary man might think that a fellow might deserve a poke in the jaw, Marsh would decide he needed a little killing.'[28] No longer believing that Williams' incarceration had been a miscarriage of justice, Bowers began to think that he had only been pardoned because of the military's interest in his inventions.

Prior to their meeting, Bowers had sketched out a liberal character study – one that juxtaposed Williams, the rugged individualist, with Captain Peoples, the cold disciplinarian in charge of the prison. James Stewart's Williams would learn social responsibility from the warden, while his redemption would inspire Wendell Corey's Peoples to challenge the cruelty of the Carolina penal system. As Bowers realised, however, the real Williams expressed no remorse and did not seem to have become a 'reformed character' – and thus failed to fit the stereotype that Bowers had derived from numerous other prison films. Instead the writer tried to apply other biopic clichés. Observing that 'at an age when other children would be perfectly satisfied with the possession of a cap pistol, Marsh felt the necessity for a gun that really worked', Bowers tried to convince himself that this could be explained 'by the young Thomas Edison theme of inquisitiveness'.[29]

Bowers hoped to develop this theme in conversation with the people who knew Williams best. Yet, Peoples offered no new insights, and Williams' wife, Maggie, was too accustomed to 'years of defending Marsh' to be of much help. Leon Williams, the inventor's younger brother, impressed Bowers as 'one of the few men in the world who can analyze Marsh openly, to his face, and get away with it', and the writer wanted to spend more time with Leon in discussion of Williams' relationship with his parents, evidently shifting towards a psychological interpretation of his subject. However, such discussion was cut short because 'Marsh was always hanging around to try and make sure we heard only the things he wanted us to hear'. In the end, Bowers admitted defeat: 'I have simply been unable to fathom the correct, underlying, true motivation... His nature seems incomprehensible even to people who have known him from childhood.'[30]

In June of 1951, Bowers passed his material on to a new writer, Art Cohn. Cohn thought he could use Maggie to voice Bowers' concerns about Williams' obsession, characterising her as one who 'misinterprets Marsh's preoccupation with guns in prison as another outlet for his violence'. The film would then correct this, with an interpretation based on Cohn's own impressions of Williams:

> To comprehend Marsh's nature, and its fundamental simplicity, one must observe the loving care with which he handles his guns. Here his true sensitivity comes out. When you see the artistry of his work, the painstaking efforts that went into the guns he made...the true character of the man unfolds.[31]

Yet, in casting Williams as 'sensitive' at heart, Cohn came up against a further problem. Following his release from prison, Marsh had continued to live apart from his wife and son, spending ten years working for the Winchester Arms Company at New Haven. Cohn therefore scripted a framing device, in which Marsh's son fights with kids who taunt him about his father's past. Fearing that his son is embarking on a similar path of delinquency to his own, Marsh asks Peoples to tell the boy his story 'as seen through impartial eyes'.[32] This idea was suggested by the pronouncement in Williams' autobiographical article, which he was writing 'because of my boy'.[33] Cohn's story would then end with the family's reconciliation as Marsh accepts the responsibilities of fatherhood. Unfortunately, Cohn soon found out that his protagonist had actually spent his wealth maintaining 'a 22-room mansion and an apartment, the latter under an assumed name, to facilitate simultaneous liaisons with two mistresses', while Maggie was left alone 'raising Marsh Junior back home in North Carolina'.[34] Having originally insisted that 'we do not have to invent' or 'dramatize' anything in Williams' life, Cohn belatedly understood that, in order to achieve 'an upbeat ending', they would have to 'ignore Marsh's actual neurosis'.[35]

Richard Blum suggests that the central 'hazards' in developing biographies lie in 'accepting a wrong or oversimplified hypothesis about what the subject is like', and 'the human tendency to assume that consistency exists in personality and that harmony is therefore required in biography'.[36] Bowers and Cohn fell into both traps, and the complications involved in writing *Carbine Williams* stemmed largely from this. Certainly they were trying to make Williams' life fit the 'highly conventionalised strategies' of the Hollywood biopic genre, but their problems were not simply the result of a formulaic historical consciousness. Their growing knowledge of Marsh as a person, conflicted with the 'authoritative' version of history that Williams himself had put into the public domain via autobiographical articles and interviews. Williams' own account suggested that he had learned his lesson, that he had been changed by his time in prison and his success in inventing something that had been of benefit to society. Williams had emplotted his life onto a neat, idealised narrative of redemption – and when Bowers and Cohn discovered that there had been no such redemption, they saw how self-serving his autobiographical accounts were. Yet, they could not tell the 'truth', partly because the public already thought they knew Marsh's 'life story', and partly because Williams necessarily had to protect his own version. And so Cohn returned to the tried-and-tested formulae of biopics that typically create characters that are 'level, decent, and unmarred by the obsessiveness of real artists, scientists or statesmen'.[37] Ultimately Cohn wrote the story of what should have happened to Williams if he had been more like Jimmy Stewart. The *Variety* review, which accused the screenplay of failing to make Marsh 'any more than a very ordinary fellow', ironically confirmed the 'success' of Cohn's efforts.[38]

'THE AUDIENCE DOESN'T KNOW WHAT WE KNOW'

When prior biographies did not exist, the work of screenwriters was more akin to being an 'authorised' biographer for contemporary celebrities. Ghostwriter Margot Strickland notes that in her experience, the writer 'is inevitably fettered, not to the truth as he sees it, but to an economy with the truth, to satisfy the big name and his view of himself'. Problems arise when the subject tries 'to exclude material damaging to him, or include trivial episodes which vain-glorify him'.[39] In Hollywood, however, economies with the truth were rarely the problem – rather the main concern of biopic writers was that accommodating the subject's 'view of himself' might compromise the dramatic story that they intended to impose upon the life of that 'big name'. Thus, in the early stages of developing a film biography, writers sought to impress firmly in the minds of their subjects that certain liberties would have to be taken.

Everett Freeman stressed this from the moment work began on the biopic of *Jim Thorpe – All American* (1951), telling the former Olympian that 'to create a picture of merit, I must be able to fictionalize and dramatize freely'.[40] The famed Native American athlete had won both the Pentathlon and Decathlon in 1912, but had been stripped of his medals for having once played professional baseball while at college. Frustrated in his ambitions, and ultimately embittered by the death of a son, Thorpe retired in 1928 and sank into personal and financial decline.[41] Freeman developed his screenplay in conjunction with Douglas Morrow, who had recently scripted the highly successful sports biopic *The Stratton Story* (1949), and cast Burt Lancaster in the title role. Their script sentimentalised Thorpe's life, treating him as a victim of circumstances, and somewhat naïve because his upbringing on the Sac and Fox reservation had sheltered him from the complexities of the 'white' world. His decline was only dealt with briefly at the end of the film, allowing him to bounce back with a positive attitude about the future.

Sadly, Thorpe's recovery in the film was entirely fictitious. As Lancaster recalled, 'his life had gone to pot'.[42] After one year of playing major league baseball, Jim drifted in and out of various sporting contracts, drank heavily, had been divorced and remarried twice, and had found occasional work in the 1930s playing Indians in Hollywood westerns. In 'pretty dire financial straits', he was reduced to working as a bouncer. Freeman made an unsuccessful bid to have Jim's medals returned, drafting letters for Thorpe to send to the American Olympic Committee, in an effort to concoct a 'real' happy ending.[43] When this failed, Morrow had to convince Warner Bros. executives that the depressing reality would not affect the film:

> You said something yesterday about Jim still being a bum. Maybe he is... I have tried to keep as uncynical about Jim as possible... The audience doesn't know what we know concerning his intimate personal life; they will only know what we tell them. And we can only tell them something if we ourselves assume, even temporarily, a greater sincerity of feeling regarding the fictitious construction in the second part of the film.[44]

However, the fiction was threatened by the 'troublesome nature' of Jim's third wife. Because of their financial problems, Patricia Thorpe desperately needed to capitalise on the film's publicity, and arranged all sorts of personal appearances and endorsements for Jim which even she recognised were incongruous (especially those for Lucky Strike cigarettes).[45] She also put pressure on Warner Bros. for greater compensation. Freeman did contract Thorpe as a 'technical advisor' on his own life, at $250 a week for the duration of the production, but Patricia had some justification for believing that the studio was taking advantage of her husband. Having sold his life story to MGM in 1931 for $1500, Jim technically did not have to be paid again in 1949 when Warner bought the rights directly from MGM. When Jack Warner received a stinging letter from Robert F. Kennedy deploring the 'monetary arrangements with Mr Thorpe as extreme a case of exploitation as we have ever heard', it was evident that Mrs Thorpe had been using her sob-story to great effect.[46] Patricia also tried to intimidate Freeman, blustering that she could 'drop the Warner Bros. deal completely and come way out ahead'.[47]

Indeed, at one stage, she threatened to sue to the studio if they 'deviate[d] from fact in any way'.[48] Her objections, though, were not entirely motivated by the need to see her husband get over 'the financial hump'. Because this was to be the first biography presented to the public, the Thorpes perceived Freeman as a ghostwriter. They could not understand why he was not relying more on Jim's memories. 'Going off half-cocked on information which is proving to be inaccurate, is going to make a mess of the Thorpe story,' complained Patricia. 'If that is the way Warners make a documentary film, why bother calling it the Thorpe Story, why not just John Doakes?'[49] Her belief that the studio was making a documentary was at odds with Hollywood's conception of biopics. Moreover, her outspoken presence was undermining Freeman's efforts. He feared that an interview Patricia had given to the *Los Angeles Examiner* about their hard times 'makes you and Jim out as avaricious characters'. 'These things appearing in print,' he warned, 'do not tally with the character we are trying to portray on the screen.' More significantly, in attempting to 'place Jim in a more sympathetic light', Freeman had fictionalised his domestic life – and Patricia's very existence was proving a problem. 'Since our film version only involves one wife in Jim's life,' noted the anxious writer, 'these statements coming from a third wife are going to make us appear ridiculous.'[50]

Freeman and Morrow had not been substantially constrained by the public memory of Thorpe, who was generally remembered for his Olympic triumph and subsequent scandal, and his Native American heritage. But to ensure that audiences accepted the biopic as 'authentic', the studio had to make sure that the real details of Thorpe's life were not widely known before the movie's release. They apparently succeeded. Five months after the film hit cinemas, Jim underwent surgery for cancer of the lip and it was only then that the media became aware of his destitute state.[51] After the struggle to contain this, Freeman must have been wryly amused when reviewers found that *Jim Thorpe – All American* possessed 'an honesty of handling felt all the way'.[52]

Ultimately, Patricia Thorpe's influence was limited because Jim had sold the rights to his story 20 years earlier. But other filmmakers faced wives who could exercise greater control as 'custodians' of their husbands' memories. In the case of *The Glenn Miller Story*, for example, the band-leader's widow was particularly concerned to protect her husband's reputation. The press dramatically pictured Helen Miller as being 'besieged' at her home in Pasadena by 'every studio in Hollywood'.[53] She certainly rejected many offers, contending that 'the scripts had not given sufficient acknowledgement to her husband's serious musicianship'. She did not want him to be remembered simply as 'a successful record seller'.[54]

Biographers are often confronted with such a 'widow's cloak', and it firmly influenced the screenplay which Valentine Davies developed for Universal.[55] Davies and producer Aaron Rosenberg addressed Helen Miller's concerns directly, with a 'blueprint' for a biopic which would eschew 'the conventional screen treatment which…sprinkles isolated musical numbers at regular intervals' and 'arbitrarily divides story from music'. Instead, 'because music was such an integral part of Glenn Miller's life', the narrative would be told as a 'quest' – the 'search for a new sound' that had existed only in Miller's mind.[56] In showing him achieve this sound, Miller's imprint on modern music would be acclaimed. This angle, com-bined with Rosenberg's ability to acquire the services of James Stewart – whom Helen had always wanted to play Glenn – secured the rights for Universal, provided they followed the treatment 'substantially in form and taste'.[57]

During writing and production, Helen Miller remained a regular presence at the studio – along with many of Glenn's associates, such as Ben Pollack, Don Hayes, Wilbur Schwartz and Chummy McGregor, all of whom lived in Southern California. Publicity put a positive spin on this, noting that 'one thing we didn't lack on this story was the availability of help on research. With so many members of his band still alive, we were able to recreate his life virtually down through the years.'[58] Jimmy Stewart apparently found this of value, drawing his portrayal from 'a dozen qualified informants on the appearance, habits, eccentricities, character and philo-sophy of Glenn Miller'.[59] Officially, it also benefited Davies, but in an article entitled 'An Author Who Found Six Characters' (referencing the satire on theatrical realism by Luigi Pirandello), he indicated that he was 'startled' by the presence of the very people he was trying to write about. As McGregor, Hayes 'and especially Helen Miller' frequently came in to read pages of the script as they were coming off the typewriter, they were apparently 'somewhat amazed to learn exactly what they had said many years ago'. This 'disturbed' Davies, who echoed Freeman's plea that he needed to be free to fictionalise:

> As I pointed out, it is not only a screenwriter's task to tell faithfully the story of a man's life – it is also his job to make a screen story that will absorb the interest of an audience and move it to a sympathetic identification with the lead characters. To achieve this, even in the case of as promising a subject as Glenn Miller, would require a considerable amount of artistic elbow room. And to be confined by the details of the exact facts as recalled by those involved, I was afraid, would magnify the difficulties of my job immeasurably.

This article, intended for publicity purposes, went on to state that Davies' 'fears were short-lived', because those involved were 'no newcomers to the world of entertainment' and understood his perspective.[60] However, in

The Widow's Cloak: The real Helen Miller checks the details as Jimmy Stewart prepares to play her late-husband in *The Glenn Miller Story* (1953). Scenarist Valentine Davies privately admitted that her constant presence had made the film 'a very difficult one to write'. (Courtesy of the Academy of Motion Pictures Arts and Sciences)

private correspondence, Davies told a different story, confessing that the film had really been 'a very difficult one to write' because Helen *et al* 'were constantly at my elbow'.[61]

Director Anthony Mann felt similarly constrained, unhappy with the film's 'sentimentality and banality', but showing 'little taste for a battle over the agreed-upon script' with 'Helen Miller hovering around'.[62] One important consequence of her presence, however, was clear in the characterisation of Helen herself, as played by June Allyson. Acknowledging that Helen's memories furnished him with the basis for numerous scenes and dialogue that he used 'almost word for word', Davies cast her as Glenn Miller's muse and inspiration.[63] In one instance, Glenn composes 'Little Brown Jug' for her, in spite of the fact that Bill Finegan actually wrote the arrangement.[64] Moreover, it is Helen who thinks about the future, and secretly saves up enough money so that when Glenn wants to start his own band, he has the funds immediately available. And it is Helen who constantly pushes him to find his sound. All the 'drive' that a man like Miller must have possessed is projected on to her instead. As a result, the 'memory' of Glenn produced by the film was one that greatly satisfied her. The portrayal developed by Davies and Stewart did not simply conform to Helen's personal memories, but also defined the image of Glenn Miller she wanted to impress on the public collective memory – recreating the bandleader as an artist untainted by worldly ambition.

'FORGED FROM FALSE RECOGNITIONS'

The experiences involved in such biopics increasingly suggested that memories, and the histories based upon them, could be untrustworthy, fractious, and already as sanitised as Hollywood's biopics were often accused of being. Directors and writers frequently encountered versions of history which they knew not to be true, while finding that the public figures involved either acquiesced, or actually insisted on the 'facts' being rewritten, as long as the film presented them as they wanted to be remembered. Resultant movies were therefore often literal screen memories – whole films like Don Lockwood's verbal life story.

Freud's contention had been that 'real' history – as experienced – was recoverable, for the truth was preserved in 'deep memory'. One strand of contemporary historiography was certainly in alignment with this. R.G. Collingwood, for instance, had argued that the 'past as it was experienced' *could* be recovered, if historians were capable of recreating 'the imagination of the past' and aimed to understand the events, actions and thoughts of people in their own historical moment. For Collingwood, the key question in history was how did people in the past derive the meaning of their lives?[65] But, for those involved in the making of biopics, it was increasingly clear that people were forever reinterpreting and rewriting their own place in history, which made it all but impossible to truly 'recreate' historical experiences.

Thus the publicity of *The Glenn Miller Story* and narratives like *The I Don't Care Girl* knowingly communicated a false image of the construction of biography. And as the 1950s progressed, the scale of biopic production made the tensions relating to subjective interpretations of the past far more prominent and difficult to ignore. Some strains were alleviated after 1955 when, following *Confidential*'s lead, biopic writers no longer felt so compelled to suppress information about the less savoury aspects of their subjects' lives. More cynical attitudes towards fame and celebrity were reflected in Jose Ferrer's production of *The Great Man* (1956) – a sour satire in which Ferrer's character prepares a eulogistic memorial show for a popular national commentator who has just died. Despite being well loved by 150 million viewers, the collective memory of him is a false image. No one who really knew the man has a good word to say about him – the star was a 'despicable phony', whose 'feet of clay' extended 'right up to the knees, at least'. By the late Fifties, scepticism about the reliability of memories – both collective and personal – had grown, and six years after *Singin' in the Rain*, another musical comedy placed the uncertainty of biographical history at the very centre of its narrative.

Sol Seigel's production of *Les Girls* (1957) concerned the fallout from the publication of a 'spicy' autobiography by retired chorus girl Sybill Wren. Her former colleagues in the 'Les Girls' show – Angele Ducros, Joy Henderson and dancer Barry Nichols – meet again when they present evidence at a trial for libel. Sybill is being sued for claiming that Angele had once attempted suicide when Nichols rejected her love for him. Under oath, both Wren and Ducros assert that their testimony represents events 'exactly as I remembered it', and thus equate personal remembrance with the truth. According to Sybill, Angele kept both her career and her romance with Nichols a secret from her fiancé, Pierre Ducros. When she unexpectedly saw Pierre in the audience one night, Angele panicked and spoilt the show – resulting in a violent row with Nichols. When Sybill returned to their shared apartment later that night, Angele was lifeless on the bed, having apparently tried to gas herself. This, however, is flatly contradicted by Angele's recollection. Her claim is that Sybill was frequently too drunk to perform. In an effort to protect her friend, Angele had told Nichols that Sybill was 'hopelessly in love' with him, and drank to console herself. Sybill's love for Nichols was then finally requited – much to the discomfort of her fiancé, Gerald Wren – until Angele's white lie was uncovered, and Nichols fired Sybill in anger. It was then Angele who found Sybill trying to kill herself in the gas-filled apartment.

As in *Singin' in the Rain*, these memories were presented as flashbacks – but the fact that these accounts are clearly irreconcilable disrupts the assumption that flashbacks represent the 'truth' of lived experience as recorded in memory. Reflecting the tenacity of that perception of memory, the judge automatically assumes that one of the women must be lying. Charges of perjury are only avoided when Nichols himself arrives to testify. He asserts that he had actually been in love with *Joy* – and plotted with Gerald and Pierre to break up the act, so that each of them could marry the girl they loved. But on the night that Les Girls disbanded, it was Nichols who found *both* Angele and Sybill unconscious in their room. Neither had tried to commit suicide, but had simply been overcome by a gas leak from a broken heater. Since the group had split, the girls never compared stories and had therefore mistakenly formed their own conclusions. Because Nichols' account rests on things that actually 'happened' but that 'neither of the girls knew about', the court accepts that his testimony restores the connection between 'true' memory and lived experience. The 'ideology of truth' is not questioned, because each of the characters told the truth in so far as they knew it, but their knowledge was partial.[66] Recourse to the memories of other participants enables a complete and consistent account of lived history to be constructed. This, then, suggests a return to the Freudian-historicist faith that we have the capacity to recover accurately the memory of all human experiences.

However, the audience is encouraged not to accept this conclusion quite as readily as the court does. As Nichols leaves the hearing, Joy – now his wife – points out that his account may explain the confusion over the suicide attempts, but not the fact that both Sybill and Angele fervently believed that he loved the other. Nicholls – played by Gene Kelly – simply shrugs off the illogic with a mock-innocent grin. Yet the fact remains that the combined memories of Les Girls clearly do not add up to the satisfactory coherent whole that is both accepted by the court and promoted by other films (*The I Don't Care Girl* in particular) as being the inevitable outcome of collective recollection. Instead, it draws attention to the artifice involved in autobiographical recollection – indicating the effort of authors to find, impose and invent patterns to explain character and behaviour in order to form a consistent story.[67] Moreover, the visual evidence presented in their flashbacks includes things that the testifier could not actually have observed. Each girl's testimony includes images of Nichols' clandestine dates with the other chorine, and Sybill is definitely not a witness to the row between Angele and Barry that she recalls. When this point is raised by the prosecutor, Sybill responds that she is repeating events 'as Angele repeated them to me', and further notes that Joy had told her of Pierre's presence in the audience on the fateful night.

This directly aligns *Les Girls* with Halbwachs, rather than Freud, in the debate over the nature of memory and history. As the sociologist noted, 'many of the remembrances that we believe genuine, with an identity beyond doubt, are almost entirely forged from false recognitions, in accordance with others' testimony and stories'.[68] By the end of the trial, a 'collective memory' has been formed, which erases the 'idiosyncrasies' of the individual memories that have been presented – conforming precisely to the workings of social memory as Halbwachs described them. This collective memory, moreover, has been accorded authoritative status by the court, which has accepted it as true, and thus, by extension, as historically accurate. However, this 'official history' is undermined by our awareness that it does not fully correspond with the 'past as it actually happened'. The collective memory remains an incomplete account of historical experience, with only a limited ability to explain the past.

Thus, by the conclusion of *Les Girls*, at least three ideas had been raised which were anathema to Hollywood's traditional imaging of autobiographical memory. It was acknowledged that memories are not fixed but malleable: to incorporate the new knowledge that Nichols provides, the individual memories of the girls would have to be refashioned – 'retrospectively redescribed' – to deal with their revised comprehension of past experience. Remembrance was also shown to be an explicitly imaginative process, and the narratives of individuals are clearly identified as self-serving constructs – including Nichols' version, since his assertion that he 'only had eyes for Joy' remains irreconcilable with the recollections of the other girls. And because of this, the realities of the past still remain elusive – which suggests that the 'truth' cannot be recovered solely through recollection, conscious or unconscious. Overall, the film might even prompt audiences to consider that 'several appropriate explanations may *viably* exist for the same phenomenon'.[69]

Indeed, many filmmakers had come to experience the discord in individual memories made apparent by the existence of multiple perspectives on any one event – an observation which itself is a crucial stimulus to genuine historical inquiry. To privilege the autobiographical memory of one historian for a moment, Daniel Gordon recalls that following his parents' divorce, he was exposed to not only different, but 'mutually contradictory' accounts of 'what really happened' when the marriage deteriorated – and thus he developed an 'acute awareness that the reports about the past that circulate in [a person's] immediate milieu cannot all be true'. 'From this discordance,' writes Gordon, 'comes the awareness that the past can be understood only through a critique of the available sources, and through a method that is not held hostage by the self-serving memories of the participants.'[70] Although filmmakers rarely engaged in evaluating historical sources, this sort of 'epiphany' – brought on by contact with Helen Miller, Marsh Williams, *et al* – could certainly explain the fissures present in *Les Girls*, and suggest why Hollywood's project of presenting biopics as a 'tidy genre...of success parables, touched by an aura of historical sanctity', was increasingly difficult to sustain.[71]

Intellectual History

A world full of ignorant people is too dangerous to live in.

Paul Verall, *Born Yesterday* (1950)

Intelligence! Nothing has caused the human race so much trouble as intelligence.

Stella, *Rear Window* (1954)

In *Blackboard Jungle* (1955), the jaded Jim Murdock introduces himself by declaring that he is 'making money under the false pretence of teaching history'. In a school dominated by delinquent youth, he asserts that the crucial lesson to be learned from history is 'Don't turn your back' on the enemy. Murdock's acerbic asides provide some humour in the often bleak narrative of the film, but associating this character with the teaching of history was a deliberate decision on the part of the filmmakers at MGM. It departed from Evan Hunter's original source novel in which the character who derides the 'garbage can of the educational system' teaches an engineering course, while the history teacher is actually an affable 'eager beaver' who believes in the students.[1] Suggestions as to why this transposition occurred can only be speculative, but it was not an isolated example of antipathy towards historians. Despite Hollywood's unprecedented level of interest in history, the image of historians, both professional and amateur, in the movies themselves was profoundly negative. Dana Polan, who has examined this representation in general terms, notes that the profession's

173

own 'traditional conception of itself as a lofty transmission of the truths of history' has often been 'at variance with the image that novels and films present' – but in the 1950s, the disparity reached an extreme.[2]

Members of the contemporary American historical profession were certainly concerned about their public image. The 'old and chronic' complaint that historians were 'failing a waiting public by making history dull, jejeune, and overly specialised' was frequently revived.[3] Allan Nevins observed that since history 'as written in our universities' had become 'compartmented into many specialities, economic, constitutional, social, political and intellectual', it had 'lost the large public authority it once possessed'.[4] This concern was strengthened by surveys such as W. Stull Holt's 1954 analysis of 'Who Reads the Best Histories?' which drew the 'disturbing conclusion' that academic texts were not only ignored by the general public, but neither were they being read by most professional historians. 'Scholarly history' was only being written 'by specialists for a small fraction of the specialists.'[5] Although the phenomenon was not exactly new, Holt's data fed the anxieties of many academics who desired to reconnect with the lay public. Key figures, like Nevins, exhorted colleagues to write with 'erudition, enthusiasm, clarity and brilliance', so that history might serve the needs of 'the great mass of the people'.[6] As president of the American Historical Association in 1950, Conyers Read explicitly blamed the situation on the 'little pedants' of the academic world who lacked the 'courage to attempt history in the grand manner'.[7]

Hollywood's perspective, however, was somewhat different. Given that filmmakers usually only dealt with historians when asking for advice on visual minutiae, or when receiving letters of complaint about 'distortion', it would be understandable had they represented historians as such pedants, working on esoteric subjects detached from public interest. But in the films that were explicitly critical of historians, this was not the case. Murdock is certainly incapable of 'reaching' the students of *Blackboard Jungle*, but it is his world-weary scepticism, rather than pedantry, that proves debilitating. *The Bad and the Beautiful* (1952) chose to chastise its history professor for lack of experience in the 'real world'. *The Charge at Feather River* (1953) and *Jupiter's Darling* (1955) presented historians as frauds who corrupt the historical record – while *Witness to Murder* (1954) took this to ever more disturbing lengths, depicting a respected historian as a psychopathic neo-Nazi, adept at covering both his own crimes and those of the Third Reich. American historians may have feared that the image of the professoriat as 'dry-as-dust' and nit-picking lay at the heart of the distance between them and the public – but this was not what filmmakers were suggesting. The antipathy displayed on the screen clearly had more complex roots.

AN IMPORTANT PUBLIC SERVICE

In fact, the depiction of academics as obscurantists was militated against because pedantic detail actually mattered a great deal to history filmmakers for whom 'authenticity was a must'. Most presented the accumulation of visual material, rather than the interpretation of evidence, as the guarantor of accuracy and the standard by which their product should be judged. Indeed, when promoting their films, a number of producers displayed an aspiration to be regarded as 'popular historians', and suggested that their dedication to detail matched the way in which professionals approach historical research. Frank McCarthy, for instance, spoke of the 'sleuthing' he undertook to find original 'props' and artefacts for *Decision Before Dawn* (1951) in order to 'reconstruct the last days of the war in Germany'.[8] Robert Rossen had 'painstakingly read through all those ancient writers who speak of Alexander the Great, as well as the works of modern writers', until he had unravelled 'the maze of often contradictory statements' and made sense of 'the mysterious and often controversial personality of his hero'.[9]

Independent producer Nat Holt was even more adamant that, in conjunction with screenwriter and novelist Frank Gruber, the history films he made were equivalent to new works of scholarship, representing the past 'as it really was'. For *Denver and the Rio Grande* (1952) Gruber apparently spent two months undertaking 'preparatory research' for his account of the building of the railroad through the Colorado Mountains, and amassed '150 pages of notes, over 4000 miles of flying, and a score of curious facts about the travel and travail west of the Mississippi'. This was allegedly derived from archival material that historians had not yet made use of: 'stacks of records, photographs and correspondence that had lain forgotten for years'.[10] Similar 'little-known records, correspondence and newspaper accounts' were drawn upon for Holt's production of *The Great Missouri Raid* (1951), in a purported attempt to 'present the first true account' of the story of Frank and Jesse James – which up until Holt's movie was supposedly more 'garbled and misunderstood' than any other 'epic in history'. *The Great Missouri Raid* was no mere film but 'the most authentic history of America's most sought-after outlaws' – a historical interpretation that supplanted all previous accounts and thus performed 'an important public service'.[11]

Never one to be outdone, DeMille not only published his 'research' for *The Ten Commandments* as if it was a serious work of scholarship, but even presented himself as qualified to deliver a public seminar. Addressing the audience of *The Buccaneer* in an on-screen introduction, he asked them to 'bear with me' since 'it may increase the enjoyment of the picture you are about to see, if you know why Jean Lafitte and his little island stronghold of Barataria...was so important to both sides of the War of 1812'. The subsequent lecture came complete with maps and a pointing stick.

This aggrandisement of the educational value of history films was encouraged by the industry's president, Eric Johnston, who counted such movies as among Hollywood's 'most valuable programs' – dramatising 'the great historical movements which have shaped the destiny of the world', and the lives of 'the great figures who have led mankind'.[12] The federal government itself agreed. A State Department report in 1953 applauded the 'day-to-day contributions of films to education', particularly with regard to 'History recreated on the Screen' – and saw propaganda value in disseminating abroad this 'American interpretation of life and the world'.[13] Cold War imperatives evidently contributed to the credit given to Hollywood's versions of history.

This elevation, however, implicitly denigrated academic histories. Not only were filmmakers as capable of constructing the past (or 'reconstructing', as they usually preferred) by the methods presumed to be employed by professional historians, they were more adept at making their histories interesting and relevant. Filmmakers did not have to directly charge historians with being 'little pedants' – it was implicit in most every history film they made. Publicity material repeatedly referred to 'the pages of history' and 'the chapters of history' from which the movies were 'torn' and 'brought to life'.[14] According to such stock phrases, history, when confined to books, did not 'come alive' as it did on the cinema screen. When Walt Disney claimed that in making *Johnny Tremain* he had 'transformed history into sparkling film fare', he did not mean that he had transformed 'the past' but rather 'history-as-written-by-historians' – which self-evidently was in sore need of his animating powers.[15] The introduction of 3-D and CinemaScope only led filmmakers to make even stronger claims about their abilities.

In this respect, 'pedantry' in detailed research was less of a problem for the image of academia than the emphasis that contemporary historians placed on 'abstract ideas' and 'impersonal pressures' as forces in historical explanation. In 1954, the founders of *American Heritage* magazine warned that history was too often 'presented in terms of vast incomprehensible forces moving far under the surface, carrying human beings along, helpless, and making them conform to a pattern whose true shape they never see'.[16] The post-war approach to historical writing in academia – classed by John Higham as the 'consensus' school or paradigm – concieved of history in terms of complex problems and impersonal socio-economic forces, 'deflating' the 'dramatic moments' of history, instead of 'paint[ing] America in the bold hues of conflict'.[17] 'Increasingly we present history,' wrote Henry Steele Commager, 'as a series of headaches – not the story of Westward movement, but the "problem of the frontier", not the winning of independence but the "problem of imperial organization", not the spectacle...but "the problem of social reform"'.[18]

Hollywood, however, continued to present history in precisely the form of stories, movement, victories and spectacle – and made conflict, not consensus, central to the drama of the past. In many ways filmmakers were producing material akin to the history in the school textbooks of their youth. David Saville Muzzey's *American History* (first printed in 1911 and retitled *A History of Our Country* in 1936) dominated American historical education for nearly half a century, and was still selling strong in the 1950s. Muzzey portrayed history as 'a personal matter', in which the main actors were not 'institutions or social forces' but individual leaders, acting 'as free agents, whose vices and virtues determined the course of history'. He drew heavily on theatrical images, depicted heroes and villains 'each of whom had his own intrinsic image as a person', and clearly 'saw history as a series of terrific dramas'. As Hollywood put human agency (in the form of actors) at the centre of historical narratives, so Muzzey provided 'many wonderful stories', which – as Frances Fitzgerald notes in her study of history textbooks – could easily have been 'a piece of movie scriptwriting'.[19]

Yet, while *American Heritage* proposed emulating this in order to regain the 'large public authority' that nineteenth-century historians like George Bancroft and J.L. Motley had possessed, the profession was divided over the intellectual value of a return to 'grand narrative' histories. The popularity of the 1947 abridgement of Arnold Toynbee's *A Study in History* suggested that a desire for 'large-scale panoramic history' still existed, but in the face of the Cold War, few contemporary historians were as enamoured of the 'conception of all human history as a single story, uniting past and future into coherent meaning'.[20] As 'the dominant position of the United States in the world quickly revealed the limits of its power', many historians, including Richard Hofstadter and C. Vann Woodward, preferred to fashion an 'ironic' interpretation of history that undercut the 'romance' of American progress and destiny associated with grand narrative.[21] Moreover, in contrast to the anxieties of Read and Nevins, the majority of contemporary historians were content not to court the popular market. Indeed, 'to write solely for one's fellow historians could be a kind of liberation', since the pressure to write 'popular' history had often been seen as 'contaminating' the pursuit of objectivity, getting in the way of studying 'the past for its own sake'. But, if many American historians no longer aimed to 'achieve a dominant position in providing history for the general reading public', this only encouraged filmmakers like Holt and DeMille to pose as new and more effective aspirants to that role.[22]

'YOU'RE NOT LIKE THE BOOKS!'

In trying to appropriate the mantle of historians for Hollywood filmmakers, the discourse surrounding history films challenged the 'prestigious place' that academics occupied in what Foucault refers to as 'the economy of knowledge'.[23] As Iwona Irwin-Zarecka notes, 'historians are often granted a special status as those with the strongest claims to the truth of the "this really happened" kind'.[24] The American public at large might not have questioned the authority of professional historians; but filmmakers did have reason to question the status accorded to academic versions of history, as they made so many history films and became aware (however superficially) of the problems inherent in constructing accounts of the past. Indeed, if they absorbed any of their own publicity, some might well have concurred with Foucault that 'there is nothing more to the difference between knowledge and ignorance than authority'.[25]

This perception was evidenced in a handful of films featuring subplots that questioned the sources of historical knowledge and the validity of the historical record. In *The Charge at Feather River*, for instance, the exploits of 'The Guardhouse Brigade' are recorded for posterity by a sketch-artist, Grover Johnson, who (according to the script) 'considers it a duty to portray the Indian fighting soldier as he really is'.[26] After Johnson's death in the eponymous charge, the last frames of the movie focus on the images in his sketchbook, as if suggesting that his work survived and contributed to histories of the events depicted in the film itself. Yet, serious doubt is cast on the reliability of this source. Johnson is introduced sketching Colonel Kilrain in his office, with the subject seen sitting astride a saddle perched on a wooden sawhorse, dressed in his uniform and hat, and flourishing his sabre. Captain Archer enters and observes the scene with incredulity, which only increases when he looks at Johnson's sketch and sees that the artist has depicted the colonel riding a fierce charger into battle against screaming and savage Indians. As the audience then realises, the account of the 'Indian fighting soldier' that Johnson is sending back to the East coast for publication is one derived from his imagination, not from reality. Declaring that director Gordon Douglas was a 'student of the pioneer west' and a 'stickler for accuracy', publicity implied that his filmic representation of history was much more realistic (and enhanced by 3-D) than the 'false' images that previous generations had relied upon.[27]

The Left-Handed Gun similarly suggested that those who originally recorded the past were not always trustworthy. Arthur Penn's film, based on a television play by Gore Vidal, was concerned with the creation of 'the legend of Billy the Kid', which it sought to contrast with a 'psychological', and hence supposedly more 'truthful', portrayal of William Bonney. Paul Newman brought Method performance techniques to his characterisation of Billy, giving him a sense of depth and complexity – while the screenplay itself provided a commentary on the inauthenticity of previous accounts. Like Jesse James in Nicholas Ray's *True Story*, Billy the Kid is shown becoming a legend in his own lifetime, already transformed into a character in dime novel escapades. But while Jesse was shown to relish and deliberately add to the 'Robin Hood' mythology accumulating about him, Billy plays no part in manufacturing his own legend. Rather, the sensationalised accounts of his exploits are created by an unsavoury character called Moultrie.

Moultrie is first seen, 'excited by Billy's energy', approaching The Kid in a bar in Missouri.[28] The suggestion that his interest in Billy is unhealthily obsessive and possibly homosexual was intensified in the casting of Hurd Hatfield, best known for playing the eponymous role in the 1945 adaptation of *The Picture of Dorian Gray*. After Billy is thought to have burned alive in an incident in the Lincoln County Range Wars, Moultrie picks through the charred ruins of his house, morbidly acquiring *momento mori*. When he later discovers that Billy survived, he uses these to begin spinning the legend to anyone who will listen:

Moultrie: I was there. I saw it! … I saw the house go boiling up in flames. But he did not die – a burning man was seen by witnesses – man made out of fire, burned to ashes! He is no common outlaw – I know it when I see it: the mark of greatness! Look here – cartridge cases from his gun, each one a human life! This buckle held his gun around his waist! This 'kercheif is stained with his blood!

Later, when Billy is in jail, Moultrie brings him copies of dime novels, with titles such as *Outlaw King, Killer of the West* and *The Luck of Billy the Kid*, which are based on letters and stories written by Moultrie for Eastern audiences. 'I let them know how you live!' he claims, asserting his status as Billy's unofficial biographer. However, these fictional versions of Billy's life have generated a reputation and notoriety that Billy cannot live down. As Pat Garrett hunts Billy, the outlaw feels trapped by the myths surrounding him, and strikes out at Moultrie. Moultrie is stunned when he 'senses

'I let them know how you live!': The legend of Billy the Kid grows in *The Left-Handed Gun* (1958), as William Bonney (Paul Newman, left) reads notices of his own death, produced by Moultrie (Hurd Hatfield, right). Eventually, Billy's failure to live up to the myths created by Moultrie is a decisive factor in his 'real' demise. (Courtesy of the British Film Institute)

fear in Billy', because this weakness betrays the idealised image that the biographer has created in his own head, and in the minds of his readers.[29]

> *Moultrie:*   I wrote letters – stories… You're not like the books. You don't wear silver studs – you don't stand up to glory. You got dirt on your coat – sweat and dirt! You're not HIM!

This realisation prompts him to betray Billy to Garrett in turn. As Jonathan Bignell notes, 'Billy's repudiation of Moultrie's rewritings of his life as a western adventure is, in a sense, the cause of his death'.[30] Further reflecting Hollywood's antipathy towards historians, it is notable that in the original teleplay Billy was betrayed by an unnamed drunk, not by his 'historian'.[31]

Although Moultrie knew the 'real' William Bonney, and had been an eye-witness to formative events in Bonney's outlawry, he knowingly constructed a history of 'Billy the Kid' that had little basis in reality. His historical writing is driven by personal, subjective reasons, yet is accorded substantial authority (however unwarranted). Hollywood, of course, was itself culpable in creating such legends – especially with regard to Billy, who had featured in at least 14 earlier movies, and two adventure serials. In this case, however, even as publicity sought to assert the truth status of the film as 'the first real story of Billy the Kid', the narrative simultaneously excused its own role in mythmaking by suggesting that the reality had been forever obscured by the misrepresentations of men like Moultrie.[32]

This pretext was made explicit in the musical comedy of *Jupiter's Darling* (1955), which concerned Hannibal's march on Rome in 216 BC. As the foreword to the movie claimed, 'The history of this great march has always been confused'. However, the next title card declared, with tongue firmly in cheek, that 'This picture will do nothing to clear it up'. The supposed lack of definition in the historical record provided an opportunity to jokingly present 'History as it should have been', rather than to suggest any plausible interpretation of accepted knowledge – resulting in what one critic described as 'a version of the Second Punic War as it might have occurred in the Land of Oz'.[33]

However, the 'confusion' over what really happened is presented as the fault of one 'Horatio the Historian', played by Richard Haydn. First introduced as an omnipresent narrator delivering the prologue in verse, Horatio is actually soon seen to be the official chronicler of Hannibal's campaign – immediately compromising the historian's detachment.

Moreover, Horatio refuses to accept the film's conclusion, which presents Hannibal's decision to turn back and not sack Rome as a result of his having fallen in love with Amytis, a beautiful Roman woman. Asserting that this is out-of-character for the God-like Carthaginian general of his history, Horatio deliberately erases this romance from his account. As the generator of a primary source, the historian-chronicler himself is made responsible for the gaps in historical records of the campaign. Intimating that such gaps then permit filmmakers to develop their own imaginative (and romantic) interpretations, this created a self-justification for Hollywood's attitude towards the past; allowing the presentation of 'some of the dizziest events that were *never recorded in the history books* on Rome'.[34]

The narrative conceit also undercut Horatio's opening verses, in which the 'truth of the story' was said to rest on his 'great sincerity' and the authority of his personal knowledge: 'For I, you will see, was a part of it'. When Hannibal takes Amytis on a tour of his encampment, she suggests that he should paint his elephants, because their natural grey is 'too dreary'. When Horatio jots this down, however, he writes that 'It was suggested by a close friend of the heroic Hannibal's that our eight hundred elephants be painted various colours'. Hearing this, and having seen only a handful of elephants, Amytis looks questioningly at Hannibal. 'Eight hundred?' Hannibal shrugs: 'We only have sixty, but you know historians!' Horatio has no qualms about adding 'a touch of colour' to his account when 'the course of history grows duller'.[35]

His readiness to exaggerate the historical truth might be attributed to filmmakers' encounters with technical advisors, who were similarly prepared to accept the 'demands of drama' and readily acquiesced in the creation of fictionalised histories. The characterisation of James Lee Bartlow, the historian in *The Bad and the Beautiful*, suggests that such experiences did have a direct affect. Bartlow is more than willing to compromise the integrity of his academic career, when he collaborates on the cinematic adaptation of his 'scholarly work about Early Virginia', in order to produce 'a botched replica of *Gone With the Wind*'.[36] In one draft of the script, movie producer Jonathan Shields asks 'why would any man want to be a Professor?' Bartlow's response, though delivered with a wry smile, may represent exactly what filmmakers believed about historians: 'So that he can write books that men like you pay a lot of money for!'[37] Yet, as Hannibal's nonchalant 'You know historians!' suggests, the ease with which historians might 'colour' their accounts was a joke that the audience was also expected to appreciate – indicating that wider cultural references were being invoked.

THE SOURCES OF ANTI-HISTORIANISM

At a general level, this corresponded with a climate of popular anti-intellectualism that vexed the academic community in the 1950s. Senator McCarthy's 'sorties against intellectuals and universities' fed on what Hofstadter identified as an 'ingrained distrust of eggheads', and promoted 'a climate in which it is easy to identify nonconformity with subversion and in which it is not easy to think critically'.[38] Attacks on Democrat candidate Adlai Stevenson, and the liberal scholars who worked on his presidential bid in 1952, led to *Time* magazine reporting Eisenhower's election victory as indicative of 'a wide and unhealthy gap between the American intellectuals and the people'. Merle Curti, as president of the American Historical Association in 1954, expanded this to a 'dangerous gulf' which, in entitling his address 'Intellectuals and Other People', he evidently considered to be endemic.[39]

Cold War anti-intellectualism was certainly rife in Hollywood's cycle of anti-Communist films – *My Son John* (1952) being the classic illustration of 'intellectual vitality' as the 'first temptation on the slippery slope towards espionage'.[40] Yet, in studying the particular representations of historians, rather than intellectuals in general, it becomes apparent that Hollywood's suspicion of the profession predated the Red Scare. Indeed, the evolution of the role of Horatio through consecutive rewrites of *Jupiter's Darling* – which had been in development at MGM since 1933 – suggests that additional barriers between historians and the public had been established during World War II. The threat of war revived the studio's interest in Robert Sherwood's 1926 Broadway play, *The Road to Rome*, as Hannibal's earlier plans to conquer central Europe suddenly acquired new relevance. And in 1939, writers Marion Parsonnet and Robert Thoeren introduced a new character to the script – originally named Scrivus – entrusted with 'writing the history of Hannibal for posterity'.[41] As the war progressed, subsequent scriptwriters then levied two charges against this character: first, they accused the historian of writing without 'real-life' experience; second, they associated him with the rewriting of history that was then being witnessed in fascist Germany and Italy.

The privileging of experience over passive intellectual observation was first evidenced in May 1940, in a terse exchange between the official historian (then named Thothmes) and the men of Hannibal's army:

Hasbudral: You've got a fine job! We fight battles, you write 'em.

Thothmes: Somebody has to do this work... You men should realise that these records of mine have intense historical value. I have here the entire story of Hannibal's march.

Hasbudral: Don't talk to me about history. I'm pretty damned sick of parading around the world making history for somebody else to read.[42]

This attitude continued into the 1950s – one of the final drafts included a scene in which Hannibal loses patience with his historian's 'scribbling', and thunders that 'Wars are won with deeds, not words'.[43] Such confrontations embodied that 'too-sharp distinction between the man of thought and the

Hostility towards Historians: As the official historian to Hannibal (Howard Keel), Horatio (Richard Hadyn), finds that men of action and deeds have little respect for his 'scribbling' – and neither does the audience when they witness him distorting the record. (Courtesy of the British Film Institute)

man of action', which Curti saw as one of the cornerstones of American anti-intellectualism.[44]

This division was reinvigorated as World War II prompted those who experienced the conflict first-hand to think differently about their own place in history. Participation in something so self-evidently historic engenders a sense of agency, and many Hollywood filmmakers had been very active in the war. Over 7000 studio employees joined the military, with Clark Gable, Tyrone Power, Jimmy Stewart and Gene Autry among the 'He-men in the movies' whose service in the war effort was widely publicised.[45] The varied skills of filmmakers were also put to use in units such as the Army Signal Corps, the Navy Photographic Unit, or the Office of War Information. Zanuck was appointed Colonel, to supervise 42 cameramen documenting the campaign in North Africa; George Stevens formed a Special Coverage Unit to film the liberation of Europe from the Nazis – and shot the only colour footage of the D-Day landings and the American arrival in Auschwitz; and John Ford was wounded while recording the Battle of the Midway for the Navy. This kind of direct engagement, as Christopher Browning has suggested in his work on representations of the Holocaust, casts the recent past as 'Experiential History' – whereby history is no longer perceived in the abstract. Memories of personal agency are subsequently placed alongside the accounts of historians 'trying to write about those events' who 'have experienced nothing in their personal lives that remotely compares'. Thus historians after World War II came to suffer from a kind of 'experiential shortcoming' – which was particularly picked up on by filmmakers, who had not only taken part but had actually 'documented' history as it unfolded.[46]

This perception was certainly unfair. American historians may not have had much battlefield experience, but they were heavily involved in the war effort. William Langer of Harvard headed the research and analysis branches of the Office of Strategic Services, and recruited many American historians 'who applied their historical training…to the problems raised for the United States government by the war'.[47] Among many notable contributions, Ernest May advised the Joint Chiefs of Staff, Gordon Wright joined the National War College, and Arthur Schlesinger, Jr., worked for both the Economic Cooperation Administration and the Mutual Security Administration.[48] Yet, research and analysis remained desk-bound and, however unjustly, Hollywood's post-war films repeatedly judged historians 'against a world of active doing' and 'found them wanting'.[49] In *Charge at Feather*

River, Johnson only fully understands what the Indian fighter goes through when he himself joins a rescue expedition. A 1948 draft of the screenplay, revealed that tuberculosis had prevented Johnson's participation in the Civil War, and his efforts to 'draw and paint soldiers [and] show what they go through' were attributed to his desire to 'make up for not being in the war'.[50] The grim violence that Johnson witnesses is then juxtaposed with the sanitised and glorified images he was originally sending to magazines 'back East'. Johnson's own death at the end of the film directly guarantees one result of his new experiential knowledge: he will never again misrepresent the 'truth'.

The Bad and the Beautiful elaborated on this perspective, suggesting that the work produced by historians was lacking in its engagement with reality. Bartlow's historical writing – entitled *The Proud Land* – is certainly good enough to attract the attention of producer Jonathan Shields. Tragedy strikes during filming, however, when Shields inadvertently causes the death of Bartlow's wife, Rosemary. Yet, out of this experience Bartlow writes his first modern novel, described as a 'sensitive, unforgettable portrait of a present-day Southern belle'. Clearly based on Rosemary, *A Woman of Taste* garners critical plaudits and even wins a Pulitzer Award – implying that after Shields has exposed him to the dramas and tragedies of 'real life', Bartlow has become a much better writer. Indeed, Bartlow's historical writing is presented as being insubstantial in comparison. Although the audience is told that it is a 'scholarly work', the cover artwork for *The Proud Land* is more in keeping with a cheap historical romance novel – further suggesting that when historical writing lacks grounding in lived experience, it is practically indistinguishable from imaginative fiction.

The naïve perception of historians as 'detached' from reality was admittedly encouraged by academics who argued that historical knowledge is 'ontology free' – that history is an independent construction upon which the personality and experience of the historian has (or should have) no bearing. As Polan notes, it is only in the moment when Bartlow punches Shields to the floor in fury, that he is defined as something 'substantial', 'something other than a professor' – and only then does his work gain substance too. Polan's essay indicates that this is common in Hollywood's imaging of professors in the humanities – that they 'can become real only through gestures that intervene in the concrete world *outside* of the classroom' or their 'ivory towers'.[51] It is a measure of the industry's skewed perceptions that Hollywood considered itself to be a more 'real' part of the 'concrete world' than academia.

This assessment, however, was relatively innocuous compared to the contrary image of historians that also emerged from World War II, as viewed through the prism of Nazi abuses of history. William Shirer's *The Rise and Fall of the Third Reich* explained how 'history was so falsified in the new textbooks' of Hitler's regime 'and by the teachers in their lectures that it became ludicrous' – while accounts such as Gregor Zeimer's *Education for Death* (1942) had made Americans aware of how bogus history was used to inculcate fascist doctrines.[52] In 1948, Frederic Lilge held German historians to account for having furnished 'proof' of the Nazi theory of the cultural superiority of the Aryan race, thus encouraging the rise of fascism. Indeed, he singled out for blame Oswald Spengler, the author of *The Decline of the West* (1918–22). Concerned with the struggle for racial survival in national destiny, Spengler's grand narrative was accused of having given

In *The Bad and the Beautiful* (1952), Professor James Lee Bartlow (Dick Powell) reflects on his historical writing just before he 'sells out' to the film industry. The contrast between the 'academic' Bartlow presented to the public through the history books, and the casual attire he wears in everyday life, prefigures the film's suggestion that Bartlow becomes more 'real' after his experiences in Hollywood. (Courtesy of the British Film Institute)

historical countenance to fears about 'the eventual loss of white supremacy in the world brought about by a receding Western imperialism weakened at home by humanitarian ideals…[and] the loss of nerve on the part of the industrial and military leadership of the West'. Such anxieties inspired the cult of 'great men' evident in many pre-war historical biographies, which implicitly called for an authoritarian leader like Hitler. According to Lilge's analysis, 'no other' Germans had done as much as historians to 'create in Germany that fatal mood in which many…people saw a course of desperate and irrational action as the only alternative to cravenly resigning themselves to an obscure place in history'.[53]

Early treatments of *Jupiter's Darling* in World War II depicted 'Scrivus' in this light, acting as a 'State Historian' who convinces 'Field Marshall' Hannibal that strong actions 'will make you immortal!'[54] Parallels to Joseph Goebbels were also made explicit in one draft, with Scrivus pompously defining himself as 'the official press agent and propagandist for Hannibal the Great – ruler of Carthage, Spain, and soon the entire world!'[55] Exploiting Hannibal's desire to be remembered throughout history, he exercises an insidious influence. Aghast when Hannibal suggests that he might 'spare the women' of Rome, Scrivus exhorts him not to undermine his historical reputation as 'a remorseless conqueror', and thus encourages his brutality.[56]

By the 1950s, the 'Red Fascism' conflation of Nazism and Stalinism ensured that Communists were condemned in the same way for their 'crimes against history'. Noting that 'the distortion of history was a deliberate Nazi policy', Pendleton Herring, president of the Social Science Research Council, asserted that it 'now continues as a propaganda device for the Soviets'.[57] Likewise, Arthur Schlesinger, Jr., contended that 'a genuinely Communistic textbook would be [as] unacceptable for its distortion of fact', as Nazi historiography had been.[58] Rather more strikingly, George Orwell's *1984* excoriated the totalitarian attitude towards history, with Winston Smith employed to rewrite history, 'turning unwanted historical actors' into 'unpersons', and stuffing truth down the 'memory hole'. But 'Red Fascism' also fed directly into American anti-intellectualism, as can be seen in one of the most extreme artefacts offered by Hofstadter as evidence of post-war attitudes, namely author Louis Bromfield's reactionary definition of the 'egghead' as a Nazi or Communist sympathiser:

A person of spurious intellectual pretensions, often a professor or the protégé of a professor... Supercilious and surfeited with conceit and contempt for the experience of more sound and able men. Essentially confused in thought and immersed in a mixture of sentimentality and violent evangelism. A doctrinaire supporter of Middle-European socialism as opposed to Greco-French-American ideas of democracy and liberalism. Subject to the old-fashioned morality of Neitzsche which frequently leads him into jail or disgrace. A self-conscious prig...[59]

Bromfield's ridiculous diatribe could be easily dismissed, and certainly would not be worth repeating, were it not for the fact that it reads like a blueprint for the character of Albert Richter, the historian in Chester Erskine's *Witness to Murder*. Indeed Richter, as portrayed with cold-blooded charm by George Sanders, represented a coalescence of anti-intellectual conceptions of historians: simultaneously detached from reality, contemptuous of the experiential knowledge of ordinary Americans, and a revisionist who distorts the facts for 'fascist' purposes.

Richter is clearly identified as a 'noted historian' from the beginning – referred to as such on the jacket of one of his books, *The Age of Violence*. When Lieutenant Mathews comes to question Richter about the accusations of murder levelled against him by his neighbour, Cheryl Draper, we are informed that he writes about 'historical possibilities', and that *The Age of Violence* is 'a collection of lectures [he] delivered in Europe'. However, when Draper and Mathews pursue their suspicions, they discover that Richter was 'a minor in the big league of Hitler's culture system'. Although he got himself 'de-Nazified in court' at the end of the war, his writing suggests that he is 'not so "ex"'. Asserting that 'violence is in the nature of progress' and is 'the well spring of growth', *The Age of Violence* defines historical destiny in terms of survival of the fittest, writing that 'the unworthy' must 'fall by the wayside, under the trampling feet of the future, unfit to live'. As Mathews notes, it is 'a hash of Hegel and Nietzsche'.

In keeping with Bromfield's definition, this particular historian's 'philosophical morality of Nietzsche' threatens to lead him to jail. Draper – and the audience – have witnessed him strangling a woman, later identified as a prostitute named Joyce Stewart. Before Richter is arrested, he reveals that he killed her because she imperilled his impending marriage to a rich widow, whose wealth he intends to use in mounting his monomaniacal plans to surpass Hitler. It is at this point that his 'violent evangelism' gets the better of him:

> Richter: That insignificant little nobody put in jeopardy my
>   life's work. Put in jeopardy the future of the world! For
>   I alone…have the key for which history awaits. The
>   gospel which may well be the religion of centuries to
>   come. With the fortune I am to marry, and with Miss
>   Stewart eliminated, we move forward. We move for-
>   ward into the future!

Most assuredly opposed to 'Greco-French-American ideas of democracy and liberalism', his rant then switches into German, announcing that 'our destiny calls us to rule the world'.

In his comments on the film, Richard Willson suggests that 'Richter is not sinister because he is a professor, but because he is a German'.[60] However, the fact that Richter is a *history* professor *is* fundamental to his villainy, because the film's dramatic tension rests on competing 'truth claims' and questions of epistemology. The police are not inclined to believe Draper when she claims to have seen Richter kill Stewart, from her window across the street. No body is found, and there are no signs of a struggle in Richter's apartment. Yet, since the camera presented Draper's perspective in the opening scenes, the audience was also witness to the murder, and so our knowledge of what happened, like Draper's, is ontological. As she repeatedly asks the sceptical Lieutenant, 'You don't expect me to deny something I actually saw with my own eyes?'

This awareness, shared by audience and Draper, fixes Richter's homicidal action as a fact. Richter, however, undermines her credibility, partly by consistently exerting an air of self-confident superiority, and exhibiting what Bromfield described as the typical intellectual's 'conceit and contempt' for a 'sound and able' woman. He is also accorded an unwarranted authority by the police simply because he is a published historian. Mathews is instantly impressed by the weighty volume, until he actually reads it. The detectives take it for granted that they share with him a mutual respect for empiricist knowledge, based on objective inference from indisputable factual evidence. Draper, on the other hand, is presented as an artist who relies on intuition. When Richter suggests that she only had a nightmare, the police are quick to agree, and dismiss her as overly 'subjective' and 'imaginative' in her interpretation of what happened. Despite his desire to believe Draper (with whom he is falling in love), Mathews cannot escape the confines of naïve empiricism, and readily accepts the 'facts' that Richter is actually defining for him. Draper pleads with him to accept what she is saying, but he remains sceptical about her perspective:

Mathews:	I believe you told the truth as you saw it. But the question is, did you see it?
Draper:	And the answer is I did not?
Mathews:	That *has* to be the answer.
Draper:	Why?
Mathews:	Because the *facts* say it is the answer.

However, the film makes it clear that 'the facts' are not actually immutable. The historian exercises control over the evidence and – worse – is fully capable of constructing false 'facts'. It is Richter's suppression of the evidence (including his disposal of Stewart's body) that casts doubt on Draper's knowledge in the first place; and then he forges new evidence in support of *his* 'interpretation' of events, which is that she is a dangerously obsessive paranoid. Writing threatening letters to himself on Draper's typewriter, he provides the police with 'proof' that she is a hysterical woman

'Supercilious and surfeited with conceit': In *Witness to Murder* (1954), shadows of doubt are cast on the eye-witness testimony of Cheryl Draper (Barbara Stanwyck), as 'not so ex' Nazi historian Albert Richter (George Sanders) distorts the evidence. (Courtesy of the Academy of Motion Pictures Arts and Sciences)

intent on taking justice into her own hands. This documentary evidence is automatically accepted as factual. Moreover, Richter ensures that his version becomes part of the 'official' record, persuading the police captain to send Draper to hospital for observation. Having controlled the way in which the recent past will be interpreted, Richter feels free to confess his crimes to Draper, now that her 'insanity' is 'recorded in police files and hospital reports'. Richter is well aware of the authority and power accorded by society to the written historical record. As a corrupt, fascist historian, he has already been exploiting this authority to persuade the public that his warped interpretation of the past is the right one. The film, however, privileges *visual* knowledge instead, suggesting a lesson (somewhat disturbingly) appropriate to Hollywood's self-perception: that you should believe what you see, not what historians tell you.

In this linking of historian and homicide, Nietzsche and Nazism, *Witness to Murder* invokes the spectres of moral and cognitive relativism. The argument of historical relativists – which in pre-war America included Carl Becker and Charles Beard – was that historical interpretations were always 'relative' to the historian's time, place, values and purposes, and that since one can never escape from societal influences, what is accepted as 'the truth' is also relative. This philosophy of history had indeed been expressed most extremely by Friederich Nietzsche in *The Use and Abuse of History* (1873), in which he asserted that 'objectivity' was just the pretence of academic 'eunuchs'. He protested that history was neither passive nor objective, but consisted of acts of interpretation and understanding performed by human beings who *always* had purposes and ideals of their own.[61] This directly challenged the empiricist claim that the 'facts spoke for themselves'. Indeed, Becker concluded that since 'it is not the undiscriminated fact, but the perceiving mind of the historian that speaks', no account could be 'true' except 'relative to the age that fashioned it'.[62] Arguing that all systems of knowledge were socially constructed, one could therefore never adjudge 'the truth' with absolute certainty.

As Peter Novick details, this philosophy was hotly debated among American historians in the 1930s. But Nietzsche had gone on to conclude that societies should have a strong sense of their own mission and importance, and that historians should abandon the fallacy of objectivity, and instead commit themselves to the study of models and examples that would inspire and encourage that mission. Put into alarming and vicious practice by Hitler's regime – which denounced 'objectivity' and insisted that all intellectual endeavours *must* purposefully serve the present day – the associated philosophy became indelibly tainted. Post-war American historians (many of whom were already hostile to the theory) moved quickly to denounce relativism as 'the doctrine to which historical writing has bowed under state pressure in Nazi Germany and Fascist Italy' – and charged that its denial of 'absolutes' was dangerous and debilitating.[63]

Witness to Murder makes Richter's self-interested exploitation of facts and interpretations very dangerous indeed, connecting his historical relativism to an absence of moral absolutes. Plainly, the film's distrust of intellect is rooted in the lack of certitude that results from relativism – and the narrative looks for an 'escape', or at least some reassurance that absolutes of truth actually exist. In one scene, Draper acknowledges the difficulties; when questioned by a psychiatrist about the emotions represented in one of her paintings she notes that 'It's what you yourself bring to it… A hundred people can *see* the same sunset, but each will be moved differently.' Yet, ultimately, what many people see is what establishes the one 'absolute' in the film – Richter's guilt as a murderer. The audience, alongside Draper, observes him strangling Miss Stewart, and it is this *shared* perspective that establishes an immutable fact in our minds, which even Richter cannot fully undermine. While unable to completely repudiate relativism, this narrative did, in part, correspond with Karl Mannheim's similar wish to avoid despairing of the problem, reflecting his assertion that 'though all knowledge was perspectival, the multiplication of perspectives, and their attempted reconciliation, could move one closer to objectivity'.[64] Indeed, one could argue that it is literally our 'common-sense' knowledge of what happened which provides the means to resist Richter's purposive relativism.

Witness to Murder's defence of 'truth' as defined by the collective perspective of 'the people' (the audience), rather than the historian, was not an isolated example. A far less anti-intellectual variation was presented in *Born Yesterday* (1950), which also suggested that the public needed a better historical education for this to work. When tycoon Harry Brock hires Paul Verall to tutor his mistress – an ex-showgirl named Billie Dawn – and make her 'culturefied', Verall decides to teach history in a very practical fashion. He takes Billie around Washington DC, to the Capitol and the Library of Congress, where she can gain knowledge through personal engagement with historical sources. She reads for herself, for example, the original Declaration of Independence, displayed under glass. However, Brock opposes her 'learning about dead people' – and he is right to fear it, for

Billie's lessons in history prompt her to declare her own independence from the 'two-bit crook' who has been dominating her.

As Verall puts it, 'education is pretty hard to control' – at least, implicitly, in a democratic society, where genuine historical knowledge can be obtained by 'the people' themselves. This conception was one that *Born Yesterday* shared with the federal government's 'Freedom Train' which, sponsored by Congress in 1947, toured the country carrying copies of the same documents that were to inspire Billie – including the Treaty of Paris, Washington's annotated copy of the Constitution, and the Bill of Rights. Attorney General Tom Clark promoted the train as making a vital contribution to the Cold War, 'by reawakening in our people their profound faith in the American historical heritage'.[65] This was not an escape from relativism, because it strongly suggested that history should 'be living history', 'intended to do work in the world'.[66] But unlike Nietzsche's conception, it was also a call to 'democratise' historical knowledge, preventing 'others' from distorting and controlling it as European fascists once had. Ironically, while Carl Becker was being pilloried within American academia for subscribing to the 'doctrine' of relativism, *Born Yesterday* and the Freedom Train seemed to applaud and echo Becker's analysis that 'Everyman' could be 'his own historian'.[67]

Yet, despite its positivity about intellect, *Born Yesterday* still did not trust a historian to explain the meaning of the past to Billie. Verall was cast as a journalist, presumed to be more in contact with the 'real' world, and thus more suited to the task of making history relevant. Historians were therefore in a no-win situation – caught between an image of being overly detached in their dedication to 'value free' objectivity, and a contrary and suspicious image associated with mindful distortions of the truth. Both images rested upon naïve understanding of what historians actually do, but the academy offered little to correct these perceptions.

Many contemporary historians *were* engaged with the social and political concerns of the nation. C. Vann Woodward's *The Strange Career of Jim Crow* (1955), supported the civil rights movement, in demonstrating that segregation laws were only recent creations, and that since the 'race problem' was made by men, it also could be undone by them. He also joined historian John Hope Franklin in helping the NAACP prepare the brief in the *Brown vs. the Board of Education* case that escalated the process of school desegregation.[68] In terms of Cold War politics, Daniel Boorstin asserted before HUAC that his *Genius of American Politics* (1953), was written in a spirit of 'opposition' to Communism, to explain 'the unique virtues of American democracy'.[69] And in a positive reaction to the political climate, many other histories similarly documented and celebrated America's 'massive stability and philosophic harmony' as rendering the nation impervious to Marxist ideology.[70] However, contemporary historians were generally far more reserved about expounding the present-day values of their studies, than the previous generation of scholars. Whereas James Robinson, in 1912, had issued a clarion call for historians to make their subject 'an institute for social progress', post-war historians were more mindful of the perceived 'danger' of relativism, and typically denied or downplayed their presentist concerns rather than embracing them.[71]

This 'retreat into quietude', coinciding with a greater emphasis on the ironies of history and a distaste for grand narrative, evidently reinforced the profession's loss of 'public authority'. At the start of the decade, Conyers Read expressed concern that 'if historians, in their examination of the past, represent the evolution of civilization as haphazard, without direction and without progress, offering no assurance that mankind's present position is on the highway, and not on some dead end, then mankind will seek for assurance in a more positive alternative'.[72] Read had the alternatives of religion and Communism in mind when he said this; he did not anticipate that Americans would turn to Hollywood instead.

Historians were far from pleased when the public did so. Echoing Boorstin's concern about the way in which films and other public history drew 'heavily upon the materials of our history, but always in a distinctly nonhistorical frame of mind', Hofstadter was explicitly critical of the 'increasingly passive and spectatorial manner' in which Americans were learning their history.[73] American society was clearly 'inquisitive about the past' to a huge degree – but historical novels, magazines like *American Heritage,* living history museums, and Hollywood films seemed, to Louis Gottschalk, to be encouraging 'nostalgia', without teaching 'the way peculiar to historians of thinking about the world's problems'.[74] Even Allan Nevins, probably the profession's most ardent campaigner for increasing the popular appeal of history, worried, with a 'certain despair', that the movies were 'guilty of some horrible distortions of the truth'.[75] In the eyes of filmmakers, however, contemporary historians had apparently abdicated their responsibility to the general public. This left a vacuum that Hollywood was pleased to fill – while chastising historians for leaving it.

Conclusion

There's one final thing I have to do and then I'll be free of the past.

Scottie Ferguson, *Vertigo* (1958)

It is true that the huge discourse about the past that engaged Hollywood in the 1950s resulted in no real equivalent to the so-called 'New History Films' beloved by postmodernists. Nor did it produce many films that could be considered 'scholarly' in their treatment of historical materials; when the integrity of the past and dramatic license conflicted, the latter always prevailed. Yet, it is just as evident that the range of accomplishment in Hollywood's history films was far greater than has previously been acknowledged, and that the industry's historical consciousness was far from monolithically 'trite'.

The arguments I have advanced have emphasised structural factors of particular importance in the Fifties – from studio economics to the limited definition of 'research' and the remit of advisors – using archival production materials as evidence of the thought processes behind the films themselves. Parallel work needs to be done on other periods before we can really start to talk about developments in Hollywood's historical consciousness over time. However, the evidence presented here would suggest that even as the studio system collapsed, it bequeathed certain approaches to depicting the past that influenced filmmakers both within and without that system. Publicity, for example, defined a realist perspective, repeatedly referring to a past that could be 'brought back to life', relived, reconstructed or returned to. In relation to widescreen technologies, advertising trumpeted the 'miraculous' achievements of filmmakers in turning back the clock. However, this dominant rhetoric also militated against direct references within history films to the constructed nature of historical representation – the illusion of reality had to be maintained. To live up to the expectations that the industry had raised, filmmakers were further compelled to prioritise the construction of an aesthetic and visceral 'experience' of the past.

Yet, filmmakers and audiences were conscious that this notion of vicarious experience was a deception, albeit one to be indulged. As Vivian Sobchack notes, the presence of stars such as Charlton Heston or Elizabeth Taylor, the glamorous sets of palaces and pirate ships, or the 'gold lamé push-up bras' worn in biblical epics, were factors which made the films compelling, yet simultaneously stopped audiences from fully believing in the highly stylised images on the screen.[1] Likewise, filmmakers knew what went into the production of history films, understood the compromises with 'truth' that they made, and so remained aware that their historical representations were constructs. The self-reflexivity of a number of history films clearly reveals this. Most filmmakers were also conscious that their intentions – to shape the past with a dramatic imagination, to make money, and to make an impact on contemporary popular culture – were very different from those of professional historians, who at least pledged to reflect accurately on the past and generally wrote for their peers.

However, an awareness that written history is itself only a representation – and not a definitive truth – was also fostered as filmmakers came into contact with historians, advisors, and self-appointed 'custodians' of historical memories. Realising that official and academic accounts involved selection, imagination and fiction, they were exposed to a perspective that was virtually deconstructionist. Here, history was not 'real', but a disputed and artificial text. And when methodologies were confused with intentions, the practices of professional historians, from this perspective, no longer seemed quite so distinct.

Filmmakers were therefore hardly restricted to a single way of contemplating the past, and were frequently (if often unwittingly) exposed to serious issues of historical epistemology. Indeed, the making of a history film could involve exposure to all these perspectives at once: having come to perceive the writing/making of historical representations as an artifice, filmmakers would still strive for 'realism' in the movie itself, which would then often be presented to the public as the definitive account of 'how it really was'. One can see the inconsistency in Hollywood's attitudes towards professional historians, representing them in films with little respect for their scholarship, yet deferring to their academic knowledge when asking for advice on how best to present a past which they then presumed to be 'real'.

Some filmmakers, at least, were prompted to think about these paradoxical positions. Certainly, few – if any – thought 'historically' in the sense that historians aim to, but even if Hollywood had possessed the same goals, its vocabulary of historical representation was inherently different. Cinematic history was distinguished by two factors that historians could rarely emulate – namely the visual and the performative. At its best, when filmmakers realised this distinction for themselves, Hollywood was capable of reflecting on this and achieving genuine historical insight.

Take, for instance, Vincente Minnelli, one of the most celebrated contract studio directors of the period, whose prime concern in any production was the 'search for an appropriate style'.[2] Formerly a theatrical set designer, costumer and art director, Minnelli's historical consciousness was expressly artistic, and he believed that paintings and works of art 'should be used as a basic source of reference' for the way in which they 'reflect their times so accurately'.[3] This is very notable in *Gigi* (1958), where his 'evocations of a bygone era' were explicitly influenced by French Impressionist artists such as Constantin Guys, Eugene Louis Boudin and the caricaturist Sem. Reporting on the production for *The New Yorker*, Genet noted that Minnelli had purposefully 'discovered elderly actresses who still resemble Sem's famous cartoons of years ago – those eccentric beak-nosed grisettes, like macaws with pompadours'.[4] As Natalie Zemon Davis comments, this use of paintings from the past as a marker of authenticity potentially signals a naïve understanding of history. While it 'enhances the beauty of the film and allows the audience the pleasure of recognition', works of art are compromised as sources of how the past actually looked by virtue of their always being 'artist's impressions'.[5] Other filmmakers may not have cared much about this problem, but in his depiction of Vincent Van Gogh's *Lust for Life* (1956), Minnelli was evidently conscious of it – and simultaneously embraced and addressed the issue in his construction of the past.

Lust for Life embodies Minnelli's 'thesis', derived from art history and study of Vincent Van Gogh's letters, that 'never did a color palette so closely parallel an artist's life'.[6] With producer John Houseman, he devised progressive changes in the tonality of the cinematography, so that the images on the screen reflected the hues that Van Gogh himself used at each particular stage of his artistic development: drab slate grey dominates the coal-mining scenes of the Borinage; the Dutch villages are picked out in dark green and blues, 'as seen in paintings of his Dutch contemporaries'; the sombre tones lighten, with sharp reds and blues and 'exuberant pastels' reflecting the influence of the Impressionist painters he met in Paris; while the concluding sequences in Arles are suffused in vibrant sunny yellows, as was Van Gogh's work during this most prolific period.[7] Then, as Stephen Harvey's perceptive reading of the film attends, 'when solitude and fatigue overtake the painter', Minnelli saturates the screen 'with tints of queasy intensity – deep sapphire for the waters of the bay where Van Gogh paints *Starry Night*; red for the *Night Café* of his absinthe stupors'.[8] According to Houseman, this not only reflected Van Gogh's art, but the narrative of his life as well, constructing his biography as 'the story of a painter who progressed from darkness to light – from the literal darkness of black, grim coal mines to the dazzling sunlight of Provence; from the murky, labyrinthine gloom of his own uncertainty and lack of confidence, to the ultimate triumph of his powers and talent'.[9]

The effect was intended to share with audiences some of the experiences and visual sensibilities that shaped Van Gogh's life and work. The film does 're-enact' works of art such as the 'Night Café', the 'Potato Eaters' and the 'Portrait of Dr Gachet', with Kirk Douglas as Van Gogh sketching the scenes in front of him. The *mise-en-scène* closely resembles the images that appear on his canvas. James Naremore has commented that 'the implication of these shots is paradoxical: Is Van Gogh a photographic realist, or is the film trying to see the world through his eyes?'[10] To answer Naremore, the filmmakers were explicit in their intent. 'Our job,' wrote Dore Schary, 'was to reconstruct what he had painted – perhaps it wasn't actual reality, but… it was the world as Van Gogh saw it – and that was what we wanted.'[11] Location footage, which captured real images such as the spring in Arles, was explicitly 'integrated into the final film not from the viewpoint of some neutral observer, but as the experience of our central figure – to whom landscapes and seasons and all manifestations of Nature meant vastly more than a series of pretty picture postcards'.[12] The historical record was thus expressly presented in subjective terms, exploring Minnelli's fascination with 'the way in which a painter transforms reality to suit his private vision'.[13]

The final film represented a unique 'mingling of art and historical incident' – consistent with the interplay between imaginary and real worlds that often characterised the director's work.[14] Gene Kelly's character in *Brigadoon* (1954), for instance, finds true happiness not in the 'real' world of present-day New York, but in the fantastic Scottish village that appears only once every hundred years, so as not to be 'in any century long enough to be touched by it'. The depiction of the past in terms of artists' visions in *Lust for Life* and *Gigi* suggested that this indeterminate boundary between the real world and imaginary pasts was very much part of Minnelli's historical consciousness – which was surely informed by his own experience of seeing frequently how that boundary was transgressed in the numerous history films produced at MGM. Minnelli may not have thought like a historian in his approach to the material, but his attitude was informed by thinking as an artistic filmmaker and a student of art history; one particularly interested in the imagination of past artists. In *Lust for Life*, this perspective produced one of the decade's most impressive biopics.

One of the best westerns of the Fifties also used its visualisation of the past to comment on the boundaries between fantasy and reality in representations of history. For *Shane*, George Stevens went to great lengths to suggest an 'objective' reality in his recreation of a Wyoming frontier community, employing Joe DeYong to research such minutiae as the difference between 'elm' shape saddles and swell-shaped saddles, or how 'cowpunchers' thinned out a horse's mane. The production team collected photographs from the descendants of Wyoming homesteaders, copied images of Fourth of July celebrations from *Harper's Magazine* and contacted the state museum for local history materials. With an eye for visual detail, Stevens was adamant that the costuming should not 'take license with nature to give an artistic effect', and quickly enjoined actor Van Heflin from wearing an Abercrombie and Fitch shirt:

> We want these people to wear the things that would have been available to them and that they would wear when they lived in the country at this time. None of these cowboys or sodbusters or women in this story were ever advised by an artist... They didn't have Western Costume Company to make them look attractive and conspicuous.[15]

He was eventually satisfied that DeYong's advice resulted in 'a quality of realism in the costuming and sets that is extraordinary' – and critics were similarly impressed with *Shane*'s authenticity, which was 'rare enough in any film' let alone a western.[16] Yet, unlike DeMille and most other directors, Stevens did not capitalise on this by promoting his film with publicity about the research effort, nor did he make aggrandised claims about 'authenticity'.[17] The convincing construction of reality was not a sales gimmick, but a crucial element in Stevens' project of interrogating the mythology of the western gunfighter.

The visuals serve to signify the 'reality' of history, which Stevens also attends to in the script with a direct lesson in history provided by the 'bad guy', cattle baron Rufus Ryker. When Ryker confronts Starrett, the leader of the homesteaders he wants to drive off the land, their dialogue specifically evokes Frederick Jackson Turner's 'frontier thesis', in explaining how Ryker's generation had 'made this country', taking the land from Native Americans and turning it into 'a safe range'. Starrett notes that 'trappers' and 'Indian traders' had been in the West before Ryker and his men, and 'they tamed the country more than you did'. He then suggests that homesteading – the building of communities – is the next and inevitable stage in a frontier that is steadily moving westwards, and that Ryker's moment has passed. This invocation of a theory of historical development is a rare moment indeed in any history film.[18]

However, while this history class is proceeding, Stevens shows us that Starrett's young son, Joey, is not paying attention, but is instead transfixed by the stuff of western legend: two gunfighters getting the measure of each other, the 'good' Shane dressed in pale buckskin, and the villainous Wilson, hired by Ryker, dressed in black. The monochrome clothing caricatures the genre's simplistic notions of 'good' and 'evil', simultaneously juxtaposing this with the complex reality that Ryker is trying to explain, in words that deter any easy condemnation of the old man's attitude. Similarly, the 'reality' suggested by the detailed visual reconstruction of frontier life seems distinctly at odds with the image of Shane himself – 'independent, forthright and noble', arriving 'mysteriously out of nowhere to mete out perfect justice'.[19] Stevens uses this contrast to suggest that we are seeing Shane, and his actions, through Joey's eyes. Joey does not see the reality of history; he idolises Shane, just as kids in the Fifties idolised the Lone Ranger and Davy Crockett. He also perceives Shane in the mould of 'Jack the Giant Killer', the fairytale we hear his mother reading to him.

Stevens uses three confrontations set in the town to convey his point. The first is explicitly from Joey's viewpoint, with him watching under the saloon door as Shane and his father take on Ryker's men in a stereotypical western bar-room brawl. The second confrontation, however, is the one scene where Joey is not present at all – and it is presented to the audience with stark realism, as Wilson takes sadistic pleasure in goading one of the homesteaders, 'Stonewall' Torrey, into drawing his gun. The shot that kills Torrey lifts him from the ground, and throws him into the mud of the gutter. Since Joey does not see this, the audience is now ahead of him in being disillusioned of the 'glamour' of western gunfights – reinforcing our awareness of the boy's fantasy. Joey's turn comes at the end, as he again is seen looking into the saloon from under the door, witness to the climatic gunfight between Shane and Wilson. This time, however, the realism of the killing of Wilson, who (like Torrey) is thrown across the barroom when the bullet enters his body, and the cut to the suddenly frightened eyes of Ryker, undermines the western clichés that Joey has been imagining. Shane may have proved himself the fastest-gun, but he too is injured, and the difference between the 'real' gun-play and Joey's imitative play-shooting, finally disrupts the romantic and idealised legend.

These examples defy many of the criticisms that have been levelled at classical Hollywood's history films. Robert Rosenstone's assertion that filmmakers tended to assume that 'mimesis is all, that history is in fact no more than a "period look"' is clearly inadequate in explaining Minnelli or Stevens' use of the past.[20] And their use of visual material to make audiences aware of subjective perspectives challenges David Herlihy's contention that the history film's illusion of visual authenticity 'undermines awareness that all historical knowledge comes to us through filters'.[21] Even though *Lust for Life* and *Shane* were strongly influenced by Hollywood's conventions of depicting history in biopics and westerns respectively, neither film was the product of a 'trite' historical consciousness.

When it came to the other distinctive component of Hollywood's historiography, namely performance, similarly self-reflexive ways were found to comment on the nature of historical representation. *Calamity Jane*, for example, emphasises role-playing, performance and false identities in a way which not only makes it clear that the film is playing fast and loose with its historical characters, but also connects this to the 'tall tales' about herself that the real Calamity, Martha Jane Canary, promoted. Indeed, the historical 'Calamity Jane' can be seen as a character that Canary constructed for public performance in the autobiographical theatrical and museum shows she gave during the 1890s. Noting in its trailer that 'there never was a glibber fibber', *Calamity Jane* justifies its attitude towards history by suggesting that it is itself 'just a good-natured whopper'.[22]

Many history films also used casting to their advantage, commenting on history through the external 'baggage' that particular stars brought to their performances. To his first starring role as Billy the Kid in Universal's *The Kid From Texas* (1950), Audie Murphy lent the image inherent in his unparalleled war record, as a 'young hero whose innocent appearance belied his lethal achievement on the battlefield'.[23] Marlon Brando's casting as Mark Antony in *Julius Caesar* raised eyebrows in 1953, but proved ideal in instantly conveying Antony's charismatic appeal, his physical energy and his ambition. As Kenneth Geist notes, 'his impassioned and sullen Antony is fascinating, and his hair style and glowering, heavy-lidded eyes give him, more than any other member of the cast, the look of a heroic Roman bust come to life'.[24] More generally, epics such as *Ben Hur* conventionally cast British actors as the ancient Romans, and Americans as Hebrews or other 'freedom fighters', allowing echoes of 'a highly simplified rendering of the American Revolution' to permeate narratives that concerned earlier struggles against imperial oppression.[25]

Yet, one of the most complex considerations of the role of performance in representing history, and the problems of knowledge (historical and otherwise), came not in a history film, but in *Vertigo* (1958) – set in contemporary San Francisco. Already exceptional, director Alfred Hitchcock was even more so among filmmakers in the 1950s for not making any history films during the decade. Advertised as 'the story of a love so strong that it broke down all barriers between past and present', *Vertigo*'s narrative directly explored the hold that the past has on the present, and problematised efforts to re-enact history as being false, deceptive and obsessive.

The inadequacy of historical reconstructions is suggested in *Vertigo*'s dismissal of 'official' histories of America as incomplete and dominated by the stories of 'dead white men'. As in other films of the Fifties, professional historians do not fare well as sources of actionable knowledge. Trying to make sense of the claim by old college friend Gavin Elster, that his wife Madeleine has been possessed by the spirit of her great-grandmother, Carlotta Valdez, detective Scottie Ferguson rejects the suggestion that he consult a history professor. Carlotta is a 'forgotten' Hispanic woman who lived in nineteenth-century California, and her official existence is only recorded by the inscription on her grave – which simply notes the years in which she lived – and by the painting of her in the Palace of the Legion of Honor. Simply entitled 'The Portrait of Carlotta', this provides no context, not even her full name. Although Professor Saunders at Berkeley is a proclaimed authority on the history of San Francisco, Scottie automatically assumes Saunders will not know the kind of 'small stuff' he needs – because her experience would be marginalised. Madeleine, supposedly 'channelling' the spirit of Carlotta, suggests this too when she examines the cross-section of a felled sequoia, which is marked with 'key' historical events. Pointing to the outer rings she murmurs, 'Somewhere here I was born and here I died. It was only a moment for you. You took no notice.' Only in discussion with Pop Liebel, 'the owner of a bookstore familiar with San Francisco lore', does Scottie discover that Carlotta had been the mistress of a rich white man and bore him a child. Yet, Carlotta was 'thrown away' by her lover, who 'kept the child' – an act that drove her mad and led to her suicide in 1857. Liebel is no professional historian – as Richard Corber observes, 'he sells rather

Making over the past: Jimmy Stewart, as Scottie Ferguson, feels the destructive allure of glamorous – but deceitful – representations of the past in Alfred Hitchcock's *Vertigo* (1958). (Courtesy of the Academy of Motion Pictures Arts and Sciences)

than writes books' – and so while he knows the truth about white patriachal oppression and the exploitation of ethnic minorities in California, 'his knowledge of the city's past remains unassimilated by official culture'.[26]

Vertigo, though, is much more overtly concerned with the specific issue of *re-enacting* the past. Scottie becomes inveigled in the plot when Elster asks if he believes that 'someone out of the past, someone dead, can enter and take possession of a human being'. That, presumably, would be the only way of truly 'bringing the past to life', excluding physical reanimation. Links to the rhetoric of Hollywood's history films and the heritage industry, are also reinforced by Hitchcock's use of the eighteenth-century Spanish mission at San Juan Bautista. This mission was a 'living history' museum, its post-war restoration financed by William Randolph Hearst's foundation, and opened to the public in 1949. Appropriately, in *Vertigo* it becomes the setting where history 'repeats' itself, and Madeleine, like Carlotta, apparently commits suicide. However, as the narrative unfolds, it becomes clear that the past has not really been 'brought back to life' – and that the re-enactment of Carlotta's suicide was quite literally an act, a duplicitous performance. The person Scottie takes to be Madeleine is actress Judy Barton, paid by Elster as part of a complicated plan to get away with the murder of his real wife. Counting on the fact that Scottie's fear of heights will prevent him from following Judy up the mission's tower, Elster had thrown the body of the real Madeleine from the top, faking her suicide; with Scottie convinced that that she killed herself because she was obsessed with re-enacting the past tragedy of Carlotta.

It is then Scottie's turn to become fixated on re-enacting the past, haunted by memories of the woman he believed to be Madeleine. His subsequent actions are therefore determined by a fallacious and performative construction of the past – which he himself then tries to reconstruct. Chancing upon Judy Barton, he at first believes she is simply a lookalike – and uses her in an increasingly domineering attempt to 'reanimate' Madeleine, making Judy over into his idealised image of the recently deceased. On this occasion, the past *is* repeating itself – with Scottie making Judy put on the 'mask' of Madeleine as Elster had done – but it only works because Judy has already been 'Madeleine'. Scottie's knowledge of past reality has been manipulated, based on false perceptions, and Judy becomes trapped in this unreal past.

In contrast to what was commonly proposed in the discourse surrounding history films, *Vertigo* questions the very possibility of depicting the 'reality' of the past, when it self-evidently cannot be accessed, 'brought to life' or exist in the present. To believe otherwise is delusional. This perspective may well have been informed by Hitchcock's own experience of making a history film, in 1949's *Under Capricorn*. A box-office disaster that contributed to the failure of his independent company, Transatlantic Pictures, Hitchcock attributed *Capricorn*'s problems to his inability to 'understand the characters' he was supposed to be 'bringing to life'. At over a century removed from the inhabitants of Australia in 1831, he could not comprehend them on the most basic levels – 'how they bought a loaf of bread or went to the bathroom' – and he vowed never to tackle another 'costume picture'.[27] *Vertigo* itself hints at this film's influence on Hitchcock's historical consciousness, specifically marking the year of Carlotta's birth as 1831 as well. It also suggests a critique of Hollywood's insistence on presenting glamorous images of the past in costume dramas – for, as the idealised portrait of Carlotta is replicated in the idealised image of Madeleine imposed upon Judy by Elster and Scottie, it becomes a 'recreation' of the past that is both overly romanticised and abused. Indeed, it is Scottie's obsession with 'recreating' such fictitious images of the past that leads inexorably to Judy's own fatal fall – making his acceptance of such representations dangerous as well as delusional.

Yet, the film also treats Scottie's compulsion to reconstruct the past as overwhelming and inescapable. This obsession continues even when he realises the deception, carrying on with the performance and taking Judy back to the scene of the crime. On this level, his attitude might again be projected on to Hollywood as a whole – as history filmmakers continued to represent their histories as 'real' even though they knew otherwise. It might also be projected onto post-war American culture in general – for Scottie's compulsion is a result his having been traumatised by the death fall of 'Madeleine'. His weakness as an individual renders him powerless to affect or change Madeleine's 'destiny' and prevent the tragedy. This acts as a constant reminder of his lack of agency in the flow of history, and determines his subsequent effort to exert some control and remake the past. Scottie's trauma brings us full circle, back to the implication of *The Story of Mankind* – that America's post-war turn to history was the response of a culture fundamentally traumatised by the ever-present nuclear threat and the ongoing uncertainties of the Cold War. Obsessing about the past was part of an effort to understand what had happened and what the new world order now meant.

As theatre critic Addison DeWitt put it, with characteristic cynicism, near the end of *All About Eve* (1950), 'the history of the world for the past twenty years' has been 'like something out of an old melodrama'. If his words are taken literally, then dramatic films themselves represented a fully appropriate mode by which to represent that past. As Hollywood constructed it, the past *was* 'melodrama' – presented as 'real', unambiguous and easily comprehended. Even the violence of historical events could be presented as 'harmless entertainment', contained within narratives which allowed individual actors to shape history and determine their own destinies (even as, paradoxically, they were simply following a pre-ordained script). This was certainly reassuring in a Cold War context – suggesting that the confusing and fearful present would one day be similarly reduced to an understandable historical drama. However, as this book has demonstrated, if we take DeWitt seriously, it also requires us to reflect on the boundaries between entertainment and history, present and past, image and reality – boundaries that filmmakers blurred with every time they produced a history film. Even when these films seemed not to take their history seriously at all, the very making of them only further problematised Hollywood's historical consciousness.

Notes

The following abbreviations are used to represent the collections consulted in the preparation of this book.

AMPAS	Margaret Herrick Library of the Academy of Motion Picture Arts and Sciences, Los Angeles, California.
AMPTP	Association of Motion Picture and Television Producers Collection, Margaret Herrick Library.
BFI	British Film Institute Library, London.
Davies-AMPAS	Valentine Davies Collection, Margaret Herrick Library.
Douglas-Madison	Kirk Douglas Collection, Madison.
Dunne-USC	Philip Dunne Collection, Doheny Library, University of Southern California.
Fox-UCLA	20th Century-Fox Produced Scripts Collection, UCLA Theatre Arts Library.
Fox-USC	20th Century-Fox Scripts Collection, Doheny Library, University of Southern California.
Freed-USC	Arthur Freed Collection, Doheny Library, University of Southern California.
Heston-AMPAS	Charlton Heston Collection, Margaret Herrick Library.
Hitchcock-AMPAS	Alfred Hitchcock Collection, Margaret Herrick Library.
Houseman-UCLA	John Houseman Collection, UCLA Special Collections Library.

Huston-AMPAS	John Huston Collection, Margaret Herrick Library.
King-AMPAS	Henry King Collection, Margaret Herrick Library.
Kramer-UCLA	Stanley Kramer Collection, UCLA Special Collections Library.
Lavery-UCLA	Emmett Lavery Collection, UCLA Special Collections Library.
Lyndon-AMPAS	Barre Lyndon Collection, Margaret Herrick Library.
Madison	The Wisconsin Center for Film and Theater Research, Madison, Wisconsin.
MGM-AMPAS	Turner-MGM Script Collection, Margaret Herrick Library.
Minnelli-AMPAS	Vincente Minnelli Collection, Margaret Herrick Library.
Negulesco-AMPAS	Jean Negulesco Collection, Margaret Herrick Library.
Nichols-UCLA	Dudley Nichols Collection, UCLA Special Collections Library.
Noerdlinger-AMPAS	Henry S. Noerdlinger Collection, Margaret Herrick Library.
Paramount-AMPAS	Paramount Pictures Scripts Collection, Margaret Herrick Library.
PCA-AMPAS	Motion Picture Association of America Production Code Administration Files, Margaret Herrick Library.
Peck-AMPAS	Gregory Peck Collection, Margaret Herrick Library.
Republic-UCLA	Republic Studios Scripts and Dialog Cutting Continuities, UCLA Special Collections Library.
Schary-Madison	Dore Schary Collection, Madison.
Stevens-AMPAS	George Stevens Collection, Margaret Herrick Library.
UCLA	University of California Los Angeles.
Universal-USC	Universal Studios Collection, Doheny Library, University of Southern California.
USC	Doheny Library, University of Southern California School of Cinema-Television, Los Angeles.
Vidal-Madison	Gore Vidal Collection, Madison.
Wald-USC	Jerry Wald Collection, Doheny Library, University of Southern California.
WB-USC	Warner Bros. Archive, University of Southern California, Los Angeles.

Wyler-AMPAS   William Wyler Collection, Margaret Herrick Library.

Wyler-UCLA   William Wyler Collection, UCLA Special Collections
                     Library.

Zinnemann-AMPAS   Fred Zinnemann Collection, Margaret Herrick
                     Library.

Introduction

1   Higham first identified this 'fundamental change of direction in the
     exploration of the American past' in 'The Cult of "American Consensus":
     Homogenizing Our History', *Commentary*, 27 (February 1959), 93–100.
     This was developed in *The Reconstruction of American History* (London:
     Hutchinson, 1963). While Higham's conclusions were widely accepted by
     socially engaged historians in the 1960s, Gene Wise challenged consensus as
     a 'descriptive label' in *American Historical Explanations* (Homewood, Ill.:
     Dorsey, 1973). Claiming that it simply did not fit the work of post-war
     historians such as Marvin Meyer, David Potter or Leo Marx, Wise suggested
     the term 'counter-Progressive' as a more accurate classification. Similar
     points were made in David Noble's *The End of History: Democracy,
     Capitalism and the Metaphor of Two Worlds in Anglo-American Historical
     Writing* (Minneapolis: Univ. of Minnesota Press, 1985). Studies of indi-
     vidual historians have also complicated the picture, including the commen-
     tary on Daniel Boorstin in J.R Pole's *Paths To the American Past* (New York:
     Oxford Univ. Press, 1979), Daniel Joseph Singal's essay 'Beyond Consensus:
     Richard Hofstadter and American Historiography', *American Historical
     Review*, 89.4 (1984), 976–1004, and John Herbert Roper's biography,
     C. Vann Woodward, Southerner (London: Univ. of Georgia Press, 1987).

2   Peter Novick, *That Noble Dream: The 'Objectivity Question' and the American
     Historical Profession* (Cambridge: Cambridge Univ. Press, 1988). See also
     Richard H. Pells, *The Liberal Mind in a Conservative Age: American Intel-
     lectuals in the 1940s and 1950s* (Middletown: Wesleyan Univ. Press, 1985).

3   Michael Kammen, *Mystic Chords of Memory: The Transformation of Tradition
     in American Culture* (New York: Knopf, 1991) and *In the Past Lane:
     Historical Perspectives on American Culture* (New York: Oxford Univ. Press,
     1997).

4   C. Vann Woodward, *American Attitudes Toward History* (Oxford:
     Clarendon Press, 1955), 7.

5   Richard Hofstadter, *The American Political Tradition* (New York: Knopf,
     1948), ix.

6   Pierre Sorlin, 'Historical Films as Tools for Historians', in John E.
     O'Connor, ed., *Images as Artefact: The Historical Analysis of Film and
     Television* (Malabar: Krieger, 1990), 42.

7   The films in question are *Jupiter's Darling* (1955), *Badman's Country* (1958), *Rogues of Sherwood Forest* (1950) and *The Conqueror* (1956).

8   Warren I. Susman, 'History and the American Intellectual: Uses of a Usable Past', *American Quarterly*, 16 (1964), 243.

9   See Mark C. Carnes, ed., *Past Imperfect: History According to the Movies* (London: Cassell, 1996) and Bruce Crowther, *Hollywood Faction: Reality and Myth in the Movies* (London: Columbus, 1984).

10   Robert Rosenstone, *Revisioning History: Contemporary Filmmakers and the Construction of a New Past* (Princeton: Princeton Univ. Press, 1995), 7.

11   Robert Brent Toplin, *History By Hollywood: The Use and Abuse of the American Past* (Urbana: Univ. of Illinois Press, 1996); Marcia Landy, ed., *The Historical Film: History and Memory in Media* (New Brunswick: Rutgers Univ. Press, 2000).

12   Robert Brent Toplin, 'The Historian and Film: A Research Agenda', *Journal of American History* (December 1991), 1160.

13   Robert Sklar, 'Scofflaws and the Historian-Cop', *Reviews in American History*, 25 (1997), 350.

14   See Kevin Sandler and Gaylyn Studlar, eds, *Titantic: Anatomy of a Blockbuster* (New Brunswick: Rutgers Univ. Press, 1999) and Martin M. Winkler, ed., *Gladiator: Film and History* (London: Blackwell, 2004).

15   Sorlin, 'Historical Films as Tools for Historians', 50.

16   Robert Brent Toplin, *Reel History: In Defense of Hollywood* (Lawrence: Univ. Press of Kansas, 2002), 90.

17   Rosenstone, *Revisioning History*, 4. Rosenstone extended this, stating bluntly that 'traditional costumes…are less important as history than a new kind of film…one that seriously deals with the relationship of past to present'(3).

18   Sorlin, 'Historical Films as Tools for Historians', 42; Leger Grindon, *Shadows of the Past: Studies in the Historical Fiction Film* (Philadelphia: Temple Univ. Press, 1994), 2.

19   Sue Harper, *Picturing the Past: The Rise and Fall of the British Costume Drama* (London: BFI, 1994), 2.

20   Sue Harper, 'Bonnie Prince Charlie Revisited: British Costume Film in the 1950s', in Robert Murray, ed., *The British Cinema Book* (London: BFI, 1997), 133.

21   Lee Clark Mitchell, *Westerns: Making the Man in Fiction and Film* (Chicago: Univ. of Chicago Press, 1996), 5.

22   See Richard Maltby, 'A Better Sense of History: John Ford and the Indians', in Ian Cameron and Douglas Pye, eds, *The Movie Book of the Western* (London: Cassell, 1996), 39.

23   Robert Rosenstone, 'Movie Reviews', *American Historical Review*, 97.4 (1992), 1138.

24   Toplin, 'The Historian and Film', 1162. Happily, Toplin has now reversed his original dismissal of the majority of period-set films, acknowledging that

'when a historian attempts to cite specific examples of such thoroughly wrong-headed interpretations from Hollywood, not many productions come to mind. Few movies qualify as comprehensive failures' (*Reel History*, 91).

Chapter 1: The Story of Mankind

1   See Rudy Behlmer, 'Deja View', *American Cinematographer* (June 1999), 128–138.
2   Review of *The Story of Mankind, Motion Picture Herald*, 26 October 1957.
3   Wherever possible, the exact chronological settings of history films have been derived from the signifiers given on screen, in forewords or narration. Otherwise, the dating has been taken from the Production Code Administration files (AMPAS) which record, on a pro-forma analysis sheet, the temporal setting and location of every movie's story. With modifications based on this research, Figure 1.1 replicates a table published by Garth Jowett in 'The Concept of History in American Produced Films Made in the Period 1950–1961', *Journal of Popular Culture*, 3.4 (1970), 799.
4   Richard Slotkin, 'The Continuity of Forms: Myth and Genre in Warner Brothers' *The Charge of the Light Brigade*', *Representations*, 29 (Winter 1990), 3.
5   Richard Slotkin, *Gunfighter Nation: The Myth of the Frontier in Twentieth-Century America* (Norman: University of Oklahoma Press, 1998), 233.
6   Homer's *Odyssey* was also adapted as *Ulysses* (1954), an Italian-American co-production directed by Mario Camerini. Other Old Testament 'histories' included *David and Bathsheba* (1951), *Slaves of Babylon* (1953) and *Solomon and Sheba* (1959).
7   George MacDonald Fraser, *The Hollywood History of the World* (London: Michael Joseph, 1988), 20.
8   *The Prodigal* pressbook, BFI.
9   Philip Dunne to Julian Johnson, 11 August 1952, *The Egyptian* Interoffice Communications, Dunne-USC: Box 6.
10   *Photoplay Studies*, 24.5, November 1959, 7, *Ben Hur* Promotional Material, Wyler-UCLA: 20.8
11   Foreword to *The Black Rose* (1950).
12   Review of *The Black Shield of Falworth, Hollywood Reporter*, 3 August 1954.
13   Sue Harper, 'Bonnie Prince Charlie Revisited: British Costume Film in the 1950s', in Robert Murphy, ed., *The British Cinema Book* (London: BFI, 1997), 138.
14   Brian Taves, *Romance of Adventure: The Genre of Historical Adventure Movies* (Jackson: Univ. Press of Mississippi, 1993), 23. Nineteen Arabian Nights fantasies were released, from *The Desert Hawk* (1950) to *The Seventh Voyage of Sinbad* (1958), with Katzman also producing *The Magic Carpet*

(1950), *The Thief of Damascus* (1951), *Siren of Bagdad* (1952) and *Prisoners of the Casbah* (1953).

15   *Ibid.*, 95, 93.

16   Examples include *Buccaneer's Girl* (1950), *The Fortunes of Captain Blood* (1950), *Against All Flags* (1952), *Pirates of Tripoli* (1955) – and the spoof *Double Crossbones* (1951) which united Blackbeard, Kidd and the fictional Captain Blood.

17   *At Sword's Point* pressbook, BFI.

18   In a less generic form, Stanley Kramer's *Cyrano de Bergerac* (1950) adapted Edmond Rostand's 1897 play.

19   Foreword to Casanova's *Big Night* (1954).

20   Walt Disney, on-screen introduction to *Johnny Tremain* on *Disneyland* television programme, broadcast 21 November 1958.

21   There was, moreover, further reflection on the Revolution in depictions of the 'cruelty and injustice' of Hanoverian rule in George I's Britain – the background to *Rob Roy, The Highland Rogue* (1953), *The Master of Ballantrae* (1953) and *The Iron Glove*. In 'Bonnie Prince Charlie Revisited', Sue Harper suggests that American producers 'deployed the romantic Scottish rebellion against British rationality as a sort of "prequel" of the American War of Independence' (138).

22   Foreword to *The Man From the Alamo* (1953). See also *Lone Star* (1951), *The Iron Mistress* (1952), *Davy Crockett, King of the Wild Frontier* (1954), *The Last Command* (1955) and *The First Texan* (1956).

23   *Band of Angels* Production Notes, n.d., WB-USC.

24   Joseph McBride, *Searching for John Ford: A Life* (New York: St Martin's Press, 2001), 596.

25   Will Wright, *Six Guns and Society: A Structural Study of the Western* (Berkeley: Univ. of California Press, 1977), 5.

26   *Ibid.*, 6.

27   Jowett, 'The Concept of History', 806.

28   Richard Maltby, 'A Better Sense of History', in Ian Cameron and Douglas Pye, eds, *The Movie Book of the Western* (London: Cassell, 1996), 41.

29   Foreword to *The Man from God's Country* (1958).

30   Advertisement copy for *Westward the Women*, Production Correspondence, 8 October 1951, Schary-Madison, 54.7.

31   Social change is affected by the press in *Fort Worth* (1951) and *Texas Lady* (1955); by doctors in *Strange Lady in Town* (1955) and *The Hanging Tree* (1959); and by clergymen in *Stars in My Crown* (1950) and *The Peacemaker* (1954). *High Noon* (1951) and *Rio Bravo* (1958) both depict strong lawmen solving a town's problems, while 'historical' figures such as Wyatt Earp and Bat Masterson are considered in *Wichita* (1955) and *Gunfight at Dodge City* (1959) respectively.

32 Douglas Pye, 'The Collapse of Fantasy: Masculinity in the Westerns of Anthony Mann', in Cameron and Pye, eds, *The Movie Book of the Western*, 168.

33 Andre Bazin, *What Is Cinema?* (Berkeley: Univ. of California Press, 1967), 151.

34 Billy the Kid also featured in *The Kid from Texas* (1950), *I Shot Billy the Kid* (1950), *The Law vs. Billy the Kid* (1954) and *The Parson and the Outlaw* (1957). Jesse James received treatment in *Kansas Raiders* (1950), *The Great Missouri Raid* (1950), *The Great Jesse James Raid* (1953) and the Bob Hope comedy, *Alias Jesse James* (1959).

35 Pye, 'The Collapse of Fantasy', 167–173.

36 *Escape from Fort Bravo* pressbook, 2, BFI.

37 Maltby, 'A Better Sense of History', 34.

38 Douglas Brode, *The Films of the Fifties* (New York: Citadel, 1992), 134.

39 George Sherman, *Chief Crazy Horse* Press Release, 17 May 1955, Universal-USC: 421.23.

40 Reflecting the derivative nature of *The Story of Mankind*, Hollywood had already produced biopics of *The Story of Alexander Graham Bell* (1939), *Young Tom Edison* (1940) and *Edison, The Man* (1940).

41 Steven Watts, *The Magic Kingdom: Walt Disney and the American Way of Life* (New York: Houghton Mifflin, 1997), 299; *Gigi* pressbook, BFI.

42 It is suggestive that the only biopic to depict a real inventor was *Carbine Williams* (1952), about the man who invented the carbine rifle used by American soldiers in World War II.

43 George Custen, *Bio-Pics: How Hollywood Constructed Public History* (New Brunswick: Rutgers Univ. Press, 1992), 89.

44 *The Buster Keaton Story* (1957), *Man of a Thousand Faces* (1957), *Valentino* (1951) and *The Story of Will Rogers* (1952).

45 Geoffrey Shurlock to Al Zimbalist, 16 July 1957, *Baby Face Nelson* file, PCA-AMPAS.

46 Foreword to *Paths of Glory* (1957). Other films set against WWI included *The African Queen* (1951), *Lafayette Escadrille* (1958), *What Price Glory* (1952), *A Farewell to Arms* (1957), *The Royal African Rifles* (1953).

47 Foreword to *The Flying Leathernecks* (1951).

48 Foreword to *Pork Chop Hill* (1959).

49 Richard Hoftstadter, *The American Political Tradition* (New York: Knopf, 1948), ix.

50 In Disney's *20,000 Leagues Under the Sea*, the Nautilus submarine apparently runs 'on the secret sources of the power of the universe'. In Jules Verne's novel, the Nautilus is destroyed in a maelstrom, but in the movie it self-destructs, consumed in a mushroom-cloud explosion. Similarly, while 'gun-cotton' is used as the rocket-launching explosive in the original novel, *From the Earth to the Moon* redefines it as atomic energy, labelled 'Power-X'.

51   Review of *The Story of Mankind, New York Post*, 10 November 1957.

52   *Time*, 17 March 1942, 32.

53   See William H. McNeill, *Arthur J. Toynbee: A Life* (New York: Oxford Univ. Press, 1989), 205–213.

54   *Story of Mankind* Press Release, n.d, WB-USC.

55   'General Information Interview with Irwin Allen', 27 September 1957, *Story of Mankind* Publicity, WB-USC.

Chapter 2: Economic History

1   *Sign of the Pagan* Press Release, Production Notes file 1, Universal-USC: 580-17808.

2   Philip Dunne to Charles Enfield, 5 November 1954, *Prince of Players* Production Correspondence 2, Dunne-USC.

3   Hortense Powdermaker, *Hollywood, The Dream Factory: An Anthropologist Looks at the Movie-makers* (London: Secker and Warburg, 1951), 88.

4   MGM's data is in *The Eddie Mannix Ledger*, held in the Howard Strickling Collection, AMPAS. The equivalent accounting for Warner Brothers is *The William Schaefer Ledger* in the William Schaefer Collection, USC. Two articles by H. Mark Glancy offer an introductory interpretation of these ledgers – 'MGM Film Grosses, 1925–1948: the Eddie Mannix Ledger', *Historical Journal of Film, Radio and Television*, 12.2 (1992), 127–144, and 'Warner Bros Film Grosses, 1921–51: the William Schaefer Ledger', *Historical Journal of Film, Radio and Television*, 15.1 (1995), 55–72. However, Glancy's discussion and data did not cover the 1950s in either case, and the data presented in this book comes directly from the ledgers themselves. Similar data exists for RKO and is discussed by Richard B. Jewell in 'RKO Film Grosses, 1929–1951: the C. J. Tevlin Ledger', *Historical Journal of Film, Radio and Television*, 14.1 (1994), 37–49; but unlike Mannix and Schaefer, Tevlin did not continue his accounting beyond 1951.

5   According to calculations based on the Mannix ledger, the 192 films released by MGM that were not set in the past generated revenues of $386 million – an average gross income of $2.1 million. The Schaefer ledger records incomes for 112 non-history films, grossing a total of $274 million – an average of $2.4 million per film.

6   Calculated from the tables of 'Box-Office Hits 1914–1986', in Joel W. Finler, *The Hollywood Story* (London: Octopus, 1988), 276–277.

7   Dore Schary, 'The Changing World of the Screen' (article prepared for the *New York Times*, 25 July 1956), Schary-Madison: 19.5.

8   Appendix V in Garth Jowett, *Film: The Democratic Art* (Boston: Little, Brown, 1976), 472.

9   See Frederic Stuart, *The Effects of Television in the Motion Picture and Radio Industries* (New York: Arno Press, 1975).

10 Quoted in James Patterson, *Grand Expectations: The United States, 1945–1974* (New York: Oxford Univ. Press, 1996), 350.

11 Jowett, *Film*, 338.

12 Michael Conant, *Antitrust in the Motion Picture Industry* (Berkeley: Univ. of California Press, 1960).

13 Appendix XIX in Jowett, *Film*, 483.

14 Glancy, 'Warner Bros Film Grosses, 1921–51', 55–72.

15 This was calculated following Glancy's lead, whereby 'expensive' films are defined as ones which cost more than 50 percent of the average production cost in any given year.

16 See Aubrey Solomon, *Twentieth Century-Fox: A Corporate and Financial History* (London: Scarecrow Press, 1988), 215–260.

17 Similarly, history films represented 66 percent of films with budgets in excess of $2 million at Fox, and 62 percent at Warner Bros.

18 Freeman Lincoln, 'The Comeback of the Movies', *Fortune*, 51 (February 1955), reprinted in Tino Balio, ed., *The American Film Industry* (Madison: Univ. of Wisconsin Press, 1976), 379.

19 The ORC's 1957 survey, *The Public Appraises Movies*, is reprinted in Jowett, *Film*, 476–480.

20 Campbell MacCulloch, quoted in Richard Maltby, 'Sticks, Hicks and Flaps: Classical Hollywood's Generic Conception of its Audiences', in Melvyn Stokes and Richard Maltby, eds, *Identifying Hollywood's Audiences: Cultural Identity and the Movies* (London: BFI, 1999), 24.

21 See, for example, review of *The Buccaneer's Girl, Variety*, 1 March 1950.

22 Review of *Ivanhoe, Variety,* 11 June 1952; review of *King Solomon's Mines, Variety,* 23 September 1950.

23 Darryl Zanuck, 'Production Survey', 12 October 1950, King-AMPAS: f.138.

24 Review of *The Flame and the Arrow, New York Times*, 15 July 1950.

25 Review of *Prince Valiant, Variety,* 2 April 1954.

26 'Memorandum on *Prince Valiant*', 20 November 1952, 2, Fox-UCLA: 157-2569.3.

27 'Conference Notes on *Prince Valiant*', 10 February 1953, Fox-UCLA: 157-2569.6.

28 Mike Steen, *Pandro S. Berman: A Louis B. Mayer Foundation – American Film Institute Oral History, Volume 1* (Los Angeles: American Film Institute, 1972), 106.

29 Review of *Flying Leathernecks, Variety,* 28 August 1951.

30 Darryl Zanuck to Robert Jacks on *The Desert Rats*, 15 October 1952, 3–4, Fox-USC: 2528.9.

31 'Comment on *Destination Gobi* Script', 5 July 1952, Fox-USC: 2522.6.

32 Fred Zinnemann to Irwin Shaw, February 15 1952, Correspondence File, Zinnemann-AMPAS: 99-1322.

33 Al Hine, 'Movies', *Holiday* (September 1950), 19–22.

34 George Custen, *Twentieth Century's Fox: Darryl F. Zanuck and the Culture of Hollywood* (New York: Basic Books, 1997), 354.

35 Solomon, *Twentieth Century-Fox*, 129.

36 *Ibid.*

37 Custen, *Twentieth Century's Fox*, 14, 224.

38 Respectively referring to *In Old Chicago* (1938), *Brigham Young* (1940) and *Alexander's Ragtime Band* (1938), see Mel Gussow, *Don't Say Yes Until I Finish Talking: A Biography of Darryl F. Zanuck* (New York: Doubleday, 1971), 75.

39 Custen, *Twentieth Century's Fox*, 202–204.

40 *Variety*, 12 February 1952.

41 Review of *Darby O'Gill and the Little People, Variety*, 29 April 1959.

42 Review of *Showboat, Variety*, 6 June 1951; Review of *Barretts of Wimpole Street, Variety,* 16 January 1957.

43 Richard Dyer McCann, 'Hollywood Faces the World (1962)', reprinted in Gerald Mast, ed., *The Movies in Our Midst: Documents in the Cultural History of Film in America* (Chicago: Univ. of Chicago Press, 1982), 667.

44 Maltby, *Hollywood Cinema*, 69.

45 At Warner Bros. 61 percent of films broke even in the domestic market; foreign sales increased this to 85 percent of films recouping their costs.

46 See review of *It Came From Beneath the Sea, Variety*, 17 June 1955.

47 See review of *The McConnell Story, Variety*, 17 August 1955.

48 Review of *Love Me Tender, Variety*, 21 November 1956.

49 Review of *Journey to the Centre of the Earth, Variety*, 9 December 1959.

50 Darryl Zanuck, 'Production Overview', 1 August 1953, 6, King-AMPAS: f.138.

51 'Conference notes on *Desiree*', 30 June 1953, Fox-UCLA: 719-25902.2.

52 *Ibid.*, my italics.

53 Stan Margulies to Roger Lewis, United Artists, 14 May 1957, *Paths of Glory* Correspondence, Douglas-Madison: 23.21.

54 David O. Selznick to John Huston, 4 March 1957, 3, Correspondence, Huston-AMPAS: Box 2.

55 Lists of the top ten bestselling books of each year can be found at htpp://www.caderbooks.com/best50.html (accessed October 2004).

56 *Alexander the Great* pressbook, 8, BFI.

57 Review of *Lady Godiva, Hollywood Reporter*, 7 October 1955.

58 Darryl Zanuck, 'Production Overview', 5 July 1952, 2, King-AMPAS: f. 138.

Chapter 3: Economic History

1   *The Charge at Feather River* pressbook, BFI.
2   See, for example, John Belton. *Widescreen Cinema* (Cambridge: Harvard Univ. Press, 1992), R.M. Hayes, *3-D Movies: A History and Filmography of Stereoscopic Cinema* (London: McFarland, 1989), and the excellent *Widescreen Museum* website by Martin Hart at http://www. widescreenmuseum.com (accessed October 2004).
3   John Houseman to Max Ophuls, 13 March 1953, Houseman-UCLA: 5-816.
4   'Vista Vision', http://www.widescreenmuseum.com/widescreen/wing vv1.htm (accessed 6 October 2004).
5   Milton Lowell Gunzberg Oral History, interviewed by Douglas Bell (Margaret Herrick Library, 1994), 110, AMPAS.
6   Review of *The Robe, Time*, 28 September 1953.
7   Andre Bazin, 'Will CinemaScope save the Cinema?', *Esprit* (October 1953), reprinted in *Velvet Light Trap*, 21 (1985), 14.
8   Darryl F. Zanuck to Philip Dunne, 1 August 1953, in Rudy Belhmer, ed., *Memo From Darryl F. Zanuck: The Golden Years at Twentieth Century Fox* (New York: Grove Press, 1993), 244.
9   John Belton, *Widescreen Cinema*, 194.
10   Vivian Sobchack, 'Surge and Splendor: A Phenomenology of the Hollywood Historical Epic', in Barry Keith Grant, ed., *Film Genre Reader II* (Austin: Univ. of Texas Press, 1995), 286.
11   *The Conqueror* pressbook, AMPAS; *Knights of the Round Table* pressbook, BFI.
12   *Knights of the Round Table* pressbook, BFI.
13   Michael Todd, Jr. and Susan McCarthy Todd, *A Valuable Property: The Life Story of Michael Todd* (New York: Arbor House, 1983), 267.
14   John Belton, *Widescreen Cinema*, 127.
15   Jack Warner, '1927, Sound – 1953, 3-D', in Martin Quigley, Jr., ed., *New Screen Techniques* (New York: Quigley Publishing, 1953), 84.
16   William Paul observes that 'like movies, [wax sculpture] has not been taken seriously as art, yet its popular appeal, like that of film, lies in its ability to recreate reality, or more accurately, create the fullness of an illusion of reality'. Paul, 'The Aesthetics of Emergence', *Film History*, 5.3 (1993), 341.
17   See Charles Musser, 'The Eden Musee in 1898: Exhibitor as Co-Creator', *Film and History*, 11.4 (December 1981), 73–83.
18   Paul, 'The Aesthetics of Emergence', 342.
19   W.R. Wilkerson, *Hollywood Reporter*, 11 December 1952, 1.
20   Paul, 'The Aesthetics of Emergence', 350.
21   Anthony Slide, *De Toth on De Toth: Putting the Drama in Front of the Camera* (London: Faber and Faber, 1996), 116.

22 *Charge at Feather River* Press Release, 7 June 1953, BFI.

23 Michael Kerbel, '3-D or not 3-D', *Film Comment*, 16.6 (November 1980), 16.

24 Quoted in Belton, *Widescreen Cinema*, 77.

25 Darryl Zanuck, 'Entertainment vs. Recreation', *Hollywood Reporter*, 26 October 1953.

26 Belton, *Widescreen Cinema*, 98.

27 Warner, '1927, Sound – 1953, 3-D', 86.

28 Belton, *Widescreen Cinema*, 187.

29 *Oklahoma!* pressbook, BFI.

30 *The Robe* pressbook, BFI.

31 *Run For Cover* pressbook, AMPAS.

32 Paul, 'The Aesthetics of Emergence', 336.

33 James Spellerberg, 'CinemaScope and Ideology', *Velvet Light Trap*, 21 (1985), 30.

34 Leon Shamroy, 'Filming *The Robe*', in Quigley, ed., *New Screen Techniques*, 177.

35 Michael Kammen, *Mystic Chords of Memory: The Transformation of Tradition in American Culture* (New York: Knopf, 1991), 539.

36 David M. Simmons, *The Wells Family and the Early Years of Sturbridge Village* (Sturbridge: Old Sturbridge Inc., 2000), 36.

37 Calico Ghost Town website, http://www.calicotown.com (accessed October 2004).

38 Kammen, *Mystic Chords of Memory*, 547.

39 Charles Barr, 'CinemaScope: Before and After', *Film Quarterly*, 16.4 (1963), 4–25.

40 Ben Schlanger, 'The Evolution of the Williamsburg System', originally in the *Journal of the Society of Motion Picture and Television Engineers* (January 1962), reproduced at http://www.widescreenmuseum.com/widescreen/williams.htm (accessed October 2004).

41 During the 1950s, 'the number of annual visitors to national parks rose from 13.9 million to 26.6 million, those to national monuments from 5.3 million to 10.7 million, and those using national parkways from 2.8 million to 8.9 million'. This 'travel binge' was aided by 'cheap gasoline, a growing network of highways, paid vacation time, and more money than ever before'. Moreover, while some 676,000 American tourists travelled abroad in 1950, this had increased to 1.6 million by 1960. See J. Ronald Oakley, *God's Country: America in the Fifties* (New York: Dembner, 1986), 259–260.

42 Behlmer, *Memo From Darryl Zanuck*, 244.

43 'Memorandum on Working Script of *Garden of Evil*', 16 June 1953, 1, Fox-UCLA: 695-2576.3.

44 *The Pride and the Passion* pressbook, BFI; *Knights of the Round Table* pressbook, BFI.

45 *Run For Cover* pressbook, AMPAS.

46 *Oklahoma!* pressbook, BFI.

47 *Around the World in 80 Days* Press Release, 23 July 1955, BFI.

48 Jack Harrison, *Hollywood Reporter*, 18 October 1956.

49 *Around the World in 80 Days* Press Release.

50 Thomas C. Renzi, *Jules Verne on Film* (London: McFarland, 1998), 23, 19.

51 James T. Patterson, *Grand Expectations: The United States, 1945–1974* (New York: Oxford Univ. Press, 1996), 313.

Chapter 4: Political History

1   Larry Ceplair and Steven Englund, *The Inquisition in Hollywood: Politics in the Film Community, 1930–1960* (Berkeley: Univ of California Press, 1983), 209–211.

2   Walter Bernstein, *Inside Out: A Memoir of the Blacklist* (New York: Knopf, 1996), 257– 258.

3   Pierre Sorlin, 'Historical Films as Tools for Historians', in John E. O'Connor, ed., *Image as Artifact: The Historical Analysis of Film and Television* (Malabar: Krieger, 1990), 51.

4   Maria Wyke, *Projecting the Past: Ancient Rome, Cinema and History* (London: Routledge, 1997), 144; Bruce Babington and Peter Evans, *Biblical Epics: Sacred Narrative in the Hollywood Cinema* (Manchester: Manchester Univ. Press, 1993), 211.

5   John H. Lenihan, 'English Classics For Cold War America', *Journal of Popular Film and Television*, 20.3 (Autumn 1992), 42–51.

6   Geoff Andrew, *The Films of Nicholas Ray* (London: Letts, 1991), 91.

7   John Belton, *American Cinema/American Culture* (New York: McGraw-Hill, 1994), 248.

8   *The Ten Commandments* pressbook, BFI.

9   Given the fact that the world premiere of *The Ten Commandments* came in the same week as Britain, France and Israel invaded Egypt, DeMille was quick to capitalise on the coincidence. See Steven Cohan, *Masked Men: Masculinity and the Movies in the Fifties* (Bloomington: Indiana Univ. Press, 1997), 137–141; Alan Nadel, *Containment Culture: American Narratives, Postmodernism and the Atomic Age* (Durham: Duke Univ. Press, 1995), 115.

10 Foreword to *Quo Vadis;* Wyke, *Projecting the Past*, 112.

11 Alan Lupack, 'An Enemy in Our Midst: *The Black Knight* and the American Dream', in Kevin J. Harty, ed., *Cinema Arthuriana: Essays on Arthurian Film* (New York: Garland, 1991), 29–40.

12 *California Conquest* is discussed in Michael Strada and Harold Troper, *Friend or Foe? Russians in American Film and Foreign Policy, 1933–1991* (London: Scarecrow Press, 1997), 86.

13 Richard Slotkin, *Gunfighter Nation: The Myth of the Frontier in Twentieth-Century America* (Norman: Univ. of Oklahoma Press, 1998), 383–396, 433–440.

14 Robert Brent Toplin, *History by Hollywood: The Use and Abuse of the American Past* (Urbana: Univ. of Chicago Press, 1996), x.

15 Harry Schein, 'The Olympian Cowboy', *American Scholar*, 24.3 (Summer 1955), 309– 320.

16 Quoted in Paul Buhle and David Wagner, *Radical Hollywood: The Untold Story Behind America's Favorite Movies* (New York: New Press, 2002), 421.

17 Phillip Drummond, *High Noon* (London: British Film Institute, 1997).

18 Dore Schary, 'There is a Tide in the Affairs of Man', Promotional Programme for *Julius Caesar*, Houseman-UCLA: Box 119.

19 I.F.Stone, *The Haunted Fifties* (Boston: Little, Brown, 1963), 69; John E. Haynes, *Red Scare or Red Menace?: American Communism and Anticommunism in the Cold War Era* (Chicago: Ivan Dee, 1996), 119.

20 Schary, 'There is a Tide in the Affairs of Man'.

21 See Kenneth L. Geist, *Pictures Will Talk: The Life and Films of Joseph L. Mankiewicz* (New York: Scribners, 1978), 173–206.

22 Lenihan, 'English Classics For Cold War America', 49.

23 Daniel Bell, ed., *The New American Right* (New York: Doubleday, 1955). The near-contemporary interpretation of the social forces behind McCarthyism was challenged in the 1970s, when attention was re-directed towards the role of the federal government and partisan politics, in David Caute's *The Great Fear: The Anti-Communist Purge Under Truman and Eisenhower* (New York: Simon and Schuster, 1978) and Robert Griffith's *The Politics of Fear: Joseph R. McCarthy and the Senate* (New York: Hayden, 1970). More recently, Ellen Schrecker's *Many Are the Crimes: McCarthyism in America* (Princeton: Princeton Univ. Press, 1998) furthers the case for seeing McCarthyism as 'primarily a top-down phenomenon'.

24 Gore Vidal, 'Notes on 'Captain Dreyfus'', 6 October 1955, MGM-AMPAS: 1441.3.

25 *Ibid.*

26 See 'HUAC Revisited', in Gore Vidal, *Rocking the Boat* (Boston: Little, Brown, 1962), 44–56.

27 'Garfield, Ferrer, "Investigate" Selves As Prelude to April 20 Red Hearings', *Variety*, 11 April 1953.

28 Ferrer's testimony appears in Eric Bentley, ed., *Thirty Years of Treason: Excerpts From Hearings Before the House Committee on Un-American Activities, 1938–1968* (London: Thames Hudson, 1971), 407–434.

29 Bruce Cook, *Dalton Trumbo* (New York: Scribner, 1977), 199.

30 Vidal, 'Notes on 'Captain Dreyfus'', 6 October 1955. The first 'Drefuysard', Bernard-Lazare, wrote in 1897: 'It was because he was a Jew that he was arrested, it was because he was a Jew he was tried, it was because he was a

Jew that he was found guilty, and it is because he is a Jew that the voice of truth and justice is not allowed to speak out on his behalf.' See Eric Cahm, *The Dreyfus Affair in French Society and Politics* (London: Longman, 1994), 43.

31   Buhle and Wagner, *Radical Hollywood*, 370.

32   'Captain Dreyfus' Screenplay, 24 April 1956, Vidal-Madison: 28.10.

33   Ceplair and Englund, *The Inquisition in Hollywood*, 294.

34   Lavery's testimony in Bentley, ed., *Thirty Years of Treason*, 171, 173.

35   Emmett Lavery, 'Draft Notes on *Court Martial*', 2, Lavery-UCLA: 4-f.4.

36   Lavery had asserted that 'in our own domestic American life, the way to meet the challenge of Communism is not repressive legislation or scareheads, but to show that we have a better way of life…' Bentley, ed., *Thirty Years of Treason*, 181.

37   Gen. William Mitchell, *Winged Defense* (New York: Putnams, 1925), 25–26.

38   Michael Sherry, *In the Shadow of War: The United States Since the 1930s* (New Haven: Yale Univ. Press, 1995), 192.

39   Michael Wilson, 'Conditioning the American Mind: War Films Show Vicious Over-All Policy', *Hollywood Review*, 1.1 (January 1953), 3.

40   John Howard Lawson, *Film in the Battle of Ideas* (New York: Masses and Mainstream, 1953), 31.

41   See Les K. Adler and Thomas G. Paterson, 'Red Fascism: The Merger of Nazi Germany and Soviet Russia in the American Image of Totalitarianism, 1930s–1950s', *American Historial Review*, 75 (April 1970), 1046–1064.

42   Cyndy Hendershot, *Anti-Communism and Popular Culture in Mid-Century America* (London: McFarland, 2003), 59.

43   Indeed, testifying before HUAC in 1947, Hoover described the Communist Party of the United States as 'far better organized than were the Nazis in occupied countries prior to their capitulation'. Quoted in Ellen Schrecker, *The Age of McCarthyism: A Brief History with Documents* (Boston: Bedford Books, 1994), 119.

44   'The Truman Doctrine, 12 March 1947', in *The Public Papers of the Presidents of the United States: Harry S. Truman: 1947* (Washington: US Government Printing Office, 1963), 176–179.

45   Ayn Rand, *Screen Guide for Americans* (Beverley Hills: Motion Picture Alliance for the Preservation of American Ideals, 1950), 2.

46   Pressbooks for *Black Shield of Falworth, The Purple Mask, Rogues of Sherwood Forest* and *Thief of Damascus* respectively, BFI.

47   See Leon Gordon and Richard Schayer, 'Temporary Complete Screenplay of *Kim*', 8 January 1942, MGM-AMPAS: 1081.265.

48   Quoted in William H. Mooring, *The Tidings*, 27 January 1950, Press Materials 2, Dunne-USC: Box 6.

49 Quoted in Whitfield, *The Culture of the Cold War*, 80, 81. For a near-contemporary assessment of Graham's impact, see William G. McLoughlin, *Billy Graham: Revivalist in a Secular Age* (New York: Ronald Press, 1960).

50 On-screen introduction to *The Ten Commandments* (1956).

51 Father Urban Nagel, 'Notes for Developing Fatima Story', n.d., *The Miracle of Our Lady of Fatima* Production Notes, WB-USC.

52 'Actual Dialogue of the Third Apparition', compiled by E.G. Dougherty, 23 January 1952, *The Miracle of Our Lady of Fatima File*, PCA-AMPAS.

53 Warner Bros. officially based their film on C.C. Martingdale's *The Meaning of Fatima* (1950), but other post-war texts on the 'miracle' included *Jacinta: The Flower of Fatima* by Rev. William F. Hill (1946), Rev. Joseph Cacella's *A Brief History of the Wonders of Fatima, Portugal* (1947), Mary Fabyan Windeatt's *The Children of Fatima* (1948) and Thomas McGlynn's *The Vision of Fatima* (1948). ('Research Breakdown', *Miracle of Our Lady of Fatima* Research File, WB-USC.)

54 E.G. Dougherty, Memo for the Files, 23 January 1952, *Miracle of Our Lady of Fatima* File, PCA-AMPAS.

55 See, for example, Antonio Henrique de Oliveira Marques, *History of Portugal. Volume II: From Empire to Corporate State* (New York: Columbia Univ. Press, 1976) and David Birmingham, *A Concise History of Portugal* (Cambridge: Cambridge Univ. Press, 1993).

56 Marques, *History of Portugal*, 133.

57 According to the Schaefer Ledger, *Fatima* grossed $4.2 million worldwide, compared to *I Was A Communist*'s meagre $1.8 million.

58 Review of *The Miracle of Our Lady of Fatima, Hollywood Reporter,* 21 August 1952.

59 'Omar Khayyam, the Astronomer-Poet of Persia', *The Calcutta Review*, January–June 1858, 149–162; copy in 'Omar Khayyam' Research File, Lyndon-AMPAS.

60 'Story Comparison' by Allida Allen, 9 August 1954, *Omar Khayyam*, Paramount-AMPAS: 3501.

61 *Omar Khayyam* pressbook, BFI.

62 J. Edgar Hoover, *Masters of Deceit: The Story of Communism in America and How to Fight It* (New York: Holt, 1958).

63 See Susan L. Carruthers, '*The Manchurian Candidate* and the Cold War Brainwashing Scare', *Historical Journal of Film Radio and Television*, 18.1 (March 1988), 75–94; John Marks, *The Search for 'The Manchurian Candidate': The Story of the CIA's Secret Efforts to Control Human Behavior* (London: Allen Lane, 1979).

64 Quoted in letter of 9 March 1953, reprinted in David Eldridge, 'Dear Owen: The CIA, Luigi Luraschi and Hollywood, 1953', *Historical Journal of Film, Radio and Television,* 20.2 (2000), 149–196.

65   Interview with Lynn Castille, entitled 'Lynn Looks at Hollywood', in *Plymouth Adventure* Miscellany, Schary-Madison: 48.1.

66   Clarence Brown, quoted in *Hollywood Citizen News*, n.d., clipping in Plymouth Adventure File, PCA-AMPAS.

67   *Time*, 9 June 1952.

68   Marian Strack, 'The Strange Case of *Plymouth Adventure*', *National Republic*, March 1953, 6, clipping in *Plymouth Adventure* Miscellany, Schary-Madison: 48.1.

69   Rand, *Screen Guide for Americans*, 3.

70   Strack, 'The Strange Case of *Plymouth Adventure*', 6. According to a report in *Variety* (26 November 1952), Chapters of the Descendants were already concerned when they heard that the screenplay 'smeared' Dorothy Bradford's reputation by suggesting an affair between her and the captain of *The Mayflower*. Strack's attack compounded their denouncement of the film.

71   Colin Shindler, 'Cold War Cinema', in Ann Lloyd, ed., *Movies of the Fifties* (London: Orbis, 1982), 23.

72   Gerry Blattner to Steve Trilling, 22 July 1950, *Captain Horatio Hornblower* Production Reports, WB-USC.

73   Review of *Scaramouche, Variety*, 14 May 1952.

74   John Steinbeck, 'Treatment of Zapata – The Little Tiger', 9 April 1949, 5, 82, Fox-UCLA: 776-2480.5a.

75   Addison Durland to Jason Joy, 1 June 1948, *Viva Zapata* File, PCA-AMPAS.

76   Steinbeck, 'Treatment of Zapata – The Little Tiger', 82.

77   'Memorandum on *Viva Zapata*', 26 December 1950, 5, 9. Fox-UCLA: 775-2480.17.

78   Sloktin, *Gunfighter Nation*, 425.

79   Elia Kazan, *A Life* (London: Andre Deutsch, 1988), 459.

80   Paul Vanderwood, 'An American Cold Warrior: *Viva Zapata!*', in John O'Connor and Martin Jackson, eds, *American History/American Film: Interpreting the Hollywood Image* (New York: Ungar, 1979), 187.

81   Review of *Bridge on the River Kwai, Hollywood Reporter*, 20 November 1957.

82   'Incomplete Screenplay of *Montezuma*', 12 October 1957, i., Douglas-Madison: 56.13.

83   Quoted in Louis Marks, 'Hood Winked', *The Listener*, 18 January 1990, 8.

84   The most thorough identification of the blacklistees working for Weinstein is Steve Neale's article, 'Psuedonyms, Sapphire and Salt, "un-American" Contributions to Television Costume Adventure Series in the 1950s', *Historical Journal of Film, Radio and Television*, 23.3 (2003), 245–257.

85   John Schulteiss, 'A Season of Fear: The Blacklisted Teleplays of Abraham Polonsky', *Literature/Film Quarterly*, 24.2 (1996), 149.

86   Abraham Polonsky, quoted in Schulteiss, 'A Season of Fear', 149.

87   Bernstein, *Inside Out*, 221.

88   Polonsky, quoted in Schulteiss, 'A Season of Fear', 149.

Chapter 5: Social History

1   Philip French, *Westerns: Aspects of a Movie Genre* (London: Secker and Warburg, 1973), 13.

2   John Lenihan, *Showdown: Confronting Modern America in the Western Film* (Urbana: Univ. of Illinois Press, 1980).

3   Dorothy Jones, 'Communism and the Movies: A Study of Film Content', in John Cogley, *Blacklisting: Volume I: The Movies* (Los Angeles: Fund for the Republic, 1956), 232.

4   Darryl Zanuck, 'Showmanship Alone No Longer Enough', *Daily Film Renter*, April 1947, 49; Darryl Zanuck, 'Film Producing: Yesterday, Today and Tomorrow', *Film Review Annual* 1946 (Englewood, NJ.: J.S. Ozer, 1945), 17.

5   Jones, 'Communism and the Movies', 232.

6   Michael Abel to Darryl Zanuck, 'Memo on 'Blood Brothers'', 1 April 1949, *Broken Arrow* Script File 1, Fox-USC.

7   Lenihan, *Showdown*, 61.

8   See Thomas Cripps, *Making Movies Black* (New York: Oxford Univ. Press, 1993), 281; and Steve Neale's reaction in 'Vanishing Americans: Racial and Ethnic Issues in the Interpretation and Context of Post-war Pro-Indian Westerns', in Edward Buscombe and Robert Pearson, eds, *Back in the Saddle Again: New Essays on the Western* (London: BFI, 1998), 8–29.

9   Gaylyn Studlar, 'What Would Martha Want? Captivity, Purity and Feminine Values in *The Searchers*', in Arthur Eckstein and Peter Lehman, eds, *The Searchers: Essays and Reflections on John Ford's Classic Western* (Detroit: Wayne State Univ. Press, 2004), 174.

10 Arthur Eckstein, 'Introduction: Main Critical Issues in *The Searchers*', in Eckstein and Lehman, eds, *The Searchers*, 3.

11 George Lewis, 'Scientific Certainty: Wesley Critz George, Racial Science and Organised White Resistance in North Carolina, 1954–1962', *Journal of American Studies*, 38 (August 2004), 231.

12 Alabama State Senator Walter Gihvan, quoted in Neil McMillen, *The Citizens' Council: Organized Resistance to the Second Reconstruction, 1954–64* (Urbana: Univ. of Illinois Press, 1971), 185.

13 David Grimstead, 'Re-Searching', in Eckstein and Lehman, eds, *The Searchers*, 296.

14 Brian Henderson, '*The Searchers*: An American Dilemma', *Film Quarterly*, 34.2 (Winter 1980), 9–23; Douglas Pye, 'Double Vision: Miscegenation and Point of View in *The Searchers*', in Ian Cameron and Douglas Pye, eds, *The Movie Book of the Western* (London: Cassell, 1996), 229–235.

15 Review of *The Searchers*, *Hollywood Reporter*, 26 May 1956.

16 Ekstein, 'Introduction: Main Critical Issues in *The Searchers*', 14.

17   See Pye, 'Double Vision', 229–230; and Tad Gallagher, 'Angels Gambol Where They Will: John Ford's Indians', *Film Comment*, September–October 1993, 70.

18   Grimstead, 'Re-Searching', 295, 317.

19   Michael Coyne, *The Crowded Prairie: American National Identity in the Hollywood Western* (London: I.B.Tauris, 1997), 93; Jon Tuska, *The American West in Film: Critical Approaches to the Western* (Westport: Greenwood Press, 1985), 146.

20   'Vital Statistics on *The True Story of Jesse James*', Production Notes in *The True Story of Jesse James* Clipping File, AMPAS.

21   See Geoff Andrew, *The Films of Nicholas Ray* (London: Letts, 1991), 140–142.

22   James Gilbert, *A Cycle of Outrage: America's Reaction to the Juvenile Delinquent in the 1950s* (New York: Oxford Univ. Press, 1986), 185, 188–189.

23   See Thomas Doherty, *Teenagers and Teenpics: The Juvenilization of American Movies in the 1950s* (London: Routledge, 1988), 182–183.

24   *The Burning Hills* pressbook, WB-USC.

25   Review of *The Burning Hills, Memphis Press Scimitar*, 23 August 1956 in *The Burning Hills* Clipping File, WB-USC.

26   Doherty, *Teenagers and Teenpics*, 189.

27   Gilbert, *A Cycle of Outrage*, 144, 15, 77.

28   An additional flashback for gang-member Cole Younger is still evident in the 'Final Script' 14 September 1956, 66–77, Fox-UCLA: 2680.8.

29   Gilbert, *A Cycle of Outrage*, 155.

30   Andrew, *The Films of Nicholas Ray*, 140.

31   'The Problem Grows Worse… What to Do When Kids Shoot Down Kids?', *Newsweek*, 16 May 1955, 34.

32   From a 1955 article by John Cogley published in *Commonweal*, quoted in Lenihan, *Showdown*, 141.

33   Russell Hughes, 'Treatment of *True Story of Jesse James*', 15 May 1956, Fox-USC: 2680.1

34   'Why the Young Kill: Prowling the Juvenile Jungles of the Big Cities', Newsweek, 19 August 1957, 26.

35   Gilbert, *A Cycle of Outrage*, 17.

36   Robert Merton, 'Social-Cultural Environment and *Anomie*', quoted in Gilbert, *A Cycle of Outrage*, 134.

37   Lenihan, *Showdown*, 141.

38   Gilbert, *A Cycle of Outrage*, 135.

39   Albert Cohen, *Delinquent Boys: The Culture of the Gang* (London: Routledge, 1956), 140.

40   '*True Story of Jesse James* Revised Script', 29 May 1956, Fox-USC: 2680.

41   Review of *The True Story of Jesse James, Hollywood Reporter*, 15 February 1957.

42   Erik Erikson's original formulation of 'identity diffusion' is reprinted in *Identity and the Life Cycle: Selected Papers* (New York: International Univ. Press, 1959), 74, 91–94.

43   Walter B. Miller, 'Lower Class Culture as a Generating Milieu of Gang Delinquency', *Journal of Social Issues*, 14.3 (1958), 14.

44   Kefauver's opinion was that delinquency was 'the rubble from crumbling social pillars of strength: the home, the school, and the church'. See Gilbert, *A Cycle of Outrage*, 154.

45   Wertham's *The Seduction of the Innocent* (New York: Kennikat Press, 1953), posited a direct connection between delinquency and crime comics, and prompted a national crusade against media representations of violence.

46   Bernard Eisenschitz, *Nicholas Ray: An American Journey* (London: Faber and Faber, 1993), 232.

47   Peter Biskind, 'Rebel Without a Cause: Nicholas Ray in the Fifties', *Film Quarterly*, 28.1 (1974), 33.

48   Quoted in Doherty, *Teenagers and Teenpics*, 184.

49   Eisenschitz, *Nicholas Ray*, 283.

50   David Riesman, Nathan Glazer and Reuel Denney, *The Lonely Crowd: A Study of the Changing American Character* (New Haven: Yale Univ. Press, 1950). The 'crisis of masculinity' and its cultural forms are discussed in Steve Cohan, *Masked Men: Masculinity and the Movies in the Fifties* (Bloomington: Indiana Univ. Press, 1997).

51   John Kenneth Galbraith, *The Affluent Society* (London: Hamish Hamilton, 1958); William H. Whyte, *The Organization Man* (London: Cape, 1957); Vance Packard, *The Hidden Persuaders* (London: Longmans, 1957); C. Wright Mills, *The Power Elite* (London: Oxford Univ. Press, 1956).

52   Louis Lyndon, 'Uncertain Hero: The Paradox of the American Male', *Woman's Home Journal*, November 1956, 41–43, 107, quoted in Cohan, *Masked Men*, 34–35.

53   David Halberstam, *The Fifties* (New York: Villard, 1993), 526.

54   Sloan Wilson, *The Man in the Gray Flannel Suit* (London: Cassell, 1956), 16.

55   See C. Wright Mills, *White Collar: The American Middle Classes* (New York: Oxford Univ. Press, 1956); Halberstam, *The Fifties*, 527.

56   See Cohan, *Masked Men*, 68–78.

57   Coyne, *The Crowded Prairie*, 93.

58   For further comments on *Gunfight*'s masculinity see Peter Lehman and William Luhr, eds, *Thinking About the Movies* (London: Blackwell, 2003), 114–115.

59   Douglas Pye, 'The Collapse of Fantasy: Masculinity in the Westerns of Anthony Mann', in Cameron and Pye, eds, *The Movie Book of the Western*, 169.

60   Helen Mayer Hacker, 'The New Burdens of Masculinity', *Marriage and Family Living*, 19 (1957), 227–233, quoted in Cohan, *Masked Men*, 60.

61   Lenihan, *Showdown*, 108.

62   Coyne, *The Crowded Prairie*, 89.

63   Riesman, *The Lonely Crowd*, 41, 23.

64   Wilson, *The Man in the Gray Flannel Suit*, 205.

65   *The Big Country* Draft Script, 108. Heston-AMPAS: Script File 52.

66   Riesman, *The Lonely Crowd*, 75.

67   'Appendix to *The Big Country* Final Screenplay', 14 August 1957, 3, Wyler-UCLA: 13.13.

68   Charlton Heston, quoted in *The Big Country* Exhibitor's Kit, Peck-AMPAS.

69   Gregory Peck to Lew Wasserman, 28 August 1958, *The Big Country* Cutting Notes, Peck-AMPAS.

70   Betty Friedan, *The Feminine Mystique* (New York: Norton, 2001, 1963), 22–24.

71   Friedan, *Feminine Mystique*, 305.

72   Rachel Bowlby, 'The Problem With No Name: Rereading Friedan's *The Feminine Mystique*', *Feminist Review*, 27 (September 1987), 62; Friedan, *Feminine Mystique*, 19.

73   Peter Biskind, *Seeing Is Believing: How Hollywood Taught Us to Stop Worrying and Love the Fifties* (London: Pluto Press, 1983), 268.

74   Copy of Stephen Vincent Benet's 'The Sobbin' Women', in *Seven Brides for Seven Brothers* Script File, MGM-AMPAS.

75   Molly Haskell, *From Reverence to Rape: The Treatment of Women in the Movies* (Chicago: Univ. of Chicago Press, 1987), 239.

76   Peter William Evans, 'Westward the Women: Feminising the Wilderness', in Cameron and Pye, eds, *The Movie Book of the Western*, 206.

77   Dr Marynia Farnham and Ferdinand Lundberg, *Modern Woman: The Lost Sex* (New York: HarperCollins, 1947), excerpted in Mary Beth Norton and Ruth Alexander, eds, *Major Problems in American Women's History* (Lexington: D.C. Heath, 1996), 403. Farnham also argued that a woman should 'accept her dependence on her husband as the source of gratification'.

78   Jean and Eugene Benge, *Win Your Man and Keep Him* (Chicago: Windsor Press, 1948).

79   Norton and Alexander, *Major Problems in American Women's History*, 404.

80   'Making Marriage Work: If You Don't Get Dates', *Ladies Home Journal*, July 1956, quoted in Elaine Tyler May, *Homeward Bound: American Families in the Cold War Era* (New York: Basic Books, 1988), 119–120.

81   'Health for Girls' (1952), quoted in May, *Homeward Bound*, 102.

82   *Calamity Jane* Screenplay, 26 November 1952, 49, WB-USC: 1824a.

83 Joanne Meyerowitz, 'Beyond the Feminine Mystique: A Reassessment of post-war Mass Culture, 1946–1958', *Journal of American History*, 794 (March 1993), 1460.

84 *Calamity Jane* Press Releases, 15 November 1952, 16 January, 20 October, and 12 January 1953, WB-USC: 702a.

85 French, *Westerns*, 24.

Chapter 6: Researching History

1   See, for example, *Lust for Life* pressbook, BFI.

2   Pressbooks for *David and Bathsheba* and *The Great Missouri Raid*, BFI.

3   *The Court Jester* pressbook, BFI.

4   Robert Brent Toplin, Reel History: *In Defense of Hollywood* (Lawrence: Univ. of Kansas Press, 2002), 48. This point is expanded upon by Daniel Walkowitz in 'Visual History: The Craft of the Historian-Filmmaker', *Public Historian*, 7 (1985), 1193–1199.

5   Natalie Zemon Davis, 'Any Resemblance to Persons Living or Dead: Film and the Challenge of Authenticity', *Historical Journal of Film, Radio and Television*, 8.3 (1988), 271.

6   Mark C. Carnes, 'Shooting (Down) the Past: Historians vs. Hollywood', *Cineaste* (Spring 2004), 47.

7   Dwight Macdonald's 1957 essay 'The Triumph of the Fact' is reprinted in his *Against the American Grain* (New York: De Capo, 1983), 393–427.

8   Peter Novick, *That Noble Dream: The 'Objectivity Question' and the American Historical Profession* (Cambridge: Cambridge Univ. Press, 1988), 299.

9   William Wyler to Ryan A. Grut, Royal Danish Vice Consulate, 1 August 1939, Wyler-AMPAS: Box 8; Foreword to *Hans Christian Andersen* (1952).

10 Quoted in Elza Schallbert, 'Details Nudge Past Into Focus in Making Films', *Los Angeles Times*, 15 March 1954, 2.6.

11 Helen G. Percey, 'Problems of a Motion Picture Research Library', *Society of Motion Picture Engineer's Journal*, 26.3 (March 1936), 253.

12 Western Personel Service, *Motion Picture Research: An Occupational Brief* (Los Angeles: 1941), 1.

13 Sara Colton and Hawley Jones, 'What's Right About the Movies', *Harpers* (July 1943), 146–151.

14 Mervyn LeRoy, *It Takes More Than Talent* (New York: Alfred Knopf, 1953), 206. Reflecting contemporary sexism, LeRoy's rationale for employing unmarried women was that 'they are less independent about their jobs' (204–205):

   This may be a rather cool appraisal of the situation, but with a limited staff, and production going at top speed, the girl who is dependable, always there, not worrying about her husband's dinner or her child's cold, makes the best researcher... This is also a department where even the head is a woman. Women are much better at detail work than men, who are usually bored by it.

15 William B. Adams, 'A Definition of Motion Picture Research', *Quarterly Review of Film, Radio and Television* (Winter 1953), 408.

16 *King Richard and the Crusaders* Research, WB-USC: 8458.

17 Requests for Research, 9 September, 16 and 27 October, 23 and 17 December 1953, *King Richard and the Crusaders* Research, WB-USC: 8458.

18 Cameron Shipp, 'Meet Hollywood's Quizmasters', *Coronet* (November 1946), 95.

19 Adams, 'A Definition of Motion Picture Research', 411.

20 See Shipp, 'Meet Hollywood's Quizmasters', 94.

21 Technical Notes for *Dianne* [sic] by Hilda Grenier, 19 January 1955, MGM-AMPAS: 765.774. Grenier was also credited as a consultant on *Great Expectations* (1934), *The Mystery of Edwin Drood* (1935), *Kitty* (1945) and *Golden Earrings* (1947).

22 *Story of Robin Hood* pressbook, BFI.

23 *Black Shield of Falworth* Production Notes, 3, Universal-USC: 925. Any reference to his renown outside of Hollywood has yet to be found, and his exact qualifications were never made clear in publicity.

24 Louis Van den Ecker, 'A Veteran's View of Hollywood Authenticity', *Hollywood Quarterly* (Summer 1950), 325.

25 'Miscellaneous Notes from Professor Gottstein', 8 June 1958, MGM-AMPAS: 280.1102. Noted for his studies of ancient Middle Eastern languages, Gottstein headed the Hebrew University Bible Project translating the Scrolls, which had been discovered in 1947.

26 Van den Ecker, 'A Veteran's View of Hollywood Authenticity', 329, 327.

27 Jerry Wald to Frank McCarthy, 25 March 1957, *Kiss Them For Me* Project Book, Wald-USC. Military advisors included Rear Admiral Rob Roy McGregor, who served on *Run Silent Run Deep*, Admiral John Dale Price on *The Wings of Eagles* and Major Raymond Harvey on *Verboten!* Universal achieved the greatest coup, persuading General Walter Bedell Smith, Eisenhower's Chief of Staff during WWII, to introduce *To Hell and Back*.

28 *Kim* pressbook, BFI.

29 Pierre Sorlin, *The Film in History: Restaging the Past* (Oxford: Basil Blackwell, 1980), 21.

30 *East of Eden* Production Notes, n.d., WB-USC.

31 Milliken joined Warner Bros. in 1936, and was instrumental in establishing the research department, becoming head of it from 1949 to 1975.

32 Carl Milliken to Elia Kazan, 20 May 1954, in *East of Eden* Research Correspondence, WB-USC.

33 Newsclipping of *Monterey Daily Cypress,* 9 May 1917, in *East of Eden* Research Correspondence, WB-USC.

34 John Steinbeck, *East of Eden* (London: Penguin, 1992), 516–517.

35 Robert Green to Carl Milliken, 27 April 1954, *East of Eden* Research Correspondence, WB-USC.

36 Milliken reported that Green's description 'pleased Mr Kazan very much', and confirmed that Schuman was the inspiration for the scene, although his profession and name would be changed to avoid 'legal complications'. Thus Schuman the tailor became Mr Albrecht, a shoemaker. (Carl Milliken to Robert Green, 29 April 1954, *East of Eden* Research Correspondence, WB-USC.)

37 Review of *East of Eden, Motion Picture Daily*, 16 February 1955.

38 Carl Milliken to Milton Sperling, 7 June 1955, *The Court Martial of Billy Mitchell* Research Correspondence, WB-USC.

39 Milliken to Sperling, 7 and 15 June 1955, *The Court Martial of Billy Mitchell* Research Correspondence, WB-USC.

40 'Obituary: Hugh Gray', *Variety*, 23 February 1981.

41 Hugh Gray, '*Quo Vadis* Research', 18 February 1949, 1, MGM-AMPAS: QV.92.

42 *Ibid.*, 67, 34.

43 John Huston, *Open Book* (New York: Alfred Knopf, 1980), 175.

44 Hugh Gray, 'Miscellaneous Script Pages for *Quo Vadis*', 18 February 1949, Huston-AMPAS: Box 12.

45 Hugh Gray, 'Notes on *Ben Hur*', 17 March 1959, 2, MGM-AMPAS: 283.1116.

46 'Interview with Hugh Gray', *Playback: UCLA Motion Picture Division Newsletter* (Fall 1965), 2.

47 *Quo Vadis* Script Revisions, 22 August 1949, Huston-AMPAS: Box 12.

48 Quoted in Lillian Ross, *Picture* (New York: Random House, 1997), 37.

49 Hugh Gray, '*Beau Brummell* Research Notes', 7 June 1951, 35–43, MGM-AMPAS: 234.677. Lewis Melville's collection, *Beau Brummell: His Life and Letters* (London: Hutchinson, 1924), contains many love letters to which Gray may have been referring.

50 Gray, '*Beau Brummell* Research Notes', 7 June 1951, 21.

51 These memoirs have been most recently edited by Christopher Hibbert in *Captain Gronow: His Reminiscences of Regency and Victorian Life, 1810–60* (London: Kyle Cathie, 1991).

52 E.A. Smith, *George IV* (New Haven: Yale Univ. Press, 1999), 119.

53 Gray, '*Beau Brummell* Research Notes', 7 June 1951, 25, 173.

54 Joseph Breen to Sam Zimbalist, 4 June 1953, *Beau Brummell* File, PCA-AMPAS.

55 In consequence, all of the events in the film are presented as happening *before* Caroline arrives in England, with the Prince secretly 'married' to Maria in defiance of the 1772 Marriage Act. The plot thus concerns Brummell and the Prince manoeuvring to find a way to prevent the official wedding – even

though, in fact, Brummell did not become an associate of the Prince until three years *after* his marriage to Caroline.

56   Hugh Gray, '*Beau Brummell* Research Notes', 10 August 1951, 47–48, MGM-AMPAS: 234.681.

57   Tony Thomas, *Ustinov in Focus* (London: Zwemmer, 1971), 90.

58   *Helen of Troy* Research Record, WB-USC.

59   Hugh Gray, 'Treatment of *Helen of Troy*', 11 April 1952, WB-USC.

60   'Interview with Hugh Gray', *Playback*, 2.

61   Gray, 'Treatment of *Helen of Troy*', 11 April 1952, 27.

62   John Twist to Research Department, 3 March 1953, *Helen of Troy* Research Record, WB-USC.

63   'Interview with Hugh Gray', *Playback*, 2.

64   Hugh Gray to Finlay McDermid, 14 January 1953, *Helen of Troy* Story Memos and Correspondence, WB-USC.

65   Gray, 'Notes on *Ben Hur*', 17 March 1959, 2.

66   *Ibid.*, 18, 1.

67   Gray, '*Beau Brummell* Research Notes', 7 June 1951, 43.

68   Gray, 'Notes on *Ben Hur*', 17 March 1959, 18.

69   Following *The Ten Commandments*, DeMille did start to remake *The Buccaneer*, but due to illness it was completed by his son-in-law, Anthony Quinn. DeMille died in January 1959.

70   'Interview with Henry Noerdlinger', n.d., Noerdlinger-AMPAS: 2.11, tape 35.5.

71   Henry Noerdlinger, 'The Bible and Motion Pictures', unpublished address, 3, Noerdlinger-AMPAS.

72   *Ibid.*

73   'Comparison of Amount of Research Material', n.d., Noerdlinger-AMPAS: 2.14.

74   *Black Shield of Falworth* Campaign Ideas, Publicity File, Universal-USC.

75   'Interview with Henry Noerdlinger', tape 35.5.

76   Alan Nadel, *Containment Culture: American Narratives, Postmodernism and the Atomic Age* (Durham: Duke Univ. Press, 1995), 95.

77   Henry Noerdlinger to Keith Seele, 5 March 1956, Correspondence with Oriental Institute, Noerdlinger-AMPAS: f.16. Publicly, of course, DeMille claimed he was publishing it at urging of 'numerous scholars and clergymen', who 'have told me, there is no other single volume which brings together all these data from biblical, archaeological, and historical sources'. (Introduction to Henry Noerdlinger, *Moses and Egypt: The Documentation to the Motion Picture 'The Ten Commandments'* (Los Angeles: University of Southern California Press, 1956), 2.)

78   Henry Noerdlinger, 'Hollywood and the Bible', address at the Hollywood Temple Bethal, n.d., Noerdlinger-AMPAS: 2.11, tape 35.2. Quoting archaeologist Ernest Heltzfeld as taking the position that 'legend contains

truth', Noerdlinger noted that 'if one considers their antiquity, one is strongly tempted to believe that some of these traditions and legends... related actual history'.

79   'Interview with Henry Noerdlinger', tape 35.4.

80   DeMille suggested that the audience 'may have wondered at Moses' Egyptian mother, Bithiah, going on the Exodus', which is not mentioned in the five books of Moses. However, assuring them that 'You will find proof of it in I Chronicles 4:18, where there is a reference to "Bithiah, the daughter of Pharaoh which Mered took"', DeMille inferred that 'Mered could not have married Bithiah, a daughter of Pharaoh, if she had not gone on the Exodus'. ('Address given at the Plaza Hotel', reprinted in *The Ten Commandments* pressbook, BFI.)

81   *The Ten Commandments* Trailer Transcript, Paramount-AMPAS.

82   DeMille's introduction to Noerdlinger, *Moses and Egypt*, 3.

83   *Ibid.*, 2.

84   Keith Seele to Henry Noerdlinger, 23 November 1956, Correspondence with Oriental Institute, Noerdlinger-AMPAS: f.16.

85   Noerdlinger complained to Seele that DeMille was fixated with John Gardner Wilkinson's *Manners and Customs of the Ancient Egyptians* (1842) – which 'gets thrown in my face all the time!' Seele – whom DeMille respected – advised that *Manners and Customs* 'must be used with great reserve and the statements checked against those of more recent writers', and suggested that Noerlinger tell his boss that 'Adolf Erman claimed that Wilkinson's ancient Egyptians did not exist!' (Henry Noerdlinger to Keith Seele, 24 March 1953; Keith Seele to Henry Noerdlinger, 31 March, 153. Correspondence with Oriental Institute, Noerdlinger-AMPAS: f.16.)

86   Henry Noerdlinger to Cecil B. DeMille, 29 June 1954, Correspondence with DeMille, Noerdlinger-AMPAS: f.6. Noerdlinger warned that the visual materials created by film designers 'can, in truth, NOT BE CALLED AUTHENTIC. But it can be called an ADAPTATION, derived from authentic material. Of course, such an ADAPTATION is still open to criticism. However, any statement issued in its behalf – as an ADAPTATION – is honest and stands for professional integrity.'

87   Henry Noerdlinger to Keith Seele, 20 April 1956, Correspondence with Oriental Institute, Noerdlinger-AMPAS: f.16.

Chapter 7: Living History

1   See First Draft Continuity by Joseph Fields, 16 September 1948; Storyline by Marion Turk, 23 October 1948; Treatment by Albert and Arthur Lewis, 25 January 1949; Screenplay by Herman J. Mankiewicz, 28 April 1949; Memo from Darryl Zanuck to George Jessel, 22 August 1949, Fox-UCLA: 1186-2513.

2   *The I Don't Care Girl* Script Conference, 26 October 1950, Fox-UCLA: 1186-2513.18.

3   *Ibid.*

4   This analysis is based on the list of biopics identified by George Custen in *Bio/Pics: How Hollywood Constructed Public History* (New Jersey: Rutgers Univ. Press, 1992), Appendix C, 242-46. Twelve percent of biopics released in the 1930s concerned persons who were still living. This rose to 24 percent in the 1940s, and then to 34 percent through the 1950s.

5   *The Wings of Eagles* (1950) was John Ford's account of naval commander Frank Wead; *The McConnell Story* (dir. Gordon Douglas, 1955) revisited the career of Captain Joseph McConnell, Jr., a jet ace in the Korean War; while *To Hell and Back* (dir. Jesse Hibbs, 1955) was Audie Murphy's story.

6   Custen, *Bio/Pics*, 85.

7   George Custen, 'The Mechanical Life in the Age of Human Reproduction', *Biography*, 23.1 (Winter 2000), 153.

8   'The Curious Craze for Confidential Magazines', *Newsweek*, 11 July 1955, 50. This is discussed by Will Straw, 'Urban Confidental: The Lurid City of the 1950s', in David B. Clarke, ed., *The Cinematic City* (London: Routledge, 1997), 110–128.

9   David Thelen, ed., *Memory and American History* (Bloomington: Indiana Univ. Press, 1990), xvi.

10   'A man must often appeal to others' remembrances to evoke his own past,' notes Halbwachs. 'He goes back to reference points determined by society, hence outside of himself.' Maurice Halbwachs, *The Collective Memory*, trans. Francis J. Ditter (New York: Harper and Row, 1980), 51.

11   See, for instance, Herbert Leibowitz, *Fabricating Lives: Explorations in American Biography* (New York: Knopf, 1989).

12   Halbwachs, *The Collective Memory,* 51.

13   Jean Negulesco to Darryl Zanuck, 27 February 1952, Negulesco-AMPAS: Box 3.

14   'Notes on First Draft of *Stars and Stripes Forever*', 11 December 1951, 1–2, Fox-UCLA: 1189-2511.8a.

15   'Interview with Adolph Green and Betty Comden', clipping in Fordin file, Freed-USC: Box 56.

16   For consideration of Freud's analysis of the workings of memory see Patrick Hutton, *History as an Art of Memory* (Hanover: Univ. Press of New England, 1993), 59–68. Freud's essay on 'Screen Memories' is reprinted in James Strachey, ed., *The Psychopathology of Everyday Life* (London: Benn, 1966) 43–52.

17   Barry Allen, 'The Soul of Knowledge', *History and Theory*, 36.1 (1997), 78.

18   Hutton, *History as an Art of Memory*, 64.

19   '*Singin' in the Rain* Production Memo', Freed-USC: Box 21.

20   Peter Wollen, *Singin' in the Rain* (London: BFI, 1997), 54.

21   Michael Frisch, 'American History and the Structures of Collective Memory', in David Thelen, ed., *Memory and American History* (Bloomington: Indiana Univ. Press, 1990), 25.

22   Respectively starring in *To Hell and Back* (1955) and the less-than-imaginatively titled *The Jackie Robinson Story* (1950) and *The Bob Mathias Story* (1954).

23   A. Scott Berg, *Lindbergh* (London: Macmillan, 1998), 501.

24   Helen Rozwadowski, 'David Marshall Williams', in John A. Garraty and Mark C. Carnes, eds, *American National Biography Volume 23* (New York: Oxford Univ. Press, 1999), 435.

25   Arthur Fitzgerald, 'Synopsis of *The Army Carbine* by David Marshall Williams', 15 March 1951, 2, MGM-AMPAS: 503.330.

26   Richard H. Blum, 'Psychological Processes in Preparing Contemporary Biography', *Biography*, 4.4 (1982), 306.

27   William Bowers, 'Treatment of *Man With a Record*', 2 June 1951, 6, MGM-AMPAS: 503.332.

28   *Ibid.*, 9.

29   *Ibid.*, 3.

30   *Ibid.*, 31–33, 1.

31   Art Cohn, '*Carbine Williams* Treatment', 10 July 1951, 2, MGM-AMPAS: 503.335.

32   Art Cohn, 'Alternate Approaches', 18 July 1951, 5, MGM-AMPAS: 503.336.

33   David Marshall Williams, *The Williams Story* (North Carolina: Ivan Tashof, 1951), copies of galley proofs, MGM-AMPAS: 503.331.

34   Cohn, 'Alternate Approaches', 18 July 1951, 8.

35   *Ibid.*, 7, 8; Art Cohn, '*Carbine Williams:* Notes', 31 October 1951, MGM-AMPAS: 505.347.

36   Blum, 'Psychological Processes', 307–308.

37   David Thomson, 'The Invasion of the Real People', *Sight and Sound*, 47.1 (Winter 1977– 78), 19.

38   Review of *Carbine Williams, Variety*, 15 April 1952.

39   Margot Strickland, 'Ghostwriting an Autobiography', *Biography*, 18.1 (1995), 67.

40   Everett Freeman to Steve Trilling, 8 September 1949, *Jim Thorpe* Correspondence, WB-USC.

41   The fullest account of Thorpe's sporting career appears in Robert Wheeler, *Jim Thorpe, World's Greatest Athlete* (Norman: Univ. of Oklahoma Press, 1971).

42   Quoted in Michael Munn, *Burt Lancaster – The Terrible-Tempered Charmer* (London: Robson, 1995), 59.

43   Despite Freeman's efforts, the honors were not restored until 1982, 30 years after Thorpe's death. Everett Freeman to Alex Evelove, 3 October 1949 and

2 November 1949, *Jim Thorpe* Story Notes and Correspondence 3, WB-USC.

44 Douglas Morrow to Steve Trilling, 1 September 1950, *Jim Thorpe* Correspondence, WB-USC.

45 Patricia Thorpe to Everett Freeman, 18 March 1950, *Jim Thorpe* Story Notes and Correspondence 1, WB-USC.

46 Robert Kennedy to Jack Warner, (c. March 1950), *Jim Thorpe* Story Notes and Correspondence 3, WB-USC.

47 Patricia Thorpe to Everett Freeman, 23 March 1950, *Jim Thorpe* Story Notes and Correspondence 1, WB-USC.

48 Freeman to Trilling, 8 September 1949.

49 Patricia Thorpe to Everett Freeman, 10 March 1950, *Jim Thorpe* Correspondence, WB-USC.

50 Freeman to Thorpe, 23 March 1950.

51 Jim's operation, and his poverty, was reported in *Time*, 19 November 1951, prompting thousands of dollars to be sent in donations. Despite this, Jim's last job was as a greeter in a Los Angeles bar, and he died at his trailer home on 28 March 1953.

52 Review of *Jim Thorpe – All American*, *Variety*, 14 June 1951.

53 *The Denver Post*, 13 July 1953, clipping in *Glenn Miller Story* Correspondence, Universal-USC: 06134.

54 Donald Dewey, *James Stewart: A Biography* (Atlanta: Turner, 1996), 353.

55 Discussions reveal that the 'widow's cloak' is often experienced during the writing of authorised biographies. The term was coined by Stephen Spackman, who discovered that the widow of American composer Henry Cowell sacked a whole succession of would-be biographers who did not conform to her 'very decided views' on Cowell's life and work. Hugh Brogan admits to serious difficulties in progressing beyond the inflexible perspective of Arthur Ransome's wife during the writing of *The Life of Arthur Ransome* (London: Pimlico, 1984). No sexism is intended in labelling this the 'widow's cloak' – the problem is intrinsic to the protection of the partner's reputation, by any survivor. But since women tend to live longer than men, widows seem to be more common in this situation.

56 'Treatment of *The Glenn Miller Story*', 27 January 1953, 1, Davies-AMPAS: 5.35.

57 M.R. Davis to William Goetz, 14 October 1952, *Glenn Miller Story* Correspondence, Universal-USC: 06134.

58 'Campaign Ideas', n.d., *Glenn Miller Story* Press Releases and Publicity, Universal-USC: 23627.

59 *Glenn Miller Story* Press Release, 29 June 1953, Universal-USC: 23627.

60 Valentine Davies, 'An Author Who Found Six Characters', draft article, *Glenn Miller Story* Correspondence File, Davies-AMPAS: 6.40.

61 Valentine Davies to Cecil Madden, 8 February 1954, Correspondence File, Davies-AMPAS: 6.40.

62 Dennis Bingham, *Acting Male: Masculinities in the Films of James Stewart, Jack Nicholson and Clint Eastwood* (New Brunswick: Rutgers Univ. Press, 1994), 70; Dewey, *James Stewart*, 354

63 Davies, 'An Author Who Found Six Characters'.

64 See George T. Simon, *The Big Bands* (London: Collier, 1974), 359.

65 R.G. Collingwood, *The Idea of History* (Oxford: Oxford Univ. Press, 1961) – see especially the chapters on 'The Historical Imagination' (231–249) and 'History as Re-enactment of Past Experience' (282–302).

66 See Maureen Turin, *Flashbacks in Film: Memory and History* (London: Routledge, 1989), 140.

67 See Albert Stone, ed., *The American Autobiography* (Englewood: Prentice Hall, 1981), 14, 57.

68 Halbwachs, *The Collective Memory*, 71.

69 Michael Kammen, 'Review Essay', *History and Theory*, 34 (1995), 251.

70 Daniel Gordon, 'Review of *History as an Art of Memory* by Patrick Hutton', *History and Theory*, 34 (1995), 350.

71 Thomson, 'The Invasion of the Real People', 18.

Chapter 8: Intellectual History

1 Evan Hunter, *The Blackboard Jungle* (London: Bloomsbury, [1955] 1997), 70.

2 Dana Polan, 'The Professors of History', in Vivian Sobchack, ed., *The Persistence of History: Cinema, Television and the Modern Event* (London: Routledge, 1996), 237.

3 John Higham, ed., *History: The Development of Historical Studies in the United States* (Englewood: Prentice Hall, 1965), 68.

4 Allan Nevins, 'Not Capulets, Not Montagus', *American Historical Review*, 65.2 (January 1960), 254.

5 Holt's data demonstrated that works of American history, even those most highly praised by the academic community, commonly sold fewer than 4000 copies. See W. Stull Holt, 'Who Reads the Best Histories?', *Mississippi Valley Historical Review*, 40.4 (March 1954), 619.

6 Quoted in Donald Sheehan and Harold C. Syrett, eds, *Essays in American Historiography: Papers Presented in Honor of Allan Nevins* (New York: Columbia Univ. Press, 1960), v.

7 Conyers Read, 'The Social Responsibilities of the Historian', *American Historical Review*, 55.2 (January 1950), 285.

8 *Decision Before Dawn* pressbook, BFI.

9 *Alexander the Great* pressbook, BFI.

10 *Denver and the Rio Grande* pressbook, BFI.

11 The Great Missouri Raid pressbook, BFI.

12 'Movies and Self-Regulation' Pamphlet, September 1955, Production Code File, AMPTP-AMPAS.

13 Orville Andersen, 'Type of General Information on Hollywood Which Should be Disseminated Abroad', March 1953, State Department File, AMPTP-AMPAS. See also David Eldridge, 'Dear Owen: The CIA, Luigi Luraschi and Hollywood, 1953', *Historical Journal of Film, Radio and Television*, 20.2 (2000), 193–196.

14 Posters for *The Eagle and the Hawk* (1950), for example, described the history as 'Ripped from the pages of America's mightiest chapter!' AMPAS pressbook.

15 *Johnny Tremain* pressbook, BFI.

16 Bruce Catton, 'What They Did There', *American Heritage*, 1.1 (December 1954), 3.

17 John Higham, 'The Cult of the "American Consensus": Homogenizing Our History', in A.S. Eisenstadt, ed., *The Craft of American History* (New York: Harper, 1966), 194, 196.

18 Henry Steele Commager, *The Commonwealth of Learning* (New York: Harper and Row, 1968), 59.

19 Frances Fitzgerald, *America Revised: History Schoolbooks in the Twentieth Century* (Boston: Little, Brown, 1979), 61, 65, 153.

20 The 'lesson' to be learned from Toynbee was noted by Louis Gottschalk in his AHA presidential address, 'A Professor of History in a Quandary', *American Historical Review*, 59.2 (January 1954), 275.

21 Dorothy Ross, 'Grand Narrative in American Historical Writing: From Romance to Uncertainty', *American Historical Review*, 100.3 (April 1995), 653, 659.

22 Peter Novick, *That Noble Dream: The 'Objectivity Question' and the American Historical Profession* (Cambridge: Cambridge Univ. Press, 1988), 373–374. Novick further notes that historians also turned away from 'potboiling popular writing' because 'works of serious scholarship' were increasingly being printed in paperback for a 'captive' audience of university and college students.

23 See Barry Allen, 'The Soul of Knowledge', *History and Theory*, 36.1 (1997), 80; Michel Foucault's analysis appears in *Archaeology of Knowledge* (London: Tavistock, 1972).

24 Iwona Irwin-Zarecka, *Frames of Remembrance: the Dynamics of Collective Memory* (New Brunswick: Transaction, 1994), 147.

25 Quoted in Allen, 'The Soul of Knowledge', 80.

26 James Webb, 'Burning Arrow – Draft Screenplay', 9 January 1948, i, *Charge at Feather River* Files, WB-USC.

27 *Charge at Feather River* Press Release, 30 March 1953, WB-USC.

28 Leslie Stevens, '*The Left-Handed Gun* Final Screenplay', 16 May 1957, WB-USC.

29 *Ibid.*

30 Jonathan Bignell, 'Method Westerns', in Ian Cameron and Douglas Pye, eds, *The Movie Book of the Western* (London: Cassell, 1996), 103.

31 See *The Death of Billy the Kid* playscript (broadcast July 1955), Vidal-Madison: 32.3.

32 *The Left-Handed Gun* pressbook, BFI.

33 Review of 'Jupiter's Darling', *Hollywood Reporter*, 24 January 1955, 6.

34 *Jupiter's Darling* pressbook, BFI (my italics).

35 Dorothy Kingsley, '*Jupiter's Darling* Screenplay Section', 16 February 1954, MGM-AMPAS: 1633.365.

36 Review of *The Bad and the Beautiful*, *New York Times*, January 1952.

37 Charles Schnee, 'Treatment of Tribute to a Heel [*The Bad and the Beautiful*]', 6 September 1952, MGM-AMPAS: 176.176.

38 Richard Hofstadter, *Anti-Intellectualism in American Life* (New York: Random House, 1962) 3, 33.

39 Merle Curti, 'Intellectuals and Other People', *American Historical Review*, 60.2 (January 1955), 270.

40 Stephen J. Whitfield, *The Culture of the Cold War* (London: Johns Hopkins Univ. Press, 1991), 138.

41 Marion Parsonnet and Robert Thoeren, 'Treatment: *Jupiter's Darling*', 13 July 1939, 1–3, MGM-AMPAS: 1628.336.

42 Leon Gordon and Reinhold Schunzel, 'Treatment: *Jupiter's Darling*', 3 May 1940, 31, MGM-AMPAS: 1630.348.

43 Dorothy Kingsley, 'Treatment: *Jupiter's Darling*', 5 August 1953, 20, MGM-AMPAS: 1631.354.

44 Curti, 'Intellectuals and Other People', 278.

45 Thomas Doherty, *Projections of War: Hollywood, American Culture and World War II* (New York: Columbia Univ. Press, 1993), 60.

46 Christopher R. Browning, 'German Memory, Judicial Interrogation, Historical Reconstruction', in Saul Friedlander, ed., *Probing the Limits of Representation: Nazism and the 'Final Solution'* (Cambridge: Harvard Univ. Press, 1992), 25–27. See also Hayden White's 'The Modernist Event', in Vivian Sobchack, ed., *The Persistence of History: Cinema, Television and the Modern Event* (London: Routledge, 1996), 30–31.

47 Leonard Krieger, 'European History in America', in John Higham, ed., *History: The Development of Historical Studies in the United States* (Englewood: Prentice Hall, 1965), 291.

48 Novick, *That Noble Dream*, 304.

49 Polan, 'The Professors of History', 249.

50 Webb, 'Burning Arrow', 9 January 1948, 13 and 78.

51 Polan, 'The Professors of History', 252, 243.

52 William L. Shirer, *The Rise and Fall of the Third Reich: A History of Nazi Germany* (London: Secker and Warburg, 1960), 345. *Education for Death: The Making of the Nazi* (London: Constable, 1942) reached an even greater audience when it was 'adapted' by Walt Disney for a 1943 propaganda short.

53 Frederic Lilge, *The Abuse of Learning: The Failure of the German University* (New York: Macmillan, 1948), 118–119.

54 Parsonnet and Theoren, 'Treatment: *Jupiter's Darling*', 13 July 1939, 3.

55 Robert Thoeren and Waldo Scott, *Jupiter's Darling* Temporary Screenplay, 15 September 1939, 2, MGM-AMPAS: 1629.340.

56 Parsonnet and Theoren, 'Treatment: *Jupiter's Darling*', 13 July 1939, 47.

57 Quoted in Novick, *That Noble Dream*, 317.

58 Arthur Schlesinger, Jr., *Vital Center: The Politics of Freedom* (London: Deutsch, 1949), 207.

59 Louis Bromfield, 'The Triumph of the Egghead', *The Freeman* (1952), quoted in Hofstader, *Anti-Intellectualism in American Life*, 9.

60 Robert F. Willson, 'Witness to Murder: Social Roles in a 50s Thriller', *Velvet Light Trap*, 16 (Autumn 1976), 10.

61 Friederich Nietzsche, *The Use and Abuse of History*, trans. Adrian Collins (New York: The Liberal Arts Press, 1957), 36–42.

62 Carl Becker, 'Everyman His Own Historian (1931)', in *Everyman His Own Historian: Essays in History and Politics* (New York: Appleton, 1935), 251.

63 Alan Nevins, quoted in Novick, *That Noble Dream*, 290. Pages 282–292 present a detailed discussion of this and other accusations of historians having 'prepared the way for Fascism'.

64 Quoted in Novick, *That Noble Dream*, 160.

65 Quoted in Michael Kammen, *Mystic Chords of Memory: The Transformation of Tradition in American Culture* (New York: Knopf, 1991), 574.

66 J.H. Hexter, 'Carl Becker and Historical Relativism', in his *On Historians: Reappraisals of Some of the Makers of Modern History* (London: Collins, 1979), 38.

67 Becker, 'Everyman His Own Historian', 252–253.

68 See C. Vann Woodward, *Thinking Back: The Perils of Writing History* (Baton Rouge: Louisiana State Univ. Press, 1986), 88–95, for discussion on whether or not *The Strange Career of Jim Crow* was 'a reversion to the instrumentalism of early progressive historians'.

69 Quoted in Novick, *That Noble Dream*, 328.

70 Higham, ed., *History*, 223.

71 James Harvey Robinson, *The New History: Essays Illustrating the Modern Historical Outlook* (New York: Macmillan, 1912).

72 Read, 'The Social Responsibilities of the Historian', 284.

73 Daniel Boorstin, *The Genius of American Politics* (Chicago: Univ. of Chicago Press, 1953), 10; Richard Hofstadter, *The American Political Tradition* (New York: Knopf, 1948), ix.

74   Gottschalk, 'A Professor of History in a Quandary', 276.
75   Nevins, 'Not Capulets, Not Montagus', 261.

Conclusion

1   Vivian Sobchack, 'The Insistent Fringe: Moving Images and Historical Consciousness', *History and Theory*, 36 (1997), 15.
2   Vincente Minnelli, 'The Tradition of the Musical', lecture delivered at the San Francisco Museum of Art, May 7, 1954, Minnelli-AMPAS: 12.109.
3   Vincente Minnelli (with Hector Acre), *I Remember It Well* (New York: Doubleday, 1974), 311.
4   Genet, 'Letter From Paris', *The New Yorker*, 7 September 1957, 70. Similarly Guy's sketches of 'fashionable people in their carriages, bowing to each other on the afternoon rides', were the visual guide for the opening sequence in the Bois de Boulogne; while the coastal landscapes painted by Eugene Louis Boudin inspired the art direction of the beach sequences of the movie. See Minnelli, *I Remember It Well*, 311.
5   Natalie Zemon Davis, 'Any Resemblance to Persons Living or Dead: Film and the Challenge of Authenticity', *Historical Journal of Film, Radio and Television*, 8.3 (1988), 272.
6   Minnelli, *I Remember It Well*, 290.
7   *Ibid.,* 291.
8   Stephen Harvey, *Directed by Vincente Minnelli* (New York: Harper and Row, 1989), 246.
9   John Houseman to J.J. Cohn, 24 February 1955, MGM-AMPAS: 1930.1464.
10   James Naremore, *The Films of Vincente Minnelli* (Cambridge: Cambridge Univ. Press, 1993), 140.
11   Transcript of promotional film narration, *Darkness Into Light*, in Production Materials, Houseman-UCLA: Box 22.
12   Houseman to J.J. Cohn, 24 February 1955.
13   Harvey, *Directed by Vincente Minnelli*, 243.
14   *Ibid.*
15   George Stevens to Joe DeYong, n.d., *Shane*/DeYong Correspondence, Stevens-AMPAS: 3001.
16   George Stevens to Joe DeYong, 18 September 1951, *Shane*/DeYong Correspondence, Stevens-AMPAS: 3001; Penelope Houston, 'Shane and George Stevens', *Sight and Sound* (October 1953), 72.
17   Indeed poster tags reinforced the 'mythology' surrounding the protagonist, noting that 'There Never Was a Man Like Shane!'
18   Edward Countryman and Evonne von Heussen-Countryman present a detailed exposition of the film's use of the Turner thesis in *Shane* (London: BFI, 1999), 35–37.

19   Bruce Petri, *A Theory of American Film: The Films and Techniques of George Stevens* (London: Garland, 1987), 165.

20   Robert Rosenstone, *Visions of the Past: The Challenge of Film to Our Idea of History* (Cambridge: Harvard Univ. Press, 1995), 60.

21   David Herlihy, 'Am I a Camera?: Other Reflections on Films and History', *American Historical Review*, 93.5 (December 1988), 1187.

22   *Calamity Jane* Trailer Dialogue Transcript, 8 October 1953, *Calamity Jane* Censorship, WB-USC: 2704a; review of *Calamity Jane, Los Angeles Times*, 19 November 1953.

23   Bob Larkins and Boyd Magers, *The Films of Audie Murphy* (New York: MacFarland, 2004), 28.

24   Kenneth Geist, *Pictures Will Talk: The Life and Films of Joseph L. Mankiwicz* (New York: Scribner, 1978), 226.

25   Michael Wood, *America in the Movies: or 'Santa Maria, It Had Slipped My Mind!'* (London: Secker and Warburg, 1975), 183–184.

26   Richard Corber, *In the Name of National Security: Hitchcock, Homophobia and the Political Construction of Gender in Post-war America* (London: Duke Univ. Press, 1993), 156.

27   Quoted in Donald Spoto, *The Life of Alfred Hitchcock: The Dark Side of Genius* (London: Collins, 1983), 309; Francois Truffaut, *Hitchcock* (London: Secker and Warburg, 1968), 156.

Index